AF560109

THE SIKKA AND THE RAJ

THE SIKKA AND THE RAJ

A History of Currency Legislations of the East India Company, 1772-1835

SANJAY GARG

MANOHAR
2013

First published, 2013

ISBN 978-81-7304-970-5

Published by
Ajay Kumar Jain *for*
Manohar Publishers & Distributors
4753/23 Ansari Road, Daryaganj
New Delhi 110 002

Typeset at
Digigrafics
New Delhi 110 049

Printed at
Salasar Imaging Systems
Delhi 110 035

Contents

Figures

Tables

Acknowledgements

Any new research work is, in itself, a tribute to all those academicians who have contributed to that subject. This work is no exception, and I owe my gratitude to all the past and present writers who have enriched this field and whose names appear in the bibliography.

However, I must put on record my special debts, both academic and individual. In first place are the libraries and archival repositories whose resources I have liberally used. These include the National Archives of India, Nehru Memorial Museum & Library, Ratan Tata Library (Delhi School of Economics, University of Delhi), Central Secretariat Library, Central Library (Jawaharlal Nehru University), all in Delhi; the Maharashtra State Archives, Mumbai; Tamil Nadu State Archives, Chennai; West Bengal State Archives, Kolkata; British Library, London, and; the International Institute of Social History, Amsterdam. Besides, there are several virtual libraries on the internet where I located some very rare and out-of-print works. The online collections that I have utilized in this work mainly came from the Internet Library of Early Journals (University of Oxford); the Online Library of Liberty and the Internet Archive, both in the USA; the Digital Library of India, and the South Asia Resources on the Internet (SARAI, Columbia University).

Next, I would like to pay homage to my late parents—Shri R.S. Garg and Smt. Omwati Garg—who always prided themselves on the smallest of my achievements and encouraged my academic pursuits. My friend, late Dr. P.C. Pradhan, too, always prodded me to complete this work.

No amount of thanks can possibly express my indebtedness towards my Ph.D. supervisor, Prof. Aditya Mukherjee. If some of his ideas are reflected in this work, it is nothing but a tribute to his deep understanding and thorough knowledge of economic history. I also gratefully thank my co-supervisor, Dr. S. Najaf Haider, who not only helped me with his invaluable comments, critiques and suggestions, but also shared his excellent library with me.

Dr. P.J.E. Stevens (UK) shared his excellent researches and immense expertise on the coinage and currencies of the East India Company, and also provided illustrations of a number of coins from his personal collection. Jan Lingen (the Netherlands), likewise, provided the illustration of an extremely rare coin included in this work. Other illustrations have been liberally drawn from an online repository—www.coinarchive.com. My old friends, Dr. S. Ejaz Hussain, Associate Professor, Department of History, Visva-Bharati University and Dr. Shailendra Bhandare, Assistant Keeper (South Asian Numismatics), Heberden Coin Room, Ashmolean Museum (University of Oxford), helped me in more ways than one in finalizing this work. I gratefully acknowledge their help.

Finally, in such works it has become customary to thank one's spouse, but I do not intend to do it for the sake of formality. With all the sincerity at my command, I record my gratitude to my wife, Nurussaba, who always was and remains my best friend, critic, supporter and help, in whatever I do.

SANJAY GARG

Abbreviations

AAR	*Asiatic Annual Register*
BNJ	*British Numismatic Journal*
BPP	*Bengal Past and Present*
CHJ	*The Calcutta Historical Journal*
CEHI	*Cambridge Economic History of India* vol. I (Raychaudhuri and Habib 1982) vol. II (Kumar 1983)
CSSH	*Comparative Studies in Society and History* (Cambridge University Press)
EJ	*The Economic Journal* [of The Royal Economic Society, London]
EHJ	*The Economic Journal* (of The Royal Economic Society)
EHR	*The Economic History Review*
FICCI	Federation of Indian Chambers of Commerce and Industry
FWIHC	*Fort William India House Correspondence*
IA	*The Indian Archives*
IBR	*Indo-British Review: A Journal of History*
IESHR	*Indian Economic and Social History Review*
IHR	*The Indian Historical Review*
IJE	*Indian Journal of Economics*
INC	*Indian Numismatic Chronicle*
IOL/IOLR	India Office Library and Records (now Asia, Pacific and Africa Collection), British Library, London
JAINS	*Journal of Academy of Indian Numismatics and Sigilliography* (Indore)
JAS/ JASB	*Journal of the Asiatic Society* [of Bengal]
JBRS	*Journal of the Bihar Research Society*
JEEH	*Journal of the European Economic History*
JEH	*Journal of the Economic History*
JEIA	*Journal of the East India Association*
JESHO	*Journal of the Economic and Social History of the Orient*

JICH	*Journal of Imperial and Commonwealth History*
JNSI	*Journal of the Numismatic Society of India*
JONS	*Journal of the Oriental Numismatic Society*
JUPHS	*Journal of the United Provinces Historical Society*
MAS	*Modern Asian Studies*
MHJ	*The Medieval History Journal*
MIQ	*Medieval India Quarterly*
MR	*Modern Review*
MSA	Maharashtra State Archives, Mumbai
NAI	National Archives of India, New Delhi
NC	*Numismatic Chronicle*
ND	*Numismatic Digest*
Num. Cir.	*(The) Numismatic Circular*
NS	*Numismatic Supplement* [of the Journal of the Asiatic Society of Bengal]
OC	Original Consultations
OR	Original Receipt
OHRJ	*The Orissa Historical Research Journal*
OIOC	Oriental and India Office Collection (now Asia, Pacific and Africa Collection), British Library, London
ONS	Oriental Numismatic Society
ONSNL	*Oriental Numismatic Society Newsletter*
PIHC	*Proceedings of the Indian History Congress*
PIHRC	*Proceedings of the Indian Historical Records Commission*
Review	*Review* (A Journal of the Fernand Braudel Center, Binghamton University, Binghamton, New York)
SCMB	*Seaby's Coins and Medals Bulletin*
SIH	*Studies in History*
TNSA	Tamil Nadu State Archive, Chennai
WBSA	West Bengal State Archives, Kolkata

Introduction

Currency has always played a key role in the economic development of human society. In India, the monetary system built by the Mughals was marked by its prime feature, viz., a centrally directed system of coinage which formed the core of the Mughal economy. The imperial coinage was unprecedented both in quantity and quality.[1] Besides, the Mughal rulers also considered the right to strike *sikka* (or the coin) as the exclusive prerogative of the sovereign. Both these factors played a deterrent role in the growth of economic activities of European trading companies in India, who had to depend on the mints of the realm for their supply of cash. Further, due to factors such as a favourable balance of trade situation, the absence of a market for European goods in India, and the metal price disparity between India and Europe, these companies were obliged to finance their investments in India by importing precious metals. In doing so, either they sold the imported bullion to Indian dealers, or took it to the imperial mints and got it converted into current coins for their own use.

By the beginning of the eighteenth century, the process of rapid decentralization of the sovereign authority in India had started. The century is described as 'a period of transition in which India had to pass through strain and agony . . . with rapid decline in her economic condition'.[2] The decline of the central authority of the Mughals is equated by some historians, with the sharp downward trend in the Indian economy, which, they hold, had reached its 'lowest ebb' by the mid-eighteenth century.[3] Others counter this 'empire-centric' view with a 'region-centric' approach and cite the development of regional economies during the pre-colonial period as evidence of the vibrancy of the Indian economy.[4] Thus, the eighteenth-century Indian economy has been described variously as symptomatic of decline, development and stasis. This work enters into this debate through an analysis of the prevailing monetary conditions in India. According to Frank Perlin, 'the history of money [in India] from about the last quarter of the 17th century, and especially of the later 18th century—much less is known, assumptions legion, and there is little discussion or research'.[5]

Amidst the decline of the Mughal empire and process of regionalization, the English East India Company emerged as a 'Dominant firm'.[6] In the process of colonization of India by the British, currency proved to be a vital weapon as it directly affected almost every aspect of the economic life of the society.

As a result of the weakness of later Mughal rulers during the eighteenth century, a number of regional powers grew all over India, each with its own distinct coinage. Thus, by the middle of the century, the Indian money market presented a very confusing picture with a large variety of coins in circulation, which were of different kinds and different denominations, minted at different places, on different dates and had no uniform standards of weight and fineness whatsoever. This situation posed a very serious problem before the East India Company for its trade transactions in India. According to K.N. Chaudhuri, 'For a trading organisation that was constantly trans-shipping money and goods from one part of India to another, and was in the position of having to make very large disbursements in local currencies, the multiplicity of rupees and other coins had very serious implications.'[7]

The situation was further aggravated by the sharp decline in the money supply of the East India Company due to 'the cessation of the import of bullion, chiefly silver, from England after 1757'.[8]

The political ascendancy of the East India Company, which started with their earliest establishments in Madras (1639), had also seen its watermark with the grant of the *Diwani* (right of revenue collection) of Bengal, Bihar and Orissa (1765). Thus, during the latter half of the eighteenth century, the ever-growing demand for money by the East India Company for investments, trade as well as other civil and military expenses, coupled with the shortage of money supply, forced it to adopt various currency reforms to cope with the situation. These measures included, the introduction of bimetallism, and curbing the menace of *batta* (agio or discount charged by money changers), etc., on the one hand, and obtaining minting rights from the Mughal ruler and/or the local authority, and procuring charters authorizing the circulation of coins struck by its own mints, etc., on the other. It had by now became crystal clear to the East India Company administrators that 'unless a procedure for standardisation [of currency] was found, its accounts and trade were likely to be in a permanent state of confusion'.[9]

Thus, passing through the phases of 'Prohibition', 'Concession' and 'Administration' of minting activities, the undercurrent of the currency policy of the East India Company was the introduction of a 'uniform currency' in the areas of their domination.

By the close of the seventeenth century, the East India Company was able to consolidate its Indian possessions into three distinct presidencies—Madras, Bombay and Bengal, each under the charge of a Governor or the President. After the Regulating Act of 1773, the Governor of Bengal was made the Governor-General of Bengal with certain supervisory powers over the other two presidencies. From then, the Bengal presidency took a leading role in striving for a uniform currency for its dominions, and its model was followed by the Madras and Bombay presidencies.

Starting from the year 1793, the Supreme Government of the Presidency of Fort William in Bengal passed a series of regulations for currency reform, which finally culminated in the Acts XVII and XXI of 1835 by which a uniform and universal coinage was adopted for the territories of the East India Company.

The study of the process of currency reforms enacted by the East India Company through its various Regulations/Acts, etc., is, therefore, one of the most important aspects for a better understanding of the impact of the changing monetary system on various aspects of the Indian economy during the period under review.

Despite immense importance attached to the subject, the present state of research in this field is less than adequate. Although there had been some excellent studies on the currency system, financial institutions, money market and credit networks during the sixteenth and seventeenth centuries, similar studies for the crucial period of the expansion and consolidation of British rule in India—which had a tremendous overall impact on the Indian economy—have rarely been made. As early as in 1858, while publishing the edited and annotated version of James Prinsep's *Useful Tables*, Edward Thomas had appended a 'Note on the History of the Gold and Silver Currencies of India'.[10] While describing the period of British influence on the currencies of India, he realized that this was 'a subject with which much misunderstanding and some misrepresentation have taken place'.[11] Later, in 1890, while preparing a catalogue of coins in the Madras Museum, Edgar Thurston tried to present a 'History of the Coinage of the Territories of the East India Company in the Indian Peninsula', by dwelling heavily on the records of the Madras mint.[12] In 1893, he contributed a 'Note on the History of the East India Company Coinage from 1753-1835'.[13]

Economic historians have shown a keen interest in unravelling the true picture of the currency situation under British rule. J.C. Sinha, for instance, wrote an article on 'Some Currency Reforms of Hastings'.[14] The results of many such interesting studies have successively been published in various research journals and sometimes included in books dealing with various aspects of economic history, viz., trade, commerce, banking, exchange, prices, agriculture, industries, etc.

An overview of published economic literature reveals that the study of currency under British rule has been either made from the numismatic point of view, where the study is primarily aimed at a detailed description of coins, including the inscriptions, weight, fineness, assay, process of minting, varieties, denominations, etc., or from the point of view of the role of currency being analysed as an essential input for trade, commerce and revenue. Rarely do the two approaches intersect. Besides, it is also felt that in available works, while the 'system' is invariably analysed, the study of the 'process' is generally neglected.

Among the first group are the contributions of Captain F. Pridmore, C.H. Biddulph, Michael Mitchner, Peter Snartt, K.W. Wiggins, Paul Stevens, Shailendra Bhandare and others, while, in the second group, the writings of Bal Krishna, J.C. Sinha, N.K. Sinha, H.R. Ghoshal, Holden Furber, C.U. Wilson, S. Bhattacharya, Sushil Chaudhary, K.N. Chaudhuri, Irfan Habib, Asiya Siddiqi, Aziza Hasan, Om Prakash, P.J. Marshal, C.A. Bayly and John Deyell may be noted as a record.[15] In the second group, the names of three works may be specifically mentioned. B.S. Mallick has published his study on the role of the currency system and indigenous fiscal practices in the English trade in Gujarat and Bengal during the seventeenth century.[16] D.B. Mitra's work on the monetary system in the Bengal Presidency during the period 1757-1835 is based upon some untapped archival sources though it is limited in scope.[17] The latest in this category is the book by Anirban Biswas, which deals with pre-colonial and transitional phase of India's monetary and commercial history, with special reference to Bengal.[18] Though the author laments about the 'paucity of source material', he has used only printed and published primary sources, whereas the vital source material for such a work lies in the unpublished, manuscript archival records.[19]

Although there can be no second thought about the imperative need for either of the two historical approaches, it is felt that the currency history of India during British rule needs to be researched singly and independently on the basis of original sources. The present study thus aims at integrating available numismatic data into the overall monetary structure that emerged under the rule of the East India Company. The study of various internal and external forces which were at work in shaping the monetary structure during the period of our review has also been undertaken with a view to understanding the role of currency in the colonization process of India.

The scheme of chapters adopted for the present work is detailed below.

Chapter 1 deals with the general background about the currency situation prevailing in India around the mid-eighteenth century. While discussing the basic features of this period, such as the collapse of the Mughal monetary system, the multiplicity of coins in circulation, the debasement in currency, the menace of *batta* (rate of discount), etc., the chapter also discusses the post-Plassey scenario and the effects of the changed political situation on the financial policies of India.

Chapter 2 discusses the monetary problems that followed the East India Company's assumption of the *Diwani* of Bengal, Bihar and Orissa in 1765. It focuses on the currency situation arising out of the cessation of bullion imports into Bengal after 1757; the increased demand for money by the East India Company for investments in trade, military expenditure, tribute to England, and funding of the China trade and other Presidencies—all leading to a contraction in money supply. The chapter also studies some of the early measures adopted by the East India Company to improve the currency situation. These include the introduction of bimetallism in 1766 and again in 1769, the establishment of the first European bank—the Bank of Hindustan (1770), and changes in coinage (1771).

The second part of this chapter, namely the diagnosis of the monetary problems of India, begins with the year 1772, when, for the first time, the results of an official inquiry into the monetary problems of Bengal were made public. Sensing the seriousness of the problem, the Directors of the East India Company decided to seek the expert guidance of the well-known political economist, Sir James Steuart (1712-80). Steuart studied the state of monetary derangement in Bengal which 'threatened the vitality of the entire system', and reported his findings to the East India Company in 1772. Steuart's Report made an inquiry into the methods to be adopted for correcting the defects of the currency, for blocking the drains which carried off coins, and for extending circulation by the means of the 'Paper-Credit'. Thus, it offered 'an agenda for economic policies in Bengal'. His recommendations were sent to the Government of Bengal in 1774, which, after the passing of the Regulating Act in 1773, had been instituted as the Supreme Government of the East India Company in India. From this period, the Government of Bengal made steady efforts to effect currency reforms. Preliminary moves towards standardization in coinage were made by it with the decision of 1775 to confine the coinage to a single mint. By 1780, the possibilities of a paper currency were being explored. In 1787, a Committee was appointed to 'Investigate into the Causes of the Scarcity of Silver Coins'. The appointment of a Mint Committee in 1792 was again aimed at the establishment of a coinage which could be commonly accepted as the medium of exchange.

Chapter 3 analyses various regulations passed by the government, and discusses their main objectives, provisions, implementation and effects. During the period between 1793 and 1833, a series of thirty-nine Regulations were passed by the Supreme Government of the East India Company in India. These regulations dealt with various currency reform measures, viz., the reintroduction of bimetallism, prohibition of the circulation of coins other than those minted by the Company, laying down standards and specifications regarding the weight, fineness and assay of coins, declaring a certain specie of coin as the sole legal tender currency within a specified territory, regularization of *batta*, prescribing the rate of exchange between various species of coins, reorganization of mints under the Company's administration, etc. Besides, a set of these regulations also dealt with the penalties for counterfeiting and debasing the coins. These regulations passed by the government had legal validity and the force of law for their effective implementation.

Chapter 4 studies how the Government finally enacted two Acts in 1835 (nos. XVII and XXI) while pursuing a policy of universalization of currency, by which a universal coinage was established for the territories of the East India Company in India. The year 1835, therefore, marks the end of one era and the beginning of another. The Presidency System of Coinage (*c.* 1642-1835) came to an end in 1835 and the era of Imperial Coinage (1835-1947) commenced. The present study also closes with the end of the first era.

Chapter 5 examines the impact that the currency regulations of the East India Company had on the monetary economy of India.

How did these currency measures affect the monetization of society; what was their impact on the fiscal administration of the Company; in what ways did the Company's measures to regulate currency circulation and discount influence the general price structure in the market; how did the Indian credit and banking system react to the growth of colonial credit and the European banking system; and finally, how were these regulations made to serve the trade interests of the Company and the credit money network—are questions that this chapter seeks to explore. Besides, it also specifically examines the socio-economic impact of the closure of mints by the East India Company in different parts of the country.

Thus, this study contrives to present a comprehensive account of the currency policy of the East India Company, which it pursued to establish a uniform currency in India. The process of currency legislations enacted by the Company, the circumstances leading to the adoption of these legislations, as well as the effects of these legislations on the prevailing economic conditions in the country have been analysed with a view to establish a relationship between the stability of the currency *vis-à-vis* the economic colonization of India by the East India Company.

The objective of the present study is not merely to have a 'cause and effect' understanding of the currency reforms carried out by the East India Company but equally, if not more importantly, to delve into the often-overlooked or neglected prognosis of the 'what and how' of its process. For this purpose, the study is based on various legislations enacted by the Company which either directly addressed issues such as currency, coinage and mints or had a bearing on the currency administration of the Company. Therefore, non-legislative currency reforms have been dealt only with relation to their relevance as regards legislative currency reforms.

This study encapsulates the story of Indian currency during the early days of colonial rule about which J.C. Sinha once wrote: 'The bark of Indian currency has sometimes sailed through calm waters but has oftener than not been tossed in stormy seas.'[20]

NOTES

1. Richards 1987: 1.
2. Datta 1978: 12-13.
3. Raychaudhuri, in Kumar 1983: 5.
4. Datta 2004.

5. Perlin 1994a: 276.
6. Kutty 1985: Ch. III – East India Company as a Dominant Firm, 61-175.
7. Chaudhuri 1978: 183.
8. Mitra 1991: 59-60.
9. Chaudhuri 1978: 183.
10. Prinsep 1858: 72-94.
11. Ibid.: 72.
12. Thurston 1890.
13. Thurston 1893: 54-6.
14. Sinha 1924: 74-8.
15. For a detailed discussion on the secondary sources, see 'Secondary Sources: Select Annotated Bibliography', under *Sources.*
16. Mallick 1991.
17. Mitra 1991.
18. Biswas 2007.
19. Ibid.: 15.
20. Sinha 1927: 166.

Money is the worst currency that ever grew among mankind. This sacks cities, this drives men from their homes, this teaches and corrupts the worthiest minds to turn base deeds.

SOPHOCLES (*c.* 497/6 BCE–406/5 BCE),
Greek Poet and Philosopher

CHAPTER 1

The Currency System during the mid-Eighteenth Century

INTRODUCTION

The eighteenth century was the age of revolutionary transformation in India. The first half of the century saw the collapse of the old world, while the second half marked the beginning of the new.[1] With the acquisition of a vast territorial empire in India by the English East India Company during the middle of the eighteenth century, the nature, direction and purpose of British activity underwent a dramatic and lasting transformation.[2] This territorial acquisition by the British has been regarded as a 'triumph' of 'mercantilist colonialism' by Irfan Habib, who links it with the Carnatic Wars (1746-63), and the battles of Plassey (1757) and Buxar (1764).[3] In 1765, the provinces of Bengal, Bihar and Orissa were made over to the East India Company by the Mughal emperor Shah Alam II, and this year has been regarded by the historians as the year of commencement of the monetary history of modern India.[4] Henceforth, the Company's primary objective was to secure as large a revenue-surplus as possible and to transfer that surplus to Britain.[5] The acquisition of the *Diwani* rights of the provinces of Bengal, Bihar and Orissa opened new vistas for the Company where monetary transactions were involved. The Company as a *Diwan* was to directly administer the revenues arising from land rents, the farming of the exclusive privileges, fines and forfeits, and custom duties. While this was the situation in eastern India, the Company's servants in its western and southern Indian possessions were still involved in brisk trading activities combined with territorial expansion. By the mid-eighteenth century, the Company had begun to assert itself over rival European companies and Indian powers alike, and this placed it in a situation from which it could begin to carve out an extended territorial and commercial empire for itself. As the area of the Company's administration and commercial interests expanded, the highly volatile money market posed greater challenges. Under these circumstances, the ability of the Company to adjust to the demands of the prevalent monetary system became one of the essential prerequisites for its successful career.

The currency situation during the mid-eighteenth century was chaotic. The Mughal currency system, which had been established for about 200 years, fragmented along with the disintegration of the Mughal empire. The first and one of the prime features of the currency situation during this period was the multiplicity of coin-types in circulation. The coins issued by various mushroom dynasties and petty states circulated along with other specie. The difference in weight and fineness of these coins was another problem, which, in turn, led to the menace of *batta* (discount) charged by money-changers on the coins of previous years and also on those of other regions/types, etc. Besides, there were some foreign specie in circulation such as crowns from England, France and Germany, ducats and sequins from the Adriatic, and dollars from North America, Spain and Batavia, which were imported by various European companies to finance their investments in India.[6]

The currency situation during the mid-eighteenth century has been described by K.N. Chaudhuri in relation to the bullion trade of the East India Company and minting activities. He, however, observes that with the currency system predominantly consisting of metallic coins, its 'monetary problems . . . could have been made much easier for the merchants to handle had India possessed a uniform currency system.'[7]

MUGHAL MONETARY SYSTEM

The Mughals had a well-organized and sophisticated monetary system. The imperial coinage was unprecedented both in quantity as well as in quality. The entire system was centrally administered and had an in-built mechanism of quality control. As the empire expanded, so did the area of circulation for the rupee, and its copper and gold counterparts.[8] An analysis of the Mughal monetary system, thus, forms a natural backdrop for any study of the monetary problems that emanated from its collapse.[9]

MAIN FEATURES

The features that characterized the Mughal monetary system were as follows:

A. SIKKA: A ROYAL PREROGATIVE

The Mughal rulers held the right to strike *sikka* as *Inter jura Majestatis* (the exclusive prerogative of the sovereign). In fact, *khutba* (the recitation of the ruler's name in the Friday prayers in mosques) and *sikka* (the right to strike coins in one's name) were considered the most unmistakable insignia of sovereignty. The Mughal rulers exercised their right of coinage with responsibility and pride. They tolerated no infringement of this royal prerogative. Thus, in 1692, when the English East India Company attempted to replace the English-style coins issued from their Bombay mint with the prototype of the Mughal coin but bearing the names of the English monarchs—King William III and Queen Mary—in Persian, it drew the displeasure of the Mughal emperor Aurangzeb (1658-1707). He took immediate steps to check this encroachment on the sovereign prerogative. A special emissary, Khafi Khan, was sent to Bombay to investigate this and various other alleged delinquencies of the Company. The Company explained their act of coining money in their own king's name by stating that they had to purchase investments at places where the Mughal money was not accepted. However, due to strong opposition from the Mughal emissary, the coinage of this new coin-type (of which a few specimens still exist), was stopped by the Company once and for all.[10]

B. TRIMETALLISM AND METALLIC STANDARD

In the standard Mughal currency system, the three basic coins were the *muhr* of gold, the rupee of silver and the *dam* of copper. However, in spite of there being a formal trimetallism with three parallel standards, there was, in actual practice, only one metal that reigned supreme at one time; it was copper in the sixteenth century and silver in the seventeenth. During the reign of Akbar (1556-1605), copper was adopted both as the money of account and the standard of value. Later, in the seventeenth century, the silver rupee firmly established itself as the chief medium of exchange in northern and eastern India. South India had a tradition of a gold-based currency system and was largely unaffected by the silver currency of northern India. The Deccan was then in a process of transition from a gold to a silver-based system. Thus, broadly speaking, gold and silver coins came to be recognized as the common measure of value in south and north India, respectively, at the time when they came under the sway of the English Company.

Copper continued to act as a subsidiary coinage both in north and south India. Besides, there were also non-metallic currencies such as *cowries* in Bengal and Orissa, and *badam* (almonds) in Gujarat and the western coast.

C. OPEN COINAGE

The mints of the Mughal empire were open to all. Anyone could get his non-official coins or bullion converted into standard coins by paying the prescribed mint charges and seignorage. In this regard, the state itself was formally no different from any member of the public except that its resource-base was naturally larger than that of any private individual and the minting of its bullion would get priority.[11] The seignorage charged on coining constituted an important source of state revenue. Aurangzeb is said to have derived a profit of Rs. 11 lakh per annum from his Surat mint alone.[12] In order to meet the requirement of standard coins, the network of Mughal mints was gradually extended to cover the entire length and breadth of the empire. Thus, by the turn of the seventeenth century, rupees bearing the name of Aurangzeb and issued from as many as ninety-four mints have been recorded so far. However, not all of these were regular mints. Some of them were Camp Mints, which accompanied the imperial armies and issued coins primarily for disbursement to the troops. The regular mints were chiefly located in port cities like Surat, provincial capitals like Ahmedabad, Ajmer and Multan, resource centres for metals like Narnol, and frontier towns like Kabul and Peshawar, as well as in all other important towns of the empire.

D. UNIFORMITY OF COIN-STANDARD

Under Mughal rule, the weight and fineness standards of coins were strictly maintained. The gold *muhr* weighed 169 grains (10.95 g) troy and was practically unalloyed. The weight of the silver rupee was initially 178 grains (11.53 g) but was later raised to 180 grains (11.66 g) by Aurangzeb. The alloy content in the rupee was never more than 4 per cent. The copper *dam* weighed 323 grains (20.93 g) till 1663-4 when its weight was reduced to 215.34 grains (13.95 g; about ⅔ of the original weight). The imperial mints located throughout the empire struck coins to the same standard.

E. CENTRALIZED CONTROL OF PRODUCTION

The managerial functions of the Mughal mints were the responsibility of the state. The mint workers were state employees and the mint an imperial *karkhana* (or workshop). However, during the reign of Farrukhsiyar, his *Diwan*, Ratan Chand, instituted the system of farming out mints to the highest bidder. This system brought with it some inherent evils which eventually led to the chaotic monetary situation witnessed during the mid-eighteenth century. A common feature in both the systems of mint-management (state and farming) was that the actual operation of the mint and its production was based on the free market's demand for the coined money as a medium of exchange.

F. HIGH VELOCITY

As coins issued from various mints maintained a uniform standard, the Mughal currency circulated freely and uniformly from Kabul to Dacca and from Surat to Madras. Besides, the land tax demand was expressed in money terms; the salary of the officials and military was paid in cash (the *jagir* system was also prevalent, but even in them, the revenue was often collected in cash); and the commodity sales 'in an intensifying network of markets must, altogether, have increased the number and velocity of coins in circulation'.[13] According to John Deyell, this universality of Mughal currency was made possible by displacement of the local coinage, though in some cases such as Malwa and Gujarat, the Mughal state assimilated the main features of the local currency in the imperial coinage.[14] The silver *mahmudis* of Gujarat and the square copper coins of Malwa issued after the annexation of these provinces to the Mughal empire can be cited as examples.[15] In this connection, the old principle that only precious metals coins travelled, while base metals coins remained confined to their locale of issue, can definitely be rejected with the overwhelming evidence of coin hoards. Mughal coinage of all denominations had universal acceptability. According to Deyell, 'Coinage of any mint was accepted without prejudice, and the product of a frontier mint might travel clear to the other end of the empire through a myriad of intermediate exchange. . . . Mughal currency *had* currency.'[16]

G. DEPENDENCE ON IMPORTS

An important feature of the Indian monetary system during the Mughal period was its overwhelming dependence on foreign sources for supplies of coinage metals. The domestic production of precious metals was negligible; and foreign trade was the principal channel through which these metals were obtained for coinage and other uses. The third coinage metal, copper, was also obtained partly through trade. Factors such as the discovery and extensive working of the silver mines in the Spanish America from the sixteenth century onwards, the favourable balance of trade position of the East, and the metal price disparity between the East and the West, all helped India to receive a lion's share of precious metals in the international trade. The increasing international trade brought even larger quantities of precious metals into India. To quote the French physician, François Bernier, who visited India during 1656-68: '. . . gold and silver, after circulating in every other quarter of the globe, came at length to be swallowed up, lost in some measure in Hindoustan'[17]—a symbolic but very significant statement indeed.

During the seventeenth and the early part of the eighteenth century, an important medium through which foreign metals flowed into India were the European trading companies—the English, Dutch and, to a limited extent, the French East India Company.[18] To finance

TABLE 1.1: QUANTITY OF SILVER AND GOLD EXPORTED BY THE ENGLISH EAST INDIA COMPANY, 1701-60

	Pure Silver (kg.)	Pure Gold (kg.)
1701-5	166,885	–
1706-10	173,833	141.11
1711-15	167,503	145.79
1716-20	250,857	–
1721-5	289,349	–
1726-30	261,401	–
1731-5	260,102	–
1736-40	260,378	
1741-5	257,882	–
1746-50	366,289	–
1751-5	398,041	–
1756-60	193,458	–

Source: Chaudhuri 1978: Table A.7, 177.

their investments in India, these companies imported large quantities of precious metals.[19] The effect of the exportation of treasure by the English East India Company on the demand and price of precious metals in England has been recorded by Sir Issac Newton, then the Master of the London Mint, in the following words: 'When ships are lading for the East Indies, the demand for silver for exportation raises the price to $5^s 6^d$ or $5^s 8^d$ per ounce or above.'[20]

As silver was generally the official standard of currency in the East Indies as well as in China, a substantial portion of the Company's treasure was either sent in silver bars or foreign silver coins.

However, the import of precious metals from other channels also continued during the same period and we find the following figures quoted in the *Annual Register*:

TABLE 1.2: EXPORT OF GOLD AND SILVER TO INDIA, 1753-64

	Silver		Gold	
	Oz.	Kg.	Oz.	Kg.
1753 to 1758	1,05,56,748	2,99,279	1,18,127	3,349
1759 to 1764	14,11,116	40,005	9,760	277

Source: Annual Register, vol. 7 (December 1764), 68.

Thus, the Mughal monetary system, 'like the state which created it . . . was powerful, flexible, pervasive and long-lived'.[21] Over two centuries of Mughal rule, the monetization of society had risen to a level that was unprecedented. During this period, the subsistence economy of Indian villages where the 'community lived by itself, peasants grew and consumed, artisans produced and bartered' steadily drifted to become an exchange economy when 'money penetrated the agrarian sector of the Mughal empire through the twin process of state driven commerce and direct production for the market'.[22] Likewise, in the urban centres, too, money use struck deeper roots.[23] Thus, the Mughal economy was highly monetized.

Collapse of Mughal Rule

'All theories of the eighteenth century must necessarily start with the problem of the economics of the Mughal Empire before its decline.'[24] Thus, it would be in the fitness of things if the factors responsible for the collapse of the Mughal monetary system are discussed before the survey of the currency situation in the mid-eighteenth century.

The collapse of the highly centralized monetary system of the Mughals during the eighteenth century is directly linked to the disintegration of the Mughal empire itself. Aurangzeb was the last of the powerful Mughal emperors. During his rule, the boundaries of the Mughal empire were stretched to their maximum extent. However, it is said that towards the end of his reign, Aurangzeb realized that his long reign of fifty years had been a colossal failure. He is reported to have uttered the morose foreboding:

Az ma-ast hamah fasad baqi
(After me will come the deluge)

Between 1707 and 1720, the centralized structure of the empire broke apart. During the next twenty-five years, the domains of the Mughal authority were squeezed to the environs of Delhi. None of the successors of Aurangzeb proved men of any ability and the throne of Delhi was occupied by a series of *rois fainéants* (lit. 'lazy kings') under whose feeble rule the disintegration of the empire proceeded rapidly. These puppet kings were neither able to curb the rebellions in the provinces nor check the foreign invasions. As a result, rival networks of power got institutionalized throughout India, and the political authority and military power shifted from the 'centre to the periphery'.

In the first group of these neo-states were the governors of the Mughal provinces of the Deccan, Bengal and Awadh, who, with the first sign of weakening of the central authority, asserted their independence.[25]

In the Deccan, the Mughal viceroy, Zulfiqar Khan, entitled Asafjah Nizam-ul-Mulk, laid the foundation of his own dynastic rule in Hyderabad. The province held by him was, at one time, estimated to yield Rs. 18 crore per annum.

In Bengal, Murshid Quli Khan (d. 1727) held the dual position of the *Nazim* (Governor) and the *Diwan* (Revenue Collector). His successors acquired hereditary authority over Bengal, Bihar and Orissa, and the sovereignty of the Mughal emperor over this region practically came to an end.

In the Gangetic plains, Muhammad Amin, entitled Burhan-ud-din Sa'adat Khan, asserted his sway over a vast area once he was appointed the Mughal *Subahdar* (Provincial Governor) of Awadh in 1720. His successor and son-in-law, Safdarjung, was appointed *Wazir* (Prime Minister) by Muhammad Shah. Henceforth, his successors hereditarily held the title *Nawab Wazir* of Awadh and dropped even this nominal allegiance to the Mughal emperor in 1819.

The second group comprised revivalist powers who were once subjugated by the Mughals but were always looking for an opportunity to reassert their independence.[26] The Sikhs in the Punjab were one such power. Punjab, the scene of many turmoils during the eighteenth century, lay in the route of foreign invaders like Nadir Shah (1738-9) and later, Ahmad Shah Abdali (1748-61). As a result, its inhabitants suffered looting and destruction over a considerable period of time.[27] However, after the removal of Abdali from the scene, the Sikhs recovered their lost territories and, by 1764, the entire tract between the Jhelum and Sutlej was being ruled by the Sikh chieftains.

The Marathas, under the able leadership of Shivaji, were able to carve out an independent kingdom during the lifetime of Aurangzeb. The armies of Shivaji reached as far as the Karnataka in 1676. After his death (1680) Aurangzeb was temporarily successful in curbing the rise of the Marathas when he captured Sambhaji, the son and successor of Shivaji. However, after the death of Aurangzeb, the Marathas consolidated their position once again under Balaji Vishwanath, the Peshwa or Prime Minister of Sambhaji's son and successor, Shahu. Later, the office of the Peshwa became hereditary. Under the Peshwas, a great Maratha confederacy with its headquarters at Pune was founded. Together, the Maratha chiefs held large territories in the Deccan, Gujarat, Malwa, Bundelkhand, lower Bengal and Orissa. In north India, the Marathas raided as far as the Punjab.[28] With the defeat of the Maratha army in the third battle of Panipat (1761), the power of the Peshwa as the head of the confederacy declined. The Marathas were now grouped into five clans with rather undefined, separate territories. These were: the Peshwa at Pune, the Bhonslas at Nagpur, the Sindhias at Gwalior, the Holkars at Indore and the Gaekwads at Baroda.

The rulers of a large number of Rajput states had served as traditional allies of the Great Mughals. They did not take much advantage of the disintegration of the Mughal empire except for seizing portions of imperial domains which were contiguous with their own territories, or by increasing their political clout in the imperial politics in Delhi. As the clan system was still a dominant factor in these Rajput states, the disappearance of the imperial authority intensified clan rivalry.

The two leading Rajput clans at the beginning of the eighteenth century were the Rathors of Marwar (Jodhpur) and the Kachhawahas of Amber (Jaipur). The Ranas of Mewar, who had enjoyed political primacy among the Rajput states in pre-Mughal times, had fallen into internal dissensions and the state itself finally submitted to British suzerainty in 1818.

The Jats were the peace-loving cultivators of the *doab* region. During Aurangzeb's reign, they rebelled several times due to the oppressive behaviour of local authorities. Later, they consolidated their position under their leader, Churaman (1695-1721), and, in due course, converted themselves into a formidable political force. They occupied an extensive tract between Agra and Delhi, and set-up their headquarters at Bharatpur. Their political ascendancy continued under Churaman's successor, Badan Singh (1721-56), who was recognized as a Raja by the Mughal emperor, Ahmad Shah (1748-54). Badan Singh was succeeded by his adopted son, Surajmal (1756-63), who formally adopted the title of *Maharaja*. At the time of Surajmal's death, his annual revenue amounted to Rs. 175 lakh and he left a reserve fund of Rs. 10 crore.[29]

Another martial race that asserted its independence from Mughal authority in north India was the Rohillas. They occupied a large tract of land north of the Ganges that extended up to the foothills of the Himalayas.

The region between the kingdom of Awadh and the Mughal capital was dominated by the Afghans and they, too, succeeded in carving out an independent principality for themselves during the period of the disintegration of the Mughal empire.[30] Muhammad Khan Bangash (d. 1743) established his seat of power at Farrukhabad and despite the Nawab of Awadh's strong opposition, the Bangash retained their status as powerful *jagirdars*.

The independence of local governors, the rise of warrior states and the re-assertion of sovereignty by regional dynasties singly and simultaneously dismembered the empire of the Great Mughals. And, to add to the confusion, the European powers that had come to India for trade now began to assume a political character by expanding their territorial possessions and strengthening their strongholds. The Portuguese, Dutch, Danes, French and the British—all took part in this eighteenth-century power struggle. On the west coast, the Portuguese held Diu, Daman, Bassien, Chaul and Goa; the English held Bombay and Surat, while the Dutch held Cochin. On the east coast, the English held Bimlipatan, Pulicat, Madras and Negapatnam; the French held Pondicherry, Arcot, Mahe, Balasore and Masulipatam, while the Danes were confined to Tranquebar. In Bengal, the English held Calcutta while the French held Chandernagore. By the mid-eighteenth century, among all the European trading companies, the English East India Company emerged to play a dominant role in the politics and economy of India.

The dissolution of the Mughal empire is seen as a notable phenomenon of the eighteenth century.[31] Yet there is a disagreement on the role played by different socio-economic and political factors in bringing about this dissolution. Historians like William Irvine and Jadunath Sarkar project this decline in terms of a personal deterioration of the kings and nobles.[32] For example, it may be argued that had Aurangzeb left successors of his own mental and moral stature, whether the process of disintegration of the Mughal empire could have been stalled? Lane-Poole answers in negative. According to him, 'The disease was too far advanced for even the most heroic surgery.'[33] However, this and several other similar 'mono-causal' theories of the decline of the Mughal empire are now being replaced by institutional, economic and organizational structure analyses of the empire.[34] These arguments clearly demonstrate that economic factors such as the bankruptcy of the Mughal government due to incessant warfare, the disruption of trade and industry due to unstable political conditions, the oppression of cultivators by zamindars by means of increased taxation, and the 'aristocratization' of the *mansabdars*, were, amongst others, no less responsible for the decline of the Mughal empire.

An important economic factor that played a catalytic role in the decline of the Mughal empire was, however, the role of the bankers—the *sahukars*, *sarrafs* and *mahajans*. Karen Leonard has argued that 'Indigenous banking firms were indispensable allies of the Mughal state, and the great firms' diversion of resources, both credit and trade in the Indian subcontinent, contributed to the downfall of the empire.'[35]

Thus, the decline of the central structure of the Mughal empire was more in the form of 'structural changes', which, in turn, were the result of a number of politico-economic factors. Once the process of decline and disintegration of the empire was set in motion, the currency system built by it could not remain unaffected.

Decline of the Mughal Empire and the Money Market

Richards observes that the 'monetary system and the state structures underwent a similar transition when the Mughal Empire broke up in the second and third decade of the eighteenth century'.[36] The fall of the Mughal empire and the political ascendancy of various Indian and European powers during the eighteenth century was almost simultaneous. In this scramble for power, *sikka*, or the right to coinage, became the 'right-most-cherished' by the Indian claimants as an expression of their *de jure* sovereignty. The European companies, on the other hand, sought this right to expand their economic activities. As a result of the fall of the Mughal empire, the number of mint-towns grew rapidly in India. In the first category were the mints that issued coins of the Mughal prototype. These included existing Mughal mints such at Agra, Lahore, Multan, Ahmedabad, Ajmer, Burhanpur, Itawah, etc., that were now controlled by neo-claimants of the territorial authority, as well as a large number of newly set-up mints like Benares, Farrukhabad, Mathura, Panipat, Jammu, Hardwar, Baroda, etc. The vast majority of these mint-towns were the headquarters of newly 'independent' regional and local rulers, who continued to produce coins in the name of Emperor Shah Alam II. Rohilkhand, Bundelkhand and the Jat territories were notable for clusters of new mint-towns of this sort. The second category of mints issued coins in the name of independent authorities, though sometimes based on the Mughal prototype. These included the Sikh mints at Amritsar and Anandgarh, as well as the Afghan mints at Kabul and Bahawalpur. Then, there were also mints that over a period of time, transcended from issuing coins in the name of the Mughal emperor, to that of the new authority.[37]

As a result of this proliferation of mints, the market was filled with a large variety of coins of different denominations, with different weights and purity—often debased and rudely fashioned, minted at different places on different dates and fetching differing values. The bullion imported by the European trading companies in the form of coined money of varied European origins also circulated in the market, making the situation worse. The Mughal currency gradually lost its basic quality of 'currency'.[38] The coins of one region were either refused in the other region, or received at a lower value. Though a majority of coins in circulation still bore the name of the Mughal emperor, these were reduced to the state of merely being 'coined bullion'.

ADVENT OF THE BRITISH RULE

The currency was 'the most supreme desiderata in the economy of the Indian people when they came, in the middle of the eighteenth century, under the sway of the British'.[39] The gradual transformation of the English traders into masters of the land is the story of their expanding control over the Indian fiscal economy. In the early years of their connection with India, the Company was obliged to finance its purchases, or 'investment', by importing precious metals, called 'treasure' in official records, both in the form of bullion as well as coined money of varied European origins.

During the early days of the East India Company's trade with India, the treasure imported by them was either sold to bullion merchants situated in the port cities, or taken to the imperial mints to be converted into the coins of the realm. Both the systems proved to be unsatisfactory for the English. While the bullion merchants were always able to strike a deal which under-valued the metal being offered for sale, the mints, on the other hand, kept the treasure idle for some time before it was converted into *sikka*. The English, who were always in the need of ready cash for their investment had, therefore, from the very early days, aspired to appropriate to themselves the minting rights in the land of their trade.

Early Minting Activities of the East India Company: Imitation and Innovation

A. THE COROMANDEL

(i) Armagaon

The first mint established by the English East India Company on Indian soil was at Armagaon in south India. The Armagaon Factory was established in January 1626 under the authority of the local Naik ruler, who also permitted the Company 'to stamp us both *pagodas* and *fanams* also in our own house, paying 1½ per cent'.[40]

(ii) Fort St. George

Soon thereafter, in 1639, the East India Company obtained from the Raja of Chandragiri the permission to build a fort and mint at Madraspatam, or Chinapatam as it was also known. The minting rights granted to the East India Company read:

> Also the said English Company shall perpetually Injoy the priviledges of mintage, without paying any Dewes [dues] or dutyes [*sic*] whatsoever, more than the ordinary wages or hire unto those that shall Quoyne [coin] the moneyes.[41]

The Company, in 1692, was able to obtain the authority to mint silver rupees at Madras from the Mughal prince, Kambaksh, though, initially, for use in its trade with Bengal.

(iii) Fort St. David/Cuddalore

In 1690, the English had purchased from the Marathas the Fort of Tegnapatam, situated on the coast about 12 miles from Pondicherry, along with its surrounding area including the township of Cuddalore. Among the other conditions of sale, the minting rights were also acquired by the Company. It was permitted to 'Coyn [coin] money either our Royall Stamp or Such other as they shall Judge convenient, both in Silver or Gold and that no imposition, Custome or Junckan be at any time lay'd thereon. . . .'[42]

The Fort was renamed Fort St. David and was placed under a deputy governor, subordinate to Fort St. George (Madras). In a short span of time, a mint was established at Cuddalore, which started minting gold *pagodas* and *fanams* referred to as *Pollicatt* and *Mullandore,* respectively, in the records. In 1692, the Cuddalore mint was shifted to Fort St. David where it worked up to 1703-4. The Fort mint, thereafter, fell into disuse and was revived only in 1731.

In 1747, another mint was opened at Pettah at Cuddalore, which mainly struck Arcot rupees for consumption in the Bengal trade.

(iv) Chintadripet

In July 1742, a mint of the Nawab of Arcot which was located at Chintadripet, about 1 mile outside the walls of Fort St. George, was acquired by the Company. Later, through a *sanad* (grant) dated 4 November 1742, issued under the seal of Nawab Sa'adat-ullah Khan of Arcot, the grant of five villages and the privilege of a mint at Chintadripet to the Company was confirmed.

During the Anglo-French War, Madras was surrendered by the British to the French on 10 September 1746 and, consequently, the minting operations of both Fort St. George (or the Town mint) and the Chintadripet mint were suspended. The Coromandel coast headquarters of the Company were shifted to Fort St. David.

B. THE WESTERN COAST: SURAT AND BOMBAY

The earliest settlement of the English East India Company on the western coast of India was at Surat. A Factory was established here in December 1612 under a Charter obtained from the Mughal emperor, Jahangir (1605-27). Under the Mughals, Surat was a mint town for gold, silver and copper coinage. However, prior to the arrival of the East India Company, the mint had been closed and the first English Factory was established in the old Mughal mint house. The Mughal mint was revived in about 1618. Consequently, the English traders who were thus far able to discharge their debt in 'reales of eight' or Spanish dollars and other acceptable foreign coins were now forced to get their treasures converted into current coins at the Mughal mint, as the 'exportation of royalls, through occation of a mint erected in this towne being utterly debarred'.[43]

On 27 March 1668, the island of Bombay, some 150 miles south of Surat, was transferred from the Crown to the East India Company. The island, earlier a Portuguese possession, already had a coin system introduced by them when the East India Company took it over. Under the authorization of the Court of Directors, a mint was established in Bombay in 1672. It produced coins in gold, silver, copper and tin, bearing English designs and legend. However, as these coins had a limited circulation, the East India Company continued to send its treasure to the Mughal mints at Surat and Ahmedabad to be converted into coins of the Mughal pattern. Besides, depending upon their expediency, they also bought Mughal rupees directly from the brokers.

In order to extend the circulation of the coins minted in their Bombay mint, the East India Company attempted to issue rupee coins on the Mughal pattern in 1693. In their attempt, the English authorities were perhaps emboldened by the permission to mint silver rupees at Madras that had been granted to them in 1692. The coins issued from Bombay bore the names and titles of the English king, William III, and Queen Mary in the Persian script. The reigning Mughal emperor, Aurangzeb, took strong objection to this encroachment on the royal prerogative of the sovereign and the English authorities had to withdraw their issue in the teeth of opposition.

In 1713, the Court of Directors instructed the Bombay government to coin silver rupees as per the Surat standard. The despatch read:

> We expect you encourage our own mint at Bombay by coining there of the same weight and fineness with those at Surat, or very near it. If you make them finer, we shall lose by it and therefore you must be very careful to prevent it. If coarser, they will get an ill character and very likely if one or two per cent worse, they will be undervalued to three or four per cent.

Therefore they should be the same; and though at first the shroffs may endeavour to decry them, yet in time the rupee will retrieve and afterwards preserve their reputation, as experience tells us those have which were coined at Madras.[44]

The instructions of the Court implied that at Bombay too, like at Madras, rupees of the Mughal prototype be coined. As the Bombay government had invited the wrath of the Mughal emperor in the not very distant past in an attempt to issue coins on the Mughal pattern, they decided to tread very cautiously this time.

To obtain minting rights at Bombay, an embassy was sent in 1715 to the court of the Mughal emperor, Farrukhsiyar (1712-19). In its petition to the emperor, the Company stated: 'That on the island of Bombay belonging to the English, European siccaes are current, they request that, according to the custom of Madras, they may at Bombay coin [Mughal] siccaes.'[45]

The coveted permission to mint Mughal-style coins at Bombay was granted on 6 January 1717. It read: 'On the island of Bombay let there be the glorious stamp on the siccaes. Coined there passing them current as all other siccaes are throughout the Empire.'[46]

The new 'Bombay Sicca' struck by the Company soon got currency and passed in the markets in and around Bombay without any objection. Encouraged by its ready acceptance, the Company, which had initially only coined its own bullion, started accepting private bullion for coinage in August 1719.

C. BENGAL

The foundations of the English establishments in Bengal can be traced back to 1651 when a factory was opened at Hughli. Earlier in 1633, two factories, Hariharpur and Balasore, were established on the Orissan coast. To meet its requirements of coined money for investments in Bengal and Orissa, the East India Company had to import coins from Madras and Surat. Besides, they also made use of the Mughal mint at Rajmahal (Akbarnagar) to get their bullion converted into coins. The English authorities, who by their experiences in Madras and Bombay had become aware of the benefits of having a mint at the seat of their establishment, thought it prudent to have a similar privilege in Bengal too. Thus, from an early date, they endeavoured to acquire minting rights in Bengal.

The first attempt in this direction was made in 1698 when one Stanley was deputed to the court of the Mughal prince, Azim-us-Shan, grandson of Aurangzeb and the governor of the Bengal Subah.

The object of his mission was to secure, among other privileges, the permission to establish a mint at Hughli. However, this mission proved abortive. Again, in 1708, an attempt was made to secure permission from Zia-ud-din, the Mughal Governor of Hughli, to establish a mint. Nothing resulted from this attempt either.

In 1717, a *sanad* was obtained from the Mughal ruler, Farrukhsiyar, which permitted the East India Company to use the Mughal mint at Murshidabad for three days in a week to coin their bullion. This scheme, however, could never be implemented due to the strong opposition of Murshid Quli Khan, the Nawab of Bengal. The local money-changers, too, exercised 'control over the currency of Bengal, thwarting the English Company's desire to establish a mint at Calcutta, even though the amounts of silver brought annually from London rose from £75,000 (*c.* 1713) to £100,000 (*c.* 1743).[47] Thus, up to 1757, almost the entire coin requirement for the Company's trade in Bengal was met by the Madras mint. Silver imported from Europe was converted into coins by employing various methods, viz.:

I. If the ship calls at Madras, the silver may be coined in the mint there into Madras rupees.
II. It may be sold at Madras in exchange for Arcot rupees.
III. It may be carried to Bengal, and there sold for sicca rupees.[48]

On 7 February 1757, the East India Company concluded a treaty with Siraj-ud-daulah, the Nawab of Bengal, who was struggling to secure his position. The treaty granted permission to the East India Company to establish a mint at Calcutta. However, before any progress could be made in this direction, Siraj-ud-daulah was deposed and replaced by Mir Jafar. The new Nawab of Bengal granted more extensive privileges to the East India Company, thus facilitating the establishment of the Calcutta mint. Consequently, in August 1757, the Company's mint was established in Calcutta.[49]

FEATURES OF INDIAN MONEY MARKET IN *c.* MID-EIGHTEENTH CENTURY

Money of Account and Currency

A. THE COROMANDEL

When the East India Company founded establishments on the Coromandel coast, the coinage of southern India consisted extensively of gold and copper coins. Of gold, there were two denominations: the *hun* (also called *varaha* or *pagoda*; 50 to 60 grains/3.23 to 3.88 g in weight) and the *fanam* (3 to 5 grains/0.19 to 0.32 g). Copper coins were called *kasu* (or 'cash' in English records). The Company's account of the Coromandel coast was kept in *pagodas* and *fanams.* Originally, cash appears to have been money of account but by the middle of the seventeenth century (1660-1), it was an actual coin. 80 cash exchanged for one *fanam* and 36 *fanams* for one *pagoda*.

Towards the close of the seventeenth century following the Mughal conquest of Golconda and Bijapur in 1687, the silver rupee was introduced into the Carnatic. With its disbursement in payment to Mughal troops, the rupee became firmly established in centres such as Arcot and Trichinopoly.

B. THE WESTERN COAST

By the mid-eighteenth century, the western coast areas had completed the transition from gold to a silver-based monetary system, which had begun in around the 1630s. V.G. Kale, writing about the money market in Maharashtra during this period, observes:

> Gold coin had almost gone out of use as currency and *mohurs* of various makes were sold and purchased merely as bullion. The gold *hon* which was extensively employed in Maharashtra in payments, as a measure of value and money of account, in the 17th century, had ceased to function in that capacity and only the rupee coin had established itself as the only metallic currency in universal use.[50]

Of the various sorts of silver rupees of native and foreign origin, the most commonly used specie was the silver rupee coined at Surat in the name of the Mughal emperor. The Surat mint was operated by the Nawab of Surat. In 1717, the English had secured the coining rights at Bombay from the Mughal emperor, Farrukhsiyar. However, the silver rupees coined at Bombay were confined to the island itself; for their trade outside Bombay, the Company either bought Mughal rupees from brokers or continued the custom of sending their silver to the Surat mint.[51]

As the importance of Bombay and its trade developed, silver rupees of different issues and varying qualities circulated in the island. Many were inferior in value to the Bombay or Surat rupee. These rupees of sorts were bought up by the shroffs on the mainland at an unreasonable discount and then imported to Bombay where they passed in payment for goods at a lesser discount or at par. This practice was put to an end by the English East India Company in 1733 by declaring the Bombay and Surat rupee as the sole tender for payment on the island. Under the new arrangement, any person having more than Rs. 10 of any coin or bullion other than Bombay or Surat was required to bring them to the Company's mint where he could exchange them at their real value, by paying 1 per cent for re-coinage.[52] This practice, however, could not continue for long because of the fact that while the English mint at Bombay, especially after 1738, issued silver rupees of standard weight (179 grain/11.60 g troy) and fineness, no such regulation was imposed on the coins minted at Surat. As a result, merchants found it more profitable to remit their holdings to Surat where they received more rupees in return than at Bombay. As the English started suffering losses, they suspended their minting activities at Bombay in 1778.

In the native money market, accounts were kept in *taka*, and, on an average, four of these were exchanged for a rupee.[53]

C. BENGAL

Sicca—Coin and the Weight: In the mid-eighteenth century, the Bengal silver rupee was the standard unit of value. The most recognized specie among the horde of rupees in circulation was the Murshidabad rupee. It had a weight of 10 *masha* (or 179.66 grain troy =11.60 g) and a fineness of 98/100. In Bengal, 10 *masha* was also a unit of bazaar weight called a *sicca*. Thus, a newly-coined rupee of full standard was both a denomination of money and a denomination of real weight. The sicca weight was divided into 16 *anna*, one *anna* being equal to 12 *pice* in exchange. A Sicca rupee, therefore, meant a coin whose weight was equal to one sicca or 16 *annas* or 10 *masha*.

Sanwat Rupee: One frequently comes across the term 'Sunaut' in the East India Company records. The origin of this term lies in the impression of the regnal year (or *San-i Julus*) of the Mughal emperor on coins. Thus, a rupee issued in the 4th regnal year of the emperor was called '4 *sun* (or *san*) sicca'. The regnal year commenced each year on the anniversary of the enthronement of the king, so it did not usually synchronize with the Hijri year, which was also inscribed on the coins. Coins issued in the same Hijri year occur with different regnal years.

When a rupee passed on from its sicca rating of the first year to 3 per cent and 5 per cent *batta* for the second and third years respectively, it was termed as *sanwat* (literally 'a coin of years', *sanwat* being the plural of *sanat* or year).

Money of Account: Faced with the problem of varying values for different specie of the same denomination, the East India Company kept its accounts in an imaginary coin termed as the Current Rupee from the early days of its commerce in Bengal.[54] To facilitate accounting, all specie of rupees of differing standards, weights and fineness, as well as siccas reduced by *batta*, were measured against this Current Rupee. Thus, 100 sicca rupees were rated equivalent to 116 Current Rupees in the first year of their circulation. In the second year, they equalled 113 Current Rupees while in the third year and thereafter, they were valued at 111 Current Rupees.

While the Current Rupee was a money of account of the East India Company, in local practice, it was expressed as *das* (ten) *masha*. It signified any rupee weighing 10 *masha* weight and having standard sicca fineness. In actual value, the *das masha* rupee was 10 per cent higher than the Current Rupee of the East India Company's accounting systems.

Multiplicity of Coins in Circulation

One of the most striking features of the currency situation during the mid-eighteenth century was the multiplicity of coins in circulation. With the disintegration of the Mughal empire, several regional powers established their independence in different parts of India.

> In the general scramble for independence . . . the right to coinage, as one of the most unmistakable insignia of sovereignty, became the right most cherished by the political adventurers of the times. It was also the last privilege to which the falling dynasties clung and was also the first to which the adventurers rising to power aspired.[55]

As a result, the market was soon filled with a large variety of circulating media.

With the worsening of the situation, there arose a condition where not only different kinds of coins circulated in different regions but, even in the same region (district or *moffusil*), different commodities had to be purchased with different kinds of coins of the same denomination. Thus, in Bengal, where the silver rupee was the standard circulating media, commodities of daily need such as rice, *ghee* and cloth were sold in different specie of rupees in different districts.[56] For example, in Jessore, trade in grains, betel-nuts, sugar, jaggery, and coconut was carried on in *siccas*; trade in cloth, oil, pepper and turmeric in Murshidabad *sanwats*; and trade in salt in French *Arcots*. In Bishnupur, *das mashas* were used for trade in grain, tobacco and jaggery; and *Arcots* for trade in cloth.[57] The economy, thus, presented a curious phenomenon where the large presence of cash in the market only restricted the exchange economy.

Debasement in Currency

The multiplicity of coins would not have been a matter of much concern had the issuers of various specie of coins maintained a common standard for the coins of the same denomination by sticking to the original Mughal coin-standard. This, however, was not expected. Thus, a large variety of coins of a single denomination were found circulating in various stages of debasement. 'Given the different degrees of debasement, the currency necessarily lost its primary quality of general and ready acceptability.'[58] The evil of debasement in the coinage manifested itself in two ways; first, by a deficient pure metal content or increased alloy content in a coin of full weight. Writing in 1775, Philip Francis noted: 'In some of them, the alloy is equal to forty per cent upon the weight. From the state of Baseness to the Purity of the Sicca, the Degrees are innumerable.'[59] The second form of debasement was by issuing underweight coins. In the former situation, the content of the coins belied the supposed value of its denomination, thus turning the coins into a commodity of merchandize, while, in the latter situation, the coin seized to be 'currency by tale' to act as a ready means of exchange.[60]

Menace of *Batta*

With the multiplicity of coins in circulation and the evil of debasement, there arose an exceedingly complicated problem of the mutual conversion of these diverse coins. Prior to Farrukhsiyar's reign, rupees remained *sicca* during the lifetime of the emperor in whose name they were struck. After the accession of a new ruler, the coin lost its *sicca* rating and became subject to a decrease in value caused by the imposition of a discount called *batta*. Such coins were not received in the royal treasury except as bullion.[61]

By the middle of the eighteenth century, *batta* on the coinage was charged for the first three years. During the first year of its circulation, the rupee retained its *sicca* rating. In the second year, it became subject to a discount of 3 per cent. During the third year, a further *batta* of 2 per cent was added and it was then known as the *sanwat* rupee.[62] In actual practice, *batta* meant the loss arising from payments or advances not being made in the specific coins that was required locally. The class of people who benefited most out of this loss was the *sarrafs* or money-changers. A *sarraf* examined every coin, graded each piece according to weight and fineness, and fixed the *batta*. He 'assumed a relationship between age, velocity of circulation and weight loss in classifying coins into three categories—*sikka*, *chalna* [or *chalni*] and *khazana*—and levied discounts [*batta*] to redeem value and reduce transaction costs'.[63] While there was some justification in levy charges to cover the cost of production (brassage) and the seignorage resulting from the *actual* loss of weight due to wear, in actual practice, even a full weight coin was given the *chalna* status after a year. Similarly, the 'underweight coins of previous mintages suffered a double discount, and coins of identical weight and fineness fetched different values'.[64] The *sarraf* provided current coins in lieu of *batta* and collected the old/non-current coins offered in exchange. These old coins were recoined by him in the mint for further transactions. As the mints were generally farmed out to individuals, a nexus was formed between the mint-masters and shroffs.

'Humble Currencies' and Non-Metallic Issues

Although the currency system was mainly that of 'metallic currency' during the mid-eighteenth century, a number of 'humble currencies'[65] of baser metals such as tin and lead, as well as non-metallic currencies such as almonds (bitter, non-edible type), some kinds of seeds and cowrie shells, were also prevalent in small regions.

TIN (TUTENAGUE)

As early as the sixteenth century, tin was used by the Portuguese to coin their monetary units called *bazarrucco*, *roda*, *solde* and *bastardo*, issued from Goa. As their minting activities spread to Diu, Daman, Bassien and Chaul, tin was put to extensive usage as currency.

Between 1672 and 1677, the English also issued tin coins called *tinnys* or *buzerook* (or *bujrook*—from the Portuguese *Bazarrucco*) from their mint at Bombay. The circulation of these *tinnys* was, however, restricted to the island of Bombay. The coins were paid out to the Company's labourers employed for fortifications, soldiers' pay and other local charges. The use of *tinnys* did not gain much acceptance with the common people and this first experiment of a tin currency by the English failed. After 1677, tin as a coinage metal ceased to be used in the Bombay mint. The practice of issuing tin coins to defray small payments was once again revived in 1716 and a new series of tin *buzerooks* were coined. From 1717 until 1793, tin coinage, interspersed with copper issues, became a regular feature of the Bombay currency.

Tin was also used by the Dutch East India Company to mint *bazaruk* coins from their mint at Cochin during 1724-95.

LEAD

Ever since their settlement in India during the seventeenth century, the Danish Trading Company extensively minted lead coins called *kas.* These coins were current in their settlement at Tranquebar on the south-east coast of India. Only the basic unit of *kas* was made of lead; its multiple denominations, viz., 2 *kas*, 4 *kas*, and 10 *kas* were made of copper. Eighty *kas* equalled to one *royaliver* (*fano* or *fanam*)—a silver coin.

The Dutch also minted lead coins which formed their smallest monetary unit at the Negapatnam mint.

BADAM (ALMONDS)

Certain types of inedible bitter almonds were imported into Gujarat where they were used as money. According to Jean de Thevenot, who visited Surat in 1666-7, these almonds passed for money at Surat and came from Persia.[66] The areas of south and central Gujarat in which *badam* circulated comprised a complex of large and small urban centres, inhabited by moneylenders, bankers, merchants and craftsmen.

COWRIES

In Bengal, Orissa and Assam, the *cowrie* shell (*cyprea moneta*) was the chief medium of small change for all transactions below a rupee.[67] In Bengal, silver or copper fractions of the rupee were seldom minted.

The usual measurement of the *cowrie* was as follows:

4 *kauris*	= 1 *ganda*		
20 *ganda*	= 1 *pan* or *pun*	=	80 shells
16 *pans*	= 1 *kahan*	=	1,280 shells
4 *kahan*	= 1 rupee	=	5,120 shells

Normally, the exchange value of the cowrie currency with the rupee was calculated upon the number of *pans*, and this varied from fifty to seventy according to the locality and period. A Report to the Council at Calcutta, dated 15 May 1758, shows purchases of cowries at the rate of 46 *pans* for the Calcutta Current Rupee.

Recognizing that the cowrie had no intrinsic or stable value, the Company made several attempts to rectify the situation. As early as in October 1757, they introduced a copper token currency for payment to labourers engaged in the fortification of Fort William.[68] They also attempted a more general introduction of small gold and silver coins by requiring a certain proportion of the bullion that was handed into the mints to be coined into fractions; in the case of private bullion, this condition was evaded. It was not until the major currency reforms of 1792 that progress was made in this aspect of currency.

By 1834, cowries had ceased to be imported for currency having been superseded by the Company's copper pice coinage.[69]

Credit Instruments

While coins represented a physical equivalent, various credit instruments helped in increasing the velocity of money circulation and facilitated inter-spatial transfers. Therefore, there existed a 'close co-existence of metallic money, credit and banking instruments'.[70] Among the major credit instruments were:

A. LOAN DEED

The loan deeds prevalent during the Mughal period were called *Dastawez* and were of two types:

i. *Dastawez-i Indultalab* which was payable on demand.
ii. *Dastawez-i Miadi* which was payable after a stipulated time.

B. PAY ORDERS OR LETTERS OF CREDIT

Another instrument in use during this period was in the form of Pay Orders or Letters of Credit and was issued from the royal treasury on one of the district or provincial treasuries. These were called *barats* (or *varats*) and were akin to present-day drafts or cheques.[71] For example, under the Gaekwads, 'whenever the Government needed money, it would issue to any one of these potedars a money warrant accompanied by a letter of credit, known as *varat*, enjoining upon some *ijaradar* to reimburse the potedar from the revenue of villages farmed out to them'.[72]

C. *HUNDIS*

The most important class of credit instruments that evolved in India were termed *hundis* or bills of exchange. During the Mughal period, we have the testimony of many foreign travellers regarding the use of bills of exchange in big commercial centres. From their writings, it may be noted that Indian bankers also issued bills of exchange on foreign countries, mainly for financing the seaborne trade. These bills were widely accepted and were traded at high discounts, as these incorporated the insurance premium covering the risk, including the safe arrival of goods. Their use has continued till today. In a sense, they represent the oldest surviving form of credit instruments. *Hundis* were used variously as remittance instruments (to transfer funds from one place to another), as credit instruments (to borrow money [IOUs]) and, most commonly, for trade transactions (as bills of exchange).

Hundis were of various kinds and each type had certain distinguishing features.

i. *Durshani hundi*: This was a demand bill of exchange, payable on presentation, according to the usage and custom of the place. These were mainly of four types:
   a. *Sah-jog*—a *hundi* transferable by endorsement and delivery but payable only to a *sah* or to his order. A *sah* was a respectable and responsible person, a man of worth and substance who was known in the market.
   b. *Dhanni-jog*—a demand bill of exchange payable only to the *dhanni*, i.e. the payee. This *hundi* was not negotiable.

c. *Farman-jog hundis* came into existence around the twelfth century. *Farman* is a Persian word meaning order and, therefore, *farman-jog hundis* were payable to the order of the person named. These *hundis* could be negotiated with a simple or conditional endorsement.

d. *Dekhavanhar*—this was a bearer demand bill of exchange payable to the person presenting it to the drawee. Thus, it corresponded to a bearer cheque.

ii. *Muddati hundi*: This was a usance bill and was payable after a stipulated time, on a given date, on a determinable future date or on the happening of a certain stipulated event. *Muddati hundis* of the *sah-jog, dhanni-jog* and *farman-jog* types had the same features as those attached to the same types of *darshani hundis.* However, the most important type of *muddati hundi* was the *jokhami hundi*, which was a documentary bill of exchange corresponding to the present-day bill of lading. This had been in use for centuries and payment was conditional on the safe arrival of goods.

Role of Money-changers or *Sarrafs* in the Money Market

As the money market was filled with a large variety of coins of differing values during the mid-eighteenth century, the money-changers or *sarrafs* assumed a role of crucial importance. In Gujarat, the *parekhs* or *parikhs* (from the Sanskrit *pariksha*, 'to examine') and *Nanavatis* (from *nana* 'coin' and *vati* 'who deals in') had developed into a special class of businessmen who dealt in money-changing and discounting. The Gujarati word *sharaf* (from the Arabic *sarraf*)—corrupted as *shroff*—was a more generic term applied to the merchants specializing in money-changing, moneylending and giving and discounting bills of exchange.[73] Initially, the *sarrafs* were appointed to examine the purity of gold and silver coming to the Mughal mints, but soon they acquired expertise in determining the weight and age of every coin.[74] These *sarrafs* then began to deal independently in money-changing. They used to change old rupees which fell below the standard weight into newly-coined rupees.

Hoarding

Another feature of the mid-eighteenth century money market in India was the hoarding propensity of the society, which had a proportionate relationship with political stability, peace and tranquillity. As one of the memorialists of the East India Company describes it: 'In India, as in all other despotic governments, mankind are bridled only by fear: this leads men to hide or dissipate their money as fast as they acquire it; both are equally injurious to trade.'[75] Or specifically, as Sir Richard Temple puts it: 'The possibility of a political revolution occurring is always present to the monetary and financial mind of the people of India. The consequence is, that their coinage is used partly for purposes of circulation and partly for hoarding.'[76] There were other considerations, too. Bayly has interpreted hoarding as 'methodical and rational responses to circumstances . . . connected with the need to have different institutions of credit for different fields'.[77] Citing the example of the Benares merchants, Bayly writes:

> Benares merchants held Mughal gold mohurs, in case of problems with silver; they hoarded family jewels in the case of the death of the family head; they kept Mughal jewels for occasions of public display, and latterly they kept Company paper to be able to operate in the arenas of the East India Company.[78]

While both silver and gold were hoarded, silver was hoarded almost entirely in specie whereas gold was partly in specie but chiefly in bullion.[79] Coming more specifically to coin hoards, these fall under two major categories—emergency hoards and saving hoards. Usually the first category comprises coins withdrawn from circulation and hidden during an emergency with the intent of later retrieval. The coins in these hoards are of random denominations. In the second category, the coins are usually of high denominations and of better quality but of limited variety. These include what are known as 'mercantile hoards' and 'bullion hoards'.[80] Other categories of coin hoards include votive or religious hoards (viz., temple offerings), accidental hoards (viz., from shipwrecks) and abandoned hoards (viz., from burial hoards, wishing wells/ponds, etc).

The size of the hoard varies; while 'a majority of hoards probably contain between 50 and 100 coins, but a fair number exceed 1,000 and a few much larger'.[81]

During the eighteenth century, there were two major foreign invasions in north India by Nadir Shah (1739) and Ahmed Shah Abdali (1758-61). The latter is said to have taken nearly Rs. 40 crore from India in the course of his three invasions. But since much of this booty was not in circulation, 'all that the Persians or Afghans were doing was to move large stores of immobilised specie from treasure hoards in India to treasure hoards of their own countries'.[82]

Thus, a large portion of the coin hoards which were stashed away through military exploits could never be brought back into circulation when intended. This sometimes caused an acute scarcity of the circulating medium. However, this was not always the case. Bayly has pointed out that 'considerable quantities of hoarded bullion were spasmodically released by rulers of central and north India to finance their military and ceremonial enterprises'.[83] Therefore, the hoarding and release of coins during this period had a variegated effect on the money economy, pushing the interest rates and the price of commodities upwards or downwards.

POST-PLASSEY (1757) SCENARIO

Plassey, a sleepy town in the Nadia district of West Bengal, has earned a most remarkable recognition in the annals of modern India. It was here that on 23 June 1757, the armies of the East India Company defeated the forces of Siraj-ud-daulah, the Nawab of Bengal. As a battle, Plassey was a miserable affair yet its consequences were enormous both for India as well as for Britain. This victory laid the foundations of the British empire in India. It is an important chronological marker in the history of modern India. According to Percival Spear, 'the date of Plassey no more obviously marked a political revolution to the contemporaries than the fall of Constantinople in 1453 marked a cultural and intellectual one to fifteenth century Europe'.[84]

Sushil Chaudhary regards this event as the beginning of British imperialism. According to him, 'Bengal became the springboard from which the British extended their territorial acquisitions in different parts of India, and gradually built-up the Indian empire'.[85]

One of the most significant economic consequences of the British conquest of Bengal was that 'one of the most prosperous *subahs* of the Mughal empire came in handy for financing the British expansion'.[86]

The 'Plassey Plunder' which began immediately after the battle of Plassey has few parallels in history. It is a unique example of the wanton extraction of the wealth and resources of a colony by an imperial power. Most of the wealth thus extracted by the East India Company and its servants was sent out of Bengal. It is estimated that during 1757-65, the Company officials received from Mir Jafar and others a sum of £2.2 million or Rs.17.6 million. This is exclusive of the monetary gains to the Company, which, in the same period, amounted to £10.7 million (Rs. 85.6 million)—£3.7 million in cash and about £7 million in territorial revenues.[87]

The 'Plassey Plunder' also revolutionized the nature of East India trade. Prior to 1757, bullion was the chief constituent of the Company's export trade with India. However, after 1757, bullion was no longer required to finance the Company's investment in India. Now expenditure on purchases in Bengal and other parts of India could be made largely out of the surplus of the territorial revenue of Bengal.

The cessation of the import of bullion, chiefly silver, had a telling effect on the currency situation of Bengal. Hitherto, almost the entire quantity of bullion imported by the Company was coined into local currencies, which, in turn, facilitated trade and commercial activities. Once this channel was cut-off, there arose an acute scarcity of silver rupees, which were the common media of exchange, not only in Bengal but also in north, central and western India.

The East India Company was not the only European trading company which stopped the import of bullion after 1757; the Dutch, the French and the Danes, among others, also discovered a local source for financing their investments. They could now raise capital by issuing bills of exchange redeemable in Europe to the servants of the English East India Company who were always too eager to remit their illegal fortunes to their homes. The European trading companies provided a safe channel to the servants of the East India Company, as they did not fear detection or confiscation of their wealth by their employers. This practice must have reached alarming proportions, as is clear from certain provisions of an Act passed by the British Parliament in 1782. By the East India Company Act, 1781 (21 Geo. III, c. 70), the Company's servants and other British subjects residing in India were prohibited from 'lending money to foreign companies or foreign European merchants, and from purchasing goods on their account, and from being concerned in such transactions and from giving credit by bills of exchange on persons in Europe'.[88] The Company's servants who violated this injunction were liable to be suspended while licensed traders found guilty of such transactions were to be deprived of their licenses and the Company's protection, and to be sent at once to England.[89]

The 'Plassey Plunder' opened up a regular stream for the drain of wealth from India. Philip Francis (1776) divided this flow into four streams:[90]

1. the East India Company 's investments
2. remittance to other presidencies
3. the transfer of private income to England, and
4. the transfer of income from private trade.

A large proportion of the drain of wealth was in the form of silver specie. Francis writes: 'It is well known that in consequence of the advanced price and reduced quality of Bengal goods, the Captains and officers do not find it advantageous to make their returns by investments on such goods . . . the alternative left is to carry home specie.'[91]

Various estimates have been given by different authorities about the volume of drain.[92] Writing in 1776, Francis gives a 'very moderate' estimate of Rs. 12 lakh (or £0.12 million) per annum exported out of Bengal in the form of specie.[93] Digby places India's total drain to Britain, between the battles of Plassey and Waterloo (1757-1815) at nearly £1,000 million.[94] Marshall estimates that before 1757 from Bengal, alone a remittance of £3 million was 'sent home' on private account, which rose to £15 million during 1757-84.[95] Hamilton puts the total drain from Bengal to England in 1757-80 at £34.5 million.[96] J.C. Sinha's total figure for the same period is £38.4 million.[97] In a recent survey, which critically analyses all the evidences at hand, the 'minimum transfers' for the period 1758-1815 have been estimated at £38 million, 'or £30.2 million once British bullion exports to India are deducted'.[98]

The loot of Plassey also revolutionized the economy of England. Brooks Adams observes:

> Before the influx of the Indian treasure, and the expansion of credit which followed, no force sufficient for this purpose existed. . . . The factory system was the child of the 'Industrial Revolution', and until capital had accumulated in masses, capable of giving solidity to large bodies of labour, manufactures were carried on by scattered individuals. . . . Possibly since the world began, no investment has ever yielded the profit reaped from the Indian plunder, because for nearly fifty years Great Britain stood without a competitor.[99]

As soon as the Plassey plunder began to arrive in London, its effects on the economy were manifested instantaneously, for all authorities agree that the Industrial Revolution, the event that has divided the nineteenth century from all antecedent times, began with the year 1760. According to William Digby: 'England's industrial supremacy owes its origin to the vast hoards of Bengal and the Karnatik being made available for her use. . . . Before Plassey was fought and won, and before the stream of treasure began to flow to England, the industries of our country were at a very low ebb.'[100]

Thus, the reduced import of bullion and increased export of specie on account of the China trade, as well as remittances to England, and other presidencies, marked the post-Plassey currency situation in Bengal, which resulted in an acute shortage of specie in the market. According to an estimate, during 1757-66, Bengal lost £8 million 'by deficiency in the usual imports of bullion and by exportation of silver'.[101]

Post-Plassey, the Company continued to consolidate its financial position in Bengal. In 1760, by espousing the claim of Mir Qasim to the governorship of Bengal, the East India Company acquired three important districts of Bengal in return—Burdwan, Midnapore and Chittagong, in addition to their old *zemindari* of Calcutta, Sutanati and Govindpur. However, after his installation on the *musnad* of Murshidabad in 1760, Mir Qasim had an estranged relationship with the Company. Open hostilities broke out between them in 1763 and, in July, the Company restored the old Nawab, Mir Jafar, on the *musnad*. The ousted Nawab, Mir Qasim, joined hands with Nawab Shuja ud-Daulah of Awadh and the refugee Mughal emperor, Shah Alam II. The combined forces of Mir Qasim and Shuja, accompanied by Shah Alam, were decisively defeated by the British in the famous battle of Buxar (22 October 1764).

SUMMING UP

The robust currency regime established by the Mughals crumbled with the decline and disintegration of their empire during the eighteenth century. As a result, the society which had become highly monetized under Mughal rule plunged into a state of chaotic confusion not because of the lack or scarcity of currency required for its multifarious economic activities but because of its abundance. In the absence of a central administrative authority, many neo-rulers sprang up and issued their own coins, albeit in the name of the Mughal emperor. These coins of different weight and fineness added to the prevailing confusion in the money market. The currency lost its velocity and became regional, even local, in nature.

To cope with the situation, the monetary structure of eighteenth-century India developed a mechanism of coin valuation based on the pure metal content of the coin. This feat was performed by a highly professional functionary—the *sarraf*—who soon assumed a formidable position in the money market. In many cases, this class controlled the operations of the mint and were, thus, able to regulate the supply of currency in the market.

During the initial phase of its commercial activities in India, the English East India Company had to depend on the Mughal mints to procure cash for their 'investments'. Gradually, it secured minting rights and, by the end of the seventeenth century, had established its own mints at several places in the Madras presidency and Bombay on the western coast. In Bengal, however, the Company's attempts to obtain minting rights were thwarted by the local Mughal governor, who had become virtually independent of the centre. Until the middle of the eighteenth century, the English Company was left to meet its demands for cash for its 'investments' in Bengal through a supply of coins from its own mints in the Madras presidency. However, around this time, one event redefined the subsequent history of the region and the entire country.

The battle of Plassey (1757) laid the foundation of the British empire in India. The most crucial economic fallouts of Plassey were the cessation of bullion import into Bengal and the opening up of a regular stream of the drain of wealth, chiefly in the form of silver specie, that left the Bengal economy in acute shortage of working capital. While Bengal faced a currency crisis the economy of England was revolutionized with the influx of 'Indian treasure', which fuelled the Industrial Revolution.

The process of empire-building that had started with Plassey was further consolidated by the victory of the English Company at the battle of Buxar (1764). Of immense political significance was the defeat of Shah Alam II, the titular head of the Mughal empire, who was now reduced to a hapless pensioner of the Company. On the economic front, one of the most noteworthy outcomes of the battle of Buxar, which was to have an everlasting impact on the currency situation in India, was the grant of the *Diwani* of Bengal, Bihar and Orissa to the East India Company.

NOTES

1. Eraly 2000: 521.
2. Bowen 1991: 5.
3. Habib 2003: 1.
4. Harrison 1893: 52.
5. Bowen 1991: 12.
6. Harrison 1893: 52.
7. Chaudhuri 1978: 183.
8. Richards 1987: 1.
9. For various aspects of the Mughal coinage and monetary system, see Habib 1961; Haider 1996 and 1999; Hasan 1969 and 1970; Moosvi 1968 and 1987; Om Prakash and Krishnamurty 1970; Om Prakash 1988; Richards 1987; and Venkateshwara 1918.
10. Gupta 1959: 174.
11. Om Prakash 1988: 478.
12. Manucci 1907-8, vol. 2: 417.
13. Richards 1987: 6.
14. Deyell 1987: 44.
15. For monetary integration of Gujarat into the Mughal empire, see Haider 2005.
16. Ibid.: 45.
17. Bernier, *Travels in the Mogul Empire, 1656-1668*, quoted in Haider 2007: 185.
18. Om Prakash 1987: 171.
19. The other ways of financing the investments adopted by these companies were by exporting European goods—for which there was practically none or very little demand in the East, and by borrowing, chiefly against bills of exchange issued in the East and payable in Europe.
20. *State of the Gold and Silver Coins*, 25 September 1717, quoted in Chaudhuri 1978: 160.
21. Richards 1987: 2.
22. Haider 1996: 298.
23. For a detailed discussion on this theme, see Perlin 1987.
24. Habib 2003: 101.
25. Ali 1975: 391.
26. Ibid.
27. Sarkar 1988: 97-100.
28. Ibid.: 34-63.
29. Sarkar 1991: 251-72.
30. Ibid.: 1988: 21-33.
31. Malik 1990: 169.
32. Irvine 1922; Sarkar 1988-92.

33. Lane-Poole 1892: 411.
34. Richards 1995: Chapter 12—Imperial decline and collapse, 1707-20, 253ff.; Hintz 1997: 13.
35. Leonard 1979: 399. This theory was refuted by Richards who challenged the evidentiary basis of Leonard's arguments (Richards 1981). For Leonard's reply to Richard's refutations, see Leonard 1981.
36. Richards 1987: 12.
37. Bayly 1983: 56-7.
38. Ali Muhammad Khan, *Mirat-i Ahmadi*, cited in Haider 2005: 140.
39. Ambedkar 1947: 2.
40. Pridmore 1975: 4.
41. Quoted in ibid.
42. Ibid.: 42.
43. Ibid.: 96.
44. Quoted in ibid.: 110-11.
45. Ibid.: 111.
46. Ibid.
47. Furber 1980: 133.
48. Pridmore 1975: 4.
49. Garg 1990.
50. Kale 1937: 243.
51. Pridmore 1975: 97.
52. Letter dated 7 December 1733, quoted in Pridmore 1975: 117.
53. Kale 1937: 243.
54. Verelst 1772: 89.
55. Ambedkar 1947: 4-5.
56. Sinha 1938: 4-5.
57. Sen 1957: 159.
58. *FWIHC*, IX 1959: xiii.
59. NAI, Public Department, OC, 13 March 1775, no. 18(a).
60. Ambedkar 1947: 5.
61. Pridmore 1975: 190.
62. See Habib 1961 on *batta* and why it was charged. For a full-scale treatment of the subject, see Haider 2008.
63. Haider 2008.
64. Ibid.
65. Richards (1987: 11-12) and Perlin (1987: 237) include copper coins too in their definition of 'humble currencies'. However, copper was an integral part of the Mughal monetary system and, though marginalized, had maintained its position in the trimetallic system. See Habib 1987.
66. Garg 2007: 246-8; Perlin 1987: 317, fn. 20.
67. For a detailed discussion on cowrie currency, see De 1952; Garg 2007 and Biswas 2007: 143-9; and Deyell 2010.
68. Rhodes 1999.

69. Garg 2007: 248-59.
70. Haider 2002: 58; Om Prakash 2002: 40-57.
71. 'A writing conferring immunity or exemption, commission, warrant, decree, assignment, letter; draught [draft], cheque', John T. Platts (1884), *A Dictionary of Urdu, Classical Hindi and English*, London: W. H. Allen & Co.: 143.
72. Tripathi 2002: 132.
73. Torri 1991: 1.
74. Singh 1975: 85.
75. Warring 1771: 34.
76. Temple 1883: 293.
77. Bayly 2004: 43.
78. Ibid.
79. Temple 1883: 291.
80. Grierson 1975: 13-16.
81. Ibid.: 130.
82. Bayly 1983: 69.
83. Ibid.: 170.
84. Spear 1978: 2.
85. Chaudhary 1995: 9.
86. Ibid.
87. Gupta 1966: 127.
88. NAI, Public, Letters from Court, dated 25 January 1782, paras 73-5.
89. Ibid.
90. NAI, Public Department, OC, 1 November 1776, no. 4.
91. Ibid.
92. Sinha 1952; Ganguli 1965; Roy 1987.
93. NAI, Public Department, OC, 1 November 1776, no. 4.
94. Digby 1901: 33.
95. Marshall 1976: 234.
96. Hamilton 1919: 135-6, 146-8.
97. Sinha 1927: 46-52.
98. Esteban 2001: 66.
99. Brooks Adams 1896: 313-17.
100. Digby 1901: 30.
101. Sinha 1927: 55-6.

CHAPTER 2

Post-1765 India and the Diagnosis of its Monetary Problems

On 12 August 1765, Shah Alam II issued a *farman* granting the *Diwani* of Bengal, Bihar and Orissa to the East India Company in perpetuity, and requiring it to pay Rs. 26 lakh annually to the imperial exchequer. The balance of the revenue of these three provinces was to be spent on 'the expenses of the administration of Bengal and maintenance of the family of the Nawab of Murshidabad (fifty lakhs), and the cost of the military defence of the provinces'.[1]

Thus, it was essentially as revenue collectors that the English began their actual occupation of the country, and it was the exigencies of the revenue service that compelled them to elaborate a system of government and, through a long process, extrude native sovereignty from its role in governance. Under the plea that they were acting within the constitution of the Mughal empire, the Company's servants built-up a system of internal government, and 'when the walls of their building reached a certain height, the sun of the British Crown rose to its meridian, and the shadow cast by the setting constellation of the Mughal empire disappeared forever'.[2] According to Firminger, 'the history of revenue administration is thus the backbone of the history of the English occupation of Bengal'.[3]

This chapter discusses how currency reforms, which were crucial for the successful career of the Company as the revenue administrator of Bengal, Bihar and Orissa, were attempted by early 'reformers' in utter ignorance of economic principles. The failure of two experiments to introduce bimetallism and to eliminate discounts on coins of older mintage by issuing coins with fixed dates prompted the Court of Directors of the East India Company to establish an official enquiry to diagnose the currency crisis of Bengal. The recommendation of this enquiry laid the agenda of currency reforms in Bengal. In Bengal, too, official committees were appointed and, on the basis of their recommendations, a number of measures were adopted.

GRANT OF *DIWANI* AND THEREAFTER: HISTORIOGRAPHY

The monetary problems that followed the East India Company's assumption of the *Diwani* of Bengal, Bihar and Orissa, and its impact on the economy, have hitherto attracted the attention of only a few scholars. In particular, the crucial phase from 1765 to 1792—the latter year when a Mint Committee was finally constituted by the Government of Bengal to suggest ways to improve the circulation of exchange media—has been left almost untouched by most economic historians who have otherwise contributed some valuable studies on various aspects of the monetary system and its role in the economic history of modern India. However, there are a few exceptions. J.C. Sinha contributed two papers: one specifically dealing with the currency reforms of Warren Hastings and the other being a general survey of currency during the latter half of the eighteenth century.[4] Later, he devoted almost one-third of his book to discussing the currency problems faced by the Company in Bengal right from 1757 to 1793.[5] More recently, D.B. Mitra and Anirban Biswas have contributed a history of the monetary system of the Bengal presidency.[6] Mitra does not bring the discussion on the currency reforms of the East India Company to the point of culmination (the year 1835, as we shall see later) but restricts it to the experimentalist approach of the early currency reformers. He, nevertheless, is able to demonstrate the overall change in the monetary economy of the Bengal presidency that was effected by various currency measures undertaken by the Company from the mid-eighteenth to the early nineteenth century. In his work, Biswas essentially deals with the transitional phase of the Bengal economy, from pre-colonial to colonial India, and devotes two of the six chapters of his book discussing monetary system of the Mughal and pre-colonial South and the Deccan. He, however, does not touch upon the subject of currency administration under the colonial rule.[7] Rajat Datta's extremely interesting study of commercialization in rural Bengal (*c.* 1760-1800) analyses the monetary problems of Bengal with relation to the availability of bullion and presents a critical reassessment of its impact.[8]

THE COMPANY RULE IN EASTERN INDIA

The grant of the *Diwani* of Bengal, Bihar and Orissa in 1765 confirmed and consolidated all the political and military advances that had been made by the East India Company during the previous decade. The new acquisition was seen as a panacea to all the financial problems lately faced by the Company. Robert Clive even predicted that the 'gain' would be able to 'defray all the expenses of investments in goods for export, furnish the whole of the China treasure, answer the demands of all other settlements in India, and leave a considerable balance in the treasury'.[9]

The developments of 1765 focused the political attention of Britain upon India and the East India Company. The first parliamentary inquiry into the East India Company's affairs was conceived and prosecuted between 1766 and 1767. However, the transformation of traders into sovereigns brought about many problems relating to the financial administration of the Company's government in India.[10]

BULLION SUPPLY AND MONETARY CONTRACTION

The basic question that was faced by the government of Bengal was how to cope with the contraction in money supply which was primarily due to the cessation of bullion import, chiefly silver, into Bengal after 1757 and its reverse flow to England. Philip Francis, writing in 1776, gives a 'moderate estimate' of the amount sent 'home' in specie at Rs. 12 lakh per annum.[11] Warren Hastings's estimate was Rs. 40 lakh per annum, but he was candid enough to accept that his calculation was 'not founded on authentic documents nor reducible to certainty'.[12] Sir John Shore also attests to the 'considerable' export of silver bullion to England after 1765, though he does not hazard any guess. In his Minute dated 18 June 1789, he writes: 'Silver bullion is also remitted by individuals to Europe; the amount cannot be calculated, but must since the Company's accession to the Dewany have been very considerable.'[13]

In his study on the monetary system of the Bengal presidency between 1757 and 1835, Mitra has discussed various causes for the scarcity of silver currency in Bengal after 1757. According to him, besides the cessation of bullion import, the decline of Bengal's trade with Iran and the Red Sea area after Plassey was another factor responsible for the low supply of money.[14]

Another related problem was of the 'Tribute' or 'Drain of Wealth' which had also started with the 'Plassey Plunder' and had caused a severe strain on the economy, which was already facing a scarcity of media of exchange. Enormous wealth began to flow into the

Company's exchequer as well as into the private purses of its servants through bribes, exactions and plunder. According to an estimate, the Company and its employees received £60,00,000 from the Indians as gifts from 1757 to 1766.[15]

Monetary disturbances were also created by the export of Bengal silver to Canton to balance the tea trade between China and England. The triangular trade between India, China and England necessitated the export of a huge amount of silver from Bengal to China. During the second half of the eighteenth century, the Company's trade with China became more valuable than its Indian investments. 'The enlargement of the Trade to China to its utmost Extent', wrote the Court of Directors in 1768, 'is an object we have greatly at heart, not only from the Advantages in prospect, by gaining a Superiority and thereby discouraging Foreign Europeans from resorting to that Market; but also from a National Concern, where Revenue is very materially interested. . . .[16] The practice of sending silver from Bengal to China commenced in 1757 and continued without remission till the year 1770.[17] The ill-effects of bullion demand for the China trade severely hit Bengal's resources.

Before the battle of Plassey, Bengal received silver in bullion and specie from the Bombay and Madras presidencies. For example, in July 1753, '50 chests of treasure' were received from Madras.[18] In September of the same year, a consignment of 4 lakh Bombay Rupees was received from the President and Council at Bombay.[19] All this changed after Plassey. On 21 July 1757, the Bengal government requested the Bombay government 'not to be supplied with more money, as by the late revolution in these provinces, the Company are to receive in specie the sum of one crore of rupees (besides other advantages)'.[20] Immediately thereafter, the reverse flow of treasure from Bengal to the Madras and Bombay presidencies started.[21] In its letter dated 8 March 1758, the Court directed the Bengal government to supply the Madras government 'from time to time with what money they shall stand in need of, . . . also for sending from thence to China. . . . Our Presidency of Bombay must also be supplied if remittances are wanted there or may be of use.'[22] These remittances became regular in subsequent years and carried away a large chunk of Bengal's monetary resources. It has been estimated that between 1761 and 1771, Bengal remitted a net amount of £23,58,298 to other settlements. About £1,60,000 (or nearly 6.78 per cent) a year was the regular remittance to Bombay alone.[23]

While the circulating media was contracting, the demand for more money was increasing.[24] As revenues were not only assessed in cash but also demanded in the form of silver and gold coins and later on in the form of the Company's rupees, the greater monetization of the economy was affected. Lack of money also led to a fall in the revenue collections of the Company.

Monetary contractions should have had a deflationary effect on the economy, an effect which awaits a serious probe. Asiya Siddiqi has done a comparative study of the monetary and price history of India and Britain during 1760-1840.[25] According to her, the government's intervention in the credit market through public loan transactions 'often gave rise to sudden contraction or expansion of money supply', resulting in sharp fluctuation of prices in India.[26] She has also argued that the gradual drift of the currency policy in India towards silver mono-metallism and that of England to establish a gold standard (by the Coinage Act of 1816) encouraged the outflow of gold from India to Britain. She says: 'At a time when reserves of gold were low in England, conditions had been fostered to divert it from India.'[27] She has also discussed the ways in which the Indian monetary and financial resources served the need of Great Britain and argues that developments in these fields were part of the process described by Irfan Habib as the 'colonisation of Indian economy'.[28]

BENGAL PRESIDENCY

The East India Company's supreme government in Bengal made several attempts to ease the monetary crisis in the Bengal presidency based upon economic doctrines prevailing in contemporary England.[29] The first measure was the introduction of bimetallism in Bengal in 1766. In this system, currencies of two metals circulate simultaneously as legal tender at a fixed rate of exchange.

Monetary Problems: Initial Adventurism of Clive, Verelst and Hastings

Between 1766 and 1771, within a short span of five years, the Company altered its monetary policy three times. The basic question that was being addressed by the successive Governors of Bengal was to find a currency model that was the best-suited to the prevailing monetary situation in Bengal.

A. INTRODUCTION OF BIMETALLISM, 1766

The scarcity of silver currency in Bengal led its government to adopt a bimetallic standard for its currency. The purpose was to supplement or substitute silver with gold and expand the total size of the currency in circulation. Thus, on 2 June 1766, the following regulations were promulgated to establish a gold currency in Bengal:

1. That the Gold Mohurs shall be struck bearing the same impression with the present Moorshedabad Sicca, and that this Mohur shall also be issued in the subdivisions of halves, quarters, and eighths.
2. That the new coin shall be of the fineness of twenty carats, or it shall contain one sixth part of an alloy, which reduces it to Rupees 16-9-4 per cent below the value of pure gold, to 14-7-7 below the mean fineness of the Sicca and Dehly Mohurs, and to 8-2-2 one-third beneath the standard of the present Arcot gold Mohurs.
3. That the gold Mohur shall be increased from fifteen Annas, the present actual weight, to sixteen Annas, the better to avoid the inconvenience of fractional numbers in the sub-divisional parts and the exchange.
4. That the par of exchange between the gold Mohurs and the Silver Sicca Rupee shall for the present be eliminated at the rate of fourteen to one reckoning upon the intrinsic value of either. Thus, a gold Mohur weighing sixteen Annas shall be deemed equivalent to fourteen Sicca Rupees.
5. That the silver Sicca Rupee shall be less than the standard of 11 oz. 15 dwt. or 13 dwt. better than English standard.
6. That all payments, whether of a public or a private nature, shall be made at the established Batta, and every attempt to create an artificial Batta, or exchange, shall be rigorously punished.
7. That a tender of payment, either public or private, shall in future be equally valid in gold and silver, and that a refusal of the established gold currency shall incur such punishments as this Board may think proper to inflict.
8. That public notice shall be given to all Zemindars, Collectors of the revenue and others, that the collections may be made indiscriminately in gold and in silver, the former to be received at the Mint and Treasury at the proposed in the 2ᵈ article.[30]

Thus, a legal tender gold *muhr* was inducted into the monetary system of Bengal. Its weight was 16 *annas* (179.66 grains =11.64 g) and its fineness 20 carats (or 149.72 grains = 9.70 g). Half, quarter and one-eighth *muhr* denominations of proportionate weight and fineness were also sanctioned. However, only full-*muhr* and half-*muhr* denominations have been reported.[31] Perhaps quarter and one-eighth *muhrs* were never minted. Curiously, on the available specimens, the English letter 'C' appears on the reverse, which, notwithstanding the mint name 'Murshidabad' appearing on these coins, is interpreted to mean Calcutta where the Company had established their own mint in 1757 (Fig. 2.1).

However, the coinage of these *muhrs* was not confined to one mint and, before their final recall in 1768, the Calcutta, Murshidabad and Patna mints struck gold coins of the 1766 standard.[32] Pridmore, therefore, suggests that the 'C' on these coins may indicate the 'Government of Calcutta', which explains the identical appearance of the gold coins of all three mints.[33]

To encourage the public to bring gold to the mint for coinage, the official exchange rate of the gold *muhrs* with sicca rupees was fixed at 1:14. The prevailing market rate of gold and silver in Bengal during this time was approximately 1:11½ *sicca* rupees and thus, the legal rate of gold *muhrs* was higher by 17½ per cent of their market value in silver. Thus, it was more profitable to make payment in gold for obligations originally agreed to in silver currency.[34] The experiment of 1766 of deliberately fixing the rate of the gold coin much higher than the market ratio had been aimed at bringing hoarded gold into circulation, as it was estimated that there were large hoards of gold in private possession. It was also conceived as 'the only practicable method' of abolishing *batta*. As the ratio of exchange between silver and gold was 'officially' fixed, it was hoped that fluctuations in their price would cease in time. This scheme was also perceived as a check against the scarcity of silver specie since gold currency would always afford alternative means of payment.[35] It has been noted by Harrison that 'with the exception of the revenue settlement of Akbar, in which the ratio of gold to silver was indirectly fixed at 10 to 1 by enunciating the ratio of each of these metals to copper, *this was the first attempt in Indian history to fix the relative values of gold and silver*' (emphasis added).[36]

Full *Muhr*, 1766 Half *Muhr*, 1766

Fig. 2.1: Full and Half *Muhrs*, 1766

Between the period 1766 and 1768, a total of 2,63,045-gold *muhrs* were minted; of these 1,77,871 were minted at Calcutta, 70,000 at Murshidabad and 15,274 at Patna. Out of this 1,34,417 *muhrs* were sent to Madras, while 1,28,728 *muhrs* were issued for general circulation in the Bengal province.[37]

In spite of such noble intentions and safeguards, the experiment of 1766 was foredoomed to failure. The consequence was that silver currency started disappearing from circulation while gold *muhrs* passed at a discount, thus altering the legal rate of exchange.[38]

The Bengal government, in a bid to enforce bimetellism more strictly, issued the following Notice, on 30 June 1766:

> Notice is hereby further given that any person or persons discovered in attempting to make a variation of the exchange here settled between gold and silver or in obstructing the currency of a new coin by refusing to accept it in payment, if natives they will be punished with utmost severity, if Europeans they will forfeit the Company's protection and be sent to England forthwith.[39]

As J.C. Sinha avers, 'Economic laws have little respect for statesmen and administrators.'[40] Even the drafters of the Scheme of 1766 had themselves realized that it could not serve 'as an effectual remedy, but as a palliative, which will obstruct the progress of the evil until a more radical cure could be discovered'.[41] The Court of Directors severely criticized both the inducement as well as the motives behind this scheme. About the expected release of the hoarded gold by raising its exchange value, the Court of Directors wrote:

> . . . no man would part with his gold but for a consideration, and that consideration could be only silver, therefore the effect was that there was so much silver hoarded up instead of the gold, not only the hoards were changed from Gold to Silver, but all the neighbouring Provinces would undoubtedly pour in their Gold for your Silver. . . .[42]

The Court also doubted the motives of the perpetrators of this scheme and minced no words in declaring that 'those who took lead in this extraordinary measure had secretly bought up large Quantities of Gold before the rise took place. . . .'[43] This was perhaps a dig at Robert Clive, who, as the Governor of Bengal (1765-7), was the man behind the scheme. In fact, one of the charges levelled against Clive during his famous trial was of fraud allegedly committed by him in the minting of gold coins in Bengal. Clive, however, claimed that not a single gold *muhr* or rupee was coined during his lifetime in Bengal as he left for England in January 1767 before the gold coins came into circulation.[44]

This attempted bimetallism proved to be a 'duometallism'.[45] In practice it meant dual pricing where the same commodity might have one price in gold and another in silver. This dual pricing system is impractical for a functioning economy. Within a year and a half of the introduction of this scheme, the discount on the gold *muhr* rose to about 38 per cent in Calcutta alone.[46]

In 1768, the government of Bengal decided to abandon this experiment. The withdrawal of gold coins issued by the government was announced. As many as 1,20,161 gold *muhrs* out of a total of 1,28,728 issued by the government were received back into the treasury at the prevailing rate of Rs. 14 to one gold *muhr*.[47]

B. RE-INTRODUCTION OF BIMETALLISM, 1769

The aborted experiment of 1766 caused greater currency problems in Bengal than before. In 1769, leading European and Armenian merchants as well as the principal residents of Calcutta petitioned the government stating that, '. . . at present the distress is so great that every merchant in Calcutta is in danger of becoming bankrupt, or running a risk of ruin by attachment on his goods, which would not sell for half their value, it being impossible to raise a large sum at any premium or bond.'[48]

The chief cause of distress was the scarcity of silver specie and this scarcity was not confined to Calcutta alone but was spread all over the province. Harry Verelst, who now headed the government of Bengal, immediately set forth to find out 'some safe, or at least temporary remedy for this growing evil'. He had a sounder knowledge of economic principles than his predecessor, Robert Clive. In his Minutes dated 1 September 1768 and 20 March 1769, he demonstrated his better understanding of monetary principles:

> It is a certain proposition that the particular increase of any species of coin will either sink its own value, or what is in fact the same, raise that of the other current coin, which may be in a smaller proportion. . . . The establishment of a gold currency was not in itself a grievance but the erroneous plan on which it was founded. . . . The original and capital error in the former currency was that of lowering the standard as a supposed encouragement to a larger importation of gold.[49]

Verelst, therefore, decided to reintroduce bimetallism in Bengal.

The Court of Directors was not in favour of changing the long-established metallic standard in Bengal, more so after the resounding failure of the 1766 scheme. In fact, in their letter dated 11 May 1769, they had restrained the Bengal government from any such experiment in the future:

We see in so strong a light dangerous consequences of making any alteration in the standard of the Coin of the Country, that we do most positively direct you do not (without our previous and express Order) under any pretence whatsoever presume to make any alteration in the Original and established Standard for weight and fineness of the Gold Mohurs and Silver Rupees which may from time to time be coined in out Mint at Calcutta, and whoever shall be guilty of a breach of this Order will incur an immediate dismission [*sic*] from our Service.[50]

But before this letter reached Calcutta, a new plan to reintroduce bimetallism was adopted.[51] Under this, the weight of the *muhr* was increased to 17 *annas sicca* weight (or 190.773 grains =12.36 g) and the fineness was restored to the old Mughal *muhr's* standard of 23 carat 3.75 grains (or 190.086 grains =12.35 g) of pure gold. Fractional denominations, viz., half, quarter, one-eighth and sixteenth of the proportional weight and fineness were also ordered, and rules for the mintage of gold bullion into various denominations were also laid down as per the following proportion:

..........................100 Mohurs.			
A number not exceeding	25	to be coined into	25 pieces
Halves	18	ditto.	36 ditto.
Quarters	18	ditto.	72 ditto.
Eighths	18	ditto.	144 ditto.
Sixteenths...........	21	ditto.	336 ditto.
Mohurs	100	ditto.	613 ditto.[52]

All gold delivered into the mint for coinage was to be minted into the full and fractional denominations in the ratio of 25:75 per cent respectively. Thus, gold worth 100 *muhrs* delivered into the mint would get its owner 25 full-*muhrs* and 588 fractional denominations, viz., 36 half-*muhrs*, 72 quarter *muhrs*, 144 one-eighth *muhrs* and 336 one-sixteenth *muhrs*. The real objective in instituting these fractional denominations of the gold *muhr* was to facilitate the use of gold currency in daily transactions. Accordingly, the exchange rate of the new *muhr* was fixed at 1:16 sicca rupee and the smallest denomination of the new coin series, the sixteenth *muhr*, was equalized with the one sicca rupee. This exchange rate, the government claimed, was 'as near as possible, to the respective value of the old standard gold and silver, throughout the empire', and, therefore, it hoped that the currency of the new gold *muhr* 'may fairly and justly be everywhere enforced. . . .[53] However, even at this rate, the gold *muhr* was overvalued 'by as much as 5.71 per cent'.[54] As a result, 'the effects of the old currency reappeared in a less severe form. . . the well-meaning currency reform of Verelst being of a palliative nature, failed to deliver the goods.'[55]

Full *Muhr*, 1769 One-eighth *Muhr*, 1769

Fig. 2.2: Full and One-eighth *Muhrs*, 1769

The new coinage came into circulation in May 1769 and, apart from Calcutta, its minting was carried out in the Patna and Dhaka mints.[56] The government of Bengal informed the Court of Directors that the new coins 'had met with a ready Circulation and were received with general Satisfaction'.[57] However, the experiment of 1769 faced a serious challenge in the very next year of its introduction. The terrible famine of 1770 raised prices higher than ever before.[58] Gradually, the area of circulation of these gold coins became restricted to Calcutta, where they were accepted as currency as late as in 1796.[59]

C. REGULATION OF 1771: ELIMINATION OF DISCOUNT BY AGE

The mid-eighteenth-century money market in India was plagued by the menace of *batta* charged by the money changers to exchange silver coinage of older mintage. As was the custom, the mintage of the coins bearing the new regnal year of the Mughal emperor was undertaken on the anniversary of his accession to the throne.

In 1771, the Company's government in Bengal decided to equate the current silver rupee bearing 11 *sun* (or the regnal year of Shah Alam II) with the new rupee bearing 12 *sun*. In normal circumstances, immediately after the issuance of the new coin (12 *sun*), the current coin (11 *sun*) would have become liable for a *batta* of 3 per cent, causing a great loss to the government as well as to the public at large. The only group benefiting from this custom, as always, was that of the money changers or *sarrafs*.

The government of Bengal, in yet another attempt to regulate the money market, sought to stabilize the sicca rupee by abolishing the distinction between the *sicca* and *sanwat* rupees. Thus, on 26 August 1771, the following Regulation was issued:

> This is to give notice to all merchants and others residing under the Honorable Company's protection at this settlement, that they have ordered Sicca Rupees of the twelfth year of his present Majesty Shah Allum's Reign to be struck in the Honorable Company's Mint and pass current at sixteen per cent Batta on the twelfth day of September next ensuing; and they likewise give public notice, that this coinage of the twelfth Sun Siccas shall not cause the eleven Sun Siccas to fall in their value, but that the eleven Sun Siccas shall pass on the same footing as they have heretofore done, that is to say at the Batta of sixteen percent; and whenever new Siccas of any future year shall be issued, the Siccas of the former years as far back as eleven Sun shall not fall in their value or be reduced to the state of Sonauts, but they shall be considered and pass in payment at the same value as the Siccas of the current year: the ten Suns Siccas are from the 12th day of September next to be considered and pass as Sonaut Rupees, and all other sorts of Rupees are to pass and be received as heretofore.[60]

The objective of this Regulation was to convert the entire currency system of Bengal to the *sicca* standard, which, according to J.C. Sinha, was 'a step towards uniformity of currency'.[61] Accordingly, the mintage of the silver rupees bearing the 12th regnal year of Shah Alam II commenced in the Company's mints on 12 September 1771. Even for the following years, i.e. the regnal years 13 and 14 of Shah Alam II, no new coins, except for the customary *nazarana*, were struck and the coins issued during this period (1771-3) continued to bear 12 *sun*. The temporary respite though failed to act as a bulwark against the impending danger. On 30 June 1773, the 15th regnal year of Shah Alam II commenced and, subsequently, new coins bearing 'regnal year (*San-i Julus*) 15' were struck.[62] It is not clear as to why the regnal year 12, which had remained fixated since 1771, was discontinued despite the regulation referred to above. Once sicca rupees of the 15th *sun* appeared in the market, the *sarrafs* immediately reduced the rupees of the 11 and 12 *sun* to *sanwats*, and the money market was plunged into more serious upheavals than those witnessed before 1771.

The real defect of this reform lay in equating *sanwat* rupees 'which might have lost a part of their bullion content through wear and tear', with the newly-coined *siccas*, and letting them pass at par, at 116 current rupees.[63] It has been argued that had steps been taken to re-coin the underweight *sanwat* rupees into the *siccas*, and 'to mark all future *sicca* rupees with one invariable date, the Regulation of 1771 would have facilitated the gradual change of the whole currency into *siccas*'.[64] But this was not to be.

By this time, a lot of dissidence against the East India Company had started brewing in England. Writing in 1771 John Scott Warring, who was very critical of the economic policies of the East India Company, observes: 'For these twelve or fourteen years past, a private body of merchants . . . have taken a principal part in the transactions of the great peninsula of India.'[65]

DIAGNOSIS OF MONETARY PROBLEMS

The Court of Directors's Initiative

The Court of Directors of the East India Company was so perturbed with the post-Plassey currency situation in Bengal that it proposed sending a team of experts to India to examine the position. William Pulteney, a Member of Parliament who had a great influence on the India House, had suggested the names of Adam Ferguson, Andrew Stuart (both MPs) and Adam Smith for a Special Commission of Supervision that the Court of Directors were contemplating to constitute to study the affairs of the East India Company. Edmund Burke was also offered a seat on this Commission but he refused. Smith was initially quite elated for being recommended 'to East India Directors as a person who could be of any use to them'. However, his *Wealth of Nations* was yet to be published and his reputation as an economist established.[66] The idea of the Commission never materialized as the Parliament intervened and forbade any such Commissions to be sent at all.[67]

The person to whom the Court of Directors of the East India Company turned for advice was the famous economist Sir James Steuart. The reputation of Sir James had already been established as an analyst of the monetary problems through his *Dissertation on German Coin* published in 1761. Subsequently, in 1767, his *magnum opus*, *Principles of Political Economy* appeared in two volumes.

Fig. 2.3: Sir James Steuart (1712-80)

In early 1772, at the suggestion of Lord Barrington, the East India Company approached Sir James for his advice. Sir James never visited India but stayed in London for three months (May-July) in 1772 to prepare his report. Originally styled as *Observations for the Court of Directors*, the report was eventually published in July 1772 under the title *Principles of Money Applied to the State of Coin in Bengal.* It is the first authoritative study on Indian currency problems ever made and is the sourcebook for several subsequent studies. This contribution made Sir James, 'first of the long series of British economists who have been called upon from time to time to advice on the economic problems of India'.[68] Soon after the publication of the report, Harry Verelst, a former Governor of Bengal, some of whose actions were censured by Sir James, published a book in which he criticized certain points in Steuart's report.[69] Steuart replied to these criticisms in an appendix written for a later edition of the report.[70] However, it is not until 1774 that this report was sent to India for implementation of its recommendations.

Sir James commences his treatise with an explanation of the basic features of metallic currencies, and definitions of the terms bullion, coin and money. According to him, bullion is 'silver or gold, the mass or weight of which is not determined, though the fineness may be known by a particular stamp'. Coins, on the other hand, have been described as 'pieces of gold or silver of determinate weights and fineness', whereas money is 'nothing more than the denomination which determines a proportion of value'.[71] Thus: 'The pounds, shillings, and pence, in a merchant's account; the pound expressed in a bond, bill or banknote, are all denominations of money, but they are not coin, any more than they are bullion.'[72]

From these basic definitions, Steuart then goes on to elaborate the uses of money. The main part of his treatise is divided into three parts—the coinage of Bengal, the causes of the scarcity of coins in Bengal and the methods for extending paper credit.

COINAGE OF BENGAL: CREATION OF A MONEY MANAGEMENT

Steuart holds that the 'Current Rupee, and not the sicca, or any coin whatever, must be the standard by which every coin or currency is to be valued and no precaution ought to be omitted, to fix and ascertain its own value.'[73] This measure, he says, is of the utmost importance to provide security to debtors and creditors.

The Current Rupee of Bengal was a money of account, much like the Pound Sterling in Britain, Livre in France, Florin in Germany, Piastre in Spain or Rupee in Portugal—none of which were real coins. The reason for having an imaginary money for accounting purposes, according to Steuart, was the variable nature of the value of metals. He says: '. . . at the first establishment of any currency, the capital and standard money of account may have been realised in a specific coin; yet the variation, in the value of metals, has obliged all states to depart from their first regulation.'[74]

Analysing the causes of the failure of bimetallism that was introduced in Bengal in 1766, Steuart writes:

> The gold mohar of 1766, was intrinsically worth no more than 11½ sicca rupees. 11½ sicca rupees were worth 13.34 current rupees. Now by carrying the denomination of this gold mohur to 14 sicca rupees, the first consequence was, that nobody would *willingly* give 14 silver sicca rupees for this gold coin, which according to the proportional value of gold and silver bullion, was worth no more than 11½ silver siccas. The silver was therefore withdrawn

from circulation, and could not be got, by fair means, in exchange for this gold coin.[75]

This measure, says Steuart, was no less harmful to the Company itself. The gold *muhr*, which was by the Regulation of 1766 equated to 14 Sicca Rupees or 16.24 Current Rupees, was tendered by the debtors of the Company whereby they could settle the debt of 16.24 Current Rupees through a single gold *muhr*, the actual worth of which was not more than 13.34 Current Rupees or $11\frac{1}{2}$ Sicca Rupees.

By the Regulation of 1771, the Company's government in Bengal attempted to adopt a similar mesure with regard to silver currency which it had adopted in respect of gold currency in 1766. By this measure, the government assigned an increased value to the coins of the 11 *sun* which were liable to become *sanwat* after the issue of new coins bearing 12 *sun*. Now 100 coins of 11 *sun* were to pass for 116 Current Rupees—at par with the newly-coined Sicca Rupees. No steps were taken by the Company's government to re-coin the *sanwat* coins, which might have lost a part of their bullion content through wear and tear.[76] Steuart says:

> Must there not be a great profit to the person who can turn these 100 sunats into 116 current rupees by the stroke of a hammer? The Company ought to have, at least, the profit of doing this; since they are to bear the loss, in the payment of their revenue every succeeding year; because all sunats will henceforth be paid to them at the rate of siccas.[77]

Thus, the Regulation of 1771 resulted in debasing the value of the Current Rupee, on the one hand, and in diminishing the revenue of the Company and the salaries of its servants, on the other—that too, without any profit upon the re-coinage of *sanwat* accruing to the Company.

Steuart then goes on to examine the 'present state of the coin in Bengal' and does so by looking at it in its historical perspective. 'The standard of Bengal money has been silver; gold has been occasionally coined', he observes. The most common silver coin in Bengal was 'the rupee of one sicca, or ten massa weight and of the fineness of 98/100 or 11.03 oz. 15 dwt. 4 gr. 0.8 dec. troy'.[78] According to Steuart, the siccas of Bengal, along with the rupees of Madras, Bombay and Surat, were 'coined by the best regulations of weight and fineness', yet the denomination—or the determinant of the proportion of value—of the Bengal sicca rupee was very different from those of

Madras or Bombay.[79] This was due to the *battas*, which, according to Sir James, was 'the first and radical defect of the Bengal currency'.[80]

The second defect of the Bengal currency, holds Steuart, was 'with respect to the accuracy of its fabrication'. The coins were issued from various mints 'where the regulations, both as to the fineness, and the weight of the coins are different, though their denomination be the same' (viz., the rupee). Then there were also malpractices such as 'punching out holes, and filling up these holes with base metal,[81] as well as wilfully diminishing the weight of the coin, after coming from the mint'.[82]

Fig. 2.4: 'Surakhi' Rupee

All these gave differing values to the currencies of various provinces. These defects introduced 'a general and insupportable abuse: namely that of the Shroffage', Steuart then describes the system of shroffage:

> When a sum of rupees is brought to a shroff, he examines them piece by piece, ranges them according to their fineness, then by weight. Then he allows for the different legal battas upon siccas and sunuts, and this done, he values in gross *by the rupee current*, what the whole quantity is worth (italics in the original).[83]

Thus, once the assessment of various species of rupees by the *sarrafs* is done, the assessed value is expressed in terms of Current Rupees because their value was 'the only thing fixed . . . and the reason is, because it is not a coin itself, and therefore can never be falsified or worn.'[84] Therefore, a regulation to determine the value of the Current Rupees, which does not get debased with the debasement of the coin was required.

SCARCITY OF COIN IN BENGAL

Coming to the second aspect of the currency crisis of Bengal, Sir James observed that the 'complaints of a scarcity of coin in Bengal . . .

are so general that *the fact can hardly be called in question*.'[85] He enumerates eight causes of drain of silver from Bengal.

The first cause was the cessation of silver imports from England. Upon the East India Company's acquiring revenue collection rights in Bengal (1765), the import of silver into India from England ceased and the investments of the Company came to be paid from the money thus collected from the revenue. According to Sir James, '. . . the goods exported from Bengal by the English having occasioned no importation of money from England in return, the importation of goods from England and from their Indian neighbours must have been paid with the money of Bengal exported, to the diminution of the general fund.'[86] Thus, according to Sir James, 'the articles of importation into Bengal as far as they are not compensated with the exportation of their own commodities and bought up with the very money of the country', constituted the first cause of drain of Bengal's silver specie.[87]

The second cause was the Company's China trade. The Company's investments in China were paid for with the revenues of Bengal. According to Sir James, 'the specie carried by the Company for the China market, which in the space of three years [1769-71] amounts to about 72,000*l* Sterling' was a major drain.[88]

Another drain of Bengal's wealth was by way of the annual subsidy paid by the East India Company to the Mughal Emperor 'which is sent out of Bengal, and never returns'.[89]

The fourth drain, according to Sir James, was 'the money laid out in buying diamonds'.[90] Diamonds were an important medium of the transfer of funds in the eighteenth century. The Company's servants, too, freely invested money in diamonds for the transfer of their surplus income to England. Sir James observed, 'there are no diamond mines in Bengal, the coin was sent out of Bengal for the purchase of the diamonds, and was virtually exported to the diminution of their wealth'.[91]

A fifth drain, according to Sir James, was 'the lending of money to foreign nations trading to India'.[92] A large chunk of Bengal's money went to the other European trading companies present in India. French, Dutch, Danish and Swedish companies borrowed money from the English East India Company's servants in return for bills of exchange drawn over Europe. Thus, while these companies acquired an additional source of income to finance their trade in India, China and other parts of Asia, the East India Company's servants found a convenient mode of transferring their ill-gotten fortunes safely to their homes.

Ever since the grant of the *Diwani* of Bengal, the East India Company set out a concrete plan of territorial acquisition and expansion. This necessitated the maintenance of a large army by the Company, and all expenditure on this account constituted a severe drain of Bengal's specie.

'Whatever raw-silk, cotton, or other merchandize fit for manufacture is imported from other nations, unless paid for by the exchange of commodities', was, according to Sir James, the seventh article of drain.[93] The manufactures from these raw materials, when exported by the Company, added to its wealth 'when realised into money, at their London sales, but still at the expense of the wealth of Bengal'.

The eighth and the last drain on the silver currency of Bengal was, according to Sir James, caused by financing of the Madras and Bombay presidencies from the Bengal's revenues. As there was a constant deficit in the income and expenditures of the East India Company's Madras and Bombay Presidencies, the surplus revenue of Bengal was regularly diverted to these establishments. According to Sir James, 'the extent, as well as the necessity of this drain is so well known to the Company, that it is here stated for the memory only'.[94]

THE REMEDIES

The remedies suggested by Sir James were threefold and followed logically from his diagnosis of the currency problems of Bengal:

1. All sources of further drain should be stopped and steps should be taken to improve Bengal's balance of trade;
2. The circulation of money within the country should be accelerated by various public finance measures; and
3. A bank should be established on the model of the Bank of England so that paper money might be issued as necessary.[95]

FOLLOW-UP MEASURES ADOPTED BY THE EAST INDIA COMPANY'S GOVERNMENT IN BENGAL

These were the times when the currency situation in Bengal was in the most supreme state of desiderata. The two experiments to introduce bimetallism to reduce pressure on the silver currency had failed. The demand for coined silver was increasing day-by-day to meet war expenditure, tribute to England and financing of the China trade, among others.

Under these circumstances, the Court of Directors, in its letter dated 30 March 1774 wrote to the Governor-General of Bengal: 'There is not any object before you which more immediately claims your attention than the state of coinage and currency of Bengal.'[96]

Along with this letter, the Court of Directors sent the treatise by Sir James Steuart to the government of Bengal for guidance in the matters of currency reform. The Court wrote:

> We earnestly recommend to you, that after availing yourselfs of every light thrown upon the subject by the records of the Company, and by a treatise compiled for our use by Sir James Steuart, herein transmitted, and also of the assistance of the most experienced persons in the province, you endeavour to establish an equitable rupee. . . .[97]

These were also the times when the Company was on the verge of bankruptcy. Ever since the acquisition of the *Diwani* of Bengal, Bihar and Orissa, the proprietors and shareholders of the East India Company persisted in believing that they had struck a gold mine. Thus, persuaded by false hopes, they continued year after year, in defiance of an exhausted treasury, to increase the amount of dividend—from 6 to 10 and from 10 to 12½ per cent.[98] As a result, on 8 July 1772, on an estimate of cash for the next three months, there appeared a deficiency of £12,93,000! On 15 July, the Directors of the Company were forced to apply to the Bank of England for a loan of £4,00,000 for two months. Within a fortnight, on 29 July, they applied for another loan of £3,00,000. The Bank, however, could not offer more than two-thirds of that amount. Unable to secure the money from the Bank of England, the Directors of the East India Company applied for a government loan of £10,00,000 on 10 August 1772.

The British government, headed by Lord North, seized this opportunity to establish its firm control over the East India Company's affairs. In November 1772, a 13-member Secret Committee of Parliament was appointed to investigate the affairs of the Company.[99] The financial recommendations of the Select Committee included the grant of a government loan of £1,400,000 at the rate of 4 per cent to the Company, reduction of the proprietors' dividend to 6 per cent, and the postponement of the government share of £400,000 per annum till the payment of the loan amount. The Company was forbidden to declare a dividend exceeding 6 per cent and was required to submit its accounts to the Treasury every six months.

The recommendations of the Select Committee were accepted by the Parliament and the result was the passing of the Regulating Act of 1773. Its arrangements concerning business at home commenced on 1 October 1773, and those concerning administration in India on 1 August 1774.

Under the provisions of the Regulating Act, the status of the Governor of Bengal was raised to that of the Governor-General of Bengal, and a Council consisting of four members was appointed to assist him. This Act was the first step towards the creation of a central authority for the territories administered by the East India Company. Hereafter, the Presidencies of Madras and Bombay were subjected to, with certain provisos, the Governor-General-in-Council in matters connected with hostilities or war against any Indian princes or powers. An offending President or the Council of these Presidencies could be suspended by the Governor-General-in-Council. Moreover, these Presidencies were to transmit regularly to the Governor-General intelligence of all transactions relating to the government, revenue or the interests of the Company.[100]

FRANCIS'S PLAN (1775)

By 1774, the failure of the measures for currency reforms adopted in 1771 was evident. The sicca rupees, upon which *batta* was discontinued by the Regulation of 1771, valued just a little more than the *sanwat* rupees of full weight in the market. This caused serious resentment among the troops of the East India Company whose salaries were paid in sicca rupees. The evil effects of this regulation were not confined to the troops alone; they were experienced in revenue administration as well.[101]

The first fruit of the despatch of the Court of Directors and Sir James Steuart's advice was the masterly Minute by Philip Francis, a prominent member of the newly-appointed Council of the Governor-General. Francis was apparently influenced by Sir James's doctrine for currency reform though he was quick to point out his difference both to the Court of Directors as well as James Steuart. He writes: 'I foresee that I shall be obliged to differ, in some degrees, from the Idea conceived . . . by the Court of Directors, and, if I am not mistaken, by Sir James Steuart.'[102] However, his difference was more in the matter of details rather than on general principles on which he is not 'found to depart materially from those great authorities'.[103]

In his Minute dated 13 March 1775, Francis laid down three important principles:

1. That there should be only one of precious metals coined as legal tender and that this coin should be [of] silver. Every other species of coin should be regarded as bullion.
2. That the disproportion between the nominal and intrinsic value of the new coin should be, no more than sufficient to answer two purposes, viz., to pay the expence [*sic*] of coinage and to make the Coin hard enough for current use.
3. That there should be but one mint.[104]

On the basis of the above principles, Francis proposed the following measures for currency reform:

1. A new rupee be struck called a Calcutta Rupee, bearing on one side the titles of the Emperor Shaw Allum as impressed on the Siccas and on the reverse the words 'Calcutta Rupee' with the year of the Christian era. Any future change in the sovereignty will make no alteration in the coin, excepting in the Titles of the Sovereign.
2. That this new Rupee be coined of the standard of England.
3. That the weight of this Rupee be the same with that of the Sicca, viz. 7 dwt. $11\frac{2}{3}$ grs [or 179.66 grains =11.64 g].
4. As the proposed alteration of standard will make near Six per cent Difference between the intrinsic value of the new Rupee and the present Sicca, that a batta of ten per cent be fixed on the Calcutta Rupee for the first year of its passing current, until a sufficient number of them be coined to answer the purposes of Circulation, when it may be expected that the Ideas of battas may in a short time be entirely obliterated, by making this one Species of Rupees the only legal tender.
5. That until a sufficient number of Calcutta Rupees can be coined, or for the Space of one year from the commencement of the Plan, the siccas of the 12 and 11 Sun be allowed to circulate at the usual batta of 16 per cent as lawful money but that the Batta of the 11 Sun be reduced to 13 per cent only, and that, after the expiration of twelve months from that time, all Rupees, whatsoever (except the new Coin) be indiscriminately considered as Bullion and only bought and sold as merchandise, not received in payment by any valuation of the shroffs.
6. That after the above term of twelve months, all receipts and payments, whether of the Revenue, or of the Civil and Military establishment, be made in Calcutta Rupees and called as many Calcutta Rupees as they turn out at the proportionate value of ten percent Batta, reduced from whatever Denomination of Specie these payments were usually made in. That the

new rupee be made the only money of account, that all the Company's Books and Accounts be kept in this Denomination of money only; by which it is proposed totally to set aside the use of Batta on Rupees.

7. That an allowance of $2\frac{1}{2}$ per cent on Silver and the 1 per cent on gold be made for the charges of Coinage and Recoinage of all bullion and that the present heavy duty of $4\frac{1}{2}$ per cent on the coinage of silver bullion be abolished. That this allowance of $2\frac{1}{2}$ per cent be made on the Quantity of the standard Metal, the Charges of refining being on account of the Proprietors; and that for the Ease of Merchants who have Rupees or other coin of a known standard to be recoined, a Table be made out of the produce of each sort of Rupees, which Table shall be kept open in the Assay Office for the inspection of any person who wishes to have Recourse to it.
8. That half and quarter Rupees be also struck of the same standard and of a weight proportionate to the Denomination and annas of a compound mass of copper and silver, weighing eight annas or half a Rupee and containing such a quantity of fine silver, as may be found necessary to proportion their intrinsic to their nominal value. Pice may also be coined of pure copper of a weight to be calculated and determined on the same principle. The two last mentioned coins shall not be enforced as legal tender. Their use and convenience will probably give them a universal currency.
9. As many conveniences arise in large trading cities from the circulation of gold coin, I recommend that Gold Mohurs be struck of the same weight as the new rupee and 23 carats fine and issued at sixteen rupees each. To avoid, however, the inconveniences which are generally felt from the fluctuations of the relative value of the precious metals, that these mohurs be not made legal tender and that the paying and receiving of them be left to a voluntary agreement between the parties.[105]
10. That there are in circulation, at present a number of Gold Mohurs bearing the Patna stamp, of very inferior value, it will be necessary to recall these, and as the Faith of Government is pledged for their Goodness, by the Stamp which gives them currency, the loss ought not to fall on Individuals but on those officers of the Mint or rather on the Juamer [? Contractor] of the Mint, who must have abused the Trust reposed in him.
11. [To enquire] whether the Patna Mohurs, now in circulation, be not received at a Discount. If so, the immediate Holders will have no just claim on Government for the Difference between the real and nominal value of those coins when recalled.[106]

Two notable features of Francis's plan were his advocacy of silver monometallism (a principle which was finally adopted by the Court of Directors in 1806) and the induction of copper currency as the third tier of the currency system. However, his scheme was impractical on many counts. For example, he was apparently unaware of the total coins in circulation and the heavy expenses on their recoinage, and recommended demonetization of all other species of rupees, except the 'siccas of the 12 and 11 sun . . . after the expiration of twelve months'. Nevertheless, several of his suggestions, viz., the establishment of a silver standard and operating only a single mint in Bengal, found place in the currency reforms initiated by Warren Hastings.

HASTINGS'S PLAN (1777)

Warren Hastings proposed a new regulation for reforming the ailing currency, which was laid before the Board on 5 May 1777:

1st. That it be resolved and declared that only one Mint shall be allowed for the Coinage of Money, for the use of the three Provinces, which shall be that of Calcutta.

2nd. That only Sicca Rupees of the present standard be struck into [*sic*] the mint.

3rd. That no Gold coins be coined after the 31st of this month.

4th. That all Sicca Rupees of the future coinage shall pass for ever, without any deduction of batta, by weight and not by tale, in all Receipts of Revenue and in all Receipts and issues of the Company's treasury.

5th. That orders be sent to the Provincial Councils and Collectors to transport to the Presidency all Rupees of whatever denomination, which may be now in their Treasuries, and from time to time such others as they shall receive, excepting Sicca Rupees of the 11 Sun and of later dates and that all such rupees as they arrive at the Presidency be sent to the mint to be recoined.

6th. That for encouragement of individuals to bring bullion to the mint, the present duty of $4\frac{1}{2}$ per cent on coinage be abolished and in lieu thereof a duty of [. . .][107] per cent in addition to the real charges be established and that the Assay Master be directed to form Tables of Rates specifying the amount of those Charges on Bullion and Specie of the different degrees of fineness and of the produce in Sicca Rupees.

7th. That for the further encouragement of the Proprietors of Bullion and Specie requiring to be recoined, the expedient proposed by the Assay Master in his letter above recorded be adopted as a fixed percentage of Regulation, that is to say, that all such Bullion or Specie as shall be tendered to the Mint, shall, after having been assayed be received into the mint on the Company's account and that the produce estimated by the preceding Regulation be immediately paid to the Proprietor

> from the Public Treasury on producing the receipt of the Mint Master for the weights of Bullion received and the Certificate of the Assay Master of its value in Sicca Rupees.[108]

Besides Hastings, only one other member of the four-Member Board, namely Richard Barwell, 'a blind supporter of Hastings', agreed with the proposal.[109] While General John Clavering, the Commander-in-Chief of the Company's forces in India and a member of the Board, sought time to consider it, and 'a few days later criticised almost all of them and suggested his own scheme instead',[110] Philip Francis, an arch critic of Hastings, recorded his disagreement on the second point of Hastings' Plan but he, too, gave his support to the proposed regulation. His main disagreement was regarding the existing standard of the Sicca Rupee, which he considered too fine for permanent circulation.[111] Nevertheless, Hastings went ahead and implemented his plan, which involved the following changes.

One of the first acts under this plan was the closure of Mints at Patna, Dacca and Murshidabad. With the grant of the *Diwani*, the control of all the three Mughal mints located in the *subahs* of Bengal and Bihar, viz., Jahangirnagar (Dacca), Murshidabad and Azimabad (Patna), passed on to the East India Company on 12 August 1765. Besides these three mints, the Company already had a mint at Calcutta. All the four mints of the Bengal presidency struck silver coins of the *sicca* standard—Patna and Dacca had the mint names as of *Azimabad* and *Jahangirnagar*, respectively, while the Calcutta mint struck these coins with the mint name *Murshidabad*. As far as the quality of coins struck at the newly-acquired mints was concerned, it was observed that the *sicca* standard was not maintained by the Patna and Dacca mints. Thus, with a view to ensuring the uniformity of standard, the Patna mint was closed in 1772, followed by that of Dacca in 1773.[112]

No sooner were the mints at Patna and Dacca shut down that the demand for their re-opening began to be raised. The Provincial Council at Patna, in their letter dated 27 March 1775 addressed to the Governor-General and the Council of Revenue, proposed the resumption of the coinage of rupees at the Patna mint.[113]

On 4 May 1775, the Governor-General in Council asked the Board of Trade and the different provincial councils to send their comments on:

a. Whether the mints at Patna and Dacca should be re-established, and
b. If so, whether the rupees of the four mints should bear the name of the

place where they were coined or should have exactly the same inscriptions so as to be indistinguishable from each other.[114]

The replies received from various public bodies presented discordant views. On the question of the re-establishment of mints, the Board of Trade and the Provincial Councils of Murshidabad did not offer any opinion of their own. The Council at Dinajpur, Patna, Burdwan and Dacca favoured the re-opening of the mints, while the Calcutta Committee of Revenue wanted a mint at Patna but not at Dacca.

As for the second point of reference, while the Dinajpur Council wanted the inscription and the name of a single mint, all other bodies advocated the insertion of the name of the mint where the coin was struck.

On 5 May 1777, Warren Hastings proposed new regulations for reforming the ailing currency, which included, among others, the closure of the Murshidabad mint and the centralization of all minting activities at Calcutta. Even before the new plan was approved by the Board, the Murshidabad mint was abolished on 9 May 1777 and the privilege of annually minting a small number of silver coins that the Dutch enjoyed here was transferred to Calcutta. On 29 May 1777, the Board gave its approval to the closure of the Murshidabad mint.[115]

The overall impact of closing the mints at Patna, Dacca and Murshidabad was a further aggravation of currency problems, as the Calcutta mint could not cope with the work of four mints.

Another measure adopted by Hastings, though it was not explicitly mentioned as such in his plan, was freezing of the regnal year appearing on the coins. Silver coins bearing the frozen regnal year 12 continued to be struck during 1771-7. However, this measure that was supposed to check the menace of *batta* proved to be self-defeating. While the regnal year appearing on the reverse of the coins was 'frozen' on the silver coins issued during this period, the obverse continued to bear its correct Hijri year. The mismatched Hijri-regnal year combination appear on the coins as:

> AH 1185/12 RY, AH 1186/12 RY, AH 1187/12 RY, AH 1188/12 RY, and AH 1189/12 RY.

This gave the money-changers ample scope to differentiate the coinages of the different years and charge a discount (*batta*) on the older coinage.

On some coins purporting to be the issues of 1773-4, the mismatched Hijri-regnal year combination is noticed, viz., AH 1189/

15 RY and AH 1190/15 RY. The Hijri year AH 1189 commenced on 4 March 1775 and continued up to 20 February 1776, while AH 1190 commenced on 21 February 1776 and continued up to 8 February 1777. On the other hand, the 15th regnal year of Shah Alam II commenced much earlier on 30 June 1773 and continued up to 18 June 1774.

To supersede coins of all these varying dates, a new coin was introduced by the East Bengal government in 1777 dating from the 19th regnal year of Shah Alam II that commenced on 17 May 1777.

One of the provisions of Hastings' currency reforms of 1777 was the abandoning of the second experiment of bimetallism that was introduced by Verelst in 1769 and reintroducing silver monometallism. Thus, the Regulation of 1777 declared that 'no gold coins be coined after the 31st of this month'. Accordingly, the minting of new gold coins was stopped with effect from 31 May 1777. However, existing *muhrs* were not withdrawn from circulation. Instead, they were allowed to pass universally 'at the usual value of 16 *sicca* rupee each, and be received and issued at the public treasuries at the same rate'.[116] Thus, instead of effectively introducing a silver monometallic standard, this provision set up something like the 'Limping Standard' in Bengal.[117]

To ensure the flow of private bullion into the government mint, Hastings's scheme proposed to encourage individuals to bring bullion to the mint. For this purpose, the duty of 4½ per cent on coinage was abolished and a duty in addition to the actual minting charges was established in its place.[118]

Until now, the owners of bullion had to deposit their metal in the mint and wait till it was assayed, refined and converted into coins. This provision acted as a deterrent to bullion owners, especially when they were in immediate need of coins to meet their requirements. Hastings's plan took care of this problem as well, and declared that all bullion tendered to the mint should be assayed and entered into the mint on the Company's account. The proprietors of such bullion were to be immediately paid the estimated produce in coin from the public treasury.

PLANS FOR INTRODUCTION OF A PAPER CURRENCY (1780)

One of the measures to overcome the shortage of specie in Bengal, which was originally recommended by Sir James Steuart, was the introduction of a paper currency. In 1780, steps were taken to adopt this recommendation. In June 1777, treasure worth 30 lakh Sicca rupees was deposited in the 'New Fort William' at Calcutta to meet the exigencies of the government. On 1 May 1780, Hastings, in his famous Minute, proposed to utilize this amount as a security for the issue of paper currency.[119] The government's plans were made public through an advertisement:

> . . . it is their [Government's] intention to issue notes from their Treasury either for ready money which shall be tendered, or in payment of demands on the Treasury, to such persons as may chuse [*sic.* choose] to receive them in lieu of the ready money, which notes shall be signed by the Governor-General-in-Council and sealed with the Seal of the Company, and be made payable on demand, either to the Bearer or Order, at the option of the parties receiving them shall be granted for any respective sum, not less than 100 Current nor more than 10,000 Current Rupees.[120]

The form of the proposed notes was to be as follows:

No.
Seal of the Company Calcutta, ...th 1780

We, the Governor-General-in-Council of Fort William, do, on behalf of the United Company of Merchants of England trading to the East Indies—promise to pay at our Treasury in Calcutta on Demand to ______________ or Bearer,* the sum of Current Rupees ________________ for value received.

* 'or Order' in case the Note was payable to Order.

Fig. 2.5: Form of a Note Payable to Bearer

This was probably the earliest scheme of a government paper currency in India. Apart from the deposit of 30 lakh sicca rupees, it seems that there was to be an additional reserve of 66 per cent against the notes actually issued to the public. It is not clear what prevented the government from implementing this scheme.

THE CONTRACT COPPER COINAGE, 1780-1784

Bengal had no copper coins of its own. For small transactions below a rupee, the chief medium of eighteenth-century Bengal was the *cowrie* shell (*cyprea moneta*), as the silver and copper fraction of the rupee were seldom minted in the Bengal mints. One of the reasons for the absence of fractional small denomination coins, especially of silver, could be the minting charges and the bullion loss in converting the metal into coins. Besides, the popularity and ready acceptability of *cowries* in the bazaars prevented the necessity of having an alternative medium for smaller monetary transactions. That the *cowrie* was a popular medium of currency can be seen from the fact that till the end of the eighteenth century, the government revenue was collected in *cowries* in many parts of the Bengal presidency.[121]

However, the availability of *cowries* in Bengal depended on their import mainly from the Maldives archipelago, a group of coral islands lying around 400 miles west of Cape Comorin.[122] Consequently, the price of *cowries vis-à-vis* the rupee often fluctuated. To overcome this difficulty, the government had tried to issue tickets made of base metals such as copper, brass and tutenagues as a means of small payments as early as in 1757. This experiment, however, was unsuccessful.

On 23 March 1780, John Prinsep, a prominent government contractor, submitted a proposal to the Bengal government to supply copper coins. In his proposal, Prinsep informed the Bengal government about his discovery of copper ore in one of the undisclosed districts of the Bengal province and requested the government to grant him exclusive rights over these mines. In return, he agreed to pay a sum equivalent to the current rent of the land to its owner and to 'deliver the whole produce of pure copper in coin at the rate of 52 Sicca Rupees per maund', to the government. On 4 April, the government entered into a contract under which John Prinsep was given the exclusive right to procure copper from the copper mines at Rohtas and Monghyr in Bihar. He was to use this metal to produce copper coins, which were then to be purchased by the Bengal government for general circulation in the province. This contract was initially for three years and was renewable for the next twenty-seven years after the expiry of this term.

Under this contract, Prinsep was to mint four denominations of copper coins. (Table 2.3)

TABLE 2.3: BENGAL: PRINSEP'S CONTRACT COINAGE, 1780-4

Denomination	Equivalent to	Relative value to		Weight	
		Sicca Rupee	*Cowries*	*Anna* Weight	Grams
Madosie	Half *Anna*	32	160	20 *Annas*	14.58
Faloos	Quarter *Anna*	64	80	10 *Annas*	7.29
Neem Faloos	Eighth *Anna*	128	40	5 *Annas*	3.64
Paw Faloos	Sixteenth *Anna*	256	20	2½ *Annas*	1.82

The news of this contractual copper coinage was welcomed by the public. James Augustus Hicky's *Bengal Gazette* records the euphoria of the public in the following words:

> We are informed that a copper coinage is now on the carpet . . . it will be of the greatest utility to the Public and will abolish the trade of Cowries, which for a long time has formed so extensive a field for deception and fraud. A grievance the poor has long groaned under. . . .[123]

John Prinsep set up a mint at Falta, a village 22 miles south of Calcutta. His partner in this new business was one Alexander Cunningham. The Falta mint was far more advanced in its mechanical equipment than the government mint at Calcutta. To further enhance the quality of his produce, Prinsep managed to secure die-engravers and other technical staff from the government mint at Calcutta. By 13 December 1780, specimen coins were struck and the design was approved by the government.

One-Eighth *Anna* Half *Anna*

Fig. 2.6: Prinsep's Contract Coinage

These coins were of superior mintage. All denominations have identical inscriptions and uniformly bear the date AH 1195/ 22 RY. The only means to distinguish between them is by their size and weight. The mint name, a permanent and prominent feature of contemporary coinage, is conspicuously absent from all these coins. Perhaps the government wanted to hide the fact that these coins were of private mintage.

The actual coinage at Falta commenced in about March 1781 and, on 30 April, forty specimens of the new copper coins of different denominations were sent to the Court of Directors in London.[124] By September, sufficient stocks had been accumulated for its general release. On 24 September 1781, the government announced the introduction of a general copper coinage and authorized its circulation.

It announced that in all government payments, 1 per cent of the total amount would be accepted in the form of copper coins.

This attempt of the Bengal government drew severe censure from the Court of Directors. In its letter dated 25 January 1782, the latter observed that 'the contracts entered into with Mr. Prinsep are highly prejudicial to our interests'. The Court of Directors regarded the granting of the right of coining to 'an individual' as 'utterly improper'. It held that: 'The Company are, and ought to be, accountable, so far as can be the case, for the purity and propriety of the coin of Bengal. Their responsibility cannot be transferred, and consequently their authority must not, on any account whatever, be delegated.'[125]

The Court of Directors directed the Bengal government to immediately serve a notice to John Prinsep that in no event would they continue the contract beyond the term of three years, after which Prinsep was to surrender the contracts for mining and coining copper.[126] Accordingly, with effect from August 1783, the coinage of copper was stopped; in 1784, the mint at Falta was closed and the contract between the government and Prinsep was cancelled in the following year.

Prinsep, however, was no loser in this game. He claimed a huge indemnity for the losses and expenses that he allegedly incurred in working the mines and minting the copper coins. The amount was settled at 1,65,389 Current Rupees, which Prinsep most obligingly accepted.[127]

DEVELOPMENT OF EUROPEAN BANKING

One of the main characteristics of the money market of the eighteenth-century India was the dictating role of the money-changers or *sarrafs* who doubled up as bankers and sometimes also as insurers. The diversity of specie in circulation and its remittance to the government in the form of revenue often led to losses to the Company by way of the *batta* charged by these money-changers for converting one specie into another.

The need for starting a bank on European lines was felt by the East India Company as early as in 1683 when its Directors at London wrote to the Madras government 'to raise capital and accept deposits'.[128] The outcome of this communication is not known but what we know for sure is that no bank based on European banking practices was established in Madras till about 1788.

(a) Bombay Presidency

Bombay was the first presidency to establish a bank on European lines. On 22 December 1720, 'after consultation with eminent black [read Indian] merchants', the BANK OF BOMBAY was established by the Government of Bombay. The management of the bank was vested in the Governor and two members of its Council. A sum of Rs. 1 lakh was furnished out of the Company's cash as the capital stock of the bank. Deposits of Rs. 100 and more were received for six months, for which the depositors received promissory notes in exchange bearing interest at a fixed amount per day. Inhabitants of Bombay, whether native, covenanted or hired servants, were allowed to borrow at a fixed rate of 9 per cent against a security of goods or the joint security of the borrower and another substantial party. Borrowers were encouraged by the facility of repayment in instalments of Rs. 100 or more. The manager of the bank was paid by a levy of 1 per cent on each loan.[129]

In 1770, the Government of Bombay faced an acute shortage of silver coins. To meet the crisis, the Governor-in-Council drew up a scheme for the payment of the debt of Rs. 8 lakh due from the treasury in bank notes. The salient feature of the scheme was the protection afforded to individual officers against the liability to repay the money promised on the notes. These bank notes were to bear an interest of 6 per cent. However, the shortage of coins became so acute that the bank note scheme could not be carried into effect and was dropped in 1771. Hereafter, the bank itself went into oblivion.[130]

(b) Bengal Presidency

Fifty years after the establishment of the Bank of Bombay, a well-known agency house in Bengal made its foray into the banking business. A bank, named the BANK OF HINDUSTAN, was established by Alexander & Co. in 1770. This bank was a pioneer in its attempt to introduce paper currency in India. It issued, for the first time in India, paper money on the pattern of notes that were current in England. These notes were in the denominations of 4, 10, 16, 20, 50, 100, 250 and a 1,000 Sicca rupees. Though these notes were not accepted in government transactions, they become increasingly popular with the public.

One of the measures adopted by Warren Hastings to improve the currency situation in Bengal was the establishment of a bank. The revenue in Bengal was not only assessed in current coins but also realized in specie. As a variety of coins circulated in various parts of Bengal, these were tendered in the district collectorates in the payment of revenue. The collectors were often at a loss to ascertain the correct amount of *batta* to be levied on various sorts of specie. This resulted in a substantial loss to the Company. Another related problem was that of the remittance of funds. The transfer of revenue collected in the form of specie from the districts to Calcutta faced the risk of dacoity and, therefore, had to be escorted by a military guard.

Hastings thought that the only expedient for meeting these difficulties was by setting up a bank which should have its head office in Calcutta and branches in district headquarters. The branches would receive the revenue payments from the collectors in the current coins of the particular district and transmit the same amount to Calcutta by issuing bills of exchange drawn on its head office. Inversely, the merchants, who were required to remit money to the *moffusil* for making payments for the investments, the purchase of trade items and so on, could purchase bills from bank's head office in Calcutta or any of its branches by making payments in the local currency. By this measure the merchants would have the advantage of having the locally current specie readily available to them in the concerned *moffusil.*

The bank, named GENERAL BANK OF BENGAL AND BEHAR, or simply GENERAL BANK, was instituted in April 1773. It had two main offices—one in Calcutta and the other at Murshidabad, and fourteen branches located at Bhagalpur, Birbhoom, Bishnupur, Burdwan, Dacca, Dinajpur, Hughli, Jessore, Malda, Midnapur, Nadia, Purnea, Rajmahal and Rangpur. The bank was a private establishment and had amongst its directors two leading bankers of the time, namely Hazarimal and Rai Durlabh. However, it had the government's patronage and the collectors of the districts were given instructions to remit their revenue collections by this bank's bills of exchange.

However, the bank failed the expectations of both the government as well as the public. The Court of Directors in its letter dated 30 March 1774 lamented that: '. . . for every 1,000,000 sunats paid to the agents of the Bank, in the various districts of Bengal, there will only be repaid to the Governor-General in Council at Calcutta rupees 94,828 of the same weight and real value. . . .'[131]

The directors, therefore, declared that 'this regulation cannot be confirmed by us'. The Court of Directors's main objection was to the arrangement of placing the entire business of the movement of the government's revenue in the hands of the managers of the bank and it felt that the government derived no benefit from its institution.

Having lost the government as its patron, the General Bank was closed down in February 1775.

The BENGAL BANK was established in Calcutta in 1784. This was the earliest European bank in Bengal not connected to any agency house. Its proprietors were employees of the English East India Company. This bank is said to have issued its own notes, though no such note has been reported so far.[132] The amount of notes it issued was about Rs. 8,00,000.[133] These notes commanded the full confidence of the Calcuttans but they did not circulate at all in the districts and *moffusils*. Holt Mackenzie has recorded the reason in his evidence before the Parliament. According to him: 'In general, indeed, payment in districts, even in the provision of the staple articles of Commerce, are made in such small sums, and the population is so poor that there is scarcely any room for a large circulation of bank paper.'[134]

The outbreak of the Third Anglo-Mysore War in 1790 adversely affected the resources of the Bengal Bank. The heavy drain of silver from Bengal to Mysore for financing the war coupled with the rumours of British reverses in the war led to a panic in Bengal in which everyone wanted to encash bank notes. Thus, in 1791, between 20 and 27 November, the Bengal Bank paid more than 8 lakh Sicca rupees.[135] Thereafter, it ran short of hard cash and was forced to apply to the government of Bengal for a loan of Rs. 5 lakh for a period of three months at the rate of 12 per cent per annum. The bank pledged the Company's papers to the full value of the loan as security. There was a similar request from the Bank of Hindustan, which, too, was facing a cash crunch. Of the two, the Government of Bengal opted to help the latter to overcome the crisis. As a result, the Bengal Bank was closed down in November 1791.

Another bank named the GENERAL BANK OF INDIA was started in Calcutta on 1 June 1786. In January 1787, the Government of Bengal extended its patronage to this bank by declaring its notes acceptable in the payment of government dues. The real reason behind extending this privilege to the General Bank was that the Government of Bengal was facing an acute financial crisis. The discount on government securities had risen up to 25 per cent and further borrowing had become virtually impossible. Lord Cornwallis, the Governor-General of Bengal, wrote to the Court of Directors in December 1786:

> . . . while the unavoidable expenses of the establishments, the interests due upon the debts, and the demand from the other presidencies, absorbed the produce of revenue, considerable investment could only be made by fresh issue of paper, by which mode the evil might be protracted, but would only be ultimately increased.[136]

At this juncture, the General Bank lent to the government of Bengal 20 lakh Current Rupees at a favourable rate of interest against which notes could be issued by the bank. These notes, in turn, could be used for settling government dues. According to J.C. Sinha, this arrangement 'alleviated the currency difficulties' of the government of Bengal in the following two ways: 'Firstly, by providing a convenient paper currency which was almost as good as legal tender, and, secondly, by holding as reserve against its issue Company's paper thus rehabilitating the value of such securities.'[137]

The General Bank, thus, became the virtual bankers of the English East India Company. However, government patronage to the bank was short-lived. By a notification published in the *Calcutta Gazette*, the government refused to recognize the notes of this bank after 30 November 1788. On 24 April 1789, orders were issued for closing the government account with the bank. The bank itself was wound up on 31 March 1791.

(c) Madras Presidency

The first joint-stock bank to be established on European lines in the Madras Presidency was the CARNATIC BANK. Amongst its eight founding members was N.E. Kendersley, who was also a member of the Board of Trade.[138] Nothing much is known about its activities except that it was to receive money, issue bills, notes and discount bills, and other securities 'after the manner of the most respectable bank in London'.[139] The bank had a capital of 1.20 lakh Star *pagodas* and had the power to issue notes to the value of three times the capital.[140] The notes issued by this bank were accepted by the Madras government.[141]

Like the Carnatic Bank, the MADRAS BANK (estb. 1795) also issued notes which were accepted by the government.[142] It must be noted that during this period, the Madras government was facing an acute shortage of coin 'due to export to Hyderabad and Mysore wars and to China and Manila on account of Company's investments'.[143] The Company, therefore, found it prudent to borrow and accept the notes of these banks.

Another bank, a contemporary of the Madras Bank, was the BRITISH BANK (estb. *c.* 1795). It was founded by five individuals, one of whom, John Hunter, worked as a cashier in the Carnatic Bank.[144] Though nothing is known about the date of its establishment, its existence in 1795 has been reported.[145] Like the preceding two banks, it is also known to have issued notes, though no specimen issued by any of them has been reported.[146]

The twin objectives of the currency reforms undertaken by Warren Hastings were 'the establishment of the sicca rupee as the standard coin of the province . . . [and] . . . to maintain a fixed ratio of exchange between the gold mohur and the sicca rupees.'[147] Hastings failed in meeting both these objectives. With a view to achieving his first objective, he had suspended the coinage of gold from 31 May 1777 but, at the same time, the closure of mints at Patna, Dacca and Murshidabad restricted the supply of silver rupees. The Calcutta mint—which still followed the minting style of the old Mughal coins—was still ill-equipped to meet the output of the four mints. As a result, in 1780, the coinage of gold *muhrs* was once again allowed at the Company's mint at Calcutta.[148] As gold currency had not gained circulation beyond the town of Calcutta, the *sarrafs* demanded *batta* on its exchange. By August 1787, the *batta* for exchanging gold *muhrs* for silver rupees, which was 5 *annas* per Rs.100 in March 1787, rose to Rs. 3 per cent at the beginning of August of the same year.[149] As John Shore later noted: '. . . the batta on gold mohurs from its augmentation became a subject of complaint, the quantity of mohurs in Calcutta had been annually increasing, and as few passed current beyond the limits of Calcutta, the accumulation exceeded the wants of the inhabitants.'[150]

One thing was clear: the diagnosis by Sir James Steuart and the measures resultant from his recommendations had not worked in Bengal. At this juncture, Cornwallis, who had assumed the office of the Governor-General of Bengal in September 1786, decided to institute his own enquiry committee to find out what ailed the currency of Bengal.

OFFICIAL DIAGNOSIS: THE COMMITTEES

Currency Committee (1787)

The monetary problems of the post-1765 era ultimately led the East India Company to adopt a 'systematic' way to find out an 'administrative' solution to what was essentially an 'economic' problem. Thus, on 25 September 1787, the Government of Bengal appointed a 'Committee for Enquiring into the Causes of the Scarcity of Silver Coin'. This was probably the earliest Currency Committee in India.[151]

The Committee ascribed the scarcity of silver in Calcutta to numerous temporary and permanent causes. Among the permanent causes were:

1. Increase in the remittance of revenue through bills: it was noted that during two years (1785-6), out of a total remittance of 7.50 crore, 3.75 crore had been sent in bills, 1.75 in *sicca* rupees and the rest (2 crore) in gold.
2. Reduced import of silver from Europe and its increased export to other presidencies and to China.
3. Over-valuation of the gold coin compared to silver.
4. Increased demand for money for investment: Money realized by way of revenue was often reinvested in purchase. Thus, very little money actually reached Calcutta.
5. War Financing: the Company's imperialist policy of territorial expansion was vigorously being followed at this time. The decade 1775-85 saw three major wars fought on Indian soil—the First Anglo-Maratha War (1775-82), the Anglo-French War (1778-83) and the Second Anglo-Mysore War (1780-4). These military exercises gobbled up Bengal's specie to a very large extent.

Besides, a temporary cause of the acute scarcity of silver at Calcutta during April to August was due to the drain of silver to the *aurangs* (or manufacturing centres) to provide for investments, with no return of rupees to Calcutta in the shape of land revenue during these months.

On the basis of the above findings, the Committee made the following major recommendations for currency reform:

1. To receive all the rupees that come into the hands of the government throughout the country, milling and subdividing them

into halves and quarters, adding an alloy equal to the English standard for the silver coin.

2. To waive the duty upon coinage for individuals.
3. To let the gold *muhrs* be milled and subdivided in a similar manner into halves, quarters and eighths, increasing the size of the subdivision beyond that now known without altering the present standard.
4. To inflict punishment upon shroffs who shall be convicted for giving anything less than sixteen new milled rupees for a new milled gold *muhr*.
5. To lower the value of copper to a more equitable standard.[152]

The recommendations of this first-ever enquiry committee on currency reforms provided only ad hoc solutions. The committee itself admitted, 'that to decide fully, and with sufficient supply [of] precaution upon so great a question as the alteration of the coinage of a country, would require a much longer and mature deliberation'.[153]

The government considered these recommendations in December 1787. Though no steps were taken immediately, practically all the recommendations were ultimately given effect to by Cornwallis. The problem of *batta* on gold *muhrs*, however, called for immediate attention. Since August 1787, the *batta* had continually risen and, by April 1788, it had doubled. As the editor of the *Calcutta Gazette* remarked: '. . . the tricks in raising the batta on gold coins called aloud for redress. The extortion which has prevailed in despite of every representation and even the scrutiny of the Committee of Enquiry [the Currency Committee] continues to gain ground, and is now as high as six per cent.'[154]

A petition from the 'respectable mercantile gentlemen' of Calcutta sought a direction from the government to its officers to receive gold *muhrs* 'indiscriminately in all payment of revenue, at their authorized value of 16 sicca rupees'.[155]

The problem once again brought a core issue before the currency administrators of the Company—that of adopting the most appropriate metallic standard for the currency of Bengal. The Board of Revenue, whose views were sought on this issue, was divided in its opinion. Two members of the Board, Thomas Graham and Richard Johnson favoured the institution of gold as legal tender, while the third member, John Mackenzie, preferred to continue with silver monometallism. According to him, 'only one precious metal should be considered as legal currency'.[156]

While the plans to introduce bimetallism were shelved for the time being, the coinage of gold *muhrs* was stopped by an order dated 3 December 1788. At the same time, it was also decided to reduce 'the duty and charges on the coinage of silver bullion at the mint, amounting to three Sicca Rupees and three Pice per cent . . . to one per cent.'[157] These measures must have definitely, though temporarily, eased the pressure on the silver currency of Bengal, as we note a jubilant Governor-General, Lord Cornwallis, writing to the Court of Directors: 'An exorbitant batta having for several months been demanded on the exchange of silver for gold, we have tried various means of stopping this abuse and with considerable success.'[158]

One decision taken by the Bengal government on the recommendation of the Currency Committee was to improve the minting process in order to fashion coins on the European model. To give effect to the Committee's recommendation of milling gold and silver coins, new machinery was commissioned at the Calcutta mint under the supervision of two engineers of the Bengal army. Lieutenants Golding and Humphries 'not only supervised the construction of machinery . . . but they also invented several parts of it.'[159] The minting of the first milled gold *muhrs* was announced on 21 July 1790 and was subsequently publicized through an advertisement:

> The Governor General in Council has directed NOTICE to be given that his Lordship has been pleased to revoke the Order that was passed on the 3rd December 1788 for suspending the Coinage of Gold Mohurs at the Mint, and that from and after the 1st of next Month, August, Gold Bullion will be received there for that purpose and coined without charge to Individuals.
>
> It is further hereby NOTICED that from and after the 1st of such Month new Milled Gold Money will be issued, of the former weight and standard, and the Gold now extant of the Calcutta Coinage will be recoined, on application at the Mint, into Gold Mohurs of the New Coinage, also into small Money, that is, into Halves and Quarters for the Convenience of Individuals, without any Expence to them, and Weight will be delivered for Weight.[160]

Soon thereafter, on 1 September 1790, another notice was issued by which new milled silver coins were commissioned (Fig. 2.7).

By now it was quite clear that monetary policy and mint reforms must go hand-in-hand, and that a supervisory establishment for

Gold *Muhr*

Silver Rupee

Fig. 2.7: First Milled Coinage, 1790

dealing with issues of currency and coinage must be set up on a permanent basis. The result was the creation of a permanent Mint Committee in 1792.

Mint Committee (1792)

The appalling currency situation in the Bengal Presidency compelled the government to institutionalize the process of currency reforms. By an Order of the Governor-General, Lord Cornwallis, dated 2 May 1792, a Committee was constituted in Calcutta for superintending the mints, and enquiring into the general state of coinage in Bengal, Bihar and Orissa. This Committee, too, was headed by Herbert Harris, and had G.H. Barlow, Abraham Caldecott and Lieutenant Golding as its members.[161] The instructions given to the Committee were:

1. To ascertain the causes of delay in coining bullion sent to the Company's mints.
2. To enquire particularly into the cause of little progress towards the establishment of the general currency of Sicca rupees.

3. To ascertain the cause of the *batta* or discount that had frequently been levied on the exchange of gold *muhr* for silver.
4. To report whether it would be advisable to declare gold *muhrs* and its multiples legal tender of payment in all public and private transactions throughout the three provinces.
5. To enquire into the state of copper currency.
6. To advise on the practicability and expediency of coining gold *muhrs*, rupee and *pice*, or any of those coins, with machinery similar to that used in the European mints. (In case this was found impracticable, the Committee was directed to inform the Board whether any alterations in the size, shape or impression of the coin can be effected with the implements procurable in India.)
7. To make a particular inquiry into the rules hitherto in use for assaying bullion sent to the mint.
8. To suggest regulations, 'best adapted to deter individuals from coining, filing, defacing and falsifying the coins'.[162]

On 26 June 1792, the Committee submitted the following measures to reform the currency:

I. That the rupees coined throughout Bengal, Behar and Orissa, and the districts of Benaras, be of the same weight, standard, size and impression [as the rupee of the 19th *san* then coined at Calcutta].
II. That the Mints of Dacca, Patna and Murshidabad be re-established.
III. That one specie of copper coin be declared current throughout the Company's dominions.[163]

With a view to drawing the old and light coins into the mints, and to establish the 19th *sun* Sicca rupees as the general currency throughout the Bengal Presidency, the Calcutta Mint Committee recommended that 'after April 10, 1794, only the 19th *sun* Sicca rupees be received at the public treasuries, or issued there from'. Besides, the Mint Committee, in order to put an end to the practice of *batta*, recommended that the rupees issued by the Company's mints at Dacca, Patna, Murshidabad or Calcutta be made as indistinguishable from each other as possible. Thus, the shape, weight and standard of these rupees were to be the same. The Hijri year on them was also to be omitted; instead, the 19th *sun* (regnal year) of the Mughal ruler, Shah Alam II, was 'frozen' on the coin-inscriptions so that the year of their issue could not be identified by money-changers.

Apart from various recommendations for currency reform, the

Calcutta Mint Committee also made a significant suggestion for improving the existing coinage. Until now the coins were struck with dies which were usually bigger than the size of the flan or the blank of the coin. As a result, a part of the contents of the die—whether a device or inscription—always remained off the flan. Thus, the coin, which was also used as a medium to communicate information, viz., the name of the ruler, year and the place of issue, etc., could not fulfil its role. The Mint Committee, therefore, recommended that 'the dies be made of the same size as the coin'.[164]

Another problem connected with the coins of precious metal was that of clipping. Some people used to remove a fractional part of the metal from the edges of the coins, thus reducing its weight. The Mint Committee was aware of this fraudulent practice and, therefore, reaffirmed the recommendation of the Currency Committe that the 'coins should be milled'. Thus, any portion of the edge of the coin that was tampered with could be easily detected.

REMEDIES ADOPTED AT THE RECOMMENDATION OF THE OFFICIAL COMMITTEES

Equipped with the expert advice of the Mint Committee, the government set forth to introduce various reform measures to streamline the currency. Among its first steps was the re-opening of provincial mints.

Enhancing Minting Capacity: Reopening of the Dacca, Patna and Murshidabad Mints

Acting upon the advice of the Mint Committee, it was notified in August 1792 that directions had already been given by the Governor-General for the re-establishment of the mints at Dacca, Patna and Murshidabad, so as to enable individuals to get their old coins or bullion converted into *sicca* rupees without delay.

Third Attempt to introduce Bimetallism, 1792

After two unsuccessful attempts in 1766 and 1769, a third attempt to reintroduce bimetallism in Bengal was made in 1792. It was observed by the government that, of late, the circulation of the gold *muhrs* was confined to Calcutta which gave rise to the *batta*. The *sarrafs* in Calcutta charged a discount from the holders of gold coins, who, in turn, were required to make payments in the *moffusil* where the silver rupee was the only current coin. Besides, due to the overrating of gold *muhrs* in Calcutta, 'the returns from Madras and the Eastward were generally made in gold'.[165]

With the objective 'to make the gold coin pass at its full value by facilitating and extending its circulation' and to discourage 'the importation of gold in preference to silver', the government passed the following Resolution on 23 November 1792:

1. That gold mohrs of full weight [viz. 17 *annas sicca* weight] coined in the Calcutta mint since the 20th March, 1769 shall be declared a legal tender of payment in all public and private transactions throughout the country at the rate of sixteen sikka rupees.
2. That certain charges were to be imposed on gold bullion sent for coinage.[166]

Up to this time, the greater part of the expense of refining gold for coinage was borne by the government. This encouraged the public to send gold in preference to silver to the mint. The second clause of the above Resolution was meant to stop this preference.

All the recommendations of the Mint Committee were finally incorporated in Regulation XXXV of 1793.

MADRAS PRESIDENCY

While giving an account of the British administration in the Madras Presidency, D.N. Banerji observes:

> In the eighteenth century complete anarchy prevailed in the land [i.e. the Madras Presidency] and the condition of the people was miserable, marked by insecurity of property, obstructions to trade, heavy taxation, *uncertainty in the value of currency* and by distressing poverty of the agricultural classes. (emphasis added).[167]

From the mid-eighteenth century, the East India Company acquired extensive territories in southern India, which, in turn, were placed under its Madras Presidency. The *jagir* or Chingleput district was acquired by the British in 1750 and 1763 under two grants from the Nawab of Arcot. By the Treaty of Masulipatnam (14 May 1759) that was concluded between the East India Company and the Nizam of Hyderabad, the *sarkars* of Masulipatnam with its eight districts and that of Nizamabad with its two districts were ceded to the East

India Company. In 1765, Robert Clive obtained a *farman* from the Mughal emperor to acquire five important *sarkars* on the eastern coast that were nominally under the control of the Nizam. These *sarkars*, viz., Sikkacole, Ellure, Rajahmundry, Mustafanagar and Murtazanagar, were formally ceded to the East India Company by the Nizam under the provisions of the Treaty of Hyderabad (12 November 1766; reconfirmed by another Treaty of Hyderabad, 23 February 1768). All this territory was later reorganized into the districts of Guntur, Masulipatnam, Rajahmundry, Visakhapatnam and Ganjam, and were collectively designated as the 'Northern Circars'.[168] By the Treaty of Seringapatnam (8 February 1792), concluded at the end of the Third Anglo-Mysore War (1790-2), the East India Company made large territorial acquisitions. Apart from Baramahal (Salem) district and Dindigul, they secured a large tract of land on the Malabar coast—from the north of Cannanore to the south of the Ponnani River—with Coorg as its defensive hinterland. Similarly, as their booty from the Fourth Anglo-Mysore War (1799), the British annexed Canara and Soondah from Mysore. In the same year, the Raja of Thanjavur resigned the administration of his territory to the East India Company. In 1800, Bellary and Cuddapah were made over to the Company by the Nizam of Hyderabad to defray the expense of an increased subsidiary force. These were designated as the 'Ceded Districts'. In 1801, the English took possession of the Carnatic from the Nawab of Arcot.

These developments necessitated wide-ranging administrative measures in these territories, which included currency reform as one of the priority areas. To meet the increased demand for coined money in the newly-acquired territories, minting activities were extended beyond the Madras mint. The Masulipatnam mint, which was earlier under the Nizam's control, was continued after the town was ceded to the East India Company, and it struck silver and copper coins of various denominations. Negapatam, which was captured from the Dutch in 1781, had a mint in which gold *pagodas* were struck; the British seem to have continued the minting of gold *pagodas* at this mint. After the cessation of Baramahal, the East India Company decided to introduce the Company's coinage in this area and, for this purpose, established two mints in 1793 at Salem and Krishnagiri. It was proposed to strike several of the Company's coins at these mints. However, both these mints were short-lived and were closed in about 1798-9.[169]

During the closing years of the eighteenth century, the Madras government faced great inconvenience due to 'the insufficiency of gold coin in circulation'.[170] While providing them immediate pecuniary aid in 1796 by sending gold bullion worth Rs. 8 lakh, the Supreme Government advised the Madras government 'to endeavor to raise money by the sale of promissory notes at a rate of discount somewhat higher that what they bore in the market in order to secure a more ready sale'.[171] They were also advised to raise money by drawing bills of exchange upon the Court of Directors as well, as they had been drawing upon the government of Bengal.[172]

All these recommendations led the Madras government to institute an official inquiry to diagnose the financial ailments of their presidency and also to look into the practicability of the various suggestions made by the Government of Bengal.

Finance Committee (1798-1800)

In 1798, the Government of Fort St. George appointed a Finance Committee to look into a variety of subjects ranging from the management of the lottery fund and the establishment of a Government Bank, to the condition of the Company's junior servants and the reorganization of the Post Office. Included in the terms of reference of this Committee was the core issue of currency reform. The Committee's Report, which was submitted to the government on 26 March 1800, is considered 'one of the important documents on the history of Madras Currency'.[173] The Committee ascribed the financial anomalies of this period chiefly to the dearth of specie because of its export to Manila and China for investments, as well as to Hyderabad and Mysore for war-financing. The Committee also discovered that the Company had suffered heavy losses due to the re-coinage of various gold and silver coins that were not current in the Madras territories. Between 1786 and 1800, a loss of 1,50,611 *pagodas* was recorded owing to the re-coinage of gold and silver coins that were received at their intrinsic value in various treasuries of the Madras Presidency. The Committee suggested that both these anomalies, namely the shortage of specie and loss due to re-coinage, could be overcome by the establishment of a general bank and the issue of bank notes. With a view to improving the working of the Madras mint, the Committee suggested the separation of duties of the Mint Master and the Assay Master, and, for the first time, laid down rules and regulations for the conduct of the mint and assay departments. These regulations were aimed at checking and preventing fraud in the mint, and also defined and classified various duties and responsibilities of the Mint and Assay Masters. They also prescribed the procedure to be adopted for the receipt and coining of bullion.[174]

The Committee concluded its report by suggesting the introduction of a currency of uniform weight and standard throughout the Carnatic. The report of the Finance Committee of the Madras government was sent to the Court of Directors but for the next five to six years, no action seems to have been taken on its recommendations.

BOMBAY PRESIDENCY

Around 1765, the island of Bombay was facing an acute shortage of silver coins. To overcome this scarcity, the Governor and Council of Bombay decided to mint the gold 'rupee' with its halves and quarters at the Bombay mint. These coins were of English design and bore the shield of arms of the East India Company on the obverse, and the mint name and year in English characters on the reverse.

Fig. 2.8: Bombay Gold 'Rupee', 1765

It was decided that coins to the value of Rs. 60,000 would be struck. On 8 January 1766, a public notice was issued stating that the gold 'rupee' (or *muhr*) should pass at Rs. 15 each and its fractions in proportion. The metal for the mintage of this new coin was to come chiefly from Venetian ducats that were imported into Bombay. This experiment was quite beneficial for the government, as, in 1770, it was noted that it was 'more advantageous to coin than sell the Gold in the Treasury'.[175] It seems, however, that the 1765 coins of English design did not meet the general acceptance of the public. In a meeting of the President and the Board of the Bombay government held on 3 July 1770 to discuss the proposal of the new gold coinage, it was noted that:

the Stamp, which the Bombay Gold Rupees coined in 1765, at present carry, viz. that of the Honble Company's small Seal on one side, is highly improper, as none but Sovereigns have a right to affix any Stamp on public Coin . . . the Honble Company's Privilege of Coining here, being derived solely from the Mogul.[176]

Perhaps the Bombay government recalled an earlier instance when, during 1693-5, they had issued coins in the name of the English rulers, King William and Queen Mary, and with the inscription *Sikka Angrez Kampani* (Coin of the English Company) from the Bombay mint. These coins incurred the displeasure of Aurangzeb and were soon withdrawn from circulation.[177] It was, therefore, decided to issue new gold coins with similar inscriptions to those on the silver coins. Curiously, the new coins were issued in the name of the dead Mughal emperor, Alamgir II (1754-9).[178] These coins were designated as the *Bombays* and bore the legend *Sikka Mubarak Sanah 9 Alamgir Badshah Ghazi Sanah* 1184 (The auspicious coin [issued in regnal] year 9 [of] Emperor Alamgir, the Warrior [and in the Hijri] year 1184 [=1770]), on the obverse and the mint name ('BOMBAY'), year ('1770') and their value ('15 Rups') all in English characters on the reverse.

Fig. 2.9: *'Bombays'* 15 Rupees, 1770

However, this experiment in bimetallism—with fixed conversion rates between gold and silver coins at 1 gold 'rupee' to 15 silver rupees—was foredoomed to failure as the market price of gold bullion constantly fluctuated. Thus, when gold was cheap, the coin was overrated; when dear, underrated.[179] In 1774, therefore, the Bombay government decided to increase the weight of the gold coin from 10.95 to 11.55 g, though there was no change in the fineness and exchange value with the silver rupees. It was also decided to gradually withdraw the old gold coins from circulation and recoin them into the new weight standard, on which the same impression as on the silver rupees would be inscribed.[180] At least one fractional denomination of the new weight standard, viz., the quarter gold 'rupee' (3.84 g), was also known. A year later, the Bombay government made another attempt to meet the demand for silver rupees by introducing a unique denomination of one-fifteenth of the gold 'Rupee' weighing 0.76 g to pass as the equivalent of one silver rupee.

Fig. 2.10: 1/15 Rupee, 1775

In its meeting on 25 April 1775, the Bombay Council noted:

> As there is at present a want of Silver currency on the island it is agreed in order to obviate the inconveniences resulting there from to coin Gold to the amount of 60,000 Rupees into Pieces of the value of one Silver Rupee each, to be in fineness exactly equal to the Gold Rupee now current at 1/15th part of the weight of a Gold Rupee.[181]

However, the high minting cost, the rampant forgery of these small gold coins and the refusal of the troops to be paid in this denomination resulted in the abandonment of the minting of these coins in March 1778. They ceased to be legal tender from 31 May 1778.[182]

Both these experiments seem to have been unsuccessful as, after 1774-5, the coinage of gold in the Bombay mint was almost non-existent. Only in November 1790 do we come across a reference to gold minting at the Bombay mint when a small quantity of counterfeit *muhrs* were recoined into 258 *muhrs* of full standard.[183]

The silver coins that were struck at the Bombay mint were issued in the name of the Mughal emperors. These included the rupee with its fractions of half, quarter, eighth and sixteenth, though not all denominations were issued concurrently. Thus, during the second half of the eighteenth century, coins in the names of Ahmad Shah (1748-54), Alamgir II (1754-9) and Shah Alam II (1759-1806) with

Fig. 2.11: 'Mumbai' Rupee in the name of Shah Alam II

the mint name 'Mumbai' (*zarb Munbai*) were struck at the Bombay mint.

However, in about 1778, the minting of silver rupees was suspended at the Bombay mint. The main reason for this was the scarcity of silver in the island of Bombay. In addition, there was another very prolific mint in the vicinity of Bombay that was producing debased silver rupees. This was the Surat mint, then under the control of the Nawab of Surat. As early as in 1733, the Surat rupee was made the sole legal tender in Bombay, at par with the Bombay rupees. Now, due to the debasement, merchants found it more profitable to send their bullion to Surat, 'where they received a greater number of rupees in return than at Bombay'.[184] It was not until 1800 when the Surat mint came under the control of the East India Company that the minting of silver rupees was restored at the Bombay mint.

Right from 1672, Bombay had followed a system of minting tin and copper coins as the third tier of the currency system. The early tin coins were called *tinnys*. In 1717, the Bombay government started a new series of tin coins called Double *Pice* (27.20 g), *Pice* (13.60 g) and Half *Pice* (6.80 g). This series continued till 1771, but on 1 December 1773, these tin coins ceased to be current and had to be exchanged at the treasury by the end of that month.[185] In August 1775, the Board was informed that the tin coins had been sold at 4 Rs. 0 *annas* 50 *pice* per Surat Maund.[186] So ended the tin coinage of the Bombay Presidency.

Fig. 2.12: Tin, Double *Pice*

Apart from the tin coinage, the Bombay government also minted copper pieces called *copperoons*. In 1705, the copper *pice* replaced the copperoons. However, the mintage of copper in the Bombay mint was stopped around 1749 and, thus, from the middle of the eighteenth century, there was a great shortage of copper pice in Bombay. Though tin pice were minted extensively between 1717 and 1771 at Bombay, these never became popular as currency and the copper pice remained in demand. In a letter recorded in the Bombay Public Consultations for 19 February 1754, John Spencer, the Mint Master of Bombay, describes the 'great want of [copper] pice' in the island. He also observes that 'the present very high price of copper would make them turn out to the disadvantage of the Honourable Company, were they to be made of that article. That tutenague [tin] is now cheaper than it has been for many years past, and that one thousand and fifteen Surat *mans* will supply the necessity of the place.'[187] Accordingly, it was decided to mint tin coins to meet the shortage of small denomination coins in Bombay. The situation does not seem to have improved on this count and three years later, in 1757, we once again hear complaints about the shortage of small change in Bombay.[188] Finally, in 1773, the minting of tin coins was permanently suspended and that of copper coins resumed.[189]

A full-fledged copper currency was thus established in 1773, with the following four denominations:

Double *Pice*	10.28 g
Pice	5.06 g
Half *Pice*	2.63 g
Quarter *Pice*	1.22 g

Fig. 2.13: *Pice*, 1773

All these denominations bear the balemark of the East India Company on their obverse; the *Pice* and Double *Pice* also bear the year of their mintage, 1773, while the half and quarter denominations simply have their fractional unit inscribed on their reverse, viz., ½ and ¼, respectively.

A few local copper coins have been found with a countermark, 'BOMB 1788'.

Fig. 2.13: *Pice*, 1788

It is suggested that this was done to meet the demand for the supply of copper pice to Tellicherry, where a great 'scarcity of pice' was reported in April 1788.[190]

Fig. 2.15: *Pice*, 1791

A new series of copper coins commenced in Bombay in 1791 when four new denominations were established. These denominations were based on the Portuguese money of accounts called 'Quarter' and *Reas*, in which 400 reas or one quarter were equal to one rupee.

TABLE 2.4: DENOMINATIONS OF BOMBAY *PICE*, 1791

Denomination	Weight		Equivalent to
	Grains	Grams	
Double *Pice*	200	12.95	8 *Reas*
One and a Half *Pice*	150	9.71	6 *Reas*
Pice	100	6.47	4 *Reas*
Half *Pice*	50	3.23	2 *Reas*

A remarkable feature of these issues is their mintage. All these coins were minted in England and then shipped to Bombay for circulation in that Presidency. According to official records, copper coins worth Rs.70,592 were transmitted to Bombay between 1791 and 1794, upon which the Company made a profit of Rs.38,194.[191]

SUMMING UP

By the end of 1792, the Supreme Government at Bengal was not only fully aware of the nature and extent of their financial ailments due to the findings of official committees, but had also learnt a lot from past experiments of currency reform. The establishment of the Mint Committee of Calcutta in 1792 institutionalized the reforms process in Bengal, and it was frequently asked to consider and advice on various aspects of currency and coinage reform in the Madras and Bombay presidencies. The recommendations of this Committee provided the foundation for a series of legislations passed by the Bengal government from 1793 onwards for better currency administration.

NOTES

1. Sarkar 1991: 326.
2. Firminger 1917: viii.
3. Ibid.: iii.
4. Sinha 1924 and 1927.
5. Ibid.: 1927.
6. Mitra 1991.
7. Biswas 2007.
8. Datta 2000: Appendix 2—The Problem of Bullion and the East India Company in Bengal: 342-63.
9. *FWIHC*, IV 1962: 145, 338-9.
10. Bowen 1991: 49.
11. NAI, Public Department, OC, 4 November 1776, no. 1.
12. Ibid.: OC, 23 November 1780, no. 61.
13. Quoted in Sinha 1927: 43.
14. Mitra 1991: Ch. 3.
15. Marx 1887: 777.
16. NAI, Public, Letters from Court, 11 November 1768, para 29.
17. Verelst 1772: 85.
18. NAI, Public Department, Proceedings dated 30 July 1753: 412-17.
19. Ibid.: 10 September 1753: 497-502.
20. Ibid.: 21 July 1757: 202-4.
21. Ibid.: 3 March 1758: 221-93.
22. NAI, Public, Letters from Court, 8 March 1758, para 14.
23. *FWIHC*, VI 1960: lix. Datta (2000: 354) gives a reduced figure of £15,91,696 as the total remittance of bullion to other presidencies during 1761-2 to 1770-1 at an annual average net of £1,51,841.4. Even without entering into the clash of figures, it is possible to agree with him that 'such transfers were indeed substantial'. However, the data provided by Datta gives interesting information that during the same period, nearly £2,25,423 was the inverse flow of bullion from other presidencies.
24. Bagchi 1985: 506.
25. Siddiqi 1981.
26. Ibid.: 245.
27. Ibid.: 240.

28. Ibid.; Habib 1975.
29. For a discussion of British economic thoughts and their implications on India, see Sinha 1925 and, more comprehensively, Barker 1975.
30. 'Regulations for Establishing a Gold Coinage, proposed by the Select Committee and approved by the President and Council on 2nd June 1769.' Colebrook 1807: 365-6.
31. Pridmore 1975: 232; Coin nos. 15 and 16.
32. Verelst 1772: 104.
33. Pridmore 1975: 200.
34. Mitra 1991: 30.
35. Verelst 1772: App.: 241.
36. Harrison 1893: 53.
37. Ibid.: 104.
38. Sinha 1927: 56-8.
39. Ibid.: 58.
40. Sinha 1927: 58.
41. NAI, Public, Letters to Court, 24 March 1766 quoted in Verelst 1772: App., 27. See also ibid.: App.: 239.
42. NAI, Public, Letters to Court, 11 November 1768, para 57.
43. Ibid.
44. Desai 1984: 213.
45. Mitra 1991: 32.
46. Sinha 1927: 58.
47. NAI, Public, Letter to Court, 25 September 1768, para 17; Verelst 1772: 104.
48. Sinha 1927: 59-60.
49. Ibid.: 59.
50. NAI, Public, Letter from Court, 11 May 1769, para 119.
51. 'Plan for the Establishment of a Gold Currency, proposed by the President and Council on the 20th March 1769, and carried into effect with the consent of the Nabob of Moorshedabad.' Colebrooks 1807: 366-7.
52. Resolution dated 20 March 1769. See Verelst 1772: App.: 243.
53. Ibid.
54. Sinha 1927: 62; Mitra pegs the difference at 5.25 per cent (Mitra 1991: 35). Pridmore follows Harrison and gives 'the ratio of silver to gold in the intrinsic contents of the coin' as 14.81 to 1 and the prevailing bazaar rate as 14 to 1 (Pridmore 1975: 201; Harrison 1893: 53).
55. Chatterjee 1939: 209.
56. Pridmore 1975: 201.
57. NAI, Public, Letters from Court, 25 September 1769, para 71.
58. Harrison 1893: 53.
59. Minute of Sir John Shore, dated 29 September 1796, quoted in Sinha 1927: 62 fn.
60. Colebrook 1807: 367.

61. Sinha 1927: 121.
62. 'Letter [nd] from the Provincial Council of Revenue at Moorshedabad, to the Governor General in Council and Council of Revenue, transmitting two mohurs and fifteen Sicca rupees of their new coinage of the 15th Sun.' NAI, Public Department, OC, 8 March 1775, no. 25.
63. Sinha 1927: 121.
64. Ibid.
65. Warring 1771: 2
66. Sen 1957: 155. It has also been suggested that had Adam Smith found a place in the Commission proposed by the Court of Directors, 'it is probable that the *Wealth of Nations* would have never seen the light'. Rae 1895: 256.
67. Rae 1895: 256.
68. Sen 1957: 16.
69. Verelst 1772: Ch. 3.
70. Steuart 1805, vol. V: 101-9.
71. Steuart 1772: 5.
72. Ibid.
73. Ibid.: 11.
74. Ibid.: 12.
75. Ibid.: 13.
76. Sinha 1927: 121.
77. Steuart 1772: 14.
78. Ibid.: 14.
79. Ibid.: 15.
80. Ibid.
81. This practice was known as *Surakhi*. See Fig. 2.4 'Surakhi' Rupee. See also Milburn 1825: 283-4.
82. This was done by a process called 'sweating' by heating the coin and extracting a small amount of silver. Cf. also Haider for the practice of rubbing and clipping (*Maalish wa jaz*) 'by ordinary users, merchants and money-changers alike' during the Mughal period (Haider 2005: 133).
83. Steuart 1772: 17.
84. Ibid.
85. Ibid.: 56.
86. Ibid.: 57.
87. Ibid.
88. Ibid.; 'Memoirs on Coinage in Bengal', IOL, Home Miscellaneous vol. 62, quoted by Rajat Datta, gives a total of £2,23,684 in silver that was sent from Bengal to China between 1768-9 and 1770-1. Datta claims that this amounted to '2.37 per cent of £ 95,22,389 which the Company earned in Bengal in those three years, and Steuart's assessment was 'no more than an inspired guess' (Datta 2000: 352). However, in another

contemporary estimate, we get £12,84,008 as 'the sums exported in silver by the English Company alone' during the five years between 1765-6 and 1770-1 (Verelst 1772: 85). This latter estimate gives an annual average of £2,56,802, which alone exceeds the three years' total given in the 'Memoirs' quoted above.

89. Ibid.: 57.
90. Ibid.: 58.
91. Ibid.
92. Ibid.
93. Ibid.: 61.
94. Ibid.
95. Sen 1957: 168-9.
96. NAI, Public, Letters to Court, 30 March 1774, para 46.
97. Ibid.: para 50.
98. Gleig 1835: 237.
99. Earlier, on 15 April 1772, a 31-member Select Committee under Lord Burgoyne was appointed by the Parliament. In November, the Select Committee was reappointed as the Secret Committee, with a scaled-down composition. See Bowen 1991: 133-42.
100. Keith 1930: 72.
101. NAI, Public Letters to Court, 30 March 1774: paras 48-9.
102. NAI, Public Department, OC, 13 March 1775, no. 18(a).
103. Ibid.
104. Ibid.
105. Francis ascribes 'the general Prejudice prevailing . . . in this country in favour of fine gold' as the reason for his deviation from the English standard of 22 carat in case of the gold coins, while he recommended the same English standard for the silver coins. At this rate, the exchange value of the new gold coin came to 1:15½ *sicca* rupees. See ibid.
106. NAI, Public Department, OC, 13 March 1775, no. 18(a).
107. Missing in the original.
108. NAI, Public Department, Body Sheet dated 5 May 1777: 171-3; Proceedings: 491-93.
109. Sinha 1927: 138.
110. Ibid.: 138-9. See NAI, Public Department, Proceedings dated 29 May 1777: 583-617.
111. Ibid.: 138.
112. There has been some confusion as to the actual date of closure of various provincial mints in Bengal. In a letter of the Mint Committee of Calcutta dated 4 August 1792, the date of abolition has been given as 1772. However, all the three mints were closed in different years (Sinha 1927: 122 ff.). See also Sinha 1924: 75; Pridmore 1975: 203.
113. NAI, Public Department, OC, 4 May 1777, no. 2.
114. Ibid.: 4 May 1775, no. 5.

115. *FWIHC*, VII 1971: 62-3.
116. NAI, Public Department, OC, 18 September 1777, no. 3.
117. Sinha 1927: 137, fn 37. The term, which draws its name from the shortness of one 'limb' (metallic standard) of the currency body, refers to a compromise bimetallism in which there is concurrent use of two metals, one being overvalued and coined only by the state authority. The quantity of this 'favoured' metal is necessarily limited in amount to avoid depreciation or the ejection of the other metal from circulation. See *Encyclopaedia Britannica*, 11th edn., 1911, q.v. 'Money'.
118. The new rate of duty which replaced the previous duty of $4\frac{1}{2}$ per cent has nowhere been given in the records.
119. NAI, Public Department, OC, 1 May 1780, no. 24.
120. Ibid.: no. 25.
121. De 1952: 1.
122. Ibid.
123. *Bengal Gazette*, 29 April 1780, quoted in Yule and Burnel 1886: 271.
124. NAI, Public, Letters to Court, 30 April 1781, paras 22-6.
125. NAI, Public, Letters from Court, 25 January 1782, para 81.
126. Ibid.: paras 79-82.
127. NAI, Public, Letters to Court, 10 December 1784, para 70. For a detailed description of Prinsep's contract copper coinage, see Wodak 1958 and 1958a and Stevens 2011.
128. Tandon 1989: 61.
129. Ibid.
130. Gupta 2000: 18.
131. NAI, Public, Letters from Court 30 March 1774: para 98.
132. Gupta 2000: 13.
133. Mitra 1991: 123.
134. Ibid.: 124.
135. Sinha 1927: 240.
136. Sinha 1968: 1.
137. Sinha 1927: 239.
138. Rau 1929: 16.
139. Ibid.
140. Ibid.
141. Gupta 2000: 21.
142. Ibid.
143. Ibid.
144. Rau 1929: 19.
145. Ibid.
146. For a discussion on the impact of currency regulations on the development of European banking in India, see Chapter V, q.v. 'Credit and Banking—European Banking'.

147. Sinha 1927: 205-6.
148. NAI, Public Department, OC, 22 September 1790.
149. Sinha 1927: 206.
150. Minute by Sir John Shore, Governor General, dated 29 September 1796, quoted in ibid.: 206.
151. Sinha 1925a.
152. NAI, Public Department, OC, 6 December 1787, no. 28.
153. Herbert Harris et al. to Charles Cornwallis, Governor General in Council, dated 15 November 1787. NAI, Public Department, OC, 6 December 1787, no. 27.
154. *Calcutta Gazette*, dated 10 April 1788, quoted in Sinha 1927: 209.
155. NAI, Public Department, OC, 16 April 1788.
156. Sinha 1927: 211.
157. NAI, Public, Letters to Court, dated 22 December 1788, para 53.
158. Ibid.
159. Pridmore 1975: 205.
160. Ibid.: 205-6.
161. Letter from Edward Hay, Secretary to Government. NAI, Public Department, OC, 2 May 1792, no. 8.
162. Ibid.
163. Thurston 1893: 59-60.
164. NAI, Financial Department, Mint Committee Proceedings, dated 4 August 1792, no. 14.
165. NAI, Public Department, OC, 23 November 1792, no. 19A.
166. Ibid.
167. Banerji 1991: 622.
168. Thornton 1854: 219.
169. Wiggins 1980: 349-50.
170. NAI, Public, Letters to Court, 11 January 1796: para 15.
171. Ibid.: para 18.
172. Ibid.: paras 19, 21.
173. TNSA, Public Sundries, MS. p. 692, quoted in Ramachandran 1970: 45.
174. Ramachandran 1970a: 37.
175. 'Proposal for new gold coinage', MSA, Bombay Public Consultations, 3 July 1770.
176. Ibid.
177. Gupta 1959: 174.
178. Alamgir II was murdered on 8 Rabi II AH 1173 (= 29 November 1759), Pridmore 1975: xxiv.
179. Pridmore 1975: 123.
180. MSA, Bombay Public Consultations, 15 June 1774.
181. Pridmore 1975: 123.
182. MSA, Bombay Public Consultations, 25 March 1778.

183. Pridmore 1975: 130.
184. Ibid.: 123.
185. MSA, Bombay Public Consultations, 1 December 1773.
186. Ibid.: August 1775.
187. MSA, Bombay Public Consultations, 19 February 1754.
188. Ibid.: 2 August 1757.
189. Ibid.: 5 October 1773; and Proclamation dated 30 November 1773.
190. Pridmore 1975: 124.
191. Ibid.: 125.

CHAPTER 3

The Currency Regulations of the East India Company (1793-1833)

The Charter Act of 1793 (33 Geo. III, c. 52) made significant changes in the East India Company's administration of its Indian possessions. The year also saw the commencement of the legislative process in the Bengal Presidency, when a series of forty-eight regulations were passed by the Governor-General-in-Council. Generally known as the 'Cornwallis Code', these regulations ranged from revenue and commercial administration to criminal and civil justice and, in a sense, 'completed the edifice of reforms'.[1] The year 1793 is also a landmark in the history of the currency legislations of the East India Company. We shall discuss various legislations passed by the three presidencies over a period of four decades (1793-1833), at the end of which a uniform currency was established in the territories of the East India Company. As most of these legislations were enacted in the Bengal Presidency, the discussion is also aimed at establishing the leading role played by this presidency in institutionalizing the currency reforms process in India.

BENGAL PRESIDENCY

On 1 May 1793, a number of regulations were passed by the Governor-General-in-Council, which laid the foundation of currency reforms, initially in the Bengal Presidency but eventually in the whole of British India.

By Regulation III of 1793,[2] aimed at 'extending and defining the jurisdiction of the Courts of Dewanny Adawluts, or Court of Civil Judicature for the trial of Civil Suits in the first instance, established in the several zillahs, and in the cities of Patna, Dacca, and Moorshedabad', the Mint and Assay Masters along with their assistants and native officers were granted immunity from trial in the zillah or city courts, for any act done in their official capacity. This step was aimed at insulating minting activities by the Company's servants from unnecessary litigation.[3]

BENGAL, BIHAR AND ORISSA: EXPANSION OF SILVER CURRENCY

Regulation VIII of 1793[4] was aimed at giving a wide circulation to the Company's rupee—the *Sicca*. Revenues in Bengal were not only to be assessed in terms of the Sicca rupees but also to be realized in that specie alone. However, as not too many Sicca rupees were in circulation, a provision was made in this Regulation to accept other specie of rupees, subject to the bazaar rate of *batta* or discount. Thus, Section XLII of Regulation VIII of 1793 read:

All engagements for the *jumma* [land revenues] whether executed by proprietors or farmers are to be for *sicca* rupees, and a clause is to be inserted, obliging them to pay Government *siccas* or the same specie of rupees as they may receive from their under farmers or *ryots*, at the *bazaar* rates of *batta*, until a sufficient number of *sicca* rupees can be circulated to make these the only legal tender. The collectors are to insert in their treasury accounts the rates of *batta* at which all rupees, not *siccas*, may be received by them.

Having made some preliminary provisions in Regulations III and VIII of 1793, the Governor-General-in-Council enacted (also on 1 May 1793) Regulation XXXV of 1793,[5] 'for the reform of the Gold and Silver Coin in Bengal, Bihar, and Orissa; and for prohibiting the currency of any Gold or Silver Coin in those Provinces, but the Nineteenth Sun Sicca Rupee, and the Nineteenth Sun Gold Mohur, and their respective divisions and sub-divisions into Halves and Quarters; and for preventing the counterfeiting, defacing, or debasing of the Coin'.

This was the first of a series of comprehensive currency regulations passed by the Governor-General-in-Council. It contains twenty-eight sections and runs into sixteen pages. Section I of this Regulation presents a vivid account of the currency situation in Bengal, Bihar and Orissa.

SILVER CURRENCY THE 19-*SUN* SICCA

The principal districts in Bengal, Bihar and Orissa had a distinct silver currency of their own which consisted either of the 19-*sun* Sicca rupee, or old or counterfeit rupees of different regnal years, coined either prior or subsequent to the Company's administration. These coins served as the standard measure of value in all transactions only in that district.

Thus, if a Sicca Rupee of the Nineteenth Sun, which is intrinsically worth about seven per cent more than an Arcot, was offered in payment in the

Dacca Province, it was either reduced, or received nearly at the same value as an Arcot; whilst the holder of Arcots, or other sorts of Rupees, who carried them into Districts in which they were not current, was subjected to similar loss.[6]

However, when the mints at Patna (Azimabad), Dacca (Jahangirnagar), and Murshidabad were shut down in 1772, 1773 and 1777, respectively, the people at large and, more particularly, proprietors and farmers of land in the interior parts of these provinces faced a lot of difficulties. Public revenue was assessed and payable in Sicca rupees, which was obtainable only from the mint at Calcutta and of which sufficient quantity was not yet in circulation. Thus, as an alternative, farmers were permitted to make their payment in older species of rupees at a fixed rate of exchange. In order to pay their rent in a particular sort of rupee, these farmers demanded it from the manufacturers in payment for their grain or raw materials, and the manufacturers, in turn, demanded the same specie of rupees from the traders who came to purchase their cloth or other commodities. The merchants and traders who generally operated across various districts, each with a specific specie of current or dominant rupee, on the other hand, were either obliged to procure the local coin from the *sarrafs* at a premium or discontinue their purchases.

Thus, various sorts of old rupees remained in circulation and soon became the established currency of the particular district. As an inevitable consequence, the value of each rupee was enhanced in the district in which it was current as it remained in demand for all transactions, while rupees current in other districts were not readily accepted and, therefore, attracted a huge *batta* or discount which the possessor was obliged to pay upon exchanging them at the house of a *sarraf*.

From the rejection of the coin current in one District, when tendered in payment in another, the Merchants and Traders, and the Proprietors and Cultivators of Land in the different parts of the country, are subjected in their commercial dealings with each other to the same losses by exchange, and all the other inconveniences that would necessarily result, were the several Districts under separate and independent Governments, each having a different coin.[7]

The profits which the *sarrafs* or money-changers derived from this disorderly state of the coin were enormous. They had their agents in different parts of the province who purchased, at a discount, all rupees which were brought into the districts in which they were not current, and sent them at a premium to those districts where they were the prevailing currency.

It was also noticed that due to the enhanced valuation of rupees of an older mintage in a particular district, the proprietors and farmers of land, or other persons concerned in making their payments to the public treasuries, derived a considerable advantage as they were able to obtain a profit while exchanging them for *siccas* at a rate considerably exceeding their intrinsic worth.

The Bengal government, therefore, concluded that unless various old and counterfeit rupees that were current in different parts of the presidency were thrown out of circulation, and one specie of rupee made the standard measure of value in all transactions between individuals, the government and its subjects, the loss that fell upon the government and the public at large would be perpetual.

Regulation XXXV of 1793 sought to establish the 19-*sun* Sicca as the established silver coin of the Bengal Presidency. As early as in 1777 (1773 in the text of the Regulation), it had taken a decision 'that all Rupees coined in future should bear the impression of the Nineteenth Sun'. However, as a temporary measure, Rupees of the 11th, 12th and 15th *sun* were also directed to be considered current at par with the 19th *sun* Sicca rupee until there was a sufficiency of the latter. Again, in 1792, on the recommendation of the Mint Committee, the Company's government in Bengal decided that 'after April 10, 1794, only the 19th *sun* Sicca rupees be received in the public treasuries, or issued there from'. These as well as other provisions of the above-mentioned Regulations were re-enacted with amendments by the Regulation XXXV of 1793.

With a view to rendering the 19-*sun* Sicca rupee generally current and making it the standard of value throughout the Bengal Presidency, the following measures were considered necessary:

First. To direct the officers employed in the provision of the investment, the manufacture of Salt, and all commercial transactions of the Company, to make their agreements with individuals for Sicca Rupees of the Nineteenth Sun; for if Government in their extensive commercial dealings, and in the provision of the Salt, make contracts with their subjects in other species of Rupees, they must necessarily continue the measure of value where those concerns are transacted, and it would be as ineffectual to declare the Nineteenth Sun Sicca Rupees the only legal currency, as it would be unjust to attempt to enforce the rule.

Secondly. To oblige individuals to estimate their property by the Nineteenth Sun Sicca Rupee, by declaring the amount of Bonds and engagements entered into after a certain period (in fixing which a time was allowed that was presumed sufficient for the introduction of the necessary number of the Nineteenth Sun Sicca Rupees into circulation) whereby any sum of money might be stipulated to be paid in any species of Rupees excepting the Nineteenth Sun Siccas, not recoverable in any Court of Judicature.

Thirdly. To prohibit the receipt of any Rupees excepting Siccas of the Nineteenth Sun, at the public treasuries after the date above alluded to. This last measure was calculated to oblige the Proprietors and Farmers of Land to require Nineteen Sun Sicca Rupees from their under Renters and Ryots, and consequently induce the latter to demand them from the Manufacturers, who for similar reasons, would necessarily require them from the Merchants, and Traders, and thus make it the interest of all descriptions of persons to receive the Nineteenth Sun Sicca Rupee, and to reject every other species of Rupee, upon the principles on which they before demanded the particular Rupee current in the respective districts.

Fourthly. To establish Mints at the cities of Patna, Dacca, and Moorshedabad, to coin precisely the same Rupee as that struck at Calcutta. Without the adoption of this last arrangement, it would have been useless to declare the Nineteenth Sun Sicca Rupee the only legal tender of payment. For unless individuals had been afforded a ready means of procuring their old coin to be converted without loss into the new, they would have been obliged to have purchased the new money from the Shroffs, who would have demanded an exorbitant exchange upon it, as well with a view to reap the immediate advantage, as to prevent the establishment of the general currency of the Nineteenth Sun Sicca Rupee. Keeping open Mints in the interior parts of the country until the circulation may be filled up with that Coin, precludes the necessity of any person applying to Shroffs for it, and consequently deprives them of their influence (which is founded on the wants and necessities of individuals) by furnishing all persons with the new money at the cheapest rate, and with the least trouble.[8]

It was hoped that by the operation of these rules, the various sorts of old and light rupees would, in course of time, fall to their intrinsic worth as compared to the *sicca* of the 19-*sun*. As these old coins would nowhere pass or be accepted as coin, they would necessarily be brought to the mint to be converted into *siccas* of the 19-*sun*.

Thus, Section II of Regulation XXXV of 1793 prescribed a silver rupee—the 19-*sun* Sicca—of 179.666 grains Troy (11.642 g) weight, with 97.916 per cent (175.923 grains/11.40 g) of pure silver and 2.083 per cent (3.749 grains/0.242 g) of alloy. This rupee, along with its half and quarter denominations of the same standard and

Fig. 3.1: 19-*sun* Sicca

proportionate weight, was thus established as the standard silver currency for the Bengal Presidency.

For the success of the new coinage, it was important that the old and light coins of an older mintage as well as bullion were drawn into the Company's mints and recoined into the 19-*sun* Siccas. To facilitate the re-minting process, this Regulation provided that no minting charges would be levied from any individual, provided the metal was equal to or more than the above-mentioned *sicca* standard (Sec. IV). However, if the metal was below this standard, only refining charges at the rate of twelve annas per cent were to be paid for getting the bullion converted into 19-*sun* Sicca rupees, half rupees or quarter rupees (Sec. V).

To facilitate a fair exchange of the different sorts of rupees circulating in Bengal, section XIV of this Regulation laid down rules and valuations according to which all rupees of older mintage were to be received in discharge of the public revenue until 10 April 1794. For this purpose, the Mint Committee at Calcutta obtained information from various district officials about different sorts of rupees then in circulation in the districts of Bengal. Based on this input, the Committee drew up a list, in which twenty-seven different types of silver rupees were recorded, which included as many as fourteen different types of Arcot rupees alone. The exchange rates for these different sorts of rupees were then calculated after ascertaining their intrinsic value through an assay in the Calcutta mint. These exchange rates were then expressed in relation to the 19-*sun* rupee as shown in the following table (Table 3.1).

It was clarified that a 100 *sicca* weight of each of the sorts of rupees specified in the first column, irrespective of the number of rupees that may go into that weight, was to be considered equal to the number of 19-*sun* Sicca rupees placed opposite to it in the second

TABLE 3.1: SORTS OF RUPEES

	Sicca Weight	*19-sun* Siccas		
Siccas of Moorshedabad, Patna and Dacca, per	100	100	0	0
Phooley Sonats	do	100	0	0
Delhy Mahomet Shai	do	99	8	0
Money Surat large	do	99	8	0
Benares Sicca	do	99	8	0
Bissun Arcot	do	97	14	6
Sonats Sabic and Duckie	do	97	8	0
Forshee Arcots	do	97	6	6
French Arcots	do	97	0	0
Patanca Arcots	do	96	9	6
Arungzebee Arcots	do	96	9	6
Gursaul	do	96	9	6
Madras Arcots new	do	96	4	9
Masulipatam and Shardar Arcots	do	96	0	0
Patna Sonats old	do	96	0	0
Benares Rupees old	do	95	14	6
Madras Arcots old	do	95	14	6
Farukabad Rupees	do	95	12	9
Jehaujee Arcots	do	95	1	3
Chaunta Arcots	do	95	11	3
Calcutta and Moorshedabad Arcots	do	95	6	6
Old Arcots	do	95	3	3
Dutch Arcots	do	95	0	0
Surat Arcots	do	94	0	0
Benares Trisolie	do	92	6	6
Viziery Rupees	do	63	0	0
Narrainy half Rupee new	do	63	0	0

Source: Regulation XXXV, 1793, Sec. XIV; see Appendix A.3.

column (Sec. XV). If any specie of rupees other than those specified in the table was tendered in payment at any of the public treasuries, the Regulation provided that:

. . . one hundred Sicca weight of them, indiscriminately taken from the sum paid in the presence of the payer or his agent, is to be sent to the nearest Mint to be assayed, and the payer shall receive credit for a number of the Nineteenth Sun Sicca Rupees equal in weight to the Silver of Sicca Standard that the Rupees so paid may be estimated to contain according to the Assay, after deducting twelve annas per cent, for the expence of refining, should the Rupees be under Sicca Standard (Sec. XVI).

After one year of the operation of Regulation XXXV of 1793, it was noticed that the number of 19-*sun* Sicca in circulation was still not sufficient to enforce it as the sole legal tender, a provision that was to come into effect from 10 April 1794. Hence, by Regulation VI of 1794,[9] passed by the Governor-General-in-Council on 30 May 1793, the provisions of sections XVIII, XIX, XX and XXIII of Regulation XXXV of 1793 were postponed for another year—to 10 April 1795.

Another year passed but there was no significant change in the currency situation. Thus, Regulation LIX of 1795,[10] passed by the Governor-General-in-Council on 29 September 1795, records: 'The reasons assigned in the preamble to Regulation VI, 1794, for suspending certain rules in Regulation XXXV, 1793, until the 10th April 1795, continuing to operate, and consequently rendering it necessary that the enforcement of those rules should be further postponed.'

The provisions of sections XVIII, XIX, XX and XXIII of Regulation XXXV of 1793 were postponed for yet another year—now to 10 April 1796. However, this Regulation directed that all specie of rupees other than the 19-*sun* Sicca, received in the public treasuries 'are not on any account to be disbursed from the said treasuries, but are to be sent to the mint to be recoined into siccas of the nineteenth sun . . . '.

The operation of the provision under section XX of Regulation XXXV of 1793, which specifically rendered void all bonds and agreements for any sum of money 'stipulated to be paid in any species of Rupees excepting Sicca Rupees, or Gold Mohurs, of the Nineteenth Sun, or the halves and quarters each', was suspended till the end of 10 April 1798 in the district of Sylhet (Regulation III, 1799[11]) and till 16 August 1803 in the district of Chittagong (Regulation LIV, 1803).[12]

Prior to the passing of Regulation VIII of 1793, all payments in silver were made by weight. This practice was aimed at keeping the circulating coin to its full standard weight by obliging the holders of the light-weight coin to carry it to the mint for re-coinage. After 1793, the demand of the government on the proprietors of estates came to be fixed in perpetuity at a specific amount of money. It was noticed that the 19-*sun* Sicca coined in the Company's mints at Calcutta and Murshidabad lost some of its weight immediately after being issued from the mints. Though this deficiency was negligible

(2 to 4 *anna* weight per 100 Sicca rupees), it invited the charging of *batta* on these light-weight coins. By virtue of *batta*, these light-weight coins remained in circulation, making Gresham's Law operative.

To overcome this difficulty which hampered the circulation of the 19-*sun* Sicca, certain orders were issued to the Board of Revenue and to the collectors of the districts on 2 October 1795, 'to obviate the loss and inconvenience that would have resulted both to the public and individuals by rejecting the new coin in payment on account of the smallest deficiency in weight, and consequently compelling the holders to return it to the mint almost immediately after its being issued from thence. . . .'[13] These orders were modified and enacted into Regulation LXI of 1795,[14] which was passed by the Governor-General-in-Council on 13 November 1795. By this Regulation, 'the salutary custom of receiving coin by weight' was preserved. It was now declared that all 19-*sun* Sicca rupees, 'which shall not have lost by wear a greater proportion of their full standard weight than six annas per cent, or six fifteenth of a rupee in one hundred rupees; shall be considered as of standard weight, and be received as such in all public and private transactions'. The catch in this Regulation was 'loss in weight by wear'; any loss in weight 'by filing, clipping, or other artificial means' was not covered by it and such light-weight coins were to be received at their intrinsic value. It was also enacted that light-weight rupees thus received at the public treasuries were not to be disbursed again but were invariably to be sent to the mint to be recoined. The Mint Master of the Calcutta mint was ordered to prepare stamped metal weights of fifty *sicca* weight for the use of the collectors of the districts.

By Regulation LXII of 1795,[15] passed by the Governor-General-in-Council on 11 December 1795, the mint at Murshidabad was abolished. The 'inconsiderable quantity of coin and bullion brought to it for coinage' was cited as the reason. There was no change in the weight and fineness standard of the 19-*sun* Sicca rupee for the next twenty-five years; its minting was now confined to the Calcutta mint.

On the basis of the experience of over a quarter of a century, it was noticed that due to the high contents of pure metal, both the 19-*sun* Sicca and 19-*sun* gold *muhr*, were easily malleable, and 'ill calculated to resist the wear and defacement to which coins are necessarily exposed'. Besides, the high purity of metals also necessitated the 'expensive process of refining, diminishing consequently the productiveness of most of the sorts of Bullion imported into the Company's territories'.[16] The Bengal government was also under pressure to achieve 'as much uniformity as can be established between the currencies circulating at the different Presidencies'.[17] Thus, by Regulation XIV of 1818, which was passed on 24 December 1818, it increased the weight of the 19-*sun* Sicca rupee, as follows:

TABLE 3.2: BENGAL: WEIGHT AND FINENESS OF 19-*SUN* SICCA RUPEE

Established by	Weight		Fineness		%
	Grs	Gms	Grs	Gms	
Reg. XXXV, 1793	179.666	11.64	175.923	11.40	97.916
Reg. XIV, 1818	191.916	12.44			91.666

Half and quarter rupees of proportionate weight and fineness were also authorized (Sec. I, *Second*). The coins of the revised standard were to circulate on par with those of the old standard throughout the provinces of Bengal, Bihar and Orissa (Sec. II).

GOLD CURRENCY

The prevailing crises of silver currency in Bengal had forced the Mint Committee of Calcutta to recommend the integration of gold currency into the monetary structure of the province. Therefore, a gold coin called the 'Nineteenth Sun Gold Mohur', weighing 190.894 troy grains (12.37 g), was established as the legal tender by Regulation XXXV of 1793 (Sec. II).[18]

Fig. 3.2: 19-*sun Muhr*

Provisions were also made for the coinage of half and quarter *muhrs*. The choice of fixing what quantity of each denomination could be coined out of bullion or light-weight coins of earlier mintage supplied by individuals was left to them (Sec. VI). A duty ranging from Rs. 2.8 *annas* to Rs. 3.12 *annas*, depending on the fineness of the metal, was imposed on gold bullion sent to the government mints for coinage (Sec. XXIV). This was done to offset the expense 'incurred in refining Gold [which was] not of Gold Mohur standard' [i.e. 99.25 per cent (189.462 grains/12.27 g) gold and 0.75 per cent (1.431 grains/0.92 g) alloy]. This was also aimed at discouraging 'the importation of Gold bullion in preference to Silver bullion' (Sec. XXIV). However, no charges were prescribed for the re-coinage of gold *muhrs*, including their halves and quarters, coined at the Calcutta mint since 20 March 1769,[19] or for those authorized to be coined at the mints of Calcutta, Murshidabad, Dacca and Patna.

The factors which necessitated an increase in the alloy contents of the 19-*sun* Sicca rupees and thereby an alteration in the overall weight of that coin in 1818 were equally applicable to the 19-*sun* gold *muhrs*. Therefore, by Regulation XIV of 1818, the standard of weight and fineness of the gold *muhrs* was altered as follows:

TABLE 3.3: BENGAL: WEIGHT AND FINENESS OF 19-*SUN* GOLD *MUHRS*

Established by	Weight		Fineness		% (in carat)
	Grs	Gms	Grs	Gms	
Reg. XXXV, 1793	190.894	12.37	189.462	12.27	23.25
Reg. XIV, 1818	204.710	13.26	187.651	12.15	22

However, unlike the silver rupee where the amount of pure metal had remained unchanged, Regulation XIV of 1818 in fact, reduced the content of pure gold in the new *muhr* by 1.811 grains (or 0.11 g). This reduction in the overall fineness of the new gold *muhr* was done with a view to bring it to the 22 carat standard, so as to make it less malleable and resistant against wear. However, as a fallout of this measure, grounds were provided for adding a premium on the gold *muhrs* of the old mintage. Half and quarter *muhrs* of proportionate weight and fineness were also authorized by this Regulation (Sec. II).

COPPER CURRENCY

Regulation XXXV of 1793 was confined to the reform of silver and gold currency, and we find no mention of the copper coin in it. The need for having a copper currency for minor transactions, however, could not remain neglected for long. In his letter dated 17 February 1795, Robert Blake, the Assay Master of the Patna mint, informed James Miller, the Mint Master at Calcutta, about the scarcity of the copper coin in Bihar. He writes: '. . . this species of coin is the principal currency amongst the manufacturing and labouring class of people in this quarter, . . . [in case of] a deficiency of this currency in circulation, whether real or artificial, the evil will fall principally on the lower classes of people.'[20]

The effect of this scarcity in money supply was directly evidenced in the exchange rate of copper *pice* with the silver rupee, which soared from 64 to 52 to a rupee.[21] To overcome this situation, the Bengal government, in 1795, authorized the minting of two denominations of copper coins, viz., 'One Pie Sikka' weighing 179.6 grains troy (= 11.64 g) and 'Half Pie Sikka' weighing 89.8 grains troy (= 5.82 g). However, the minting of these coins was confined to the Calcutta mint. Both these coin denominations were made legal tender for fractions of a half rupee and were to pass at the rate of one-fourth and one-eighth of an *anna*, respectively, throughout the provinces of Bengal, Bihar and Orissa. It was also decided that these coins of these two denominations would be struck for an equal value 'until it could be ascertained which coin was in greatest demand'.[22]

One *Pie Sikka*

Half *Pie Sikka*

Fig. 3.3: One *Pie* and Half *Pie Sikka*

After a few months of the coinage of these two denominations, in May 1796, their weights were reduced to 134.7 grains troy (= 8.73 g) and 67.3 grains troy (= 4.36 g), respectively.

In 1817, the Bengal government passed a regulation 'for fixing the weight of the Pice struck at the Calcutta Mint, and for giving circulation to Pice struck at any of the Mints subordinate to this Presidency' (Regulation XXV of 1817).[23] By this regulation, the weight of the Calcutta *pice* was further reduced to 100 grains troy (= 6.47g; Sec. II), and its rate of exchange was fixed at 64 = 1 *sicca* rupee. To augment the supply of copper coins in the ever-expanding boundaries of the Bengal Presidency, the copper coins struck at the Benares and Farrukhabad mints under the provisions of Regulations X of 1809,[24] VII of 1814[25] and XXI of 1816[26] were also authorized to circulate at par with the Calcutta *pice* throughout these provinces (Sec. IV).

In 1831, the Bengal government passed another regulation 'for legalising the circulation of Copper Half Ana and Single pie pieces' (Regulation III of 1831).[27] The need for introducing other divisions of the copper coinage can be attributed to the increasing monetization of the markets and a shift from cowries to metallic currencies for minor transactions. According to Pridmore:

> The gradual extension of the Company's rule in India and a stable currency policy increased the demand for coin, including the need for smaller copper denominations. . . . For smaller fractions, the cowrie shell had served the need. By 1830 the situation had changed. The cowrie shell had no intrinsic value, nor was its import under any regulation. Consequently, for several years a steady influx had taken place and the shells no longer possessed the stability of value of former years.[28]

Thus, by Regulation III of 1831, two new denominations were added. These were: the half *anna pice* weighing 200 grains troy (= 12.95 g; Sec. III) and a *pie*, or one-twelfth of an *anna*, weighing 33.33 grains troy (= 2.16 g; Sec. IV).

Pie Half *Anna*

Fig. 3.4: *Pie* and Half *Anna*

The rates of exchange of various copper coins were now fixed as follows:

3 *pie* = 1 *pice*
2 *pice* = 1 half *anna*
2 half *anna* = 1 *anna*

Both the pie and half *anna* denominations were, likewise, legal tender at these rates throughout all the provinces under the Bengal Presidency (Sec. V). One interesting feature of these coins is that while all other coins struck by the East India Company during this period (1793-1835) were issued in the name of the Mughal emperor, his name is conspicuously absent on these coins.

CUTTACK

When Cuttack came under the control of the East India Company in 1805, the rules relating to the coinage of Bengal, Bihar and Orissa were extended to this district. As a result, the 19-*sun* Sicca rupees and 19-*sun* gold *muhrs* were introduced in the district of Cuttack (including the *pergunnahs* of Puttispore, Kummardichour and Bograe, which were earlier part of the Midnapore district of Bengal) by Regulation XII of 1805,[29] which was passed on 5 September 1805. It was stipulated by section XIII of Regulation XII that 'all engagements for the payment of the public revenue by the zemindars, talookdars, farmers and other holders of land, shall be made in Calcutta Sicca Rupees of the nineteenth sun'. However, in order to facilitate a smooth transition, various sorts of rupees were allowed to be received in the payment of public revenue until the end of 1808. The rates of exchange for rupees of various sorts were to be calculated in accordance with the table of rates contained in section XIV of Regulation XXXV of 1793, which list twenty-seven different types of silver rupees. As this table was not exhaustive, the collector of Cuttack was asked to collect specimens of 'any other specie of rupees' that might be current in that district. These specimens were then to be forwarded to Calcutta for assay and a supplementary table of rates was to be drawn up for use in the transition period.

In Cuttack, as in other parts of Orissa, cowries were a popular medium of exchange and an accepted medium for the payment of public revenue. For the transition period, their acceptance in the public treasuries was also allowed at the rate of four *kahans* per Sicca rupee.

Apart from the payment of public revenue in 19-*sun* Sicca, Regulation XII of 1805 also provided that all bonds, writings or other agreements made 'prior to the expiration of Willaity year 1213 (= AD 1806), whereby a sum of money is stipulated to be paid in any specie of rupees, excepting the nineteenth sun sicca, or the gold mohur of the nineteenth sun' may be liquidated (Sec. XIV), and all new agreements may be made in Calcutta (19-*sun*) Sicca rupees or the 19-*sun* gold *muhr* (Sec. XVI). After the stipulated date (i.e. 1806), persons were to forfeit the right to realize any payment under a bond or agreement, 'by which any sum of money shall be stipulated to be paid in any species of rupees, excepting Calcutta Sicca rupees, or gold mohurs of the nineteenth sun, or the halves or quarters of each' (Sec. XV). This provision was, however, rescinded in 1807 (Sec. III, Regulation XIII of 1807[30]). The Regulation also prohibited all proprietors and farmers of land 'from concluding engagements with their under-farmers, ryots, or dependent talookdars, after the expiration of the Williaity year 1213 (= AD 1806) in any specie of rupees or gold mohurs, excepting the Calcutta Sicca rupees and the gold mohurs of the nineteenth sun' (Sec. XVI). Defaulters were to face the penalty 'of not being permitted to recover any arrears, that may become due to them under such engagement' (Sec. XVI). Hereafter, all regulations that were framed for the provinces of Bengal, Bihar and Orissa were also made applicable to Cuttack (see, e.g., Secs. IV, VI, VII & XV of Regulation XIII of 1807).

The Williaity year 1215 (= AD 1808) was fixed as the cut-off year for the settlement of revenue in Cuttack. After the expiry of 1808, this revenue settlement was to be made in Calcutta 19-*sun* Sicca rupees and, thereafter, 'no rupee excepting Calcutta Siccas' were to be received in the public treasuries (Sec. IX of Regulation IV of 1807).[31]

During the intervening period, such portions of rupees of different mintage received into the government treasury at Cuttack as could be withdrawn 'without impeding the general circulation of the district' were to be sent to the Calcutta mint to be recoined into *siccas* (Sec. IX of Regulation IV of 1807). The *pergunnahs* of Puttispore, Kummardichour and Bograe, however, were ordered to remit their entire revenue receipt in rupees of different mintage to the Calcutta mint for similar recoinage into *siccas* (Sec. X, Regulation IV of 1807).

Ceded Provinces: Awadh

In 1801, a large tract of land in the doab region was ceded to the East India Company by the Nawab Wazir of Awadh, who obtained, in return, a yearly subsidy for his maintenance. By the Treaty of Lucknow signed on 10 November 1801, the districts of Gorakhpur (including Azamgarh and Basti), Allahabad (including Fatehpur), Kanpur, Etawah, Etah, Mainpuri, Bareilly and Muradabad were taken over by the East India Company.

To manage the affairs of the new territories, a 'Board of Commissioners for the Management of the Ceded Province' was constituted on 14 November 1801 and Henry Wellesley, younger brother of the Governor-General Lord Richard Wellesley, was appointed as 'Lt. Governor of Ceded Provinces (of Oudh)'. Bareilly was selected as the seat of the new administration. The territories ceded by the Nawab of Awadh in 1801 were further augmented by another cession by the Nawab of Farrukhabad, who, in 1802, surrendered his territories to the East India Company and obtained an annual subsidy in return.

Henry Wellesley's commission was dissolved on 21 February 1803, 'with all its offices, authorities and power'. In its place, a new division called 'Provinces Ceded by the Nawab Vazir' was created, which comprised seven districts designated as follows:

1. Muradabad
2. Bareilly
3. Etawah
4. Farrukhabad
5. Kanpur
6. Allahabad
7. Gorakhpur

John Fombelle was appointed 'Secretary to the Government for the Affairs of the Ceded Provinces'.

Having settled the administration, the government now turned its attention to the state of currency in this new territory. On 24 March 1803, Regulation XLV of 1803[32] was passed by the Governor-General-in-Council 'for the Reform of the Gold, Silver, and Copper Coin of the Provinces ceded by the Nawaub Vizier. . . .' The reasons for promulgating this Regulation are spelt out in its preamble. These included the circulation of 'rupees of various denominations, differing in weight and standard' throughout the ceded provinces. Before the cession to the East India Company, land revenue in these territories as well as other transactions, whether with the government or between individuals themselves, were carried on 'in the currency of the *zillah*'. However, the 'continually fluctuating' relative current or nominal value of these currencies caused much inconvenience and loss to the transacting parties. Thus, with a view to withdrawing various sorts of rupees from circulation and instituting a standard silver rupee throughout the ceded provinces, Regulation XLV of 1803 was issued.

SILVER CURRENCY, PARTIAL STANDARDIZATION: THE 45-*SUN* SICCA RUPEE

The silver rupee, which Regulation XLV of 1803 sought to institute as the 'legal silver coin' in the ceded provinces, was modelled on the weight and standard of the Lucknow rupee coined by the Nawab of Awadh at the Lucknow mint. Though the East India Company's proposed silver rupee was to be struck at the Farrukhabad mint, they preferred to call it the 'Lucknow Sicca rupee of the forty-fifth *sun*' (Sec. II). However, the specific weight and standard of the proposed Lucknow Sicca rupee was not immediately laid down but deferred to a later date (Sec. III). The Lucknow Sicca rupee was to adopt the size of the Company's 19-*sun* Sicca rupee struck at the Calcutta mint (Sec. V). Apart from rupees of full denomination, the minting of fractional silver coins, viz., the half-rupee and the quarter-rupee of proportionally less size but with the same inscription as the rupee, was also authorized (Sec. VI). All these denominations of silver coins were declared legal tender throughout the ceded provinces.

GOLD CURRENCY

Under Regulation XLV of 1803, while the silver rupee was installed as the legal tender general currency, no attempt was made to either establish a gold coinage on the lines of the silver rupee or to fix any relative value or official exchange rate between coinages of these two metals. Instead, gold coins or *muhrs* were allowed to circulate as before, as per the 'established usage of the country' (Sec. XLII). However, the status of 'legal tender of payment, in any public or private transaction' was not granted to these *muhrs* under this Regulation.

COPPER CURRENCY

On the other hand, Regulation XLV of 1803 did envisage a copper currency to substitute silver rupees in small transactions, usually those under a rupee. Thus, a copper pice of 284.50 grains (18.43 g) and its half-denomination was established by this Regulation (Sec. XLIII). These copper coins were also to bear the '45-*sun*' legend, similar to those of their silver counterparts (Sec. XLIV). With a view to ensuring the proper and extensive circulation of these copper coins throughout the ceded provinces, the Regulation provided for their free minting, and also for their receipt and issue at all public treasuries (Sec. XLIX). However, no copper coins established under Regulation XLV of 1803 were ever issued and these provisions remained only on paper. Later, it was noticed that no application from private individuals for minting copper coins had been received at the Farrukhabad mint.[33] In 1806, therefore, the government decided to withdraw its offer of free minting of copper coins and restrict copper coinage only on its own account. By Regulation III of 1806,[34] it was laid down that 'pice shall only be coined on account of Government, and in such quantities and at such times, as the Governor-General-in-Council may direct' (Sec. III).

In 1816, the weight of the copper coin was reduced to 200 grains (12.96 g) for the full denomination or 'double pie' and 100 grains (6.48 g) for its half or 'single pie'.[35] Later, by Regulation XXV of 1817,[36] it was decided to mint copper coins of 100 grains (6.48 g) at the Calcutta mint was and declare it legal tender throughout the Bengal Presidency at the rate of 64 *pie* to a rupee (Sec. IV). The copper coins of Benares and Farrukhabad mintage were equalized with the Calcutta *pie* (Sec. V), and, thus, a uniform copper currency was established throughout the Bengal Presidency.

When a copper currency was conceptualized for the ceded provinces in 1803, no attempt was made by the government to fix any official exchange rate between silver and copper coins. Section XLIX of the Regulation XLV of 1803 clearly stated that copper *pice* 'shall be received and issued according to the rate at which pice may be current in the *bazaar*'. However, by Regulation III of 1806, the exchange rate of the copper coin was fixed at 26 *pice* to one Lucknow Sicca rupee. Later, when two new denominations of copper coins were approved in 1816, their exchange rate was fixed at 32 double *pice* = 64 single *pice* = 1 rupee (Sec. IV of Regulation XXI of 1816). The new exchange rates are significant as they indicate an appreciation in the price of copper in comparison with that of silver. In 1806, one Lucknow Sicca rupee fetched 7,397 grains (479.31 g) of copper at the rate of 26 *pice* to one rupee; a decade later, in 1816, one rupee fetched only 6,400 grains (414.71 g) of copper at the rate of 32 double *pice* to one rupee. These copper coins were made legal tender for payments under a rupee and any refusal to receive these coins was made punishable.

ESTABLISHMENT OF THE FARRUKHABAD MINT

The provisions for substituting the multiple species of silver rupees with one standard 45-*sun* Lucknow Sicca and introducing a subsidiary coinage in copper entailed a large minting infrastructure, capable of producing large quantities of coins of the prescribed weight and standard. Any shortage of supply of the coins was bound to result in the very abuses that these measures were pitched against, namely hoarding, inflation, and premiums or discounts in monetary transactions. Therefore, under Regulation XLV of 1803, a new mint was set-up at Farrukhabad (in U.P.).[37]

Besides, this Regulation gave the Governor-General the right 'to increase or reduce the number of mints in the Ceded Provinces, or to remove the mint or mints to any other place or places, within the dominion of the Company' (Sec. IV). Under this provision, the mint at Bareilly was abolished (Sec. XL).

MINT MANAGEMENT AND TECHNOLOGY

For the supervision of the mint, a Mint Committee was also established at Farrukhabad, which had the District Magistrate and District Collector as its members. This Mint Committee was to function under the overall supervision of the Mint Committee at Calcutta. The Farrukhabad Mint Committee was also required to conduct surprise checks at the mint and collect random samples of the coins for onward transmission to the Calcutta Mint where these were to be examined and assayed (Sec. XIII). To ensure that the coins struck at the Farrukhabad mint were of a consistently identical weight standard and appearance, Regulation XLV of 1803 stipulated that 'the dies for striking silver coin in the ceded provinces shall be cut in the mint at Calcutta' (Sec. VIII). Broken or unserviceable dies were required to be returned to the Calcutta mint so as to avoid their misuse. The silver coin that was made legal tender in the ceded provinces by Regulation XLV of 1803 was the '45-*sun* Sicca'. The '45-*sun*' or the forty-fifth regnal year of the Mughal emperor, Shah Alam II, in whose name these coins were to be struck, commenced on 9 August 1802 and terminated on 28 July 1803, whereas the actual striking of these coins in the Farrukhabad mint commenced only in 1806.[38]

With the institution of the 45-*sun* Sicca, mechanized minting was also introduced in the ceded provinces. Uptil now, all the coins struck in various mints in this territory were hand-minted. Due to its being struck by a machine (press = *kal*), the Farrukhabad rupee soon acquired the sobriquet *kaldar rupiya*. The establishment of a mechanized mint at Farrukhabad was aimed at meeting the supply needs for replacing existing multiple currencies.

Another improvement that the 45-*sun* Sicca had over the hand-minted coins was the appearance of the coin legend. In the hand-minted coins, the dies of the coins were slightly larger than their flan and as a result, part of the die-impression remained 'off-the-flan'. Regulation XLV of 1803 prescribed that the dies of the 45-*sun* Sicca were to be made 'of the same size as the coin, so that the whole of the impression may appear upon the surface of it' (Sec. VII).

Thus, we see that by Regulation XLV of 1803, the East India Company aimed at substituting multiple hand-minted coins of differing weights and fineness with its own machine-struck standard rupee of uniform weight and fineness throughout the newly-acquired territories designated as the 'Ceded Provinces'. However, any overnight switchover of this kind was impossible and the Company was aware of this fact. They had tried a similar experiment while introducing the '19-*sun* Sicca' in Bengal, Bihar and Orissa through Regulation XXXV of 1793. The implementation of that Regulation had to be postponed twice—once in 1794 (Regulation VI of 1794) and again in 1795 (Regulation LIX of 1795)—due to the insufficient circulation of that specie in the designated territories. Therefore, we find that in Regulation XLV of 1803, a sufficient time cushion was granted to maintain the status quo in the payment of revenue, by accepting 'various sorts of rupees, current in those provinces' (Sec. XVIII). This arrangement was to continue till the end of the harvest (Fasli) year 1215 (AD 1808), after which no other rupee but the 45-*sun* Sicca was to be the legal tender of payment in any public or private transactions (Sec. XXIII). To make the usage of the 45-*sun* Sicca universal throughout the ceded provinces, Regulation XLV of 1803 made ample provisions for its use not only as currency but also as a money of account. Thus, all 'bonds, or writings, or other agreements, whether written or verbal entered prior to the commencement of the year 1216 Fussily (1809 AD)', whereby a sum of money was pledged in any other currency except the 45-*sun* Sicca, were to be liquidated (Sec. XXIV). The same cut-off date was stipulated for all proprietors and farmers of land who were prohibited 'from concluding engagements with their under-farmers, *ryots*, or dependent *talookdars*, in any (other) specie of rupee' (Sec. XXVI).[39]

Regulation XLV of 1803 finally aimed at drawing all other circulating specie to the mint for re-coinage into the 45-*sun* Sicca, and, therefore, prohibited the government officers 'from issuing, from public treasuries, rupees of sorts which may be received at the same . . . excepting in instances in which the exigencies of the public service shall render the issuing of such rupees indispensably necessary' (Sec. XXII).

To facilitate the stipulated short-term co-existence of rupees of different mintage along with the newly-established 45-*sun* Sicca, Regulation XLV of 1803 conceptualized a table prescribing the exchange rates between the 45-*sun* Sicca and various other rupees then circulating in the ceded provinces (Sec. XVII). The conversion rate was to be fixed on the basis of the intrinsic value of such rupees, 'as ascertained by assay in the Calcutta Mint'. This table was published under Regulation III of 1806 wherein forty-nine specie of silver rupees were listed and their conversion rate into the 45-*sun* Sicca laid down.

Before we analyse other provisions of Regulation III of 1806, let us turn to some political developments that ultimately had a bearing upon it.

CEDED AND CONQUERED PROVINCES

The opening years of the nineteenth century saw the expansion of the territorial possessions of the East India Company. After securing a large tract of land in the doab from the Nawab of Awadh in 1801, the Company concluded the Treaty of Deogaon on 17 December

1803 with the Bhonsla ruler, Raghuji II of Nagpur, by which the province of Orissa, and the country west of the river Wardha and south of Narnalla and Gwaligarh, was annexed to the Company's territories. A few days later, on 30 December, the Company concluded the Treaty of Surji Anjangaon with Daulat Rao Sindhia. By this treaty, all territories lying between the Yamuna and Ganga; those situated between the north of Jaipur, Jodhpur and Gohad; those between Ajanta and Godavari, as well as the towns of Ahmednagar and Bharoch, came into the Company's hands.[40]

To take care of the administrative responsibilities of the newly-acquired territories, the Department of Ceded Provinces, created in 1801, was reorganized and came to be known as the 'Department of Ceded and Conquered Provinces' from 27 November 1804.

With a view to establishing the currency of the yet-to-be-issued 45-*sun* Sicca in the newly-acquired territories, the Company, issued Regulation XI on 15 August 1805, 'for extending to the conquered provinces, situated within the Doab and on the right bank of the river Jumna; and to the territories ceded to the Honorable the English East India Company in Bundelcund by the Peishwah; . . .'[41]

This Regulation abolished the operation of any mint within these territories, except for 'the coinage of whatever silver bullion and silver coin may be deposited in such mint or mints for coinage' (Sec. III), thus centralizing the minting activities at the Farrukhabad mint.

Now it was high time that the much-discussed 45-*sun* Sicca was minted and pushed into circulation. While Regulation XLV of 1803 had laid down the rules for its general appearance, its weight and standard were not fixed until 17 March 1806 when Regulation III of 1806 was issued, 'for defining the weight and standard of the silver coin, established in the Ceded and Conquered Provinces. . . .'[42]

The weight of the silver rupee was fixed at 173 grains (11.21 g) of which 95.5 per cent was pure silver and 4.5 per cent the alloy.

Fig. 3.5: 45-*sun* Sicca

Similarly, the weight of the copper coin of 284.50 grains (18.43 g) established by Regulation XLV of 1803 was also expressed in Lucknow and Calcutta *sicca* weights, so as to fix their conversion rates *vis-à-vis* these silver coins (Sec. III). Accordingly, twenty-six copper pice were equalled to one Lucknow (45-*sun*) Sicca rupee (Sec. IV).

The most important component of the Regulation III of 1806 was the table of rates 'for determining the receipt and payment of different descriptions of rupees, not being the rupees declared [viz., 45-*sun* Sicca]':

TABLE 3.4: TABLE SHOWING THE INTRINSIC COMPARATIVE VALUE THAT EACH SPECIE OF RUPEE BEARS TO THE LUCNOW SICCA RUPEE, OR IN OTHER WORDS, THE NUMBER OF LUCNOW SICCA RUPEES INTRINSICALLY EQUAL TO ONE HUNDRED LUCNOW SICCA WEIGHT OF EACH OF THE DIFFERENT SORTS OF RUPEES SPECIFIED IN THE TABLE

Sorts of Rupees	Lucnow Sicca Weight	Lucnow Sicca Rupee		
Siccas of Lucnow, Troy weight grains 173, fine silver, grains 165 22,	100	100	0	0
Calcutta, Moorshedabad, Patna, and Dacca, 19-*sun* sicca rupees,	ditto.	10	9	9
Furruckabad rupees,	ditto.	97	10	3
Bareilly rupees,	ditto.	97	6	0
Nudjeebabad rupees,	ditto.	96	5	3
Lucnow rupees coined at Allahabad	ditto.	96	13	8
Old 18 suns Lucnow,	ditto.	95	8	9
Viziery rupees,	ditto.	89	4	2
Benares rupees,	ditto.	101	0	8
Corah 12 suns,	ditto.	91	9	11
--------20 suns,	ditto.	91	1	6
--------12 suns,	ditto.	92	14	10
Furruckabad 31 and 39 suns,	ditto.	97	6	0
Etawah rupees,	ditto.	95	4	6
Saharunpore old rupees,	ditto.	96	9	6
Saharunpore new rupees,	ditto.	96	13	8
Panniput rupees,	ditto.	95	12	1
Samlie rupees,	ditto.	94	12	2
Kerhanah rupees,	ditto.	96	5	3
Lundowrah rupees,	ditto.	95	12	11
Thannah rupees,	ditto.	94	12	2
Ruckaby rupees,	ditto.	91	1	6
Sirdannah rupees	ditto.	96	5	3

Delhi siccas,	ditto.	101	0	8
Delhi 38 suns,	ditto.	96	9	6
Bhurtpore rupees,	ditto.	100	12	6
Khotah rupees,	ditto.	95	8	8
Ghutsun 29 suns,	ditto.	99	7	6
Mahomed Shahee 19-suns,	ditto.	101	0	8
Gocul 46 suns,	ditto.	96	13	8
Jeend rupees,	ditto.	84	13	0
Siccas of Lucnow,	ditto.	100	0	0
Gourshahee 7 suns,	ditto.	95	4	6
------------- 8 suns,	ditto.	95	12	11
------------- 9 suns,	ditto.	93	3	0
------------ 10 suns,	ditto.	93	3	0
------------ 11 suns,	ditto.	92	6	5
------------ 12 suns,	ditto.	91	5	8
Siringury rupees,	ditto.	93	7	2
Tamboshahree rupees,	ditto.	91	9	11
Ballashahee rupees, coined at Culpie,	ditto.	93	11	5
Hattrass rupees,	ditto.	99	7	6
Bindrabunsee rupees,	ditto.	87	6	10
Generally struck by Perron	ditto.	90	9	2
Deeg rupees,	ditto.	91	9	11
Gourshahee 7 rupees,	ditto.	98	11	0
Bombay rupees,	ditto.	96	5	3
Old Arcots, Moorshedabad, Calcutta,	ditto.	97	10	3
French Arcots,	ditto.	99	7	6
Madras Arcots,	ditto.	98	11	0

Source: Regulation III of 1806, Sec. V, Appendix A.16.

This table lists forty-nine varieties of silver rupees and their conversion rate in Lucknow (45-*sun*) Sicca rupees. Of these, only five were found intrinsically superior to the 45-*sun* Sicca. These were 19-*sun* Siccas struck at the Company's mints at Calcutta, Murshidabad, Patna and Dacca; Benares rupees, also struck by the Company; Delhi Siccas; Bharatpur rupees; and Muhammad Shahi 19-*sun* (i.e. rupees struck in the nineteenth regnal year of the Mughal ruler Muhammad Shah).

The rupees struck at Jind (in Haryana) and at Vrindavan (near Mathura in UP) had the poorest conversion rates in comparison to the Lucknow (45-*sun*) Sicca rupees. For the purpose of conversion, various sorts of rupees were first equated to 100 Lucknow *sicca* weights (173 grains or 11.21 g) and then their equivalence to the number of Lucknow (45-*sun*) Sicca rupees was fixed according to the assay.

The enactment of Regulation III of 1806 provided a sound basis for the efficient monetary administration of the Ceded and Conquered Provinces. However, the calculation and settlement of revenue of this vast tract of land in terms of the newly-established legal currency was a tedious and time-consuming process. Regulation XLV of 1803 had provided that after the expiry of the ongoing triennial settlement of the land revenue of the ceded provinces in 1212 Fasli (AD 1805), 'all future settlements of the land revenue in those provinces, shall be made in the Lucknow forty-fifth *sun* sicca rupee' (Sec. XVII).

However, due to the fast-changing political situation and the consequent territorial expansion of the East India Company, the triennial settlement of land revenue could not be effected. As a result, by Regulation IV of 1807[43] which was passed on 19 March 1807, the operation of clause 1 of section XVII of Regulation XLV of 1803 was suspended in the Ceded and Conquered Provinces till the end of 1215 Fasli (AD 1808) and in Bundelkhand till the end of 1216 Fasli (AD 1808/09) (Sec. II). During the intervening period, all sorts of rupees current in these provinces were to be received in payment of government dues, as per the table prescribed by Regulation III of 1806.

Meanwhile, another measure introduced by Regulation XLV of 1803 was posing hurdles in the spread of money use in the society. Section XXII of this Regulation had ruled that rupees of various sorts that might be received at the public treasuries should not, on any account, be re-issued but were to sent to the mint at Farrukhabad to be recoined into the Lucknow 45-*sun* Siccas. Regulation IV of 1807 realized that this measure 'might not be practicable' because it substantially reduced the quantum of money in circulation and, at the same time, the Farrukhabad mint, which had commenced its operations in 1806, was unable to cope with the recoinage of a 'large proportion of rupees of sorts' that were thus withdrawn from circulation. It was, therefore, decided that only 'mintable quantities of different specie will be withdrawn from circulation and sent for recoinage' (Sec. IV).

The minting of the Farrukhabad rupee was initially confined to the Farrukhabad mint. Although its minting was also authorized at the Delhi (Shahjahanabad) mint in 1813, the production of ***kaldars*** could never be effected at Delhi and that mint was finally shut down in 1818.[44] However, in 1817, the Bengal government resolved to extend the right of minting the Farrukhabad rupees to the mints of Calcutta and Benares, and to any future mint to be established by the Company. Thus, by Regulation XXVI of 1817,[45] dated 16 December 1817, the Farrukhabad rupee minted at any of the Company's mints was declared to be 'the established and legal silver coin in the Ceded and Conquered Provinces' (Sec. II). As a follow-up to this decision, the Calcutta mint was declared open for the coinage of Farrukhabad as well as the Benares rupee on account of individuals, and an advertisement in this regard was published in September 1818 for general notice.[46]

By Regulation XI of 1819,[47] the Farrukhabad rupee, irrespective of its mintage, was declared 'a legal tender in all the territories under the Bengal Government', except the provinces of Bengal, Bihar and Orissa (Sec. IV). The weight of the Farrukhabad rupee was raised from 173 grains (11.21 g) to 180.234 grains (11.67 g) though there was no change in the weight of the pure content, which remained constant at 165.215 grains (10.70 g), thus retaining the proportion of $^{11}/_{12}$ part of pure metal and $^{1}/_{12}$ part of the alloy (Sec. III).

By Regulation II of 1824[48] dated 5 February 1824, the government decided to abolish the Farrukhabad mint (Sec. II) and, thereafter, the minting of the Farrukhabad rupees was carried out in the mints at Calcutta and Benares. The total value of the silver coinage struck at the Farrukhabad mint throughout its existence (1806-24) was Rs. 7,75,42,114.[49] With a view to augment the production of the Farrukhabad rupee, a mint was opened in Saugor in the same year (1824) where the minting of Farrukhabad rupees commenced in 1825. In the next year, the area of circulation of the Farrukhabad rupee was officially extended to the Saugor and Nerbudda territories, which the East India Company had acquired from Peshwa Baji Rao II after the Third Anglo-Maratha War (1817-18).[50] The total value of the silver coinage of the Saugor mint during the entire period of its operation (1825-35) was Rs. 53,27,503.[51]

Benares

The mint at Benares was first established in the fifteenth regnal year of Muhammad Shah (1732-3).[52] Till 1748, it remained under the charge of the Mughal emperor but was usually farmed out. From 1748 to 1751, it remained under the charge of Raja Balwant Singh of Benares.[53] Even after the cession of this district to the East India Company in May 1775, the control of the Benares mint remained in the hands of the Raja of Benares, Chait Singh. However, after the expulsion of the Raja in 1781, the Company took direct control of the mint, but it continued the mintage of gold, silver and copper coins on the existing pattern.

In 1812, a Mint and Assay Master was formally appointed for the Benares mint. The control of the mint was vested in the Board of Commissioners of the Ceded and Conquered Provinces.[54] By Regulation VII of 1826,[55] this control was transferred to a local committee.

SILVER CURRENCY

At the time of the cession of Benares to the East India Company, the rupee coined at the Benares mint weighed 630 *chowals* (or grains = 11.29 g approx.) and had a alloy of 18 *chowals* (or 0.32 g).[56] These bore a mint mark—that of a fish—on the obverse, and were, thus, popularly known as the *Machhlidar* Rupees.

In 1812, the East India Company took steps to regulate the mintage of silver rupees at the Benares mint. By Regulation II of 1812, the weight of the Benares rupee was fixed at 175 grains (11.34 g). It was to contain 96.5 per cent pure silver and 3.5 per cent alloy (Sec. XI). Though it was somewhat inferior in weight and standard when compared to the 19-*sun* Sicca (179.66 grains = 11.64 g) struck at the Calcutta mint, it was to adopt the size and form of the latter (Sec. XIII). To facilitate this provision, it was decided that the dies for striking these coins would be prepared at the Calcutta mint, and all broken or unserviceable dies would be returned to that mint (Sec. XIV).

The Benares rupee, including its halves and quarters, was declared legal tender throughout the province of Benares (Sec. XX). A

Fig. 3.6: Benares (*Machhlidar*) Rupee

deficiency in weight up to 'six annas per cent, or six-sixteenth of a rupee in one hundred rupee' by way of usual wear was permitted (Sec. XXI) beyond which these coins were to be sent to the mint for recoinage.

In 1818, the Bengal government decided that, along with the Farrukhabad rupee, the minting of the Benares rupee must be extended to the Calcutta mint as well. Though the minting of the Farrukhabad rupee did take place at the Calcutta mint, the proposal to mint Benares rupees at Calcutta remained on paper.

GOLD CURRENCY

The mintage of gold *muhrs* at the Benares mint was not regular. In September 1811, the quantity of gold coined in the Benares mint since 1782 was reported to be only 1,21,949 *muhrs*.[57] Weighing 168.44 troy grains (10.91 g) and with the fineness of 23 carat 1 grain, it was inferior both in weight and standard to the Calcutta *muhr*.[58] Like the silver rupees, the gold *muhrs* of Benares, too, bear the mint mark of a fish on their obverse.

Fig. 3.7: Benares (*Machhlidar*) Muhr

COPPER CURRENCY

When the East India Company assumed control of the Benares mint in 1781, a copper pice weighing 138.490 grains troy (8.47 g) was coined there. In 1786, the weight of this coin was raised to 155.333 grains troy (10.06 g) and a mark of a trident (*trishul*) was added. Henceforth, the copper pice of Benares was popularly known as the *trishuli paisa*. However, this change seems to have been effected at the local level without the express authority of any official regulation, for, in 1806, we find Dr. Thomas Yeld, the Mint Master at Benares, reporting that 'there is no regulation for the weight, size, or impression of pice'.[59] A large quantity of these *trishuli* coins was manufactured in 'Oudh, the Riwa Raja's country, and other places and smuggled into circulation'.[60] Yeld, therefore, suggested a plan to establish a copper coinage for the Benares province, according to which four denominations were contemplated:

TABLE 3.5: PROPOSED DENOMINATIONS OF COPPER COINS FOR THE BENARES PROVINCE, 1806

Denomination	Weight		Exchange rate with a rupee
	Grs	Gms	
Double *Pice*	240	15.55	32
Single *Pice*	120	7.77	64
Half *Pice*	60	3.88	128
Quarter *Pice*	30	1.94	256

Yeld did not recommend the minting of these pieces at any other place but Benares, conceding to the 'prejudices of the natives of Benares', though he suggested that 'the machinery of the Calcutta mint could be used in laminating the *derabs* [coin blanks]'.

No immediate steps were, however, taken to adopt this plan but eventually the minting of the first three denominations was undertaken at the Calcutta mint between 1807/8 and 1809/10 for circulation in the Benares province. The weights of these three denominations were slightly less than those initially recommended by the Mint Master of the Benares mint.

TABLE 3.6: COPPER COINAGE FOR THE BENARES PROVINCE, 1807-8 TO 1809-10

Denomination	Weight		Exchange rate with a rupee
	Grs	Gms	
Do-Pai Sikka (Double *Pice*)	192.298	12.46	32
Ek-Pai Sikka (Single *Pice*)	96.149	6.43	64
Ādha-Pai Sikka (Half *Pice*)	48.074	3.11	128

Fig. 3.8: *Do-Pai Sikka*

The mint mark trident was omitted from these coins. To give currency to these copper pieces of Calcutta mintage in the Benares province, the East India Company, on 15 December 1809, enacted

Regulation X of 1809 for the establishment of a copper coinage in the province of Benares. It was to be of pure copper, weighing 'Sicca weight eight annas nine pie each' (= 6.23 g) (Sec. III). It was denominated as '*one pie sicca*' and bore the name and the thirty-seventh regnal year of Shah Alam II in Persian. Its exchange rate was fixed at 'sixty-four pice for one Benares sicca rupee', and it was declared legal tender payment in the province of Benares 'for any sum being the fractional part of a rupee' (Sec. IV).

With a view to deter counterfeiters and fraudulent money-changers, the Regulation declared the 'melting, counterfeiting, clipping, filing, drilling, defacing, or debasing' of the copper pie a criminal act liable for prosecution (Sec. V).

A transition period of six months was allowed for the acceptance of various other sorts of copper coins then circulating in Benares, after which only the *one pie sicca* alone was to be accepted as legal tender (Sec. VI). However, even this time-bracket was found to be impractical to call in other copper coins then circulating in the province of Benares. Hence, the implementation of this section was further postponed by XII of 1810 which declared that:

> . . . copper coin, which has been hitherto current in the province of Benares, shall continue to be received in discharge of all private and public demands, until the Governor-General-in-Council or Vice President in Council, shall signify by proclamation, that an adequate supply of copper coin of the size and weight prescribed by the Section III, of that Regulation [Regulation X, 1809], has been introduced in the province of Benares.[61]

It is, thus, clear that the supply of copper coins from Calcutta fell far short of the demand for that specie in the Benares province. To worsen the effects of this supply crunch, the *sarrafs* of Benares found it more profitable to export the new *pice* intended for Benares to neighbouring Bihar where the demand for copper money was much greater.[62] The worst-hit by this situation were people belonging to the 'lower classes of the community' who were subject to 'the impositions and hardship . . . by the monopoly and combination of the shroffs and money changers.'[63] The Mint Master of Benares, therefore, urged the government to 'accelerate the introduction of a new copper coinage into this Province, by allowing such copper as may be brought by Individuals to be coined in the Benares Mint'.[64] It was also noticed that the *sarrafs* of Benares had devised a novel way to depreciate the exchange value of the old *trishuli pice* that was still current in the Benares province:

> . . . since the 'trisoolee pisa' was originally established as the copper currency of Benares, no measures had been adopted to renew it, and the inscription had, by the process of time, become more or less indistinct, and the shroffs had reduced the value of the pice in which the trisul was defective by reducing it 11 per cent in current value for no other reason than the defectiveness of the trisul.[65]

The government responded to the need for establishing a copper currency for the Benares province by passing a regulation for the purpose. Accordingly, Regulation VII of 1814[66] was passed on 29 April 1814, which superseded the provision laid down in Section II of Regulation X of 1809 requiring the pice to be struck at the Calcutta mint, and provided for their minting at the Benares mint. While there was no change in the weight of these coins (*pice* = 6.23 g), the mint mark trident was reintroduced in the design: 'In compliance with established usage, the figure of a Trisool shall be impressed upon all the copper coin which may hereafter be struck at the city of Benares.'[67]

Fig. 3.9: *Trishuli Pice*

By retaining the *trishul* on the copper *pice*, the government hoped that 'the coin cannot circulate in any other Province'.[68] At the same time, this move was also aimed at obtaining 'for the copper coin of the Benares mint, a local currency and circulation which the pice coined in Calcutta did not possess'.[69]

To undertake the minting of a large quantity of copper, new machinery fabricated at the Calcutta mint was installed at Benares in early 1815 and the production of the *trishuli paisa* commenced by May. Though initially restricted for circulation in the Benares province alone, the circulation of *trishuli pice* was extended to all the provinces of Bengal Presidency by Regulation XXV of 1817, giving it legal parity with the Farrukhabad and Calcutta *pice*. The legal tender, however, as in other instances, was restricted to the fractional parts of a rupee and the exchange rate of 64 *pice* to a rupee was retained (Sec. V).

The minting of *trishuli pice* at the Benares mint continued till the mint was abolished in September 1829. The circulation of these coins was again restricted to the province of Benares by Act XIII of 1836. They were demonetized from 1 August 1844 by Act XIII of 1844.

MINTING CHARGES

All the mints of the Company were open to the reception of bullion for coinage on private account. All bullion intended for coinage was brought to the office of the Mint Master, where it was examined by the processes of cutting and burning so as to ascertain that there was no fraudulent admixture. After examination, a receipt for the weight of the bullion was issued to its proprietor. A specimen of the bullion was then taken to the Assay Office where it was assayed to ascertain its fineness. A deduction was made 'from the assay produce of bullion to cover the expenses of coinage'.[70] After the assay, the proprietor exchanged his mint receipt for a certificate 'of the standard value of the bullion in gold or silver money'.[71] This certificate was then converted into cash at the treasury as soon as the new coins were transmitted there from the mint.

Minting charges varied at the different mints of the East India Company. Till 1812, no charges were levied on the bullion sent to the East India Company's mints in Bengal for coinage; only a small charge for refining metal of an inferior standard was levied. For all silver bullion, or old or light silver coins which were below the *sicca* standard (i.e. having alloy contents of more than 2.089 per cent), a refining charge of 12 *annas* per cent was levied under Regulation XXXV of 1793 (Sec. V). Similarly, with gold bullion which was below the gold *muhr* standard fixed by Regulation XXXV of 1793 (i.e. having alloy contents of more than 0.75 per cent), its proprietors were charged a refining duty depending on its alloy contents (Regulation XXXV of 1793, Sec. XXIV). While there was no refining charge on gold or bullion which was of or above the gold *muhr* standard, a duty of Rs.2.8 *annas* per cent ($2\frac{1}{2}$ per cent) was imposed by Regulation XXXV of 1793 'with a view to discourage the importation of Gold Bullion in preference to Silver Bullion' (Sec. XXIV). Thus, a coining charge or seignorage did exist on gold coins under Regulation XXXV of 1793. However, the receipts on these counts were negligible and the entire expenditure on the mint establishment was borne by the government. According to a statement dated 27 April 1787 prepared by the Auditor of Indian Accounts at the East India House, the Bengal Presidency suffered a loss of Rs. 93,670 on the mint establishment for four years between 1781/2 and 1786/7.

TABLE: 3.7: BENGAL: MINT ACCOUNTS FOR 1781-2 TO 1786-7

Year	Receipts (in Rs.)	Disbursements (in Rs.)	Net (+/-)
1781-2	25,789	44,777	-18,990
1782-3	39,214	58,538	-19,324
1783-4	11,861	37,138	-25,277
1784-5	*	*	*
1785-6	*	*	*
1786-7	15,319	45,398	-30,079
Total	92,183	1,85,853	-93,670

Note: *Figures not available.
Source: NAI, Home Miscellaneous, vol. 87: 102-3; NAI, Public, Letters from Court, dated 20 August 1788.

With a view to turning government mints into possible sources of revenue, or at least offset a part of the mint charges, the Bengal government, on 21 March 1812, passed Regulation II of 1812[72] that instituted a duty of 2 per cent on silver and $2\frac{1}{2}$ per cent on gold, exclusive of the refining charges that were levied earlier. This Regulation incorporated tables of produce of various sorts of silver bullion at the Calcutta, Farrukhabad and Benares mints, and a similar table for gold coinage at the Calcutta mint.[73] An additional duty of 1 per cent was charged if the proprietor wanted his silver bullion converted into the halves and quarters of a rupee (Sec. II: *Third*).

TABLE 3.8: BENGAL: MINT ACCOUNTS FOR 1814-15

Mint	Receipts (in Rs.)	Disbursements (in Rs.)	Net (+/-)
Calcutta	1,37,719	1,39,422	-1,703
Benares	77,803	75,648	+2,155
Farrukhabad	7,865	74,695	-66,831
Total	2,23,387	2,89,765	-66,378

Source: Adapted from Harrington 1814-15: 647-8.

The rate of refining silver was now fixed at 12 *annas* for Rs. 100 (Sec. II: *Fifth*).

As can be seen from the accounts of subsequent years, the mints of the Bengal Presidency were able to reduce their liability on the government.

MADRAS PRESIDENCY: BENGAL LAWS AND THE MADRAS PRESIDENCY

The process of passing regulations and legislations concerning coinages and currencies, that is so manifestly witnessed in the case of the Bengal Presidency ever since the passing of the Regulating Act of 1793 (33 Geo. III, *c.* 52), was apparently absent in the case of the Madras and Bombay presidencies. To quote Edward Thomas:

> The Madras and Bombay Governments seem to have pertinaciously abstained from legislating on coinages and currencies, and their Statute Books are altogether silent on these subjects, until the action of the Supreme Government [i.e. Bengal] is brought to bear on them in 1835.[74]

The reasons for this situation are not far to seek. By the Regulating Act of 1773 (which came into operation in October 1794), the Madras and Bombay Presidencies were subjected to the Bengal Presidency as far as commencing of hostilities or declaring war against any Indian power, or entering into any treaty of peace or other treaty, were concerned. For these actions, they were required to seek the prior approval of the Governor-General of Bengal and his Council.[75] Though these two presidencies were in no way legally subordinate to the Bengal Presidency for their internal administration, including currency management, they did look upon it for guidance and support, and, therefore, constantly and diligently transmitted true and exact copies of all orders, resolutions and their acts in Council to the government of Bengal.

The position of the 'Supreme Government' (Bengal) *vis-à-vis* the 'Subordinate Governments' (Madras and Bombay) was further strengthened by the Pitt's India Act of 1784, which now empowered the Governor-General-in-Council 'to superintend, control and direct' the subordinate governments in matters relating to the application of revenues or forces in times of war. To make the subordination of the Madras and Bombay presidencies complete, the Pitt's India Act provided that these presidencies must obey the Governor-General unless they had received different orders from the Court of Directors which were not known to the Governor-General. According to Keith, 'this new rule for the first time established a real subordination'.[76]

The dependency of the Madras and Bombay governments on the Bengal Presidency in matters concerning currency reforms in India was established by the famous despatch of the Court of Directors in 1806. In their letter dated 25 April 1806, the Court directed the governments of Madras and Bombay to transmit their reports to Bengal 'with all convenient dispatch, and that our Governor-General lose no time in reporting to us on the plan herein detailed [about the currency reforms in India] as it applies to the several countries comprising British India; and also on such parts of the reports from Madras and Bombay as may appear to require their notice'.[77]

That the Madras and Bombay presidencies were guided in their actions concerning coinages and currencies by the Bengal Presidency can also be illustrated by citing the case of the Mint Committee of Calcutta that was initially constituted in 1792 and reconstituted in 1813 under an order of the Court of Directors (dated 3 September 1813). This Committee was 'referred to upon questions connected with the mints at Fort St. George and Bombay'.[78]

Committee of Finance (1805)

In 1805, the Madras government appointed a second Committee of Finance to review its financial stringency resulting from the failure of its attempt to raise a 10 per cent loan earlier that year.[79] This Committee, composed of T. Oakes, C. Smith, G. Buchan and J. Taylor, also dwelt upon various problems of coinage, especially the multiple varieties of coin-types and denominations that plagued the Madras Presidency. In its report submitted to Lord William Bentinck, the Governor-in-Council of Fort St. George on 12 October 1805, the Committee recommended the introduction of the coinage of Bengal as the sole currency of the Madras Presidency.[80] In its findings, it had noted that the market rate of gold and silver was higher than the official rate between the gold *pagoda* and the silver Arcot rupee which stood at 100:350. As a result, silver coins had disappeared from the market. The Committee, therefore, believed that the introduction of the coinage of Bengal would simultaneously introduce the exchange rate of Bengal. Had their recommendation been accepted, a greater part of the Company's territories in India would have seen the introduction of a uniform coinage. But this was easier said than done.

The idea of having a uniform coinage throughout India was questioned by Benjamin Roebuck, the Assay Master of the Madras mint, on the grounds that there was no evidence to prove that it would immediately establish a standard rate of exchange between gold and silver throughout India. Dismissing the whole idea as 'laughable', Roebuck asserted that it would 'no more effect the relative exchange between the different Presidencies, than it would the exchange between Madras and China, or Madras and London'.[81]

Meanwhile a general reform of the coinage of India was actively being debated in the meetings of the Court of Directors in England. The results of these deliberations were embodied in their despatch dated 25 April 1806 to the government of the three presidencies in India, which settled the question of choosing the most appropriate metallic standard for India. However, no time-frame was prescribed by the Court to implement its recommendations.[82]

Madras Mint Committee (1808)

The 1806 despatch of the Court of Directors set the process of currency reform in motion in the Madras Presidency. Acting upon these directives, the Madras government appointed a three-member Madras Mint Committee in 1808 to suggest the steps required to implement the currency reform recommended by the Court of Directors.[83] Besides, the Committee was also asked to submit its recommendations for the interior management of the Madras mint.[84]

SILVER CURRENCY

In its report, the Madras Mint Committee recommended that in compliance with the directives of the Court of Directors, the currency system of their presidency should adopt silver monometallism. The Madras silver currency at this time consisted of coins struck under two different standards, viz., the *pagoda* standard and the rupee standard.

Earlier, by a proclamation dated 15 July 1807, the Madras government had approved eight denominations of silver coins—four each under the two weight standards.

TABLE 3.9: MADRAS: DENOMINATIONS OF SILVER COINS UNDER *PAGODA* AND RUPEE STANDARDS, 1807

Pagoda standard		Rupee standard	
Denomination	Weight (in gms)	Denomination	Weight (in gms)
1 *Fanam*	0.91	$\frac{1}{4}$ Rupee	3.02
2 *Fanam*	1.83	$\frac{1}{2}$ Rupee	6.04
3 *Fanam*	-*	1 Rupee	12.09
5 *Fanam*	4.65	2 Rupees	24.19

Note: *Never seems to have been issued for general circulation.

Fig. 3.10: 5 *Fanam*

Two new denominations, viz., the half *pagoda* (21.17 g) and quarter *pagoda* (10.58 g), were approved under the *pagoda* standard by another proclamation of the Madras government dated 22 August 1807. Another denomination, namely one-eighth of a rupee or two *annas* (1.51 g), was added to the coin series under the rupee standard by a proclamation dated 28 November 1807 though it did not achieve general circulation.

The *pagoda* standard coins display distinct English design elements and have their denominations inscribed upon them in four different languages—English, Persian, Telugu and Malayalam, which is indicative of their area of circulation. A proclamation dated 28 November 1807 declared that the area of circulation of the silver half and quarter *pagoda* was extended to include 'every part of the Dominions of the Honorable Company, subject to the Government of Fort St. George'.

All these coins were struck from silver obtained from imported Spanish dollars and had the fineness of the dollar standard. The adoption of the dollar standard for the silver coins of Madras in place of the Arcot Sicca standard was apparently based on two premises. First, that it was harder and, therefore, less likely to wear, and second, that large denomination silver coins, viz., the half *pagoda* and silver double rupee which were of nearly the same size as the dollar, could be struck without melting the dollars, thereby assuring the dollar fineness without the necessity of assaying all the silver.[85] However, the assay and experiments of these coins conducted in the Tower Mint, London, soon established that the dollar standard coin wears faster than the English standard and that not all dollars had a uniform standard of silver. The Court, therefore, felt that the standard should have remained the same as that of the old Arcot rupee.[86] However, a large quantity of silver coins was already minted at Madras with the help of new machinery obtained from Calcutta. The Madras mint, which was shifted from inside Fort St. George to a new location on Mint Street at George Town, minted over 79.38 lakh pieces of silver coins of varying denominations between April 1807 and March 1808.[87] Recalling this huge quantity of recently-issued coins was found impracticable and, therefore, these were allowed to remain in circulation. The question of altering the standard of fineness of the silver coins was postponed to a later date.

Meanwhile, the new coinage of 1807/8 came under the sharp criticism of the Court of Directors. In its letter dated 6 March 1810 to Fort St. George, it expressed its serious objection to the multiplicity of the types of coins that comprised the new coinage at Madras.[88] The Court, therefore, ordered that the coinage of Madras should consist of a silver rupee coinage composed only of the following four denominations: the single rupee, 8 *annas*, 4 *annas* and 2 *annas*.[89]

This letter, somehow, did not reach Madras till December 1811.[90] However, in compliance with the Court's instructions, the next major step for currency reform was taken by the Madras government in 1812 when, by a Proclamation dated 19 June, the coinage of double rupees as well as of various denominations of the *pagoda* standard was discontinued, and the silver currency was now confined to rupees, half rupees and quarter rupees. The proclamation also laid down the weight and fineness of the surviving denominations as follows:

TABLE 3.10: MADRAS: WEIGHT AND FINENESS OF SILVER COINS, 1812

Denomination	Weight (in gms)	Fineness			
		Pure Silver		Alloy	
		Weight (in gms)	%	Weight (in gms)	%
Rupee	11.66	10.78	92.45	0.87	7.46
½ Rupee	5.83	5.39	92.45	0.43	7.37
¼ Rupee	2.91	2.69	92.43	0.21	7.21

Another denomination, the one-eighth rupee weighing 1.46 g with proportionate fineness, seems to have been added in 1813, which was to pass at the rate of 28 to one *pagoda*.[91]

Though the weight of these coins was less than that of those issued under the proclamation dated 15 July 1807—where the weight of the rupee was fixed at 12.09 g, their fineness was slightly better. The new rupee, in fact, had 0.001 g more of pure silver. However, this fraction was so miniscule that it was decided to treat the old coins at par with the new ones. Accordingly, old coins, both of the *pagoda* as well as the rupee standards, were allowed to remain in circulation 'and be issued and received at the treasuries at the same rate and value as heretofore'.[92] The exchange rate of the old and new coin, designated in the proclamation as the 'Arcot' and 'Company' rupee, respectively, with the gold coin—the Star *pagoda*, was fixed at Rs. 350 to 100 Star *pagodas*.[93]

Having abolished the *pagoda* standard from the silver coinage, the Madras government now decided to institute the Arcot rupee as the standard of value and money of account in the territories subordinate to the Madras Presidency, and thus establish the silver monometallism that was urged by the Court of Directors in their despatch dated 25 April 1806.

By a proclamation dated 9 December 1817, the Madras silver rupee was declared 'the standard circulating medium'.

Fig. 3.11: Madras (Arcot) Rupee, 1817

By another proclamation dated 7 January 1818, the fineness of the Madras rupee was re-adjusted. While it retained the old weight of 11.66 g, the standard of fineness or the pure silver content was reduced to 10.69 g. The same weight and standard of fineness was also adopted for the gold currency—the Gold Rupee—which then superseded the long-established Star *pagoda*.

Thus, the Madras silver rupee became the standard circulating medium of the Madras Presidency and retained its characteristics when it was assimilated in a general plan to establish a uniform currency for all the three presidencies of the East India Company in 1833.

It is also interesting to note that the Madras rupees were extremely popular as a circulating medium in the Chittagong and Dacca districts of the Bengal Presidency. Till 1757, the Company did not possess any mint in Bengal and, therefore, all its requirements for coined money were met by the Madras mint, where silver rupees bearing the mint name *Chinapatan* were regularly coined from 1692.[94] As south India had a predominantly gold-based currency regime, most of the silver output of the various mints of the Madras Presidency was shipped to Bengal. Bengal also subsumed a large quantity of Arcot rupees, initially struck by the Nawab of Arcot but also later coined by the English and French companies. The Arcot rupee was 'lower in value than the Bengal Sicca rupee, but despite this, it was imported by the merchants of Calcutta in large quantities'.[95] Prinsep notes that 'from some reason or other, perhaps from commerce between two places, the Chittagong and Dacca currency formerly consisted of Arcot rupees'.[96] It is quite likely that economic factors such as the easy liquidity of Arcot rupees in Bengal as well as the profit due to the metal price disparity between the two regions must have contributed significantly in popularizing their use in Bengal. We have evidence that during 1823-5, the Madras rupee of the 1818 standard were also minted at the Calcutta mint for circulation in these districts.

GOLD CURRENCY

Since 1740, the established gold currency of Madras was the Star *pagoda* of 3.40 g, which derived its name from the five-pointed star which occupied the dotted or granulated field on the reverse. The obverse showed a standing figure of Vishnu.

Fig. 3.12: Star *Pagoda*

This coin is referred to in official records as the 'Madras current or Star Pagoda'. To encourage people to bring their gold bullion to the mint to be coined into the Star *pagoda*, the half per cent mintage was suspended for six months in 1742.[97] The Star *pagoda* soon became the principal circulating medium of the gold coin in the Madras Presidency, except for the Northern Circars and Hyderabad, where an old variety, the '3 Swami' *pagoda*, was more popular.

For nearly seven decades, the Star *pagoda* minted at the Madras mint remained the only denomination of the gold coin. In 1808, two new denominations, the Two *pagoda* of 5.94 g and a *pagoda* of 2.97 g, were added to the gold currency by a proclamation dated 3 February 1808.

Two *Pagoda*, 1808 *Pagoda*, 1808

Fig. 3.13: *Pagodas*, 1808

However, the Madras Presidency was working towards the implementation of the Court of Directors's recommendation to establish a general silver currency. Even since the introduction of the Arcot rupee into the general currency of Madras in 1749, the established exchange rate of one Star *pagoda* was $3\frac{1}{2}$ Arcot rupees, or 42 silver *fanams.*[98] However, the pure silver content in the exchanged value of Arcot rupees and silver *fanams* ($3\frac{1}{2}$ and 42, respectively) varied as $3\frac{1}{2}$ Arcot rupees contained 0.51 g more fine silver than 42 silver *fanams*, both of which exchanged for one Star *pagoda*—which, in turn, was the money of account in all transactions. It was, therefore, felt that all public accounts should be kept in the same denomination of rupees, *annas* and *pice.*[99] The Committee of Reform established by the Madras government in 1799, therefore, recommended (para 54 of their report) that their accounts of the Madras government 'might be assimilated as much as possible to the Government accounts of Bengal and Bombay', where the silver rupee was the money of account.

No action seems to have been taken on the recommendations made by the Committee of Reforms in 1800, until its plan was endorsed by the Court of Directors in their despatch of 1806.[100] Even, thereafter, there was a lapse of over a decade till finally, in 1817, a proclamation was issued on 9 December by which the coinage of the Star *pagoda* was discontinued and the Madras (Arcot) silver rupee was declared as the standard circulating medium. By a further proclamation dated 7 January 1818, a gold 'rupee' or *muhr* equivalent in weight and fineness to the silver rupee, each weighing 11.66 g and containing 10.69 g of fine metal, was established as the gold currency. The gold 'rupee' also had two fractional denominations: the half rupee/*muhr* (5.88 g) and quarter rupee/*muhr* (2.91 g).

In a major move to establish the Company's sovereign position through its coins, the gold rupee, which till now bore the name and titles of the Mughal ruler, were ordered to be redesigned so as to bear the name, arms and crest of the East India Company. On 7 August 1818, the Mint Master of the Madras Mint submitted specimens of the new designs which were immediately approved by the Governor of the Madras Presidency. The redesigned gold coin was denominated as *Ashrafi*, and bore the arms of the East India Company on the obverse, and the value and name of the Company—*Ashrafi Kampani Angrez Bahadur*—in Persian on the reverse:

Fig. 3.14: *Ashrafi*, 1817

The half and quarter denominations were called *Nim Ashrafi* and *Pau Ashrafi*, respectively, and bore the crest of the East India Company on the obverse and the value in Persian on the reverse. All these denominations were announced to the public by a proclamation dated 9 March 1819.

The last change in the gold currency of the Madras Presidency was in 1820. It was then recommended by the Mint Committee that for the convenience of computation, the gold rupee should be divided into thirds instead of halves and quarters, so that $\frac{1}{3}$ gold *ashrafi* would be equivalent to 5 silver rupees. Thus, the fractional denominations of half and quarter gold *ashrafi* were replaced by a new one called *Panj Rupiya* or 5 rupees, weighing 3.88 g and equivalent to $\frac{1}{3}$ of a gold *ashrafi*.

This measure had its precedent in the Bombay Presidency where $\frac{1}{3}$ gold *muhr*, called *Panchia* and weighing 3.86 g was introduced

Fig. 3.15: 5 Gold 'Rupees', 1820

in 1801, primarily due to the scarcity of silver. The Madras *Panj Rupiya* was similar in design to the half and quarter *ashrafis* that it had replaced, i.e. it had the crest of the East India Company on the obverse and the value written in Persian on its reverse. Henceforth, the gold coinage of the Madras Presidency, except for a small coinage of gold half rupees struck during 1822-3, consisted entirely of the *ashrafi* and its $\frac{1}{3}$ fraction.

COPPER CURRENCY

The Madras Presidency had a large variety of copper coins. The various denominations can be grouped under three nomenclatures: *Dudu*, *Cash* and *Dub*.

The weight of the *dudu* was regularized in the middle of the eighteenth century, and was fixed at 6.30 g for the full and 3.14 g for the half *dudu* piece. The copper coinage of Madras underwent a change in 1803 when four new denominations called '*Cash*' were introduced.

TABLE 3.11: MADRAS: DENOMINATIONS OF '*CASH*' COINS, 1803

Denomination	Weight (in gms)
XX *Cash*	12.95
X *Cash*	6.47
V *Cash*	3.23
I *Cash*	0.64

All these coins were struck at a private mint, Matthew Boulton at Soho, Birmingham. Their design—showing the arms of the Company with the date '1803' on the obverse of XX, X and V Cash and the crest of the Company on the I Cash denomination, along with the value of the coin in Persian and English on the reverse, was prepared by the Company's librarian, Charles Wilkins, and the dies were engraved by John Philip of Matthew Boulton.

XX *Cash*

X *Cash*

V *Cash*

I *Cash*

Fig. 3.16: *Cash* Copper Coins

The reason for this experiment of the European minting of copper coins for the Madras Presidency can be traced to 1786 when the Court of Directors entered into a contract with Messrs Boulton and Watt of Soho, Birmingham, for the supply of copper coinage for the British settlement on the west coast of Sumatra. According to Pridmore, 'struck by machinery developed by Boulton, the Directors had evidently decided that the supply of minor copper coinage could be effectively executed in England, and produced equally as cheaply as in their mints in India, notwithstanding the higher price of copper in Europe and the freight costs'.[101]

These coins of four denominations were sent to Madras where they were immediately pushed into circulation. However, shortly thereafter, when a general reform in the currencies of the Madras Presidency was made in 1807, the copper coinage also underwent a change. It appears that the copper coins of European minting were in short supply and had limited circulation. Consequently, proclamation of the Madras government was issued on 22 August 1807 'with a view to remedy the inconveniences which have hitherto been felt from the want of a proper copper coinage in the Honorable Company's Districts under this Presidency' (para 1). The proclamation issued the 'New Copper Coinage' under two series: the first series (*dubs*) was meant for the Northern Circars while the second series (*cash*) was for other districts of the Madras Presidency.

Dubs (called *fulus*, lit. 'a copper coin', on the coins) were struck at the new Madras mint, which began operations in the spring of 1807. The following denominations were struck:

Double *dubs*	20.61 g @ 24 to the rupee or 84 to a *pagoda*
Single *dub*	10.31 g @ 40 to the rupee or 168 to a *pagoda*
Half *dub*	5.15 g @ 96 to the rupee or 336 to a *pagoda*
Quarter *dub*	2.57 g @ 192 to the rupee or 672 to a *pagoda*
Regulating *dub*	7.56 g @ 229½ to one *pagoda*

Double *Dub*

Regulating *Dub*

Half *Dub*

Fig. 3.17: *Dub* Copper Coins

The Regulating *dub* was essentially for computation purposes and to facilitate payments made in copper *dubs*. In the same proclamation, the exchange rate of various *dub* coins with the new silver *fanam* (0.92 g) was fixed as follows:

1 *fanam* = 3 single *dubs* + one Regulating *dub*
= 6 half *dub* + one Regulating *dub*
= 12 quarter *dub* + one Regulating *dub*

Interestingly, the inscription on the Regulating *dub* mentions the value as well as its exchange rate with the silver *fanam*, viz. *In sikka wa seh falus yak falam khurd ast* or 'this coin and three *falus* are [equal to] one small *falam* [*fanam*]'.

TABLE 3.12: MADRAS: DENOMINATIONS OF '*CASH*' COINS, 1807

Denomination	Weight (in gms)
XL *Cash*	19.31
XX *Cash*	9.65
X *Cash*	4.82
V *Cash*	2.41
2½ *Cash*	1.21

It can be seen that while the exchange rate of the *dub* and the silver and gold currency was officially fixed, no such attempt was made with regard to the coins issued under the '*cash*' series.

As expected, this led to confusion in the money market and shortly thereafter, an agreement was reached with the *sarrafs* of Madras to fix the exchange rate as follows:

TABLE 3.13: MADRAS: EXCHANGE RATES, 1807

Denomination	Silver	Copper
One *pagoda*	44	70
Half *pagoda*	22	35
Quarter *pagoda*	11	17½
One rupee	12	65
Half rupee	6	32½

The government agreed to supply adequate quantities of *fanams* and copper coins of different denominations to the shroffs to enable them to carry on their business of money exchange smoothly. The details of this agreement were announced through a proclamation dated 28 November 1807.

Coins of both the series (*dub* and *cash*) were minted at the new mint erected in the Black Town in Madras. Between August 1807 and March 1808, a total of 84.34 lakh pieces of different denominations of the above-mentioned copper coins were minted.[102] Now the '*Cash*' series of European mintage and the '*Cash*' series of Madras mintage with three common denominations (XX, X and V *Cash*) that followed two different weight standards circulated indiscriminately, since the former was not withdrawn from circulation before the latter was issued. In a bit to rationalize their weights, those of the two denominations of European mintage (XX and X *Cash*) were reduced in 1808.

TABLE 3.14: MADRAS: COMPARATIVE WEIGHTS OF '*CASH*' COINS—EUROPEAN AND MADRAS MINTAGE

Denomination	European Mintage		Madras Mintage
	1803-8 (Old Weight)	1808 (New Weight)	
XX *Cash*	12.95 g	9.33 g	9.65 g
X *Cash*	6.47 g	4.66 g	4.82 g
V *Cash*	3.23 g	3.23 g	2.41 g

Yet the weights of the coins of the two mintages were still not at par.

During 1824, copper coins of altogether different denominations were struck for the Madras Presidency. These coins called 4 *pice*, 2 *pice* and one *pice* were struck at the royal mint at London, and showed the arms of the Company on the obverse and the value in Persian on the reverse. According to an estimate, a total of 19,003,880 pieces were minted between 1824 and 1825.

TABLE 3.15: MADRAS: MINTAGE OF COPPER *PICE*, 1824-5

Denomination	Number of pieces minted
4 *Pice*	71,36,448
2 *Pice*	71,26,104
1 *Pice*	47,41,328
Total	19,003,880

However, all denominations remained in circulation until 1835 when a universal copper coinage was finally introduced.

The statute books of the Madras government commenced from

the year 1802 when, on the model of the Bengal Presidency, a regular code for all regulations passed by the government of Fort St. George was established. However, as has been noted in the beginning of this section, these books are generally silent on the question of coinage and currency. These issues, as we have seen, were regulated over the years by issuing proclamations under the authority of the Governor-in-Council of the government of Fort St. George.

The earliest regulations passed by the Madras government nevertheless included some provisions as far as trade in bullion, both internal and external, was concerned.

BOMBAY PRESIDENCY

As noted under the Madras Presidency, the silence of the statute books on the subject of coinage and currency legislation is also witnessed in the Bombay Presidency. Most of the changes which were introduced in the coins and currency system of this presidency were by way of proclamations issued under the authority of the Governor-in-Council, as was the case in the Madras Presidency.

Silver Currency

After the minting of silver rupees was suspended in Bombay in 1778, the Bombay mint was practically shut down and all minting activities were conducted at the Surat mint. However, in May 1800, the East India Company secured the control of the Surat mint and following this move, 'the Surat Rupee was adopted by the Company as the standard currency unit for western India'.[103] From November 1800, the Bombay government started minting a silver rupee of the Surat standard—11.60 g with 92.03 per cent (10.67 g) pure silver and 7.97 per cent (0.92 g) alloy—at the Bombay mint. These rupees were called '46-*san* Surat rupees'.[104] Shortly thereafter, this standard was regularized by a proclamation dated 27 January 1801.

Fig. 3.18: 46-*san* Surat Rupees

The move to adopt silver monometallism and a rupee of uniform weight and fineness throughout the territories of British India, which was declared the most important agenda for currency reforms in India by the 1806 despatch from the Court of Directors, played a catalytic role in the Bombay Presidency as well.

The views of the Court on the introduction of silver monometallism and the uniformity of coinage throughout India, however, drew sharp criticism from H. Scott, the Assay Master of the Bombay mint, who argued that unlike the Bengal Presidency, silver was no longer the principal circulating medium in the Bombay Presidency and 'most of the ordinary business of the place was carried on without the assistance of silver'.[105] Describing the monetary economy of western India as the one based on the gold standard, Scott notes that 'silver has really lost here one of the great qualities that usually attend the precious metals the straitness [*sic* straightness] of their value at all times and by which they are so fitted to become the measure of value of every other kind of property'.[106]

During this period, apart from the presidency mint at Bombay, the East India Company had the mints at Surat and Broach under its control, which it had taken over from the local rulers in 1800 and 1803, respectively.[107] In a bid to establish greater control over the quality of coin production, the Bombay government pursued a policy of suppressing the mints in the region. In this process, the coinage of silver was closed at the Broach mint in 1814.[108] In the next year, the Surat mint, too, was closed and all its minting operations were transferred to Bombay. This change was announced through a public notice published in the *Bombay Gazette* dated 31 October 1815.

With the closure of the Surat mint, the Bombay mint came under heavy pressure to meet the demand for silver currency. With a view to easing this pressure, plans were finalized to get the Bombay 'Surat' Rupee minted at Calcutta. Between the financial years 1822-3 and 1824-5, a total of 30 lakh rupees were minted at the Calcutta mint on account of the Bombay government. The first lot of these rupees was released some time towards the end of 1823, as we learn from a notice dated 19 December 1823 issued to the collectors of various districts under the Bombay Presidency.[109] In this notice, the collectors were informed about the rupees of the new coinage being in circulation. No fractional divisions of this type were minted.

These rupees were of superior mintage and machine-struck, as compared to the hand-struck or hammered coinage of Bombay/ Surat mintage.

Fig. 3.19: Surat Rupee (Calcutta Mintage)

However, it was soon found that these coins were susceptible to counterfeiting. In a letter dated 7 November 1829, Major John Hawkins of the Bombay Engineers drew the attention of the Bombay Mint Committee towards the 'great and increasing want of the silver currency and . . . extensive counterfeits of the old rupees in the Deckan.' According to Hawkins, 'I have seen several of the milled Bombay Rupees struck in Calcutta counterfeited in this side of India, and accordingly well executed.'[110]

This experiment of the government of Bombay to meet its demand for silver currency from Calcutta proved to be a failure. It was then decided to augment the minting operations of the Bombay mint. A plan to construct a new mint at Bombay, which was to be half the capacity of the proposed mint at Calcutta, was prepared in 1824. The plan was approved by the Governor-in-Council on 10 November 1824 and the construction work was assigned to Captain John Hawkins who had earlier successfully completed the construction of the Town Hall building, following the death of its architect, Colonel Thomas Cowper.[111]

Meanwhile, the Bombay government also decided to implement the recommendation of the Court of Directors. The successful example of the Madras government where an Arcot rupee of 11.66 g was adopted as the standard currency in 1818 was also before them. By a proclamation dated 6 October 1824, the Surat rupee of the Bombay Presidency was assimilated to the Madras standard. It was to weigh 180 grains (11.66 g) with 165 grains (10.69 g) or 91.66 per cent of pure silver and 15 grains (0.97 g) or 8.33 per cent of alloy. The new rupee was designated as the Bombay Rupee and, along with its subdivisions, was declared 'at par with the present Bombay rupee and its subdivisions, within the territories subordinate to this Presidency, and as such receivable wherever the present Bombay rupee and its subdivisions are current as a legal tender in all public and private transactions'.

Following the completion of the new mint in Bombay in 1829, suggestions were made to adopt a new design for the silver currency. Hawkins was of the opinion that the design should be such that would render its counterfeiting most difficult. In his letter dated 7 November 1829 to J.D. Devitre, President of the Bombay Mint Committee, Hawkins writes: '. . . a well engraved human head, is the most difficult to be imitated by the Natives of India, and next to it, the human figure, or that of animals.'[112]

However, on the question of a new design the Court of Directors, had already communicated their views in their despatch of 27 May 1829 wherein they had ordered that the gold and silver coins should continue to have 'the present inscriptions and of the same denomination'. The Mint Committee, therefore, refused to deviate from the instructions of the Court and, by July 1832, all preparations were completed to issue the Bombay rupee of 'improved form and impression, but of the same weight and standard as the present current money'. The prototype for these coins was the Bombay Rupee minted at Calcutta during 1823-4. The minting of these coins of 'improved' design commenced at the Bombay mint in September 1832 and they were declared current by a proclamation dated 17 October 1832. By this proclamation, four denominations of silver currency were announced:

The Bombay Rupee
The Bombay Half Rupee
The Bombay Quarter Rupee
The Bombay Eighth of a Rupee or the two *anna* piece

The last-named denomination, however, remained on paper and was never minted.

Coinage of this new, improved silver currency continued at Bombay until December 1835 when the Company's universal rupee replaced it.

Gold Currency

At the time of the reopening of the Bombay mint for the coinage of silver in 1800, a recommendation was made in the report prepared by the Mint and Assay Master that the exchange rate between gold and silver be fixed as one to fifteen, and that the weight and fineness of the gold *muhr* and the silver rupee be the same, viz., weight 179 grains (11.60 g) with 164.74 grains (10.67 g) of pure metal and

14.26 grains (0.92 g) of alloy.[113] The minting of gold coins recommenced at the Bombay mint in 1801 when gold *muhrs* were allowed to be coined for a private firm, Bruce Fawcitt and Company. This full denomination was also supplemented by fractional denominations. The first of these was authorized in May 1801. It was called the $\frac{1}{3}$ *muhr* (3.86 g). As it passed at the rate of Rs. 5, it soon acquired a popular name, *panchia*. The second fractional denomination was the same as the $\frac{1}{5}$ *muhr* of 1775 mintage. It weighed 0.77 g and was declared legal tender and equal to one silver rupee. Thus in 1801, a gold currency was established in the Bombay Presidency with the following three denominations:

TABLE 3.16: BOMBAY: DENOMINATIONS OF GOLD COINS, 1801

Denomination	Weight		Fineness	Value in Silver Rupee
	Grs	Gms		
Muhr	179.0	11.59	92%	15
$\frac{1}{3}$*Muhr* or *Panchia*	59.6	3.86		5
$\frac{1}{5}$*Muhr*	11.9	0.77		1

Bombay (Surat) *Muhr*

Bombay (Surat) $\frac{1}{5}$ *Muhr*

Fig. 3.20: Bombay (Surat) *Muhrs*

By a government order dated 3 February 1802, the fineness of the above-mentioned denominations was increased by 2 per cent. In a move to assimilate the gold coins to the new weight standard of the silver coins that was established in 1824, their weights were increased slightly in 1825 as follows:

TABLE 3.17: BOMBAY: DENOMINATIONS OF GOLD COINS, 1825

Denomination	Old Weight		New Weight	
	Grs	Gms	Grs	Gms
Muhr	179.0	11.59	180	11.66
$\frac{1}{3}$*Muhr* or *Panchia*	59.6	3.86	60	3.88
$\frac{1}{15}$*Muhr*	11.9	0.77	12	0.77

With the new weight standards, these three denominations continued to be minted at Bombay till 1833.

Copper Currency

The supply of copper coins from England stopped after the last shipment in 1794 and, by the turn of the century, the demand for copper currency was soaring in the Bombay Presidency once again. In 1802, a proposal to revive the coinage of copper coins in the Bombay mint was submitted to the government by the Mint and Assay Masters. They noted that if the same weight standard as that of the copper coins of English mintage was adopted, there would be a great loss since the price of copper had gone up. They, therefore, suggested that the weight of the full denomination should be reduced to 164 grains (10.62 g). They also recommended scrapping of the denomination of one and a half *pice*, as it was frequently mistaken either for the Double *pice* (8 *reas*) or the Single *pice* (4 *reas*), and was hardly necessary for the purpose of accounts. Both these recommendations were accepted by the government on 15 November 1802 and a new series of copper *pice* commenced at the Bombay mint. The design of these coins was copied from the 1791-4 series but the execution was much cruder. The new series initially had four denominations to which another one, the Quarter *pice* was added later.

TABLE 3.18: BOMBAY: DENOMINATIONS OF COPPER COINS, 1802

Denomination	Weight	
	Grs	Gms
4 *Pice*	656	42.51
2 *Pice*	328	21.25
1 *Pice*	164	10.62
$\frac{1}{2}$ *Pice*	82	5.31
$\frac{1}{4}$ *Pice*	41	2.65

It was soon realized that even at the reduced weight, the minting of copper coins at Bombay was still an expensive and unprofitable affair. In a letter dated 12 December 1802, the Mint and Assay Masters recommended that it was 'desirable to have the Copper Money sent hither from England'. The Bombay government accordingly wrote to the Court of Directors requesting them to send copper coins worth one lakh rupees.

The Court placed orders for this supply with the Soho mint at Birmingham. For these coins, the denomination and weight standard of the 1791-4 mintage was adopted but with a modified design. Though the reverse of these coins was the same as the earlier series, the obverse now bore the arms, motto and titles of the East India Company instead of their balemark.

Bombay 2 *Pice*, 1804

Bombay 1 *Pice*, 1804

Fig. 3.21: Bombay Pice Series (Soho Mintage), 1804

However, unlike the 1791-4 series, only three denominations of the copper coins of Soho mintage are known; the one and a half *pice*, though mentioned in the mint records, has not been traced so far.

TABLE 3.19: BOMBAY: DENOMINATIONS OF COPPER COINS (SOHO MINTAGE), 1804

Denomination	Weight	
	Grs	Gms
Double *Pice*	200	12.95
$1\frac{1}{2}$ *Pice**	150	9.71
Pice	100	6.47
Half *Pice*	50	3.23

*Not traced

These coins would have only temporarily offset the pressure on the copper coins of Bombay mintage whose minting is reported to have continued, though not all denominations were struck each year. The huge quantities of copper coins minted at Bombay can be estimated by a report dated 15 September 1819, according to which copper coins worth Rs. 2,77,357, producing 1,71,79,650 pieces of *pice*, half *pice* and quarter *pice*, were struck during 1809-19.

In 1819, the minting process of the Bombay mint underwent a change with the installation of new machinery. At the same time, plans were also formulated to replace the existing copper coins of twin-weight standards (100 grain English minting and 164 grain Bombay minting) with a uniform weight. The new weight was to equate the *pice* to a quarter of an *anna*, resulting in a change in its exchange rate from 50 to 64 *pice* per silver rupee. Under this scheme, four denominations were suggested: *Anna*, Half *Anna*, Quarter *Anna* and *Pice*.

Specimens of these denominations struck with the machinery installed at the Bombay mint in 1819 were submitted to the government on 5 December 1821. Patterns of half *anna* and quarter *anna* denominations have also been noticed.[114] However, these coins were never struck for general currency and the plan was shelved, though temporarily, as we shall see.

The issue of copper coinage at the Bombay Presidency was scrutinized by the Court of Directors and, in their despatch dated 27 March 1829, they authorized the following three denominations for copper coins:

TABLE 3.20: BOMBAY: DENOMINATIONS OF COPPER COINS, 1829

Denomination	Weight	
	Grs	Gms
Half *Anna*	200	12.95
Quarter *Anna*	100	6.97
Pice or $\frac{1}{12}$ *Anna*	$33\frac{1}{3}$	2.15

By 1829, the construction of the new building of the Bombay mint was complete and production began in November 1830 with the issue of the new copper coin authorized by the Court of Directors. By a proclamation issued on 29 November 1830, the above-mentioned denominations were declared 'legal tender to the amount of a rupee and its fractional parts, in all public and private transactions throughout the provinces subject to this Presidency'. Their value in terms of exchange was fixed as follows:

32 Half *Anna* or 64 Quarter *Anna* = 1 Rupee
12 *Pie* = 1 *Anna*

The design of these coins was adopted from the *pice* series that was struck in England during 1804, with the addition of the value of the coin in English characters on the reverse. The same denominations of copper coins continued to be struck and circulated in Bombay till well after the introduction of the universal currency by the East India Company. It was only in 1844 that it was replaced by the universal copper coins of the East India Company.

Thus, for regulating coinage and currency, the Government of Bombay, like that of Madras, resorted to issuing proclamations. The only pieces of legislation regarding questions of coinage and currency in the Bombay Presidency relate either to the transit, import or export of treasure (coin or bullion), or checking the menace of coin counterfeiting. The coinage of Bombay during this period shows a phase of transition from a gold-based economy to silver.

OTHER MEASURES

Customs, Transit and Town Duties and Monetary Policies

After the grant of the *Diwani* of Bengal, Bihar and Orissa, the Company had developed its own tariff system. However, all the three presidencies were independent of each other as far as the regulation of customs and transit duties was concerned.[115] As Banerjea observes: 'The result was that not only did each Presidency administer its own customs department, but had its separate tariff.'[116] However, the fact that all these regulations passed by the presidency governments were subject to the final approval of the Court of Directors and the Board of Control ensured some degree of similarity in the tariff structure, though uniformity was still elusive.[117]

BENGAL

In Bengal, the customs and transit duties were administered by a Board of Customs under the Revenue Department. In 1793, it was transferred to the Commercial Department of that government. In 1797, the Company introduced a duty of 1 per cent on all imports and exports from the Calcutta port. This levy was in addition to the existing duty of 2.5 per cent charged on a large variety of goods, including those that were then exempt from duties. However, all bullion and coins imported or exported from the Calcutta port were exempt from this new levy (Regulation I of 1797, Sec. III).[118]

Similarly, when a cess known as the 'Calcutta Town duties' was abolished in 1795 and re-introduced in 1801, the exempted list included 'bullion and coins' as well as copper imported from Madras (Regulation V of 1801, Sec. II: *Sixteenth*).[119]

In 1803, while organizing the ceded provinces, it was decided by the East India Company that all *rahdary* or transit duties in these territories should be abolished and government customs and *gunj* (market) duties may be levied on goods instead. Once again, an exemption was made for bullion, whether imported into or exported from the ceded provinces. However, in a clever move to keep a tab on the quantity of bullion movement, a provision was made in section XIII of Regulation XXXVIII of 1803[120] that the value and quantity of these articles must be regularly entered into the Custom House books. This measure was later found to be impractical and was, therefore, rescinded by Regulation IX of 1810.[121]

By Regulation XV of 1825,[122] the import of bullion and coins from Britain, Europe and the United States of America was also declared free from any duties or levies.

While bullion and treasure was exempt from customs, transit and town duties in the Bengal Presidency, a duty of 5 per cent *ad valorem* was levied on *cowries* imported by sea at Calcutta, Chittagong and Balasore.[123] This was obviously aimed at supporting the currency policy of the Company, which sought to substitute the *cowrie* currency of Orissa and Bengal with a metallic currency.

MADRAS

In Madras, too, right from the beginning, bullion and treasure were kept out of the tariff net. Here, the revision of customs regulations took place in 1781 and again in 1786.[124] A series of regulations aimed at regulating the import and export of varied merchandise, both by the sea and land routes, were passed by the Madras government in 1803. A common feature of these regulations was that treasure and bullion were placed in the exempted list and no duty whatsoever was levied on the trade of these commodities (1803: Regulation IX, Sec. XXVV; Regulation XI, Sec. XXIII and Regulation XII, Sec. XXX).[125]

Similarly, when 'Town duties' were introduced in Madras by Regulation X of 1803,[126] the exemption list included treasure and bullion (Sec. XIX). However, like the regulations of Bengal, the quantity and value of all treasure and bullion, whether imported or exported, was required to be registered at the customs house or at the checkposts situated at transit points.

BOMBAY

The earliest legislation concerning the export and import of bullion that appears in the statute books of the Government of Bombay is dated 14 May 1805. By Regulation I of 1805,[127] the Bombay government ruled that all treasure imported into that presidency would be opened and examined at the customs house. Though no import duty was to be levied on the bullion thus imported, the regulation prescribed that no bullion would be permitted to be imported or exported without a manifest (Sec. XVII).

In 1810, the Bombay government also decided to reintroduce the 'town duties' which had ceased to exist from April 1805 (Regulation I of 1810).[128] However, bullion was exempt from this duty.

In 1813, an export duty was introduced on coin or bullion exported to foreign nations. Regulation X of 1813[129] prescribed a duty 'to be levied on all coin or bullion exported from Bombay or from any part subordinate thereto, either to America or Europe, at the rate of three percent if exported on British vessels and six percent if exported on foreign bottoms' (Sec. IX).

Thus, while bullion and treasure was generally free from various duties under the Company's government, some measures were undertaken to record and quantify their movement, both within and outside India. The reason for this free movement of precious metals was perhaps the objective of the currency administrators of the Company to keep their supply for coinage purposes unhindered.

Laws on Counterfeiting: Assertion of Sovereignty or Sound Monetary Policy?

Precious metal coins were always prone to some fraudulent practices: whether it was debasing the coin by reducing its fine metal content, or reducing its weight by sweating, or punching holes in it and filling it with base metal, or issuing a base metal coin with silver plating or gilding as the case may be. The practices varied. In fact, the history of counterfeiting the official coin is as old as the history of the coin itself, and this phenomenon was common both in the East as well as in the Western world. Counterfeit coins of the Bactrian, Shaka and Kushana rulers have been reported,[130] while clay moulds of punch-marked coins have been discovered in India.[131] Similarly, moulds for counterfeiting die-struck Roman imperial coins have been found in many parts of the Roman Empire.[132]

The Islamic rulers considered the *Sikka* and *Khutba* as the exclusive prerogative of sovereignty and any incidence of counterfeiting the royal *sikka* was viewed as a crime against the state. The English Company in India had no such privilege. Officially, they were the *Diwans* of the Mughal emperor whose name and titles their coins bore. The Company, therefore, resorted to technological improvements in coin production to check material injury to the coins and prevent their counterfeiting. Thus, milled coinage was established at the Calcutta mint in 1790 as an attempt by the Company to secure its coins against the fraudulent practice of clipping them from the edges. Now, the milling on the edge made such an attempt easily detectable. With its high workmanship, it was also seen as a bulwark against counterfeiting. However, soon after the new gold *muhrs* were released in the market, the counterfeiters set to work and one incident of the detection of counterfeit a gold *muhr* came to light in July 1791.[133] While examining the accused, G.C. Myers, the Preparer of Reports in the Revenue Department, suggested that in the absence of any penal law to punish the manufacturers of counterfeit coins, the provisions of an Act passed in 1572 [14 Eliz. I, c. 3] and entitled 'An Act against the forging and counterfeiting of foreign coin, being not current within this Realm' could be extended to India. He also suggested that the government should 'issue Public Notice that all offenders against this act will be prosecuted with the utmost severity in the Supreme Court of Judicature, and an adequate reward may be offered by the Government to any person who shall give information against them, so that they may be apprehended, and convicted according to law'.[134] The Advocate General of the Company, however, opined differently. According to him, no statute pertaining to coins extended 'to the offence of counterfeiting the coin of this country current in Calcutta; tho' undoubtedly the uttering of such coin knowing it to be forged, and with an intent to defraud, might be prosecuted and punished as a fraud by indictment'.[135]

We, therefore, find that the earliest currency regulation (Regulation

XXXV of 1793) that formed part of the 'Cornwallis Code' in Bengal incorporated some pointed directions as to how this menace was to be tackled.

BENGAL

Regulation XXXV of 1793 prescribed that the 'Persons charged with counterfeiting, clipping, filing, drilling, defacing, or debasing, the Gold or Silver Coin, are to be committed to the Criminal Courts, and punished according as the law may direct' (Sec. XII).

The menace of counterfeiting of coins was quite widespread. The town of Calcutta, the districts of Burdwan, 24-Parganas, Kishennagar, Midnapore, Murshidabad and Chandernagore under the Bengal province, and Birbhoom and Bhagalpur in the Bihar province were reportedly the production centres for counterfeit coins.[136] However, the writ of the Supreme Court of Judicature, which was established in Calcutta in 1773 under the provisions of the Regulating Act, did not prevail outside the town of Calcutta. Therefore, for apprehending counterfeiters outside Calcutta, something analogous to the 'Backing Warrants' of England was contemplated.[137] However, even that possibility was ruled out by the Advocate General of the Company: 'a Proceeding analogous to . . . which in England is described by the expression of Backing Warrants [as they] may from the situation of this country and the peculiar constitution of the Supreme Court be subject to some Difficulties and Delays. . . .'[138] The problem in prosecuting offenders was grave as none of the existing laws treated the counterfeiting of coins as a 'capital offence'. In the opinion of the Advocate General and the Standing Counsel of the Company, 'the persons guilty may be prosecuted for a misdemeanour, but if convicted will not be subject to any heavier punishment than fine and imprisonment, unless the circumstances appearing against them shall be sufficient to maintain an Indictment for a conspiracy'.[139]

Like Regulation XXXV of 1793, Regulation XLV of 1803, too, provided that instead of the existing hand-minted coins, the new 45-*sun* Sicca of the Farrukhabad mint should have milled edges to guard against 'counterfeiting, drilling, filling, defacing or debasing' (Sec. VII). Any person charged with these acts was to be committed to the criminal courts (Sec. XIV). But, once again, any specific legislation for punishing the act of counterfeiting coins was absent from the lawbooks.

Finally, by Regulation XVII of 1817,[140] certain penal provisions were introduced to check the counterfeiting of coins. Any person convicted of having forged or having procured to forge any coin in imitation of the gold, silver or copper coins of the British governments in India, or of any coin usually received as money in the British possessions in India, or being involved in 'clipping, filing, drilling, defacing, or debasing' these coins, was liable 'to receive thirty stripes with a corah [whip], and to be imprisoned in banishment from the district, for the period of seven years; or for the term of fourteen years' (Sec. IX, *Second*). The same penalties were also extended for counterfeiting and forging credit instruments such as bank notes, promissory notes and public securities.

MADRAS

The counterfeiting of gold *pagodas* was not confined to India alone. In a letter dated 24 September 1796, the Secret Committee of the Court of Directors informed the Governor-General that 'counterfeit Pagodas were making [*sic*] in this country, for the purpose of being sent to India'.[141] The Committee noted that 'considerable quantities' were ordered 'for the purpose of taking them out as private ventures', and, therefore, cautioned the Indian authorities to 'be upon its Guard' and take such steps, 'previous to the arrival of the Fleet from Europe, as may prevent these counterfeit Pagodas becoming current'.[142] The Indian government was also directed to take adequate measures for 'detecting and bringing to punishment the Persons who may attempt to circulate them [counterfeit Pagodas] in India'.[143]

However, in the regulations for the administration of criminal justice in the Madras Presidency, the counterfeiting and debasing of the legal coin was made a cognizable offence as late as in 1827. By Regulation VI of 1827,[144] provisions against the counterfeiting of coin were made and even 'making, mending, buying, selling, concealing, or having possession of implements for coining' was declared a punishable offence (Sec. IV. *First*). An interesting part of this legislation was that under the scope of this offence, all 'gold, silver, or copper coins of the British government in India, or any coin usually received as money in the British possessions in India' were included.[145]

BOMBAY

To curb the menace of the counterfeiting of coins, a legislation was issued by the Bombay government on 25 March 1812,[146] under the authority of an Act of British Parliament—An Act for the Better Government of the Settlements of Fort St. George and Bombay, 1807 (47 Geo. III, c. 68). It prohibited the manufacturing of any coin current in the island of Bombay without the authority of the government. The act of debasing the current coins was, likewise, brought under the definition of 'criminal misdemeanour' and all violators were made liable for trial by the 'Court of Petty Sessions' (Regulation I of 1812, Title Ninth: *Of Coining*, Article I).

The provisions of this regulation which were reiterated in a comprehensive legislation for 'defining crimes and offences, and specifying the punishments to be inflicted for the same' was passed by the Government of Bombay on 1 January 1827. By Regulation XIV of 1827,[147] persons convicted of illegal coining, counterfeiting or debasing the coin were 'punishable with fine, ordinary imprisonment not exceeding eight years, or flogging, or any of these combined' (Sec. XVIII and XIX). For petty crimes concerning counterfeiting where the amount was limited to ten rupees, the fine was limited to three times of the sum involved, 'commutable to ordinary imprisonment, without labour, for a period to two days for each rupee of fine' (Sec. XIX, *Second*).

The laws on counterfeiting coins that were enacted by the governments of the three presidencies could not eliminate this evil, which now spread to territories falling outside the Company's domains. Thus, as late as in 1831, we notice coiners in Oudh counterfeiting the coinage of the Company.[148] Many of these counterfeiters were patronized by the local *zamindars* and other officials, who, in turn, received a hefty amount as 'tax' from them. Apart from penalties imposed in the legislations mentioned above, the government also tried to tackle the problem of counterfeiting through technological improvements of the coin device. As we shall see in Chapter IV, the change in the device of the coin which the Company ultimately choose to install as the common currency in its territories was aimed both as an assertion of its sovereign status in India as well as an ultimate check against its possible counterfeiting.

ESTABLISHMENT OF A UNIFORM CURRENCY THROUGHOUT BRITISH INDIA

As early as in 1799, the Committee of Reforms set up by the Madras government had proposed a regulation for the adoption of the Bengal coinage comprising the 19-*sun* Sicca and 19-*sun Muhr* and their fractional denominations as the general coinage throughout British India.[149] Had this plan been accepted, a uniform currency throughout British India would have come into effect from 1 January 1802—the date proposed by the Committee.[150]

A general plan for establishing a uniform currency throughout British India was later laid down in a despatch from the Court of Directors dated 25 April 1806 and addressed to the presidencies of Bengal, Madras and Bombay. The Court referred to a letter from the Earl of Liverpool to the king on the coins of the realm wherein he had propounded a principle of monometallism for a sound monetary system.[151] The Earl noted that 'the money or coin which is to be the principal measure of property ought to be of one metal only'.[152] The Court, therefore, concluded that 'In applying this argument to the general use in India, there cannot be a doubt, in our opinion, that such coin must be of silver.'[153]

The decided preference of the Earl of Liverpool in favour of monometallism and the subsequent decision taken by the Court on that basis was nothing new for India. In his Minute dated 29 September 1796, the then Governor-General of India, Sir John Shore, had dwelt at length on the question of currency reforms in Bengal and had proposed that a coin of only one metal should be legal tender and that metal should be silver.[154]

The next question was to decide on the weight for the proposed silver coin. The Court noted that the standard weight of the Mughal rupee 'was uniformly one sicca, or 10 massa, being 179⅔ troy grains or 179.5511 [11.63 g]'.[155] The Court, though inclined to adopt the weight of the former Mughal rupee for their proposed uniform coin for British India, chose to 'fix the gross weight in whole numbers' and, therefore, adopted '180 troy grains as the nearest to the sicca weight'.[156]

Having decided upon the metal and the weight of the proposed uniform coin for India, the Court then considered the question of the fineness of this coin. This question was already deliberated upon, albeit in a different context, by the Committee of Privy Council appointed in January 1803 'to take into consideration the state of coins of this country [England] and the present establishment and constitution of His Majesty's mint'. In its Report, the Committee had recommended the ratio of $\frac{11}{12}$ pure metal and $\frac{1}{12}$ alloy as the 'best proportion'. The Court decided to adopt this proportion for the proposed coin of India as follows:[157]

Troy grains	180
Deduct one-twelfth	15
And contain of fine silver, troy grains	165

Coming to the adoption of the foregoing principles of a standard weight and fineness in India, the position regarding the principal units of silver currencies circulating in the three presidencies presented a very divergent picture. In Bengal alone, there were three different silver coins, viz., the 19-*sun* Sicca, the Farrukhabad rupee and the Benares (*Machhlidar*) rupee, which had different weights and pure metal contents. In Madras, there was the Arcot rupee while the Surat rupee was the principal currency in Bombay, which again had a weight and fineness that was different from each other. The overall picture emerged as follows:

TABLE 3.21: PRINCIPAL UNITS OF SILVER CURRENCY IN BRITISH INDIA (*c.* 1806)

Issued by the Govern-ment of	Territory in which it circulated	Date and Authority of Issue	Silver Coins		
			Name	Gross Weight (in gms)	Pure Contents (in gms)
Bengal	Bengal, Bihar and Orissa Cuttack	Regulation XXXV of 1793 Regulation XII of 1805	Sicca (19-*sun*) Rupee	11.64	11.40
	Ceded and Conquered Provinces	Regulation XLV of 1803	Farrukhabad (Lucknow 45-*sun* Sicca) Rupee	11.21	10.77
	Benares Province	Regulation III of 1806	Benares (*Machhlidar*) Rupee	11.34	10.94
Madras	Madras Presidency		Arcot Rupee	11.43	10.78
Bombay	Bombay Presidency	Proclamation, 27 January 1801	Surat Rupee	11.60	10.67

Source: Despatch from the Court of Directors to the governments of Bengal, Madras and Bombay, dated 25 April 1806, British Parliamentary Papers, 1898, no. 127, para 6; Ambedkar 1947: 17.

In order to reduce all these silver currencies to a common standard, except for the 19-*sun* Sicca, only a slight adjustment in their fineness was required:

TABLE 3.22: DEVIATIONS OF THE PROPOSED STANDARD OF FINENESS FROM THAT OF THE PRINCIPAL RECOGNIZED RUPEES

Silver Coins recognized as Principal Units and their Fineness		Standard Fineness of the proposed Silver Rupee (in gms)	More valuable than the proposed Rupee		Less valuable than the proposed Rupee	
Name of the Coin	Its Pure Contents (in gms)		(in gms)	By %	(in gms)	By %
Sicca (19-*sun*) Rupee	11.40	10.69	0.708	6.211	–	–
Farrukhabad (Lucknow 45-*sun* Sicca) Rupee	10.77		0.073	0.683	–	–
Benares (*Machhlidar*) Rupee	10.94		0.253	2.511	–	–
Arcot Rupee	10.78		0.095	0.887	–	–
Surat Rupee	10.67		–	–	0.026	0.157

Source: Ambedkar 1947: 17.

Thus, except for the Sicca (19-*sun*) and Benares Rupee, all other principal units adhered closely to the new standard of fineness, viz., 165 grains (10.69 g) of pure silver. Even in the case of the Sicca Rupee, where the proportion of pure metal was much higher than the proposed standard, the Court of Directors did not 'apprehend any objection on the part of the people of Bengal' and remarked that 'no objection but what a very short experience of the advantages of the general currency would remove'.[158]

The Court also contemplated the fractional units of the principal coin as follows:[159]

Half rupee weighing troy grains		90
Quarter rupee	do.	45
Anna	do.	$11\frac{1}{4}$

For small monetary transactions, the Court recommended a copper coinage consisting of the following three denominations:[160]

6 *pice* or half *anna*
3 *pice* or quarter *anna*
1 *pice* or one-twelfth *anna*

The *pice* was to be the smallest currency unit. To guard against the clandestine melting of this specie, the Court directed that: '. . . the weight of this coin to be so adjusted, according to the price of copper and expenses of coining, as to leave a profit on its issue; which would have the good effect of preventing the melting of the coin, as its value in currency would be something more than the value of the metal, with all the export charges upon it.'[161]

While establishing the silver rupee and its fractional denominations as the principal monetary unit and a copper coinage as a subordinate currency medium for small transactions, the Court also considered the issue of gold coinage and noted that they were 'by no means desirous of checking the circulation of gold, but of establishing a gold coin on a principle fitted for general use'.[162]

The gold coin, according to the Court, was to be modelled on the same standard of weight and fineness as that of the proposed silver rupee, 'viz. 180 troy grains, gross weight, and 165 troy grains, fine gold'.[163] It was to be called 'gold rupee' and was to have half and quarter denominations of proportionate weight and fineness. However, the gold coinage was not to have any fixed value with regard to the silver coin 'but left to find its own level according to . . . the market value of the metals'.[164]

As for the general device of the new coinage, the Court recommended the following pattern:[165]

Obverse: Company's arms and motto with an inscription 'English East India Company', as also the denomination and value of the coin with the year of coinage, viz. Sicca Rupee, 1806/Half Rupee or $\frac{1}{2}$ Rupee, 1806/Anna, 1806.

Reverse: Persian inscription expressing the English one on the obverse, with the value and denomination of the coin, together with the date of coinage.

It was also mentioned that 'If the smaller gold and silver coins (perhaps below the half rupee) do not present surface sufficient for a clear impression, it would be proper to substitute for the arms, the Company's crest, the inscriptions to remain alike in all.'[166] No device was prescribed for the copper coins. No time-frame was prescribed for the adoption of these measures in India and the three presidencies were left to carry these recommendations into effect at their discretion.

The task of reducing the existing units of currency to that proposed by the Court was first accomplished in Madras.[167] By a proclamation issued by the government of Fort St. George on 7 January 1818, a gold rupee and a silver rupee, each weighing 180 grains troy and containing 165 grains of pure metal, was established. Six years later, the Bombay government followed suit. By a proclamation issued on 6 October 1824, the Surat rupee of the Bombay Presidency was re-designated as the 'Bombay Rupee' and assimilated to the Madras standard. The gold *muhr* of Bombay was, likewise, assimilated to the new standard in 1825.

In the Bengal Presidency, three principal currencies were established:

TABLE 3.23: BENGAL: PRINCIPAL SILVER CURRENCIES AND THEIR AREAS OF CIRCULATION, *c.* 1819

Denomination	Area of Circulation
Sicca Rupee	Provinces of Bengal, Bihar and Orissa
Farrukhabad Rupee	Upper Provinces, Lower Provinces, Saugor and Nerbudda Territories
Benares Rupee	Benares Province

As a first step to reduce the coin types, the Benares rupee was abolished by Regulation XI of 31 December 1819 and the circulation of the Farrukhabad rupee was extended to the province of Benares. Second, the weight of the Farrukhabad rupee was altered as follows:

TABLE 3.24: BENGAL: WEIGHT AND FINENESS OF FARRUKHABAD RUPEE

Established by	Weight		Fineness	
	Grs	Gms	Grs	Gms
Reg. III, 1806	173	11.21	165.215	10.70
Reg. XI, 1819	180.234	11.67		

Thus, while there was no change in the content of pure metal, Regulation XI of 1819 brought the weight of the Farrukhabad rupee within close proximity of the standard prescribed by the Court of Directors. However, even now, two measures of value prevailed in the Bengal presidency in contrast with the Madras and Bombay presidencies where the Arcot and Bombay rupees, respectively, had been established as the measure of value by now.

TABLE 3.25: BENGAL: SICCA AND THE FARRUKHABAD RUPEE, *c.* 1819

Coin	Weight		Fineness	
	Grs	Gms	Grs	Gms
Sicca Rupee	191.916	12.44	175.923	11.40
Farrukhabad Rupee	180.234	11.67	165.215	10.70

Standardization and Revenue Collection

The question of having only one silver coin for the Bengal Presidency was now contemplated and the option of having either the Farrukhabad (or the *Kaldar* Sicca) or the Sicca Rupee, both of which had different weights, was debated in several consecutive meetings of the Mint Committee. Holt Mackenzie, Secretary to the government and a Member of the Calcutta Mint Committee, recorded his observations in his Minute dated 12 May 1825, where he writes: 'This question resolves itself into the discussion, whether the Calcutta Sicca or the Furruckabad Rupee shall be our standard of value.'[168]

The chief hindrance in adopting the Calcutta Sicca Rupee as the general standard was the potential loss of revenue from areas where the revenue assessment had been done as per the Farrukhabad (or Arcot/Bombay) Rupee standard, which was $\frac{1}{16}$ (or 6.25 per cent) less in intrinsic value. Mackenzie estimated this loss to the tune of Rs. 52 lakh:

> In the land revenue of the Western Provinces, and of Madras and Bombay, a remission to the extent of $6\frac{1}{4}$ per cent must be made amounting to about Rupees 52,00,000. This would be a dead loss to the Government . . . the sacrifice of the revenue would be so great as to oppose an insuperable bar to the adoption of this branch of alternative.[169]

On the other hand, if the Farrukhabad rupee was adopted as the standard measure of value, it would have clashed directly with the provisions of the Permanent Settlement of Bengal, Bihar and a portion of Orissa, where annual revenue of Rs. 2.85 crore had been fixed in the Calcutta Sicca. As Mackenzie observes:

> If we continue to demand the same nominal amount of Rupees, we shall sustain an annual loss of about Rupees 17,80,000 by taking Farruckabad instead of the Sicca Rupees. If we increase the nominal amount of the Revenue in proportion to the reduced value of the coinage, we shall ostensibly enhance a demand, which the nation is so solemnly pledged to continue unaltered.

We shall thus probably give occasion to much complaint, and for a time at least may actually injure the zemindars.[170]

In spite of the obvious difficulties, Mackenzie was in favour of adopting the Farrukhabad rupee as the uniform currency for the Bengal Presidency. In subsequent years, while efforts were made to regularize the minting operations of the different mints of the Bengal Presidency and to facilitate the circulation of various sorts of old and new currencies, no breakthrough was apparently made either in reducing the two principal silver currencies of the Bengal Presidency to a single coin type, or in assimilating either of the two to the principal units of the other presidencies, namely Madras and Bombay.

The principal individual who spearheaded the task of assimilating the Farrukhabad rupee to the Bombay and Arcot rupees and, thus, achieving uniformity in the weight and fineness of the principal silver rupees of the three presidencies was James Prinsep (1799-1840), the son of John Prinsep, who, during 1780-4, had supplied copper coinage to the Bengal government from his private mint at Falta. Thus, James had the genes of a coiner in his blood.[171]

JAMES PRINSEP

James Prinsep had earlier served as the Assay Master and the Secretary of the Mint Committee at Benares (1820-9) and, after the abolition

Fig. 3.22: James Prinsep (1799-1840)

of the Benares mint in 1829, as Deputy Assay Master at the Calcutta mint (1830-2). In January 1833, when the Assay Master, Dr. H.H. Wilson, left for England to take up his new assignment as the Boden Professor of Sanskrit at the University of Oxford, James Prinsep succeeded him as the Assay Master of the Calcutta mint and Secretary of the Mint Committee.

Immediately after assuming these responsibilities, Prinsep got an opportunity to review the question of the weights and measures of India and formulate a plan for establishing uniformity in the weight and fineness of the principal silver currencies of British India. The occasion was provided by an error which he discovered in the table of weights of various coins that was prepared by H.H. Wilson before his departure for England. This table was printed by the order of the government and circulated for the guidance of the revenue officers of the Bengal Presidency. In his letter dated 11 April 1833 that was addressed to the Mint Committee of Calcutta, Prinsep pointed out that in this table, the new Farrukhabad rupee had been 'inserted as weighing 180 grains troy [11.66 g] instead of 180.234 [grains = 11.67 g] as provided by Reg. XI of 1819, Sec. 5'.[172]

Prinsep then described the existing twin weight and fineness standard for the same specie, viz., the Farrukhabad rupee, coined at the Farrukhabad, Calcutta and Benares mints, on the one hand, and at the Saugor mint, on the other.

TABLE 3.26: BENGAL: MINTING OF THE FARRUKHABAD RUPEE (1819-33)

Mint	Years	Weight		Fineness	
		Grs	Gms	Grs	Gms
Farrukhabad	1819-24*				
Calcutta	1819-33$	180.234	11.67	165.215	10.70
Benares	1820-29*				
Saugor	1825#-33$	180	11.66	165	10.69

Notes: *Mint abolished #New Mint established $Minting continued till 1833

While the Farrukhabad, Calcutta and Benares mints followed the weight and fineness standard prescribed by Regulation XI of 1819, the Farrukhabad rupee coined at Saugor followed the weight and fineness standard of the Arcot rupee established in 1818 right from its inception, and to which the standard Bombay rupee was assimilated in 1829. Thus, by 1829, a uniformity of weight and fineness of the principal silver currency circulating in a large part of British India was virtually established.

However, the existence of two differing weight and fineness standards of the same specie caused both loss and confusion, as noted by Prinsep in his letter to the Mint Committee, referred to above. He records: '. . . it is a waste of silver to coin heavier money to circulate at par with them [lighter coins]' and adds that 'confusion at the Collector's office will prevail in ascertaining when the current coin is to be deemed of short weight what are still issuable at one Treasury will have caused to be so at another and vice versa as long as the two weights remain'.[173]

Referring to the 'expressed desire' of the Court of Directors 'to equalize the coin of the whole of their Indian possessions, both in weight and standard', Prinsep advocated the adoption of 180 grains (11.66 g) as the standard weight for the Farrukhabad rupees minted at Calcutta in the hope that 'the adoption of the smaller weight will tend to keep the present currency afloat for a longer period'.[174]

As the weight of 180 grains was $\frac{15}{16}$th of 192 grains (12.44 g)—the weight of the Calcutta Sicca,[175] comprising 16 *annas*, the problem of conversion was also expected to be simplified, 'since the commonest understanding could comprehend the calculation of one anna per rupee which would be leviable upon all fixed settlements in excess of their jumma [revenue] if paid in new Farrukhabad Rupee'.[176]

Prinsep hoped that if this arrangement was adopted, 'the abolition of the [Calcutta] Sikka Rupee (or the suspension of any further coinage of it) might be at once effected'.[177] Thus, his plan was twofold: first, to reduce the two principal currencies of the Bengal Presidency to one and, second, to assimilate it to the weight and fineness standard of the Arcot and Bombay rupees, and thereby complete the process of uniformity of currency that was started in Madras in 1818 in accordance with the roadmap laid down in the Court of Directors's despatch of 1806.

Associated with the reform of the coin was the problem of weights that were in general usage. During this time, weights throughout the country were expressed in terms of the principal coin and, thus, *ser* and *man* were simply multiples of the principal coin current in that area. Prinsep notes: '. . . throughout the Marathi states, the ser is referred to the Puna or Ankusi rupee: in Gujarat, to the Baroch rupee: in Ajmir to Salimsahi; in Bengal, to the old Murshidabad rupee . . .' .[178]

In Bengal, two systems of weights were prevalent. The first was the Factory weight, based on the English avoirdupois pound system, while the second, called the *bazaar* or *sicca* weight, was based on the old Murshidabad rupee weighing 176.666 grains (11.64 g). In those parts of the Bengal province where the Farrukhabad rupee was in circulation, the *ser* and *man* were expressed as multiples of that coin. Prinsep was aware that any change in the weight system was not an easy task. He writes: 'However desirable it may be, in theory, to reduce the system of weights throughout the vast continent of India to order and uniformity; in practice, it is well known that insuperable difficulties oppose the execution of such a project.'[179]

To start with, such a change required a corresponding adjustment in all the weights in use at the mint, the customs house, the treasury, the banks, the collector's offices and a number of other government offices. Undeterred by the apparent difficulties, Prinsep, by his mathematical calculations and statistical analysis, successfully demonstrated that by a slight modification in the *sicca* weight, it could be adopted as the standard unit for weights as well as for the new rupee coins.

When the weight of the Calcutta Sicca rupee was increased from 179.666 grains (11.64 g) to 191.916 grains (12.43 g) by Regulation XIV of 1818, a corresponding alteration to the weights of general use was not carried out. Prinsep writes: '. . . it was not deemed expedient to extend the alteration to the weight founded upon the old coin and consequently a Sikka weight was retained as the unit of weight contradistinguished from the Sikka Rupee of the new currency.'[180]

Prinsep found a great opportunity in this anomaly as the old *sicca* weight (179.666 grains) was 'but a trifling fraction of a grain lighter than the proposed Rupee of 180 grains'.[181] This difference of 0.333 grains (21 mg) or a nearly six hundredth part was negligible and, therefore, readily adaptable 'without the smallest difficulty or inconveniences in commercial or revenue transactions'.[182]

Having studied the coin and currency systems of India through the ages, Prinsep was also aware of the fact that the traditional Indian weight of the *tola* was, in fact, the weight of the silver rupee, 80 of which went for a *ser*. The *tola*, in turn, closely matched the weight of the Farrukhabad rupee (180 grains) that was proposed by Prinsep as the sole silver currency unit for the Bengal Presidency. On the other hand, the multiples of the *tola* also synchronized with the English troy weights:[183]

8 *rattis*	= 1 *masha*	= 15 grains troy		= 0.97 g
12 *mashas*	= 1 *tola*	= 180 grains troy		= 11.66 g
80 *tolas*	= 1 *ser*	= $2\frac{1}{2}$ lbs. troy		= 933.1 g
40 *sers*	= 1 *man*	= 100 lbs. troy or *bazaar maund*		= 37.32 kg

Prinsep, therefore, wanted the weights to be fabricated on this system for general use. He also preferred the use of 'the universal Hindi word *tola*' in contrast with '*sikka* weight' which he found objectionable—'. . . it is an English compound and cannot be translated into the native language.'[184]

The plan proposed by Prinsep was forwarded to the Governor-General on 12 April 1833.[185] In a reply dated 1 July 1833, G.A. Bushby, Officiating Secretary to the government in the Financial Department, informed the Mint Committee of Calcutta about the decisions of the Governor-General in this regard.[186] First of all, the proposed alteration in the weight of the Farrukhabad rupees to be coined at the Calcutta mint from 180.234 to 180 grains, as well as that of the Calcutta Sicca rupees from 191.916 to 192 grains, was approved. Similarly, the assimilation of the Sicca weight, 'contradistinguished to the Sicca Rupee', with the weight of the Farrukhabad rupee (180 grains), as well as the substitution of the term *tola* for *sicca* weight, was also approved. However, regarding the enforcement of 'the general use of the uniform weights and measures' in all public transactions, the Governor-General observed that the same 'could not be effected without prescribing penalties for employing others than those of the Regulation standard'. As an alternative, therefore, he suggested that 'where application is made to the Mint and Assay Offices for the verification or manufacture of Sicca weights, that a standard of 180 grains ought to be adopted'.[187]

Subsequently, on 13 July 1833, Regulation VII of 1833[188] was passed which converted Prinsep's proposals into a legislation. By this Regulation, the weight of the Farrukhabad rupee—one of the principal coins of northern India, was fixed at 180 grains troy, corresponding to the traditional Indian weight for the silver rupee, i.e. 1 *tola* of 12 *mashas*. This coin was then adopted as the unit of a general system of weights for government transactions throughout India.

At the same time, by this alteration in weight, the Farrukhabad rupee was also assimilated to the weights of the Bombay and Arcot rupees—the principal coins of the Bombay and Madras Presidency, respectively. Now all the three presidencies of the East India Company had their principal coins of a uniform weight. A uniform coinage was a *fait accompli*.

TABLE 3.27: UNIFORMITY OF SILVER RUPEE AT THE END OF 1833

Presidency	Silver Rupee			Fineness		
	Denomination	Weight		Grs	Gms	%
		Grs	Gms			
Bengal	Sicca Rupee	192	12.44	176	11.40	91.63
	Farrukhabad Rupee	180	11.66	165	10.69	91.68
Bombay	Bombay Rupee	180	11.66	165	10.69	91.68
Madras	Arcot Rupee	180	11.66	165	10.69	91.68

Source: Adapted from Ambedkar 1947: 17.

Prinsep, at the same time, was also convinced that such a wide-ranging change that touched almost every aspect of public life could not be effected by force. Thus, we find that the Regulation expressly avoided any penal provision for default. The decision of the government as well as a copy of Regulation VII of 1833 was forwarded to the Court of Directors by the Governor-General's letter dated 9 September 1833.[189]

A uniformity of currency thus achieved, the next target in the plan for currency reforms was the introduction of a universal coinage throughout the Indian possessions of the East India Company.[190]

SUMMING UP

Based on the recommendations of the Mint Committee of the Bengal Presidency, the Bengal government had initiated a systematic process of reforming the colonial currency. The regulations passed by the Governor-General-in-Council in 1793 established the Company's silver coin—the Sicca Ruppee—as the principal currency of the Bengal Presidency. As new territories were added into the presidency, new currencies were standardized for these regions—the Farrukhabad rupee for the Ceded and Conquered Provinces, and the Benares rupee for the Benares province. Initially, the currency system was modelled on bimetallism but, in 1806, the Court of Directors decided in favour of monometallism and, consequently, the silver rupee was not only standardized but also firmly established in regions like those under the Madras Presidency which traditionally had a predominantly gold-based currency system. By 1824, the principal rupees of the Madras and Bombay presidencies—the Arcot rupee and the Bombay rupee—had been assimilated in weight and fineness to establish a uniform currency within a large part of the Company's territorial possessions in India. In 1825, the same weight and fineness was adopted for the Farrukhabad rupee coined at the newly-established mint at Saugor, which catered to the monetary requirements of the Saugor and Nerbudda territories. Finally, in 1833, the Farrukhabad rupee coined in the Company's mints at Farrukhabad, Calcutta and Benares, and the principal currency of northern India, was also assimilated with the Arcot and Bombay rupee. Thus, a uniform currency was established in the territories of the East India Company, except the Bengal province, where the Sicca rupee of a slightly higher weight but lesser fineness was retained.

The process of currency reforms that was carried out by the East India Company between the years 1793 and 1833 addressed the liquidity crisis faced by it in its multifarious activities ranging from revenue collection to military campaigns. With the establishment of a uniform standard (silver monometallism) and the assimilation of the weight and fineness of the principal currencies of different regions, the velocity of money was greatly enhanced, which, in turn, helped the Company to meet a currency crunch in one region by mobilizing surplus money from the other regions. These reforms also struck down the menace of *batta* charged by the money-changers, which resulted in streamlining the rates of exchange between the different specie of rupees circulating in a particular region.

The currency reforms also addressed the need for the technological upgradation of the minting process in India. Screw presses were introduced for the first time in Indian mints, which resulted in a manifold increase in their output. This quantum leap in mint production greatly facilitated the replacement of various sorts of currencies in the region by the Company's coins. It also helped in meeting the demands of an expanding area of money use in the society.

Finally, by exempting the import and export of bullion from duty, the Company encouraged its free flow into its mints. Incidents of counterfeiting the established coin were curbed, to a large extent, by incorporating provisions for strict penalties for violators in legislations dealing with the administration of criminal justice in British India.

Thus, within a short span of four decades, the East India Company was able to integrate the currencies of its dominions and secure the currency administration firmly in its hands. This provided the Company a powerful tool which not only helped it transform from traders to full-fledged administrators—a role bestowed upon it by virtue of the Charter Act of 1833—but also in establishing an imperial currency to serve as the facilitator of imperial finances.

NOTES

1. *FWIHC* XII, 1978: 2.
2. Appendix A.1.
3. Even today, most legislations have a similar clause granting immunity to public servants for any action done by them in 'good faith'.
4. Appendix A.2.
5. Appendix A.3.
6. Regulation XXXV, 1793, Sec. I, Appendix A.3.
7. Ibid.
8. Ibid.
9. Appendix A.4.
10. Appendix A.5.
11. Appendix A.9.
12. Appendix A.13.
13. Regulation LXI of 1795, Sec. I, Appendix A.6.
14. Appendix A.6.
15. Appendix A.7.
16. Regulation XIV of 1818, Preamble, Appendix A.30.
17. Ibid.
18. Appendix A.3.
19. In 1769, the mintage of gold *muhrs* weighing 17 *annas sicca* weight or 190.773 troy grains (12.36 g) and having a fineness of 99.63 per cent was authorized. With a view to easing the pressure due to the scarcity of the silver coin, this *muhr* was declared legal tender and, thus, for the second time since 1766, a bimetallic currency was established in the Bengal Presidency. However, as the exchange rate between the silver and gold coins that was officially fixed by the government was overvalued, this measure (like the previous one in 1766) was doomed to failure.
20. NAI, Finance Department, Mint Proceedings, vol. 1795: 29.
21. Ibid.
22. Pridmore 1975: 209.
23. Appendix A.28.
24. Appendix A.19.
25. Appendix A.24.
26. Appendix A.25.

27. Appendix A.38.
28. Pridmore 1975: 213.
29. Appendix A.15.
30. Appendix A.18.
31. Appendix A.17.
32. Appendix A.12.
33. Pridmore 1975: 223.
34. Appendix A.16.
35. Sec. III of Regulation XXI of 1816, Appendix A.25; and Pridmore 1975: Coin Nos. 335 and 335A.
36. Appendix A.28.
37. The Farrukhabad mint was first established during the sixth regnal year of Farrukhsiyar (1716-17) by the first Bangash Nawab of Farrukhabad, Muhammad Khan Bangash (d. 1743). On the coins issued subsequent to AH 1167 (AD 1753-4), the mint name appears as *Ahmadnagar Farrukhabad*. The Bangash Nawabs later became tributaries of the Nawab of Awadh. This mint was located at Fatehgarh, the administrative headquarters of Farrukhabad. See Prinsep 1858: 26.
38. The new Farrukhabad mint started production in 1806 and continued its operations till 1824. It was finally abolished by Regulation II of 1824.
39. However, even before the expiration of the cut-off date, this order was rescinded in 1807 (Sec. IX of Regulation XIII of 1807; see Appendix A.18).
40. By a separate treaty, the Treaty of Mustafapur concluded on 21 November 1805 with Daulat Rao Sindhia, the town of Gohad and the fort of Gwalior was restored to him. In return he renounced his claims on the territories north of the river Chambal in favour of the Company.
41. Appendix A.14.
42. Appendix A.16.
43. Appendix A.17.
44. Garg 1990: 233-40.
45. Appendix A.29.
46. NAI, Financial Department, OC, 4 September 1818, no. 25.
47. Appendix A.32.
48. Appendix A.35.
49. Pridmore 1975: 257.
50. NAI, Financial Department, OC, 19 January 1826, nos. 1-3 and 16 March 1826, no. 2.
51. Pridmore 1975: 257.
52. Report of G.H. Barlow, Sub-Secretary to the Government of Bengal, dated 24 August 1787. NAI, Mint Committee, vol. 1792: 79.
53. Mishra 1975: 177.
54. Regulation II of 1812, Sec. XV, Appendix A.23.

55. Appendix A.37.
56. The local jewellers' weights at Benares were based on the following metrology:
    8 *chowals* (or grains of rice) = 1 *ratti*
    64 *chowals* = 8 *ratti* = 1 *masha* (1 *masha* approx. 17.7 troy grains)
    768 *chowals* = 96 *ratti* = 12 masha = 1 *tola*
57. Thurston 1893: 70.
58. Pridmore 1975: 215.
59. Thurston 1893: 67.
60. Ibid.
61. Regulation XII of 1810, Sec. III, Appendix A.21.
62. Thomas Yeld, Mint Master, Benares Mint, to Sir J.E. Colebrook and John Deane, Board of Commissioners, Province of Benares, dated 18 December 1812: NAI, Finance Department, Mint Committee, Letters Received, vol. 1811-13: 269.
63. Ibid.: 270.
64. Ibid.: 275.
65. Thurston 1893: 72.
66. Appendix A.24.
67. Ibid.: Sec. III.
68. Pridmore 1975: 219.
69. Harrington 1814-15: 632.
70. Prinsep 1858: 9.
71. Ibid.: 8.
72. Appendix A.23.
73. Some inaccuracies were noticed in the calculations of the produce of gold bullion at the Calcutta mint, which were later removed by passing Regulation XIV of 1817 on 9 September 1817.
74. Prinsep 1858: 79.
75. Keith 1937: 71-2.
76. Ibid.: 97.
77. British Parliamentary Papers, 1898, no. 127, para 41.
78. Harrington 1814-15: 616-17.
79. Ramachandran and Gupta 1971: 33.
80. Reform of the Coinage—Report of the Committee of Finance. IOL Coll. F/4/188, no. 123, quoted in Stevens 2004: 123.
81. Ibid.
82. British Parliamentary Papers, 1898, no. 127.
83. The three members were Cecil Smith, John Hodgson and Edward Greenway. However, the composition of the Committee changed from time to time; Stevens 2004: 136.
84. Ramachandran 1970a: 37.
85. Letter from the Court to Fort St. George, dated 6 April 1808. IOL Coll. F/4/477, no. 11486, quoted in Stevens 2004: 134.

86. Ibid.
87. Stevens 2004: Tables 3-5, 126-8.
88. IOL Coll. F/4/477, No. 11486, quoted in Stevens 2004: 138-9.
89. Ibid.: 139.
90. Ibid.: 142.
91. Pridmore 1975: 37.
92. Thurston 1890: 44.
93. Ibid.: 45.
94. Pridmore 1975: 23.
95. Ibid.: 8.
96. Prinsep 1858: 24.
97. Pridmore 1975: 27.
98. Despatch from the Court of Directors to the governments of Bengal, Madras and Bombay, dated 25 April 1806, British Parliamentary Papers, 1898, no. 127: para 26.
99. Ibid.: para 21.
100. Ibid.
101. Pridmore 1975: 34.
102. Stevens 2004: 126 and 129, Tables 3 and 6.
103. Pridmore 1975: 126.
104. Anon. 1986: 9.
105. H. Scott to F. Warden, Secretary to the Government of Bombay, 7 December 1806, para 14. NAI, Home, Public, Proceedings Volume, 22-9 January 1807: 327.
106. Ibid.: 330-1.
107. Stevens 2004d: 25-32.
108. Ibid.
109. Pridmore 1975: 134.
110. NAI, Mint Committee, Letters Received, vol. 1826-1830: 489.
111. Anon 1986: 4.
112. NAI, Mint Committee, Letters Received, vol. 1826-1830: 490.
113. Report of the Assay and Mint Master, dated 28 November 1800—quoted in Pridmore 1975: 130.
114. Pridmore 1975: 178, Coin nos. 334-5.
115. The term 'Customs duty' has been used in this work to denote the duties on importing into and exporting outside India, while 'Transit duty' has been used for duties levied on the inland trade of India. However, in the sources, the words 'Customs duty' are frequently used to describe the duties on inland trade as well, sometimes distinguishing the two by using 'Sea customs' for duties on export/ import and 'Land customs' for duties on inland trade. Both Banerjea and Borpujari agree that 'the British deliberately confused these terms so as to apply to the inland trade of India the concessions they had acquired from native Indian rulers regarding the payment of customs duty on the foreign trade of India.' Banerjea 1928: 209; Borpujari 1973: 218.

116. Report of the Select Committee on the Affairs of the East India Company, 1810, quoted in Banerjea 1922: 8.
117. Banerjea 1922: 8-9.
118. Appendix A.8.
119. Appendix A.10.
120. Appendix A.11.
121. Appendix A.20.
122. Appendix A.36.
123. Milburn 1825: 264.
124. Banerjea 1922: 32.
125. Appendix B.1, B.3 and B.4.
126. Appendix B.2.
127. Appendix C.1.
128. Appendix C.2.
129. Appendix C.4.
130. Cunningham 1840 and 1840a; Kala 1947.
131. Prasad and Gupta 1956.
132. Grierson 1975: 158.
133. NAI, Home Department, Public Branch, Proceedings, 20 July 1791, nos. 9-11.
134. Ibid.: 29 July 1791, no. 16.
135. T.H. Davies, Advocate General to the Governor-General in Council giving his opinion on the applicability of statutes to the offence of counterfeiting coin in India, letter dated 8 September 1791. NAI, Home Department, Public Branch, OC, 14 September, 1791, no. 4.
136. NAI, Home Department, Public Branch, OC, 2 September, 1793, no. 2 and 7 October 1793, no. 21; Datta 1968: 215-16, 219-20, 222-3, 290, and 292-3.
137. Backing Warrants were issued by the Justices of Peace in England for apprehending persons residing outside the jurisdiction of their county. These warrants required the endorsement (or 'backing') of the Justice of Peace of the county where the accused resided.
138. W. Burroughs, Advocate General, to E. Hay, Secretary to the Government, Fort William, giving his opinion as to the prosecution of coiners guilty of circulating base coins, letter dated 8 February 1793. NAI, Home Department, Public Branch, OC 11 February, 1793, no. 10.
139. W. Jackson, Company's Attorney, to C. Shakespeare, Sub-Secretary, Fort William, embodying the opinion of the Advocate General and the Standing Counsel on the punishment to be awarded to the persons concerned in counterfeiting gold *muhrs*, letter dated 17 August 1793. NAI, Home Department, Public Branch, OC, 19 August 1793, no. 9.
140. Appendix A.27.
141. NAI, Foreign Department, Secret Branch, Letters From Court, dated 24 September 1796.

142. Ibid.
143. Ibid.
144. Appendix B.5.
145. Ibid.: Sec. IV. *First.*
146. Appendix C.3.
147. Appendix C.5.
148. NAI, Foreign Department, Political Branch, OC, 11 February 1831, nos. 72-3.
149. NAI, Financial Department, Mint Committee, Letters Received, vol. 1811-13: 153-65.
150. Ibid.
151. Liverpool 1805.
152. Despatch from the Court of Directors to the governments of Bengal, Madras and Bombay, dated 25 April 1806, British Parliamentary Papers, 1898, no. 127: para 6.
153. Ibid.
154. Referred to in NAI, Public, Letters from Court, dated 25 May 1798, para 25.
155. Despatch from the Court of Directors to the governments of Bengal, Madras and Bombay, dated 25 April 1806, British Parliamentary Papers, 1898, no. 127: paras 6 and 8.
156. Ibid.
157. Ibid.: para 9.
158. Ibid.: para 10.
159. Ibid.: para 14.
160. Ibid.
161. Ibid.: para 15.
162. Ibid.: para 16.
163. Ibid.
164. Ibid.: para 18.
165. Ibid.: para 37.
166. Ibid.
167. Ambedkar 1947: 16.
168. NAI, Financial Department, OC, 26 July 1826, no. 10.
169. Ibid.
170. Ibid.
171. See Garg 2001.
172. NAI, Financial Department, Mint Proceedings, 1 July 1833, no. 2.
173. Ibid.: para 20.
174. Ibid.
175. Its weight was actually 191.916 grains or 12.43 g, as fixed by Regulation XIV of 1818.
176. NAI, Financial Department, Proceedings, 1 July 1833, no. 2.
177. Ibid.

178. Prinsep 1858: 109.
179. Ibid.
180. Prinsep to the Mint Committee, dated 11 April 1833. NAI, Financial Department, Proceedings, 1 July 1833, no. 2.
181. Ibid.
182. Ibid.
183. Ibid.
184. Ibid.
185. Mint Committee to Secretary to Government in General Department. NAI, Financial Department, Proceedings, 1 July 1833, no. 1.
186. NAI, Financial Department, Mint Committee Proceedings, July 1833, no. 15.
187. Ibid.
188. Appendix A.39.
189. Bengal Letter to Court, no. 16 of 1833. NAI, Financial Department, Letters to Court, vol. 1833: 125-38.
190. The term 'universal coinage' used here and subsequently has been discounted from the literal meaning of the word denoting 'beyond the frontiers of one country and pertaining to the universe'. The applied meaning of this term in this work is restricted to the territorial possessions of the English East India Company in India.

CHAPTER 4

From a Uniform Currency to a Universal Coinage (1833-1835)

By the middle of 1833, the East India Company had successfully integrated the principal currencies of the three presidencies to conform to a uniform weight and purity. In a parallel development, the British Parliament sought 'to replace the existing multiplicity in the systems . . . by a uniform system . . . common as far as possible to the whole of India. . . .'[1] In this process, the uniformity of currency provided a solid foundation on which administrative structures were built not only for the civil and military government, but also for the management of revenue and commerce throughout British India. Thus 'an all-powerful Central Government, legislating for and controlling the affairs of India as a whole' was established by the Charter Act of 1833.[2]

The Charter Act of 1833 (3 & 4 Will. IV, c. 85) gave wide-ranging powers to the government of India.[3] The Governor-General of Bengal now became the Governor-General of India. He was empowered to legislate without seeking the prior approval of the Parliament.[4]

> . . . the Governor-General in Council (at Fort William in Bengal) shall have power to make laws and regulations for repealing, amending, or altering any laws or regulations, whatever, now in force or hereafter to be in force in the said territories or any part thereof, and to make laws and regulations for all persons, whether British or native, foreigners or others, and for all Courts of Justice, whether established by His Majesty's Charters or otherwise and the jurisdictions thereof, and for all places and every part of the said territory, and for all servants of the said Company within the dominions of princes and states in alliance with the said Company. . . .[5]

The imperial system of government that was thus established by the Charter Act of 1833 required an imperial currency, not merely as the stamp of its authority but also as a facilitator of imperial finances. The uniformity of currency, more specifically that of the principal unit of the circulating medium—the Rupee, having being established by Regulation VII of 1833, the next logical step was to establish a universal coinage, which was not only of the same weight and standard but which also bore the same device and impression. However, in India, where coins were traditionally regarded as the insignia of sovereign power, any change in their device or appearance was a risky preposition. There were also issues relating to technology for ensuring the production of identical coins from all the mints of the East India Company. This chapter studies how all this and more was achieved by the East India Company with remarkable rapidity within a short span of two years.

BACKGROUND

Having made the Mughal emperor its pensioner, the East India Company had been contemplating altering the device of the coins issued from its mints for a very long time. In its despatch dated 25 April 1806, the Court of Directors had mooted the idea of having a coinage with its own impression (para 37). However, in India, the impression on the coinage was always linked with sovereignty. Nominally, the English Company was still the *Diwan* of the titular Mughal ruler, Shah Alam II. Even after his death on 18 November 1806, the Company's government in India was not disposed to shed the cloak of the nominal overlordship of the Mughal ruler, Akbar Shah II, who succeeded his father, Shah Alam II, on 19 November 1806. The views of the government in this regard are embodied in a letter dated 10 December 1806 from Thomas Brown, Chief Secretary to the government, to the Mint Committee at Calcutta. He writes:

> . . . supposing the Plan of one General Coinage for the Company's possessions in India as directed by the Hon'ble Court or any other Plan to be adopted, the Governor General in Council is of the opinion that the coins should be struck in the name of the King of Delhi as heretofore and not in the Company's with their arms as proposed by the Court.[6]

The use of the Company's arms and crest on the coins issued by it was not altogether an alien phenomenon in India. On the copper coins of Madras (Cash series) struck at England in 1803 and 1808, both the arms and crest of the East India Company were used. Later, in 1819, both these motifs were used on the gold coins of the Madras Presidency where, besides the English characters, the name of the Company was also inscribed in Persian as *Kampani Angrez Bahadur* (the Honourable English Company). Similarly, the *pice* series of

Madras (1824-5) also bore the Company's arms. In the Bombay Presidency, too, coinage in all the metals, viz., gold, silver, copper and tin, bore the Company's arms, shield of arms, balemarks and the crown at different points in time ever since the commencement of its minting activities in about 1672. The case of the Bengal Presidency was, however, altogether different as all the regular coinage was struck in the name of the Mughal emperor.

Therefore, we find that the impression on the coinage struck by the East India Company was not governed by any general policy but was left to the judgement of the individual presidency, subject only to the general acceptability of the coins that were struck.

In 1818, the question of adopting a new device for the coins resurfaced and the Mint Committee recommended that 'it would be more consistent with the dignity of the British Government of India to authorise its own currencies by its own peculiar stamp and impression'.[7] However, once again, a final decision in this regard was postponed to a later date.

In the next year, treading upon the roadmap laid down in the 1806 despatch from the Court of Directors for the introduction of a uniform coinage for British India and to centralize the minting activities at the Calcutta mint, the Mint Committee at Calcutta recommended the construction of a new mint, equipped with modern machinery to undertake large coinage.[8] As part of this plan, Lieutenant W.N. Forbes of the Bengal Engineers was deputed to England to oversee the construction of machinery for the new mint; his brief included instructions 'to bring the subject of the Device for the coin to the notice of the Honorable the Court of Directors'.[9]

In 1824, the Court of Directors once again expressed their desire to have 'the most appropriate impression for the obverse and the reverse of the coinage of the new mint'.[10] Throughout 1825, the issue of adopting an appropriate impression on the coins of the Bengal Presidency was hotly debated in the Mint Committee meetings at Calcutta and their final recommendations in this regard were communicated to Lord Amherst, the Governor-General of Bengal, on 2 November 1825.[11] By this time, the uniformity of weight and fineness of the principal silver currencies of the Madras and Bombay presidencies was already established, and even the Farrukhabad rupee was in close approximation to their standard (see Chapter III). The next logical move, therefore, was to graduate from a uniform to a universal currency and this is what the Mint Committee was convinced about. It wrote:

The advantages of having one currency for the whole of British India are fully appreciated by us, and we concur in expressing an opinion of the expediency of such an arrangement. . . . In consistency with the establishment of one currency we concur in considering it advisable to adopt a uniform impression and in recommending the abolition of all the existing forms.[12]

Regarding the repercussions of the proposed alteration in the impression on the coinage, we find a complete change in the perception of the Company. While in 1806, the Company's government in India was absolutely adamant on maintaining a status quo, the issue had completely receded into insignificance by 1825. The wording of the Mint Committee's letter to the Governor-General is worth noticing in this connection: '. . . we are satisfied that the nature of the impression [on the coins] is a subject on which the people of India are in general wholly indifferent and that any alteration compatible with task or utility may be made without the fear of offending religious or political prejudices.'[13]

Earlier, H.H. Wilson, the Acting Mint Master of the Calcutta Mint, in a separate communication, had called the existing coin impression 'an absurdity and falsehood' which offered no kind of security 'against fraudulent imitation'.[14] While the members of the Mint Committee were unanimous in their view that the new device on the coinage should 'render illicit fabrication as difficult as possible', they held divergent views as to what exactly new device and the inscriptions should be.[15] Ultimately, the question of choosing the appropriate impression on the coins was left to the Court of Directors.[16] The Court, in its reply dated 11 March 1829, deferred any decision on this question once again and wrote: 'We have particularly considered the subject relating to the impressions on the coinage of our mints; and on the whole we are not disposed, at present, to authorize any alteration in that respect, therefore the several coins must continue to be struck with the same impression with which they are now issued.'[17]

In 1829, a new mint was nearing completion in Bombay, and it was once again thought advisable to determine 'the important question of the impression of the new coinage' to be produced at that mint. On 18 February 1830, the Bombay government wrote to the Governor-General of Bengal, emphasizing that a 'uniformity [of coin-impression] should prevail throughout the British territories in India'.[18] However, the Governor-General found himself restrained by the direct orders of the Court of Directors via their despatch dated 11 March 1829 not to take any decision in this regard.

In the Bengal Presidency, the building of the new mint at Calcutta was completed by the end of 1829 and the mint itself was fully commissioned by the end of 1833. There were now five hydraulic presses, costing Rs. 11 lakh. Of these, two were of 40 horse power each, and three were of 24, 20 and 14 horse power, respectively. Their total capacity was 10.03 million pieces per annum. For the production of a large coinage, a large number of dies were also required, not only for the one at Calcutta mint but also for the Bombay and the other *moffusil* mints.

With both the mints at Calcutta and Bombay fully equipped to undertake extensive coinage for the British territories in India, as contemplated in the 1806 despatch of the Court of Directors, dies for the new coinage were required to be prepared expeditiously.

JAMES PRINSEP AND A UNIVERSAL COINAGE

James Prinsep, who had played a key role in bringing about the uniformity of currency in a greater part of the British territories by assimilating the Farrukhabad rupee to the Arcot and Bombay rupees earlier in 1833, decided to impress upon the government the need to establish a universal coinage throughout the British India. Having studied the records of the Mint Committee, Prinsep knew that one major hurdle in adopting a uniform device for this universal coinage was the total dependency of the Indian government on skilled die-engravers from England.

As early as in 1829, the Court of Directors had ordered the centralization of die manufacture at the Calcutta mint. In its letter dated 29 March 1829, the Court had directed the Bengal government that 'all the dies which might be required for the mints of Madras and Bombay also should be executed in the Calcutta mint'.[19] Prinsep was convinced that the deputation of an English die-engraver would always be suspect and, therefore, indigenous skills must be tapped for this purpose. On 1 October 1833, he submitted a note to the Mint Committee, entitled 'On expediency of establishing a die and copy work plate engraving office at the new mint (at Calcutta)', where he proposed to have a permanent establishment for die engraving.[20]

By now, the general agreement was 'that it was desirable that the device [of the coins] should be altered and reformed, but that references [to] home were requisite and that an English die cutter was absolutely necessary to carry on such reform into effect'.[21] However, against many of his compatriots, Prinsep had full faith in the capabilities of his Indian co-workers. Thus, while the hunt for the chief die-engraver was on, he short-listed three names, two of which were of Indians:

1. Dela Combe, the engraver of the map of Calcutta;
2. Kashi Nath, the engraver of the device for the government promissory notes; and
3. Hari Mohun Roy, a seal engraver.

These three engravers were given a pair of blank steel dies and specimens of the coins, viz., the half *anna*, *paisa* and *pie*, respectively, to demonstrate their artistic skills. Being an accomplished artist himself, Prinsep was able to choose the best; his choice was Kashi Nath. He writes: 'There can be no hesitation however, in pronouncing Kashinauth's engraving to be superior to the other two, and indeed his skill as the engraver for copy work is without an equal in Calcutta.'[22]

Prinsep, thus, preferred to employ an Indian rather than an English die-engraver. He informed the Mint Committee that: 'I cannot but pronounce that we have ample means for executing any device that may be selected in Calcutta: that native artists are fully equal to it; that they are much cheaper, much more manageable and more easily replaced upon death or removal.'[23]

Apart from the reasons given above, Prinsep had another hidden agenda, in pronouncing his preference for an Indian die-engraver. He believed that by removing talented die-engravers from the private domain, the 'avenues to illicit coinage' would be shut down.[24] Prinsep, therefore, recommended the extension of the die department of the Calcutta mint and suggested that the services of a 'school of mint engravers' might be most profitably employed for the preparation of plates for government securities, treasury notes, drafts, etc.[25]

Coming to the device of the new coinage, Prinsep regretted that it was not reformed on the opening of the new mint at Calcutta but hastily added that 'it is needless to expatiate on what cannot now be remedied'.[26] He, therefore, wrote to the Mint Committee that:

> . . . now that the Bombay Mint is also completed and the prior step of equalizing the weights of the currencies of the three Presidencies has happily

been effected, a simultaneous movement of the two mints [Bombay and Calcutta] might easily be commanded for the issue of a British Indian coin uniform in device and in every respect worthy of the British name.[27]

As an immediate step in bringing about uniformity in the coinages of the three presidencies, Prinsep recommended the adoption of the armorial bearings of the East India Company that were found on the Bombay and Madras copper coins by the new copper coins of the Bengal Presidency. He urged the government for an immediate decision on the point as the Calcutta mint was in the process of issuing a large copper coinage to replace the *trishuli pice* then circulating in the Bengal Presidency. The question on the device of the silver coins was left 'for more mature consideration'.[28]

Prinsep, meanwhile, studied the Mint Committee records on the subject and on 8 November 1833, shot another note to the Mint Committee 'on the device of Indian coin'.[29] Summarizing 'all that has been said and written on the subject' of the alteration of the device on the coins, Prinsep called upon the government for 'the immediate reform of the device here [in India] without waiting longer for the reply of Hon'ble Court of Directors to the reference made in 1829,[30] which has doubtless been lost sight of in the numerous discussions of more weight and importance that have lately engaged the Indian Government'.[31]

Before taking any decision on the subject, the Mint Committee solicited the opinions of Robert Saunders, the Mint Master, and Captain W.N. Forbes, Superintendent of Machinery of the Calcutta Mint.[32]

By this time, unanimity had emerged in the government on the general impression for the proposed coinage. All were in favour of a pictorial design, though there was some difference of opinion on whether it should be the Company's arms, an emblematic device, the head of the king of England, or a combination of the three. As not everyone was confident about the skills of an Indian engraver in executing a human face, Prinsep decided to give practical evidence of his own conviction. He engaged Kashi Nath for preparing a pair of matrix dies for a specimen coin with the head of King William IV on the obverse, which was adopted from the English sovereign. The reverse had a laurel wreath with the name and date of the coin, 'One Rupee 1834', in the centre. The same was expressed in Devanagari, Persian and Bengali on the margin. However, the die prepared by Kashi Nath cracked in the process of hardening. Even this did not

Obv. Bust of the King facing right. Surrounded by the legend: GULIELLMUS IV D:G: BRITANNIAR: REX F:D: All within a raised, toothed rim.

Rev. The value in English: ONE/RUPEE/1834 with a lotus flower above and the date below. All within a wreath of laurel. Around this is the legend and the value (one rupee) in Hindi एक रूपया (*Ek Rupiya*), Persian یک روپیہ (*Yek Rupiya*)/and Bengali এক রূপয়া (*Ek Rupiya*) EAST INDIA COMPANY all within a raised, toothed rim.

Fig. 4.1: Silver Rupee Pattern, 1834 (by Kashi Nath)

dampen the spirits of Prinsep, who notes: '. . . although [the die has] thus materially injured, enough of the face remains to enable one experienced in such matters to judge of the execution.'[33]

Prinsep submitted the result of Kashi Nath's endeavours to the Mint Committee on 6 April 1834, along with his other note entitled 'On the Device of the British Indian Rupee'.[34] In this note, Prinsep saw a tacit declaration of 'the rule of the British monarch without any assumption of a title which might be obnoxious to political discussion' in this coin [35] and, in its larger role, conceived of it as a 'colonial currency' not only for India but also for other British colonies at its intrinsic value of two shillings. He, therefore, preferred the use of the English name of this denomination as 'One Rupee', without any indication of the place of its minting. Thus, for the first time, the denomination was used on the rupees struck by the East India Company.[36] As Prinsep noted later, 'the great object in equalizing the rupee of the three presidencies was to remove all distinction and make "Rupee" in British India what the term "Pound" or "Shilling" is in England, that it should have but one meaning'.[37] These rupees were also popularly called 'Badshahi', indicating the head of King William IV on the obverse of these coins.[38] In fact, the idea behind the introduction of a universal rupee with an English design, and showing the portrait of the king of England, was also to establish it as a universal colonial currency in the possessions of the East India Company.[39] Shailendra Bhandare has studied the process of the outward flow of the Indian rupee into the colonial possessions of the

English and the Dutch where it was established as the principal, and sometimes sole, currency.[40] For example, from about the 1820s, the 'principal rupees to enter circulation in Ceylon were the "Surat" (Bombay) and "Arcot" (Madras) rupees of the East India Company', and these 'continued to circulate freely and officially in Ceylon' until her independence in 1948.[41] The Murshidabad Sicca rupee, likewise, finds frequent mention in the official correspondence of Java after the Company wrested it from the Dutch in 1811, so much so that 'when a local striking of rupee was considered, the engraver was asked to model the design on that of the "Bengal Rupees"'.[42] It was with this background that Prinsep suggested the adoption of a coin nomenclature, 'One Rupee', for the proposed universal silver coin. In his note dated 6 April 1834, he writes: 'Another advantage of having the name in English is that the coin may, with the permission of His Majesty's Government, be allowed to circulate in other British Colonies at its intrinsic value of two shillings.'[43]

For the gold coins, Prinsep was of the opinion that their design should be altogether different from the silver rupee, so as to 'prevent the fraudulent practice of gilding the Rupee'. He, therefore, suggested a design comprising the king's head (as on the rupee) on the obverse, and a lion and palm tree on the reverse. This reverse pattern was originally suggested by Captain Forbes in his report dated 27 June 1825, where he describes the solitary lion 'as a symbol of an appropriate type of sovereignty and as an emblem known and respected wherever British rule has been extended'. According to him: '. . . the ease and dignity and strength which he [lion] so nobly personified . . . would be still more consistent and characteristic when applied to India. . . . Moreover, that he might be completely localized by the ever flourishing palm—an Asiatic altho' ancient tasteful emblem of perpetuity.'[44]

Prinsep, at the same time, impressed upon the Mint Committee the great advantage of adopting the same weight and fineness standard for the gold coin as for the silver, as had been contemplated as early as in 1806 by the Court of Directors. It had already been effected in Bombay and Madras, and therefore, its adoption was strongly recommended by Prinsep for the Bengal Presidency.

For the copper coins, Prinsep proposed the adoption of the Company's armorial bearings for the obverse as against the head of the king 'in preventing the copper coin from bearing whitened or gilded over and passed on the unawary as a silver or gold coin'.[45]

Prinsep wanted that these 'designs for the equalized currency of

British India' be brought into operation 'upon the promulgation of the new charter'—the Charter Act of 1833, which came into force on 22 April 1834. According to him:

> . . . it would answer every purpose were the public notification of the intentions of Government [to introduce a universal currency for its Indian possessions] to be made coeval with that Epoch of British Indian Rule.[46]

This, however, was too ambitious a deadline to follow. Nevertheless, the plan submitted by Prinsep was endorsed by the Mint Committee and, along with the specimen and sketch prepared by Kashi Nath, it was forwarded to Sir C.T. Metcalfe, the Vice-President-in-Council at Fort William on 15 April 1834.[47] In its letter, the Mint Committee sought the sanction of the government on the following points:

> I. That there should be a common device for the coins of the three presidencies,
> II. That this shall differ on the three metals, so as fully to distinguish them from one another and prevent impositions and fraud from gilding or silvering inferior coins,
> III. That the device shall be pictorial and essentially English,
> IV. That the Gold Mohur of Bengal shall in future be equalized with that of Bombay and Madras, and
> V. That the coinage of the Sicca rupee shall be discontinued from the commencement of the new Charter and the reformed device be restricted to the new universal coin. . . .[48]

Besides, it was also left to the government to approve the specific designs submitted for the silver and copper coin and that proposed for the gold coin, or to recommend others of a different description.[49] The most important part of this letter, however, was the Mint Committee's recommendation to go ahead with the proposed alteration in the device of the coinage, notwithstanding the injunction prescribed by the Court of Directors in their letter dated 11 March 1829. The letter of the Mint Committee, thus records: '. . . under the enlarged powers conferred upon the Supreme Government by the Act [the Charter Act of 1833], which will immediately come under force, we hope that a further previous reference to the Hon'ble Court of Directors will not be considered indispensable.'[50]

In its reply dated 5 May 1834, the government, while fully concurring with the views of the Mint Committee and expressing entire satisfaction with the proposed design, did not agree that it could overrule the injunction placed upon it by the 1829 despatch of the Court of Directors—'prohibiting any alteration of the device or character of the coin of this Presidency without the previous sanction of the Court'.[51] They, therefore, decided to refer the matter to the Court of Directors for an early decision in this regard. At the same time, the government authorized the Mint Committee to continue making preparations under the assurance that the alteration of the coinage would shortly take place.[52]

On the same day, a letter was addressed to the Court of Directors where they were urged for an early sanction of the proposed alteration. The letter records:

> Should any intermediate orders of your Honorable Court remove the interdict which at present restrains us from acting in this matter, we shall gladly enter upon the prosecution of measures to effect so great and beneficial a reform of this Department as we deem the changes contemplated to be calculated to introduce.[53]

The letter recounted the absurdity of the government continuing to issue coins 'stamped with the Persian distich of Shah Alum and purporting to be coined at Moorshedabad in the 19th year of his reign though all the world well knows that this nominal sovereign of India died near thirty years ago *and the dynasty he represented has since been falling everyday into greater insignificance*'.[54]

There was also apprehension regarding acceptance by the Muslim populace of India of a coin bearing a facial image since Islam forbids the use of pictorial images of any living being. However, in their letter to the Court of Directors, the Bengal government assured the home authorities that they 'do not apprehend any mischief from this objection'.[55]

Thus, while reference was made to the Court of Directors to obtain their sanction for the proposed alteration of the device on the coinage, dies were simultaneously authorized for the new coinage. The appointment of Kashi Nath as the Head Die-cutter and Copper Plate Engraver at the Calcutta mint was earlier approved by the government, and he now engaged himself in preparing the matrices of various dies for the approval.[56]

Universal Silver Coinage

On 18 November 1834, the Mint Committee submitted five specimens of coins struck from a fresh die prepared by Kashi Nath.[57] The obverse showed the head of King William IV, adapted from an English sovereign—a coin of considerably smaller dimensions.

Obv. Bare head of the King facing right. Divided legend: GULIELMUS IIII D:G: BRITT. ET IND. REX enclosed in a wavy circle. All within a raised, toothed border.

Rev. The value in English with a lotus flower above: ONE/ RUPEE/1834 all within a wreath of laurel. Around this is the legend and the value (one rupee) in Hindi एक रूपया (*Ek Rupiya*), Persian یک روپیه (*Yek Rupiya*)/and Bengali এক রূপয়া (*Ek Rupiya*)/EAST INDIA COMPANY all within a wavy circle line and surrounded by a raised, toothed rim.

Fig. 4.2: Silver Rupee Pattern, 1834 (by Kashi Nath)

In its reply dated 25 November, the government informed the Mint Committee that the Governor-General of India-in-Council was prepared to take immediate steps to change the device of the coin of India and to confine the coinage to rupees of 180 grains of the standard current in the Madras, Bombay and Agra presidencies, and in the new territory of the Bengal Presidency, and discontinue issuing of the Calcutta Sicca rupees bearing the nineteenth regnal year of Shah Alam.[58] However, in the proposed design, Governor-General, Lord William Bentinck was not appreciative of the Latin legend on one side and the English one on the other. The Mint Committee was, therefore, asked to submit 'designs of other devices adapted to the coin of India of every metal so as to afford the Supreme Government the means and opportunity of selection'.[59]

Prinsep, who was a man in a hurry by this time, felt that the preparation of fresh dies to strike specimens of alternative designs for the final approval of the Governor-General would further delay a decision in this regard. He, therefore, on 2 January 1835, submitted sketches of various designs as a prototype for the new coinage. These included:

a. Three designs in pencil by James Atkinson prepared some years ago.
b. Eight designs in outline by James Prinsep:
   1. Britannia from the English penny

2. A Lion from an antique Greek coin
3. An elephant (this device is adopted on the coins of Ceylon)
4. A Ship, emblematical of British commerce
5. A British Senator, between a Hindu and a Musalman, presenting the Charter
6. An emblematical figure of Justice and Plenty
7. Typical figures of Britannia and India
8. The Banyan tree, taken from the seal of the Royal Asiatic Society of London
9. The finely sculptured Lion of Flaxman large medallic die reduced to the dimension of the new rupee.[60]

Three days later, on 5 January 1835, Prinsep submitted a lengthy Note entitled 'Reasons for Reforming Currency' to the government.[61] In this note, Prinsep put up a strong case for an immediate change in the device of the Company's rupee and argued that 'the grounds of hesitation stated by the Honorable Court do not exist at present'. He lists numerous disadvantages that were being felt due to the multiple coins in circulation. These included 'trouble to the public officers in calculation of Batta for the adjustment of receipts and payments . . . and the rogueries, frauds and impositions practiced by the money changers and others'.[62]

He also notes that the circulation of the government of India's coin in other British colonies like Singapore and Mauritius was prevented since the 'Persian legend of the different coins is not legible and the difference between each [rupee] such as the Moorshedabad and Farruckabad is not distinguishable'.[63] As for the expediency of such a change, he writes: 'The sovereignty of the King of England over India has now been broadly declared and promulgated over the world, after which to continue striking coins with the unmeaning distich of Shah Alum is ridiculous, if it be not lese.'[64]

Various sketches and engravings along with Prinsep's note were forwarded to the Governor-General on 5 January 1835.[65]

The argument put forth by Prinsep had the desired result. The change of device for the new Company Rupee was approved by the Governor-General and a Resolution was passed on 27 May 1835. This Resolution pronounced the determination of the government of India 'to establish one uniform rupee corresponding in value, weight and standard with the present Farruckabad, Madras and Bombay rupee, but of a new device, and to declare and make the same current in all the Presidencies and possessions of the British nation in India'.

The provisions of this Resolution were subsequently incorporated in Act XVII of 1835,[66] which was passed on 17 August 1835. On 2 September, a proclamation was issued where weight, standard of fineness and size of the various denomination of the new currency were announced.

TABLE 4.1: UNIVERSAL RUPEE, 1835

Denomination	Weight		Fineness Pure Silver			Size (diameter)
	Grs	Gms	Weight		Percentage	
			Grs	Gms		
Double Rupee*	360	23.32	330	21.38	91.66%	1.5″
Rupee	180	11.66	165	10.69		1.2″
½ Rupee or 8 *anna*	90	5.83	82.5	5.34		0.95″
¼ Rupee or 4 *anna*	45	2.91	41.25	2.67		0.75″

Note: * Never issued.

All the magistrates, collectors and other public officers were directed to promulgate this proclamation throughout their respective districts and 'particularly to notify to all moneychangers, shroffs, podars and others, the provision in the aforesaid Act XVII of 1835,

Obv. Head of the King facing right. R.S. incuse on the truncation of the neck. Surrounded by the divided legend: WILLIAM IIII, KING. All within a raised, toothed border.

Rev. The value in English and Persian: ONE/RUPEE یک روپیه / All within a wreath of laurel.
Around this the legend: EAST INDIA COMPANY 1835 all within a raised, toothed rim.

Fig. 4.3: King William IV, Silver Rupee, 1835

against clipping, filing, punching or otherwise defacing the new coins. . . .'[67]

UNIVERSAL GOLD COINAGE

In the resolution passed by the Governor-General of India on 27 May 1835, a decision was taken to coin four denominations of gold coins. Subsequently, the decisions of the resolution were embodied in section VII of Act XVII of 1835. This section laid down the weights and standards of the gold coins, while the impression on these coins and their legal status were prescribed in sections VIII and IX, respectively.

TABLE 4.2: UNIVERSAL *MUHR*, 1835

Denomination	Weight		Fineness Pure Silver			Equal to
			Weight		Percentage	
	Grs	Gms	Grs	Gms		
Double *Muhr*	360	23.32	330	21.38	91.66%	30 Rupees
Muhr	180	11.66	165	10.69		15 Rupees
$\frac{2}{3}$ *Muhr*	120	7.77	110	7.12		10 Rupees
$\frac{1}{3}$ *Muhr*	60	3.88	55	3.56		5 Rupees

It was also resolved that preparations must be made at the government mints for coinage of new gold pieces of various denominations. Section VIII laid down the design of these coins as follows:

Obverse: Head and name of the reigning sovereign of the United Kingdom and Great Britain and Ireland.

Reverse: Designation of the coin in the English and Persian languages and the word 'East India Company' in English, with such embellishment as shall from times to time be ordered by the Governor General in Council, which shall be different from that of the silver coinage.

Earlier, on 31 March, the Mint Committee had submitted a specimen of the proposed double *muhr*, which showed the king's head on the obverse and a lion of the reverse (Fig. 4.4).

The government in its reply dated 8 April 1835 called for further reports and suggestions on the 'correspondent change in the Gold and Copper currency of British India'. No final decision was taken on the device of the proposed gold coinage of British India.[68]

Obv. Bust of the King facing right. R.S. or F incuse, or no initial, on the truncation of the neck.
Surrounded by the legend: WILLIAM IIII, KING. The date below. All within a raised, toothed border.

Rev. A lion standing, facing left with a palm tree above. The legend above: EAST INDIA COMPANY and the value in English and Persian ONE MOHUR/يك اشرفى (*Yek Ashrafi* = one *muhr*) below: All within a raised, toothed rim.

Fig. 4.4: King William IV, Gold *Muhr*, 1835

Meanwhile, the government of India saw a change of guard. Lord William Bentinck, who was earlier away on tour, returned to Calcutta in March 1835 and left for England immediately thereafter. After his departure, his deputy, Sir Charles Theosophilus Metcalfe, who had been conducting all the business in the presidency during Bentinck's absence, was made the Governor-General of India.

On the question of adopting a new device for the proposed coinage for British India, Metcalfe had earlier, as Vice-President-in-Council, refused to authorize any change without the approval of the Court of Directors.[69] As the Governor-General, too, he deemed himself precluded from sanctioning the measures repeatedly recommended by the Mint Committee by the positive terms in which any change in currency or of the device of the coin had been prohibited by the Court of Directors's despatch of 1829. He, therefore, decided to make another reference to the Court of Directors for soliciting their approval.[70]

The matter rested at that point, and both the Mint Committee and the government of India busied themselves in deciding upon the new silver coinage for British India. Once this issue was settled with the enactment of Act XVII of 1835, the question of selecting an appropriate device for the gold coinage, which was now part of this Act, resurfaced.

Some delay was experienced in submitting specimens of the

proposed designs for the gold coinage due to the 'employment of the die-engraver on the silver matrices' and in their letter dated 1 September 1835 to the government, the Mint Committee expected 'to furnish them in the course of 15 days'.[71]

Finally, on 24 October 1835, a specimen struck with another design for the gold coin (double *muhr*) was submitted to the Governor-General 'to form an opinion of the general appearance'.[72] The design was in conformity with the provisions of Act XVII of 1835 (Sec. VIII). For the embellishment on the reverse, it had the figure of a lion and palm tree, same as had been submitted for the approval of the Governor-General in March 1835.

In this letter, the Mint Committee raised a very interesting question about the nomenclature of the fractional denominations, i.e. of the one-third and two-third *muhr* respectively. This question of choosing an appropriate nomenclature emanated from Section IX of the above Act which provided that 'no gold coin shall henceforth be a legal tender of payment in any of the territories of the East India Company'. It was earlier resolved that the gold coins would have no legal ratio to the silver coins and would be left to circulate 'at whatever rate of value to the legal silver currency of the country they may bear to that currency'.[73] However, to facilitate transaction in gold coins, it was further resolved to introduce a fixed ratio between the two currencies:

> The Governor General in Council will from time to time fix the rate by Proclamation in the Calcutta Gazette at which they [gold coins] shall be received and issued at the public treasuries in lieu of the legal silver currencies of British India. Until further notice that rate will be as the names of the tokens denote. The gold mohur for fifteen rupees, the five rupee piece for five rupees, the ten rupee piece for ten rupees and the thirty rupee for thirty rupees.[74]

This measure required constant alteration of the official rates of exchange between coins of the two metals so as to correspond to the prevailing rates of the two metals in the market. In the volatile market of precious metals, a slight change in their relative prices was bound to offset this bimetallic arrangement.

The Mint Committee, therefore, felt that in a continually fluctuating bullion market, the coin terms to be inscribed on the gold coins should not have 'any direct reference to the silver unit of value'. The Committee preferred the usage of the terms 'one-third Mohur' and 'two-third Mohur' on the small denomination gold coins 'in lieu of the more simple designation 'ten rupees' and 'five rupees', respectively.[75] Apart from the comparative denominational term for these coins, the Committee also faced some difficulty in rendering these expressions into Persian. They communicated their preference for 'the Hindustanee term "Tihai" to the Arabic "Suls" as being more generally intelligible to the people at large'.[76]

Both these points—selecting an appropriate embellishment for the reverse of the gold coins as well as the usage of silver rupee equivalents (or one-third and two-third *muhrs*)—were deliberated upon in the Supreme Council headed by C.T. Metcalfe, the Governor-General of India. Metcalfe was not in favour of 'the representation of any animal upon the gold coin' and, therefore, the design submitted by the Mint Committee was not approved. The Committee was, accordingly, directed to 'prepare a device for each of the gold coins ordered, containing on the reverse the name of it in English and Persian with an ornamental wreath or other embellishment easily distinguishable from the rupee'.[77]

As for the second question, the Governor-General observed that: '. . . the 5 and 10 rupee pieces are so specifically named in the act recently passed and if the designation of the coin is to be borne on the reverse it will be necessary that the name shall correspond with that used in the law under which it is coined.'[78]

Pending a decision on the new gold coinage, the minting of private bullion into old standard *muhr* was continued to be allowed at the Calcutta mint. However, with the notification of Act XVII of 1835 on 2 September providing for the new gold coinage, there was a rapid escalation in the price of the gold *muhr* of the old standard. The Mint Committee was asked by the government to report on the matter and the situation was summarized as follows:

> The promulgation of the act for the new gold coinage caused a considerable rise in the market price of the old standard gold mohur and many merchants speculating thereon bought up fine gold to send into the mint in the time limited or purchased old mohurs already coined at enhanced prices with a view to their resale at a profit.
>
> The postponement of the date of issue of the new coin caused an immediate fall in the price of the old standard mohurs and it is to save themselves from loss that the holders now seek to hasten the order against which they have hitherto uniformly protested.[79]

In November 1835, Raj Kishan Nundee, Anand Mohan Dalal and

some other merchants of Calcutta petitioned the government for the speedy adoption of the new gold *muhrs.* They requested that the mint certificates to be issued to them in lieu of the gold bullion that they deposited in the Calcutta mint should be 'payable in Gold Mohurs of the new value and device'.[80] The Mint Committee once again urged the government to sanction the design already submitted, viz., the lion and the palm tree, since the preparation of any new design was ruled out for the next couple of months due to the pre-occupation of the Head Engraver, Kashi Nath with the silver dies and the plates for the new 4 per cent loan in the Company's rupees.[81]

The government finally gave up. In a letter dated 25 November 1835, the Mint Committee was informed that the Governor-General 'has been induced to waive his objection to the representation of an animal upon the gold coins of India, and to approve the adoption of this device'.[82]

On the receipt of these instructions, dies for the double *muhr* and *muhr* were prepared, and the minting of gold commenced by the end of the year.[83] These two denominations of gold coins of the new device were issued from 1 January 1836.

Universal Copper Coinage

In the scheme of introducing a universal currency for all of British India, copper coinage was included right from the beginning. As early as in 1829, the Court of Directors had instructed that the copper coinage of the Bengal Presidency should consist of only three denominations: half *anna*, quarter *anna* and one *pie*. This tri-denominational formula for the copper coinage was congruous with the plan of a uniform gold and silver currency laid down in the Court's 1806 despatch, prescribing three pieces: the whole, halves and quarters for gold and silver.

Later, when a note entitled 'On the expediency of establishing a die and copper plate engraving office at the new mint (at Calcutta)' was submitted by James Prinsep on 1 October 1833, he noted:

> The question of the copper currency now under agitation affords a strongly corroborative argument in favor of a new device for that metal. The pyce now circulating are of such variable form and appearance that one large portion of the currency is absolutely discredited and the public is suffering great inconvenience from the doubt whether the coin is or is not spurious.[84]

Prinsep, therefore, recommended that the armorial bearings of the East India Company that had already been adopted on the copper coins of Bombay and Madras should immediately be introduced in Bengal. Though not very impressed with this design ('it has no great beauty', he writes), Prinsep agreed to its adoption in Bengal for the sake of establishing homogeneity of device between the copper coins of the three presidencies.[85] For the reverse of the proposed copper coin of Bengal, he suggested a 'small deviation from the Bombay coin', namely inscribing the name or value of the coin in English, Devanagari and Persian enclosed in a wreath instead of the device of a scales in equilibrium with the Persian world '*adl* (or justice) found on the copper pieces of Bombay and which Prinsep regarded as 'not in very good taste'.[86]

Prinsep urged the government to take an immediate decision on this subject as a large copper coinage was then being contemplated at the new mint at Calcutta to replace the *trishuli pice*, which was authorized to circulate throughout the Bengal Presidency under the provisions of the Regulation XXV of 1817. Had his suggestion been accepted by the government of Bengal, a uniform copper coin would have been established in the three presidencies in 1833 itself. However, this feat was not achieved until a couple of years later.

No decision, however, was taken for the reform of the device of the copper coin. The succeeding months saw a rapid change in the administrative structure of the Company and priority was given to the reform of the device of the silver currency. This matter, therefore, receded into the background. It came to the fore once again when a proposal to reform the coinages was submitted to the Mint Committee on 2 January 1835.[87] Though a decision on the device of the copper coin was kept in abeyance, the government was convinced by now that a large quantity of copper coins of new mintage would be required to replace the old ones, which were continued to be produced at the Calcutta mint. Therefore, preparatory to the issue

Fig. 4.5: Quarter *Anna*, Pattern

of the new copper coins, the minting of the double *pice* or half *anna* denomination was stopped at the Calcutta mint in January 1835.[88]

Prinsep, in the meantime, got a sketch prepared of the modified design of the Bombay copper coin that he had proposed for Bengal. This sketch of a quarter *anna* was executed by his protégé, Kashi Nath, and was submitted to the Mint Committee along with his note dated 6 April 1834.[89]

Once again, no decision was taken on the device of the coin.

The money market during this period was facing a heavy influx of copper coins. There were several reasons for this situation. In conformity with the instructions contained in the despatch of the Court of Directors dated 11 March 1829, the Bengal government had authorized the coinage and issue of two new denominations of copper coins by Regulation III of 1831,[90] the half *anna* and one *pie* or one-twelfth *anna*. These two denominations were in addition to the one *pice* and half *pice*, that were then in circulation. In fact, during the next three years, over 87 million pieces worth Rs. 12,38,508 were thrown into circulation by the Calcutta mint alone.[91] Added to these four denominations minted at the Calcutta mint were the *trishuli pice* of Benares, Farrukhabad and Saugor mintage, which circulated concurrently with the old and new Calcutta copper coins. Thus, with the supply of copper coins being greater than the demand, a great depreciation of copper coins ensued. The government treasuries were flooded with old and depreciated copper *pice* by means of receipts in fractional payments of the *abkari* (a tax on spirituous liquors), stamp, post-office and custom revenues.[92] The Calcutta mint, where all the old and light-weight coins were ultimately turned in, had to undertake the tedious process of defacing these coins by passing them through laminating machine rollers, lest these found their way into circulation once again. In a statement submitted by the Mint Master of the Calcutta mint, it was revealed that on Rs. 10,000 worth of *trishuli pice* received at the rate of 64 pice per rupee, a loss of over Rs. 6,277 was sustained by the government.[93] The Mint Master estimated a loss of Rs. 5,71,340 in withdrawing all of the old coins from circulation, which would have absorbed all the profits not only of the Calcutta mint, but of the provincial ones as well.[94] The Mint Committee, on the other hand, was convinced that the only way to ameliorate this appalling situation was to replace the existing multiple copper coins with one of a universal standard and appearance. To facilitate the selection of a suitable device for the reverse of the proposed copper coins, the Committee submitted the following proposal:

For the reverse we have proposed a single wreath and denomination of the Coin in English and in the Native languages, in lieu of the Balance with the word *Adal* of Bombay, or the *ek fuloos panj Kas ust* of Madras as being the more elegant and consistent with the general appearance of the new Silver Coinage.[95]

The government, obviously, was not willing to sanction such a huge expenditure at this juncture. In his reply dated 20 May 1835, the secretary to the government informed the Mint Committee that:

The expence of withdrawing the existing coin which would be depreciated by the issue of an entire new coinage of copper money, protected by a Device, the skill of which will preclude its imitation at the Native mints and by clandestine fabricators in our own Provinces, is an objection to that measure. . . .[96]

Therefore, no decision was taken immediately on the device of the copper coins. However, with a view to curbing the supply of copper coins, the minting of the *pie* or $\frac{1}{12}$ *anna* denomination was stopped at the Calcutta mint in May 1835. Shortly thereafter, on 1 July 1835, the entire matter was again reviewed and a resolution was passed by the government of India to stop the minting of copper coins in the name of Shah Alam. It was decided that like other currencies, an English device would be adopted for the copper coins.[97]

However, a general introduction of the new copper currency was not immediately contemplated. It was decided that the '*pyce*' of the present Calcutta coinage may be supplied to the treasuries in the provinces till they exhausted the existing stores available for that purpose. Later, when the mint was required to provide for a deficiency and to prepare new coins, they would be struck and issued with an English device. At the same time, the Accountant General was made responsible for regulating the supply of copper coins in the market and thereby preventing the depreciation of the copper currency. Finally, the Mint Committee was given a go-ahead to prepare and submit specimens of the proposed new copper coins with the English device on the reverse that was suggested by them.[98]

After some initial failures in preparing the matrices for the proposed design, specimens were prepared and, along with the Mint Committee's report on the proposed copper currency, these were submitted to the Governor-General on 10 October 1835.[99] This was the same design as initially suggested by James Prinsep in his note dated 8 November 1833, and Kashi Nath's sketch of which was submitted for the approval of the government on 23 April 1835.[100] With the enactment of Act XVII of 1835, the Governor-General was now fully empowered 'to prescribe the devices and inscriptions of the copper coins issued from the mints . . .' (Sec. X). These designs were, thus, finally approved by Governor-General, Metcalfe and the Mint Committee was asked to 'take steps to prepare the necessary dies for commencing a coinage of copper with the Device of the Company's Arms, whenever ordered.'[101]

By 2 December 1835, the draft of another Act to give circulation to the new copper coinage was ready.[102] This draft curiously did not include any reference to the existing copper currency, which was allowed to circulate alongside the new copper coins of the Company. The Mint Committee was asked 'to cause a supply of pice, double pice and pies to be immediately struck' as the government desired that the 'first issue of this coin should be made as soon after the fifteenth instant [15 December 1835], as possible'.[103] On 7 December, Act XXI of 1835[104] was passed by the Legislative Council of India which established the following three denominations for the copper coins:

TABLE 4.3: UNIVERSAL COPPER COINAGE, 1835

Denomination	Weight		Legal Tender for
	Grs	Gms	
Double *Pice*	200	12.95	$\frac{1}{32}$ of Company's Rupee
Pice	100	6.97	$\frac{1}{64}$ of Company's Rupee
Pie or $\frac{1}{12}$ of an *Anna*	$33\frac{1}{3}$	2.16	$\frac{1}{192}$ of Company's Rupee

This Act had only three sections: the first and second dealt with the weight and value of the various denominations of copper coins to be issued from the mints in the Bengal Presidency, while the third one prescribed that no copper coins would be legal tender, in 'any part of the territories of the East India Company . . . except for fractions of a rupee'. All these provisions were to become effective from 20 December 1835.

Initially, only one denomination, the quarter *anna*, was issued from the Calcutta mint.

The other denominations were added a few years later.

With the adoption of a uniform design for the copper coins of

Obv. Arms of the Company, with the date between the scroll and the ribbon. The ribbon bears the abbreviated Latin motto: AUSP: REG: & SEN: ANG: All within a plain, raised rim.

Rev. The value within a wreath of laurel: ONE/ QUARTER/ ANNA Between the tips of the wreath is the value in Persian یک پای (*Yek Pai* = one *pice*): Around this the legend: EAST INDIA COMPANY All within a raised, plain rim.

Fig. 4.6: Quarter *Anna*, 1835

Bengal, the process initiated by James Prinsep in 1833 to establish a uniform currency and a universal coinage was complete.

TABLE 4.4: UNIVERSAL COINAGE FOR BRITISH INDIA, *c.* 1835

Mint	Metal	Denomination	First Issued
Calcutta Mint	Silver	Rupee	
		Half Rupee	September 1835
		Quarter Rupee	
	Gold	Double *Muhr*	
		Muhr	December 1835
	Copper	Quarter *Anna*	

The monetary integration of the British India was, thus, effected.

The year 1835 marks the end of the Presidency coinage and heralds the era of Imperial coinage in India. The minting of the imperial coinage commenced at the Calcutta mint in 1835 and soon the Bombay and Madras mints followed suit.

TABLE 4.5: UNIVERSAL COINAGE STRUCK AT OTHER MINTS[105]

Mint	Metal	Denomination	First issued
Bombay Mint	Gold	*Muhr*	August 1839
	Silver	Rupee	January 1837
		Half Rupee	January 1837
		Quarter Rupee	January 1837
Madras Mint	Copper	Half *Anna*	April 1838
		Quarter *Anna*	July 1837
		Twelfth *Anna*	June 1839

SUMMING UP

With the replacement of the gold and silver coins bearing the name and titles of the phantom Mughal ruler, Shah Alam II, by those depicting the head of the English sovereign, William IV, the culmination of the political ascendancy of the East India Company was declared to the masses. Apart from correcting 'an absurdity and falsehood' of issuing coins in the name of the dead Mughal ruler, this attempt is also seen as a security against the 'fraudulent imitation' of the Company's coins. The currency reformers of the Company were convinced that the new coins with their pictorial device would be difficult to imitate.

The new rupee with its 'pictorial and essentially English' design was also seen in the context of its larger role of serving as a universal colonial currency in the other colonies of Britain. For this purpose, the English name of its denomination—One Rupee—was inscribed on the coin with no indication of the place of its minting. The centralization of matrix die production at Calcutta after 1835 meant that identical coins could be uttered from any mint of the East India Company. To facilitate the free flow of colonial finances into the British coffers, the exchange value of the new rupee with the English pound/sterling was pegged at two shillings.

The process of currency reforms that had begun in 1793 and culminated in 1835 affected various aspects of the economic life of the people. Although the real assessment of the effects and influences of this monetary integration is to be seen in subsequent years of the nineteenth century, a fair appraisal of its implications for the period terminating with 1835 can be made in the following pages.

NOTES

1. Ambedkar 1925: 1.
2. Ibid.: 3.
3. 'An Act for Effecting an Arrangement with the East India Company and for the Better Government of His Majesty's Indian Territories'. It came into effect on 22 April 1834.
4. Keith 1930: 183-8.
5. Ibid., Sec. 43.
6. NAI, Home, Public, OC, 11 December 1806, no. 1, para 2.
7. Thurston 1893: 74-5.
8. NAI, Financial Department, OC, 17 September 1819, nos. 6 and 9.

9. Report of Lt. Forbes, dated 27 June 1825, para 18, NAI, Financial Department, OC, 26 July 1826, no. 7.
10. NAI, Financial Department, Letters from Court, 23 April, 1824, para 4.
11. NAI, Financial Department, Proceedings Volume, July-August 1826: 63-5.
12. Ibid.: paras 4 and 6.
13. Ibid.: para 6.
14. H.H. Wilson to Mint Committee, 26 November 1826, para 2. NAI, Financial Department, Proceedings Volume, July-August 1826: 65-6.
15. Minutes by H. Wood dated 13 February 1825; W. Money, dated 18 February 1825 and by Holt Mackenzie dated 21 February 1825, ibid.: 68-72.
16. NAI, Financial Department, Letters to Court, 26 July 1826.
17. NAI, Territorial Finance Department (Mint), Letters from Court, 11 March 1829, para 37.
18. J.P. Willoughby, Acting Secretary to the Bombay government to Holt Mackenzie, Secretary to the government of Bengal in the Territorial Finance Department, dated 18 February 1830. NAI, Mint Committee Letters Received, October 1826-August 1830: 382.
19. NAI, Territorial Finance Department, Letters from Court, dated 11 March 1829, para 44.
20. NAI, Financial Department, Mint Committee Proceedings, November 1833, no. 18.
21. Ibid.
22. Ibid.
23. Ibid.
24. Ibid.
25. Ibid.
26. Ibid.
27. Ibid.
28. Ibid.
29. Ibid., no. 19.
30. NAI, Financial Department, Letter from Court, 11 March 1829.
31. NAI, Financial Department, Mint Committee Proceedings, November 1833, no. 19.
32. Ibid.
33. NAI, Financial Department, Mint Proceedings, 15 April 1834, no. 3.
34. Ibid.
35. Ibid.
36. The word '15 Rupees' appear on gold *muhrs* struck in 1770 at the Bombay Presidency but never had this term (rupee) been inscribed on any silver coin of the East India Company.

37. James Prinsep, 'Note on the Name of the New Rupee', dated 6 September 1835. IOR, Bengal Consultations, P/162/86.
38. Ibid.
39. James Prinsep, 'Note on the Device of the British Indian Rupee'. NAI, Financial Department, Mint Proceedings, April 1834, no. 3.
40. Bhandare 2007: 206-44.
41. Ibid.: 216-17.
42. Ibid.: 219-20.
43. NAI, Financial Department, Mint Proceedings 15 April 1834, no. 3.
44. NAI, Financial Department, Proceedings, 26 July 1826, no. 7, para 24.
45. Ibid., Mint Proceedings, 15 April 1834, no. 3.
46. Ibid.
47. NAI, Finance Department, Mint Committee Proceedings, April 1834, no. 5.
48. Ibid.
49. Ibid.
50. Ibid.
51. H.T. Prinsep, Secretary to Government to the Mint Committee dated 5 May 1834, para 3. NAI, Financial Department, Mint Committee Proceedings, May 1834, no. 27, para 5.
52. Ibid.: para 6.
53. NAI, Financial Department, Letters to Court, no. 11, dated 5 May 1834, para VI.
54. The italicized portion was deleted from the final draft; ibid.: para 7.
55. This letter seems to be heavily moderated. The words *we attach no weight to* in the original draft were changed to *we do not apprehend* . . . in the final version; ibid.
56. H.T. Prinsep, Secretary to Government to the Mint Committee dated 5 May 1834, para 3. NAI, Financial Department, Mint Committee Proceedings, May 1834, no. 27.
57. Mint Committee to Lord William Bentinck, Governor-General of India, dated 18 November 1834. NAI, Financial Department (India), Mint Proceedings, 25 November 1834, no. 1.
58. H.T. Prinsep, Secretary to Government, to the Mint Committee dated 25 November 1834; ibid.: no. 3.
59. Ibid.
60. Ibid.: 12 January 1835, no. 2.
61. Ibid.: no. 3.
62. Ibid.
63. Ibid.
64. Ibid.
65. Mint Committee to H.T. Prinsep, Secretary to Government, dated 5 January 1835; ibid.: no. 1.

66. Appendix A.40.
67. NAI, Financial Department (India), Mint Proceedings, 2 September 1835, no. 1.
68. H. Torrens, Officiating Deputy Secretary to Government to Mint Committee, dated 8 April 1835. NAI, Financial Department (India) Mint Proceedings, 8 April 1835, no. 4.
69. NAI, Financial Department, Letters to Court, dated 5 May 1834.
70. Letters to Government No. 10 of 1835, dated 8 April 1835. NAI, Financial Department, Letters to Court, vols. 35-7: 55-9.
71. Mint Committee to G.A. Bushby, Secretary, Government of India, Financial Department, dated 1 September 1835. NAI, Financial Department (India), Proceedings, dated 2 September 1835, no. 9.
72. Mint Committee to Governor General of India, 24 October 1835. NAI, Financial Department, Mint Committee Proceedings, 4 November 1835, no. 1.
73. Resolution passed by the Supreme Council of India, 27 March 1835. NAI, Financial Department (India) Mint Proceedings, 27 May 1835, no. 1.
74. Ibid.
75. Mint Committee to Government, dated 24 October 1835. NAI, Financial Department (India) Mint Proceedings, 4 November 1835, no. 1.
76. Ibid.
77. G.A. Bushby, Secretary, Government of India, Financial Department to the Mint Committee, dated 28 October 1835. NAI, Financial Department (India) Mint Proceedings, 28 November 1835, no. 3.
78. Ibid.
79. Mint Committee to G.A. Bushby, Secretary, Government of India, Financial Department, dated 16 November 1835. NAI, Financial Department (India), Proceedings, 25 November 1835, no. 3.
80. Petitions of Raj Kishan Nundee and others, dated 3 November 1835, and Anand Mohan Dalal and others, dated 16 November 1835; ibid.: nos. 1-2.
81. Mint Committee to G.A. Bushby, Secretary, Government of India, Financial Department, dated 16 November 1835; ibid.: no. 3.
82. Secretary, Government of India, Financial Department to Mint Committee, dated 25 November 1835; ibid.: no. 4.
83. Pridmore 1980: 8.
84. NAI, Financial Department, Mint Proceedings, November 1833, no. 18.
85. Ibid.
86. Ibid.: 570.
87. R. Saunders, Mint Master, and James Prinsep, Assay Master, Calcutta Mint, dated 2 January 1835 to the Mint Committee. NAI, Financial Department (India), Mint Proceedings, 12 January 1835, no. 2.

88. Pridmore 1980: 7.
89. James Prinsep's Note 'On the Device of the British Indian Rupee' dated 6 April 1834. NAI, Financial Department, Mint Committee Proceedings, 15 April 1834, no. 3.
90. Appendix A.38.
91. NAI, Financial Department, Letters from Court, no. 13 of 1836, dated 12 October 1836, para 4.
92. C. Morley, Accountant General to G.A. Bushby, Secretary to Government in Financial Department, dated 29 April, 1835. NAI, Bengal, Financial Department, Mint Proceedings, 13 May 1835, no. 1.
93. R. Saunders to C. Morley, dated 20 April, 1835; ibid.: no. 4.
94. R. Saunders to the Mint Committee, dated 22 April 1835; ibid.: no. 2.
95. Pridmore 1980: 7.
96. G.A. Bushby to the Mint Committee, dated 20 May 1835, para 2. NAI, Bengal, Financial Department, Mint Proceedings, 20 May 1835, no. 4.
97. Resolution dated 1 July 1835. NAI, Financial Department (India), Mint Proceedings, 1 July 1835, no. 2.
98. Ibid.
99. Mint Committee to Government: Report on the Subject of the New Copper Currency for British India; ibid.: 10 October 1835, no. 10.
100. Mint Committee to Sir C.T. Metcalfe, Governor General of India, dated 10 October 1835. Ibid.: 11 November 1835, no. 1.
101. H.T. Prinsep, Secretary to the Government of India in the Financial Department, to Mint Committee, dated 11 November 1835; ibid.: no. 4.
102. H.T. Prinsep, Secretary to the Government of India in the Financial Department, to Secretary, Government of Bengal, dated 2 December 1835; ibid.: no. 1A.
103. H.T. Prinsep, Secretary to the Government of Bengal, to Mint Committee, dated 2 December 1835; ibid.: no. 2.
104. Appendix A.41.
105. Pridmore 1980: 18.

CHAPTER 5

Currency Regulations and Monetary Economy

In the administration of colonial finances, the monetary policy of the imperial power for their dependencies had a tremendous impact on the colonial economy. According to Dietmar Rothermund, 'this impact has not yet been studied adequately'.[1] The currency reforms of the East India Company affected the contemporary society in more ways than one. The ways and the extent to which these measures influenced or were influenced by the changing economic structure of India have been discussed in the following pages. On the basis of an understanding of the monetization level that emerged during the crucial period when currency measures were undertaken by the East India Company, it has been argued that the aim of these regulations was to facilitate the colonization of the Indian economy.

MONETIZATION

Level of Monetization

The eighteenth century saw the spread of the use of money in Indian society. According to Perlin, 'Wages were being paid in cash. Even small cultivators in many areas paid their taxes in cash, which they acquired by selling a portion of their crop.'[2] Frank Perlin interprets the incidence of 'gimcrack coinages, privatization of mints and multiplication of both mints and coin types' that characterizes not only the eighteenth but also the early decades of the nineteenth century in relation to 'the contemporary needs of a commercializing economy'.[3]

Amongst various factors that substantially induced the growth of monetization levels in society were revenue collection and military expenditure. In addition, the transition of certain areas like Bengal and Orissa from *cowries* to metallic currency was encouraged and facilitated by a series of regulations passed by the East India Company.

Among the chief causes that contributed to the shift 'from kind economy to cash economy', Ambedkar gives the first place to 'the British system of revenue and finance'.[4] First of all, the British adopted a system where not only the land revenue but also various other taxes such as customs, salt tax, *abkari*, *sayer* duties and so on were collected in cash. As territory after territory came under the the Company, 'the first step taken was to substitute in place of the rural militia of the feudatories a regularly constituted and a well disciplined standing army located at different military stations, paid in cash. . . .'[5] The civil establishment was also extended to these new acquisitions by appointing 'a host of revenue collectors and magistrates with their extensive staff, all paid in current coin'.[6] In addition, there were other charges such as 'Home charges' and 'Interest Public Debt', which were all realized on a cash basis. Thus, a cycle was formed which gave momentum to the monetization process. Ambedkar writes, 'The State, having undertaken to pay in cash, was compelled to realize all its taxes in cash, and as each citizen was bound to pay in cash, he in his turn stipulated to receive nothing but cash, so that the entire structure of the society underwent a complete transformation.'[7]

Introduction of Copper Coinage in Eastern India

When the English Company assumed the *Diwani*, it discovered that Bengal and Orissa had no copper currency. In Bengal, *cowries* were used for small transactions, generally below a rupee, while in Orissa, *cowries* seem to have been unlimited legal tender.[8] Much against the general belief that *cowries* were necessarily and universally used only for petty transactions, there is evidence to prove that these were used even in large transactions in Orissa.[9] In these areas of non-metallic currencies, metallic currency was gradually introduced. In Bengal, a concrete step was taken when John Prinsep was contracted to supply copper coins for the province in 1780. Between 1780 and 1784, Prinsep minted a large number of copper coins at his mint at Falta. However, 'a general reluctance on the part of the people to accept this new copper coinage in lieu of their familiar and popular cowrie shell' posed a great hindrance.[10] Nevertheless, in order to exhaust the large stocks of this contract copper coinage, the Government of

Bengal 'established a practice of issuing one percent (of all its payments) in copper money'.[11] By replacing *cowries*, the Company also expected to save 'the quantity of specie that was annually exported to the Maldives for [purchasing] cowries'.[12]

Following the currency reforms initiated in 1793, a regular copper coinage was established in 1795 and 'it was declared legal tender throughout all three provinces of lower Bengal'.[13] By Regulation XXV of 1817, the circulation of the Calcutta copper coins was extended 'to all areas under the presidency of Fort William'.[14] Thus, in about twenty years, large areas under the Bengal Presidency saw the replacement of *cowries* with a copper currency.

In Orissa, too, attempts were made to introduce a copper coinage. On 8 May 1804, George Harcourt, First Commissioner in Cuttack, apprised the Bengal government about the 'considerable inconvenience . . . experienced in the Province of Cuttack from the want of some current coin of small value.'[15] The Commissioner solicited the government's orders to issue 'a copper coinage for the use of the Province of Cuttack' and even submitted a sample of the proposed coinage, showing, on the obverse, 'the figure of Juggernaut and on the reverse the value of the coin . . . in Persian and Oriah characters, together with the year of coinage.'[16]

By Regulation XII of 1805, the East India Company declared that *cowries* would no longer be received in the payment of revenue at the government treasuries. A grace period of three years was fixed (till 1808) for the receipt of *cowries* in official payments and then it was to be replaced by the Sicca rupees. It is interesting to note that *cowries* were not replaced by copper coins in Orissa, as was the case with Bengal, but by the silver rupee. In fact, Orissa did not adopt a copper currency till it was made legal tender throughout the Bengal Presidency by Regulation XXV of 1817.

Bullion Supply and (De)monetization in Western India

The bullion influx during the seventeenth century had resulted in the growth of the monetized market economy in western India. The expansion of the Surat rupee as a money of account during this period facilitated 'internal trade throughout the subcontinent'.[17] This growth pattern sustained a severe blow when the international supply of silver bullion, both on the western and eastern coasts of India, touched its lowest ebb following the Company's assumption of political power in Bengal. It did affect the process of monetization. Citing the case of Surat, Torri observes: '. . . in an economy at the stage of development prevailing in the eighteenth-century Surat, bullion was the indispensable fuel for the whole economic system. Without it, any kind of trading and financial activity was bound to grind to a halt or, at least, to be severely hampered.'[18]

It may be argued that the import of bullion did not altogether stop on the western coast, and Bombay and Surat's trade with the Persian Gulf and China regularly fed the bullion coffers of the region. However, the question is, did it lead to an overall demonetization?

Earlier, in his antithesis of the monetization theory, Perlin had argued that 'till the mid-19th century . . . India's integration into a colonial empire was marked by a broad-based process of underdevelopment of which deindustrialisation was merely a part, and including, a process of *relative de-monetization* (emphasis added).'[19] Evidence of the large-scale import of copper and *cowries* in India during the sixteenth and seventeenth centuries were seen by Perlin as symptomatic of 'the need of economies growing in size'.[20] On the basis of the 'remarkable involvement in monetary relationship by humble people' of the Maharashtra villages during the eighteenth century, Perlin argued that:

> By contrast, in the 19th century, after occupation by the English East India Company, the displacement of local elites from the countryside, the more ruthless and efficient exploitation of peasant populations and the large-scale export of taxed wealth, left Maharashtra's villages suffering a relative demonetisation of local economy.[21]

There are many flaws in Perlin's hypothesis. The first and most apparent is his generalization of 'relative demonetization' for the entire region on a sample test of Maharashtra's villages. The money economy in different parts of India was characterized by different patterns of money use. Therefore, monetization in this context would mean a shift from barter trade to money use, or even a shift from a non-metallic currency to a metallic one, as one seen in Orissa during the early decades of the nineteenth century. The extent of monetization of a society can best be judged from the output of coins from various mints. Several scholars who have worked on the quantity theory during the sixteenth and seventeenth centuries have based their findings on the output of the Mughal mints.[22] Later, Perlin himself contributed an excellent study on the productivity of several mints in India from the sixteenth to the nineteenth century.[23]

MINT PRODUCTION AND MONETIZATION

Any increase in the mint output can directly be linked with a proportionate increase in money use, though the entire output may not circulate. In its diagnosis of the currency situation of Bengal, the Mint Committee that was set up in 1792 pointed out that the Calcutta mint with its traditional minting techniques was unable to meet currency demands and, as a result, there was an inordinate delay in coining the bullion sent to the mint.[24] The Committee, therefore, recommended an enlargement of the mint establishment and an improvement in minting techniques in all the mints under the Company.

By this time, the Industrial Revolution of the 1750s had already revolutionized the mode of coin production in England. In 1778, Matthew Boulton established a modern mint at Soho, Birmingham, with steam-powered machinery. Boulton's partner in this enterprise was none other than James Watt (1736-1819), the Scottish inventor and engineer whose improvements to the steam engine were fundamental to the changes wrought by the Industrial Revolution. The Soho mint undertook the mass production of English copper pennies during 1797 (about 4,200 tons), and also the minting of copper coins for Madras and Bombay. This mode of production was cheap and involved minimum wastage of metal. The Soho mint was commissioned to install coining machinery for the Tower mint, London, at the royal mints in Russia, Spain and Denmark, and also for Mexico before it were asked to construct modern minting machines for the Calcutta and Bombay mints whose modernization took place during the 1820s.[25]

If we compare the output of the two mints of Bengal, viz. Murshidabad and Calcutta, we find that as against a daily output of 48,660 coins by the Murshidabad mint in 1722, the daily output of the fully-mechanized Calcutta mint stood at 3,08,000 in 1833.[26] Thus, with an increase in minting capacity, these mints were turned into 'factories for coin production' and greatly helped in elevating the monetization of Indian society. Similarly, the total value of gold coins in circulation in Bengal stood at 2.45 crore when its withdrawal was contemplated in 1796.[27] This figure is interesting also because of the fact that the gold coins were declared legal tender only four years before, in 1792. The argument that the gold coins constituted the 'elite currency' also stands invalidated as a considerable abatement in the demand for quarter *muhrs* was recorded in 1795. In his letter dated 17 February 1796, Thomas Myers, the Accountant General of the Bengal Presidency, informed Sir John Shore, the Governor-General of Bengal, that 'the quarter mohurs are in much greater request amongst the lower order of the people to whom advances are made by the agents of the Board of Trade. . . '.[28] The production of copper *pice* in 1796 stood at 22,000 to 26,000 pieces per day.[29] This figure, too, is quite significant considering the fact that the copper currency had only been introduced in 1795 and was still struggling to make inroads into the non-copper Bengal economy.

Such instances can be cited from other regions as well, which go on to prove that the incidences of the 'relative demonetization' of India 'till the mid-19th century' could at best be a temporary and localized phenomenon that could not be generalized to represent an increasingly monetized money economy under the period of our review. Perlin seems to have agreed with this later.[30]

Thus, the overall picture of the Indian economy in the nineteenth century presented a picture of high monetization, supported by extensive money supply in the form of:

i. Copper and silver coins openly coinable at the government mints;
ii. Gold *muhrs* of limited tender;
iii. Bank paper currency backed by metallic reserves;
iv. Bank deposits of the western type;
v. Indian credit instruments (*hundis*); and
vi. Credit created by Indian bankers and moneylenders.[31]

FISCAL SYSTEM

The initial years of the Company's direct administration of Bengal's finances were marked by 'the abysmal failure of the new state to effect a viable system of currency administration'.[32] In a monetized revenue regime, the state of the currency played a crucial role and, therefore, it immediately seized the attention of the new *Diwans* of Eastern India.

Revenue

When the East India Company acquired the *Diwani* rights over Bengal, Bihar and Orissa in 1765, its revenue was estimated at over Rs. 30 million.[33] For the first seven years, the revenue was collected through a system of Dual Government instituted by Robert Clive wherein 'native' collectors, Mohammad Reza Khan for Bihar and Shitab Rai for Bengal, were appointed under European supervisors. As land revenue was collected in silver specie, there was a seasonal surge in the demand for that currency. But after an initial increase in revenue collections, it was soon realized that due to the growing scarcity of silver currency in Bengal, the collection of revenue was becoming increasingly difficult. On 21 November 1768, the Government of Bengal wrote to the Court of Directors:

> You may be convinced that the value of your Territorial acquisitions has not been decreasing since the Collections are now greater than they ever have been since your Dewanee. But be assured the benefits expected from them must be of short duration whilst a scarcity of Specie prevails as at present and is daily encreasing [*sic*] you must expect unless the evil is speedily removed to collect your revenues in the commodities produced in the Country, without having a prospect of vending them at any rate, as the Merchants will be totally deprived of the means to purchase them.[34]

A year later, the import of silver specie was strongly recommended 'as a certain mode of securing the future payment of the Revenues in silver'. The Court of Directors was informed in no uncertain terms that the scarcity of silver specie might lead to the demonetization of a portion of revenue collections in the future:

> . . . the Terror of a Scarcity of silver is by no means confined to this Presidency; and now we must inform you that the Ministers [the *Naib Diwans*] find the utmost difficulty in Collecting the Revenues; and this difficulty does not arise from any deficiency in the Harvests but from a real Scarcity of Current Coin; so that altho' we may be able to collect the whole of this years Revenues in Specie, yet unless the Importation of Silver is soon and that too considerably increased, we may venture to assure you, that the day is not very distant, when part of the Revenues must of necessity be received in the Produce of the lands.[35]

After two unsuccessful attempts to establish bimetallism in 1766 and 1769, currency reforms were initiated by Warren Hastings in 1771 by which *batta* on the Sicca rupees of 1770 mintage (11-*sun*) onwards was abolished. However, even this measure did not have the expected result. It was soon discovered that with the Sicca rupees of current and old mintage (11-*sun*) being equalized, people preferred to pay their revenues in Sicca rupees, which passed 'at market very little more than sunaut rupees of full weight'.[36] A less number of

Sicca rupees now fulfilled the revenue demands for which, in normal circumstances, a greater number of *sanwat* rupees were required.[37] This entailed a loss in the Company's net income from revenue. In its letter dated 30 March 1774, the Court noted: '. . . the loss upon the revenue is alarming. The rents are ascertained in sicca rupees but the amount of the revenues, paid specifically in that coin, will be nearly 13 lakhs per annum less than if paid in sunaut rupees.'[38]

The Governor-General of Bengal chose to blame 'the natural repugnancy inherent in the subjects of any country to a material innovation in its current coinage' for the continuance of the practice of *batta*.[39]

The twenty-year period from 1772 to 1792 has been referred to as 'a period of currency confusion and official bungling'.[40] The institution of the Permanent Settlement for land revenue and the commencement of a series of currency regulations in Bengal on the same date show the importance of currency in a monetized revenue regime. It is, therefore, not surprising that after a third attempt to establish bimetallism in 1792, it was later incorporated in the 'Cornwallis Code' of 1793 to give it a legal status, which earlier attempts to introduce bimetallism lacked. As a result, in 1795, it was noted that 'the circulation of the Gold Coin [is] daily increasing, in consequence of its being received in Payment of Revenue throughout all the Collectorships. . . .'[41] However, this situation changed once the import of bullion was resumed in around 1784. The share of gold in the revenues of Bengal steadily declined in subsequent years while that of silver increased. During 1796-7, the share of gold as a percentage of Bengal's revenue stood at about 74 per cent which fell to below 10 per cent by 1808-9. During the same period, the share of silver rose from 25 per cent to above 90 per cent.[42]

In the Madras Presidency, too, the introduction of the Ryotwari system in 1796 entirely changed the nature of land revenue from '*warrum* (share in the crop) into *teerva* (money tax)'.[43] With the contraction of money supply during the first half of the nineteenth century, the prices of agricultural produce showed a downward trend and, as a result, the peasantry suffered not only from the low income but also due to 'the additional loss of converting the Government's share into money . . . '.[44] Here too, as in the case of Bengal, the monetization of land revenue made the currency reforms inevitable. For the Company, the maximization of land revenue was imperative to increase their profits.[45]

INVESTMENTS OF THE COMPANY

The purchases made by the East India Company in India were called 'investments'. Initially, up to the mid-eighteenth century, the Company followed a system of advancing money to the merchants called *dadani*.[46] Under this system, the merchants were given advances ranging from 50 to 75 per cent of the total cost of investments, a part of which used to be in cash and the rest in bills of debt. The full and final settlement of investments was done at the time of the delivery of goods.[47] In lieu of this advance, the *dadani* merchants undertook to supply the Company 'a specific quantity of export commodities by a certain date'.[48] During the first half of the eighteenth century, the most prominent *dadani* merchants in Bengal were the Seths and Basaks of Sutanati and Amichand (Omichand) of Calcutta. Around 1751-2, the Company's investment through the *dadani* system in Bengal was about Rs. 3.36 lakh.[49]

Apart from *dadani*, investments were also made through ready money. Here too, the *dadani* merchants appropriated the privilege of supplying ready money goods to themselves through their network of agents in different production centres throughout the province. In both the systems, the Company often found itself with little or no choice but to accept the price quoted by these merchants because in most of the cases, the producers and cultivators of these goods were indebted to them. The Company, therefore, decided to abandon the system of indirect investment through *dadani* and ready money, and replace it with a system in which *gomashtas* (brokers or paid agents) were appointed to make purchases under the direct supervision of the European servants of the Company.[50]

The state of currency had a direct impact on the Company's investments in the new investment regime. Now, the requirements of cash were to be met directly by the Company rather than by the merchants. The effects of the post-Plassey currency situation on the Company's investments in Bengal have been discussed by Mitra, who notes that 'the acute scarcity of silver throughout the period and the consequent batta on gold mohurs adversely affected Company's "investment"'.[51] This statement apparently stands in contrast with known theories of Bengal's 'surplus revenue' especially during the first three decades of Plassey, which 'not only provided for the Company's "investment" but furnished also the sinews of the various wars which brought the greater part of India under British rule'.[52]

The manner in which the Company's investments in Bengal

suffered due to the want of silver currency can be judged from the following extract from a letter that Harry Verelst, the Governor of Bengal, wrote to the Court of Directors in 1768:

> The increasing scarcity of silver has been so fully set forth in the proceedings of the Council and Committee that nothing but the urgent Necessity of the Settlement could tempt me to remind you of it in this Letter. Gold is not current at the Aurangs and *we shall with difficulty be enabled to raise sufficient quantity of Silver for the Province of the ensuing Years investment* (emphasis added).[53]

By September 1769, the prospects of increased investments appeared to be dismal and not even Rs. 15 lakh were available 'in advance for the space of a Month' in the Company's treasury.[54]

Apart from the general scarcity of silver currency, another factor that affected the investments of the Company was the local circulation of different specie of rupees. The fact remains that due to the prevalence of numerous varieties of silver currency in different parts of Bengal, any shortage of a particular specie in a district directly and immediately affected its investments in that district. Thus, we find the Resident at Lakhipur, where only Arcot rupees were accepted by artisans, writing to the Board of Trade in 1777 that the purchase of piece goods had almost come to a stop for want of a suitable currency.[55] Similar requests poured in from other quarters as well. In its letter dated 21 November 1777, the Government of Bengal informed the Court:

> We have received many Applications from the Board of Trade to make the advances for the Investment at particular Factories in Specific Coins stated in their letters and when we have not had such Coins in the Treasury they have desired us to purchase them in the Buzar for the Supply required. If we have been able to procure such Species as they are applied for without loss We have constantly supplied them but when a discount on the Exchange has been demanded which is most frequently the Case We thought it would be improper to comply with their request and have Ordered the Advances to be made them in Sicca Rupees or in such Coins as were actually in our possession leaving it to them if necessary to purchase others for their advances to the Manufacturers. . . .[56]

Thus, in spite of the several currency reforms introduced in 1777, the circulation of the Sicca rupee remained circumscribed and the specific silver currencies of different districts continued to dictate the investment needs of the Company. To reduce the mounting loss in the Commercial Department, the Court, on 23 December 1778, decided to book all loss on account of the exchange of money in a specific coin in the Revenue Department.[57] Even this measure did not solve the problem of specific coins being required for investments. Instead, it caused further inconvenience as the advances in Sicca and other available species of coin that were issued from the treasury had to be 'transported through a country infested by dacoits' and only through 'a very dangerous navigation' reached Dacca, where these were exchanged into Arcot or other desired specie.[58]

None of these measures seem to have worked for, in 1784, we still find the Resident at Lakhipur demanding the speedy and timely supply of a 'usable' currency which was 'the essential pre-requisite for securing the full quota of the "investments"'.[59] The attempts of the Company to introduce the Sicca rupee in Lakhipur and other areas dotted with the circulation of a specific currency were thwarted by stiff resistance, unwillingness and a popular prejudice against any other specie of coin. As a result, in order to finance its investments in different districts, the Company was forced to take the help of money-changers and sustained a considerable loss in the process. Thus, during 1786-7, when 'the Court of Directors were expecting an investment of at least Rs. 94 lakhs, investment of only Rs. 66 lakhs could be made'.[60] Even Lord Charles Cornwallis's plan for establishing a General Bank in India was aimed at securing the 'assistance of ready money' for investment.[61]

The preamble of Regulation XXXV of 1793 sums up the prevailing currency situation in Bengal but, as we have seen, even after officially establishing the 19-*sun* Sicca as the sole legal tender silver currency of Bengal in 1793, it could not supplant the regional circulation of specific currencies in Bengal. In places like Dacca and Chittagong, the Arcot rupees continued to remain a popular circulating medium till as late as 1825.

However, other currency reforms undertaken by the Company in Bengal from 1793 did help it in reducing the pressure on investments due to the scarcity of silver specie. One such measure was the re-introduction of bimetallism in 1792, which was formally established by Regulation XXX of 1793 by which gold coin was declared legal tender for all government payments at the rate of 16 Sicca rupees for one gold *muhr*. To aid the circulation of gold coins for smaller payments, the coinage of half and quarter *muhrs* was also authorized. In 1795, the government declared that 'in the Salt and Commercial Departments, all payments under four Rupees, and fractional parts of larger payments, as are too small to be made in gold, be issued in silver'.[62] All other payments were to be made 'in gold and silver indifferently, excepting in the month of April, May and June, when . . . payments are to be made half in silver and half in gold'.[63] The collectors of the districts were also empowered to buy a stock of silver to keep the commercial residents in full supply.[64]

All these measures were intended to extend the circulation of gold coins in the interior parts of the Bengal Presidency where *aurangs* were located. However, it gave birth to a fraudulent practice which is recorded in the Bengal government's letter to the Court, dated 2 November 1795:

> . . . individuals who received large payments in it (gold coin) from the Treasury, and had occasion to employ the money in the interior parts of the country, were obliged to sell the money to the Shroffs for silver, or what was the same in effect, to take bills from them for Rupees payable in the Districts . . . the Gold was returned to the treasury at par, by the operations of the Shroffs. . . .[65]

As a result, a loss 'from $2\frac{1}{2}$ to 6 or 7 per cent, varying in proportion to the demand for silver' was sustained 'thereby operating as a tax upon the Company, upon individuals and upon the industry and commerce of the country.'[66]

Apart from monetary factors, the investments of the Company were also influenced by political developments. For example, in 1804-05, the total allocation for investments was reduced from 105 lakh to a mere 60 lakh rupees due to the war with Jaswant Rao Holkar in India and with Napoleon in Europe.[67]

PRICES

The prices and price movements of the commodities of mass consumption have always been vital for all sections of society. In the pre-modern economy, apart from the monetary factors, price fluctuations were usually caused by local non-monetary factors such as the scarcity of food supply, droughts, famines and disruption in the means of transport. However, British rule entailed a close connection of the local price movement with the rest of the world and with Europe, in particular. As a result, the course of prices also now came to be determined by conditions outside India, which had a direct bearing on the quantum of money available for monetary use.

Irving Fisher has theorized the effects of the quantum of money on its purchasing power. According to him, the quantum of money (*M*) and deposits (*M′*), their velocity (*V*), the volume of trade (*Q's*) and the price (*P*)—all these five elements of a monetary economy are related to each other.[68] Thus, an increase in the quantity of money (*M*) tends to increase deposits (*M′*) proportionally, and an increase in these two (*M* and *M′*) tends to increase prices proportionally. Similarly, an increase in deposits (*M′*) or velocities (*V*) compared with money tends, likewise, to displace the coin and raise prices. An increase in the volume of trade (*Q's*), tends not only to decrease prices (*P*) but also to increase velocities (*V*) and deposits (*M′*) relatively to money and, through them, to neutralize, partly or wholly, the decrease in prices (*P*).[69]

From this basic theoretical plane, we can attempt to study the impact of currency measures on the general price structures in the presidencies of Bengal and Madras, where the East India Company was directly involved with revenue administration and, thus, with the agricultural mode of production.

Currency Measures and Inflation/Deflation

We have noticed that after the Company assumed the *Diwani* rights in Bengal, there was a general scarcity of silver currency. According to Irfan Habib, the impact of the scarcity of silver currency can also be studied from the depression of the prices of food grains—a commodity of mass consumption—'not only in Bengal but in other parts of India as well'.[70]

In Bengal, the price movement of food grains during the period 1757-92 was very volatile, the chief reason being recurrent famines.[71] Thus, during the famine of 1769-70, the price of rice which sold at the rate of 10 to 20 *sers* a rupee at Murshidabad shot up to 3 *sers* per rupee in July 1770.[72] Failed crops in 1777 and 1779, likewise, resulted in an exceptional rise in prices. In 1787-8, a serious famine followed by an inundation disrupted normal life in all of eastern Bengal.[73] As a result, in Rangpur, 'rice which sold at three to four maunds a rupee before the famine, sold at only one maund per rupee in June, 1789 and in July, it sold at 30 seers a rupee and in September sold at 23 to 25 seers a rupee'.[74]

There were no major famines in Bengal from 1790 till the close of our study.[75] For the period between 1792-3 and 1822-3, Mitra has analysed data on the price of rice in different districts of the Bengal Presidency; he reveals that, during this period, the price of rice rose nearly everywhere though the increase was not uniform in all places.[76] According to Mitra's analysis, the 'prices rose despite scarcity of rupees in circulation, at least in some periods during the period under review [1792/93-1822/23].[77] This, he points out, was due to the fact that, during this period, the demand for rice was greater owing to a rise in population and because new lands had not been brought under cultivation.[78]

However, in our study, we have seen that the currency crisis of Bengal started improving after 1792 when bimetallism was re-introduced for the third time. The gradual extension of gold currency coupled with the resumed inflow of bullion through imports certainly eased the pressure on the currency of Bengal. As the benefits of these currency reforms were at least initially confined to Calcutta and its immediate neighbourhood, we may as well compare the prices of rice at Calcutta with those in other districts of the Bengal Presidency. During 1793-4 and 1798-9, the price of coarse rice at Calcutta remained fixed at 36 *sers* per rupee.[79] Other documented articles such as oil, *ghee* and *gur*, too, either showed a remarkable stasis or even a downward trend during the period 1793-4 to 1812-13. Thus, in the case of Calcutta, a direct connection can be seen between currency reforms and stability of prices. However, certain non-monetary factors such as the static cultivation area *vis-à-vis* a rise in consumption due to an increase in population must have caused a price rise in the districts, as revealed by Mitra's analysis.

A similar analysis of the price movements of rice in different districts of the Madras Presidency during the first half of the nineteenth century is available to us in a remarkable study by Sarada Raju where he has listed four varieties of rice, viz., Paddy (first sort), Paddy (second sort), Ragi and Cholam, and computed their prices in rupees per Madras Garce (= 3,200 measures).[80] Between the period 1801-2 and 1834-5, for which prices are included in this analysis, 1806-7, 1812-13, 1824-5, 1825-6 and 1833-4 were famine years in the Madras Presidency. Taking 1801-2 to 1810-11 as the base year for the index number, Sarada Raju has demonstrated that after the famine of 1807, prices were persistently low and rose above the base only during subsequent famine years.[81] He has noted that 'up to the close of the eighteenth century and for some years later, the exports of piecegoods and spices ensured a steady supply of money'.[82] Thus, large payments by way of investments directly entered into circulation and tended to keep the prices high. However, with the decline of the textile trade from the early years of the nineteenth century, these large investments were discontinued and there was a great reduction in the circulating medium. During the same period, great confusion prevailed in the currencies of the Madras Presidency, which was grappling between the *pagoda* standard and the rupee standard, and was in the transition phase from a gold standard to a silver one. The silver standard was finally adopted in Madras in 1818 but the number of silver coins remained in short supply. As a result, general prices—if we accept the price of rice as a test sample—remained low.

Another factor responsible for the deflationary trends in the Madras Presidency 'was the increasing issue of Bills by the Court of Directors for payments due to the presidency'.[83] According to Sarada Raju, 'before 1819-20 these bills were negligible but they assumed very large proportions during the third and the fourth decade of the nineteenth century . . . the value of Bills drawn on Madras rose from Rs. 9,427 in 1819 to Rs. 2,66,412 in 1835-36.'[84] The rates of these bills were deliberately fixed below the bullion rate of remittances and, as a result, it prevented the import of bullion not only from England but also from the countries with which England had an adverse balance of trade.[85] This arrangement caused a great diminution of bullion imports into Madras and resulted in contraction of the currency in circulation.

Reporting in 1813, the Board of Revenue attributed the fall of prices to the withdrawal of currency from the Madras Presidency for 'meeting public demands as well as in other parts of Asia, as in Europe, while the supplies which had been customarily derived by means of importation had not . . . been continued of late to any considerable extent.'[86] Later, in another report, the Board warned the government about the evil effects of the contraction of money supply on prices:

> If in this way the currency of India should be diminished in quantity, the *money prices of agricultural produce* must in consequence be lower than they otherwise would be, and the Board see [*sic*] no reason to feel assured that the fall may not be in such degree and permanency as to render it a matter of very serious importance. (emphasis added)[87]

A third example of the price of an agricultural product of mass consumption can be drawn from Delhi. Here, we have a list of the prices of wheat for seventy-two years (1763-1835).[88] Jevons made this list the very keystone of his theory of commercial crisis, which, in the case of Delhi, occurred in the years 1763, 1772-3, 1783, 1804 and, after a gap of about twenty years, in 1825-6 and again in 1836. This, according to Jevons's theory, 'fell into a regular series of decennial cycles' of price escalation.[89] Now, if we analyse these prices in the perspective of the monetary history of Delhi, we notice that from the time Delhi came into the hands of the Company (1803) till 1818, it did not disturb the local circulating medium. The Delhi (or Shahjahanabad) mint continued striking silver rupees in the name of the Mughal emperor. However, in 1818, the Delhi mint was abolished and the Farrukhabad rupee was established as the currency of Delhi.[90] The price of wheat, which was Rs. 38 for 1,000 *sers* in 1818, rose to Rs. 42 in 1819 and Rs. 46 in 1820. Thereafter, except for the crisis years of 1825 and 1826 when the prices of wheat were recorded as Rs. 39 and Rs. 48, respectively, the average price up to 1835 remained around Rs. 30 per 1,000 *sers.* Once again, these deflationary trends could be partly attributed to the slow penetration of the Farrukhabad rupee into the money market of Delhi after the abolition of the Delhi mint in 1818.

Irfan Habib ascribes some credit for the stability of prices to the decline in the world production of silver, which fell from an annual peak of 28.7 million oz. in 1801-10 to 14.8 million oz. in 1821-31 and 19.2 million oz. in 1831-40.[91] Thus, reduced production led to an overall contraction of silver currencies, forcing the prices down. For the agricultural classes, a fall in prices occasioned great distress and hardship since their income dwindled greatly while their expenses and other charges remained undiminished.[92] This, in turn, resulted in the decline of government revenue in the Madras Presidency, which fell from Rs. 4,16,40,810 to 3,79,19,310 in 1819-20.[93] In the Mahalwari areas of northern India, the rural population suffered miserably because 'the land revenue collections went on increasing while prices remained stable or even declined'.[94]

Thus, the course of prices during the period of our review was greatly influenced by the changing currency policies of the colonial government and, due to a general deflationary tendency, adversely affected the agricultural economy of the country.

Currency Circulation and Discount

In the economy that was marked by multiplicity of coinage, exchange rates played an important role in facilitating circulation and increasing the velocity of money. Rajat Datta has discussed the problem of the disappearance of bullion from the Bengal market after 1765 on the basis of the monthly rates of *batta* on the Arcot rupees in the bazaars of Dhaka between 1769 and 1773. According to him, for the thirty-eight documented months between 1769 and 1773, the *batta* on Sicca rupees averaged 7.06 per cent and for thirty-five documented months of the same period, it was 3.2 per cent on *sanwat* rupees.[95] Contrasting these rates with those charged on Sicca rupees 'during the silver "crises" of 1729', when it was as high as 12.5 per cent, Datta questions the notions of 'a great scarcity of silver and silver currency'.[96] Other historians like Om Prakash seem to agree with his analysis and 'strongly discount the likelihood of any serious shortage of money being there in the region at this time'.[97] Datta utilized the data of the monthly rate of *batta* on the Arcot rupees to prove his theorem that fluctuations in its rate indicate variations in the quantities of bullion in circulation in the economy.[98] In the absence of any specification of the specie of rupee intended by the generic use of the term 'sicca' by Datta, we can only conjecture that he has used this term to denote the two varieties of the *same* specie of silver rupee, viz., the Arcot Sicca and Arcot *sanwat*. In this connection, we have another contemporary evidence which allows us to compare the rates of *batta* on *different* specie of silver rupees that were prevalent in Calcutta, during 1768.

A diary of the price of silver in Calcutta (June-August 1768), records:

> . . . the established Battas are as follows:
>
> | | | |
> |---|---|---|
> | viz. | 9 Sun Siccas, being the coin struck in that year | 16 per Cent. |
> | | 8 Suns, the coin of the preceding year | 13 per Cent |
> | | Sunats, being the third year in circulation, are | 11 per Cent |
> | | Arcots, are | 8 per Cent.[99] |

These rates were quoted by Verelst to demonstrate 'the extraordinary discount on the gold mohurs of 1766', where a 'deviation from these numbers express the rise and fall of Batta'.[100] However, taking these numbers as indicative of their relative value, we can test the relationship between the Sicca and *sanwat* rupees, on the one hand, and the 9-*sun* Sicca and Arcot rupee on the other. It is, thus, evident from the above rates that coins of the current year passed at the full rate of 16 *annas* per rupee; one-year-old coins lost 3 *annas* (or 18.75 per cent) of their value and were good for only 13 *annas* (or 87.75 per cent) of the Sicca rate; the *sanwat* rupees lost 5 *annas* (or 31.25 per cent) of their value as compared to the Sicca rupees and their value dropped to 11 *annas* (or 68.75 per cent). The Arcot rupee, on the other hand, equalled only 50 per cent as compared to the Sicca rupee of 16 *annas* in Bengal.

It needs to be remembered that the Arcot rupees were the chief circulating medium in the Dhaka and Chittagong region, and the Company's mints at Chintadripet and Madras had been supplying this specie of coin for circulation in this region since 1742. Apart from the Company's mints, the Arcot rupee was also minted by the Nawab of Arcot, and by the Dutch and French East India Companies until 1825.[101] In fact, the table included in Regulation XXXV of 1793 lists as many as fourteen different types of Arcot rupees circulating in the Bengal Presidency. As the principal currency in south India consisted of the gold *pagoda* and silver *fanams*, the rupees minted by the Nawab of Arcot, as well as the English and French Companies, were pumped into the Bengal trade. Looking at the popularity of the Arcot rupees in the Bengal trade in 1761, their minting was started in the Calcutta mint and 'from 1761 until the introduction of the 19 san sicca rupee in May 1777, the greater part of the output of the Calcutta mint consisted of the Arkaṭ silver rupee'.[102] The circulation of this 'foreign' coin in Bengal had prompted the Court of Directors to ask the government of Bengal to explain why the 'Arcot Rupees should be the only currency in several parts of the Province' and whether they 'cannot by degrees establish the Currency' of the Sicca rupees.[103] However, the Arcot rupees continued to dominate the money market in these regions of the Bengal Presidency.

The returns of the Calcutta mint for the year 1775 show that the total value of Arcot coinage coined in that mint was Rs. 47,28,253.8.9 as compared to Rs. 270.3.6 for the Sicca coinage.[104] An earlier report of 1774 mentions that the rate of coining Arcot rupees in the Calcutta mint was 25,000 a working day.[105] Therefore, the adequacy or sufficiency of the Arcot rupees, which led to a lowering in the rate of *batta* on Arcot Sicca and *sanwat* rupees in the markets of Dhaka between 1769 and 1773 to an average of 7.06 per cent for Sicca rupees and 3.2 per cent for *sanwat* rupees, cannot be used as evidence for the generalization made by Datta and Om Prakash that the post-1765 silver crisis was due to a 'temporary disruption in Bengal's money market . . . do not reflect an absolute reduction or shortage of currency'.[106]

The fact remains that whether it was due to 'the gap between financial requirements (of the Company) and the revenue surplus of Bengal'[107] or due to the cessation of bullion imports from Europe or the demands of an expanding money market, there *was* a shortage of silver currency in Bengal for at least about twenty years between 1765 and 1784, and this contraction of currency supply adversely impacted the discount rates for various sorts of coins circulating in different regions.

CREDIT AND BANKING

Credit System: Indian and Colonial

The elaborate credit network that indigenously developed in India supported a monetized system of exchange 'by allowing claims to money to be used for making payments and settling obligations'.[108] The most popular Indian credit instrument was the *hundi*.[109] It not only facilitated the transfer of money between places as distant as Calcutta and Bombay or Benares and Nasik, but also served as an 'important source of banking capital'.[110] The English Company, like their other European competitors in India, made extensive use of *hundis* for cash remittances. During the period between 1757 and 1797 when the scarcity of silver specie remained a cause of concern for the East India Company, inter-presidency as well as intra-presidency remittances were largely carried out through *hundis*. Thus, for remittances of funds, proceeds and the profits of trade, *hundis* were the most central and characteristic instruments of the Indian banking system.[111]

During the period of our review, the traditional system of credit was challenged not only by the entry of European players but also by the Company's repressive actions. Agency houses and European private merchants carried out trade and financed manufacturers, also making inroads into the banking and credit networks. In 1790, for example, there were fifteen agency houses in Calcutta alone which ran three banks and four insurance companies there and speculated in public securities. As a result, though the *hundi*-based credit network of the Indian merchant bankers lost some of its turf to new players, the credit instrument itself was able to sustain the challenge.

The Company, too, came into direct clash with the *sarrafs* on a number of occasions. There are numerous instances which attest to the growing discordance between the Company and the indigenous bankers during the period of our review. Lakshmi Subramanian and Michelgulielmo Torri list many incidents that took place in western India especially from 1760 onwards where questions of raising the standard of the rupee, the exchange rate between the Surat rupee and rupees of other mintage, the rate of *batta* on old coins, etc., widened the chasm between the two.[112] However, in spite of the Company's efforts to bring these indigenous *sarrafs* and bankers under their control, 'their control over credit remained unimpaired'.[113]

In a bid to extend their control over financial and credit transactions, in Bengal, the Company imposed heavy restrictions in 1814 when elaborate Stamp Duty rules were passed via Regulation I (of 1814). This Regulation prescribed that after 1 May 1814,

> every bond, promissory note, bill of exchange, letter of credit, or other obligation for payment of money, every receipt or acquaintance . . . every deed of gift, sale, devise, or other transfer of property, real or personal, every lease, deed of mortgage, or other limited assignment of land; every deed of contract, partnership agreement, security, or engagement . . . shall be written on paper . . . impressed with the government stamp. (Sec. XI)

However, the *hundis* then operated not on any legal obligation but on trust as they do even today. They did not bear any seal or signatures, or even had an envelope, and yet they enjoyed universal acceptance throughout the country. The dishonouring of *hundis* was rare and was seen as a sign of loss of the credit of its drawer. Thus, *hundis* continued to play a major role in the Indian money market in private and official transactions. In fact, during the twentieth century, a number of Indian princely states, the British government and the government of independent India adopted *hundis* as an 'official' credit instrument (see Figs. 5.1 and 5.2), though these are still not covered under the Negotiable Instruments Act, 1881.

Speaking at the Institute of Bankers, London, in May 1881, Sir Richard Temple had this to say about the popularity and extensive circulation enjoyed by the *hundis*:

> These *hundys*, I assure you, circulate from one end of India to the other, that is, from the Himalayas down to Ceylon, and some Native merchants can give you a draft upon any place in the world, upon Constantinople, upon the Levant, upon London, and now, I almost regret to say, upon New York, and they have long been able to do so upon San Francisco. Of course, the total amount of these *hundys* depends upon the internal trade, the value of which . . . cannot be exactly estimated; but if I were to say that an amount

of from fifty to an hundred million sterling worth of these *hundys* must be in circulation in India at one time, I should hardly be guilty of any exaggeration.[114]

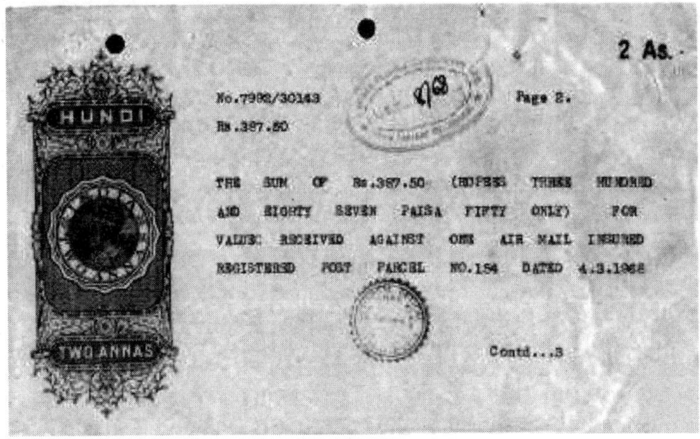

2 As.

HUNDI

TWO ANNAS

No.7998/30143 Page 2.

Rs.387.50

THE SUM OF Rs.387.50 (RUPEES THREE HUNDRED AND EIGHTY SEVEN PAISA FIFTY ONLY) FOR VALUE RECEIVED AGAINST ONE AIR MAIL INSURED REGISTERED POST PARCEL NO.154 DATED 4.3.1968

Contd...3

Fig. 5.1: British Government *Hundi*

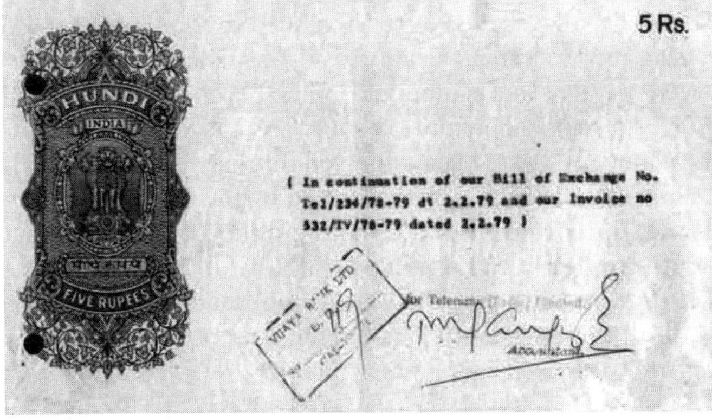

5 Rs.

HUNDI

INDIA

FIVE RUPEES

(In continuation of our Bill of Exchange No. Tel/234/78-79 dt 2.2.79 and our Invoice no 532/TV/78-79 dated 2.2.79)

Fig. 5.2: Government of India *Hundi*

The *hundis*, thus, served as a vital organ of the money market and played a crucial role in increasing the velocity of money and in the expansion of money supply, both being lifelines of a growing economy.

The growing pressure on the Company's revenues due to increased exports, military expenses, remittances to the Madras and Bombay

Presidencies, and to China and Manila as well as to England on account of 'Home Charges', on the one hand, and the scarcity of silver currency in Bengal during the decade following the grant of *Diwani*, on the other, forced the Company to adopt an elaborate network of European credit instruments and to introduce a public debt system in India.

Thus, we find the extensive use of bills of exchange—the colonial cousins of the indigenous *hundi*, which were issued to Indian as well as English traders against receipts in specie. This system soon became a convenient mode of raising capital at the presidencies to which the surplus revenue of Bengal was otherwise pledged. For example, to obviate the need for remittances in specie or bullion, the Bombay and Madras presidencies were authorized to 'enter into engagements with Native shroffs or British Agency Houses, who would pay regular monthly sums at the treasury and receive bills at a favourable rate of exchange on Benares or Calcutta, i.e. wherever they liked to transfer their money'.[115] Similarly, if the merchants of Bengal 'desired to get back returns of trade or military contract from Bombay and Madras safely, they would pay the returns at the Bombay and Madras treasuries for bills on Benares or Calcutta'.[116]

These bills of exchange were also issued to the English and other European private traders against cash receipts in Indian currencies, and were payable in London and other European capitals. By this measure, substantial quantities of rupee receipts were obtained locally by the Company. It has been estimated that between 1757 and 1784, the value of the bills of exchange issued by the East India Company on its headquarters in London, including those drawn at Canton, amounted to nearly £11.8 million.[117]

The drawing of the bill of exchange on London was regulated by the Court of Directors in 1774 and the rates of exchange of various currencies were fixed as follows:[118]

TABLE 5.1: EXCHANGE RATES OF PRINCIPAL CURRENCIES, 1774

Presidencies	Denominations	Exchange Rate
Bengal	Current Rupee (CR)	2s 1d.
Madras	Star *Pagoda*	7s 4d.
Bombay	Bombay Rupee	2s. 3d.

By this rate, the internal exchange rates of the three currencies were fixed thus: 100 star *pagoda* = 350 Bengal CR and 108 Bengal CR = 100 Bombay rupees.[119]

The bills of exchange gradually became a most popular and trusted means of the intra-presidency remittances of the Company's financial resources. In 1788, for example, we find the Governor-General of Bengal informing the Court that the Government of Bengal had 'engaged a Remittances of Bills to Bombay for three lacs of Sicca Rupees, and advertised for proposals to remit a further sum to that Presidency'.[120]

The bills of exchange drawn by the presidencies of Madras and Bombay on the Bengal Presidency, thereby locally securing the supply of the circulating medium, was not always advantageous to the Company for the rates of interests for these bills were usually high. In their letter to the Bengal government in 1790, the Court expressed its concern over 'the loss arising from money being taken up there [Madras] for Bills on your Presidency at a disadvantageous rate of exchange'.[121]

In 1827, certain banks started issuing 'post bills'. These were inland promissory notes issued by the bank on a distant place, the holder of which would be paid on acceptance after a specified number of days (seven days' sight or thirty days' sight), and were similar to *muddati hundis*. These bills had a much smaller currency limit than bank notes, mainly because the government refused to authorize their receipt in the payment of public dues. They were mainly used by European businessmen for purposes of internal remittances.

A question may be asked as to what extent the bills of exchange displaced the indigenous credit instrument, viz., the *hundi*, for long-distance remittances within India. A direct answer to this question is elusive considering the fact that no quantification of monetary transactions through credit instruments is available for this period. However, through some evidences, trends can be ascertained. The fact remains that despite the extensive usage of bills of exchange by the Company during the last quarter of the eighteenth century, the role of indigenous banking houses in large-value remittances could not be wished away by it. In the 1790s, remittances from Bengal to Bombay, amounting to Rs. 3 lakh per month, were affected through the house of Bhawani Das Manohar Das of Benares.[122] In 1795, Khushal Chand, a *gumashta* of another banker family of Benares—Gopal Das Harkishan Das—proposed to the Bengal government that he would advance Rs. 36 lakh at Bombay by instalments of Rs. 3 lakh per month on the condition that for every Rs. 96 paid at Bombay, the firm should receive 100 Sicca rupees at Benares after 51 days.[123] The loss through this mode of remittance was a cause of concern to the Company and we find the Court's instructions to the Bengal government to explore some alternative mode of remittance to Bombay. In their letter dated 8 February 1792, the Directors wrote: 'The Company are liable to considerable loss by remittances made through Benares, we direct that you endeavour to devise some more eligible mode of effecting these remittances from the next season!'[124]

The Bengal government also remitted funds to Bombay by drawing bills on prominent *sarrafs*. Those who redeemed these bills despatched by the Fort William Council were Surat-based 'Arjunji Nathji Tarvady, Atmaram Jagjeevandas, Tapidas Laldas, Goculdas Brandavandas, Maya Shankar and Atmaram Bhucandas'.[125] These *sarrafs* accepted the Bengal bills at Surat and then conveyed the amount pledged therein to Bombay through '*hundis* drawn on their agents in the island city'.[126] Thus, in spite of the prevalence of bills of exchange for the transfer of government money, *hundis* were integrated into the new credit network.

With the increase in expenditure, the Company decided to seek additional resources in 1783 by raising money on loan from the public. Under this scheme, the Company issued promissory notes (bonds or certificates) bearing fixed rates of annual interest. These notes were to mature after a specified period but were tradable at a discount even before their maturity, something like a modern-day debenture. Another type of credit instrument was the remittance bond, primarily meant for the Company's servants who wanted to transfer their incomes home. These bonds bore an interest at half the rate of a common loan and were repayable in a term of no less than five years. These remittance bonds were precursors of the modern-day traveller's cheques. Regarding the two loans floated by the government of Bengal, the Court of Directors were informed:

> The first loan received upon common interest notes at 8 per cent per annum was certainly the most simple, but the others were intended to be more beneficial to the Company at the same time that they tended to accommodate particular individuals who otherwise would not have subscribed to them. The 4 per cent remittance loan produced on immediate supply repayable in a term of no less than five years, with an interest of only half the rate of the common loan, and in fact was not to be an additional burthen [*sic*] upon your treasury in England. . . .[127]

The scheme of promissory notes was quite successful, and in 1793, encouraged by a steady rise in the sale of these notes, the Company decided to slash the interest by 2 per cent and offer the new notes to the public at 6 per cent interest.[128]

Banking: Indigenous and European

Indigenous Banking

The terms indigenous banking, indigenous bankers or indigenous banks are generally used to denote 'all kinds of private bankers, moneylenders, banking or moneylending firms, with the distinction that the "banker", individual or private firm, in addition to making loans, received deposits and dealt in *hundis*... while the "moneylender", also an individual or private firm, made only loans, and did not usually receive deposits or deal in *hundis*.'[129]

Ever since the commencement of their commercial activities in India, all the European trading companies depended on the highly-developed indigenous money and credit network of India for their requirements of cash, money transfer, short-term loans and the conversion of bullion into coins. All these functions were performed by the *sarrafs*, who served not only as money-changers but also as full-fledged bankers by discounting *hundis*, accepting deposits and lending money.[130] After establishing themselves as revenue collectors, first in Bengal and later in other parts of India, the East India Company utilized the services of these indigenous bankers for their multifarious financial requirements, the chief of which was the transfer of revenue from the *moffusil* towns to their headquarters, and also for intra-presidency remittances.

However, slowly, the power wielded by Indian bankers began to wane and they went through a complex and gradual process of re-deployment.[131] By the 1820s, a treasury system was established by the East India Company and, as a result, 'Indian merchants were not needed as guarantors, and district treasury bills had begun to replace the *hundi* as the basic instrument of official transaction'.[132]

This change was fast and sudden in some places such as the Bengal Presidency, as well as slow and gradual in various pockets of western India and in the Madras Presidency. In both cases, a direct connection can be seen between the monetary integration, stabilization and standardization of the currency established by the East India Company, on the one hand, and the decline of the Indian merchant bankers, on the other.

The formulators of the colonial currency policy were always

sceptical about the enormous powers wielded by the *sarrafs* of India. James Steuart considered them as 'parasites whose activities in weighing, measuring and assaying slowed the velocity of circulation', and his remedy for the ailing currency of Bengal was aimed at saving the wealth of the country from being 'swallowed up' by these *sarrafs*.[133] The relations of the *sarrafs* of Bengal with the East India Company have been studied by Mitra, who argues that the tension started between the two 'mainly over batta on Madras coin'.[134] It may be noted that as the English did not have minting rights in Bengal until 1717, they had to finance their investments by importing silver coins from Madras and Surat.[135] Even though the Company was able to obtain a *farman* from the Mughal emperor, Farrukhsiyar, permitting them to use the Murshidabad mint to coin their bullion on payment of the customary charges, they were unable to implement this arrangement due to the strong opposition of Murshid Quli Khan.[136] Mitra observes that the English Company could not use the mint (at Murshidabad) primarily because of the influence of Jagat Seth Fateh Chand,[137] whom Robert Orme described as 'the greatest shroff and banker in the known world'.[138] The Jagat Seths enjoyed a very cordial relationship with the Nawab of Murshidabad, which, according to K.N. Chaudhuri, 'stemmed from the mutual advantage they gained from the maintenance of a *quasi-monopoly of currency* . . .' (emphasis added).[139] The house of the Jagat Seths commanded the bullion market to the extent that no purchaser could dare to offer a price higher than that offered by them. They fixed the rates of exchange of various species of coins, which were accepted by all concerned.[140]

Regarding Fateh Chand's monopolistic control over the bullion market and the mint at Murshidabad in around 1721, we have the following statement from the Company's officials at Cassimbazar: '. . . he [Fateh Chand] alone having the sole use of the mint, nor dare any shroff or merchant buy or coin a rupee's worth of silver.'[141] In spite of his commanding role in the money market, Fateh Chand did not take 'an unscrupulous advantage of the monopoly he possessed', and on many occasions offered a better price for the Company's treasure than what they would have willingly accepted.[142]

Fateh Chand died in 1744 but his house continued to flourish. Captain Fenwick, who wrote about the affairs of Bengal in *c.*1747-8, describes Fateh Chand's grandson, Mehtab Rai, as 'a great Banker than all in Lombard Street joined together'.[143] Mehtab Rai further consolidated his hold over the bullion market when he obtained in 1750 the exclusive rights to purchase bullion from the Nawab of Murshidabad. In their letter dated 9 January 1750, the Company's servants at Cassimbazar informed the Governor at Fort William that 'the Seats [*sic Seths* = Jagat Seths] have lately obtained from the Nawab [an order] which forbids all persons besides themselves from purchasing any silver or taking any Arcot rupees'.[144]

The relations of the Company with the Jagat Seths underwent a change once it was able to establish its own mint at Calcutta in 1757.[145] According to an estimate prepared in 1757, the house minted Rs. 50 lakh annually, on which its profit at 7 per cent amounted to Rs. 3.50 lakh. This, however, was only a small portion of the total income of the Jagat Seths which stood close to Rs. 50 lakh per annum.[146] Their main source of profit was through the receipt of the revenue of Bengal and other payments made to the Nawab. It is estimated that their commission stood at 10 per cent, which, according to the Resident at Murshidabad, gave the Jagat Seths an annual income of Rs. 40 lakh.[147] Even this source of profit was insignificant in comparison to their earnings by way of the discount charged on the exchange of specie. As the Nawab received his revenues only in the Siccas of current years, the Jagat Seths made a huge profit by way of 'shroffing the revenues—examining, sorting, and weighing of various kinds of rupees and settling the batta upon all in terms of sicca rupees'.[148]

However, after the establishment of the Calcutta mint, the Company was no longer dependent on Jagat Seth to get its bullion converted into coins. It has been noted by Mitra that 'the prosperity of the House of Jagat Seth began to decline from 1750s and the *decline became more rapid after 1757*' (emphasis added).[149] Many other factors would certainly have contributed to the decline of the Jagat Seths but the fact remains that a chink in their monopoly over the bullion market and, more specifically, their control over the mint at Murshidabad was caused by the establishment of the Calcutta mint in 1757. Though 'the establishment of a mint at Calcutta did not, for some years, do them [Jagat Seths] any harm, owing to their command of the specie of the province and the operation of the practice of batta',[150] the subsequent extension of the East India Company's minting activities in the other mint towns of the Bengal Presidency, viz., Murshidabad and Patna, after the grant of *Diwani* rights in 1765, made the downfall of this house imminent. In fact, in 1789, Jagat Seth sought the permission of the Company to establish his own mint at Murshidabad but his request was turned down.[151] Now, the Company was able to meet its requirements of coined money by sending its bullion directly to its own mints.

Thus, once the Company was able to get a foothold in Bengal politics, it gradually worked to wrest control of the money market from the hands of the Jagat Seths. By establishing its own mint at Calcutta and extending its minting activities in other mints, the Company was able to break the Jagat Seths' monopoly over the bullion market. The new revenue regime of the Company after 1765, especially after the establishment of the treasury system for the transfer of revenue from the districts to Calcutta, resulted in a huge loss of profit that was previously earned by the Jagat Seths. Various currency reforms of the Company, especially the two early attempts (in 1766 and 1769) to introduce bimetallism and, thus, reduce the dependence on silver currency, which was the sole source for exacting *batta*, also depleted the income of the Jagat Seths. Finally, the business of the house as the provider of commercial credit to European merchants also suffered a setback after 1757. In the post-Plassey scenario, while the servants of the Company were able to finance their private trade out of their earnings from presents and other perquisites, 'the Dutch, the French (after 1763) and the Danes [too] no longer depended on the financial support of the Seths'.[152] They now met their credit and investment requirements largely by receiving liquid cash from the Company's servants in exchange for bills of exchange drawn on Europe. Joint-stock banking on the European pattern that emerged in Bengal from the 1770s also eroded the firm base that the Jagat Seths had in the money market. As a result of these developments, control over the money market of Bengal passed into the hands of the Company and their protégés.

In her analysis of the relationship between the *sarrafs* of Bengal and the East India Company, Shubra Chakrabarti has emphasized 'the crucial centrality of the shroffs in the prevailing currency system and the Company's attempts to dispense with them through repeated, though unsuccessful, currency reforms'.[153] Kumkum Chatterjee stresses that the duality of this relationship was marked by both collaborations and conflicts.[154] The period selected by Chakrabarti (1757-1800) and Chatterjee (1757-1813) was the one in which the role of the Bengal *sarrafs* was becoming increasingly marginalized as far as the financial management of the Company's funds was concerned. However, they still held a considerable sway in the currency market due to the 'continuation of traditional business practices, methods of revenue collection, and the persistence of indigenous institutions'.[155]

The growth of European banking, the establishment of the treasury system, an increase in the Company's minting capacity, the establishment of the 19-*sun* Sicca and the Farrukhabad rupee as the sole legal tender currencies in Bengal, the extensions of the bills of exchange system, the adoption of new modes of public finance (viz., government bonds and promissory notes) and, finally, the establishment of a uniform currency in 1833 and a universal coinage in 1835 'created an unprecedented division of the economic space between *la blanc et le noir* [lit. the white and the black]'.[156]

Thus, in the final conflict to re-draw economic space, the indigenous business of banking, moneylending, and the exchange and transfer of funds suffered a fatal blow at the hands of the Company-led European banking and currency management.

In south India, the prevalence of a bi-metallic currency system consisting of gold and silver provided fertile ground for the *sarrafs* and bankers to alter the exchange value of the currencies to whet their caprice. Different relative values of gold and silver prevailed in the Northern Circars and Madras, which, in turn, established a nefarious link between the *zamindars* and *sarrafs*. As Raman Rao notes, 'The system of differential ratio established between gold and silver coins was responsible for all the chaotic fluctuations, the shroffs, the zamindars and merchants trying to take advantage of the situation.'[157]

In about 1740, the largest banking house of the south was that of a Gujarati family, Bukanji Kasidas, frequently referred to as 'Sarkar's *Sowkar* and the chief shroff of the Province'.[158] Besides, there were local Chettis (or Chettiars) who carried on banking activities mostly in the small towns and cities.

The indigenous bankers of south India were combined in their opposition to an 'organized' banking. Even Tipu Sultan's attempt to establish *Mullicutyal Coties*—a network of state-sponsored banking houses all over the south, backed and funded by a central bank at Srirangapattanam, was thwarted by these indigenous bankers, 'who preferred to operate without any restrictions from an external authority'.[159] Even the three private banks, viz., the Carnatic Bank (established in 1788), the Madras Bank (established in 1795) and the Asiatic Bank (established in 1806), could not enjoy the full benefits of their resources due to 'collusion of interests, competition and mutual rivalries'.[160]

The process of currency reforms in the Madras Presidency, as we have seen in Chapter III, did not actually begin till almost the close of the eighteenth century, even though the government was facing tremendous financial stringency due to frequent wars, political disorder and the chaotic currency situation for the last several decades. The First (1798-1800) and the Second (1805-8) Finance Committees set up by the Madras government to examine the state of government finance were unanimous in their opinion that 'the scarcity of the medium of exchange or the current coin could, at best be overcome by the establishment of a general bank on a large scale and the issue of bank notes'.[161]

With the slow pace of currency reform and the refusal of the Court of Directors to approve a plan for a government bank in the Madras Presidency, the indigenous bankers survived for a longer period even after the establishment of joint-stock banks like the Bank of Madras (established in 1843). While some of them shifted to Burma, a majority continued to play their traditional role in the south Indian economy.

Western India was dominated by a horde of Gujarati merchant bankers during this time, who 'operated as traders, brokers, shroffs or currency dealers, bankers, insurance agents and shop-owners'.[162] Surat, which was the principal mint town on the western coast until its closure in 1815, was the seat of one of the very important houses of the merchants of Gujarat: Virji Vora (*c.* 1590-1670) and later, the Travadis. The Parsis, Jews and Armenians were other players in the field.[163] There were Muslims as well, 'even if their role as bankers or money changers was extremely limited and in no way comparable to the one they played as merchants'.[164] Ahmedabad, another mint town, was, likewise, dominated by the house of Shantidas Zaveri (1587-1659). There were other mint towns at Broach and Cambay, which became clusters of banking activities of numerous indigenous merchants, traders and bankers.[165] While big merchant-princes like Virji Vora and Shantidas Zaveri engaged themselves in trade and financing, or occasionally competing 'with the sarrafs by offering a higher price for bullion',[166] there were numerous others—Parekhs, Nanawatis and Shroffs—who were closely connected with the business of bullion and the mint.

Lakshmi Subramanian has discussed how the Surat *sarrafs* formed themselves into a 'pressure group' during the 1760s and 1770s, and thwarted all the attempts of the Bombay government to raise the standard of the Surat rupee or to regulate the *batta*.[167] Regarding the dominant role of the *sarrafs* in the money market at the turn of the eighteenth century, very interesting evidence is available in a report dated 7 December 1806, submitted by H. Scott, the Assay Master of the Bombay Mint, where he writes:

> No man without considerable experience in this country can form an opinion of the influence and the arts of shroffs. They hold in their hands almost the whole specie of the country; their houses are connected in every part of India; their whole life is spent in the trade of gaining money by exchange and by every other means connected with this art. They follow the same trade from generation to generation, they are subtle and acute from long and early habit and are divided from the rest of the people, not more by their cast [*sic* caste], than by their means of living in which they are allow none to participate. Their influence is great and extensive nor is it even in the power of Government on many occasions to protect itself against their combinations.[168]

Scott cautioned the government that the exchange rate between the silver and gold currencies should be officially fixed, as in a bimetallic economy, rather than adopting silver monometallism as suggested by the Court of Directors in its despatch of 1806. The reasons cited by him for advocating bimetallism further establishes the leading role of the *sarrafs* in the money market:

> If any denomination of the coin were left here to find its value in the market instead of being fixed by Government, it is certain that this would be done by the shroffs, as their own interest might dictate. No other part of this community would have any influence in fixing the rates, for the shroffs hold in their hands almost all the specie and would be the entire masters of the exchange.[169]

Scott's assertions about the ability of the *sarrafs* to fix the exchange rates and relative value of the coins of two different metals 'as their own interest dictate' may not be entirely true for they, too, were guided by the principle of demand and supply, and the floating exchange rates, especially in a bimetallic regime, were a problem in all pre-modern economies. Yet it nevertheless attests to their enormous influence in the money market.

The establishment of silver monometallism in the Bombay Presidency, Scott's objections notwithstanding, and the extension of the minting activities of the Company through the acquisition of several silver mints of the region, such as: Broach (1772)[170] and nearby Jambusar (1775),[171] Surat (1800), Ahmedabad (1817), Bagalkot, Belgaum-Shahpur, Nasik, Chandor and Poona (all in 1818), largely reduced the Company's dependence on *sarrafs* to meet their requirements of coined money. Subsequently, the Company adopted a policy of closing down all *moffusil* mints and of centralizing its minting activities at the Presidency mint at Bombay.[172] The large-scale extension of the Bombay Mint in the 1820s was also an attempt to break the monopolistic role of the Indian money merchants in the bullion market and currency circulation in western India.

Right from the beginning, the administrators of the Company were aware that any attempt to regulate the Indian currency market would be fiercely opposed by local players. Their main task was of abolishing the agio (discount) charged by the *sarrafs* on coins of an older and/or different mintage. This, the government noted, was 'a very intricate subject'. The Governor of Bengal informed the Court in September 1769 that it will require 'very mature deliberations, particularly the Measures to be pursued for breaking through the Combination that will doubtless be formed against abolishing a custom that hath been so long established by which Number of Persons are supported'.[173]

Several years later, in its letter dated 28 April 1790 to the Governor-General of Bengal, the Court of Directors noted:

> We are aware that the measures [of establishing 'only one single coin throughout the country'] will meet with the great obstruction from the Shroffs and others who have hitherto reaped considerable advantage in exchanging the various species of Rupees that have hitherto passed Current in the several Districts.[174]

The Court, therefore, directed the Government of Bengal that once they decided to implement their plan, 'most vigorous measures must be adopted in order to render it effectual'.[175] The government, as we have seen in Chapter III, adopted all-out measures to push its agenda of regulating the currency. The 'pressing preoccupation of the British administration . . . [was] to clip the wings of the malicious Indian shroffs'.[176]

EUROPEAN BANKING

The emergence of European banking in India (called 'Anglo-Indian' banking by Bagchi)[177] during the second half of the eighteenth century has been discussed in Chapter II. This phase was marked by the dominance of joint-stock banks established by English agency houses. However, 'mixing trading with banking took its toll, for all of them failed with the collapse of their parent agency house'.[178] By the turn of the century, the Indian money market had become quite extensive and it was repeatedly felt that in order to support the administration of the enlarging territories of the Company as well as its trade and commercial enterprise, banks founded on European lines were indispensable. It was also realized that the banking business could not be left entirely in the private domain. The advantages of state support for banking institutions were obvious but this idea was not initially appreciated by the Court of Directors. In its letter dated 10 January 1787, it ordered local authorities in India not to have any dealings with private banks or encourage them in any way. They held that the agency houses and indigenous banking were better fitted to meet the banking needs of the community than the European banks.[179]

With particular reference to a proposal of the government of Bengal to support setting up a bank 'under the denomination of the General Bank of India', the Court of Directors once again repeated its sentiments in its letter dated 27 March 1787:

> We have very great doubts upon our minds respecting the utility of such an Establishment in India. You are therefore to give no countenance or encouragement to any plan or plans that have been or may hereafter be laid before you by individuals for any such establishment and *you are not to admit or receive any notes or other engagements from the private Banks as a payment in the collection of our Revenues or in any other department of our publick* [sic] *or commercial concern* (emphasis added).[180]

The government of Bengal had, in anticipation of the Court of Directors' approval, lent its support to the proposal (see Chapter II). However, in view of the Court's instructions, government support was withdrawn after 1788 and in another six months, all government accounts with the banks were closed. However, as the incidence of the failure of early joint-stock banks especially in Bengal increased, the idea of setting up a government-supported bank was strengthened.

The Finance Committees set up by the government of Madras in 1798 and 1805, respectively, were unanimous in their recommendation of the establishment of a government bank and the extensive issue of bank notes as the most effective means for overcoming the scarcity of the circulating medium in the Madras Presidency. Even as the government contemplated implementing the recommendations of the First Finance Committee, another joint-stock bank was established in Madras.

The Asiatic Bank was established in Madras in 1804 with a capital of 2.50 lakh *pagodas.*[181] As with other joint-stock banks of the Madras Presidency, the Asiatic Bank also issued notes. Four denominations of these notes have been reported: 5, 10, 100 and 500 star *pagodas.* These notes also bear the equivalent amount expressed in Arcot rupees at the rate of $3\frac{1}{2}$ Arcot rupees for one star *pagoda*. What the volume of issue of these notes was is not known but it is certain that their issue continued at least till 1820.[182] However, unlike the notes of the other banks of Madras, those of the Asiatic Bank were not accepted by the Company.

Meanwhile, in June 1805, the Second Finance Committee was constituted by Lord William Bentinck, the Governor of Madras. The terms of reference for this Committee included the question of establishing a government bank in Madras.[183] The Committee in its report (October 1805) recommended the establishment of a bank with the power to issue paper currency 'with authority derived from the government'.[184] A government bank was, thus, established at Madras with a capital of 8 lakh *pagodas.* This bank, which started its operations from 1 February 1806, was also authorized to issue notes that were thrice the amount of its coin holdings.[185] The plan of this bank was not approved either by the Supreme government at Bengal or by the Court of Directors and this action of the government of Madras drew the severe censure of both these authorities. Yet the Madras Government Bank continued to operate till 1843 when it was superseded by the presidency bank called the Bank of Madras.

By establishing the Madras Government Bank, Bentinck was able to ease the financial stringency of the Madras government to a considerable extent by reducing government borrowings, which, during the period 1801-5, amounted to 63.32 lakh *pagodas* at an interest of 8 to 10 per cent.[186]

P.L. Gupta has observed that the notes issued by the Madras Government Bank 'were more like treasury bills by which the Government raised funds'.[187] This statement gets corroborated if we notice that at the end of the first year, the bank had issued notes worth 57.67 lakh *pagodas* against a net holding of specie worth 11.67 lakh *pagodas.*[188] This also indicates that the denominations of the bank notes must have been very high. However, the surviving specimens of the bank notes issued by the Madras Government Bank stand in sharp contrast to this premise. Only two denominations of notes issued by this bank are known, viz., 2 star *pagodas*/Rs. 7 and 5.[189]

The idea of establishing a joint-stock bank with the tacit support of the government was also germinating in Bombay at about the same time. In 1807, Robert Rickards, a member of the Governor's Council who was also involved in large-scale private trade, submitted a plan for setting up an all-India bank with head-offices in the three presidencies and subordinate banks around the country.[190] However, his plan was rejected both by the Supreme Government at Bengal and also by the Court of Directors.

No further measures were taken in Bombay to establish a joint-stock bank on European lines, much less one with government support, till about 1836 when the idea of establishing a government-sponsored bank was mooted, which ultimately led to the establishment of the Bank of Bombay in 1840.[191]

In Bengal, the idea of a government-supported bank with the power to issue notes was conceived by Henry St. George Tucker, the Accountant General of the Supreme Government. During the opening years of the nineteenth century, the financial situation of the Company was quite precarious due to the constant wars 'unleashed by Wellesley' and increased demands for 'investments'.[192] The government's '12 per cent' treasury notes sold at a discount of 3 to 4 per cent in 1801. The collection of revenue suffered because of the scarcity of silver coins and, when collected in gold coins, an additional loss of 6 to 7 per cent was sustained.[193] Against this backdrop, Tucker forwarded his scheme of establishing a government-supported bank to the Governor-General on 17 October 1801.

The capital of the proposed bank was to be Rs. 50 lakh divided into 500 shares of Rs. 10,000 each. Pending the approval of the Court of Directors, a provisional bank named the Bank of Calcutta was set up in May 1805 and, after obtaining government sanction on 27 February 1806, it opened on 27 March 1806.[194] Henry St. George Tucker, Richard Becher, a member of the Board of Trade, and Richard Waite Cox, a member of the Board of Revenue, were appointed the government directors of the bank.[195]

This bank was empowered to issue bank notes of a value of not less than Rs. 10 and not exceeding 10,000. The bank consequently issued notes in the denominations of Sicca rupees 10, 50, 100, 250, 500, 1,000, 5,000, and 10,000. Notes under Rs. 250 were payable 'at all times at the Bank in specie'.[196]

In May 1807, the government of Bengal decided to replace the Bank of Calcutta with a full-fledged Bank of Bengal. This scheme was later approved by the Court of Directors and, on 1 January 1809, the Bank of Bengal was established. During its existence of about thirty-three months, the Bank of Calcutta issued notes of the value of Rs. 91,37,500.[197]

The Bank of Bengal was the first charter bank of India. It was constituted under the authority given to the Indian governments by an Act of Parliament (47 Geo. III, c. 68).[198] Henry St. George Tucker, R.W. Cox and W. Egerton were appointed government nominees in the nine-member Board of Directors. The offices of the Secretary and Treasurer were held by a covenanted civilian.[199] The East India Company, in turn, contributed one-fifth of its total capital of 50 lakh Sicca rupees.

The charter of the Bank of Bengal authorized it to issue 'Promissory Notes for not less than 10 or more than 10,000 Sicca Rupees payable on demand'.[200] The bank accordingly issued notes in the denominations of 10, 15, 20, 25, 50, 100, 250, 500, 1,000 and 10,000 Sicca rupees. Later, on 8 August 1816, a new denomination of 16 Sicca rupees was added 'to facilitate the exchange of gold mohurs'.[201] During the first six years (1809-15), the bank issued notes worth Rs. 1,25,95,000.[202] The limit for issuing notes was raised to Rs. 2 crore in August 1822.

Apart from the government-supported Bank of Bengal, a few other joint-stock banks were privately established in Bengal during the first half of the nineteenth century. These included the Commercial Bank (1819-31), the Calcutta Bank (1824-9), the Bank of India (1828) and the Union Bank (1828-48). Besides, the Bank of Hindustan which was established by Alexander and Company in 1770 continued its operations till 1831. All these banks issued their own notes.

It may, thus, be seen that in the nineteenth century, a new phase of government-supported banks dominated the economic scene, especially in Madras and Bengal. Under the new arrangement, indigenous banking failed to meet the challenge of organized banking and suffered greatly as a consequence. Notes issued by the government-supported as well as other joint-stock banks provided 'a medium of circulation which was acceptable to the government'.[203] The success of these bank notes had a far-reaching impact on the Indian economy as it prepared the ground for the introduction of a full-fledged government paper currency in India in 1861.

TRADE: INTERNAL AND EXTERNAL

Trade is recognized as an important apparatus of a society without which the distribution of specialized products of labour would be difficult.[204] In this distribution of products, money always played a crucial role not only by obviating the difficulties of barter but also by facilitating sustained production.

The state of currency on the eve of the reforms initiated by the Company was no better than a 'barter economy' due to the lack of a common medium of exchange. The multiplicity of coinage almost always necessitated the elusive 'double coincidence' which characterizes the barter economy.[205] This obviously had a telling impact on trade which was compelled to divert a portion of its trading capital to the payment of discounts or premium (*batta*) while dealing with different species of coins within its areas of operation. As one Chinese adage suggests, ten exchanges eat up one's capital. The constant need for exchanging one specie of coins with another throughout the trading circle proved to be a major impediment to the extension of trade.

The Company soon realized that, on the one hand, 'diseased money is worse than want of money',[206] while, on the other, that its trade would suffer permanently if it were to deal with diseased money or the absence of money. Thus, the trade interests of the East India Company played a major role in forcing it to introduce various measures for evolving good money out of the bad.

Internal Trade and the Problem of Weights and Measures

During the second half of the eighteenth century, the internal trade of Bengal steadily declined.[207] However, during the 1790s, especially after the process of currency reforms was initiated in 1792, with the 'alleviation of financial and currency distress, the inland trade showed signs of revival'.[208] Bengal had a well-established internal trade, both local (between towns and rural areas) and also inter-regional (within and outside the Bengal Presidency). Rice was the chief agricultural produce of eastern and southern India. It was exported in large quantities 'from the districts of South Bihar to Benares, Murshidabad and Calcutta'.[209] South Bihar and Patna regularly received large quantities of wheat and tobacco from north Bihar. Dacca, Calcutta and Murshidabad supplied betel-nut and salt to different parts of Bengal, Bihar, Benares and the Upper Provinces. Other commodities of internal trade included '*pasari* goods' or spices, herbs and drugs, and a vast variety of mineral products including copper, zinc, lead, tin and certain other items.[210] Overall, the increasing monetization of the economy facilitated a 'cash-nexus' between market centres linked by trade routes and the countryside, and, as a result, internal trade flourished.[211]

If we leave aside other articles of trade such as textile fabrics and raw silk, we notice that one of the defects from which internal trade in these commodities constantly suffered was 'the bewildering variety of weights and measures prevalent in the country'.[212] As these weights were based upon the principal coin of that region, a difference in coin weights resulted in a difference in the weighing measures of various commodities. Thus, a *ser* (or *seer*) in Malwa comprised 80 Bhopal rupees; in Baroda 42 Babashahi rupees; in Belgaum 24 Shahpuri rupees; in Calicut 20 Surat rupees; in Indore 82 Ujjaini rupees and so on.[213]

Similarly, there was a difference in the ratio between a *ser* and a *man* (or maund): in Malwa a *man* comprised 40 *sers*; in Baroda 42 *sers*; in Belgaum 44 *sers*; in Calicut 68 *sers*; while in Indore, there were two sets of *mans*—one of 20 *sers* for grains and the other of 40 *sers* for opium, etc.[214] Around 1825, a great number of commodities were sold in Bombay 'by Surat maund, which, notwithstanding it is said to contain only 40 seers, is sometimes 41, 42, 43, through all the intermediate gradation up to 46 [*sers*]'.[215]

In southern and western India, the principal weight for large quantities was expressed in candy.[216] It weighed 20 *man*, and, therefore, varied according to the weight of *man* in different localities. Around 1760, the candy weights of different regions on the western coast and in the Coromandel were as follows:

TABLE 5.2: CANDY WEIGHTS, *c.* 1760

Region	Number of *Mans* per Candy	Weight of Each *Man*		Total Candy Weight	
		lbs. troy	kg.	lbs. troy	kg.
Bombay[217]	20	20	7.465	560	209
Surat	20	37.33	13.93	746.66	278.7
Anjengo	20	25	9.33	500	186.6
Carwar	20	28.75	10.73	575	214.6
Coromandel	20	25	9.33	500	186.6

Source: John Henry Grose, *A Voyage to the East Indies*, 2 vols., London, 1772, quoted in Yule and Burnell 1886: 155.

In south India, the candy weight was also equalized with another weight called *bahar*.[218] However, different kinds of *bahar* were in use for different articles of merchandise; or rather, each article had a special surplus allowance in weighing, which practically made a different *bahar*.[219] Besides, *bahar* had different values in different locations thus:

Honawar: 201.96 kg.; Bhatkal: 212.058 kg. (usually), 192.78 kg. (for sugar); Cannanore: 205.63 kg.; Calicut 208.15 kg.; Cochin and Kollam: 166.27 kg. (here the *khanḍi* used to measure rice was distinct from *bahar* and weighed 214.267 kg.); Kayal: 211.14 kg.; Nagapattinam and Pulicat: . . . 229 kg. . . . ; Masulipatnam: 238 kg.; Bimilipatnam 247 kg.[220]

In fact, as early as in 1775, Philip Francis described 'the Regulation of Weights and Measures . . . as an object of the utmost Importance to society' and had stressed upon the 'necessity of an early Reformation [of weights and measures]' in India.[221] He advocated the adoption of the same weights and measures throughout the country.

Therefore, reducing various denominations of coins to a uniform weight was a matter of crucial importance to facilitate internal trade. Similarly, the prevalence of numerous currencies in the country with no standard or fixed rate of conversion also hampered trade. Therefore, the establishment of uniformity in weights and measures and of the principal coin current in the territories of the Company was one of the main objectives of the currency reforms that were launched in Bengal in 1793 and later emulated in other presidencies.

Despite the severe handicap of differing weights and measures that were prevalent throughout the country, internal trade was carried out with remarkable ease and market centres throughout the countryside soon developed a cash nexus.[222] Various regulations that were passed by the Company to impose taxes on the movement of different commodities, including customs, town duties, and the transit tax of *gunje* (market), purportedly kept the movement of bullion and coins out of the tax net so as to ensure the free flow of capital from surplus to deficient markets.

External Trade

India's external trade during the period of our review was one of the 'abiding concerns' of the East India Company.[223] The years between 1757 and 1813 marked both the high point of the Company's monopoly as well as the beginning of its end.[224] Until 1813, the foreign trade of India 'retained its pre-modern character'.[225] According to K.N. Chaudhuri:

> . . . the far more important characteristic of the half a century following the revolution of 1757 was the fact that Indian trade still continued to flow along the traditional channels and its composition was based on an exchange of fine textiles, foodstuffs, and other raw materials for precious metals and certain manufactured products.[226]

The Charter Act of 1813 which threw open the East India trade gave a great impetus to the private trade between India and England. As a result, several structural changes took place in the Company's trade pattern in subsequent years. With the passing of the Charter Act of 1833, the Company lost its monopoly of the tea trade in India and of its trade with China. Chaudhuri ascribes 'the imposition of British rule in the greater part of the sub-continent and . . . the increasing dominance by Britain of the international money market' as the main factors in bringing about these structural changes.[227] Thus, from the mid-1790s, commodity exports from India included almost all the indigo that Britain either used or re-exported.[228] Similarly, 'more than half of the raw silk in 1772-1820, a bewildering variety of cotton goods for re-export or domestic manufacture, and the superior grade of saltpetre that gave British cannon an edge' comprised the other export commodities.[229] In return, India, which had traditionally been receiving bullion, saw the pattern of her imports undergoing a change. As bullion played a crucial role in 'international monetary transactions, both directly as a medium of payment and a measure of value',[230] the subsequent discussion centres round this particular article of India's external trade.

BULLION TRADE AND CURRENCY REGULATIONS

During the first half of the eighteenth century, the external trade of India was dominated by bullion imports and as this commodity was directly linked with coinage and currency, any change in its trading pattern almost instantaneously affected the money market. Barendse counters this view by holding that the trade in precious metals was 'trade in just another kind of merchandize' and that 'an increase in the imports of silver did not have an immediate impact upon the amount of money in circulation and thus on the price of commodities'.[231] While it is true that the entire quantity of precious metals imported into a country are seldom converted into coins (some of it always goes to non-currency usage like jewellery, household ware, luxury items, etc.), the increasing monetization of the Indian economy during this period subsumed an ever-increasing proportion of bullion for coinage purposes.

The efforts of the East India Company 'to integrate its import of treasure into the India's monetary system went through several distinct historical stages'.[232] The establishment and expansion of mints in the three presidencies was one such effort by the Company to maximize bullion use for coinage purposes. This situation changed after Plassey. One of the features of India's foreign trade from this time onwards was its near-total dependence on local revenues. In the words of the Parliamentary Select Committee of 1783:

> In all other countries, the Revenue following the natural course and order of things, arises out of their commerce. Here [in Bengal], by a mischievous inversion of that order, the whole Foreign, Maritime Trade, whether English, French, Dutch or Danish arises from the Revenues; and these are carried out of the Country, without producing any thing to compensate so heavy a loss.[233]

Thus, a shift from the centuries-old 'bullion for goods' character of Indo-European trade to 'revenues for trade' created a currency panic everywhere. The cession of bullion import chiefly silver, by the Company, in turn, led to a 'silver famine' and contraction of money supply. The Company was forced to introduce the various currency reforms that we discussed in Chapter 3. The initial currency reforms—from the 1760s to 1790s in Bengal and till a little later in the Madras and Bombay presidencies, resulted in resounding failures (such as the introduction of bimetallism in Bengal, Madras and Bombay).[234] This bullion crisis was further aggravated due to the Company's trade with China. From the 1760s to 1790s, the annual bullion remittances from Bengal to China ranged between Rs. 20 and 24 lakh.[235]

The scarcity of silver continued to dominate not only Bengal but also the Bombay Presidency. The minting of silver rupees at the Bombay mint had to be abandoned in around 1778. By 1793, a proposal to purchase dollars to be coined into the Siccas was being considered as the Accountant General of Bengal suggested that 'the consequent loss would be less than by yielding batta on gold'.[236] It is, therefore, not surprising that the establishment of 19-*sun* Sicca as the sole legal tender in Bengal under the provisions of Regulation XXXV of 1793 had to be postponed twice till 1795.

Therefore, the stream of bullion flow to India that had almost dried up since 1757 was revived by the East India Company in 1784 and, from 1795-6, regular consignments of bullion started arriving in India. Between 1795-6 and 1805-6, the Company imported a total treasure worth Rs. 8.60 crore into Bengal at an annual average of Rs. 78.16 lakh.[237] Private traders, too, replenished the bullion coffers of Bengal by importing bullion worth Rs. 4.58 crore at an annual average of Rs. 45.78 lakh between 1796-7 and 1805-6.[238] One of the reasons that compelled the Company to resume the export of bullion to India was that even the third attempt to introduce bimetallism in Bengal by Regulation 1793 was not successful. After postponing the implementation of this Regulation twice, first in 1774 and then in 1795, the Company noticed that there was still an insufficient quantity of silver rupee in circulation. Later, after the Charter Act of 1813 ended the Company's trade monopoly over India, bullion cargoes regularly arrived in India both on account of the Company as well as private merchants.

Between 1813/14 and 1833/4, while Calcutta and Bombay had a negligible quantity of net bullion export, Madras, on the other hand, had a net bullion export of 24.16 per cent as against a net import of 75.84 per cent.

Thus, during these twenty years (1813/14 to 1833/4), the net import of treasure into India by the East India Company, as well as on private account, amounted to a staggering 99 per cent as against a total net export of 1 per cent on the Company and private account during the same period[239] (see Figs. 5.3 and 5.4, and Table 5.3).

BULLION TRADE AND BALANCE OF PAYMENT

India's currency regulations can also be studied with reference to the bullion trade and the balance of payment that India had with Britain. India's external trade with Britain underwent a complete transformation owing to the 'military conquest of India by the East India Company, and to the fact that Britain was fast becoming the world's leading industrial nation, and her capital city the dominant centre of international trade and finance'.[240]

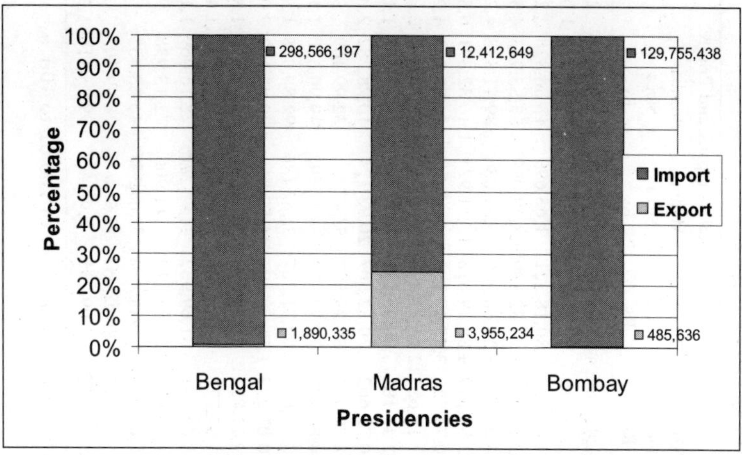

Fig. 5.3: Net Export/Import of Treasure by India (in Sicca Rupees) 1813/14-1833/4

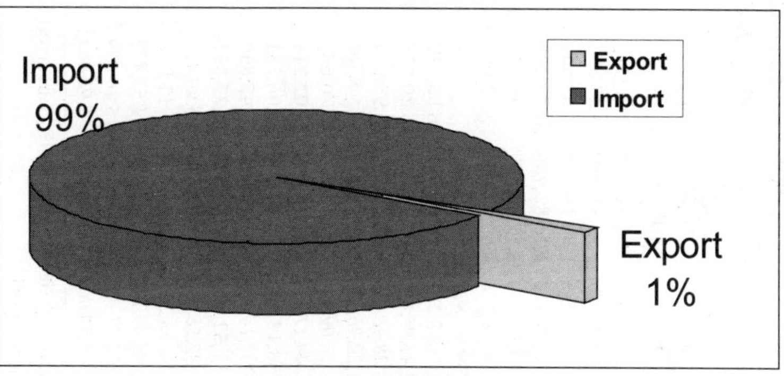

Fig. 5.4: Net Export/Import of Treasure by India 1813/14-1833/4

As is clear from the above table, bullion exports to India stood at 4 per cent of the total India transfers to Britain during 1772-5. This was the period when, armed with the expert recommendations of Sir James Steuart, the Bengal government was grappling with the scarcity of silver and alternative measures, such as accelerating the circulation of money by various public finance measures and establishing a paper currency so as to reduce the dependence on metallic currency, were

TABLE 5.3: NET IMPORT OR EXPORT OF TREASURE INTO OR FROM THE 3 PORTS OF CALCUTTA, FORT ST. GEORGE AND BOMBAY, 1813/14-1833/4

Years	Company's Account				Private Account				Total Company and Private			
	Bengal Sicca Rs.	Madras Sicca Rs.	Bombay Sicca Rs.	Total Sicca Rs.	Bengal Sicca Rs.	Madras Sicca Rs.	Bombay Sicca Rs.	Total Sicca Rs.	Bengal Sicca Rs.	Madras Sicca Rs.	Bombay Sicca Rs.	Total Sicca Rs.
1813/14	–	*22,97,880*	–	*22,97,880*	54,41,288	2,28,117	*485636*	51,83,769	54,41,288	*20,69,763*	*4,85,636*	28,85,889
1814/15	–	*4,69,243*	39,216	*4,30,027*	95,31,819	4,28,891	11,78,005	1,11,38,715	95,31,819	*40,352*	12,17,221	1,07,08,688
1815/16	–	*161*	1,36,486	1,36,325	1,80,18,321	1,63,860	42,20,342	2,24,02,523	1,80,18,321	1,63,699	43,56,828	2,25,38,848
1816/17	76,99,554	*144*	–	76,99,410	3,16,82,985	8,73,203	55,53,943	3,81,10,131	3,93,82,539	8,73,059	55,53,943	4,58,09,541
1817/18	9,51,130	*88*	80,034	10,31,076	3,17,09,779	9,31,124	88,61,504	4,15,02,407	3,26,60,909	9,31,036	89,41,538	4,25,33,483
1818/19	19,76,657	*1,081*	–	19,75,576	4,69,12,956	17,13,002	1,46,32,391	6,32,58,349	4,88,89,613	17,11,921	1,46,32,391	6,52,33,925
1819/20	61,86,415	*2,543*	*2,26,974*	59,56,898	3,13,60,689	–	47,10,836	3,60,71,525	3,75,47,104	*2,543*	44,83,862	4,20,28,423
1820/1	12,17, 282	*2,366*	*2,17,698*	9,97,218	2,12,60,596	16,83,310	41,74,719	2,71,18,625	2,24,77,878	16,80,944	39,57,021	2,81,15,843
1821/2	*1,13,16,410*	*28,13,819*	*67,670*	*1,41,97,899*	2,03,74,551	16,20,825	32,51,805	2,52,47,181	90,58,141	*11,92,994*	31,84,135	1,10,49,282
1822/3	–	*2,510*	*28,46,239*	*28,48,749*	1,70,52,507	20,95,634	39,24,521	2,30,72,662	1,70,52,507	20,93,124	10,78,282	2,02,23,913
1823/4	*62,94,526*	*51,38,476*	*8,63,145*	*1,22,96,147*	1,17,24,118	*8,780*	41,62,614	1,58,77,952	54,29,592	*51,47,256*	32,99,469	35,81,805
1824/5	*9,27,221*	*17,82,029*	–	*27,09,250*	87,19,973	7,70,637	49,90,620	1,44,81,230	77,92,752	*10,11,392*	49,90,620	1,17,71,980
1825/6	1,57,968	*45,69,399*	–	*44,11,431*	1,01,13,299	9,02,214	92,88,098	2,03,03,611	1,02,71,267	*36,67,185*	92,88,098	1,58,92,180
1826/7	4,2,61,976	10,51,084	–	53,13,060	69,11,320	1,06,731	79,83,172	1,50,01,223	1,11,73,296	11,57,815	79,83,172	2,03,14,283
1827/8	*18,81,822*	*28,29,090*	–	*47,10,912*	1,15,40,417	7,45,850	1,06,25,615	2,29,11,882	96,58,595	*20,83,240*	1,06,25,615	1,82,00,970
1828/9	14,33,984	*2,81,373*	–	11,52,611	33,61,349	1,37,351	96,49,071	1,31,47,771	47,95,333	*1,44,022*	96,49,071	1,43,00,382
1829/30	7,92,747	*40,50,834*	–	*32,58,087*	73,77,185	*3,90,413*	78,16,069	1,48,02,841	81,69,932	*44,41,247*	78,16,069	1,15,44,754
1830/1	4,93,322	--	–	4,93,322	22,13,790	11,900	72,13,938	94,39,628	27,07,112	11,900	72,13,938	99,32,950
1831/2	*73,89,815*	*21,10,298*	–	*95,00,113*	*5,10,823*	*11,53,479*	46,73,352	30,09,050	*79,00,638*	*32,63,777*	46,73,352	*64,91,063*
1832/3	*12,82,940*	*2,40,964*	–	*15,23,904*	*13,79,512*	*15,10,079*	28,99,407	9,816	*26,62,452*	*17,51,043*	28,99,407	*15,14,088*
1833/4	*50,000*	–	–	*50,000*	32,59,255	*8,92,483*	99,45,416	*1,23,12,172*	32,09,255	*8,92,483*	99,45,416	1,22,62,188

Notes: 1. In this account, Madras and Bombay [Sicca rupees] are converted into Sicca rupees at the Bullion rate of 106.62 to 100.
2. The sums in italics denote the net export.

Source: NAI, Financial Department, Letters from Court, no. 8, dated 15 April 1835, paras 8-15; and no. 10, dated 5 July 1837, para 6.

TABLE 5.4: INDIA TRANSFER *VS.* BULLION EXPORT TO INDIA (IN £ '000)

Years	Total Years	Minimum India Transfers	Annual Average	Bullion Export to India	Annual Average	Bullion export to India as % of India Transfer	Nett India Transfers (C-E)
A	B	C	D	E	F	G	H
1772-5	3	420	140	18	6	4%	403
1776-83	7	507	72.42	8	1.14	1.57%	499
1784-92	8	1,112	139	98	12.25	8.8%	1,014
1793-1802	9	587	65.22	326	36.22	55.53%	261
1803-7	4	587	146.75	645	161.25	109.88%	-58
1808-15	7	480	68.57	3	0.42	0.62%	477
1816-20	4	300	75	377	94.25	125.66%	-77

Sources: Figures up to 1811: 'An Account of Bullion and Merchandise exported . . .', Parliamentary Papers (PP), 1812-13, VIII, MS, p. 416.
Figures since 1812 compiled and calculated from: 'Invoice Amounts' PP, 1830, XXVIII, MSS, pp. 80-1, and 'Totals of . . . Bullion exported . . .', IOLR, Accountant General's Records: Bullion, 3, vol. 1, MSS, pp. 69-70.
Quoted in: Esteban 2001: Table 1, 60-1.

being explored. One definite result of Steuart's recommendation—'all sources of further drain [from Bengal] should be stopped'—seems to be reflected in the minimum India transfer figures for the next seven years (1776-83) when the annual average dropped from £140,000 for 1772-5 to £72,420 during 1776-83. During the same set of years, bullion exports to India, too, dropped from an annual average of £6,000 to £1,140, which aggravated the currency crisis in Bengal. By 1780, plans to introduce a paper currency on the basis of a proportional cash reserve and to introduce a copper currency as well were already afoot in Bengal.

Between 1784 and 1792, the India transfers to Britain rose to an annual average of £1,39,000 and we see a revival of the almost dried-up stream of bullion inflow into India with the annual average rising from £1,140 during 1776-83 to £12,250 during 1784-92. The figures for 1793-1802 and 1803-7 show a quantum jump in Britain's bullion exports to India. The terminal years in the above two sets are important landmarks in the history of currency regulations in

India. In 1793, the process of currency legislation was started in Bengal by which the bimetallic currency regime that was introduced in 1792 was legally established in British India's most prosperous province. The intervening period saw the consolidation and spread of the 19-*sun* Sicca rupee and the Farrukhabad rupee in the Bengal Presidency, and that of the Company's Surat rupee in the Bombay Presidency. In fact, between 1803-7, India's net transfers to Britain recorded a negative figure with the total bullion exports to India (£6,45,000) exceeding the total India transfers (£5,87,000). Both these developments subsumed and were supported by the increased bullion inflow into India. Meanwhile, in 1806, the Court of Directors had laid down the roadmap for all future currency regulations in India by declaring silver monometallism as the ultimate goal for India's currency.

Between 1808 and 1815, the bullion export to India dropped to an all-time low, recording an annual average of £420! The reason for this drastic reduction can be found in the decisive phase of the Napoleonic War (1803-15) being fought in Europe, the expense for which stood at a staggering aggregate of £1,01,62,000.[241] England's total war expense during this period (1808-15) reached £1,62,37,000.[242] Once the war was over, bullion exports to India were resumed with greater vigour and we find that during 1816-20, the total bullion exports to India (£3,77,000) exceeded the total India transfers (£3,00,000) once again. However, this increased figure might actually have brought a lesser amount of bullion to India. This, as we shall see, was due to the establishment of a gold standard in Britain. By the Coinage Act of 1816, the gold coin became the sole standard measure of value in Britain. The silver content of the shilling was reduced. One pound troy of standard silver was, henceforth, to be coined into 66 shillings instead of 62.[243] According to Asiya Siddiqi, 'this altered ratio . . . affected the value of remittances from India to England . . . [and] helped to keep up the value of bullion in Britain and provided support to the English money market'.[244] As silver was fast replacing gold in India, it seems logical that the bullion imported into India after 1816 largely consisted of this metal.

Bullion continued to dominate the balance of payment accounts between India, Britain and China. Between 1828-9 and 1836-7, we notice a fluctuating movement in the inflow and outflow of bullion into India:

TABLE 5.5: NET EXPORT/IMPORT OF BULLION, 1828/9-1836/7 (IN MILLION RS.)

Years	Net Export (–)/Import (+)		
	Britain	China	Total
1828-9	–3.1	+10.8	+7.7
1829-30	–8.1	+13.7	+5.6
1830-1	–5.3	+9.6	+4.3
1831-2	–16.9	+5.6	–11.6
1832-3	–11.6	+5.9	–5.7
1833-4	–4.7	+13.1	+8.4
1834-5	–0.5	+12.1	+11.6
1835-6	–0.1	+12.1	+12
1836-7	–0.0	+12.3	+12.3

Source: OIOC, *Reports on the External Commerce of Bengal, Madras and Bombay, 1828-29 to 1839-40.* Quoted in Chaudhuri 1966: Table 4, 358.

It is clear from this table that India enjoyed a largely advantageous position in the bullion trade. Except for two consecutive years—1831-2 and 1832-3, the bullion trade was in India's favour. It is interesting to note that after the establishment of a universal coinage in 1835, India's export of bullion to Britain was greatly reduced and it recorded a nil account in 1836-7, while bullion imports from China continued which helped in the large-scale minting of the 1835 rupee.

Thus, a direct link can be seen between the bullion trade and currency measures undertaken by the East India Company in India, which, during a period of forty years—between 1793 and 1833—switched from bimetallism to silver monometallism, largely facilitated by the resumed bullion imports from 1784 onwards.

Barendse suggests that the 'impact of the import of bullion on the Indian economy should be viewed in a political context rather than one of price history or the growth in output'.[245] Though he makes this suggestion with reference to seventeenth-century India and, more specifically, to the bullion imported by the Dutch East India Company (VOC), the generalization made by him does provide a point of view. In arranging the finances required for various battles that resulted in the territorial expansion and political ascendancy of the East India Company, its capacity to support a large army on cash salaries and to move cash expeditiously from a surplus zone to the war zone proved to be one of the decisive factors in the outcome of many battles that were fought and won by it. There are other interlinked issues as well. Asiya Siddiqi cites the 'fruits of conquest and dominion: war indemnity and forced loans' as one of the sources of the Company's bullion supply.[246] In 1792, Tipu alone is said to have paid Rs. 1.30 crore worth of coins and bullion; in 1826, Bharatpur silver and, in the same year, Pegu gold 'flowed into the treasury following the annexation of the Jat state . . . and the war with Burma'.[247] The Company's policy of arm-twisting the Indian princely states to secure loans continued and, in 1826-7, it procured Rs. 1 crore from the Sindhia of Gwalior and Rs. 20 lakh from the ruler of Patiala.[248] Other measures such as the reduction of the allowance of the Nawab of Bengal from Rs. 32 to 16 lakh; withholding of the annual tribute of Rs. 36 lakh due to the Mughal king; and the sale of Kora and Allahabad to the Nawab of Awadh for Rs. 50 lakh definitely resulted from the currency crisis faced by the Company. Yet it would be difficult to agree with Barendse's proposition in its entirety as the availability or scarcity of currency did affect the price of commodities and the interest rates, and resulted in inflationary or deflationary trends in the market.

Finally, an idea about the international trade of India around the turn of the eighteenth century can also be formed from Table 5.2 of the Calcutta customs where the rates of exchange of coins of different countries *vis-à-vis* the sicca rupee were fixed.

Amales Tripathi cites 1793 and 1833 as the polar years during which Bengal's foreign trade, mainly with Britain, greatly improved.[249] Incidentally, both these years are also landmarks in the history of currency reforms in India—in the former year, the legislative process for currency reforms commenced in Bengal, while in the latter year, uniformity of the circulating media was established throughout the British territories in India.

CLOSURE OF MINTS AND ITS IMPACT ON THE SOCIETY

With the territorial expansion of the East India Company during the eighteenth and nineteenth centuries, many mints that were operating in these areas came under its control. In a sustained policy of centralizing its minting activities, the Company shut down a majority of these mints 'before the introduction of the uniform currency system in 1835'.[250] The closure of these mints affected the lives of

TABLE 5.6: RATES OF EXCHANGE FOR FOREIGN CURRENCIES FOR CALCUTTA CUSTOMS

Countries	Coins	Rate of Exchange	
		1796	1810
Great Britain	Pound Sterling	10 Sicca Rupees	10 Sicca Rupees
Germany	Crown	–	2 Sicca Rupees
Denmark	Rix Dollar	2¼ Sicca Rupees	at Sicca Rupees 1-10
Ceylon	Rix Dollar	–	14 *annas*
France	Livre Tournois	24 for 10 Sicca Rupees	at 24 for 10 Sicca Rupees
France	Mauritius Livre	48 for 10 Sicca Rupees	48 for 10 Sicca Rupees
Spain	Spanish Dollar	2¼ Sicca Rupees	2¼ Sicca Rupees
Portugal and Madeira	Milerea	2¾ Sicca Rupees	2¾ Sicca Rupees
Bussroh	Raize Peastre	–	12 *annas*
China	Tale	2⅓ Sicca Rupees	3⅓ Sicca Rupees
Madras	Star *Pagoda*	3¾ Sicca Rupees	3¾ Sicca Rupees
Madras	Swamy *Pagoda*	4 Sicca Rupees	4 Sicca Rupees
America	Currency to be converted into Pound Sterling as follows:		
New England		By multiplying by 3 and dividing by 4*	By multiplying by 9 and dividing by 16*
Virginia		… Ditto …	… Ditto …
New York		By multiplying by 9 and dividing by 16	By multiplying by 9 and dividing by 16
Pennsylvania		By multiplying by 3 and dividing by 5	By multiplying by 3 and dividing by 5
South Carolina		By deducting 1/27 part	By deducting 1/27 part
Georgia		… Ditto …	… Ditto …

Source: For rates of 1796: NAI, Separate Revenue Department, Letters to Court, 9 January 1797, para 26.
For rates of 1810: Regulation IX of 1810, Section LX.

Note: *'The Pound Sterling to be rated as above, at 10 Sicca Rupees. Where the invoices are in Dollars, the Dollars to be rated at 2¼ Sicca Rupees'.

people belonging to different strata of society—from merchants and traders to labourers and artisans. Thus, when the closure of the Surat mint was contemplated in the wake of the Court of Directors' despatch of 1806, Dr. H. Scott, the Assay Master of the Bombay mint, was quick to point out the fallouts of this measure. In his report to F. Warden, Secretary to the government of Bombay, dated 7 December 1806, Scott writes:

> One of the most material objections to the plan of a General Mint is the inconveniency that will arise to many classes of Men on this side of India, from the want of Mints in their neighbourhood. The natives from time immemorial have been accustomed with their Princes of every cast [*sic* caste] to the conveniency of mint in which they could convert their Silver or Gold into the ordinary Coin of the Country. . . . Holders of Bullion on this side of India, would have very real cause of Complaint from the Suppression of all our Mints. The fair Trader and even the Cultivator would find his trade injured and his profits diminished. Suppose for instance (as is the Case in a thousand situations) that they sell their goods or their Crops for Silver or Gold brought from the interior of India, from China or the Red Sea or Persian Gulph. This Silver and Gold is in Ingots or Dollars or in the form of foreign Coins. To render those Metals as much as possible productive to them they frequently turn them into the Coin of the Country. If they can no longer do this a part of their value is instantly lost. The metals can no longer answer the whole of the purposes on which their value depends. Loss and disappointment to a certain and even to a considerable extent must arise and a diminished degree of the general prosperity of the community must be the consequence.[251]

Native mints in the Bombay Presidency, the majority of which such as those at Poona, Bagalkot, Nasik and Shahpur were acquired by the Company after the Third Anglo-Maratha War (1817-18), and continued to operate under the Company's administration. However, by 1833, practically all of them were shut down leaving only the Presidency mint at Bombay to meet the demands of coined money in western India.[252]

In the Bengal Presidency, the Company acquired a large number of mints by virtue of the *Diwani* grant of 1765. Imperial Mughal mints such as those at Agra (Akbarabad) and Delhi (Shahjahanabad); provincial mints at Dacca (Jahangirnagar), Patna (Azimabad), Murshidabad as well as local mints at Allahabad, Bareilly, Hathras, Saharanpur, etc., were all successively shut down by the Company.[253] There were a few other native mints such as those at Farrukhabad and Benares, which were reorganized by the East India Company by mechanizing the minting process and authorizing an establishment usually headed by the Company's officials. However, mints of the later categories were also subsequently abolished[254] and, by 1833, when uniformity of the principal silver rupees of all the three presidencies was established by Regulation VII of 1833, the only mints operating in the Bengal Presidency were at Calcutta and at Saugor (established in 1825). Later, before the introduction of the universal silver rupee in 1835, the Saugor mint was also shut down in June 1835, thus leaving only the Calcutta mint in operation.

The closure of mints affected the merchant class directly and other classes, mostly the poor people, indirectly. Thus, when the mint at Dacca was closed down in 1796, the prominent bankers and merchants of Dacca petitioned the government for its re-establishment of the mint.[255] In their petition entitled, '*Derkhast* [petition] of all the Bankers, Merchants, Fotadars, and Shroffs inhabitants of and residing in the City of Dacca', they wrote:

> Lately, there was a Mint for the coinage of money established in the said city which is now stopped. . . . By stopping the coinage our Trade and Business in money, by which we supported and maintained ourselves, will be greatly injured. . . . Poor people in distress for Bread sold their gold and silver jewels to us to the amount of two or four Rupees and we immediately paid them in Sicca coin and these jewels when collected to a hundred or two hundred Rupees weight in twenty days or a month we delivered to the Mint and immediately received the amount in Sicca coin. By stopping the coinage the subsistence of us and of those poor people is stopped.[256]

The government, however, stuck to its decision and the petition was rejected.[257]

There were another class of people—the artisans and other workers of the mints—who were rendered jobless by the closures. When the closure of the Delhi mint was announced in 1818, many of its workers desperately sought relief both from the titular Mughal ruler and the British Resident at Delhi. In their *Urzee* (petition) to Akbar Shah II, Baqar Ali, Noor Muhammad and Dhaukal Singh of the Delhi mint wrote:

> From the time of His Majesty Ameer Tymoor, we have been generation after generation, nurtured the Office of the Mint, and from the same source, have celebrated the Acts of Festivity and of Grief and the mint of Shahgehanabad never ceased. . . . Our ancestors taught us no other Business besides the mint, to earn our livelihood. . . . Should the Business of the Mint be [re] established thro' Your Royal Favour, it will be well; it not, vouchsafe to order some provision for us from the presence.[258]

In a separate petition addressed to Sir David Ochterlony, the Resident at Delhi, the workers of the Delhi mint narrated their plight:

> It is now 5 months since the Mint has been stopped, and we have sold our property for Food—we are now arrived at the verge of starvation, our women and children are dying and reduced to the want of a Nightly Meal . . . if nothing is to be done, premature Death is inevitable.[259]

In the case of the Delhi mint, the government finally agreed to grant 'small pensions to such persons as having served for a long period, and having no other means of support, may now be prevented, by extreme old age and infirmity, from acquiring a maintenance by their own industry',[260] but mint workers in other parts of the country were not as fortunate.

In the Madras Presidency, apart from the Madras mint, the only mints that were operating towards the close of the eighteenth century were at Masulipatam and Visakhapatnam. Both these mints were closed in 1808 and 1809, respectively.

In his analysis of the effect of the closure of mints on the agricultural economy, Bayly noted that this also resulted in the fall of grain prices in north India:

> . . . between 1827 and 1832 grain prices had fallen in the Aligarh region compared with silver by not less than 30 per cent, while in Rohilkhand, the stoppage of the bullion trade as a result of the abolition of the Farrukhabad mint had dealt a revenue blow to the once thriving grain trade. Boulderson, the Collector of Bareilly, estimated that at least 8 per cent of the price fall had resulted from the abolition of the mints.[261]

Under normal circumstances, the fall in the prices of grain, a commodity of mass consumption, should have burnt a hole in the pockets of the big landholders and grain merchants by slashing their profit margins, and acted as a welcome reprieve for the labouring masses. The feedback received from the district officers also affirms that as a result of 'the abolition of western mints', a '. . . great fall in the money price of produce and commodities' had generally occurred.[262] But the fact remains that the *zamindars* increased their revenue collection from the small cultivators 'as high as 8½ per cent for the premium on the Government Coin'.[263] The price of silver appreciated up to 22 per cent and the combined effect of the premium on government coin and the high price of silver was passed on 'with most severity on those whose condition least qualified them to endure the burthen [*sic* burden]'.[264]

During this period, a general scarcity of legal coinage was felt in the western provinces. The exchange value of the government coinage against 'foreign coin or bullion' was 5 per cent above its bullion value in Agra and Farrukhabad, $6\frac{1}{4}$ per cent in Saharanpur; between 5 and 7 per cent in Moradabad; $8\frac{1}{2}$ per cent in Bareilly and the highest, 10 per cent in Aligarh.[265] But then, as the Sudder Board of Revenue at Allahabad reported, 'the foreign currency had superseded the use of the Government coin except in transactions with Government, and that at the time when the Government coin was in demand for the payment of land revenue there was a general scarcity throughout these provinces'.[266]

Bayly has also argued that the closure of the Farrukhabad mint (1824) and the Benares mint (1829) contributed to the 'lack of money' which precipitated the depression.[267] The supposed 'lack of money' in the first instance contrasts with the fact that though the mint at Farrukhabad was abolished, the minting of the 45-*sun* Farrukhabad rupee, which became the standard coin of all territories under the Government of Bengal under Regulation XI of 1819 (except in the provinces of Bengal, Bihar and Orissa), was not stopped. Rather, it was augmented with both the Calcutta and Benares mints undertaking its coinage. A year after the abolition of the Farrukhabad mint, a mint was opened in Saugor in 1825 to meet the demand for the Farrukhabad rupee. During its existence of nearly a decade (1825-35), the Saugor mint, had a coinage of the value of Sicca rupees 99,04,436[268] (Table 5.7).

The fact that out of the total output of the Saugor mint, the coinage on account of the Company was only 18.19 per cent while the rest was on the account of individuals shows that the new mint was productively used and that adequate supply of specie was maintained. In the second instance (abolition of the Benares mint), it may be seen that by August 1829, the construction of the new mint at Calcutta was completed. Its installed capacity was to 'enable it to supply two-thirds of the coin required for the circulation of India' and it was the intention of the Court of Directors that 'the new Calcutta mint would immediately or eventually have to perform the work of the Calcutta mint, and of the mints of Benares, Farrukhabad, and Sagar'.[269] Thus, when the abolition of the Benares

TABLE 5.7: COINAGE AT THE SAUGOR MINT (IN SICCA RUPEES)

Years	Company's Coinage	Individuals' Coinage	Duty
1825/6	1,14,089	11,450	1 per cent
1826/7	4,38,419	41,477	
1827/8	72,403	7,56,959	
1828/9	13,966	5,35,538	
1829/30	1,02,097	5,75,679	2 per cent
1830/1	4,85,069	4,43,859	
1831/2	2,95,923	5,06,948	
1832/3	1,51,960	10,46,784	
1833/4	91,716	20,36,610	
1834/5	36,548	21,46,982	
Total	18,02,180	81,02,256	
Company's Coinage		18,02,180	
Grand Total		99,04,436	

Source: NAI, Financial Department, Letters to Court, no. 10, 29 June 1836, para 4; Pridmore 1975: 224-5.

mint was finally effected (February 1830), all-out measures were taken to ensure the continuous and unrestrained supply of silver currency—the 45-*sun* Farrukhabad rupee—from the Calcutta mint, where it was being minted since 1818. Another factor which proved the futility of having a mint establishment at Benares was the induction of high-speed iron steamers in the river link between Calcutta, Benares and Allahabad, which 'could make the voyage in any reasonable time, say a month or five weeks to Allahabad or Farrukhabad'.[270] Therefore, a 'decided advantage' was in favour of 'the whole coinage being made at Calcutta'.[271]

The question, therefore, at this point, is whether the 'lack of money' was the lack of government coin, which resulted from the abolition of government mints, or was it a lack of specie in general. The evidence of a general fall in prices especially of food grains would indicate that despite extensive coinage in the Company's mints, as noted above, there was a lack of circulating medium. Coupled with a seasonal demand in payment to the government, this scarcity of coins would have led to an appreciation in the premium on government or the 'legal' coin in these provinces. This evidence also attests to the growth of the monetized economy and the increasing use of money in transactions.

SUMMING UP

The currency measures of the East India Company emanated primarily from its commercial interests. Initially, in order to finance its investments, the Company sought to monetize its bullion imports. Later, as revenue administrators in different parts of the country, it used currency as a tool for maximizing profits. For example, the continuance of the Sicca rupee even after 1833 when all other silver currencies were assimilated to a uniform weight and fineness cannot be explained without reference to the Permanent Settlement of land revenues in Bengal, whereby the government demands were fixed in this specie. Monetized revenues and cash salaries for the large and increasing civil and military establishment of the Company were the twin forces that propelled the growth of monetization of the economy during the period of our study.

The extraction of money by way of revenue and its redeployment through investments and remittances served the best economic interests of the Company. However, as this arrangement severely contracted the working capital in the Indian economy, there was a general depression in prices. As a result, a large mass of the Indian population that depended on agriculture suffered miserably under the Company's rule.

The pre-colonial economy of India was also supported by a thriving system of credit and banking, which augmented the capital without necessarily increasing the quantum of money. This area, too, was penetrated by the Company and, in the conflict of interests that ensued between the Indian and European systems of credit and banking management, the Indian credit system survived while the Indian banking system almost lost to its European rival.

The currency measures of the Company also resulted in a uniformity of weights, which, as we have seen, were based on the principal coin of the region. This, in turn, should have facilitated the internal trade of a large number of trade articles, especially agricultural products. However, a general scarcity or erratic supply of trading capital together with an overall deflationary trend in prices acted as recalcitrant factors and spelt doom both for Indian agriculture and the rural markets.

India's external trade in bullion played a very vital role during this period and even before the legislative process of currency reforms was set in motion, the once-dried-up channel of bullion inflow into India was revived not because of the East India Company but in spite of it. Here, as we have noted, private traders, both in India and

Europe, played an important role in replenishing the bullion coffers of India.

Finally, the Company's policy to abolish a large number of mints throughout India was aimed at monopolizing the currency supply—the life-blood of a monetized economy. With this measure, it consolidated its hold over variegated economic activities.

It is said that the currency of a country not only reflects but also influences the economic life of its people.[272] The currency regulations of the East India Company influenced almost every aspect of India's colonial economy. On the basis of our discussion, it may be argued that the impact of currency reforms on various aspects of the economic life of Indian society was both short-term and permanent. The disruption or decline of trade due to the want of trading capital or the dislocation of rural industries due to the erratic supply of money could be viewed as direct impacts, whereas the rise of European banking and the decline of indigenous banking houses; the establishment of a new public debt system and the acceleration of the drain of India's capital resources; or the extension of monetization levels in society especially when the limits of the induction of a metallic currency were realized and the introduction of a fiduciary currency was planned can be seen as factors which had a more permanent and lasting impact.

Besides, these impacts also varied in intensity—from negligible to moderate and from extreme to devastating. Thus, the whole picture during this period presents a 'patch-work quilt' of regional money economies in various stages of transition rather than a 'wall-to-wall carpet' of a uniform and standard pattern for the whole of India. The turning point was the universalization of the Company's coinage in 1835 which laid the foundation of future currency administration in India.

NOTES

1. Rothermund 1970: 91.
2. Marshall 2003: 14.
3. Perlin 2003: 57.
4. Ambedkar 1947: 28.
5. Ibid.
6. Ibid.
7. Ibid.
8. Garg 2007: 249-51.

9. Ibid.: 252-3.
10. Pridmore 1975: 204.
11. NAI, Public, Letters to Court, 10 December 1784, para 69.
12. Ibid.
13. Pridmore 1975: 210.
14. Ibid.
15. NAI, Financial Department, Mint Committee, Proceedings dated 10 May 1804, no. 2.
16. Ibid.: paras 2 and 3.
17. Barendse 2002: 228.
18. Torri 1991: 376.
19. Perlin 1983: 27.
20. Ibid.: 31.
21. Ibid.
22. Deyell 1976; Haider 1999; Hasan 1968, 1969 and 1970; Moosvi 1987; and Om Prakash and Krishnamurty 1970.
23. See Appendix 4: Mintability: Imported metal, Mint Productivity and Circulating Coins; Perlin 1987: 342-66.
24. NAI, Public, Letters to Court, 3 September 1792, para 122.
25. Stagg 1930: 18.
26. Perlin 1987: Tables 4.1.2 and 4.1.4, 352, 355.
27. NAI, Public, Letters from Court, 25 May 1798, para 25.
28. NAI, Financial Department, Mint Proceedings, 19 February 1796, no. 1.
29. James Miller, Mint Master, Calcutta to Sir John Shore, Governor-General of Bengal; ibid.: 24 June 1796, no. 1.
30. Perlin 2003: 57.
31. Chaudhuri 1968b: 47.
32. Datta 2000: 350.
33. *FWIHC*, VI 1962: xxv.
34. NAI, Public, Letters to Court, 21 November 1768, para 14.
35. Ibid.: 25 September 1769, para 32.
36. NAI, Public, Letters from Court, 30 March 1774, para 47.
37. 100 newly-minted Murshidabad Sicca rupees were equivalent to 116 Current Rupees (a money of account); after one year's circulation, their value came down to 113; in the third year of circulation and thereafter, their value was 111; *FWIHC*, VI 1960: 485; See also NAI, Public, Letters from Court, 30 March 1774, para 99.
38. NAI, Public, Letters from Court, 30 March 1774, para 48.
39. NAI, Public, Letters to Court, 20 November 1775, para 37.
40. Sinha 1965: 129-56.
41. Ibid.: 28 August 1795, para 29.
42. Datta 2000: 360, App. 2, Fig. 21.
43. Gupta and Ramachandran 1973: 84.

44. Sarada Raju 1941: 240.
45. Habib 1975: 26.
46. Sinha 1954: 25.
47. Chaudhury 1988: 75-6.
48. Ibid.: 75.
49. Ibid.
50. Ibid: 27. To facilitate the Company's investments in 1774, a Board of Trade was constituted in Calcutta but corruption soon gripped the system of procuring investments through European and Indian contractors and, as a result, 'a steady decline in both the quality and quantity of homeward cargoes' was noticed; *FWIHC*, X 1972: 6.
51. Mitra 1991: 171.
52. Sinha 1927: i.
53. NAI, Public, Letters to Court, 28 March 1768, para 55.
54. Ibid.: 25 September 1769, para 38.
55. WBSA, Proceedings of the Board of Trade, 4 July 1777, no. 45, quoted by Mitra 1991: 171.
56. NAI, Public, Letters to Court, 21 November 1777, para 12.
57. NAI, Public, Letters from Court, 23 December 1778, para 147.
58. Ibid.
59. WBSA, Proceedings of the Board of Trade, 28 December 1784, no. 60, quoted by Mitra 1991: 173.
60. *FWIHC*, X 1972: 8.
61. NAI, Public, Letters to Court, 11 January 1781.
62. Ibid.: 28 August 1795, para 29.
63. Ibid.
64. Ibid.
65. NAI, Public, Letters to Court, 2 November 1795, para 106.
66. NAI, Public, Letters from Court, 25 May 1798, para 25.
67. WBSA, Board of Trade, Proceedings, vol. 196, dated 29 April 1806, no. 23, quoted in Mitra 1991: 179.
68. Fisher 1911: Chapter VIII—Influence of Quantity of Money and Other Factors on Purchasing Power and on Each Other. For an interpretation of the 'Fisher equation', see Haider 1999: 318-19. See also Habib in Raychaudhuri and Habib 1982: Chapter XII—The Monetary System and Prices, 365-6.
69. Fisher 1911: Chapter VIII.
70. Habib 1987: 36.
71. For prices of certain agricultural products in Bengal during 1740-65, see Datta 1931.
72. Mitra 1991: 220.
73. Ibid.
74. Ibid.

75. Kumar 1983: Appendix 5.2: Famines in the Indian subcontinent during 1750-1947, 528-9.
76. Mitra 1991: Table 1—the price of rice at the several Residencies from 1792-3 to 1822-3, per maund of 80 sicca weight, 222-3.
77. Ibid.: 224.
78. Ibid.
79. *Asiatic Researches*, vol. 12 (1818): 567-8.
80. Sarada Raju 1941.
81. Ibid.: Table—Prices in Rupees per Madras Garce, 228-9, Graph, 230; 232.
82. Ibid.: 233.
83. Ibid.: 234.
84. Ibid.: 234-5.
85. Ibid.: 235.
86. Board of Trade, General Report, vol. 18, 163, quoted in ibid.: 237.
87. Ibid.: vols. 46-9, 156, quoted in Sarada Raju 1941: 237.
88. The original work containing these prices was a paper by the Rev. Robert Everest ('On the Famines that have devastated India and the probability of their being periodical', *Journal of the Statistical Society of London*, vol. 6 (1843), 246-8). This list of the prices of wheat (*ser* per rupee) was reworked by the famous British economist, Professor W. Stanley Jevons, who, in 1878, calculated it per rupees per 1,000 *sers*. The full table and Prof. Jevon's letter has been reproduced in Roy 1972.
89. Roy 1972: 92.
90. Garg 1992.
91. Habib 1987: 38.
92. Sarada Raju 1941: 340.
93. Ibid.: 341.
94. Habib 1987: 38.
95. Datta 2000: 350.
96. Ibid.: 348-50.
97. Om Prakash 2002: 11.
98. Datta 2000: 248.
99. Fort William Consultations, dated 17 June 1769, quoted in Verelst 1772: 245.
100. Verelst 1772: 245.
101. Sinha 1927: 113-14, fn 8.
102. Pridmore 1975: 225.
103. NAI, Public, Letters from Court, 20 November 1767, para 125.
104. Ibid.: 194.
105. Ibid.: 226.
106. Datta 2000: 350; Om Prakash 2002: 11.
107. Datta 2000: 350.

108. Haider 2002: 58.
109. Mirza 1956; Habib 1972; Haider 2002.
110. Haider 2002: 67.
111. Cooke 1863: 82-3.
112. Subramanian 1985, 1987 and 1991; Torri 1987 and 1991.
113. Subramanian 1985: 214.
114. Temple 1883: 301.
115. *FWIHC*, XI 1974: 18.
116. Ibid.
117. Om Prakash 2000: 11.
118. NAI, Public, Letters from Court, 23 December 1774, para 30.
119. NAI, Public, Letters to Court, 3 July 1786, para 11.
120. Ibid.: 22 December 1788.
121. NAI, Public, Letters from Court, 15 December 1790, para 51.
122. Ibid.: 4 August 1791, para 76.
123. NAI, Foreign Depratment, Persian Branch, OR no. 228, dated July 1795.
124. NAI, Public, Letters from Court, 8 February 1792, para 10.
125. Subramanian 1987: 490.
126. Ibid.
127. NAI, Public, Letters to Court, 5 April 1783, para 87.
128. Ibid.: 12 August 1793, para 118.
129. Tandon 1989: 50; see also Haider 2002: 59.
130. Moosvi 1999: 75.
131. Markovits 2000: 13.
132. Bayly 1983: 299.
133. Steuart 1772: 73.
134. Mitra 1991: 100.
135. Garg 1990: 383.
136. Ibid.: 384
137. Mitra 1991: 101.
138. IOL, Orme Mss., vol. I, f. 1455: quoted by Chaudhury 1988: 91.
139. Chaudhuri 1978: 188.
140. Chaudhury 1988: 93.
141. Little 1967: 43.
142. Little 1967: 43-4.
143. IOL, Orme Mss., vol. VI, f. 1525, quoted by Chaudhury 1988: 91.
144. Bengal Consultations, dated 11 January 1750, quoted in Little 1967: 150.
145. Garg 1990.
146. Luke Scrafton, Political Resident at Murshidabad, to Clive, dated 17 December 1757. IOL, Orme Mss., vol. XVIII, f. 5043: quoted by Chaudhury 1988: 93 and 96.
147. Little 1967: 151.

148. N.K. Sinha in Little 1967: Introduction, xv.
149. Mitra 1991: 104.
150. Little 1967: 203.
151. NAI, Public Department, OC, 1 May 1789, no. 9.
152. N.K. Sinha in Little 1967: Introduction, xiv.
153. Chakrabarti 1997: 70.
154. Chatterjee 1993.
155. Chakrabarty 1997: 70.
156. Ray 2002: 118.
157. Raman Rao 1958: 97.
158. Tandon 1989: 53.
159. Ibid.: 59
160. Ramachandran and Gupta 1971: 34.
161. Ibid.
162. Mehta 1991: 22.
163. Torri 1991: 371.
164. Ibid.
165. For a discussion on the role of the *sarrafs* in minting activities during the Mughal rule, see Haider 1996: 326-35.
166. Haider 1996: 327-8, fn. 125; see also Gokhale 1973: 24.
167. Subramanian 1991: 337.
168. NAI, Home, Public Proceedings, 29 January 1807, no. 16 (encl.), para 11.
169. Ibid.
170. Under the Treaty of Salbai (1782), Broach was made over to the Sindhias by the East India Company. It came under the control of the Company once again by virtue of the Treaty of Bassein (1803). See Stevens 2004d: 27.
171. The British occupied Jambusir from 1775 to 1783; ibid.
172. Wiggins 1996: 329-35.
173. NAI, Public, Letters to Court, 25 September 1769, para 96.
174. NAI, Public, Letters from Court, 28 April 1790.
175. Ibid.
176. Subramanian 1987: 473.
177. Bagchi 1987: 26.
178. Tandon 1989: 66.
179. Quoted by Rau 1929: 18-19.
180. NAI, Public, Letters from Court, 27 March 1787, para 314.
181. Bagchi 1987: 36.
182. Gupta 2000: 21-46.
183. Bagchi 1987: 36.
184. Ibid.
185. Ibid.: 37.
186. Bagchi 1987: Table 3.1, 34-5.

187. Gupta 2000: 22.
188. Bagchi 1987: 37.
189. Gupta 2000: 47.
190. Bagchi 1987: 47.
191. Gupta 2000: 18.
192. Bagchi 1987: 62.
193. Ibid.
194. Gupta 2000: 14.
195. Bagchi 1987: 66.
196. Ibid.: 67.
197. Gupta 2000: 14.
198. 'An Act for the better Government of the Settlements of Fort St. George and Bombay, for the Regulation of Public Banks, and for amending so much of an Act passed in the Thirty-third Year of His Present Majesty, as relates to the periods at which the Civil Servants of the East India Company may be employed in their Services abroad'.
199. Gupta 2000: 14.
200. Bagchi 1989: 89.
201. Gupta 2000: 14.
202. Bagchi 1989: 103.
203. Ibid.: 108.
204. Ambedkar 1947: 1.
205. The double coincidence is the situation where the supplier of good A wants good B and the supplier of good B wants good A. The phrase 'double coincidence of wants' was used by William Stanley Jevons: 'The first difficulty in barter is to find two persons whose disposable possessions mutually suit each other's wants. There may be many people wanting, and many possessing those things wanted; but to allow of an act of barter there must be a double coincidence, which will rarely happen.' See Jevons 1875: Chapter I: Barter.
206. Ambedkar 1947: 8.
207. Ghoshal 1950: 179.
208. Ibid.: 180.
209. Ibid.
210. Ibid.: 180-1.
211. Wink 1986: 332.
212. Ibid.: 185.
213. See 'Table of the Commercial weights of India, and of other trading places in Asia, compared with the British-Indian Unit of weight, and with the Avoirdupois system of England' in Prinsep 1858: 115-21.
214. Ibid.
215. Milburn 1825: 143.
216. Derived from Sanskrit *Khaṇḍi*, 'to divide'. Also *Khaṇḍi* in Telugu and *Kaṇḍi* in Tamil and Malayalam; Yule and Burnell 1886: 155.

217. The number of *man* per candy also varied—'... nor is candy [weight in Bombay] uniformly confined to 20 maunds'. See Milburn 1825: 143.
218. Derived from Sanskrit *bhāra*, 'a load'. Also *bhāram* in Malayalam; Yule and Burnell 1886: 47-8.
219. Ibid.: 48.
220. Subrahmanyam 1990: 371.
221. Philip Francis's Minute on Weights and Measures, dated 13 March 1775. NAI, Public Department, OC, 13 March 1775, no. 19.
222. Wink 1986: 332.
223. Siddiqi 1995: 1.
224. Ibid.: 4.
225. K.N. Chaudhuri in Kumar 1983: 813.
226. Ibid.: 806.
227. Chaudhuri 1966: 345.
228. Esteban 2001: 65.
229. Ibid.
230. Siddiqi 1995: 18.
231. Barendse 2002: 214.
232. Chaudhuri 1978: 189.
233. Ninth Report from Select Committee Appointed to Take into Consideration the State of Administration and Justice in Bengal, Bahar and Orissa. 25 June 1783. OIOC, L/Parl/2/15.
234. Sinha 1938: 8-9.
235. *FWIHC*, XII 1978: 6-7.
236. NAI, Public Letters to Court, 12 August 1793, paras 126-7.
237. K.N. Chaudhuri in Kumar 1983: 823.
238. Datta 2000: Table 66, 346.
239. NAI, Financial Department, Letters from Court, no. 8, dated 15 April 1835, paras 8-15; and no. 10, dated 5 July 1837, para 6.
240. Chaudhuri 1971: 1.
241. Esteban 2001: Table 1, 60.
242. Ibid.
243. Siddiqi 1981: 237.
244. Ibid.
245. Barendse 2002: 228.
246. Siddiqi 1995: 19.
247. Ibid.: 19-20.
248. NAI, Territorial Finance Department, Letters to Court, 19 July 1827, para 20.
249. Tripathi 1979: 208.
250. Pridmore 1975: ix.
251. NAI, Home, Public Proceedings, 29 January 1807, no. 16 (encl), paras 25-7.

252. Wiggins 1996: 328-34; Stevens 2004a: 28-32; Stevens 2004c: 24-9; Stevens 2004d: 25-32.
253. Wiggins 1996: 335-44; Stevens 2006: 18-23; Garg 1992: 233-40.
254. Stevens 2006b: 37-43.
255. NAI, Financial Department, Mint Proceedings, 28 April 1797, no. 4.
256. Ibid.
257. 'Ordered that the Judge [W. Camac, Judge and Magistrate of the City of Dacca] be informed that the Vice President in Council does not think proper to comply with the application of the Bankers respecting the re-establishment of the Mint.' See ibid.
258. NAI, Foreign Department, Political Branch, OC, 13 March 1819, no. 37.
259. Ibid.
260. C.T. Metcalfe, Secretary to the Government, to Sir David Ochterlony, Resident at Delhi, dated 13 March 1819; ibid.: no. 38.
261. Bayly 1983: 271. See also NAI, Finance Department, Letters to Court, 27 January 1834, para 64.
262. NAI, Finance Department, Letters to Court, 27 January 1834, paras 59 and 60.1.
263. Ibid.: para 78.
264. Ibid.: para 68.
265. Ibid.: para 60.2.
266. Ibid.: para 76.
267. Bayly 1983: 274.
268. Apart from the coinage of the silver rupee (45-*sun* Sicca), the Saugor mint also undertook the minting of the *trishuli pice* (45-*sun pice*) between 1826 and 1835.
269. Thurston 1893: 78.
270. NAI, Finance Department, Letters to Court, 27 January 1834, para 94.
271. Ibid.
272. Ghoshal 1950: 271.

CHAPTER 6

Conclusion

Currency played a vital role in the colonization of India by the British. For a trading company that was always in need of liquid cash for the procurement of goods and other commercial activities in India, control of the channels of money supply was crucial for its successful career. At the same time, this was a subject that was linked with a number of internal and external factors. For example, the inflow and outflow of bullion through international trade directly resulted in the expansion and contraction of money supply, which, in turn, led to inflationary or deflationary price trends affecting the entire society. The Company's capacity to pay cash salaries to its troops contributed to the success of its military expeditions against a number of Indian powers, which resulted in large territorial acquisitions that formed the nucleus of its colonial empire. Its revenue collection from a large part of the country financed its investments in India and opened up a regular stream of the drain of wealth from the country. Once again, the Company's capacity to realize this revenue in cash was determined by the state of the currency in these regions. It was through its control over currency that the Company entered India's larger money market, which, during the pre-colonial regime, had supported a thriving economy through its remarkable credit and banking networks. These networks suffered a severe blow through the Company's sustained policy of supplanting them with institutions fashioned on the European model.

Thus, currency was one of the most potent tools in the hands of the colonizers for effecting the economic subjugation of the country. The process of the standardization and consolidation of the circulating medium and the upgradation and modernization of the minting process was aimed at facilitating a variety of the Company's activities ranging from revenue collection, war financing and trade to remittances to other presidencies and its overseas establishments such as China, Manila, Fort Marlborough, Bancoolen, etc., as well as to England on account of home charges.

The drain of India's wealth by the Company, coupled with the utilization of revenues for investments without augmenting the quantum of circulating media, resulted in a serious financial crisis for the Company, which had reached the verge of bankruptcy in 1772. Currency reforms in India became imperative and an agenda was laid down in Sir James Steuart's treatise on the currency of Bengal.

Britain's economic dominion in the east and her political power was built upon the foundations of Indian land revenues. Due to the monetization of land revenue, the currency reforms became inevitable. Therefore, it was natural that these reforms originated in the Bengal Presidency where the Company had secured the revenue collection rights in 1765. From then on, Bengal became the central piece of both the tributary and the commercial empire of the Company, with a ripple effect on the other two presidencies. This was due to the vantage position of Bengal established through legislations of Parliament starting with the Regulating Act (1773).

The reforms also reflected the impact of contemporary economic opinion in England, which was opposed to bimetallism at that time. Thus, by 1806, a clear case in favour of silver monometallism was laid down which guided the future course of currency reforms in India.

Our study makes it clear that the currency measures adopted by the East India Company were part of a larger policy adopted by the British empire with regard to India right from the Parliament's first direct intervention in the affairs of the Company through the Regulating Act, 1773. It is, therefore, no coincidence that the results of the first enquiry into the ailing currency system of Bengal that was commissioned by the Court of Directors in 1772, were sent for implementation only after the Regulating Act came into operation in 1774. As a result of this Act, the supremacy of the Bengal Presidency over the two others in India was established and it is not surprising that from this point onwards, all currency reforms were centred in Bengal and emulated by the presidencies of Madras and Bombay. Similarly, when the Charter Act of 1793 confirmed and consolidated the supremacy of the Bengal Presidency, the process of currency reforms through legislative enactments was instituted as part of the 'Cornwallis Code'.

The imperial system of administration of India dates from 1833. The Charter Act of 1833 created a central government in Bengal and empowered the Governor-General to make laws and regulations for India without seeking the prior approval of the British Parliament. The imperial government needed an imperial currency, not just as an assertion of its sovereign status but also as a facilitator of imperial finances. Our study reveals that from this point onwards, the objective of the currency policy of the East India Company was not merely to create a uniform currency for its territorial possessions under the presidencies of Bengal, Madras and Bombay, but to establish a *common* currency—a universal coinage—for its entire Indian empire. These twin objectives were pursued by the Company with remarkable rapidity and, by the end of 1835, a monetary union was established in British India.

The monetary integration of British India, affected in 1835, was probably the earliest attempt by a colonial power to establish a monetary union in its colonies. The abolition of the minting rights of a number of Indian princely states and the extension of the British rupee into their territories was done simultaneously in later years. The colonial government even proposed to undertake the minting of the coins of the princely states in the government mints if they chose to close down their own.[1] The Native Coinage Act, 1876, sought to give a definite form to this monetary union by ensuring that coins circulating in the princely states followed the weight and fineness standards of the British Rupee. The universalization of coinage in 1835, therefore, laid the foundation of a gradual but sustained unification of currencies in India. A question that becomes quite obvious in this context is how far the Company's institution of an imperial currency in its possessions in India abetted the expansion of colonial rule in subsequent years. The British territorial expansion during the post-1835 period saw the simultaneous introduction of the Company's Rupee (which superseded local currencies) in the newly-acquired territories. With the supply of this coin firmly secured in its hands, the Company was able to dominate regional economies. Everywhere the Sicca followed the Flag.

Finally, this work also aims at underlining the importance of integrating numismatic researches into the study of economic history. At the same time, it raises a number of related questions which though outside the scope of the present study, await serious probe by researchers. Thus, how did changing patterns of money supply and credit practices affect wages and employment in different parts of India over a period of time; or how did the establishment of a monetary union by the East India Company in India influence currency administration in the other colonies of the British empire; or, further still, how did India sustain a silver monometallic currency during the post-1835 period of colonial rule when most of the Western world followed a gold standard? These and many other questions that emanate from the present work have the potential of being researched independently for a still more comprehensive understanding of the economic history of colonial India.

NOTE

1. Garg 1998.

CHAPTER 7

Epilogue

By Act XVII of 1835, a silver rupee of uniform weight, size, fineness and appearance called the 'Company's Rupee' (CR) was established in the Indian territories of the East India Company. On 10 February 1836, orders were issued by the Governor-General, Charles Metcalfe that all government accounts in the different presidencies should be kept in the Company's Rupee.

However, the enactment of Act XVII of 1835 that introduced a universal silver rupee for all of the East India Company's Indian territories did not bear the stamp of approval of the Court of Directors. The Court apprehended that the prevailing confusion due to the existence of multiple species of coins in India would worsen by the addition of another and entirely new currency.[1] The Court of Directors was more appalled by the fact that a 'change so extensive and important' was determined upon merely in anticipation of their approval and without waiting for their formal orders. The Directors, nevertheless, grudgingly granted their *ex-post facto* approval to the enactments of Act XVII and Act XXI of 1835. Their reluctance in granting approval is reflected in a letter dated 27 July 1836:

> We are aware of the inconvenience and confusion which would now result from the abandonment or suspension of the ***plan you have thus prematurely and unadvisedly determined to adopt***. We shall not, therefore, at present direct any departure from it, though we cannot but entertain the apprehension that the course you have pursued . . . may yet involve your Government in very serious embarrassment, while the alteration of the currency in which your accounts are stated will unquestionably occasion great inconvenience and confusion. (emphasis added)[2]

In his reply, Lord George Eden Auckland (1836-42), who had, in the meantime, succeeded Sir Charles Metcalfe (1835-6) as the Governor-General of India, allayed the fears and apprehensions of the Court of Directors. On 8 February 1837, he wrote:

4th. Your Honorable Court has not expressed doubts as to the importance of the object of the benefits expected from it nor do we find that you attach blame to the specific measures adopted by us for its accomplishment. Your animadversion is directed mainly against your Government for having determined upon effecting so important a change in opposition to the instructions contained in a despatch from your Honorable Court dated 11 Mar 1829 which forbade the Government to proceed in the matter without previous communication with you. . . .

7th. The necessity of acting in contravention of your expressed wishes although thus of old date and founded on views which your Government had reason to believe you could not still entertain was doubtless the least defensible part of the proceedings adopted on this occasion, and your Government felt that in determining not to delay the measure longer for the expected result of that prohibition they were incurring a heavy responsibility. But your Honorable Court's prohibition rested on doubts as to the success of any attempt to make the desired reform, and on a view of difficulties in the execution, all which your Government having a nearer view of circumstances felt to be without foundation. In the assurance therefore of certain and complete success of the measures they were about to undertake your Government relied upon the present to justify them for hazarding your displeasure.[3]

The Court also did not approve of the government of India's action of issuing a new copper coinage from the Calcutta mint under Act XXI of 1835, especially at a time when copper coinage was witnessing a great depreciation in the Calcutta *bazaar* owing to its excessive supply. In a strongly-worded letter addressed to the Governor-General of India, the Court noted that, 'in the three-year ending with 1832/33, Coins to the value of 12,38,508 Rupees and amounting in number to more than 87 millions of pieces were worked up at the Presidency and for the most part put in circulation'.[4] It regretted that 'the serious inconveniences were not foreseen and duly appreciated' by the government before they pushed a fresh supply of copper coinage into circulation.[5]

The gold *muhr*, although it lost its legal tender status in 1835, remained in high demand. In 1837, we find Anand Mohan Seal, a bullion merchant of Calcutta, offering to pay a premium of 5 to 8 per cent on the purchase of 'New Company's Muhrs' from the Calcutta mint.[6]

However, as later events showed, the universalization of currency was a *fait accompli* and, the Court's remonstration notwithstanding, there was no going back on that issue.

The deathknell for the old Calcutta Sicca rupee was sounded by Act XIII of 1836 which declared that after 1 January 1838, it would cease to be legal tender but would be received at public treasuries by weight, subject to a charge of one *pie* for recoinage. However, various old specie of rupees remained in circulation for quite some time. For example, in 1847, J. Thornton, Secretary to the government of the North-Western Province, gleefully reported to the government of India that 'the new Company's Rupee has superseded the old currencies throughout almost the whole of these Provinces, and the inconveniences . . . [arising] out of the state of the circulating medium have entirely disappeared'.[7] But later, by a first-hand experience, the Lieutenant-Governor of the North-Western Provinces found that in Rohilkhand, the Farrukhabad Rupee was 'still extensively in circulation throughout the parts of that district which are farthest removed from the River Ganges'.[8]

Within two years of their issue, the new gold and silver coins bearing the image of King William IV came in for a change with the accession of Queen Victoria in 1837. The problems involved in the change of device and the issuing of new coins led to the passing of Act XXXI of 1837, which suspended those parts of Act XVII of 1835 that referred to the issue of coins bearing 'the head and the name of the *reigning* sovereign of the United Kingdom of Great Britain and Ireland'. It was not until 1840 that rupees bearing the head of Queen Victoria were ushered from Indian mints.

The universalization of copper coins was also eventually established by Act XXII of 1844 by which the provisions of Act XXI of 1835 were extended to 'all the territories of the East India Company'.

The legacy of universal coinage established by the East India Company continued even after the transfer of its powers and property to the Crown of England by an Act of Parliament passed on 2 August 1858. From 1 November 1858, when the assumption of the government of India by Queen Victoria was formally announced in India by a royal proclamation, until 30 October 1862, coins issued from the three mints at Bombay, Calcutta and Madras continued to bear the designs and titles of the East India Company. On 23 April 1862, the British government of India enacted Act XIII of 1862—'An Act to provide for a new silver and a new copper coinage'. Under its provisions, new silver and copper coins were issued from the British mints in India from 1 November 1862 and a new era of imperial coinage finally began.

NOTES

1. Dayal Das 1958: 70.
2. NAI, Finance General, Letters from Court, no. 9, 27 July 1836, para 4.
3. NAI, Finance General, Letters to Court, no. 6, 8 February 1837, paras 4 and 7.
4. NAI, Finance General, Letters from Court, no. 13, 12 October 1836, para 4.
5. Ibid.: para 10.
6. NAI, Financial Department, Mint Committee, Proceedings dated 19 April 1837, no. 17 and 22 April 1837, no. 19.
7. J. Thornton to J.A. Dorin, Secretary to the Government of India, Financial Department, dated 25 November 1847, Agra, para 2. *Selections from the Records of the Government, North-Western Provinces: Mr. Thompson's Despatches*, vol. 1, 342.
8. Ibid.: dated 18 March 1848, para 3, in *Selections*, op. cit.: 348.

APPENDICES

NOTE ON APPENDICES

The first part of the appendices includes the full texts of various currency legislations passed by the presidencies of Bengal, Madras and Bombay, between 1793 and 1835. For other legislations that have a bearing on the currency measures, only the relevant extracts have been provided.

The second part of the appendices includes details of the weight system used in the sources consulted for this work.

List of Appendices

I. REGULATIONS/ACTS (1793-1835)

I. REGULATIONS/ACTS (1793-1835)

A. Bengal Regulations

Appendix A.1

A.D. 1793 REGULATION III

A REGULATION for extending and defining the jurisdiction of the Courts of Dewanny Adawlut, or Court of Civil Judicature for the trial of Civil Suits in the first instance, established in the several Zillahs, and in the cities of Patna, Dacca, and Moorshedabad.—PASSED by the Governor-General-in-Council on the 1st of May, 1793, corresponding with the 21st Bysaak 1200 Bengal era; the 6th Bysaak 1200 Fussily; the 21st Bysaak 1200 Willaity; the 6th Bysaak 1850 Sumbut and; the 19th Ramzan 1207 Higeree.

xx xx xx xx	
X. Collectors of Revenue, and their Assistants and Native Officers, Commercial Residents and Agents and their Assistants and Native Officers employed in the provision of the Investment, Salt Agents and their Assistants and Native Officers concerned in the Manufacture of Salt, the Collectors of the Customs and their Assistants and Native Officers employed in the collection of customs, the Mint and Assay Masters and their Assistants and Native Officers, are declared amenable to the Zillah or City Court in the jurisdiction of which they may reside or carry on the public business committed to their charge for any acts done in their official capacity in opposition to any Regulation printed and published in the manner directed in Regulation XLI, 1793.	Collectors of Revenue and Custom, Commercial Residents, Salt Agents, Mint and Assay Masters and their respective officers, amenable to the Courts for acts done in their official capacity.
xx xx xx xx	

Appendix A.2

A.D. 1793 REGULATION VIII

A REGULATION for re-enacting with modifications and amendments, the Rules for the Decennial Settlement of the Public Revenue payable from the Lands of the Zemindars, Independent Talookdars, and other Actual Proprietors of Land in Bengal, Behar and Orissa, passed for those Provinces respectively on the 18th September 1789, the 25th November 1789, and the 10th February 1790, and subsequent dates.—PASSED by the Governor-General-in-Council on the 1st of May, 1793, corresponding with the 21st Bysaak 1200 Bengal era; the 6th Bysaak 1200 Fussily; the 21st Bysaak 1200 Willaity; the 6th Bysaak 1850 Sumbut and; the 19th Ramzan 1207 Higeree.

	xx xx xx xx
All engagements for the *jumma* to be for *Sicca* Rupees subject for the present to a provisionary clause.	XLII. All engagements for the *jumma* whether executed by proprietors or farmers are to be for *sicca* rupees, and a clause is to be inserted, obliging them to pay Government *siccas*, or the same specie of rupees as they may receive from their under farmers or *ryots*, at the *bazar* rates of *batta*, until a sufficient number of sicca rupees can be circulated to make these the only legal tender. The collectors are to insert in their treasury accounts the rates of *batta* at which all rupees, not *siccas*, may be received by them.
	xx xx xx xx

Appendix A.3

A.D. 1793 REGULATION XXXV

A REGULATION for re-enacting with amendments, the Rules passed on the 20th October, and 31st November 1792, and subsequent dates, for the reform of the Gold and Silver Coin in Bengal, Behar, and Orissa; and for prohibiting the currency of any Gold or Silver Coin in those Provinces, but the Nineteenth Sun Sicca Rupee, and the Nineteenth Sun Gold Mohur, and their respective divisions and sub-divisions into Halves and Quarters; and for preventing the counterfeiting, defacing, or debasing of the Coin.—PASSED by the Governor General in Council, on the 1st May 1793; corresponding with the 21st Bysaak 1200 Bengal Era; the 6th Bysaak 1200 Willaity; the 6th Bysaak 1850 Sumbut; and the 19th Ramzan 1207 Higeree.

THE principal Districts in Bengal, Behar, and Orissa, have each a distinct Silver currency, consisting either of the Nineteenth Sun Sicca Rupee, or old or counterfeit Rupees of different Suns or Years, coined previous or subsequent to the Company's Administration, which are the standard measure of value in all transactions in the Districts in which they respectively circulate. The local circulation of these different sorts of Rupees, originated chiefly in the following circumstances. Under the native Government, it was customary to insert upon the Rupees, the year in which they were struck, and the Rupees coined at Patna, Dacca and Moorshedabad, (at each of which Cities there was art established Mint) borc different inscriptions, which in fact rendered the Rupees issued in each year from the respective Mints, a distinct species of Coin. Upon the Mints at Patna, Dacca, and Moorshedabad, being withdrawn soon after the commencement of the Company's administration, the Proprietors and Farmers of Land in the interior parts of the Country, who were bound by their engagements to pay the Public Revenue in Sicca Rupees, experienced considerable difficulty in obtaining those Rupees, from	[Preamble]

the coinage of them being confined to Calcutta, at which place the only Mint that remained in the Provinces was established. They were in consequence compelled to collect the Rents from the Ryots, in the species of Sonant, or other old Rupees, of which there happened to be the greatest number in their respective Districts, and which they were permitted to pay into the Public Treasuries at a fixed exchange. In consequence of the Ryots being required to pay their Rent in a particular sort of Rupee, they of course demanded it from the Manufacturers in payment for the grain, or raw materials, whilst the Manufacturers, actuated by similar principles with the Ryots, required the same species of Rupee from the traders who came to purchase their cloth, or other commodities. The various sorts of old Rupees accordingly soon became the established currency of particular Districts, and a necessary consequence, the value of each Rupee was enhanced in the District in which it was current, from being in demand of all transactions. As a further consequence, every other sort of Rupees brought into the District was rejected, from being a different measure of value from that by which the inhabitants had been accustomed to estimate their property, or, if it was received, discount was exacted upon it, equal to what the receiver would have been obliged to pay upon exchanging it at the house of a Shroff for the Rupee current in the District, or to allow upon passing it in payment to any other individual. Thus, if a Sicca Rupee of the Nineteenth Sun, which is intrinsically worth about seven per cent ore than an Arcot, was offered in payment in the Dacca Province, it was either reduced, or received nearly at the same value as an Arcot; whilst the holder of Arcots, or other sorts of Rupees, who carried them into Districts in which they were riot current, was subjected to similar loss. The Proprietors and Farmers of Land, or the persons concerned in making their payments to the Public Treasuries, derived a considerable advantage from this enhanced valuation of the particular species of Rupees current in their respective Districts, as they were enabled to obtain credit for them in exchange for Siccas, in which their Revenues were payable, at a rate considerably exceeding their intrinsic worth. The profits which the Shroffs or money changers derive from this disordered state of the coin is necessarily enormous. Their Agents in the different parts of the country, buy up all Rupees which are brought into Districts in which they are not current, and consequently at a depreciated value, and send them for sale to Districts where they are the prevailing currency, and in which the dispose of them at an enhanced Value to persons who have payments or purchases to make in those Districts. The Merchants and Traders are under the necessity of submitting to the imposition, for no other Rupee but the Nineteenth Sun Sicca feeing coined at the Mints, the old Rupees are procurable only from the Shroffs, and consequently they must either pay the exchange demanded, or discontinue their purchases. From the rejection of the coin current in one Districts, when tendered in payment in another, the Merchants and Traders, and the Proprietors arid Cultivators of Land in the different parts of the country, are subjected in their commercial dealings with each other to the same losses by exchange, and all the other inconveniences that would necessarily result were the several Districts under separate and independent Governments, each having a different coin. The money changers are the only description of people who derive any benefit from this disordered state of the coin. The loss falls upon Government and the public at large, and must be perpetual, unless the various old and counterfeit Rupees now current in the different parts of the country, can be thrown out of circulation, and one species of Rupee made the general standard measure of value in all transactions between individuals, and between Government and its subjects. The Sicca Rupee of the Nineteenth Sun is the established Silver Coin of the country and the Rupee in which the public Revenues are payable. It was with a view to render it the general measure of value, that Government determined in the year 1773, that all Rupees coined in future should bear the impression of the Nineteenth Sun, or year, of the reign of Shah Aulum, and no other species of Rupee (with the exception of some Arcots) has since been coined in the Calcutta Mint. The Rupees of the Eleventh, Twelfth, and Fifteenth Sun, were indeed directed to be considered current equally with the Nineteenth Sun Sicca Rupee. But this was a temporary measure, intended to be continued in force only until there should be a sufficiency of the Nineteenth Sun Sicca Rupee introduced into circulation. The number however of these three descriptions of Rupees, is of course inconsiderable compared with the number of the Nineteenth Sun Sicca Rupees that have been coined since the abovementioned year, and they are to much worn as to be no longer fit for circulation. The preceding remarks evince, that it is the interest of individuals of every description, excepting the money-changers, to cooperate with Government to render the Nineteenth Sun Sicca Rupee generally current, and the Standard of value throughout the country. Amongst the measures considered necessary to effect this important object, the following were the principal. First. To direct the officers employed in the provision of the investment, the manufacture of Salt, and all commercial transactions of the Company, to make their agreements with individuals for Sicca Rupees of the Nineteenth Sun; for if Government in their extensive commercial dealings, and in the provision of the Salt, make contrails with their subjects in other species of Rupees, they must necessarily continue the measure of value where those concerns are transacted, and it would be as ineffectual to declare the Nineteenth Sun Sicca Rupees the only legal currency, as it would be unjust to attempt to enforce the rule. Secondly. To oblige individuals to estimate their property by the Nineteenth Sun Sicca Rupee, by declaring the amount of Bonds and engagements entered into after a certain period (in fixing which a time was allowed that was presumed sufficient for the introduction of the necessary number of the Nineteenth Sun Sicca Rupees into circulation) whereby any sum of money might be stipulated to be paid in any species of Rupees excepting the Nineteenth Sun Siccas, not recoverable in any Court of Judicature. Thirdly. To prohibit the receipt of any Rupees excepting Siccas of the Nineteenth Sun, at the public treasuries after the date above alluded to. This last measure was calculated to oblige the Proprietors and Farmers of Land to require Nineteen Sun Sicca Rupees from their under Renters and Ryots, and consequently induce the latter to demand them from the Manufacturers, who for similar reasons, would necessarily require them from the Merchants, and Traders, and thus make it the interest of all descriptions of persons to receive the Nineteenth Sun Sicca Rupee, and to reject every other species of Rupee, upon the principles on which they before demanded the particular Rupee current in the respective districts. Fourthly. To establish Mints at the cities of Patna, Dacca, and Moorshedabad, to coin precisely the same Rupee as that struck at Calcutta. Without the adoption of this last arrangement, it would have been useless to declare the Nineteenth Sun Sicca Rupee the only legal tender of payment. For unless individuals had been afforded a ready means of procuring their old coin to be converted without loss into the new, they would have been obliged to have purchased the new money from the Shroffs, who would have demanded an exorbitant exchange upon it, as well with a view to reap the immediate advantage, as to prevent the establishment of the general currency of the Nineteenth Sun Sicca Rupee. Keeping open Mints in the interior parts of the country until the circulation may be filled up with that Coin, precludes the necessity of any person applying to Shroffs for it, and consequently deprives them of their influence (which is founded on the wants and necessities of individuals) by furnishing all persons with the new money at the cheapest rate, and with the least trouble. By the operation of these rules the various facts of old and light Rupee must in a course of time fall to their intrinsic worth compared with the Sicca of the Nineteenth Sun as they will produce no more in the Mint, and to which they will necessarily be brought to be converted into Siccas, as they will be no where passable or in demand as coin, from being no where a measure of value. The Rules by which the gold coin has been regulated, have been productive of evils similar to those which have prevailed with regard to the silver coin. Under the native administrations, and until the year 1766, the Gold Mohur was, not considered as a legal tender of payment in any public or private transaction, nor was the number of Rupees for which it was to pass current, ever fixed by the Government. It was struck for the convenience of individuals, and the value of it in the markets fluctuated like other commodities, silver being the metal which was the

	general measure of value throughout the country. In the year 1766 the value of the Gold coin with respect to the Silver, was first fixed, and the former coin declared a legal tender of payment. A Gold Mohur was struck, and ordered to pass for fourteen Sicca Rupees. But as this coin (calculating according to the relative value of the two metals) was much below the worth of the silver in the number of Rupees for which it was ordered to pass, it was found impossible to render it current, and it was accordingly called in, and a new Gold Mohur, being that now current, was issued in 1760, which was directed to pass as a legal tender of payment for Sixteen Sicca Rupees. The intrinsic worth of this coin, was estimated to be equal to the nominal value of it, or as nearly so as was deemed necessary to render it current at the prescribed rate. But whether owing to the effect of the orders for the introduction of the over rated Gold coin of 1766, the considerable value of the new Gold Mohur, and the want of divisions of it, so as to render the coin calculated for the dealings of the lower orders of the people in the interior parts of the country, or other causes, the currency of it has been confined almost entirely to Calcutta, where it has been received and paid in all public and private payments at the fixed value of Sixteen Sicca Rupees. But this partial currency of the Gold coin, has enabled the money changers to practice an abuse upon the public and individuals, of a nature similar to that which has prevailed regarding the Silver. Individuals are obliged to receive Gold Mohurs at the full value in all payments made to them from the Treasury at Calcutta. But as the coin will not pass in the interior parts of the country, the receivers are under the necessity, when they have occasion to make purchases or advances out of Calcutta, to fell heir Gold Mohurs to a Shroff for Silver of the currency of the District in which their purchases are to be made, or, what is the same for a bill on his house in the District payable in that currency, as the Shroff in the latter case exacts the discount in fixing the exchange. The Shroffs pay the Gold which they thus purchase at a discount, into the Treasury at Calcutta at par, whenever they have payments to make to Government. The Gold Mohurs are in this manner immediately thrown back upon the Treasury whenever

an opportunity offers, and the Shroffs levy a discount on them as often as they are issued from it. The obstruction to the circulation of the Gold Coin out of Calcutta, necessarily affects its value in purchases in the markets within the town, where also discount is frequently exacted upon it. The means which appear best calculated to render the Gold Mohur generally current, are to declare it receivable at all the public Treasuries and in all public payments throughout the Provinces, at the rate of Sixteen Sicca Rupees; to make it a legal tender of payment in private transactions; to coin a great proportion of halves and quarters, and lastly, to impose a duty upon all Gold Bullion tent to the Mint to be coined, to as to prevent too large a proportion of Gold being introduced into circulation, by diminishing in tome degree the advantage at present derived from the importation of it in preference to Silver. Upon the above grounds, the Regulations of the 20th June, 24th October, and 21st November 1792 were adopted, and this detail of them, by apprizing individuals of the principles on which the coin of the country is regulated, will enable them to guard against the impositions of the money changers, who alone derive advantage from the want of a uniform Gold and Silver currency. The Regulations above mentioned, are hereby re-enacted with amendments.

Mints established at Patna, Moorshedabad, and Dacca, in addition to the Calcutta Mint.

II. Mints have been established at the Cities of Patna, Moorshedabad, and Dacca, in addition to the Mint at Calcutta, in which Sicca Rupees and Gold Mohurs of the Nineteenth Sun, of the following weight and standard, and half and quarter Rupees and Gold Mohurs, of the same standard, and proportionate weight, will be coined:

Coins to be struck in the Mints.

NINETEENTH SUN GOLD MOHUR

Troy Weight,	Grains,	190.894	
		Carat	Grs.
Assay compared with English standard Gold better,		1	$3\frac{1}{4}$
Bengal weight,	Annas,		17
Bengal Assay { Touch, or parts of fine Gold, in 100,			$99\frac{1}{4}$
Bengal Assay { Alloy,			$\frac{3}{4}$

	NINETEENTH SUN SICCA RUPEE Troy Weight, Grains, 179 $\frac{2}{3}$ Assay compared with English standard Silver; better, Dwts. 13 Bengal Weight, Annas, 16 Bengal Assay { Touch, or parts of fine Silver, in 100, $97\frac{11}{12}$ Alloy, $2\frac{1}{12}$
Gold Coin of full weight and standard coined since the 20th March 1769, to be a legal tender of payment at the rate of Sixteen Sicca Rupees. Native Officers liable to dismission and to pay costs & damages upon being convicted of refusing to receive the gold coin.	III. All Gold Mohurs of the weight and standard specified in Section II, coined in the Calcutta Mint since the 20th March 1769, or which may be coined in that Mint, and in the Mints of Patna, Dacca, and Moorshedabad, after the date of this Regulation, and also their halves and quarters, are to be considered legal tender of payment in all public and private transactions throughout the Provinces of Bengal, Behar, and Orissa, at the rate of Sixteen Sicca Rupees of the Nineteenth Sun, for each Mohur and the half and quarter Mohur in proportion. If a Native Officer, of any public Treasury shall be convicted before the Court of Dewanny Adawlut of any Zillah or City, of refusing to receive in payment any such Gold Mohurs or the, halves or quarters of them, at the rates directed in this Section, the Court shall adjudge offender to be dismissed from his office, and further compel him pay to the complainant his cost of suit, and such damages as the Court may seem proper upon a consideration of the circumstances of the case.
For all Silver Bullion, or coin of, or above Sicca standard, Coin equal to the weight of the Standard Bullion to be returned without any charge.	IV. For all Silver Bullion, or old or light Silver coin, equal to, or above, Sicca standard, which may be delivered into the Mints, a number of the Nineteenth Sun Sicca Rupees, or halves or quarters of such Rupees, equal in weight to the Silver of Sicca Standard contained in such Bullion or old or light Coin, shall be returned to the Proprietor without any charge whatsoever.
Twelve annas per cent to be charged for refining to Sicca Standard, Bullion or old or light Coin under that Standard.	V. All Silver Bullion, or old or light Silver Coin, under Sicca Standard, which may be delivered into the Mints, is to be refined to the Sicca Standard, and a number of the Nineteenth Sun Sicca Rupees, or halves or quarters of such Rupees, equal in weight to the refined Bullion, shall be returned to the proprietor after deducting twelve annas per cent for the expence of refining.

VI. It shall be at the option of individuals to have their old or light Coin or Bullion if Gold, coined into Gold Mohurs, or half or quarter Gold Mohurs, and if Silver, into the Nineteenth Sun Sicca Rupees, or half or quarter Rupees, or into such proportions of each as they may think proper.	Option given to Individuals to have their old Gold or Silver Bullion or money, coined into Gold Mohurs or Rupees or halves or quarters in any proportion.
VII. To guard as far as possible against the counterfeiting, clipping, drilling, filing, defacing, or debasing the coin, the edges both of the Gold and Silver coin are to be milled, and the dies are to be made of the same size as the coin, so that the whole of the impression may appear upon the surface of it.	Coin to be milled and to be of the same size as the die, so as to receive whole impression upon it.
VIII. The Nineteenth Sun Sicca Rupees, and the Nineteenth Sun Gold Mohurs, and the halves and quarters of each, which may be coined at the Mints established at Dacca, Patna and Moorshedabad, and at the Calcutta Mint, are to be precisely of the same shape, weight, and standard, and to bear the same impression both on the surface and the edges; and with a view to the effectual attainment of the last mentioned object, the dies for striking and milling the Gold and Silver Coin, are to be cut in the Calcutta Mint, and distributed by the Mint Master to the three subordinate Mints, and when there dies are broken, or no longer serviceable, they are to be returned to the Calcutta Mint.	Coins struck in several Mints to be precisely of the same shape, weight, and standard, and to have same impression. Precaution to be taken for preventing any difference in the impression or milling of the Coins struck in the three Mints.
IX. The Gold and Silver Coin struck at the different Mints, is to be received and paid indiscriminately at the prescribed value in all public and private Transactions.	Coin struck at the different Mints, to be received and paid indiscriminately.
X. The Mint Master is to cause, a private mark to be put upon all dies which may be prepared for the several Mints, but in such a manner as not to be distinguishable by the naked eye. These marks are to be varied as often as the Mint Mailer may judge proper upon new dies being made, and he is to keep a Register of them that in the event of any debased or defective coin being found in circulation, he may be able to ascertain from what Mint it may have been issued.	Mint Master to have private marks put up on the dies.

Further precaution for preventing bad or defective Coin being issued from the Mints.	XI. The Magistrates of the Cities of Dacca, Patna, and Moorshedabad respectively, are required to proceed in person once every fortnight, or as often as they may judge it proper, to the Mints at Dacca, Patna, and Moorshedabad, without previously apprizing the Superintendent of the Mint, at the time when the Money is usually struck off, and with their own hand, to take indiscriminately out of the heaps at the foot of the striking presses three pieces of each description of Coin that may have been struck off, and transmit them to the Mint Master at Calcutta who is to cause the Coin to be examined and assayed, and it shall not be of the proper standard, or if it shall be defective in the workmanship, or in any other respect, he is to report the circumstances to the Governor General in Council.
Persons charged with counterfeiting the Coin or other offences herein specified, to be committed to the Criminal Courts.	XII. Persons charged with counterfeiting, clipping, filing, defacing, or debasing, the Gold or Silver Coin, are to be committed to the Criminal Courts, and punished according as the law may direct.
All persons prohibited affixing marks to the Coin. Coins so marked not to be legal tender of payment, and to be rejected at the Public Treasuries.	XIII. All Officers, Agents, Gomastahs, or others employed in the collection or payment of the Public Revenue, or the Rents of Individuals, or the provision of the Investment, the manufacture of Salt, or Opium, and all Proprietors and Farmers; of Land, Dependent Talookdars, under Farmers and Ryots, and all, persons whomsoever, are prohibited affixing any mark whatever to the Gold or Silver Coin, and all Rupees or Gold Mohurs, or half or quarter Rupees or Gold Mohurs; that may be so marked, are declared not to be legal tenders of payment in any public or private transaction, and the Officers of Government are directed to reject any Rupees or Gold Mohurs; or any half or quarter Rupees or Gold Mohurs, so marked, that may be tendered at the public Treasuries.
Rules and valuation according to which all Rupees not being	XIV. As the number of the Nineteenth Sun Sicca Rupees in circulation in some Districts, may not be sufficient to enable the Proprietors and Farmers of Land to pay such part of their Revenues as they may not pay in Gold, in Rupees of that description, the various sorts of Rupees

current in the several Districts, will be received at the public Treasuries from the Proprietors and Farmers of Land in payment of their Revenue until the 10th April 1794, corresponding with the 30th Chyte 1200 Bengal Era, the 25th Chyte 1201 Fussily, the 30th Chyte 1201 Willaity, the 25th Chyte 1851 Sumbut, and the 9th Ramzaan 1208 Higeree, at the fixed rates specified in the following table, which are calculated agreeably to the difference, of the intrinsic value, that each species of Rupee bears to the Nineteenth Sun Sicca Rupee, as ascertained by Assay in the Calcutta. Mint.

Nineteenth Sun Sicca are to be received in discharge of the public Revenue until the 10th April 1794.

SORTS OF RUPEES

	Sicca Weight	19-*sun* Siccas		
Siccas of Moorshedabad, Patna and Dacca, per	100	100	0	0
Phooley Sonats,	do	100	0	0
Delhy Mahomet Shai,	do	99	8	0
Money Surat large,	do	99	8	0
Benares Sicca,	do	99	8	0
Bissun Arcot,	do	97	14	6
Sonats Sabic and Duckie,	do	97	8	0
Forshee Arcots,	do	97	6	6
French Arcots,	do	97	0	0
Patanca Arcots	do	96	9	6
Arungzebee Arcots,	do	96	9	6
Gursaul,	do	96	9	6
Madras Arcots new,	do	96	4	9
Masulipatam and Shardar Arcots,	do	96	0	0
Patna Sonats old	do	96	0	0
Benares Rupees old;	do	95	14	6
Madras Arcots old,	do	95	14	6
Farukabad Rupees,	do	95	12	9
Jehaujee Arcots,	do	95	1	3
Chaunta Arcots	do	95	11	3
Calcutta and Moorshedabad Arcots,	do	95	6	6
Old Arcots,	do	95	3	3
Dutch Arcots,	do	95	0	0
Surat Arcots,	do	94	0	0
Benares Trisolie,	do	92	6	6
Viziery Rupees,	do	63	0	0
Narrainy half Rupee new	do	63	0	0

Explanation of the mode of receiving the Rupees agreeably to the above table.	XV. To prevent misconception of the mode of receiving Rupees of sorts under the above Table, it is to be understood, that one Hundred Sicca Weight of each of the sorts of Rupees specified in the first column (whatever number of the Rupees may go to that weight) is to be considered equal to the number of Nineteen Sun Sicca Rupees placed opposite to it in the second column.
Rules for the Rupees tendered at the Public Treasuries which are not specified in the table.	XVI. If any other species of Rupees be fides those specified in the Table, are tendered in payment at any of the Public Treasuries, One hundred Sicca weight of them, indiscriminately taken from the Sum paid in the presence of the payer or his agent, is to be sent to the nearest Mint to be assayed, and the payer shall receive credit for a number of the Nineteenth Sun Sicca Rupees equal in weight to the Silver of Sicca Standard that the Rupees so paid may be estimated to contain according to the Assay, after deducting twelve annas per cent. for the expence of refining, should the Rupees be under Sicca Standard.
Rupees of sorts received at the Public Treasuries to be sent to the Mints.	XVII. Rupees of sorts which may be received at the Public Treasuries agreeably to the table in Section XIV, or under Section XVI, are not on any account to be issued therefrom, but are to be sent to the Mints, and coined into Siccas of the Nineteenth Sun.
After the 10th April, 1794, no Silver or Gold Coin excepting Rupees or Gold Mohurs of the Nineteenth Sun or their respective divisions and subdivisions to be considered a legal tender for payment.	XVIII. After the 10th April 1794, no other Rupee but the Nineteenth Sun Sicca, and no other Gold Mohur but the Nineteenth Sun Gold Mohur, or the halves and quarters of each, shall be received at any of the Public Treasuries or issued therefrom, on any account whatsoever; and no other Rupees or Gold Mohurs, excepting the Rupees and Gold Mohurs of the Nineteenth Sun, and the halves and quarters of each, shall be legal tenders of payment in any public or private transaction.
Bonds or Agreements for money, executed prior to the 10th April, 1794, to be dischargeable	XIX. Bonds or writings or other agreements whether written verbal; entered into prior to the 10th April 1794, whereby a sum money is stipulated to be paid in any species of Rupee or Gold Mohur excepting the Nineteenth Sun Sicca or the Gold Mohur of the Nineteenth Sun,

and which may not be discharged previous to the abovementioned date, may be liquidated at the option the debtor, either in the Rupee specified in the instrument, or the Nineteenth Sun Sicca Rupee at the valuation specified in the Table, in Section XIV, or in the Nineteenth Sun Gold Mohur.	prior to that date either in the Com stipulated in the deed, or in Nineteenth Sun Siccas at the rates in the table.
XX. After the 10th April 1794, no person shall recover in any Court of Judicature in the Provinces of Bengal, Behar, or Orissa, any sum of money under a Bond, or other writing, or any agreement, written or verbal, entered into after the abovementioned date, by which any sum of money shall be stipulated to be paid in any species of Rupees excepting Sicca Rupees, or Gold Mohurs, of the Nineteenth Sun, or the halves and quarters of each.	Agreements executed after the 10th April, 1794, stipulating for the payment of money in any other specie excepting Rupees or Gold Mohurs of the Nineteenth Sun, or the halves or quarters of them, not recoverable in any Court of Judicature.
XXI. All engagements hereafter entered into on the part of the Government for the provision of the investment, or the manufacture of Salt, are to be made in the Sicca Rupee, or the Gold Mohur of the Nineteenth Sun, and all Proprietors and Farmers Rupee, or the Gold Mohur of the Nineteenth Sun, and all Proprietors and Farmers of Land are prohibited from concluding engagements with their under Farmers, Ryots or Dependent Talookdars, after the 10th April 1794, in any species of Rupees or Gold Mohur excepting the Sicca Rupees and the Gold Mohurs of the Nineteen Sun, under the penalty of not being permitted to recover any arrears that may become due to them under such Engagements.	All engagements on the part of the Government for the provision of the Investment, or Salt, to be made in the Nineteenth Sun Sicca Rupee or Gold Mohur. Engagements for Rent and Revenue to be made in the same coin. Arrears on engagements stipulating the payment of any other Coin not recoverable.

Punishment for Native Officers at any of the Treasuries refusing to receive the Nineteenth Sun Gold Muhur or Rupee in payment.	XXII. If Sicca Rupees or the Nineteenth Sun of full weight, the halves or quarters of such Rupees, shall be tendered at any of the Public Treasuries, and any of the Native Officers shall refuse to receive them in payment of any public demand, and shall require any other species of Rupees, or if any of the species of Rupee mentioned in the Table in Section XIV, shall be tendered at the Public Treasuries prior to the date specified in Section XVIII, at the valuation specified in the Table, and any Native Officer shall refuse to receive them at such valuation, upon proof of such offence before the Dewanny Adawlut of the Zillah or City in which the complaint may be cognizable, the Court shall dismiss the Offender from his Office, and oblige him to pay costs of suit, and damages to the party complaining.
Native Officers at any of the Public Treasuries liable to fine and dismission for receiving any Coin but the Nineteenth Sun Rupee or Gold Mohur after the 10th April 1794.	XXIII. After the date specified in Section XVIII, if any Native Officer at any of the Public Treasuries shall be convicted of receiving in payment of a public demand any Gold or Silver Coin, excepting the Gold Mohur or the Sicca Rupees of the Nineteenth Sun, or the halves and quarters of each, the Court shall dismiss him in his office, and adjudge him to pay such fine to Government as may appear to them adequate to the offence.
Duty to be levied at the several Mints on Gold Bullion.	XXIV. In consideration of the expence incurred in refining Gold, not of Gold Mohur standard, and with a view to discourage importation of Gold Bullion in preference to Silver Bullion, following duty is to be levied, on Gold Bullion sent to the Mints for Coinage. Bullion of, or above, Gold Mohur Standard; 2 8 per Cent. Do. $\frac{3}{4}$ to 5 per cent. worse than that Standard; 2 12 do. Do. from 5 to 10 per cent. do. 3 4 do. Do. from 10 to 20 per cent. do. 3 12 do.
No duty to be levied on the recoinage of old Gold Mohurs, halves or	XXV. No duty is to be charged on the re-coinage of old or light Gold Mohurs, or half or quarter Gold Mohurs, coined at the Calcutta Mint since the 20th March 1769, nor on the re-coinage of any Gold Mohurs, or half or

quarter Gold Mohurs, which may coined in the Mints at Patna, Dacca, Moorshedabad, or Calcutta, after this date.	quarters, coined in the Calcutta Mint since the 20th March, 1769, or which may hereafter coined in any of the Mints.
XXVI. All Bullion delivered into the Mints, is to be assayed in the order in which it may be received; refined in the order in which may be assayed, and coined in the order in which it may be refined. Standard Bullion delivered into the Mints is to be registered as refined Bullion, on the date on which it may be assayed.	Order in which Bullion delivered into the Mints, is to be assayed, refined and coined.
XXVII. *First.* The following Registers are to be kept open at the Mints of Calcutta, Patna, Dacca, and Moorshedabad, for public inspection. *Second.* A Register of unassayed Bullion delivered into the Mint, specifying the quantity delivered, the date on which it was received, and the name of the Proprietor. *Third.* A Register of Bullion assayed and refined, specifying the date on which it was assayed, and the date on which it was refined, the name of the Proprietor, and the produce in Sicca Rupees or Gold Mohurs, together with the date of the Certificate granted for the produce, and the date on which such Certificate was discharged.	Registers to be kept for public inspection in the several Mints.
XXVIII. Collectors of the Revenue, Commercial Residents or Agents, Salt Agents, the Mint Master at Calcutta, the Superintendents of the subordinate Mints at the Cities of Patna, Dacca and Moorshedabad, and their respective Officers, are to be liable to be sued for damages in the Zillah or City Court to which they may be amenable, for any breach of this Regulation, or any other Regulation which may be enacted respecting the Coin.	European and Native Officers of Government herein specified liable to be sued for any breach of the Regulation respecting the coinage.

Appendix A.4

A.D. 1794 REGULATION VI

A REGULATION for postponing to the 10th April, 1795, the operation of such parts of Sections XVIII, XIX, XX, and XXIII, Regulation XXXV, 1793, as regard to the Silver Coin.—PASSED by the Governor General in Council, on the 30th May, 1704; corresponding with the 19th Jeyte 1201 Bengal era; the 16th Jeyte 1201 Fussily; the 19th Jeyte 1201 Willaity; the 16th Jeyte 1851 Sumbut; and the 29th Showal 1208 Higeree.

[Preamble]	BY Section XVIII, Regulation XXXV, 1793, it was enacted, that after the 10th April 1794 corresponding with the 30th Chyte 1200 Bengal era, the 25th Chyte 1201 Fussily, the 30th Chyte 1201 *Willaity,* the 25th Chyte 1851 Sumbut, and the 9th Ramzaan 1208 Higeree, no other rupee excepting the Sicca of the nineteenth sun; should be received at any of the public treasuries, or issued therefrom, or be considered as a legal tender of payment, in any public or private transaction. This rule was a confirmation of a rule to the same effect, passed on the 24th October 1792, at which time it was presumed, that by the above-mentioned period, a sufficient number of Sicca rupees of the nineteenth sun would have been introduced into circulation for rendering it the only legal tender of payment, and enforcing the other rules in that regulation, that were to take place from the same date. The Governor General in Council having received representations from different parts of the country, that the number of sicca rupees of the nineteenth sun now in circulation is not sufficient for the purposes above-mentioned, and that rejecting all other species of rupees at the treasuries in the different zillahs at present, would impede the collection of the revenue, and be productive of much inconvenience to the people at large, the following rule has been enacted.

II. Such parts of Sections XVIII, XIX, XX, and XXIII, Regulation XXXV, 1793, as regard the silver coin, are not to be considered to be, or to have been, in force, until the 10th of April 1795, corresponding with the 30th Chyte 1201 Bengal era, the 6th Bysaak 1202 Fussily, the 30th Chyte 1202 Willaity, the 6th Bysaak 1802 Sumbut, the 19th Ramzaan 1209 Higeree, after which period, all the rules contained in those sections are to be considered in full force. Until the arrival of that period, rupees of forts are to be received at the public treasuries, and to be current under the rules that were in force regarding them previous to the 10th April, 1794.	Operation of the rules in Regulation XXXV 1793, herein specified, postponed to the 10th April 1795.

Appendix A.5

A.D. 1795 REGULATION LIX

A REGULATION for further postponing to the 10th April, 1796, the operation of such parts of Sections XVIII, XIX, XX, and XXIII, Regulation XXXV, 1793, as regard to the Silver Coin.—PASSED by the Governor General in Council, on the 29th September, 1795; corresponding with the 15th Assin 1202 Bengal era; the 1st Assin 1203 Fussily; the 15th Assin 1203 Willaity; the 1st Assin 1852 Sumbut; and the 15th Rubbee ul Awul 1210 Higeree.

[Preamble]	THE reasons assigned in the preamble to Regulation VI, 1794, for suspending certain rules in Regulation XXXV, 1793, until the 10th April 1795, continuing to operate, and consequently rendering it necessary that the enforcement of those rules should be further postponed; the Governor General in Council has enacted as follows.
Operation of the rules in Regulation XXXV, 1793, herein specified, postponed to the 10th April 1796.	II. Such parts of Sections XVIII, XIX, XX, and XXIII, Regulation XXXV, 1793, as regard the silver coin in the provinces of Bengal, Behar, and Orissa, shall not have effect until the 10th of April 1796, corresponding with the 31st Chyte 1202, Bengal era; the 18th Chyte 1203 Fussily; the 31st Chyte 1203 Willaity; the 18th Chyte 1853 Sumbut; and the 1st Showal, 1210 Higeree; after which period, all the rules contained in those sections are to be considered in full force. Until the arrival of that period, rupees of sorts shall be received at the public treasuries in those provinces, and shall be current therein, under the rules that were in force regarding them previous to the 10th April 1794; but the rupees which may be so received, are not on any account to be disbursed from the said treasuries, but are to be sent to the mint to be recoined into siccas of the nineteenth sun, as prescribed in Section XVII, Regulation XXXV, 1793.

Appendix A.6

A.D. 1795 REGULATION LXI

A REGULATION for determining what sicca rupees of the nineteenth sun shall be considered as of standard weight in payments in the provinces of Bengal, Behar, and Orissa.—PASSED by the Governor General in Council on the 13th November 1795; corresponding with the 30th Kautick 1202 Bengal era; the 17th Kautick 1203 Fussily; the 30th Kautick 1203 Willaity; the 17th Kautick 1853 Sumbut; and the 30th Rubbee us Sanee 1210 Higeree.

AGREEABLY to the ancient usage of the country, all payments in silver are made by weight. This usage was established to keep up the circulating coin to its full standard weight by obliging the holders of light coin to carry it to the mint for recoinage; and as the demand of Government on the proprietors of estates with whom a settlement has been made, is fixed in perpetuity at a specific amount in money; it is essential to the interests of the state, that this, as well as all other rules calculated to prevent the circulation of light coin, should be adhered to as strictly as may be possible. A practice however obtained under the native administration, and which continued to prevail under the British Government, of receiving light rupees in payment of private, and not unfrequently of public demands, with an allowance or batta adequate to the deficiency; individuals often finding it more convenient or advantageous to make good this deficiency, than to fend their light coin to the mint, or to dispose of it to a shroff for coin of full weight. By the abuse of this practice, in progress of time the circulation became filled with coin rendered deficient in its weight by wear, or artificial means. The landholders and farmers of the revenue, availed themselves of this defective state of the currency to exact large sums from their ryots and tenants, on account of the deficiency in its weight, urging that similar demands would be made	[Preamble]

	on them when they tendered it in discharge of their revenue and the shroffs levied similar impositions in private transactions. To obviate these and other abuses, it was determined by Regulation XXXV, 1793, that after a certain period, no rupees should be considered as a legal tender of payment excepting the rupees of the nineteenth sun of the weight and standard specified in that regulation. In weighing however the rupees received into the treasuries, against standard weights, with a view to a strict adherence to the letter of the regulation, instead of a specific number of the newest coin procurable, as had been generally the practice, it was found that the nineteenth sun sicca rupees, almost immediately after their introduction into circulation, were generally from two to four annas per cent deficient in weight; and on inquiry, it was ascertained that from the number of points in the inscription and the fineness of the silver, this deficiency invariably arose on the first introduction of new coin into circulation, although it would circulate several years without suffering any further considerable diminution in its weight. In order therefore to preserve the salutary custom of receiving the coin by weight, and at the same time to obviate the loss and inconvenience, that would have resulted both to the public and individuals by rejecting the new coin in payment on account of the smallest deficiency in weight, and consequently compelling the holders to return it to the mint almost immediately after its being issued from thence, certain orders were issued and communicated to the board of revenue and to the collectors on the 2nd October 1795. These orders, with modifications, are now enacted into a regulation, which is to be in force from the date of its receipt in the several zillah and city courts in the provinces of Bengal, Behar, and Orissa.
Sicca rupees of the nineteenth sun which may not have lost by wear more than six annas per cent to be received as of full weight.	II. All sicca rupees of the nineteenth sun, which may not have lost by wear a greater proportion of their full standard weight than six annas per cent or fix sixteenths of a rupee in one hundred rupees shall be considered as of standard weight, and be received as such in all public and private transactions.

III. The above rule however is to be considered applicable to those nineteenth sun rupees only, in which the loss of weight has been occasioned by wear. Whenever rupees of the above description may have lost any part of their full weight, although such loss shall not exceed fix annas per cent by filing, clipping, or other artificial means, they shall not be considered as of standard weight, and, if tendered in payment at any of the public treasuries, or offices, they shall be received at their intrinsic value as hereafter directed, and the podars, or examiners of the public money, are required to separate all such rupees.	The above rule applicable only to loss of weight by wear.
IV. *First.* Rupees of the nineteenth sun deficient in weight from any other cause excepting wear, or deficient in weight from wear in a greater amount than fix annas per cent are to be received agreeably to the following rule.	And in cases where the loss of weight by wear shall exceed six annas per cent.
Second. For one hundred sicca weight of such light nineteenth sun sicca rupees, the payer is to receive credit for one hundred nineteenth sun sicca rupees. The light rupees thus received at the public treasuries, are not to be disbursed again, but are invariably to be sent to the mint to be recoined.	How such rupees shall be received. Not to be disbursed again.
V. The mint master at Calcutta is required to furnish the board of revenue for the use of the collectors, with stampt metal weights, of fifty sicca weight each, or such other weight as may he required by them, and all receipts and payments at the public treasuries are to be regulated agreeably to such standard weights.	Mint Master to furnish standard weights.
VI. The foregoing rules are to be considered equally applicable to the halves and quarters of the nineteenth sun sicca rupee.	Rules to apply to the quarter and halves of rupees.

Appendix A.7

A.D. 1795 REGULATION LXII

A REGULATION for withdrawing the Mint established at Moorshedabad under Regulation XXXV, 1793.—PASSED by the Governor General in Council on the 11th December 1795; corresponding with the 28th Aughun 1202 Bengal era; the 15th Aughun 1203 Fussily; the 28th Aughun 1203 Willaity; the 15th Aughun 1852 Sumbut; and the 28th Jumaud ul Awul 1216 Higeree.

[Preamble]	THE continuance of the Mint established at Moorshedabad being deemed unnecessary, in consequence of the inconsiderable quantity of coin and bullion brought to it for coinage, the Governor General in Council has enacted as follows.
Moorshedabad Mint withdrawn.	II. The Mint established at Moorshedabad, under Regulation XXXV, 1793, is hereby directed to be withdrawn.

Appendix A.8

A.D. 1797 REGULATION I

A REGULATION for collection of a new duty of one per cent, to be levied on all imports into, and exports from, the port of Calcutta, excepting money and bullion; and for prohibiting the importation of opium from the territories of the Nabob Vizier, or from any foreign country.—PASSED by the Governor-General-in-Council on the 2nd January, 1797, corresponding with the 21st Poose 1203 Bengal era; the 19th Poose 1204 Fussily; the 21st Poose 1204 Willaity; the 19th Poose 1853 Sumbut and; the 2nd Rajeb 1211 Higeree.

xx xx xx xx	
II. All goods paying the present duties of two and a half per cent shall pay in future, an addition of one per cent, making in all three and a half per cent.	New duty of one per cent payable on goods now chargeable with duty, and also
III. All goods at present exempted from duties, are to pay a duty of one per cent, whether on importation, or exportation. This rule is not to extend to money and bullion.	on all goods now exempted from duty, money and bullion exempted.
xx xx xx xx	

Appendix A.9

A.D. 1799 REGULATION III[1]

A REGULATION for postponing to the end of the Bengal year 1204, or to the 10th April 1798, the operation of Section XX. Regulation XXXV. 1793, within the Zillah of Sylhet.—PASSED by the Vice-President in Council on the 19th April 1799, corresponding with the 9th Bysaak 1206 Bengal era; the 29th Cheyte 1206 Fussily; the 9th Bysaak 1206 Willaity; the 29th Cheyte 1856 Sumbut; and the 12th Zekaad 1213 Higeree.

Section XX, of Regulation XXXV, 1793, not to have effect in Zillah Sylhet until the 10th April 1798.	WHEREAS it appears by a representation from the judge of Zillah Sylhet, that Regulation XXXV, 1793, prohibiting the currency of any gold or silver coin after the 10th April 1794, except the nineteenth sun gold mohur and nineteenth sun sicca, was not promulgated in the above district before the month of September 1797, or Assin 1204 B.S. and that in consequence bonds and other engagements were contracted till that period in the various species of rupees current within the Zillah aforesaid, the amount of which by Section XX, of Regulation XXXV, 1793, is declared irrevocable in any court of judicature; the Vice-President in Council has therefore passed the following rule, to prevent injury from ignorance of the Regulations in such cases; and to be in force in the above Zillah only.
	II. Section XX, of Regulation XXXV, 1793, shall not have effect in the zillah of Sylhet until the 10th April 1798, corresponding to the 30th Cheyte 1204 B.S. the 22nd Shawal 1212 Higeree; and the 10th Bysaak 1855 Sumbut; after which period the provisions contained in the said section and Regulation, are to be considered in full force in that Zillah, as in other parts of the province of Bengal.

[1] This Regulation is to be considered null and void, as that part of Regulation XXV [*sic.* XXXV], of 1793, which it treats of, has been rescinded by Regulation XIII of 1807, Section II. Besides, the time, till which the suspension of Regulation XXXV, of 1793, Section XX, was to remain in the zillah of Sylhet, has long ago expired. Ref. White 1820, vol. III.

Appendix A.10

A.D. 1801 REGULATION V

A REGULATION for re-establishing, with certain exceptions, of the Calcutta town duties, abolished by Sec. II, Regulation XXXIX, 1795.—PASSED by the Governor-General-in-Council on the 14th May, 1801, corresponding with the 2nd Jeyte 1208 Bengal era; the 16th Jeyte 1208 Fussily; the 2nd Jeyte 1208 Willaity; the 16th Jeyte 1858 Sumbut and; the 30th Zeelhej 1215 Higeree.

<table>
<tr><td colspan="2">xx   xx   xx   xx</td></tr>
<tr><td>IV. Import by Sea

Sixteenth. The under mentioned articles are exempted from duty:
Timber
Horses
Bullion and Coin
Copper imported from Madras with a certificate specifying that it has been taken from the government of that presidency in payment of advances due on contracts with the Honorable Company.</td><td></td></tr>
<tr><td colspan="2">xx   xx   xx   xx</td></tr>
</table>

N.B.: The Regulation does not mention of any duty/or exemption from duty on import by land.

Appendix A.11

A.D. 1803 REGULATION XXXVIII

A REGULATION respecting the Abolition of all Rahdary or Transit Duties in the Provinces ceded by the Nawab Vizier to the Honorable the East India Company, and for the collection of Government Customs, and the Gunje Duties in the said Provinces.—PASSED by the Governor-General-in-Council on the 24th March, 1803, corresponding with the 12th Chyte 1209 Bengal era; the 16th Chyte 1210 Fussily; the 12th Chyte 1210 Willaity; the 16th Chyte 1860 Sumbut and; the 29th Zekaad 1217 Higeree.

	XX XX XX XX
No duties whatever to be levied on grain, bullion and jewels.	XIII. Grain, bullion, and jewels, of every description, shall be exempted from all duties, either on importations into, or exportation from the Ceded provinces. The value and quantity of these articles must, however, regularly entered in the custom house book.
	XX XX XX XX

N.B.: The whole of this Regulation was rescinded by Sec. 2, Regulation XI, 1804, and by Clause second, Section 2, Regulation IX, 1810.

Appendix A.12

A.D. 1803 REGULATION XLV

A REGULATION for the Reform of the Gold, Silver, and Copper Coin of the Provinces ceded by the Nawaub Vizier to the Honorable the English East India Company.—PASSED by the Governor-General-in-Council, on the 24th March, 1803; corresponding with the 12th Chyte 1209 Bengal era; the 16th Chyte 1210 Fussily; the 12th Chyte 1210 Willaity; the 16th Chyte 1860 Sumbut; and the 29th Zekaad 1217 Higeree.

WHEREAS the silver coin, in circulation in the provinces ceded by the Nawaub Vizier to the English East India Company, consists of rupees of various denominations, differing from each other in weight and standard: And whereas the settlement for the payment of the land revenue in the said provinces, and all other engagements with Government, as well as the private engagements between individuals,—have been hitherto necessarily made in the currency of the *zillah* in which the engagements have been concluded, in conformity to the usage of the country: And whereas the present state of the silver coin, in the provinces aforesaid, is equally injurious to the Government, and to individuals in general: And whereas it is necessary, for the purpose of relieving the Government and individuals from the inconvenience and loss which they sustain, from the circulation of different descriptions of silver coin, continually fluctuating in their relative current or nominal value, that the various sorts of rupees, now in circulation throughout the ceded provinces, should be withdrawn from circulation, and that one species of rupee should be rendered the general standard measure of value in all transactions between individuals, and between Government and its subjects: And whereas the copper coin, at present current in the said provinces, consists of pice of various denominations, differing in weight and standard: And whereas the convenience of the public at large will be materially promoted by the establishment of one copper coin in the provinces aforesaid: And	Preamble

	whereas it is expedient that the gold coin, or gold mohurs, current in the provinces aforesaid, should continue to circulate conformably to the existing usages of the country; the following rules have been accordingly enacted.
A silver coin, to be denominated the Lucknow sicca rupee of the forty-fifth *sun,* of the weight and standard of the Lucknow rupees, declared the established legal silver coin in the ceded provinces.	II. A silver coin, to be denominated the Lucknow sicca rupee of the forty-fifth *sun*, struck in the mint at Furruckabad, corresponding in weight and standard with the sicca rupee at present struck at Lucknow, in the dominions of the Nawaub Vizier, and thence denominated the Lucknow rupee, is hereby declared to be the established and legal silver coin in the provinces ceded by the Nawaub Vizier to the English East India Company.
A specification of the weight and standard of the Lucknow rupee, as now established, will be hereafter published.	III. A specification of the weight and standard of the Lucknow sicca rupee, as now established, will be inserted in a regulation which will be hereafter published.
A mint established at Furruckabad for coining rupees and halves and quarters of rupees, of the prescribed weight and standard. Mints to be increased, reduced, or removed, according to the pleasure of the Governor General in Council.	IV. A mint shall be established at, or in the immediate vicinity of, the town of Furruckabad, in which Lucknow sicca rupees of the forty-fifth *sun,* and of the prescribed weight and standard, and half and quarter rupees, of the same standard and proportionate weight, will be coined. It shall be competent to the Governor General in Council, by an order in Council, to increase or reduce the number of mints in the ceded provinces, or to remove the mint or mints to any other place, or places, within the dominions of the Company, according as he shall judge proper; and every mint which shall be established shall he subject to the rules contained in this regulation, regarding the mint directed to be established at Furruckabad, or such other regulations as may be hereafter enacted.

V. The Lucknow forty-fifth *sun* sicca rupee, as established by this regulation, shall be of the same size and form as the nineteenth *sun* sicca rupee, struck in the mint at Calcutta, and shall bear the following impression: ON THE FACE: الم حامی دین محمد / سایہ فضل شاہ عالم بادشاہ / سکہ زد بر هفت کشور ON THE REVERSE: میمنت مانوس / سنہ ۴۵ جلوس / ضرب فرخ آباد	Prescribed size and form of the Lucknow forty-fifth *sun* sicca rupee, and to bear what impression.
VI. The half and quarter rupee shall be proportionally less in size than the rupee, according to their respective value; and shall bear the same impression as the rupee.	Size and impression of the halves and quarters of rupees.
VII. To guard as far as possible against counterfeiting, clipping, drilling, filing, defacing, or debasing the silver coin, the edges of such coin shall be milled; and the dies shall be made of the same size as the coin, so that the whole of the impression may appear upon the surface of it.	Coin to be milled, and to be of the same size as the die, so as to receive the whole impression on it.
VIII. The dies for striking the silver coin in the ceded provinces shall be cut in the mint at Calcutta, and shall be sent by the mint master at Calcutta to the mint master at Furruckabad. When the dies are broken, or no longer serviceable, they shall be returned to the Calcutta mint.	The dies to be cut in the Calcutta mint. To be returned to the Calcutta mint, when no longer serviceable.
IX. A mint committee shall be established at Furruckabad, consisting of the magist rate, and the collector of the revenue, of that *zillah,* or the persons holding those offices for the time being, for the superintendence of the business of the mint at that station. The mint committee at Furruckabad: shall conform to such instructions as they shall receive from the mint committee at the presidency; such instructions not being contrary to this or any other regulation published in the manner prescribed in Regulation I. 1803.	A mint committee established at Furruckabad for the superintendence of the mint at that station. Of whom the committee shall consist.

The immediate business of the mint to be conducted by an officer, to be denominated the mint and assay master.	X. The immediate conduct of the business of the mint at Furruckabad shall be committed to an officer, to *be* denominated the mint and assay master, with an adequate establishment of native officers. The mint and assay master shall be subject to the authority of the mint committees at Furruckabad and Calcutta respectively.
The mint and assay master subjected to the authority of the mint committee at Furruckabad and Calcutta. *The judge of circuit to report to the Governor General in Council the manner in which the business of the mint is conducted, in holding a general jail delivery at Furruckabad.*	*XI*. It shall be the duty of the judge of the court of circuit for the division of the ceded provinces, who shall hold the half yearly general jail delivery in the* zillah *of Furruckabad, at the periods prescribed by the regulations, to visit the mint at that station, at each session, and to make such inquiries as he shall consider necessary to satisfy himself of the manner in which the business of the mint is conducted; reporting the result of his inquiries to the Governor General in Council. The mint and assay master, and the mint committee, at Furruckabad, shall furnish the judge of the court of circuit with whatever information he may require, relative to the business of the mint at that station.* *Superseded by clause second, Section 9, Regulation II. 1812.
Mint master at Calcutta to have private marks put upon the dies prepared for the mint at Furruckabad.	XII. The mint master at Calcutta shall cause a private mark to be put upon all dies which may be prepared for the mint at Furruckabad, but in such a manner as not to be distinguishable by the naked eye, or by persons unacquainted with it. These marks shall be varied as often as the mint master at Calcutta shall judge proper, upon new dies being made, and he shall keep a register of them, in order that he may be enabled to discover any debased or defective coin which may be hereafter found in circulation.
A register of new dies to be kept by the mint master at Calcutta. Precaution for preventing bad or defective coin being issued from the mint.	XIII. One of the members of the mint committee at Furruckabad shall proceed, in person, once in every fortnight, or oftener if the committee shall judge proper, at the time when the money is usually struck of, without previously apprizing the officers of the mint; and shall take indiscriminately, out of the heaps at the foot of the striking presses, three pieces of each description of coin that may have been struck off, and transmit them to the mint committee at the presidency, who shall send the

same to the mint master at Calcutta, in order that he may cause the coin to be examined and assayed. If the specimens of coin, so transmitted, shall be found not to be of the proper standard; or if the coin shall be defective in the workmanship, or in any other respect; the mint master shall report the circumstances to the mint committee at the presidency, for the orders of the Governor-General in Council.	Mint committee and mint master at Calcutta how to proceed on such occasions.
XIV. Persons charged with counterfeiting, clipping, filing, drilling, defacing, or debasing the silver coin, struck in the mint at Furruckabad, under this regulation, shall be committed to the criminal courts, and shall be punished as the law may direct.	Persons charged with counterfeiting the coin, how to be dealt with.
XV. All Lucknow forty-fifth *sun* sicca rupees, struck in the mint at Furruckabad, of the prescribed weight and standard, which shall be coined in that mint, after the promulgation of this regulation; and also the halves and quarters of such rupees, shall be considered to be a legal tender of payment, in all public and private transactions, throughout the provinces ceded by the Nawaub Vizier to the English East India Company, according to their prescribed value. If a native officer of any public treasury shall be convicted, before the court of *adawlut* of any *zillah*, of refusing to receive in payment any such rupees, or the halves or quarters of such rupees, according to their established value, the court shall adjudge the offender to be dismissed from his office; and shall further compel him to pay to the complainant his costs of suit, and such damages as to the court may seem proper, upon a consideration of the circumstances of the case.	All Lucknow forty-fifth *sun* sicca rupees, struck at Furruckabad under this regulation, to be a legal tender of payment in all public and private transactions after the promulgation of the regulation. What penalty incurred for refusing to receive such rupees.
XVI. All officers, agents, *gomashtas*, or others employed in the collection or payment of the public revenue, or the rents of individuals, or the provision of the investment; and all proprietors and farmers of land, dependent *talookdars*, under-farmers, or *ryots*, and all persons whomsoever; are prohibited affixing any mark whatever to the silver coin struck under this regulation. All rupees, or halves, or quarters of rupees, which may be so marked, are declared not to be legal tenders of payment, in any public or private transaction; and the officers of Government are directed to reject any rupees, or halves, or quarters of rupees, so marked, which may be tendered at the public treasuries in the ceded provinces.	All persons prohibited affixing marks to the silver coin. Coin so marked not to be legal tenders of payment, and to be rejected at the public treasuries.

The ensuing settlement, and all future settlements of the land revenue in the ceded provinces, to be made in the rupee established by Section 2. The Board of Revenue and the collectors how to determine the rent or *jumma* in forming the settlement. Exception.	XVII. *First.* The ensuing triennial settlement of the land revenue in the ceded provinces, which will be formed on the expiration of the Fussily year 1212, and all future settlements of the land revenue in those provinces, shall be made in the Lucknow forty-fifth *sun* sicca rupee, as established by this regulation. In determining the amount of the rent or *jumma* to be paid to Government by the proprietors and farmers of land in the ceded provinces, on the formation of the ensuing or any future settlement, (with the exception stated in the following clause,) the Board of Revenue and the collectors of the revenue will be guided by the table of rates to be inserted in a regulation, which will be hereafter published. The difference of the intrinsic value between the species of rupee in which the existing settlement has been made, and the Lucknow forty-fifth *sun* sicca rupee, as now established, shall be calculated, according to the table above mentioned; and, after deducting such difference, the settlement shall be concluded for the residue in the said forty-fifth *sun* Lucknow sicca rupee.
Rules for the payment of the revenue, in instances in which engagements shall be entered into with Government previously to the publication of the table of rates above-mentioned, and previously to the commencement of the new coinage at Furruckabad.	*Second.* In instances in which engagements with Government shall be executed by proprietors of land, or farmers of land, for the ensuing settlement of the land revenue, previously to the publication of the table of rates mentioned in the preceding clause, and previously to the commencement of the new coinage in the mint at Furrackabad, as established by this regulation, a clause shall be inserted, binding such proprietors, or farmers, to pay to Government Lucknow sicca rupees, struck at Lucknow, of the usual weight and standard; or the same species of rupees as they may receive from their under-renters or *ryots,* at the *bassai*-rates or *batta,* for the time being, which may regulate the relative value of such rupees, when compared with the Lucknow sicca rupee struck at Lucknow; until the said table of rates shall be published. From and after the publication of the table of rates aforesaid, and from and after the commencement of the new coinage in the mint at Furruckabad, as established by this regulation, the Lucknow sicca rupee, struck at Lucknow, shall be received only according to its intrinsic value, during the period prescribed by Section 23, for receiving rupees, not being the rupees declared by this regulation to be the established and legal silver coin within the provinces ceded by the Nawaub Vizier

to the English East India Company. In the event of the commencement of the new coinage in the mint at Furruckabad, previously to the publication of the table of rates above-mentioned, the public revenue shall be paid to Government, either in the silver coin established by this regulation, or in the species of rupees received by the proprietors or farmers of land from their under-renters or *ryots,* at the *bazar* rates of *batta*, for the time being, which may regulate the relative value of such rupees, when compared with the Lucknow forty-fifth *sun* sicca rupee, struck in the mint at Furruckabad, under this regulation, until the said table of rates shall be published. The collectors shall insert in their treasury accounts the rates of *batta* at which all rupees, not being Lucknow siccas struck at Lucknow, or Lucknow forty-fifth *sun* siccas struck at Furruckabad, (according as either of those descriptions of rupees may be received under this clause,) may be received by them.	
XVIII. *First.* As a sufficient number of the Lucknow forty-fifth *sun* sicca rupees, to be struck in the mint at Furruckabad, may not be introduced into circulation, for a considerable period of time, to enable the proprietors and farmers of land, in the ceded provinces, to pay their revenue in rupees of that description, the various sorts of rupees, current in those provinces, will be received at the public treasuries, from the proprietors and farmers of land, in payment of their revenue, until the commencement of the year 1216 Fussily, at the fixed rates specified in the table which will be published in a future regulation; which rates will be calculated conformably to the difference of the intrinsic value which each species of rupee bears to the Lucknow forty-fifth *sun* sicca rupees established by this regulation, as ascertained by assay in the Calcutta mint.	Rules and valuation according to which all rupees not being forty-fifth *sun* Lucknow siccas struck at Furruckabad, are to be received in discharge of the public revenue, until the commencement of the year 1216 Fussily.
Second. Immediately after the publication of the table of rates mentioned in the preceding clause, a copy of the same, in the Persian and Hindoostanee languages, shall be fixed up by the mint master, in a conspicuous part of the mint at Furruckabad, and by the judges and magistrates, and collectors of the revenue, throughout the ceded provinces, in a conspicuous part of their respective *cutcherrees*, under their signature respectively.	A copy of the above-mentioned table to be affixed up in the mint, and in the *cutcherrees* of the judges, magistrates, and the collectors.

The preceding section applicable to all issues of money made by Government in any other than the prescribed specie, until the commencement of the year 1214 Fussily.	XIX. The rule prescribed in the first clause of the preceding section, shall be held applicable to all other transactions between Government and individuals, until the commencement of the year 1214 Fussily. It is accordingly declared, that all issues of money which may be made, on account of Government, from and after the promulgation of the table of rates, mentioned in the preceding section, until the period of time above-mentioned, in any other descriptions of rupees than the Lucknow forty-fifth *sun* sicca rupee, struck in the mint at Furruckabad shall be regulated by the table of rates aforesaid.
Explanation of the mode of receiving rupees of sorts, according to the table mentioned in Section 18.	XX. To prevent misconception of the mode of receiving rupees of sorts, under the table of rates mentioned in Section 18, it is to be understood, that one hundred sicca weight of each of the sorts of rupees which will be specified in the first column, (whatever number of the rupees may go to that weight,) shall be considered equal to the number of Lucknow forty-fifth *sun* sicca rupees, struck in the mint at Furruckabad, placed opposite to it in the second column.
Rule for receiving rupees tendered at the public treasuries which are not specified in the table mentioned in Section 18. Twelve annas per cent to be deducted for the expense of refining, when below the prescribed standard.	XXI. If any other species of rupees, besides those specified in the table mentioned in Section 18, are tendered in payment, at any of the public treasuries, before the period specified in Section 23, one hundred sicca weight of them, indiscriminately taken from the sum paid, in the presence of the payer or his agent, shall be sent to the mint at Furruckabad to be assayed; and the payer shall receive credit for a number of the Lucknow forty-fifth *sun* sicca rupees, of the prescribed weight and standard, equal in weight to the silver of sicca standard which the rupees so paid may be estimated to contain, according to the assay, after deducting twelve annas per cent for the expense of refining, should the rupees be under the prescribed standard.
Rupees of sorts received at the public treasuries to be sent to the mint. Officers of Government not to issue rupees	XXII. Rupees of sorts, which may be received at the public treasuries, agreeably to the table mentioned in Section 18, or under Section 21, shall not, on any account, be issued therefrom, from and after the commencement of the year 1214 Fussily; but shall be sent to the mint at Furruckabad, and be coined into siccas of the Lucknow forty-fifth *sun*. The officers of

Government are also prohibited from issuing, from the public treasuries, rupees of sorts which may be received at the same, between the date of the promulgation of this regulation and the period of time above-mentioned, excepting in instances in which the exigencies of the public service shall render the issuing of such rupees indispensably necessary.	of sorts from the public treasuries between the promulgation of this regulation and the commencement of the year 1214 Fussily, excepting in cases of indispensable necessity.
XXIII. From and after the commencement of the year 1216 Fussily, no other rupee, but the Lucknow forty-fifth *sun* sicca, or the halves and quarters of the same, struck in the mint at Furruckabad, shall be received at any of the public treasuries, or issued therefrom, on any account whatsoever; and no other rupees, excepting the rupees above-mentioned, and the halves and quarters of the same, shall be legal tenders of payment in any public or private transaction.	After the commencement of the year 1216 Fussily, no silver coin excepting Lucknow sicca rupees of the 45th *sun*, or their respective divisions and subdivisions, to be considered a legal tender of payment.
XXIV. Bonds, or writings, or other agreements, whether written or verbal, entered into prior to the commencement of the year 1216 Fussily, whereby a sum of money is stipulated to be paid in any species of rupee, excepting in the Lucknow forty-fifth *sun* sicca rupee, as established by this regulation, and which may not be discharged previously to the above-mentioned date, may be liquidated, at the option of the debtor, either in the rupee specified in the instrument, or in the Lucknow forty-fifth *sun* sicca rupee, at the valuation specified in the table of rates mentioned in Section 18. In instances in which an agreement for the payment of money shall be adjusted, previously to the publication of the table of rates above-mentioned, and previously to the commencement of the new coinage in the mint at Furruckabad, the money shall be paid, at the option of the debtor, either in the rupee stipulated by the agreement, or according to the rule prescribed in clause second, Section 17 of this regulation.	Bonds or agreements for money executed prior to the commencement of the year 1216 Fussily to be dischargeable prior to that date, either in the coin stipulated in the deed, or in 45th *sun* Lucknow sicca rupees, at the rates specified in the table mentioned in Section 18. Exception from the foregoing rule.

Agreements executed after the commencement of the year 1216 Fussily, stipulating for the payment of money in any other specie excepting the prescribed Lucknow sicca rupee of the 45th sun, or the halves or quarters of them, not recoverable in any court of justice.	*XXV*. From and after the commencement of the year 1216 Fussily, no person shall recover, in any court of judicature in the ceded provinces, any sum of money, under a bond, or other writing, or any agreement, written or verbal, entered into within the limits of the provinces aforesaid, after the above-mentioned date, by which any sum of money shall be stipulated to be paid in any species of rupee, excepting in the Lucknow sicca rupee, of the forty-fifth* sun, *as established by this regulation, or the halves and quarters of the same.* *Rescinded by Section 9, Regulation XIII. 1807.
All engagements, on the part of Government, for the provision of the investment, to be made in the rupee prescribed in Section 2. Engagements for rent and revenue to be made in the same coin. All engagements between proprietors and farmers of land, and their under-renters of whatever description to be made in the Lucknow 45th *sun* sicca rupee, from the commencement of the year 1216 Fussily.	XXVI. All engagements hereafter entered into, on the part of Government, for the provision of the investment, shall be made in the Lucknow forty-fifth *sun* sicca rupee, as established by the present regulation; and all proprietors and farmers of land are prohibited, from the commencement of the year 1216 Fussily, from concluding engagements with their under-farmers, *ryots,* or dependent *talookdars*, in any species of rupee, excepting the rupee of the description above-mentioned, under the penalty of not being permitted to recover any arrears which may become due to them, under such engagements. Proprietors and farmers of land are expected, in all practicable cases, to conclude any engagements, which they may have occasion to form with their under-farmers, *ryots*, and dependent *talookdars*, between the date of the publication of this regulation and the commencement of the year 1216 Fussily, in the Lucknow rupee of the forty-fifth *sun,* as established by this regulation.
Penalty for acting contrary to the rules above prescribed.	XXVII. If the Lucknow sicca rupees of the forty-fifth *sun,* established by this regulation, of full weight, or the halves or quarters of such rupees, shall be tendered at any of the public treasuries; and any of the native officers

shall refuse to receive them, in payment of any public demand, and shall require any other species of rupees; or if any of the species of rupees to be inserted in the table mentioned in Section 18, shall be tendered at the public treasuries, prior to the date specified in Section 23, at the valuation specified in such table; or if any of the species of rupees in which the collections are made from the under-renters, or *ryots,* shall be tendered at the public treasuries at the *bazar* rates of *batta* for the time being, under clause second of Section 17, and any native officer shall refuse to receive them at such valuation; upon proof of such offence, before the court of *adawlut* of the *zillah* in which the complaint may be cognizable, the court shall dismiss the offender from his office, and shall adjudge him to pay costs of suit, and damages to the party complaining.	Proprietors and farmers of land expected, in all practicable cases, to form settlements with their under-renters, between the publication of this regulation and the period above specified, in the Lucknow 45th *sun* sicca rupee.
XXVIII. After the date specified in Section 23, if any native officer, at any of the public treasuries, shall be convicted of receiving, in payment of a public demand, any silver coin, excepting the Lucknow sicca rupee of the forty-fifth *sun,* established by this regulation or the halves and quarters of the same, the court shall dismiss him from his office, and shall adjudge him to pay such fine to Government as may appear to the court to be adequate to the offence.	Punishment for native officers at any of the treasuries refusing to receive the rupee established by Section 2.
XXIX. For all silver bullion, or old or light silver coin, equal to, or above, the standard of the Lucknow forty-fifth *sun* sicca rupee, (to be inserted in a regulation which will be hereafter published) which may be delivered into the mint at Furruckabad, a number of the Lucknow forty-fifth *sun* sicca rupees, or halves, or quarters, of such rupees, equal in weight to the silver of the prescribed standard contained in such bullion, or old or light coin, shall be returned to the proprietor, without any charge whatever.	Native officers at any of the public treasuries liable to fine and dismission for receiving any coin but that prescribed by Section 2. For all silver bullion or coin of, or above, the prescribed standard, coin equal to the weight of the standard bullion to be returned without any charge whatever.

Twelve annas per cent to be charged, for refining to the prescribed standard, bullion, or old or light silver coin, under that standard.	XXX. All silver bullion, or old or light silver coin, under the prescribed standard, which may be delivered into the mint at Furruckabad, shall be refined to the prescribed standard; and a number of the Lucknow forty-fifth *sun* sicca rupees, of the prescribed weight and standard, or halves, or quarters, of such rupees, equal in weight to the refined bullion, or coin, shall be returned to the proprietor, after deducting twelve annas per cent for the expense of refining.
A written notification to be affixed up in the mint, and in the *cutcherees* of the judges and magistrates, and of the collectors of the revenue, and to what effect. Changes in the rate of charge for refining or relating to the expense of coinage, to be notified in a similar manner.	XXXI. A written notification, under the signature of the mint master at Furruckabad, and of the judges and magistrates, and collectors of the revenue, of the several *zillahs*, declaring that all silver bullion, or old or light silver coin, equal to, or above, the prescribed standard, which may be delivered into the mint, at Furruckabad, for coinage, will be converted into the silver coin, established by this regulation, without any charge whatever to the proprietor; and specifying the rate of duty to be paid by persons bringing silver bullion, or old or light silver coin, below the prescribed standard, to the mint, for coinage, for the expense of refining the same; shall be fixed up in a conspicuous part of the mint at that station, and in the *cutcherrees* of the several judges and magistrates, and of the collectors of the revenue, throughout the ceded provinces. Any change which may be hereafter made in the rate of charge for refining silver, below the prescribed standard, or in any manner relating to the expense of coinage shall be notified to the public in a similar manner.
Option given to individuals to have their silver bullion, or old or light silver coin, coined into rupees, or halves or quarters of rupees.	XXXII. It shall be at the option of individuals to have their old or light silver coin, or silver bullion, coined into the Lucknow forty-fifth *sun* sicca rupees, or half or quarter rupees, or into such proportions of each, as they may think proper.
All Lucknow forty-fifth *sun* sicca rupees, which shall not have lost by wear more than six	XXXIII. All Lucknow sicca rupees of the forty-fifth *sun*, struck in the mint at Furruckabad, which shall not have lost by wear a greater proportion of their full standard weight than six annas per cent or six sixteenths of a rupee in one hundred rupees, shall be considered as of

standard weight, and shall be received as such in all public and private transactions.	annas per cent or six sixteenths of a rupee in a hundred, to be considered of standard weight, and to be received as such in all transactions.
XXXIV. The rule prescribed in the preceding section shall be considered applicable to those Lucknow forty-fifth *sun* sicca rupees only, struck in the mint at Furruckabad, in which the loss of weight has been occasioned by wear. Whenever rupees of the above description may have lost any part of their full weight, although such loss shall not exceed six annas per cent by filing, clipping, or other artificial means, such rupees shall not be considered as of standard weight; and, if tendered in payment at any of the public treasuries, or offices, they shall be received at their intrinsic value, as hereafter directed; and the *podars*, or examiners of the public money, are required to separate all such rupees.	The foregoing rule not applicable to rupees in which the loss of weight shall not have been occasioned by wear, but by artificial means.
XXXV. *First.* Lucknow rupees of the forty-fifth *sun*, struck in the mint at Furruckabad, which may be deficient in weight, from any other cause excepting wear, or deficient in weight from wear in a greater amount than six annas per cent shall be received conformably to the following rule.	Such rupees to be received at their intrinsic value.
Second. For one hundred Lucknow sicca weight of such light forty-fifth *sun* sicca rupees, the payer shall receive credit for one hundred Lucknow forty-fifth *sun* sicca rupees. The light rupees, thus received at the public treasuries, shall not be again disbursed, but shall be invariably sent to the mint at Furruckabad to be recoined.	Rule to be observed in receiving rupees deficient in weight from any other cause excepting wear, or from wear exceeding six annas per cent.
XXXVI. The rules contained in Sections 33, 34, and 35, of this regulation, shall be considered equally applicable to the halves and quarters of the forty-fifth *sun* Lucknow sicca rupee, struck in the mint at Furruckabad.	The rules contained in Sections 33, 34, and 35, applicable to halves and quarters of rupees.

The mint master at Calcutta to furnish standard weights, for the use of the collectors.	XXXVII. The mint master at Calcutta shall furnish the Board of Revenue, for the use of the collectors in the ceded provinces, with stampt metal weights of fifty Lucknow sicca weight each, or such other weights as may be required by them; and all receipts and payments, at the public treasuries, shall be regulated conformable to such standard weights.
Order in which silver bullion, and old or light silver coin, delivered into the mint, is to be assayed, refined, and coined.	*XXXVIII*. All silver bullion, and old or light silver coin, delivered into the mint at Furruckabad, for coinage, shall be assayed in the order in which it shall be received; refined in the order in which it may be assayed; and coined in the order in which it may be refined. Standard silver bullion, delivered into the mint, shall be registered as refined bullion, on the date on which it may be assayed.* *Rescinded by Section 7, Regulation II, 1812.
Registers to be kept for public inspection in the Furruckabad mint.	XXXIX. The following registers shall be kept open, at the mint of Furruckabad, for public inspection; viz. A register of unassayed silver bullion, delivered into the mint; specifying the quantity delivered, the date on which it was received, and the name of the proprietor. A register of silver bullion, assayed and refined; specifying the date on which it was assayed, the date on which it was refined, the name of the proprietor, and the produce in the Lucknow forty-fifth *sun* sicca rupees; together with the date of the certificate granted for the produce, and the date on which such certificate was discharged.
The mint master at Furruckabad to transmit copies of the foregoing registers to the mint committee at the presidency.	XL. English copies of the registers mentioned in the foregoing section, shall be sent by the mint master at Furruckabad, on the fifth day of every month, for the month preceding, to the mint committee at the presidency.
The operation of the mint at Bareilly, and the coinage of Furruckabad rupees in the Furruckabad mint, to be discontinued,	XLI. *First.* The operation of the mint at Bareilly shall be discontinued, from the date of the promulgation of this regulation; with the exception of the coinage of whatever silver bullion and silver coin may be deposited in the mint of that station, for coinage, when the regulation shall be promulgated. It shall be left to the option of the proprietors of such bullion and coin, either to withdraw the same, or to have it converted into the

silver coin hitherto struck in the mint at Bareilly, and denominated the Bareilly rupee, as they shall think proper.	and from what periods.
Second. The coinage of the silver specie, hitherto struck in the mint at Furruckabad, and denominated the Furruckabad rupee, shall be discontinued, from the time when the mint master at that station shall be furnished with the necessary machinery and dies for commencing the new silver coinage established by this regulation. Immediately on being enabled to commence the new silver coinage, the mint master at Furruckabad shall fix up a written notification, under his signature, in a conspicuous part of the mint, declaring that no silver bullion or silver coin will be received at the mint, for coinage into any other description of rupee than the rupee established by this regulation, from and after the date of such notification. The mint master shall also transmit copies of the said notification, under his signature, to the several judges and magistrates, and to the collectors of the revenue, in the ceded provinces, in order that the same may be fixed up in their respective *cutcherrees*, for general information. It shall be left to the option of the proprietors of whatever silver bullion, and silver coin may be deposited in the mint at Furruckabad, for coinage, at the time of the publication of the notification above-mentioned, either to withdraw the same, or to have it converted into the silver coin hitherto struck in the mint of that station, and denominated the Furruckabad rupee, or into the new silver coin established by this regulation, as they shall think proper.	Rule respecting bullion or coin deposited in those mints for coinage, at the periods above-mentioned.
XLII. Whereas the gold coin denominated gold mohurs, have never obtained an extensive circulation in the ceded provinces, in consequence of silver having been the general measure of value in those provinces, from time immemorial: and whereas during the government of the Nawaub Vizier, the value of the gold mohurs in circulation, with relation to the silver coin, was never fixed: and whereas the coinage of gold mohurs has been long discontinued by the native Government of the said provinces, as well as in the adjacent foreign states: it is not, therefore judged necessary, at present, to establish a gold coinage in the provinces in question. The gold	The establishment of a gold coinage in the ceded provinces not considered necessary. Gold coin to continue in circulation as heretofore. Not to be considered a legal tender of payment in any transactions.

	mohurs shall be permitted to be circulated, in the ceded provinces, as heretofore, according to the value which individuals, receiving and paying the same, shall determine; but gold mohurs shall not be considered to be a legal tender of payment, in any public or private transaction; nor shall they bear any fixed rate of value, compared with reference to the silver coin, or Lucknow forty-fifth *sun* sicca rupee, struck in the mint at Furruckabad, as established by this regulation; but they shall continue to circulate, as heretofore, agreeably to the established usage of the country.
A copper coin of an uniform weight, and of pure copper, established in the ceded provinces.	*XLIII*. A copper coin, of the forty-fifth sun, weighing two hundred and eighty-four and a half grains troy, and consisting of pure copper, shall be established, in the provinces ceded by the Nawaub Vizier to the English East India Company. The corresponding Lncknow and Calcutta sicca weight of the copper coin above-mentioned will be inserted in a future regulation.* *Rescinded by Section 2, Regulation XXI, 1816.
	XLIV. The form, size, and impression of the copper coin, established by the foregoing section, shall correspond with those prescribed by Section 5 of this regulation, for the Lucknow forty-fifth *sun* sicca rupee; but the edges of such copper coin shall not be milled, nor have any mark or impression thereon.
Form, size, and impression, which the copper coin shall bear. The edges not to be milled. Copper pice and half pice, will be coined in the mint at Furruckabad.	XLV. Copper pice, of pure copper, and of the weight prescribed by Section 43; and half pice of the same standard and proportionate weight and size; will be coined in the mint established at Furruckabad, under Section 4 of this regulation. The half pie shall bear the same impression as the whole pie. A smaller division of the pie than the half pie shall not be coined.
Individuals at liberty to send or bring to the Furruckabad mint, pure, copper or copper coin of pure	*XLVI*. Individuals are at liberty to send, or bring, to the mint at Furruckabad, pure copper, or old pice or other copper coin consisting of pure copper, to be coined into pice, or half pice, of the prescribed weight and standard.*

*Rescinded by Section 2, Regulation VI, 1820.	*copper, to be coined into pice or half pice of the prescribed weight.*
XLVII. It shall be at the option of individuals to have their copper, or copper coin, coined into whole pice, or half pice, or into such proportions of each, as they may think proper.	*Individuals at liberty to have, their copper, or copper coin, coined into whole or half pice.*
XLVIII. For all pure copper, or old copper coin consisting of pure copper, which may he delivered into the mint at Furruckabad for coinage, a number of the pice, established by this regulation, or halves of such pice, equal in weight to the copper produced from such copper or copper coin, shall be returned to the proprietor, without any charge whatever. None but pure copper shall be received at the mint for coinage into pice.	*For all copper, or copper coin, pice or half pice of equal weight to that produced, and of the prescribed weight, shall be returned to the proprietor, without any charge whatever.* *None but pure copper to be received at the mint for coinage.*
XLIX. The copper coin, established by Section 43 of this regulation, struck in the mint at Furruckabad, shall be received at, and issued from, the public treasuries, and shall also be paid and received, in private transactions between individuals, in the ceded provinces, for the payment of any sum, being the fractional part of a rupee. Pice received, or issued, under this section, shall be received and issued, according to the rate at which pice may be current in the *bazar*, with reference to the established silver coin, at the time when the payment may be made, unless any other rate shall be mutually agreed upon by the parties.	Copper coin, for any sum below, the value of one rupee, to be considered a legal tender of payment, in all transactions. To be received and issued in the foregoing case at what rate.
L. Any public officer, or other person, convicted, before a court of *adaulut*, of refusing to receive in payment the fractional part of a rupee in the copper coin now established, in adjustment of an account, as directed in the foregoing section, shall be liable to pay to the complainant his costs of suit, and such damages as to the court may seem proper, upon a consideration of the	Penalty incurred by a disobedience of the rule prescribed in the foregoing section.

If the offender be an officer of Government, to be dismissed from his office.	circumstances of the case. If the offender shall be a native public officer of Government, the court shall further adjudge him to be dismissed from his office.
The rules prescribed by Sections 11, 13, 14, and 31, applicable to the copper coinage established by Section 44.	LI. *First.* The rules prescribed by Sections 11, 13, 14, and 31, of this regulation, respecting the silver coinage in the ceded provinces, are declared to be applicable to the copper coinage established in those provinces, by Section 44 of this regulation.
Registers of copper coinage to be kept for public inspection. A copy to be sent monthly to the mint committee at the Presidency.	*Second.* A register shall be kept in the mint at Furruckabad (to be open for public inspection) of all copper, or old copper coin, which may be brought to the mint for coinage. Such register shall also specify the name of the proprietor, and the produce in the pice established by this regulation; together with the date of the certificate granted for the produce, and the date on which such certificate was discharged. An English copy of the above-mentioned register shall be transmitted, on the fifth day of every month, for the month preceding, to, the mint committee at the presidency.
European and native officers of Government herein specified liable to be sued for any breach of this or any future regulation, respecting the coinage.	LII. Collectors of the revenue, commercial residents, or agents, the mint and assay master at Furruckabad, and their respective officers, shall be liable to be sued for damages, in the *zillah* courts to which they may be respectively amenable, for any breach of this regulation or any other regulation which may be enacted respecting the coinage in the ceded provinces.

Appendix A.13

A.D. 1803 REGULATION LIV

A REGULATION for postponing the Operation of Section 20, Regulation XXXV. 1793, within the Zillah of Chittagong.—PASSED by the Governor General in Council, on the 24th of November 1803; corresponding with the 10th Aughun 1210 Bengal era; the 25th Aughun 1211 Fussily; the 10th Aughun 1211; Willaity; the 25th Aughun 1860 Sumbut; and the 8th Shabuan 1218 Higeree.

THE reasons stated in the preamble to Regulation III. 1799, for postponing the operation of Section 20. Regulation XXXV. 1793, in the *zillah* of Sylhet, being equally applicable to the *zillah* of Chittagong, until the 1st Bhadoon of the Bengal year 1210, corresponding with the 16th August A.D. 1803, when the regulation above-mentioned was first promulgated and enforced in this district; the Governor General in Council has passed the following rule, to be in force in the *zillah* of Chittagong only.	Preamble
II. Section 20; Regulation XXXV. 1793, shall not have effect in the *zillah* of Chittagong until the 1st Bhadoon of the Bengal year 1210, or 16th August A.D. 1803; after which period the provisions in the said section and regulation are to be considered in full force in that *zillah*, as in other parts of the province of Bengal.	Section 20, Regulation XXXV. 1793, not to have effect in *zillah* Chittagong until the 1st Bhadoon 1210, B.S. or 16th August 1803, E.S.

Appendix A.14

A.D. 1805. REGULATION XI

A REGULATION for extending to the conquered provinces, situated within the Dooab and on the right bank of the river Jumna; and to the territories ceded to the Honorable the English East India Company in Bundlecund by the Peishwah; Regulation XLV, 1803, entitled, a regulation for the reform of the gold, silver, and copper coin, in the provinces ceded by the Nawaub Vizier to the Honorable the English East India Company: also for providing for the appointment of the native officers of government, employed in the mint, established at Furruckabad, under Regulation XLV, 1803; and for extending to such native officers such parts of Regulation V, 1804, as provide for the appointment and removal of the native officers of government in certain departments.—PASSED by the Vice President in Council, on the 15th August 1805; corresponding with the 1st Bhadoon 1212 Bengal era; the 5th Bhadoon 1212 Fussily; the 1st Bhadoon 1212 Willaity; the 5th Bhadoon 1862 Sumbut; and the 13th Rubbee-u-Sany 1220 Higeree.

[Preamble]	WHEREAS Regulation XLV, 1803, provides rules for the reform of the gold, silver, and copper coin, in the provinces ceded by the Nawaub Vizier to the Honorable the English East India Company: And whereas it is expedient, that the regulation abovementioned should be extended to the conquered provinces situated within the Dooab and on the right bank of the river Jumna, and to the territories ceded to the Honorable the English East India Company in Bundlecund by the Peishwah: And whereas it is advisable, that rules should be provided for the appointment and removal of the native officers of government, employed in the mint at Furruckabad, the following rules have been accordingly enacted.
Regulation XLV, 1803, extended to the conquered provinces, and to the territories ceded to the	II. Regulation XLV, 1803, is hereby extended to the conquered provinces situated within the Dooab, and on the right bank of the river Jumna, ceded to the Honorable the English East India Company by Dowlut Rao Scindiah; and to the territories situated in Bundlecund on the right bank of the river Jumna, ceded to the

Honorable the English East India Company by the Peishwah; to which the laws and regulations of the British government have been extended by Regulation IX, 1804, and Regulations VIII and IX, 1805: and the periods prescribed for the operation of the said regulation, in the provinces ceded by the Nawaub Vizier to the Honorable the English East India Company, are also hereby declared to be applicable to the provinces and territories aforesaid.	Company in Bundlecund by the Peishwah.
III. The operation of the mint at Saharunpore, and of any other mint or mints within the provinces and territories mentioned in Section II, the operation of which shall not have already ceased, shall be discontinued, from the date of the promulgation of this regulation; with the exception of the coinage of whatever silver bullion and silver coin may be deposed so such mint or mints, for coinage, when the regulation shall be promulgated. It shall be left to the option of the proprietors of such bullion and coin, either to withdraw the same, or to have it converted into the silver coin hitherto struck in the mint in which it may be deposited, for coinage, as they, shall think proper.	The operation of the mint at Saharunpore, and of any other mint or mints in the conquered provinces, to be discontinued, and from what period.
IV. First. The native officers of government, forming the fixed establishment in the mint at Furruckabad, shall be nominated, in the first instance, by the mint and assay master, subject to the confirmation of the mint committee at that station, or of the Governor General in Council, according as such officers may come within the descriptions of officers specified in Regulation V, 1804, providing rules for the appointment and removal of native officers; which regulation, as far as it relates to the appointment and removal of native officers, is hereby extended to the native officers of government, employed in the mint at Furruckabad. All references, regarding the appointment, resignation, suspension, or removal, of the native officers of government, employed in the mint at the above station, whose salary shall amount to or exceed ten rupees per month, shall be made by the mint and assay master, in the first instance, to the mint committee at that station, who will act therein, in the same manner as the other intermediate authorities mentioned in the regulation aforesaid.	Native officers, employed in the mint at Furruckadab, to be nominated, in the first instance, by the mint and assay master. Rules contained in Regulation V, 1804, respecting the appointment and removal of native officers, extended to the native officers, employed in the mint at Furruckabad. References regarding the removal and appointment of native officers to

be made in the first instance to the mint committee at Furruckabad. The mint committee at Furruckabad empowered in certain cases, to direct the dismission or suspension of native officers employed in the mint, without a previous reference being made to them by the mint and assay master.	*Second.* It shall be competent to the mint committee at Furruckabad, whenever they shall see good and sufficient cause, to direct the demission or suspension of any native officer of government, employed in the mint at that station, according to the nature of the office and the amount of the salary, although a previous reference shall not be made to them, reflecting such officer, by the mint and assay master; and the mint and assay master is enjoined to obey such requisitions as may be received by him from the mint committee to the above effect. The mint committee are, however, required to report to the Governor General in Council every instance in which they shall exercise the power veiled in them by the present clause, accompanied by a translation of their proceedings, and of the defence of the officer dismissed or suspended.

Appendix A.15

A.D. 1805 REGULATION XII

A REGULATION for the settlement and collection of the public revenue in the zillah of Cuttack, including the pergunnahs of Puttespore, Kummardichour, and Bograe, at present included in the zillah of Midnapore.—PASSED by the Vice President in Council, on the 5th of September 1805; corresponding with the 22nd Bhadoon 1212 Bengal era; the 26th Bhadoon 1212 Fussily; the 22nd Bhadoon 1212 Willaity; the 12th Bhadoon 1862 Sumbut; and the 10th Jumadee-us-Sany 1220 Higeree.

xx xx xx xx	
XII. The regulations established in the province of Bengal, for raising a revenue by means of stamp paper, are hereby extended to the province of Cuttack (in common with the other regulations extended to that zillah by Section XXXVI, of this regulation), provided nevertheless that the provisions enacted respecting pleadings and other papers (which are considered to be of the nature of pleadings) under the regulations established in the province of Bengal, shall not be in force in the province of Cuttack, until the expiration of one year from the date of this regulation; and provided also, that the provisions regarding obligations for the payment of money, law papers, and generally all other stamp papers, shall not be in force until the expiration of two years from the date of this regulation.	Regulations respecting stamp paper in force in Bengal extended to Cuttack, with provisions as to the period of their being in force there.
XIII. All engagements for the payment of the public revenue by the zemindars, talookdars, farmers, and other holders of land, shall be made in Calcutta sicca rupees of the nineteenth sun; but as the zemindars, talookdars, farmers, and other holders of land, may not immediately have the means of paying their revenue in that species of rupees, the various rupees of sorts will be received at the treasures in payment of the public revenue until the expiration of the Willaity year 1215, according to the table of rates contained in Section XIV, Regulation	All engagements for the payment of the revenue to be made in Calcutta sicca rupees. Rules for the receipt of rupees of sorts until the expiration of the year 1215

Willaity, after which no money but Calcutta sicca rupees, or gold mohurs of the nineteenth sun, and their parts shall be received in payment of the public revenue.	XXXV, 1793; and cowries will be received at the rate of four cawons per sicca rupee, until the expiration of that period of time. Should any other species of rupees exclusive of those specified in Section XIV, Regulation XXXV 1793, be current in the zillah of Cuttack, the collector shall forward specimens of them, as soon as may be practicable, to the Secretary to Government in the Revenue Department, for the purpose of being forwarded to the assay mailer to be assayed; and the persons from whom such rupees may have been received, shall receive credit for the same at their intrinsic value, as ascertained by actual assay, after deducting twelve annas per cent for the expense of refining, should the rupees be under sicca standard. A supplementary table of rates of the value of each description of such rupees (prepared on the principle of the table of rates contained in Section XIV, Regulation XXXV, 1793) shall be fixed up at the cutcherry of the collector, and at the court house of the judge and magistrate. After the expiration of the Willaity year 1215 no money will be received in payment of the public revenue, excepting Calcutta sicca rupees, or gold mohurs of the nineteenth sun, or the halves and quarters of those coins.
Option left to the debtor in liquidating bond, &c. entered into for payment of different species of rupees, and not discharged prior to the expiration of the year 1213 Willaity.	XIV. Bonds, or writings, or other agreements, whether written or verbal, entered into prior to the expiration of the Willaity year 1213, whereby a sum of money is stipulated to be paid in any species of rupee, excepting the nineteenth sun sicca, or the gold mohur of the nineteenth sun, and which may not be discharged previous to the abovementioned date, may be liquidated, at the option of the debtor, either in the rupee specified in the instrument, or in the nineteenth sun sicca rupee, at the valuation specified in the table, in Section XIV, Regulation XXXV, 1793; or in the nineteenth sun gold mohur.
No money due on any bond or agreement entered into after the expiration of the year 1213 Willaity, and	XV. After the expiration of the Willaity year 1213, no person shall recover in any court of judicature in the province of Bengal, Behar, or Orissa, any sum of money under a bond, or other writing, or any agreement written or verbal, entered into after the abovementioned date, by which any sum of money shall be stipulated to be paid in any species of rupees, excepting Calcutta sicca

rupees, or gold mohurs of the nineteenth sun or the halves or quarters of each.	stipulating payment in any other specie than the Calcutta sicca rupee or gold mohur of the nineteenth sun, and their parts shall be recoverable in any Court of justice.
XVI. All engagements hereafter entered into on the part of government for the provision of the investment, or the manufacture of salt, are to be made in the Calcutta sicca rupee, or the gold mohur of the nineteenth sun; and all proprietors and farmers of land are prohibited from concluding engagements with their under farmers, ryots, or dependent talookdars, after the expiration of the Willaity year 1213 in any species of rupees or gold mohurs, excepting the Calcutta sicca rupees, and the gold mohurs of the nineteenth sun, under the penalty of not being permitted to recover any arrears, that may become due to them under such engagements.	All future engagements of government for the provision of the investment or manufacture of salt are to be made in the Calcutta sicca rupee, or the gold mohur of the nineteenth, sun and proprietors and farmers of land prohibited from entering engagements with their under farmers &c. after the expiration of the year 1213 Willaity in any other species of rupees.
xx xx xx xx	

Appendix A.16

A.D. 1806 REGULATION III

A REGULATION for defining the weight and standard of the silver coin, established in the, ceded and conquered provinces, by Regulation XLV, 1803, and Regulation XI, 1805; and the weight of the copper coin established in the said provinces by the regulations abovementioned; also for fixing a table of rates for regulating the receipt and payment of rupees of different descriptions, during the periods prescribed by Regulation XLV, 1803, for the receipt and payment of rupees not being the rupees declared by that reputation and by Regulation XI, 1805, to be the established and legal silver coin within the ceded and conquered provinces.—PASSED by the Governor General in Council, on the 27th of March 1806; corresponding with the 15th Chyte 1212 Bengal era; the 23rd Chyte 1213 Fussily; the 15th Chyte 1213 Willaity; the 7th Chyte 1863 Sumbut; and the 6th Mohurrum 1221 Hegiree.

Preamble	WHEREAS it is declared in Sections III and XLIII, Regulation XLV, 1803, that a specification of the weight and standard of the Lucnow sicca rupee, established by Section II, of that regulation, and of the corresponding Lucnow and Calcutta sicca weight of the copper coin established by Section XLIII, of the regulation aforesaid, would be published in a future regulation: And whereas it is declared in the said regulation, that a table of rates would be inserted in a future regulation, for determining the receipt and payment of rupees of different descriptions, during the periods prescribed by the regulation abovementioned, for the receipt and payment of rupees, not being the rupees declared by that regulation, to be the established and legal silver coin in the provinces ceded by the Nawaub Vizier to the Honorable the English East India Company: And whereas Regulation XLV, 1803, has been extended by Regulation XI 1805, to the conquered provinces, situated within the Doab, and on the right bank of the river Jumna, ceded to the Honorable the English East India Company by Dowlut Rao Scindiah, and to the territories in Bundlecund, ceded

<table>
<tr><td>to the Honorable the English East India Company by the Peishwah; the following rules have been therefore enacted, to be in force in the ceded and conquered provinces.</td><td></td></tr>
<tr><td>II. The following is a specification of the weight and standard of the Lucnow sicca rupee of the forty-fifth sun, struck in the Mint at Furruckabad, established by Section II, Regulation XLV, 1803, and Regulation XI 1805.

Troy Weight, one hundred and seventy three Grains.

Touch, or parts of fine Silver, in 100, 95 5
Assay Alloy, ... 4 5</td><td>Specification of weight and standard of the Lucnow sicca rupee, struck at the mint at Furruckabad, established by Regulation XLV, 1803, and Regulation XI, 1805.</td></tr>
<tr><td>III. The following is a specification of the weight of the copper coin, established by Section XLVI, Regulation XLV, 1803, and Regulation XI 1805

Troy Weight, – – Grains 284½

Rupees. Annas. Pice.
Lucnow sicca weight, – Annas 1 10 3½
Calcutta sicca weight, – Annas 1 9 4

It is to be understood, however, that pice shall only be coined on account of government, and in such quantities and at such times, as the Governor General in Council, on receipt of information on the subject from the Mint Committee at Furruckabad, may direct.</td><td>Specification of the weight of copper coins, established by the same regulation.</td></tr>
<tr><td>IV. The pice will be issued from the treasury of government at the rate of twenty six, for a Lucnow sicca rupee.</td><td>Rate at which pice will be issued from the Treasury.</td></tr>
<tr><td>V. The following is the table of rates referred to in Regulation XLV, 1803, for determining the receipt and payment of different descriptions of rupees, not being the rupees declared by that regulation, and by Regulation XI 1805, to be the established and legal silver coin in the ceded and conquered provinces, during the periods limited for the receipt and payment of such rupees by the said regulations.</td><td>Table of rates for determining the receipt and payment of different descriptions of rupees, not being the established and legal currency</td></tr>
</table>

during the period limited for the receipt and payment of such rupees, by the regulations above-mentioned.	

TABLE SHOWING THE INTRINSIC COMPARATIVE VALUE THAT EACH SPECIE OF RUPEE, BEARS TO THE LUCNOW SICCA RUPEE, OR IN OTHER WORDS, THE NUMBER OF LUCNOW SICCA RUPEES, INTRINSICALLY EQUAL TO ONE HUNDRED LUCNOW SICCA WEIGHT OF EACH OF THE DIFFERENT SORTS OF RUPEES SPECIFIED IN THE TABLE.

Sorts of Rupees	Lucnow Sicca Weight	Lucnow Sicca Rupee		
Sicca of Lucnow, Troy weight grains 173, fine silver, grains 165 22	100	100	0	0
Calcutta, Moorshedabad, Patna, and Dacca, 19 *sun* Sicca rupees,	ditto.	102	9	9
Furruckabad rupees,	ditto.	97	10	3
Bareilly rupees,	ditto.	97	6	0
Nudjeebabad rupees,	ditto.	96	5	3
Lucnow rupees coined at Allahabad	ditto.	96	13	8
Old 18 suns Lucnow,	ditto.	95	8	9
Viziery rupees,	ditto.	89	4	2
Benares rupees,	ditto.	101	0	8
Corah 12 suns,	ditto.	91	9	11
--------20 suns,	ditto.	91	1	6
--------12 suns,	ditto.	92	14	10
Furruckabad 31 and 39 suns,	ditto.	97	6	0
Etawah rupees,	ditto.	95	4	6
Saharunpore old rupees,	ditto.	96	9	6
Saharunpore new rupees,	ditto.	96	13	8
Panniput rupees,	ditto.	95	12	1
Samlie rupees,	ditto.	94	12	2
Kerhanah rupees,	ditto.	96	5	3
Lundowrah rupees,	ditto.	95	12	11
Thannah rupees,	ditto.	94	12	2
Ruckaby rupees,	ditto.	91	1	6
Sirdannah rupees	ditto.	96	5	3
Dehli siccas,	ditto.	101	0	8
Delhi 38 suns,	ditto.	96	9	6
Bhurtpore rupees,	ditto.	100	12	6
Khotah rupees,	ditto.	95	8	8

Ghutsun 29 suns,	ditto.	99	7	6
Mahomed Shahee 19 suns,	ditto.	101	0	8
Gocul 46 suns,	ditto.	96	13	8
Jeend rupees,	ditto.	84	13	0
Siccas of Lucnow,	ditto.	100	0	0
Gourshahee 7 suns,	ditto.	95	4	6
------------- 8 suns,	ditto.	95	12	11
------------- 9 suns,	ditto.	93	3	0
------------ 10 suns,	ditto.	93	3	0
------------ 11 suns,	ditto.	92	6	5
------------ 12 suns,	ditto.	91	5	8
Siringury rupees,	ditto.	93	7	2
Tamboshahee rupees,	ditto.	91	9	11
Ballashahee rupees, coined at Culpie,	ditto.	93	11	5
Hattrass rupees,	ditto.	99	7	6
Bindrabunsee rupees,	ditto.	87	6	10
Generally struck by Perron	ditto.	90	9	2
Deeg rupees,	ditto.	91	9	11
Gourshahee rupees,	ditto.	98	11	0
Bombay rupees,	ditto.	96	5	3
Old Arcots, Moorshedabad, Calcutta,	ditto.	97	10	3
French Arcots,	ditto.	99	7	6
Madras Arcots,	ditto.	98	11	0

Appendix A.17

A.D. 1807 REGULATION IV

A REGULATION for determining the rates, at which rupees of sorts shall be received and issued in the ceded and conquered provinces, during the existence of the depending settlement of the land revenue in those provinces.—PASSED by the Governor General in Council on the 19th March 1807; corresponding with the 7th Chyte 1213 Bengal era; the 25th Phaugun 1214 Fussily; the 7th Chyte 1214 Willaity; the 10th Phaugun 1863 Sumbut; and the 9th Mohurrum 1222 Higeree.

Preamble	WHEREAS it was enacted in Clause First, Section XVII, Regulation XLV, 1803, that the depending triennial settlement in the ceded provinces should he made in Lucnow sicca rupees, and that the difference between the several descriptions of rupees in which the former settlement had been made, and the Lucnow sicca rupees should be calculated according to a table of rates of the intrinsic value of all such descriptions of rupees, compared with the Lucnow sicca rupees; And whereas the said rules were extended by Section XXVIII, Regulation VIII, 1805, to the conquered provinces, situated on the right and left banks of the river Jumna, and to that part of the province of Bundlecund, in which the general laws and regulations of the British Government have been declared to be in force; And whereas the delay which unavoidably occurred in publishing the said table of rates, has precluded a general adherence to that rule in the formation of the depending settlement; the following rules have been enacted, to be in force from the time of their promulgation in the ceded and conquered provinces.
The operation of Clause First, Section XVII. Regulation XLV, 1803, and provisions	II. The operation of Clause First, Section XVII, Regulation XLV, 1803, and of the provisions contained in Regulation III, 1806, is hereby suspended during the existence of the depending triennial settlement, as follows: In the ceded and conquered provinces lying on the right and left banks of the river Jumna, until the

expiration of the Fussily year 1215; In the province of Bundlecund, until the expiration of the year 1216.	contained in Regulation III, 1806, suspended during the existing settlements.
III. Until the expiration of the periods above specified, the zemindars, farmers, and others paying revenue to government, shall discharge the demands upon them, either in the species of rupees specified in their existing engagements, or in any other species of rupees which may be current in the different districts, at the rates of batta at which they were received and paid, previously to the promulgation of the table of rates contained in Regulation III, 1806.	In what species of rupees the revenues may be paid.
IV. It is provided in Section XXII, Regulation XLV, 1803; that rupees of sorts which may be received at the public treasuries, shall not on any account be issued therefrom, from and after the commencement of the year 1214, but shall be sent to the mint at Furruckabad, and be recoined into siccas of the Lucnow forty-fifth sun. But as it might not be practicable, in consequence of the large proportion of rupees of sorts current in the ceded and conquered provinces, to coin those rupees into Lucnow siccas immediately they should be sent; and as inconvenience might in consequence be experienced from the retention of considerable sums of money from circulation, such quantity only of the rupees of sorts which may be received into the treasuries of the collectors, shall be sent from time to time to the mint at Furruckabad, as can be immediately recoined into Lucnow Siccas. It shall accordingly be the duty of the officer entrusted with the distribution of the funds, applicable to the pay of the troops serving in the upper provinces, to keep himself constantly informed respecting the quantity of money which the mint and assay-master may be able to recoin, and to regulate, in conformity to such information, the remittances of rupees of sorts from the treasuries of the collectors, for the purpose of being recoined. The mint and assay-master is accordingly hereby required to furnish that officer with any periodical reports or other information which he may require to enable him to perform that duty.	Rules contained in Section XXII, Regulation XLV, 1803, altered, and rupees of sorts allowed to be reissued from the public treasuries when they cannot be immediately recoined. Public officers to regulate their remittances of rupees of sorts to the mint for recoinage, by the quantity which can be recoined without delay.

At what rates rupees of sorts shall be reissued.	V. Such portion of the rupees of sorts as cannot be immediately recoined into Lucnow siccas, and as may be required for the pay of the troops or other exigencies of the public service, shall be issued at the rates at which they may have been or may be received into the treasuries of the collectors, under the provisions contained in the present regulation.
Rules contained in Section XVII, Regulation XLV, 1803, and Regulation III, 1806, to be in full force and effect after the expiration of the existing settlements. The ensuing settlements to be made in the Lucnow rupees.	VI. At the expiration of the present depending triennial settlement, viz. at the close of the year 1216 in Bundlecund, and 1215 in the other parts of the ceded and conquered provinces, the rule contained in Section XVII, Regulation XLV, 1803; and the provisions contained in Regulation III, 1806, shall be considered to be in full force and effect. The ensuing settlements in the ceded and conquered provinces shall accordingly be made in Lucnow sicca rupees, to be adjusted according to the table of rates contained in Section V, of the latter regulation.
None but the Lucnow rupees to be received in to the public treasuries, after the expiration of the existing settlement unless authorized by a public proclamation of the Governor General in Council.	VII. As it may likewise be expected, that at the expiration of those periods, a sufficient quantity of Lucnow sicca rupees will be generally current, to answer the ordinary purposes of circulation, no rupees of sorts shall after that time be received into the public treasuries, unless the Governor General in Council shall deem it advisable to authorize by a public proclamation, the receipt of such rupees in particular districts, for a limited specific period of time.
The principle of the foregoing provisions extended to Cuttack, and the operation of Section XIII, Regulation XII, 1805, suspended.	VIII. The principle of the foregoing provisions shall be considered to be in force in the district of Cuttack. The operation of the rule contained in Station XIII, Regulation XII, 1805, which directs, that the various rupees of sorts shall be received at the treasuries in payment of the public revenue, until the expiration of the Willaity year 1215, according to the table of rates contained in Section XIV, Regulation XXXV, 1793, is accordingly suspended; and such rupees shall be received until the expiration of that period, at the rates of batta at which such rupees have hitherto been respectively received.

IX. On the expiration of the Willaity year 1215, the ensuing settlement of Cuttack shall be made in Calcutta sicca rupees, to be adjusted according to the table of rates contained in Section XIV, Regulation XXXV, 1793. On the principle likewise stated in Section IV of this regulation, the collector of Cuttack shall send from time to time such portion of the rupees of sorts which may be received into his treasury, to the mint at Calcutta to be recoined into siccas, as can conveniently be done without impeding the general circulation of the district; and the remainder shall be issued at the rates at which they may have been received by government. On the expiration of the year 1215, no rupees excepting Calcutta siccas of the nineteen sun shall be received into the public treasury, unless the Governor General in Council deem it necessary to dispense with the observance of that rule by a public proclamation for a specific and limited period of time.	After the expiration of the existing settlement, the ensuing settlement of Cuttack to be made in Calcutta sicca rupees to be adjusted according to the table of rates contained in Section XIV, Regulation XXXV, 1793. Rules as to remitting rupees of sorts for recoinage, and the reissue of such as may be necessary. None but Calcutta sicca rupees to be received after the expiration of the existing settlement, unless authorized by public proclamation.
X. The rules ordered to be observed in the district of Cuttack, shall likewise be considered to be in force in the pergunnahs of Pattaspore and other late dependencies of that district now annexed to the zillah of Midnapore, in so far as regards the receipt of rupees of sorts from the landholders and farmers; but as the rupees of sorts which may be received on account of the revenue of those mohauls, cannot be very considerable, the whole shall be immediately remitted to the mint at Calcutta, to be recoined into siccas.	The above rules as to Cuttack, to be in force in the late Marhatta pergunnahs annexed to Midnapore, but all rupees of sorts received from those pergunnahs to be remitted for recoinage.

Appendix A.18

A.D. 1807 REGULATION XIII

A REGULATION for modifying certain parts of Regulation XXXV, 1793, Regulation XLV, 1803, and Regulation XII, 1805; relative to engagements for rupees, or gold mohurs, not being of the established coinage.—PASSED by the Governor General in Council, on the 25th June 1807; corresponding with the 12th Assaur 1214 Bengal era; the 5th Assaur 1214 Fussily; the 12th Assaur 1214 Willaity; the 5th Assaur 1864 Sumbut; and the 18th Rubbee us-Sanee 1222 Higeree.

[Preamble]	In Section XX, Regulation XXXV, 1793, it is declared, that after the tenth of April 1794 (extended by Regulations VI, 1794, and LIX, 1795 to the 10th April 1796) no person shall recover in any court of judicature, in the provinces of Bengal, Behar, or Orissa, any sum of money, under a bond or other, writing, or any agreement, written or verbal, entered into, after the above-mentioned date, by which any sum of money shall be stipulated to be paid in any species of rupees excepting sicca rupees or gold mohurs of the nineteenth sun, or the halves and quarters of each. By Section XXI, of the same regulation, all proprietors and farmers of land are prohibited from concluding engagements with their under farmers, ryots, or dependent talookdars, after the tenth of April 1794 (extended as above to 10th April 1796) in any species of rupees, or gold mohurs, excepting the sicca rupees and gold mohurs of the nineteenth sun; under the penalty of not being permitted to recover any arrears that may become due to them under such engagements: By Sections XV and XVI, Regulation XII, 1805, the same provisions are extended to the zillah of Cuttack, from the expiration of the Willaity year 1213, Sections XXV and XXVI, Regulation XLV, 1803, relative to the ceded provinces, and extended to the adjacent conquered provinces, as well as to the zillah of Bundlecund, by Section XXVIII, Regulation VIII, 1805, contain similar provisions respecting the Lucnow forty-fifth sun sicca rupee, which has been established as the legal coinage

of those provinces, to be in force from the commencement of the Fussily year 1216. The object of these provisions, and of others enacted by the regulations referred to, was to remedy, the ill consequences produced by the circulation of various rupees, of different and fluctuating value; and to establish one rupee, of fixed weight and fineness, to be the general standard and measure of Value, viz. the nineteenth sun sicca rupee (with its correspondent gold mohur of the same sun) described in Section II, Regulation XXXV, 1793, for the provinces of Bengal, Behar, and Orissa including Cuttack; and the Lucknow forty-fifth sun sicca rupee, described in Section II, Regulation III, 1806, for the provinces ceded by the Nuwaub Vizier, the conquered provinces in the Doab and on the right bank of the Jumna, and the zillah of Bundlecund. The period specified for the operation of the provisions in question in the ceded and conquered provinces is not yet expired; but since the expiration of the period fixed for the operation of them in the provinces of Bengal, Bahar and Orissa; many engagements and agreements have been entered into, within those provinces, for rupees of local currency, or used as a known and accustomed measure of value though no longer current. In some instances this has been ascertained to proceed from an insufficient promulgation of the regulations, and in general the party receiving for money or value due to him, an engagement declared invalid by the regulations, must be presumed not to have been aware of the existence of such a provision, at the time of his taking the nugatory engagement. In such cases, the penalty of non-recovery by judicial process is not only a hardship to the individual, but is repugnant to the ends of justice It is therefore expedient that the provisios above-mentioned, should be modified, in such manner as may be confident with the object of policy intended by them. The following rules have accordingly been enacted for that purpose by the Governor General in Council, to be in force from the periods therein specified, throughout the whole provinces immediately subject to the Presidency of Fort William, except the province of Benares, for the coinage of which no regulation has been yet published;	
II. Section XX, Regulation XXXV, 1793, and so much of Section XXI, of the same regulation, as declares a	Section XX and part of Section

XXI, Regulation XXXV, 1793, and parts of Regulation VI, 1794, and LIX, 1795 rescinded.	penalty of non-recovery upon engagements in any species of rupees or gold mohurs, excepting those of the nineteenth sun, together with such parts of Regulations VI, 1794, and LIX, 1795, as relate to the rule contained in Section XX, Regulation XXXV, 1795 and the penalty declared in Section XXI, of that regulation, are hereby rescinded.
Section XV and part of Section XVI, Regulation XII, 1804, rescinded.	III. Section XV, Regulation XII, 1805, relative to the zillah of Cuttack, and so much of Section XVI, of the same regulation, as declares a penalty of non-recovery upon engagements in any species of rupees or gold mohurs, excepting the Calcutta sicca rupees and gold mohurs of the nineteenth sun, are also rescinded.
How bonds or other engagements or agreements written or verbal, entered into in the provisions herein specified stipulating for the payment of money in any other species of rupee or gold mohur, than the sicca rupee or gold mohur of the nineteenth sun, may be liquidated at the option of the debtor.	IV. Bonds, or other engagements, and all agreements written, or verbal, which have been or may be entered into, within the provinces of Bengal, Bihar, or Orissa, including Cuttack, stipulating for the payment of money in any other species of rupee or gold mohur than the sicca rupee or gold mohur of the nineteenth sun, described in Section II, Regulation XXXV, 1793, may be liquidated at the option of the debtor, in the gold mohur of the nineteenth sun, or in the nineteenth sun sicca rupee, at the valuation stated in the table of sicca and other rupees, contained in Section XIV, Regulation XXXV, 1793.
How bonds or other engagements or agreements stipulating for the payment of any species of rupee not specified in the table referred to in the preceding section, may be liquidated at the option of the debtor.	V. If the bond, or other engagement, or agreement, stipulate for the payment of any species of rupee, not specified in the table referred to in the preceding section it shall be at the option of the debtor to pay in rupees or gold mohurs of the nineteenth sun, the intrinsic value of the rupees stipulated, to be ascertained by assay at the nearest mint, in the manner provided by Section XVI, Regulation XXXV, 1793, and Section XIII, Regulation XII, 1805.

VI. The courts of judicature within the provinces of Bengal, Bihar and Orissa, (including Cuttack) in giving judgment upon bonds, or other engagements, stipulating for the payment of money in any other species of rupee or gold mohur, than the sicca rupee or gold mohur of the nineteenth sun, shall adjudge the amount to be payable in gold mohurs or sicca rupees, of the nineteenth sun, according to the table of valuation contained in Section XIV, Regulation XXXV, 1793; or if the stipulated species of rupee be not specified in that table, according to the intrinsic value to be ascertained by assay in the manner prescribed by the preceding section.	How the courts of judicature are to give judgment in the provinces herein specified, on bonds or other engagements stipulating for the payment of money in any other species of rupee or gold mohur, than the sicca rupee or gold mohur of the nineteenth sun.
VII. All bonds and other engagements, or agreements for the payment of money, which may be entered into after the promulgation of this regulation, in any part of the provinces of Bengal, Bahar and Orissa, (including Cuttack,) are required to be in the sicca rupee or gold mohur of the nineteenth sun; under penalty, for disobedience to this requisition, of a fine to government, to be levied from the person taking such engagement, not exceeding one fourth of the amount stipulated to be paid in any other species of rupee or gold mohur.	All engagements for payment of money entered into in the provinces herein specified after promulgation of this regulation, to be in the sicca rupee or gold mohur of the nineteenth sun. Penalty for breach of this rule.
VIII. The civil courts of judicature shall enforce the penalty provided for in the preceding section, in all cases judicially before them, wherein any bond, engagement or agreement, executed after the promulgation of this regulation, may be found to stipulate for the payment of any other species of rupee or gold mohur than those of the nineteenth sun.	Civil courts to enforce the penalty in all cases judicially before them after the promulgation of this regulation, wherein a breach, of the above rule may appeal.
IX. Section XXV, Regulation XLV, 1803, relative to the Ceded provinces, and extended to the adjacent conquered provinces, as well as to the zillah of Bundlecund, by	Section XXV, Regulation. XLV, 1803, and

part of Section XXVI, Regulation XLV, 1803, rescinded.	Section XXVIII, Regulation VIII, 1805, together with such part of Section XXVI, Regulation XLV, 1803, as declares a penalty of non-recovery upon engagements in any species of rupee, except the Lucnow forty-fifth sun sicca rupee established by the said regulation are hereby rescinded.
How bonds or other engagements or agreements, written or verbal, entered into within the provinces herein specified, stipulating for the payment of money in any other species of rupee than the Lucnow forty-fifth sun sicca rupee, may be liquidated at the option of the debtor.	X. Bonds or other engagements, and all agreements; written or verbal, which have been or may be entered into, within the ceded provinces (including the several zillahs specified in Section II, Regulation II, 1803), or within the conquered provinces and Bundlecund (including the zillahs specified in Section III, Regulation VIII, 1805), stipulating for the payment of money in any other species of rupee than the Lucnow forty-fifth sun sicca rupee, established as the legal coinage of the said provinces by Section II, Regulation XLV, 1803, and Section XXVIII, Regulation VIII, 1805, may be liquidated, at the option of the debtor, in the Lucnow forty-fifth sun sicca rupee, described in Section II, Regulation III, 1806, at the valuation stated in the table of Lucnow sicca and other rupees, contained in Section V, of that regulation.
How bonds or other engagements or agreements stipulating for the payment of any species of rupee not specified in the table referred to in the preceding Section, may be liquidated at the option of the debtor.	XI. If the bond or other engagement, or agreement, stipulate for the payment of any species of rupee not specified in the table referred to in the preceding section, it shall be at the option of the debtor to pay in Lucnow sicca rupees of the forty-fifth sun, the intrinsic value of the rupees stipulated, to be ascertained by assay at the Furruckabad mint, in the manner provided by Section XXI, Regulation XLV, 1803.
How the courts of judicature in the provinces herein specified, are to give judgment, after the	XII. After the commencement of the Fussily year 1216, the period fixed by Section XXIII, Regulation XLV, 1803, for the exclusive currency of the Lucnow forty-fifth sun sicca rupee, the courts of judicature within the ceded and conquered provinces, and Bundelcund (including the zillahs specified in Section II, Regulation

II, 1803, and Section III, Regulation VIII, 1805), in giving judgment upon bonds, or other engagements, or agreements, stipulating for the payment of money in any other species of rupee than the Lucnow forty-fifth sun sicca rupee, described in Section II, Regulation III, 1806, shall adjudge the amount to be payable in the prescribed Lucnow forty-fifth sun sicca rupee, according to the table of valuation contained in Section V, Regulation III, 1806 or, if the stipulated species of rupee be not specified in that table, according to the intrinsic value to be ascertained by assay in the manner prescribed by the preceding section.	commencement of the Fussily year 1216, upon bonds or engagements stipulating for the payment of any other species of rupee than the Lucnow forty-fifth sun sicca rupee.
XIII. All bonds and other engagements, of agreements, for the payment of money, which may be entered into, after the commencement of the Fussily year 1216, in any part of the provinces described in the preceding section, are required to be in the Lucnow forty-fifth sun sicca rupee, established as the legal coinage of the said provinces; under penalty for disobedience to this requisition, of a fine to government; to be levied from the person taking such engagement, not exceeding one fourth of the amount stipulated to be paid in any other species of rupee.	After what period all engagements entered into in the provinces specified in the preceding section, are required to be in the Lucnow forty-fifth sun sicca rupee. Penalty for breach of this rule.
XIV. The civil courts of judicature shall enforce the penalty provided for in the preceding section, in all cases judicially before them, wherein any bond, engagement, or agreement, executed after the commencement of the Fussily year 1216, may be found to stipulate for the payment of any other species of rupee than the Lucnow forty-fifth sun sicca.	After what period the court of judicature are to enforce the penalty in cases, judicially before them, wherein breach of the above rule may appear.
XV. Nothing in this regulation shall be construed to affect the provisions contained in Regulation IV, 1807, for determining the rates at which rupees of sorts are to be received and issued in the ceded and conquered provinces (including Cuttack) during the existence of the depending settlement of the land revenue in those provinces.	Nothing in this regulation to be construed to affect the provisions in Regulation IV, 1807.

Appendix A.19

A.D. 1809 REGULATION X

A REGULATION for the eslablishment of a copper coinage in the province of Benares.—PASSED by the Vice President in Council, on the 15th December 1809; corresponding with the 2nd Poose 1216 Bengal era; the 23rd Aughun 1217 Fussily; the 2nd Poose 1217 Willaity: the 9th Aughun 1866 Sumbut; and the 7th Zekaad 1224 Higeree.

Preamble	WHEREAS it is expedient, that fixed and defined rules should be established for regulating the copper currency of the province of Benares, the following rules have been enacted by the Vice President in Council, to be in force in that province from the period of their promulgation.
The copper coin for Benares shall be pice of pure copper, and of only one size, coined at Calcutta.	II. The copper coin struck for the province of Benares shall be of pure copper, and shall be confined to pice of one size only, to be coined at the Calcutta Mint.
Size and weight of the coin. Inscription.	III. The pice shall be 19-20th parts of an inch in diameter, and shall weigh sicca weight eight annas nine pie each, and shall bear the following inscription, in the Persian and Nagree characters; On one side, in Persian, "The 37th year of the reign of Shah Allum Badshah." On the Reverse, in both Persian and Nagree, "One Pie Sicca."
To be a legal tender for any fractional part of a rupee.	IV. The copper coin established by this regulation, shall be considered to be a legal tender of payment in all money transactions, whether between government and its subjects, or between individuals in the province of Benares, for any sum being the fractional part of a rupee, at the rate of sixty-four pice for one Benares sicca rupee.

V. Persons charged with melting, counterfeiting, clipping, filing, drilling, defacing, or debasing the copper coin, established under this regulation, will be liable to be prosecuted in the criminal courts, and to be punished as the law may direct.	Persons liable to prosecution for melting, counterfeiting or otherwise debasing the coin.
VI. The copper pice of all denominations at present in circulation in the province of Benares, shall be received as heretofore in all public and private transactions for the period of six months, from and after the promulgation of this regulation; but after the expiration of that period, no copper coin, except that established by this regulation, shall be considered as a legal tender in payment of any proportion of any public or private demand.	Limitation of time as to the currency of copper pice now in circulation.

Appendix A.20

A.D. 1810 REGULATION IX

A REGULATION for rescinding the whole of the Regulations at present in force, for the collection of the Government Customs, in the Provinces of Bengal, Behar, Orissa and Benares, and in the Ceded and Conquered Provinces and for establishing those Customs, with amended Rules, for the collection of them.—PASSED by the Vice President-in-Council on 10th April 1810.

	xx xx xx xx
	XII. *First.* Duties, under the denomination of Government customs shall be levied at the following rates on the goods specified in this Section.
Enumeration of Goods	Rates of Duty
	xx xx xx xx
Copper and Brass	Ten per cent on a fixed valuation of twenty rupees per maund on importation by sea, whether wrought or unwrought; the same on inland importation, but to be levied on unwrought metal only. If imported from Nepaul, two and a half percent, whether wrought or unwrought.
Cowries	Five per cent ad valorem on the importation at Calcutta, Chittagong, or Balasore only
	xx xx xx xx
	LX. The following rates of exchange shall be adopted in the adjustment of the Calcutta Customs.
	xx xx xx xx

TABLE OF EXCHANGE FOR THE SETTLEMENT OF THE CALCUTTA CUSTOMS.

Countries	Coins	Rate of Exchange
Great Britain	Pound Sterling	at 10 Sicca Rupees
Germany	Crown	at 2 Sicca Rupees
Denmark	Rix Dollar	at Sicca Rupees 1-10
Ceylon	Ditto ditto.	at 14 annas
France	Livre Tournois	at 24 for Sicca Rupees
Ditto	Mauritius Livre	at 48 for Sicca Rupees
Spain	Spanish Dollar	at $2\frac{1}{4}$ Sicca Rupees
Portugal and Madeira	Milerea	at $2\frac{3}{4}$ Sicca Rupees
Bussroh	Raize Peastre	at 12 annas
China	Tale	at $2\frac{1}{3}$ Sicca Rupees*
Madras	Star Pagoda	at $3\frac{3}{4}$ Sicca Rupees
Ditto	Swamy ditto.	at 4 Sicca Rupees
America	Currency to be converted into Pound Sterling as follows:	
New England	By multiplying by 9 and divided by 16	The Pound Sterling to be rated as above, at 10 Sicca Rupees. Where the invoices are in Dollars, the Dollars to be rated at $2\frac{1}{4}$ Sicca Rupees.
Virginia	Ditto. ditto.	
New York	By multiplying by 9 and divided by 16	
Pennsylvania	Ditto. by 3 and do. by 5	
South Carolina	By deducting $\frac{1}{27}$ part	
Georgia	Ditto	

*Changed to $3\frac{1}{3}$ by Regulation I of 1812 (Sec. XIX).

Appendix A.21

A.D. 1810 REGULATION XII

A REGULATION for modifying the rules contained in Section II, Regulation. 1809; and Section VI, Regulation. X, 1809.—PASSED by the Vice President-in-Council on the 4th May, 1810; corresponding with the 23rd Bysaak 1217 Bengal era; the 15th Bysaak 1217 Fussily; the 24th Bysaak 1217 Willaity; the 15th Bysaak 1867 Sumbut and; the 29th Rubee-ul-awul 1225 Higeree.

[Preamble]	WHEREAS . . . ; and whereas obstacles have occurred to the general introduction of the new copper coinage into the province of Benares within the period prescribed by Regulation X, 1809 the following rules have been enacted to be immediately in force.
	XX XX XX XX
Section VI, Regulation X, 1809, rescinded. Copper coin hitherto current in the province of Benares shall continue to be received until further orders.	III. Section VI, Regulation X 1809, which prescribes, that after the expiration of six months from the period of the promulgation of that Regulation, no copper coin excepting that established by the said Regulation, shall be considered to be a legal tender of payment, is hereby rescinded, and copper coin which has been hitherto current in the province of Benares, shall continue to be received in discharge of all private and public demands, until the Governor General in Council, or Vice President in Council, shall signify by proclamation, that an adequate supply of copper coin of the size and weight prescribed by Section III, of that Regulation, has been introduced into the province of Benares.
	XX XX XX XX

Appendix A.22

A.D. 1812 REGULATION I

A REGULATION for modifying certain parts of Regulation IX, 1810; for imposing a duty on horses, imported from Europe; and for prohibiting the exportation of woollens from Bengal to China.—PASSED by the Governor-General-in-Council on the 13th January, 1812, corresponding with the 1st Maug 1218 Bengal era; the 15th Maug 1219 Fussily; the 2nd Maug 1219 Willaity; the 14th Maug Budee 1868 Sumbut and; the 27th Zeheja 1226 Higeree.

xx xx xx xx

XIX. An error having been made in the rates of exchange of the Portuguese and China coins; the following rates are to be submitted in lieu of those specified in the Section LX, Regulation IX, 1810.

How Portuguese and Chinese coins shall be valued in exchange.

Countries	*Coins*	*Rates of Exchange*
Portugal and Madeira	Milrea	at 2E Sicca Rupees
China	Tale	at 3B Ditto

xx xx xx xx

Appendix A.23

A.D. 1812 REGULATION II

A REGULATION for levying a duty on the coinage of silver bullion and on the recoinage of rupees and other coins, with certain exceptions, at the mints established at Calcutta, Farruckabad, and Benares; for defining the weight and standard of the Benares rupee; for modifying the rates of duty at present levied on the coinage of gold bullion in the mint of Calcutta; and also for establishing certain rules for the conduct of the business of the above-mentioned mints respectively.—PASSED by the Governor General in Council, on the 21st March 1812; corresponding with the 10th Chyte 1218 Bengal era; the 23rd Chyte 1219 Fussily; the 11th Chyte 1219 Willaity; the 9th Chyte 1869 Sumbut; and the 7th Rubbi-ul Awul 1227 Higeree.

Preamble	WHEREAS it has been deemed advisable to establish a duty on the coinage of silver bullion, and on the recoinage of rupees and other coins, with certain exceptions, at the mints established at Calcutta, Furruckabad, and Benares, for the purpose of defraying the expense to which government is subject on that account, and to modify the duty at present levied on the coinage of gold bullion at the Calcutta mint; and whereas it is necessary to define the weight and standard of the Benares rupee; and whereas it has been further thought expedient to prescribe additional rules for the conduct of the business of the above mints respectively; the following regulation has been passed to be in force, except in the instances hereafter specified, from the period of its promulgation.
Section IV, V, & VI, Regulation XXXV, 1793 modified.	II. First. Sections IV, V, and VI, Regulation XXXV, 1793, shall be subject to the following modifications.
All silver bullion or coin (not struck at the	Second. From and after the first day of May 1812, all silver bullion or coin, not being rupees struck at the Calcutta mints which may be delivered into that mint

for coinage, shall be subject to a duty at the rate of two per cent on the produce of such bullion or coin in sicca rupees of the Calcutta weight and standard, and the amount of the said duty shall be accordingly deducted from the return to be made to the proprietor.	Calcutta mint) delivered at the mint for coinage, to pay a duty of 2 per cent.
Third. Individuals, who may be desirous of it, shall be at liberty to have their bullion or coin converted into halves or quarters of a rupee, on condition of paying a duty at the rate of one per cent in addition to the duty of two per cent established by the preceding clause.	If coined into halves and quarters of a rupee, to pay an additional duty of one per cent.
Fourth. Should the coin however brought to the mint for that purpose, consist of Calcutta siccas, the proprietors shall only be subject to the additional duty of one per cent and not to the duty payable under the second clause of this section, on all other coin and bullion.	Calcutta siccas so coined to pay only the last mentioned duty.
Fifth. All silver bullion and coin, being inferior to the Calcutta sicca standard, which may be brought to the mint for coinage shall be refined to that standard; and the proprietors shall be subject, in addition to the duties established by the preceding sections, to a charge at the rate of twelve annas per cent on account of the loss and expence of refining, exclusive of the established deduction on account of inferiority of standard.	All silver bullion or coin of inferior standard to pay 12 annas per cent for the expense of refining.
Sixth. On delivery of the silver bullion or coin into the mint, the mint mailer shall grant to the proprietor a receipt, entitling him to a certificate from the allay mailer, for the net produce of such bullion or coin agreeably to the table, subjoined to this regulation, and marked No. I, payable at the general treasury at Calcutta, at the expiration of ten days if the produce be deliverable in whole rupees; and at the expiration of twenty days, if the produce be deliverable in halves or quarter of a rupee from the date of such certificate. In the latter case, the additional duty established by Clause Third, Section II, of this Regulation, is of course to be deducted from the net produce.	Rules as to receipt and certificates to be granted to the proprietors of bullion, &c. and the payment thereof.
III. Such part of Section XIII, Regulation XXXV, 1793 as declares that rupees and the halves, or quarters of a rupee, to which any mark may have been affixed, shall not be considered a legal tender of payment in any public	Rules in Regulation XXXV 1793, declaring

marked rupees not a legal tender rescinded, and such rupees to be received if not more than 6 annas per cent deficient in weight.	or private transaction, is hereby rescinded; Such marked rupees, halves, and quarters being of the nineteenth sun, shall be in future receivable in all public and private transactions provided that, when separately weighed, the deficiency in point of weight, be not more than six annas per cent or six-sixteenths of a rupee in one hundred rupees.
Section XXIV, Regulation XXXV, 1793, rescinded.	IV. Section XXVI, Regulation XXXV, 1793, respecting the order, in which bullion and coin received into the Calcutta mint, is to be assayed, refined, and coined, is hereby rescinded.
Section XXVI, Regulation XXXV, 1793, rescinded.	V. First. Section XXIV, Regulation XXXV, 1793, is hereby rescinded;
A duty of two rupees and eight annas per cent to be levied on all gold bullion or coin except those specified in Section XXV, Regulation XXXV, 1793.	Second. A duty shall be levied at the rate of two rupees and eight annas per cent at the Calcutta mint, on the produce of all gold bullion and on all gold coin, with the exception of the mohurs, half mohurs, and quarter mohurs mentioned in Section XXV, Regulation XXXV, 1793, on the recoinage of which no duty shall be levied.
Rules as to the return to be made for gold bullion &c. equal to or above the Calcutta standard.	Third. For all gold bullion or coin, equal to or above Calcutta standard, which may be brought to the mint for coinage, a number of the nineteenth sun gold mohurs, or of the halves and quarters of such mohurs, equal in weight to the gold of the established standard contained in such bullion, shall be returned to the proprietor, after deducting the duty mentioned in the preceding clause.
Rules to gold bullion or coin being under mohur standard.	Fourth. All gold bullion or gold coin, being under mohur standard, which may be delivered into the Calcutta mint for coinage, shall be refined to the established gold mohur standard; and in addition to the duly of two rupees eight annas per cent fixed by Clause Second of this section of the present regulation, all such bullion

or coin shall be subject to a charge on account of the loss and expense of refining Agreeably to Table No. II, in addition to the established deduction on account of the inferiority of standard.	
Fifth. The mint master on the delivery of gold bullion or coin into the mint of Calcutta for coinage, shall grant to the proprietor a receipt, entitling him to a certificate from the assay matter for the net produce of such bullion or coin, according to the Table noticed in the preceding clause, payable at the general treasury at Calcutta, at the expiration of ten days from the date of such certificate.	Rules as to receipts and certificates to be granted to the Proprietors of bullion and payment of the amount.
VI. The proprietor of any gold or silver bullion or coin, brought to the Calcutta mint for coinage, who may be dissatisfied with the assay matter's report of its value, shall be at liberty to withdraw such bullion or coin without being subject to the duties on coinage established by the present regulation.	Proprietors of bullion dissatisfied with the assay master's report, may withdraw it without the payment of duties.
VII. Section XXXVIII, Regulation XLV, 1803, respecting the order in which bullion and coin received into the mint at Furruckabad, shall be assayed, refined, and coined, is hereby rescinded.	Section XXXVII, Regulation XLV, 1803, rescinded.
VIII. First. From and after the first day of May 1812, all silver bullion or coin, not being rupees (truck at the mint of Furruckabad which may be brought to that mint for coinage, shall be subject to a duty at the rate of two per cent on the produce of such bullion or coin in sicca rupees of the Lucknow weight and standard and the amount of the said duty shall be accordingly deducted from the return to be made to the proprietor.	Silver bullion or coin not being struck at Furruckabad, liable to a duty of a per cent on coinage there.
Second. Individuals, who may be desirous of it, shall be at liberty to have their bullion or coin converted into halves or quarters of a rupee, on condition of paying a duty of one per cent in addition to the duty of two per cent established by the preceding clause. Should the coin however brought to the mint for that purpose consist of Furruckabad sicca rupees, the proprietors shall only be subject to the additional duty of one per cent	Persons requiring halves and quarters of rupee to pay an additional duty of 1 per cent but Furruckabad rupees so coined, not to

pay the duty prescribed in the preceding clause	and not the duty of two per cent. payable under the preceding clause, on all other coin and bullion.
Rules as to bullion &c. of an inferior standard.	Third. All silver bullion and coin, being inferior to the Lucknow sicca standard, as established by Section II, Regulation III, 1806, shall be refined to that standard; and the proprietors shall be subject, in addition to the duties established by the preceding section, to a charge of twelve annas per cent on account of the loss and expense of refining, exclusive of the established deduction on account of inferiority of standard.
Rules as to receipts and certificates to be delivered to the proprietors, and the discharge thereof.	Fourth. On delivery of the bullion or coin into the mint, the mint master shall grant to the proprietor, a receipt, entitling him to a certificate from the assay mailer for the net produce of such bullion or coin agreeably to the Table subjoined to this regulation, and marked No. 3, payable at the treasury of the collector of Furruckabad, at the expiration of fifteen days, if the produce be deliverable in whole rupees; and at the expiration of twenty-five days, if the produce be deliverable in halves or quarters of a rupee from the date of such certificate. In cases in which the produce may be deliverable in halves or quarters of a rupee, the additional duty established by Clause Second, Section VIII, of this regulation, is of course to be deducted from the amount payable to the proprietor.
Persons dissatisfied with the assay master's report, may withdraw the bullion free of duty.	Fifth. The proprietor of any bullion or coin brought to the Furruckabad mint for coinage, who may be dissatisfied with the assay master's report of its value, shall be at liberty to withdraw such bullion or coin, without being subject to the duties on coinage established by the present regulation.
The Magistrate of Furruckabad to visit the mint monthly, and to transmit specimens of the coinage.	IX. First. It shall be the duty of the magistrate of Furruckabad, to visit the mint monthly, and to make such enquiries as he shall consider necessary, to satisfy himself of the manner in which the business of the mint is conducted, reporting the result of his enquiries, in cases appearing to him to require it, to the Governor General in Council. The magistrate may at the same time take indiscriminately out of the heaps of coin at

the foot of the striking presses, twenty pieces of each description of coin which may have been struck off, and transmit ten of each to the secretary to Government in the public department, for the purpose of being forwarded to the Honorable the Court of Directors, and the other ten to the assay master at Calcutta, in order that he may cause the coin to be examined and assayed. If the specimens of coin so transmitted shall be found not to be of the proper standard, or if the coin shall be defective in workmanship, or in any other respect, the assay master shall report the circumstance to the Governor General in Council for his orders.	
Second. The foregoing rule shall be considered to supersede the provision contained in Section XI, Regulation XLV, 1803.	Section XI, Regulation XLV, 1803 declared superseded.
X. The silver coin now current in the province of Benares, under the denomination of the muchleedar rupee, commonly called the Benares rupee, shall continue to be the established coin of that province; and shall be received as such in all public and private transactions.	The Benares rupees to be the established coin of that province.
XI. The Benares rupee shall continue of the following weight and standard, and halves and quarters of a rupee shall be coined of the same standard and proportionate weight. Troy weight, grains 175 Touch, or pure silver 168.875 Alloy – – 6.125 Assay Touch, or parts of pure silver in 100 96.5 Alloy – – – 3.5	Its weight and standard.
XII. First. The Benares rupee shall hereafter be struck of the same size and form as the nineteenth sun sicca rupee struck in the mint of Calcutta, but shall bear the same impression as is now in use in Benares.	Size, form, impression of the Benares rupee.
Second. The halves and quarters of a rupee shall be proportionably less than the rupee, according to their respective value, and shall have the same impression as the rupee.	And of halves and quarters.

The edges to be milled.	XIII. To guard as far as possible, against counterfeiting, clipping, drilling, filing, defacing or debasing the coin, the edges of it shall be milled, and the dies shall be made of the same size as the coin, so that the whole of the impression may appear on the surface of the coin.
The dies to be cut in the Calcutta Mint, and returned when broken or unserviceable.	XIV. The dies for striking the silver coin at the mint of Benares shall be cut in the mint at Calcutta, and shall be sent by the mint master at Calcutta to the mint master at Benares. When the dies are broken or no longer serviceable, they shall be returned to the Calcutta mint.
The conduct of the Benares mint committed to a mint and assay master subject to the authority of the Board of Commissioners, and the native officers subject to the existing regulations for native mints.	XV. The immediate conduct of the mint at Benares may be committed to an officer, to be denominated the mint and assay master, with an adequate establishment of native officers. The mint and assay master shall be subject to the authority of the Board of Commissioners for the Ceded and Conquered Provinces, and the native officers shall be subject to all the rules of the existing regulations in common with all other natives in the service of Government.
The mint and assay master and native officers amenable to the dewanny adawlut of the city of Benares.	XVI. The mint and assay master and the native officers of the mint may be amenable to the Dewanny Adawlut of the city of Benares, and may be liable to be sued for damages for any breach of this regulation, or of any other regulations, which may be enabled respecting the coin.
The Magistrate to visit the mint monthly and transmit specimens of the coinage.	XVII. It shall be the duty of the magistrate of the city of Benares to visit the mint monthly, and to make such enquiries as he may consider necessary to satisfy himself of the manner in which the business of the mint is conducted, reporting the result of his enquiries in cases appearing to him to require it, to the Governor General in Council. The magistrate shall at the same time take indiscriminately out of the heaps of coin, at the foot of the striking presses, twenty pieces of each description of coin, which may have been struck off, and transmit ten of each to the Secretary to Government in the Public Department, for the purpose of being forwarded to the

Honorable the Court of Directors, and the other ten to the assay master at Calcutta, in order that he may cause the coin to be examined and assayed. If the specimens of coin so transmitted shall be found not to be of proper standard, or if the coin shall be defective in workmanship, or in any other respect, the assay master shall report the circumstance to the Governor General in Council for his orders.	
XVIII. The mint master at Calcutta shall cause a private mark to be put upon all the dies, which may be prepared for the mint at Benares, but in such a manner as not to be distinguishable by the naked eye, or by persons unacquainted with it. These marks shall be varied as often as the mint matter at Calcutta shall judge proper on new dies being made, and he shall keep a register of them, in order that he may be enabled to discover any counterfeit coin which may hereafter be circulated.	Private marks to be put on the dies.
XIX. Persons charged with counterfeiting, clipping, filing, drilling, defacing, or debating the silver coin of Benares, shall be committed for trial to the criminal courts, and shall be punished as the law may direct.	Persons charged with counterfeiting, clipping, &c. to be committed for trial to the criminal courts.
XX. All Benares rupees of the prescribed weight and standard, or the halves and quarters of such rupees according to the established value, shall be considered to be a legal tender of payment in all public and private transactions throughout the province of Benares. If a native officer of any public treasury shall refuse to receive in payment any such rupees, or the halves or quarters of such rupees according to the established value, the offender shall be liable to be dismissed from his office, and should the circumstances of the case appear to require it, to be declared incapable of again serving Government in any public capacity.	Benares rupees or their parts to be a legal tender there. Penalty for native officers refusing to receive them.
XXI. All Benares rupees which shall not have lost individually by wear, a greater proportion of the full weight than six annas per cent or six-sixteenths of a rupee in one hundred rupees, shall be considered as of standard weight, and shall be received as such in all public and private transactions.	Rupees to be considered as of standard weight if not deficient more than six annas per cent.

How light Benares rupees may be received.	XXII. First. Benares rupees which may be deficient in weight in a greater amount than six annas per cent shall be received conformably to the following rule.
To be received weight for weight but such light rupees not to be again disbursed, but recoined.	Second. For one hundred Benares sicca weight of such light rupees, the payer shall receive credit for one hundred Benares rupees. The light rupees thus received at the public treasury, shall not be again disbursed, but shall be invariably sent to the mint at Benares to be recoined.
The rules in the preceding section applicable to halves and quarter of rupees.	XXIII. The rules contained in the preceding Section of this Regulation, shall be considered equally applicable to the halves and quarters of a rupee.
The collector of Benares to be furnished with stampt metal weights.	XXIV. The mint master at Calcutta shall furnish the collector of Benares, with stampt metal weights of fifty Benares sicca weight each, or such other weights as may be required by him; all receipts and payments at the public treasury shall be regulated according to such standard weight.
Registers to be kept at the Benares mint.	XXV. The following registers shall be kept open at the mint of Benares for public information, viz. a register of unassayed silver bullion delivered into the mint, specifying the quantity delivered, the date on which it was received, and name of the proprietor. A register of silver bullion assayed and coined, specifying the date on which it was assayed, the date on which it was refined, the name of the proprietor, and the produce in Benares rupees, together with the date of the certificate granted for the produce.
English copies to be sent when required, to the Board of Commissioners.	XXVI. English copies of the registers prescribed in the foregoing Section, shall be sent when required to the Board of Commissioners.
All duties, fees, &c. hitherto levied at the	XXVII. All duties, fees, perquisites, or other imposts hitherto levied by Government or by individuals, under the names of Russoom, Dustooree, Salamee, Nuzurannah,

or any other denomination, shall immediately cease and determine, and the native officers and artificers who have been hitherto permitted to levy such fees, or perquisites, shall hereafter receive such personal salaries, or be remunerated for their labour in such manner as Government may direct.	Benares mint, to be discontinued.
XXVIII. Every native officer or artificer, or other person employed in the mint at Benares, who may be convicted in a court of judicature of receiving any fee, gratuity, or perquisite whatever, in virtue of his office, shall be adjudged to make restitution of the fee, or perquisite so received by him, with double damages to the party from whom it may have been received, and a fine according to the circumstances of the cafe, not exceeding however fix months salary. Persons offending in the manner above noticed, will likewise be of course liable to be dismissed from their offices, and should the circumstances of the cafe appear to require it, to be declared incapable of again serving Government in any public capacity.	Penalties prescribed for native officers &c. convicted of receiving any such in future.
XXIX. First. From and after the first day of May 1812, all silver bullion or coin, not being rupees struck at the mint of Benares, which may be brought to that mint for coinage, shall be subject to a duty at the rate of two per cent on the produce of such bullion or coin in sicca rupees of the Benares weight and standard; and the amount of the said duty shall be accordingly deducted from the return to be made to the proprietor.	A duty of 1 per cent to be levied on all silver bullion or coin not being Benares rupees, brought to the mint to be coined.
Second. Individuals, who may be desirous of it, shall be at liberty to have their bullion or coin converted into halves or quarters of a rupee, on condition of paying a duty of one per cent in addition to the duty of two per cent established by the preceding clause.	An additional duty of 1 per cent for halves and quarters of rupees.
Third. Should the coin however brought to the mint for that purpose consist of Benares rupees, the proprietors shall only be subject to the additional duty of one per cent and not to the duty of two per cent payable under the first, clause of this section on all other coin and bullion.	Benares rupees recoined into halves and quarters only to pay the last mentioned duly of 1 per cent.

Rules as to bullion of inferior standard.	XXX. All silver bullion and coin being inferior to the Benares sicca standard, shall be refined to that standard and the proprietors shall be subject, in addition to the duties established by the preceding section, to a charge of twelve annas per cent on account of the loss and expense of refining, exclusive of the established deduction on account of inferiority of standard.
Rules as to and certificates and the payment of them.	XXXI. On delivery of the bullion or coin into the mint, the mint master shall grant to the proprietor a receipt, entitling him to a certificate for the net produce of such bullion or coin, agreeably to the Table subjoined to this regulation, and marked No. 4, payable at the treasury of the collector of Benares, at the expiration of fifteen days, if the produce be deliverable in whole rupees; and at the expiration of twenty-five days, if the produce be deliverable in halves or quarters of a rupee, from the date of such certificate. In cases in which the produce may be deliverable in halves or quarters of a rupee, the additional duty established by Clause Second, Section VIII, of this regulation, is of course to be deducted from the amount payable to the proprietor.
Persons dissatisfied with the assay master's report, may withdraw their bullion free of duty.	XXXII. The proprietor of any bullion or coin brought to the mint at Benares for coinage, who may be dissatisfied with the assay master's report of its value, shall be at liberty to withdraw such bullion or coin, without being subject to the duties on coinage established by the present regulation.
Manufacturers of gold and silver wire &c., shall not be subject to any control on the part of the mint and assay master.	XXXIII. It is hereby declared, that the manufacturers of gold and silver wire or leaf, and of flattened gold and silver, shall not be subject to any control on the part of the mint and assay master, notwithstanding any usage which may have hitherto existed to the contrary at the mint at Benares.

NO. I.

TABLE OF THE PRODUCE OF SLIVER BULLION IN THE CALCUTTA MINT, COMMENCING THE 1ST OF MAY 1812

Sicca Weight	Assay compared with English Standard	Assay compared with Sicca Standard	Allowance for loss in refining	Charges for refining	Total Reduction	Assayed Produce Sa. Rs.	Duty of 2 per cent on Coinage	Nett Produce Sa. Rs.
	Dwts.	Pr. Cnt.						
100	13Br.	Sa. Std.	0	0	0	100	2	98.000
–	12¾	.106	.224	0	.330	99.670	1.993	97.677
–	12½	.213	.297	0	.510	99.490	1.990	97.500
–	12¼	.319	.371	0	.690	99.310	1.986	97.324
–	12	.425	.445	.75	1.620	98.380	1.967	96.413
–	11¾	.532	.518	.75	1.800	98.200	1.964	96.236
–	11½	.638	.592	.75	1.980	98.020	1.960	96.060
–	11¼	.745	.665	.75	2.160	97.840	1.956	95.884
–	11	.851	.744	.75	2.345	97.655	1.953	95.702
–	10¾	.957	.823	.75	2.530	97.170	1.949	95.521
–	10½	1.064	.901	.75	2.715	97.285	1.945	95.340
–	10¼	1.170	.980	.75	2.900	97.100	1.942	95.158
–	10	1.277	1.058	.75	3.085	96.915	1.938	94.977
–	9¾	1.383	1.061	.75	3.194	96.806	1.936	94.870
–	9½	1.489	1.064	.75	3.303	96.697	1.934	94.763
–	9¼	1.596	1.068	.75	3.414	96.586	1.931	94.655
–	9	1.702	1.072	.75	3.524	96.476	1.929	94.547
–	8¾	1.809	1.075	.75	3.634	96.366	1.927	94.439
–	8½	1.915	1.078	.75	3.743	96.257	1.925	94.332
–	8¼	2.021	1.082	.75	3.853	96.147	1.923	94.224
–	8	2.128	1.088	.75	3.966	96.034	1.920	94.114
–	7¾	2.234	1.094	.75	4.078	95.922	1.918	94.004
–	7½	2.341	1.100	.75	4.191	95.809	1.916	93.893
–	7¼	2.447	1.106	.75	4.303	95.697	1.914	93.783
–	7	2.553	1.112	.75	4.415	95.585	1.911	93.674
–	6¾	2.660	1.118	.75	4.528	95.472	1.909	93.563
–	6½	2.766	1.125	.75	4.641	95.359	1.907	93.452
–	6¼	2.873	1.131	.75	4.754	95.246	1.905	93.341
–	6	2.979	1.138	.75	4.867	95.133	1.902	93.231
–	5¾	3.086	1.144	.75	4.980	95.020	1.900	93.120
–	5½	3.192	1.150	.75	5.092	94.908	1.898	93.010
–	5¼	3.298	1.157	.75	5.205	94.795	1.896	92.899
–	5	3.405	1.161	.75	5.316	94.684	1.893	92.791
–	4¾	3.511	1.168	.75	5.429	94.571	1.891	92.680
–	4½	3.618	1.173	.75	5.541	94.459	1.889	92.570

Sicca Weight	Assay compared with English Standard	Assay compared with Sicca Standard	Allowance for loss in refining	Charges for refining	Total Reduction	Assayed Produce Sa. Rs.	Duty of 2 per cent on Coinage	Nett Produce Sa. Rs.
100	4¼	3.724	1.180	.75	5.654	94.346	1.887	92.459
–	4	3.830	1.186	.75	5.766	94.234	1.884	92.359
–	3¾ Br.	3.937	1.191	.75	5.878	94.122	1.882	92.240
–	3½	4.043	1.196	.75	5.989	94.011	1.880	92.131
–	3¼	4.149	1.202	.75	6.101	93.899	1.878	92.021
–	3	4.255	1.208	.75	6.213	93.787	1.875	91.912
–	2¾	4.362	1.214	.75	6.326	93.674	1.873	91.801
–	2½	4.468	1.220	.75	6.438	93.562	1.871	91.691
–	2¼	4.574	1.226	.75	6.550	93.450	1.869	91.581
–	2	4.681	1.233	.75	6.664	93.336	1.866	91.470
–	1¾	4.787	1.241	.75	6.778	93.222	1.864	91.358
–	1½	4.894	1.250	.75	6.894	93.106	1.862	91.244
–	1¼	5.000	1.259	.75	7.009	92.991	1.859	91.132
–	1	5.106	1.268	.75	7.124	92.876	1.857	91.019
–	¾	5.213	1.277	.75	7.240	92.760	1.855	90.905
–	½	5.319	1.287	.75	7.356	92.644	1.852	90.792
–	¼	5.425	1.297	.75	7.472	92.528	1.850	90.678
–	Eng. Std.	5.532	1.305	.75	7.587	92.413	1.848	90.565
–	¼ W.	5.638	1.313	.75	7.701	92.299	1.846	90.453
–	½	5.745	1.321	.75	7.816	92.184	1.843	90.341
–	¾	5.851	1.330	.75	7.931	92.069	1.841	90.228
–	1	5.957	1.339	.75	8.046	91.954	1.839	90.115
–	1¼	6.064	1.348	.75	8.162	91.838	1.836	90.002
–	1½	6.170	1.357	.75	8.277	91.723	1.834	89.889
–	1¾	6.277	1.364	.75	8.391	91.609	1.832	89.777
–	2	6.383	1.373	.75	8.506	91.494	1.829	89.665
–	2¼	6.489	1.389	.75	8.628	91.372	1.827	89.545
–	2½	6.596	1.404	.75	8.750	91.250	1.825	89.425
–	2¾	6.702	1.420	.75	8.872	91.128	1.822	89.306
–	3	6.809	1.434	.75	8.993	91.007	1.820	89.187
–	3¾	6.915	1.450	.75	9.115	90.885	1.817	89.068
–	3½	7.021	1.466	.75	9.237	90.763	1.815	88.948
–	3¾	7.128	1.481	.75	9.359	90.641	1.812	88.829
–	4	7.234	1.496	.75	9.480	90.520	1.810	88.710
–	4¼	7.341	1.511	.75	9.602	90.398	1.808	88.590
–	4½	7.447	1.526	.75	9.723	90.277	1.805	88.472
–	4¾	7.553	1.542	.75	9.845	90.155	1.803	88.352
–	5	7.660	1.555	.75	9.965	90.035	1.800	88.235
–	5¼	7.766	1.571	.75	10.087	89.913	1.798	88.115

Sicca Weight	Assay compared with English Standard	Assay compared with Sicca Standard	Allowance for loss in refining	Charges for refining	Total Reduction	Assayed Produce Sa. Rs.	Duty of 2 per cent on Coinage	Nett Produce Sa. Rs.
100	5½ W.	7.873	1.585	.75	10.208	89.792	1.795	87.997
–	5¾	7.979	1.601	.75	10.330	89.670	1.793	87.877
–	6	8.086	1.615	.75	10.451	89.549	1.791	87.758
–	6¼	8.192	1.632	.75	10.574	89.426	1.788	87.638
	6½	8.298	1.649	.75	10.697	89.303	1.786	87.517
	6¾	8.405	1.665	.75	10.820	89.180	1.783	87.397
–	7	8.511	1.683	.75	10.944	89.056	1.781	87.275
–	7¼	8.617	1.700	.75	11.067	88.933	1.778	87.155
–	7½	8.724	1.717	.75	11.191	88.809	1.776	87.033
–	7¾	8.830	1.734	.75	11.314	88.686	1.773	86.913
–	8	8.937	1.751	.75	11.438	88.562	1.771	86.791
–	8¼	9.043	1.775	.75	11.568	88.432	1.768	86.664
–	8½	9.149	1.800	.75	11.699	88.301	1.766	86.535
–	8¾	9.255	1.825	.75	11.830	88.170	1.763	86.407
–	9	9.362	1.850	.75	11.962	88.038	1.760	86.278
–	9¼	9.468	1.875	.75	12.093	87.907	1.758	86.149
–	9½	9.574	1.900	.75	12.224	87.776	1.755	86.021
–	9¾	9.681	1.925	.75	12.356	87.644	1.752	85.892
–	10	9.788	1.950	.75	12.488	87.512	1.750	85.762
–	10¼	9.894	1.979	.75	12.623	87.377	1.747	85.630
–	10½	10.000	2.010	.75	12.760	87.240	1.744	85.496
–	10¾	10.106	2.038	.75	12.894	87.106	1.742	85.364
–	11	10.213	2.068	.75	13.031	86.969	1.739	85.230
–	11¼	10.319	2.098	.75	13.167	86.833	1.736	85.097
–	11½	10.425	2.128	.75	13.303	86.697	1.734	84.863
–	11¾	10.532	2.155	.75	13.437	86.563	1.731	84.832
–	12	10.638	2.183	.75	13.571	86.429	1.728	84.701
–	12¼	10.745	2.211	.75	13.706	86.294	1.725	84.569
–	12½	10.851	2.240	.75	13.841	86.159	1.723	84.436
–	12¾	10.957	2.268	.75	13.975	86.025	1.720	84.305
–	13	11.064	2.296	.75	14.110	85.890	1.717	84.173
–	13¼	11.170	2.324	.75	14.244	85.756	1.715	84.041
–	13½	11.277	2.349	.75	14.376	85.624	1.712	83.912
–	13¾	11.383	2.374	.75	14.507	85.493	1.709	83.784
–	14	11.489	2.398	.75	14.637	85.363	1.707	83.656
–	14¼	11.596	2.422	.75	14.768	85.232	1.704	83.528
–	14½	11.702	2.444	.75	14.896	85.104	1.702	83.402
–	14¾	11.809	2.464	.75	15.023	84.977	1.699	83.278
–	15	11.915	2.485	.75	15.150	84.850	1.697	83.153

NO. II.
TABLE OF THE PRODUCE OF GOLD BULLION IN THE CALCUTTA MINT, COMMENCING THE 1ST OF MAY 1812

Sicca Weight	Assay per Cent	Loss and charges in refining	Total Reduction	Standard Quantity	Assayed Produce Gold Mohurs	Duty of 2½ per cent on Coinage	Nett Produce Gold Mohurs
100	¾Br.	0	0	100¾	94.82352	2.37058	92.45294
–	⅝	0	0	100⅝	94.70588	2.36764	92.33824
–	½	0	0	100½	94.58823	2.36470	92.22353
–	⅜	0	0	100⅜	94.47058	2.36176	92.10882
–	¼	0	0	100¼	94.35294	2.35882	91.99412
–	⅛	0	0	100⅛	94.23529	2.35588	91.87941
–	G.M. Std.	0	0	100	94.11764	2.35294	91.76470
–	⅛W.	0	⅛	99⅞	94.00000	2.35000	91.65000
–	¼	½	¾	99¼	93.41176	2.33529	91.07647
–	⅜	½	⅞	99⅛	93.29411	2.33235	90.96176
–	½	½	1	99	93.17647	2.32941	90.84706
–	⅝	½	1⅛	98⅞	93.05882	2.32647	90.73235
–	¾	½	1¼	98¾	92.94117	2.32352	90.61765
–	⅞	½	1⅜	98⅝	92.82352	2.32058	90.50294
–	1	½	1½	98½	92.70588	2.31764	90.38824
–	1¼	½	1¾	98¼	92.47058	2.31176	90.15882
–	1½	½	2	98	92.23529	2.30588	89.92941
–	1¾	½	2¼	97¾	92.00000	2.30000	89.70000
–	2	½	2½	97½	91.76470	2.29411	89.47059
–	2¼	½	2¾	97¼	91.52941	2.28823	89.24118
–	2½	½	3	97	91.29411	2.28235	89.01176
–	2¾	½	3¼	96¾	91.05882	2.27647	88.78235
–	3	½	3½	96½	90.82352	2.27058	88.55294
–	3¼	½	3¾	96¼	90.58823	2.26470	88.32353
–	3½	½	4	96	90.35294	2.25882	88.09412
–	3¾	½	4¼	95¾	90.11764	2.25294	87.86470
–	4	½	4½	95½	89.88235	2.24705	87.63530
–	4¼	½	4¾	95¼	89.64705	2.24117	87.40588
–	4½	½	5	95	89.41176	2.23529	87.17647
–	4¾	½	5¼	94¾	89.17647	2.22941	86.94706
–	5	½	5½	94½	88.94117	2.22352	86.71765
–	5¼	1	6¼	93¾	88.23529	2.20588	86.02941
–	5½	1	6½	93½	88.00000	2.20000	85.80000
–	5¾	1	6¾	93¼	87.76470	2.19411	85.57059
–	6	1	7	93	87.52941	2.18823	85.34118
–	6¼	1	7¼	92¾	87.29411	2.18235	85.11176
–	6½	1	7½	92½	87.05882	2.17647	84.88235

Sicca Weight	Assay per Cent	Loss and charges in refining	Total Reduction	Standard Quantity	Assayed Produce Gold Mohurs	Duty of 2½ per cent on Coinage	Nett Produce Gold Mohurs
100	6¾ W	1	7¾	92¼	86.82352	2.17058	84.65294
–	7	1	8	92	86.58823	2.16470	84.42353
–	7¼	1	8¼	91¾	86.35294	2.15882	84.19412
–	7½	1	8½	91½	86.11764	2.15294	83.96470
–	7¾	1	8¾	91¼	85.88235	2.14705	83.73530
–	8	1	9	91	85.64705	2.14117	83.50588
–	8¼	1	9¼	90¾	85.41176	2.13529	83.27647
–	8½	1	9½	90½	85.17647	2.12941	83.04706
–	8¾	1	9¾	90¼	84.94117	2.12352	82.81765
–	9	1	10	90	84.70588	2.11764	82.58824
–	9¼	1	10¼	89¾	84.47058	2.11176	82.35882
–	9½	1	10½	89½	84.23529	2.10588	82.12941
–	9¾	1	10¾	89¼	84.00000	2.10000	81.90000
–	10	1	11	89	83.76470	2.09411	81.67059
–	10¼	1½	11¾	88¼	83.05882	2.07647	80.98235
–	10½	1½	12	88	82.82352	2.07058	80.75294
–	10¾	1½	12¼	87¾	82.58823	2.06470	80.52353
–	11	1½	12½	87½	82.35294	2.05882	80.29412
–	11¼	1½	12¾	87¼	82.11764	2.05294	80.06470
–	11½	1½	13	87	81.88235	2.04705	79.83530
–	11¾	1½	13¼	86¾	81.64705	2.04117	79.60588
–	12	1½	13½	86½	81.41176	2.03529	79.37647
–	12¼	1½	13¾	86¼	81.17647	2.02941	79.14706
–	12½	1½	14	86	80.94117	2.02352	78.91765
–	12¾	1½	14¼	85¾	80.70588	2.01764	78.68824
–	13	1½	14½	85½	80.47058	2.01176	78.45882
–	13¼	1½	14¾	85¼	80.23529	2.00588	78.22941
–	13½	1½	15	85	80.00000	2.00000	78.00000
–	13¾	1½	15¼	84¾	79.76470	1.99411	77.77059
–	14	1½	15½	84½	79.52941	1.98823	77.54118
–	14¼	1½	15¾	84¼	79.29411	1.98235	77.31176
–	14½	1½	16	84	79.05882	1.97647	77.08235
–	14¾	1½	16¼	83¾	78.82352	1.97058	76.85294
–	15	1½	16½	83½	78.58823	1.96470	76.62353
–	15¼	2	17¼	82¾	77.88235	1.94705	75.93530
–	15½	2	17½	82½	77.64705	1.94117	75.70588
–	15¾	2	17¾	82¼	77.41176	1.93529	75.47647
–	16	2	18	82	77.17647	1.92941	75.24706
–	16¼	2	18¼	81¾	76.94117	1.92352	75.01765
–	16½	2	18½	81½	76.70588	1.91764	74.78824

Sicca Weight	Assay per Cent	Loss and charges in refining	Total Reduction	Standard Quantity	Assayed Produce Gold Mohurs	Duty of 2½ per cent on Coinage	Nett Produce Gold Mohurs
100	16¾ W.	2	18¾	81¼	76.47058	1.91176	74.55882
–	17	2	19	81	76.23529	1.90588	74.32941
–	17¼	2	19¼	80¾	76.00000	1.90000	74.10000
–	17½	2	19½	80½	75.76470	1.89411	73.87059
–	17¾	2	19¾	80¼	75.52941	1.88823	73.64118
–	18	2	20	80	75.29411	1.88235	73.41176
–	18¼	2	20¼	79¾	75.05882	1.87647	73.18235
–	18½	2	20½	79½	74.82352	1.87058	72.95294
–	18¾	2	20¾	79¼	74.58823	1.86470	72.72353
–	19	2	21	79	74.35291	1.85882	72.49412
–	19¼	2	21¼	78¾	74.11764	1.85294	72.26470
–	19½	2	21½	78½	73.88235	1.84705	72.03530
–	19¾	2	21¾	78¼	73.64705	1.84117	71.80588
–	20	2	22	78	73.41176	1.83529	71.57647
–	20¼	2½	22¾	77¼	72.70588	1.81764	70.88824
–	20½	2½	23	77	72.47058	1.81176	70.65882
–	20¾	2½	23¼	76¾	72.23529	1.80588	70.42941
–	21	2½	23½	76½	72.00000	1.80000	70.20000
–	21¼	2½	23¾	76¼	71.76470	1.79411	69.97059
–	21½	2½	24	76	71.52941	1.78823	69.74118
–	21¾	2½	24¼	75¾	71.29411	1.78235	69.51176
–	22	2½	24½	75½	71.05882	1.77647	69.28235
–	22¼	2½	24¾	75¼	70.82352	1.77058	69.05294
–	22½	2½	25	75	70.58823	1.76470	68.82353
–	22¾	2½	25¼	74¾	70.35294	1.75882	68.59412
–	23	2½	25½	74½	70.11764	1.75294	68.36470
–	23¼	2½	25¾	74¼	69.88235	1.74705	68.13530
–	23½	2½	26	74	69.64705	1.74117	67.90588
–	23¾	2½	26¼	73¾	69.41176	1.73528	67.67648
–	24	2½	26½	73½	69.17647	1.72941	67.44706
–	24¼	2½	26¾	73¼	68.94117	1.72352	67.21765
–	24½	2½	27	73	68.70588	1.71764	66.98824
–	24¾	2½	27¼	72¾	68.47058	1.71176	66.75882
–	25	2½	27½	72½	68.23259	1.70581	66.52678
–	25¼	3	28¼	71¾	68.00000	1.70000	66.30000
–	30	3	33	67	63.05882	1.57647	61.48235
–	30¼	3½	33¾	66¼	62.35294	1.56082	60.79212
–	35	3½	38½	61½	57.88235	1.44705	56.43530

NO. III.
TABLE OF THE PRODUCE OF SILVER BULLION IN THE FURRUCKABAD MINT, COMMENCING THE 1ST OF MAY, 1812

Sicca Weight	Assay compared with English Standard	Assay compared with F. Sicca Standard	Allowance for loss in refining	Charges for refining	Total Reduction	Assayed Produce	Duty of 2 per cent on Coinage	Nett Produce F. Sa. Rs.
100	Dwts.	Pr. Cnt.						
–	7¼Br.	F. Sa. Std.	.0	.0	.0	100	2	98
–	7	.109	.224	.0	.333	99.667	1.993	97.674
–	6¾	.218	.297	.0	.515	99.485	1.989	97.496
–	6½	.327	.371	.0	.698	99.302	1.986	97.316
–	6¼	.436	.445	.75	1.631	98.369	1.967	96.402
–	6	.545	.518	.75	1.813	98.187	1.963	96.224
–	5¾	.654	.592	.75	1.996	98.004	1.960	96.044
–	5½	.763	.665	.75	2.178	97.822	1.956	95.866
–	5¼	.872	.744	.75	2.366	97.634	1.952	95.682
–	5	.981	.823	.75	2.554	97.446	1.948	95.498
–	4¾	1.090	.901	.75	2.741	97.259	1.945	95.314
–	4½	1.199	.980	.75	2.929	97.071	1.941	95.130
–	4¼	1.308	1.058	.75	3.116	96.884	1.937	94.947
–	4	1.417	1.061	.75	3.228	96.772	1.935	94.837
–	3¾	1.526	1.064	.75	3.340	96.660	1.933	94.727
–	3½	1.635	1.068	.75	3.453	96.547	1.930	94.617
–	3¼	1.744	1.072	.75	3.566	96.434	1.928	94.506
–	3	1.853	1.075	.75	3.678	96.322	1.926	94.396
–	2¾	1.962	1.078	.75	3.790	96.210	1.924	94.286
–	2½	2.071	1.082	.75	3.903	96.097	1.921	94.176
–	2¼	2.181	1.088	.75	4.019	95.981	1.919	94.062
–	2	2.290	1.094	.75	4.134	95.866	1.917	93.949
–	1¾	2.399	1.100	.75	4.249	95.751	1.915	93.836
–	1½	2.508	1.106	.75	4.364	95.636	1.912	93.724
–	1¼	2.617	1.112	.75	4.479	95.521	1.910	93.611
–	1	2.726	1.118	.75	4.594	95.406	1.908	93.498
–	¾	2.835	1.125	.75	4.710	95.290	1.905	93.385
–	½	2.944	1.131	.75	4.825	95.175	1.903	93.272
–	¼	3.053	1.138	.75	4.941	95.059	1.901	93.158
–	Eng. Std.	3.162	1.144	.75	5.056	94.944	1.898	93.046
–	¾W.	3.271	1.150	.75	5.171	94.829	1.896	92.933
–	½	3.380	1.157	.75	5.287	94.713	1.894	92.819
–	¼	3.489	1.161	.75	5.400	94.600	1.892	92.708
–	1	3.598	1.168	.75	5.516	94.484	1.889	92.595

Sicca Weight	Assay compared with English Standard	Assay compared with F. Sicca Standard	Allowance for loss in refining	Charges for refining	Total Reduction	Assayed Produce	Duty of 2 per cent on Coinage	Nett Produce F. Sa. Rs.
100	Dwts.	pr. Cnt.						
–	1¼	3.707	1.173	.75	5.630	94.370	1.887	92.483
–	1½	3.816	1.180	.75	5.746	94.254	1.885	92.369
–	1¾	3.925	1.186	.75	5.861	94.139	1.882	92.257
–	2	4.034	1.191	.75	5.975	94.025	1.880	92.145
–	2¼	4.143	1.196	.75	6.089	93.911	1.878	92.033
–	2½	4.252	1.202	.75	6.204	93.796	1.875	91.921
–	2¾	4.361	1.208	.75	6.319	93.681	1.873	91.808
–	3	4.470	1.214	.75	6.434	93.566	1.871	91.695
–	3¼	4.579	1.220	.75	6.549	93.451	1.869	91.582
–	3½	4.688	1.226	.75	6.664	93.336	1.866	91.470
–	3¾	4.797	1.233	.75	6.780	93.220	1.864	91.356
–	4	4.907	1.241	.75	6.893	93.102	1.862	91.240
–	4¼	5.016	1.250	.75	7.016	92.984	1.859	91.125
–	4½	5.125	1.259	.75	7.134	92.866	1.857	91.009
–	4¾	5.234	1.268	.75	7.252	92.748	1.854	90.894
–	5	5 343	1.277	.75	7.370	92.630	1.852	90.778
–	5¼	5.452	1.287	.75	7.489	92.511	1.850	90.661
–	5½	5.561	1.297	.75	7.608	92.392	1.847	90.545
–	5¾	5.670	1.305	.75	7.725	92.275	1.845	90.430
–	6	5.779	1.313	.75	7.842	92.158	1.843	90.315
–	6¼	5.888	1.321	.75	7.959	92.041	1.840	90.201
–	6½	5.997	1.330	.75	8.077	91.923	1.838	90.085
–	6¾	6.106	1.339	.75	8.195	91.805	1.836	89.969
–	7	6.215	1.348	.75	8.313	91.685	1.833	89.852
–	7¼	6.324	1.357	.75	8.431	91.569	1.831	89.738
–	7½	6.434	1.364	.75	8.543	97.452	1.829	89.623
–	7¾	6.543	1.373	.75	8.666	91.334	1.826	89.508
–	8	6.652	1.389	.75	8.791	91.209	1.824	89.385
–	8¼	6.761	1.404	.75	8.915	91.085	1.821	89.264
–	8½	6.870	1.420	.75	9.040	90.960	1.819	89.141
–	8¾	6.979	1.434	.75	9.163	90.837	1.816	89.021
–	9	7.088	1.450	.75	9.288	90.712	1.814	88.898
–	9¼	7.197	1.466	.75	9.413	90.587	1.811	88.776
–	9½	7.306	1.481	.75	9.537	90.463	1.809	88.654
–	9¾	7.415	1.496	. 75	9.661	90.339	1.806	88.533
–	10	7.524	1.511	.75	9.785	90.215	1.804	88.411

Sicca Weight	Assay compared with English Standard	Assay compared with F. Sicca Standard	Allowance for loss in refining	Charges for refining	Total Reduction	Assayed Produce	Duty of 2 per cent on Coinage	Nett Produce F. Sa. Rs.
100	Dwts.	pr. Cnt.						
–	10¼	7.633	1.526	.75	9.909	90.091	1.801	88.290
–	10½ W	7.742	1.542	.75	10.034	89.966	1.799	88.167
–	10¾	7.851	1.555	.75	10.156	89.844	1.796	83.048
–	11	7.960	1.571	.75	10.281	89.719	1.794	87.925
–	11¼	8.069	1.585	.75	10.404	89.596	1.791	87.805
–	11½	8.178	1.601	.75	10.529	89.471	1.789	87.682
–	11¾	8.287	1.615	.75	10.652	89.348	1.786	87.562
–	12	8.397	1.632	.75	10.779	89.221	1.784	87.437
–	12¼	8.506	1.649	.75	10.905	89.095	1.781	87.314
–	12½	8.615	1.665	.75	11.030	88.970	1.779	87.191
–	12¾	8.724	1.683	.75	11.157	88.843	1.776	87.067
–	13	8.833	1.700	.75	11.283	88.717	1.774	86.943
–	13¼	8.942	1.717	.75	11.409	88.591	1.771	86.820
–	13½	9.051	1.734	.75	11.535	88.465	1.769	86.696
–	13¾	9.160	1.751	.75	11.661	88.339	1.766	86.573
–	14	9.269	1.775	.75	11.794	88.206	1.764	86.442
–	14¼	9.378	1.800	.75	11.928	88.072	1.761	86.311
–	14½	9.487	1.825	.75	12.062	87.938	1.758	86.180
–	14¾	9.596	1.850	.75	12.196	87.804	1.756	86.048
–	15	9.705	1.875	.75	12.330	87.670	1.753	85.917
–	15¼	9.814	1.900	.75	12.464	87.536	1.750	85.786
–	15½	9.923	1.925	.75	12.598	87.402	1.748	85.654
–	15¾	10.032	1.950	.75	12.732	87.268	1.745	85.523
–	16	10.141	1.979	.75	12.870	87.130	1.742	85.388
–	16¼	10.250	2.010	.75	13.010	86.990	1.739	85.251
–	16½	10.359	2.038	.75	13.147	86.853	1.737	85.116
–	16¾	30.468	2.068	.75	13.286	86.714	1.734	84.980
–	17	10.578	2.098	.75	13.426	86.574	1.731	84.843
–	17¼	10.687	2.128	.75	13.565	86.435	1.728	84.707
–	17½	10.796	2.155	.75	13.701	86.299	1.725	84.574
–	17¾	10.905	2.183	.75	13.838	86.162	1.723	84.439
–	18	11.014	2.211	.75	13.975	86.025	1.720	84.305
–	18¼	11.123	2.240	.75	14.113	85.887	1.717	84.170
–	18½	11.232	2.268	.75	14.250	85.750	1.715	84.035
–	18¾	11.341	2.296	.75	14.387	85.613	1.712	83.901
–	19	11.450	2.324	.75	14.524	85.476	1.700	83.767

NO. IV.
TABLE OF THE PRODUCE OF SILVER BULLION IN THE BENARES MINT, COMMENCING THE 1ST OF JANUARY, 1812

Sicca Weight	Assay compared with English Standard	Assay compared with Bs. Sicca Standard	Allowance for loss in refining	Charges for refining	Total Reduction	Assayed Produce	Duty of 2 per cent on Coinage	Nett Produce F. Sa. Rs.
	Dwts.	Pr. Cnt.						
100	9½Br.	Bs.Sa. Std.	.0	.0	.0	100	2	98
–	9¼	.108	.224	.0	.332	99.668	1.993	97.675
–	9	.216	.297	.0	.513	99.487	1.989	97.498
–	8¾	.324	.371	.0	.695	99.305	1.986	97.319
–	8½	.432	.445	.75	1.627	98.373	1.967	96.406
–	8¼	.540	.518	.75	1.808	98.192	1.963	96.229
–	8	.648	.592	.75	1.990	98.010	1.960	96.050
–	7¾	.756	.665	.75	2.171	97.829	1.956	95.873
–	7½	.864	.744	.75	2.358	97.642	1.952	95.690
–	7¼	.972	.823	.75	2.545	97.455	1.949	95.506
–	7	1.080	.901	.75	2.731	97.269	1.945	95.324
–	6¾	1.188	.980	.75	2.918	97.082	1.941	95.141
–	6½	1.296	1.058	.75	3.104	96.896	1.937	94.959
–	6¼	1.403	1.061	.75	3.214	96.786	1.935	94.851
–	6	1.511	1.064	.75	3.325	96.675	1.933	94.742
–	5¾	1.619	1.068	.75	3.437	96.563	1.931	94.632
–	5½	1.727	1.072	.75	3.549	96.451	1.929	94.522
–	5¼	1.835	1.075	.75	3.660	96.340	1.926	94.414
–	5	1.943	1.078	.75	3.771	96.229	1.924	94.305
–	4¾	2.051	1.082	.75	3.883	96.117	1.922	94.195
–	4½	2.159	1.088	.75	3.997	96.003	1.920	94.083
–	4¼	2.267	1.094	.75	4.111	95.889	1.917	93.972
–	4	2.375	1.100	.75	4.225	95.775	1.915	93.860
–	3¾	2.483	1.106	.75	4.339	95.661	1.913	93.748
–	3½	2.591	1.112	.75	4.453	95.547	1.910	93.637
–	3¼	2.699	1.118	.75	4.567	95.433	1.908	93.525
–	3	2.807	1.125	.75	4.682	95.318	1.906	93.412
–	2¾	2.915	1.131	.75	4.796	95.204	1.904	93.300
–	2½	3.023	1.138	.75	4.911	95.089	1.901	93.188
–	2¼	3.131	1.144	.75	5.025	94.975	1.899	93.076
–	2	3.239	1.150	.75	5.139	94.861	1.897	92.964
–	1¾	3.347	1.157	.75	5.254	94.746	1.894	92.852
–	1½	3.455	1.161	.75	5.366	94.634	1.892	92.742
–	1¼	3.563	1.168	.75	5.481	94.519	1.890	92.629

Sicca Weight	Assay compared with English Standard	Assay compared with Bs. Sicca Standard	Allowance for loss in refining	Charges for refining	Total Reduction	Assayed Produce	Duty of 2 per cent on Coinage	Nett Produce F. Sa. Rs.
	Dwts.	Pr. Cnt.						
100	1Br.	3.671	1.173	.75	5.594	94.406	1.888	92.518
–	$\frac{3}{4}$	3.779	1.180	.75	5.709	94.291	1.885	92.406
–	$\frac{1}{2}$	3.887	1.186	.75	5.823	94.177	1.883	92.294
–	$\frac{1}{4}$	3.995	1.191	.75	5.936	94.064	1.881	92.183
–	Eng.Std.	4.103	1.196	.75	6.049	93.951	1.879	92.072
–	$\frac{1}{4}$W.	4.211	1.202	.75	6.163	93.837	1.876	91.961
–	$\frac{1}{2}$	4.319	1.208	.75	6.277	93.723	1.874	91.849
–	$\frac{3}{4}$	4.427	1.214	.75	6.391	93.609	1.872	91.737
–	1	4.535	1.220	.75	6.505	93.495	1.869	91.626
–	$1\frac{1}{4}$	4.643	1.226	.75	6.619	93.381	1.867	91.514
–	$1\frac{1}{2}$	4.751	1.233	.75	6.734	93.266	1.865	91.401
–	$1\frac{3}{4}$	4.859	1.241	.75	6.850	93.150	1.863	91.287
–	2	4.967	1.250	.75	6.967	93.033	1.860	91.173
–	$2\frac{1}{4}$	5.075	1.259	.75	7.084	92.916	1.858	91.058
–	$2\frac{1}{2}$	5.183	1.268	.75	7.201	92.799	1.855	90.944
–	$2\frac{3}{4}$	5.291	1.277	.75	7.318	92.682	1.853	90.829
–	3	5.399	1.287	.75	7.436	92.564	1.851	90.713
–	$3\frac{1}{4}$	5.507	1.297	.75	7.554	92.446	1.848	90.598
–	$3\frac{1}{2}$	5.615	1.305	.75	7.670	92.330	1.846	90.484
–	$3\frac{3}{4}$	5.723	1.313	.75	7.786	92.214	1.844	90.370
–	4	5.831	1.321	.75	7.902	92.098	1.841	90.257
–	$4\frac{1}{4}$	5.939	1.330	.75	8.019	91.981	1.839	90.142
–	$4\frac{1}{2}$	6.047	1.339	.75	8.136	91.864	1.837	90.027
–	$4\frac{3}{4}$	6.155	1.348	.75	8.253	91.747	1.834	89.913
–	5	6.263	1.357	.75	8.370	91.630	1.832	89.798
–	$5\frac{1}{4}$	6.371	1.364	.75	8.485	91.515	1.830	89.685
–	$5\frac{1}{2}$	6.479	1.373	.75	8.602	91.398	1.827	89.571
–	$5\frac{3}{4}$	6.587	1.389	.75	8.726	91.274	1.825	89.449
–	6	6.695	1.404	.75	8.849	91.151	1.823	89.328
–	$6\frac{1}{4}$	6.803	1.420	.75	8.973	91.027	1.820	89.207
–	$6\frac{1}{2}$	6.911	1.434	.75	9.095	90.905	1.818	89.087
–	$6\frac{3}{4}$	7.019	1.450	.75	9.219	90.781	1.815	88.966
–	7	7.127	1.466	.75	9.343	90.657	1.813	88.844
–	$7\frac{1}{4}$	7.235	1.481	.75	9.466	90.534	1.810	88.724
–	$7\frac{1}{2}$	7.343	1.496	.75	9.589	90.411	1.808	88.603
–	$7\frac{3}{4}$	7.451	1.511	.75	9.712	90.288	1.805	88.483
–	8	7.559	1.526	.75	9.835	90.165	1.803	88.362

Sicca Weight	Assay compared with English Standard	Assay compared with Bs. Sicca Standard	Allowance for loss in refining	Charges for refining	Total Reduction	Assayed Produce	Duty of 2 per cent on Coinage	Nett Produce F. Sa. Rs.
100	Dwts.	pr. Cnt.						
–	8¼W.	7.667	1.542	.75	9.959	90.041	1.800	88.241
–	8½	7.775	1.555	.75	10.080	89.920	1.798	88.122
–	8¾	7.883	1.571	.75	10.204	89.796	1.795	88.001
–	9	7.991	1.585	.75	10.326	89.674	1.793	87.881
–	9¼	8.099	1.601	.75	10.450	89.550	1.791	87.759
–	9½	8.207	1.615	.75	10.572	89.428	1.788	87.640
–	9¾	8.315	1.632	.75	10.697	89.303	1.786	87.517
–	10	8.423	1.649	.75	10.822	89.178	1.783	87.395
–	10¼	8.531	1.665	.75	10.946	89.054	1.781	87.273
–	10½	8.639	1.683	.75	11.072	83.923	1.778	87.150
–	10¾	8.747	1.700	.75	11.197	83.803	1.776	87.027
–	11	8.855	1.717	.75	11.322	88.678	1.773	86.905
–	11¼	8.963	1.734	.75	11.447	88.553	1.771	86.782
–	11½	9.071	1.751	.75	11.572	88.428	1.768	86.660
–	11¾	9.179	1.775	.75	11.704	88.296	1.765	86.531
–	12	9.287	1.800	.75	11.837	88.163	1.763	86.400
–	12¼	9.395	1.825	.75	11.970	88.030	1.760	86.270
–	12½	9.503	1.850	.75	12.103	87.897	1.757	86.140
–	12¾	9.611	1.875	.75	12.236	87.764	1.755	86.009
–	13	9.719	1.900	.75	12.369	87.631	1.752	85.879
–	13¼	9.827	1.925	.75	12.502	87.498	1.749	85.749
–	13½	9.935	1.950	.75	12.635	87.365	1.747	85.618
–	13¾	10.043	1.979	.75	12.772	87.228	1.744	85.484
–	14	10.151	2.010	.75	12.911	87.089	1.741	85.348
–	14¼	10.259	2.038	.75	13.047	86.953	1 739	85.214
–	14½	10.367	2.068	.75	13.185	86.815	1.736	85.079
–	14¾	10.475	2.098	.75	13.323	86.677	1.733	84.944
–	15	10.583	2.128	.75	13.461	86.539	1.730	84.809
–	15¼	10.691	2.155	.75	13.596	86.404	1.728	84.676
–	15½	10.800	2.183	.75	13.733	86.267	1.725	84.542
–	15¾	10.908	2.211	.75	13.869	86.131	1.722	81.409
–	16	11.016	2.240	.75	14.006	85.994	1.719	81.275
–	16¼	11.124	2.268	.75	14.142	85.858	1.717	81.141
–	16½	11.232	2.296	.75	14.278	85.722	1.714	84.008
–	16¾	11.340	2.324	.75	14.414	85.586	1.711	83.875
–	17	11.448	2.349	.75	14.547	85.453	1.709	83.744

Sicca Weight	Assay compared with English Standard	Assay compared with Bs. Sicca Standard	Allowance for loss in refining	Charges for refining	Total Reduction	Asayed Produce	Duty of 2 per cent on Coinage	Nett Produce F. Sa. Rs.
100	Dwts.	pr. Cnt.						
–	17¼W.	11.556	2.374	.75	14.680	85.320	1.706	83.614
–	17½	11.664	2.398	.75	14.812	85.188	1.703	83.485
–	17¾	11.772	2.422	.75	14.944	85.056	1.701	83.355
–	18	11.880	2.444	.75	15.074	84.926	1.698	83.228
–	18¼	11.988	2.464	.75	15.202	84.798	1.695	83.103
–	18½	12.095	2.485	.75	15.330	84.670	1.693	82.977

Appendix A.24

A.D. 1814 REGULATION VII

A REGULATION for modifying a Part of a Provisions contained in Regulation X, 1809, respecting the copper coinage of the Province of Benares.—PASSED by the Vice President-in-Council on the 29th April, 1814; corresponding with the 18th Bysaak 1221 Bengal era; the 25th Bysaak 1221 Fussily; the 19th Bysaak 1221 Willaity; the 10th Bysaak 1871 Sumbut and; the 8th Jumaadi-ul-awul 1229 Higeree.

Preamble	Whereas it is enacted in Section II, Regulation X, 1809 that the copper coin required for the province of Benares shall be struck at the Calcutta mint; and whereas inconvenience has been experienced from the delay incident to that arrangement; the following rules have been enacted to be immediately in force in the province of Benares.
Part of Section II, Regulation X, 1809, rescinded	II. *First.* So much of the Section II, Regulation X, 1809, as prescribes that the copper coin required for the province of Benares, shall be struck at the Calcutta mint, is hereby rescinded.
Copper coin required for the province of Benares, to be struck at that city.	*Second.* The copper coin required for the province, shall be in future struck at the city of Benares.
The figure of a trisool to be impressed on the copper coin.	III. In compliance with established usage, the figure of a trisool shall be impressed on the copper coin, which may hereafter be struck at the city of Benares.

N.B.: Superseded by Acts XIII and XXII of 1844.

Appendix A.25

A.D. 1816 REGULATION XXI

A REGULATION for modifying Section XLIII, Regulation XLV, 1803, which prescribes a specified weight for the copper Pice to be coined at the Mint of Furruckabad.—PASSED by the Governor General in Council on the, 8th November 1816; corresponding with the 24th Cartic 1223 Bengal era; the 3d Aughun 1224, Fussily; the 25th Cartic 1224, Willaity; the 3rd Aughun 1873 Sumbut; and the 17th Zilhij 1231 Higeree.

WHEREAS it has been deemed advisable to reduce the weight of the copper coinage intended to be introduced into the ceded provinces by Section XLIII to Section LI, Regulation XLV, 1803, extended to the conquered provinces by Regulation XI. 1805, the following rules have been enacted, to be in force from their promulgation.	[Preamble]
II. Section XLIII, Regulation XLV, 1803, is hereby rescinded.	Section XLIII, Regulation XLV, 1803, rescinded.
III. A copper coin shall be struck at the mint of Furruckabad weighing two hundred grains troy for the whole or double pice and one hundred grains troy for the half or single pice.	Weight of the copper coin to be struck at the mint at Furruckabad.
IV. Such copper coin shall be issued from the mint at the rate of thirty-two whole or double pice, and of sixty-four half or single pice for each Rupee.	Rate at which such, coin is to be issued.

Appendix A.26

A.D. 1817 REGULATION XIV

A REGULATION for amending certain parts of Regulation II, 1812.—PASSED by the Vice-President in Council on the 9th September 1817, corresponding with the 26th Bhadoon 1224 Bengal era; the 14th Bhadoon 1224 Fussily; the 17th Bhadoon 1224 Willaity; the 13th Bhadoon 1874 Sumbut; and the 26th Sawul 1232 Higeree.

[Preamble]	WHEREAS it has been found that some inaccuracies of calculation exist in the table No. 2, annexed to Regulation II, 1812, by which the produce of gold bullion is calculated in the Calcutta mint; the following rules have been enacted, to be in force from the date of their promulgation.
Such part of Regulation II, 1812, as relates to table No. 2, annexed to that Regulation, rescinded.	II. So much of Regulation II of 1812, as relates to the table of the produce of gold bullion in the Calcutta mint, annexed to that Regulation, is hereby rescinded.
The table of the produce of gold bullion annexed to this Regulation, to be in force in lieu of the table No. 2, alluded to in the preceding Section.	III. Instead of the table referred to in the above Section, the assay produce, duties and net produce of gold bullion delivered for coinage into the Calcutta mint, shall be hereafter calculated agreeably to the table annexed to this Regulation, and the certificates granted by the assay master shall be made out accordingly.

TABLE OF THE PRODUCE OF GOLD BILLION IN THE CALCUTTA MINT.

Sicca Weight	Assay per cent.	Deduction for worseness	Allowance for the refining charges	Total Reduction	Standard Quantity	Assay produce, Gold Mohurs	Duty at $2\frac{1}{2}$ per cent.	Nett produce Gold Mohurs
100	$\frac{3}{4}$ Br.	0 756	–	–	100 756	94 829	2 371	92 458
–	$\frac{5}{8}$ Br.	0 630	–	–	100 630	94 711	2 368	92 343
–	$\frac{1}{2}$ Br.	0 504	–	–	100 504	94 592	2 365	92 227
–	$\frac{3}{8}$ Br.	0 378	–	–	100 378	94 473	2 362	92 111
–	$\frac{1}{4}$ Br.	0 252	–	–	100 252	94 355	2 359	91 996
–	$\frac{1}{8}$ Br.	0 126	–	–	100 126	94 236	2 356	91 880
–	Standard.	–	–	–	100 0	94 118	2 353	91 765
–	$\frac{1}{8}$ Wo.	0 126	–	0 126	99 874	93 999	2 350	91 649
–	$\frac{1}{4}$ Wo.	0 252	0 5	0 752	99 248	93 410	2 335	91 075
–	$\frac{3}{8}$ Wo.	0 378	0 5	0 878	99 122	93 291	2 332	90 959
–	$\frac{1}{2}$ Wo.	0 504	0 5	1 004	98 996	93 173	2 329	90 844
–	$\frac{5}{8}$ Wo.	0 630	0 5	1 130	98 870	93 054	2 326	90 728
–	$\frac{3}{4}$ Wo.	0 750	0 5	1 256	98 744	92 936	2 323	90 613
–	$\frac{7}{8}$ Wo.	0 882	0 5	1 382	98 618	92 817	2 320	90 497
–	1 Wo.	1 008	0 5	1 508	98 492	92 698	2 317	90 381
–	$1\frac{1}{4}$ Wo.	1 260	0 5	1 760	98 240	92 461	2 311	90 150
–	$1\frac{1}{2}$ Wo.	1 512	0 5	2 012	97 988	92 224	2 306	89 918
–	$1\frac{3}{4}$ Wo.	1 764	0 5	2 264	97 736	91 987	2 300	89 687
–	2 Wo.	2 016	0 5	2 516	97 484	91 750	2 294	89 456
–	$2\frac{1}{4}$ Wo.	2 268	0 5	2 768	97 232	91 512	2 286	89 224
–	$2\frac{1}{2}$ Wo.	2 520	0 5	3 020	96 980	91 270	2 282	88 993
–	$2\frac{3}{4}$ Wo.	2 772	0 5	3 272	96 728	91 038	2 276	88 762
–	3 Wo.	3 024	0 5	3 524	96 476	90 801	2 270	88 531
–	$3\frac{1}{4}$ Wo.	3 275	0 5	3 775	96 225	90 565	2 264	88 301
–	$3\frac{1}{2}$ Wo.	3 526	0 5	4 026	95 974	90 328	2 258	88 070
–	$3\frac{3}{4}$ Wo.	3 778	0 5	4 278	95 722	90 091	2 252	87 839
–	4 Wo.	4 030	0 5	4 530	95 470	89 854	2 246	87 608
–	$4\frac{1}{4}$ Wo.	4 282	0 5	4 782	95 218	89 617	2 240	87 377
–	$4\frac{1}{2}$ Wo.	4 534	0 5	5 034	94 966	89 380	2 235	87 145
–	$4\frac{3}{4}$ Wo.	4 786	0 5	5 286	94 714	89 143	2 228	86 915
–	5 Wo.	5 038	0 5	5 538	94 462	88 905	2 223	86 682
–	$5\frac{1}{4}$ Wo.	5 290	1 0	6 290	93 710	88 198	2 205	85 993
–	$5\frac{1}{2}$ Wo.	5 541	1 0	6 541	93 459	87 961	2 199	85 762
–	$5\frac{3}{4}$ Wo.	5 793	1 0	6 793	93 207	87 724	2 193	85 531
–	6 Wo.	6 045	1 0	7 045	92 955	87 487	2 187	85 300

Sicca Weight	Assay per cent.	Deduction for worseness	Allowance for the refining charges	Total Reduction	Standard Quantity	Assay produce, Gold Mohurs	Duty at $2\frac{1}{2}$ per cent.	Nett produce Gold Mohurs
100	$6\frac{1}{4}$ Wo.	6 297	1 0	7 297	92 703	87 250	2 181	85 069
–	$6\frac{1}{2}$ Wo.	6 549	1 0	7 549	92 451	87 013	2 175	84 838
–	$6\frac{3}{4}$ Wo.	6 801	1 0	7 801	92 199	86 776	2 169	84 607
–	7 Wo.	7 053	1 0	8 053	91 947	86 538	2 163	84 375
–	$7\frac{1}{4}$ Wo.	7 305	1 0	8 305	91 695	86 301	2 159	84 143
–	$7\frac{1}{2}$ Wo.	7 557	1 0	8 557	91 443	86 064	2 152	83 912
–	$7\frac{3}{4}$ Wo.	7 809	1 0	8 809	91 191	85 827	2 146	83 681
–	8 Wo.	8 060	1 0	9 060	90 940	85 591	2 140	83 451
–	$8\frac{1}{4}$ Wo.	8 312	1 0	9 312	90 688	85 353	2 134	83 219
–	$8\frac{1}{2}$ Wo.	8 504	1 0	9 564	90 436	85 116	2 128	82 988
–	$8\frac{3}{4}$ Wo.	8 816	1 0	9 816	90 184	84 879	2 122	82 757
–	9 Wo.	9 068	1 0	10 068	89 932	84 642	2 116	82 526
–	$9\frac{1}{4}$ Wo.	9 320	1 0	10 320	89 680	84 405	2 110	82 295
–	$9\frac{1}{2}$ Wo.	9 572	1 0	10 572	89 428	84 168	2 104	82 064
–	$9\frac{3}{4}$ Wo.	9 824	1 0	10 824	89 176	83 930	2 098	81 832
–	10 Wo.	10 075	1 0	11 075	88 925	83 694	2 092	81 602
–	$10\frac{1}{4}$ Wo.	10 327	1 5	11 827	88 173	82 986	2 075	80 911
–	$10\frac{1}{2}$ Wo.	10 579	1 5	12 079	87 921	82 749	2 069	80 680
–	$10\frac{3}{4}$ Wo.	10 831	1 5	12 331	87 669	82 512	2 063	80 449
–	11 Wo.	11 083	1 5	12 583	87 417	82 275	2 057	80 218
–	$11\frac{1}{4}$ Wo.	11 335	1 5	12 835	87 165	82 038	2 051	79 987
–	$11\frac{1}{2}$ Wo.	11 587	1 5	13 087	86 913	81 800	2 045	79 755
–	$11\frac{3}{4}$ Wo.	11 839	1 5	13 339	86 661	81 563	2 039	79 524
–	12 Wo.	12 091	1 5	13 591	86 409	81 326	2 033	79 293
–	$12\frac{1}{4}$ Wo.	12 342	1 5	13 842	86 158	81 090	2 027	79 063
–	$12\frac{1}{2}$ Wo.	12 594	1 5	14 094	85 908	80 853	2 021	78 832
–	$12\frac{3}{4}$ Wo.	12 846	1 5	14 346	85 654	80 616	2 015	78 601
–	13 Wo.	13 098	1 5	14 598	85 402	80 378	2 009	78 369
–	$13\frac{1}{4}$ Wo.	13 350	1 5	14 856	85 150	80 141	2 004	78 137
–	$13\frac{1}{2}$ Wo.	13 602	1 5	15 102	84 898	79 904	1 998	77 906
–	$13\frac{3}{4}$ Wo.	13 854	1 5	15 354	84 646	79 667	1 992	77 675
–	14 Wo.	14 106	1 5	15 606	84 394	79 430	1 986	77 444
–	$14\frac{1}{4}$ Wo.	14 358	1 5	15 858	84 142	79 193	1 980	77 213
–	$14\frac{1}{2}$ Wo.	14 610	1 5	16 110	83 890	78 955	1 974	76 981
–	$14\frac{3}{4}$ Wo.	14 862	1 5	16 362	83 638	78 718	1 968	76 750
–	15 Wo.	15 113	1 5	16 613	83 387	78 482	1 962	76 520
–	$15\frac{1}{4}$ Wo.	15 365	2 0	17 365	82 635	77 774	1 944	75 830
–	$15\frac{1}{2}$ Wo.	15 617	2 0	17 617	82 383	77 537	1 938	75 599
–	$15\frac{3}{4}$ Wo.	15 869	2 0	17 869	82 131	77 300	1 933	75 367

Sicca Weight	Assay per cent.	Deduction for worseness	Allowance for the refining charges	Total Reduction	Standard Quantity	Assay produce, Gold Mohurs	Duty at $2\frac{1}{2}$ per cent.	Nett produce Gold Mohurs
100	16 Wo.	16 121	2 0	18 121	81 879	77 063	1 927	75 136
–	16¼ Wo.	16 373	2 0	18 373	81 627	76 826	1 921	74 905
–	16½ Wo.	16 625	2 0	18 625	81 375	76 588	1 915	74 673
–	16¾ Wo.	16 876	2 0	18 876	81 124	76 352	1 909	74 443
–	17 Wo.	17 128	2 0	19 128	80 872	76 115	1 903	74 212
–	17¼ Wo.	17 380	2 0	19 380	80 620	75 878	1 897	73 981
–	17½ Wo.	17 632	2 0	19 632	80 368	75 646	1 891	73 749
–	17¾ Wo.	17 884	2 0	19 884	80 116	75 403	1 885	73 518
–	18 Wo.	18 136	2 0	20 136	79 864	75 166	1 879	73 287
–	18¼ Wo.	18 388	2 0	20 388	79 612	74 929	1 873	73 056
–	18½ Wo.	18 640	2 0	20 640	79 360	74 692	1 867	72 825
–	18¾ Wo.	18 892	2 0	20 892	79 108	74 455	1 861	72 594
–	19 Wo.	19 144	2 0	21 144	78 856	74 218	1 855	72 363
–	19¼ Wo.	19 395	2 0	21 395	78 605	73 981	1 849	72 132
–	19½ Wo.	19 647	2 0	21 647	78 353	73 744	1 844	71 900
–	19¾ Wo.	19 899	2 0	21 899	78 101	73 507	1 838	71 669
–	20 Wo.	20 151	2 0	22 151	77 849	73 270	1 832	71 438
–	20¼ Wo.	20 403	2 5	22 903	77 097	72 562	1 814	70 748
–	20½ Wo.	20 655	2 5	23 155	76 845	72 325	1 808	70 517
–	20¾ Wo.	20 907	2 5	23 407	76 593	72 088	1 802	70 286
–	21 Wo.	21 159	2 5	23 659	76 341	71 850	1 796	70 045
–	21¼ Wo.	21 410	2 5	23 910	76 090	71 614	1 790	69 824
–	21½ Wo.	21 662	2 5	24 162	75 838	71 377	1 784	69 593
–	21¾ Wo.	21 914	2 5	24 414	75 586	71 140	1 778	69 362
–	22 Wo.	22 166	2 5	24 666	75 334	70 903	1 772	69 131
–	22¼ Wo.	22 418	2 5	24 918	75 082	70 665	1 767	68 898
–	22½ Wo.	22 676	2 5	25 170	74 836	70 428	1 761	68 667
–	22¾ Wo.	22 922	2 5	25 422	74 578	70 191	1 755	68 436
–	23 Wo.	23 174	2 5	25 674	74 326	69 954	1 749	68 205
–	23¼ Wo.	23 426	2 5	25 926	74 074	69 717	1 743	67 974
–	23½ Wo.	23 678	2 5	26 178	73 822	69 480	1 737	67 743
–	23¾ Wo.	23 929	2 5	26 429	73 571	69 243	1 731	67 512
–	24 Wo.	24 181	2 5	26 681	73 319	69 006	1 725	67 281
–	24¼ Wo.	24 433	2 5	26 933	73 067	68 769	1 719	67 050
–	24½ Wo.	24 685	2 5	27 185	72 815	68 532	1 713	66 819
–	24¾ Wo.	24 937	2 5	27 437	72 563	68 295	1 707	66 588
–	25 Wo.	25 189	2 5	27 689	72 311	68 057	1 701	66 356
–	25¼ Wo.	25 441	3 0	28 441	71 559	67 350	1 684	65 666
–	25½ Wo.	25 693	3 0	28 693	71 367	67 112	1 678	65 434

Sicca Weight	Assay per cent.	Deduction for worseness	Allowance for the refining charges	Total Reduction	Standard Quantity	Assay produce, Gold Mohurs	Duty at $2\frac{1}{2}$ per cent.	Nett produce Gold Mohurs
100	$25\frac{3}{4}$ Wo.	25 945	3 0	28 945	71 055	66 876	1 672	65 204
–	26 Wo.	26 196	3 0	29 196	70 804	66 639	1 666	64 973
–	$26\frac{1}{4}$ Wo.	26 448	3 0	29 448	70 552	66 402	1 660	64 742
–	$26\frac{1}{2}$ Wo.	26 700	3 0	29 700	70 300	66 165	1 654	64 511
–	$26\frac{3}{4}$ Wo.	26 952	3 0	29 952	70 048	65 928	1 648	64 280
–	27 Wo.	27 204	3 0	30 204	69 796	65 690	1 642	64 048
–	$27\frac{1}{4}$ Wo.	27 456	3 0	30 456	69 544	65 453	1 636	63 817
–	$27\frac{1}{2}$ Wo.	27 708	3 0	30 708	69 292	65 216	1 630	63 586
–	$27\frac{3}{4}$ Wo.	27 960	3 0	30 960	69 046	64 979	1 624	63 355
–	28 Wo.	28 212	3 0	31 212	68 788	64 742	1 618	63 124
–	$28\frac{1}{4}$ Wo.	28 463	3 0	31 463	68 537	64 505	1 613	62 892
–	$28\frac{1}{2}$ Wo.	28 715	3 0	31 715	68 285	64 268	1 607	62 661
–	$28\frac{3}{4}$ Wo.	28 967	3 0	31 967	68 033	64 031	1 601	62 430
–	29 Wo.	29 219	3 0	32 219	67 781	63 794	1 595	62 199
–	$29\frac{1}{4}$ Wo.	29 471	3 0	32 471	67 529	63 557	1 589	61 968
–	$29\frac{1}{2}$ Wo.	29 723	3 0	32 723	67 277	63 320	1 583	61 737
–	$29\frac{3}{4}$ Wo.	29 975	3 0	32 975	67 025	63 082	1 577	61 505
–	30 Wo.	30 227	3 0	33 227	66 773	62 845	1 571	61 274
–	$30\frac{1}{4}$ Wo.	30 479	3 5	33 979	66 021	62 137	1 553	60 584
–	$30\frac{1}{2}$ Wo.	30 730	3 5	34 230	65 770	61 901	1 547	60 354
–	$30\frac{3}{4}$ Wo.	30 982	3 5	34 482	65 518	61 664	1 542	60 122
–	31 Wo.	31 234	3 5	34 734	65 266	61 427	1 536	59 891
–	$31\frac{1}{4}$ Wo.	31 486	3 5	34 986	65 014	61 190	1 530	59 660
–	$31\frac{1}{2}$ Wo.	31 738	3 5	35 238	64 762	60 952	1 524	59 428
–	$31\frac{3}{4}$ Wo.	31 990	3 5	35 490	64 510	60 715	1 518	59 197
–	32 Wo.	32 242	3 5	35 742	64 258	60 478	1 512	58 966
–	$32\frac{1}{4}$ Wo.	32 494	3 5	35 994	64 006	60 241	1 506	58 735
–	$32\frac{1}{2}$ Wo.	32 746	3 5	36 246	63 754	60 004	1 500	58 504
–	$32\frac{3}{4}$ Wo.	32 997	3 5	36 497	63 503	59 768	1 494	58 274
–	33 Wo.	33 249	3 5	36 749	63 251	59 530	1 488	58 042
–	$33\frac{1}{4}$ Wo.	33 501	3 5	37 001	62 999	59 293	1 482	57 811
–	$33\frac{1}{2}$ Wo.	33 753	3 5	37 253	62 747	59 056	1 476	57 580
–	$33\frac{3}{4}$ Wo.	34 005	3 5	37 505	62 495	58 819	1 470	57 349
–	34 Wo.	34 257	3 5	37 575	62 243	58 582	1 464	57 118
–	$34\frac{1}{4}$ Wo.	34 509	3 5	38 009	61 991	58 344	1 459	56 885
–	$34\frac{1}{2}$ Wo.	34 761	3 5	38 261	61 739	58 107	1 453	56 664
–	$34\frac{3}{4}$ Wo.	35 013	3 5	38 513	61 487	57 870	1 447	56 423
–	35 Wo.	35 264	3 5	38 764	61 236	57 634	1 441	56 193

Appendix A.27

A.D. 1817 REGULATION XVII

A REGULATION for the more effectual administration of Criminal Justice in certain cases.—PASSED by the Governor-General-in-Council on the 16th September, 1817, corresponding with the 2nd Assin 1218 Bengal era; the 21st Bhadoon 1224 Fussily; the 3rd Bhadoon 1224 Willaity; the 6th Bhadoon 1874 Sumbut and; the 4th Zekaedda 1226 Higeree.

xx xx xx xx	
IX. *First.* The provisions contained in Regulation II, 1807, for the punishment of persons convicted of wilful perjury, or subornation of perjury, or of forgery, or procuring forgery, are hereby declared subject to the following modifications.	The provisions in Regulation II, 1807, for the punishment of wilful perjury or Subornation of perjury, or of forgery or procuring forgery, modified.
Second. The judge of Circuit, before whom a prisoner may be convicted of any of the offences specified in the above clause, as defined in Regulation II, 1807, or in the present Regulation, provided he concur with the law officer in the conviction of the prisoner, shall sentence him to be publicly exposed in the mode commonly denominated tusheer, to receive thirty stripes with a corah, and to be imprisoned in banishment from the district, for the period of seven years; or for the term of fourteen years, if the prisoner be convicted of having forged or procured to be forged any counterfeit coin in imitation of any of the gold, silver or copper coins of the British Governments in India, or of any coin usually received as money in the British possessions in India; or of having forged, or procured to be forged, any counterfeit stamp, or stampt paper in imitation of any public stamp established by the British governments in India; or any counterfeit note, or other security for	Sentence to be passed on persons convicted before the Court of Circuit of any of the above offences as defined in Regulation II, 1807, or in the present Regulation. Enhanced penalty on persons convicted of having forged or procuring to be forged counterfeit coin, &c.

Power of the judge of Circuit to mitigate the prescribed punishment, to a certain extent, in cases of extenuation.	money, in imitation of any of the public securities of the British Governments in India; or of the bank notes issued by any public bank in the British possessions in India, unless the judge of Circuit, on consideration of all the circumstances of the case, shall be of opinion that any part of the prescribed punishment is too severe; in which case he is authorized to mitigate the sentence to imprisonment, with or without tusheer, for any period not less than seven years, in the abovementioned cases of forgery of counterfeit coin, public stamps, securities or bank notes, and procuration of such forgery, and to imprisonment, with or without tusheer, for any period not less than three years, in all other cases within the provisions of Regulation II, 1807, and the present Regulation.
If a further mitigation of punishment appear proper, the judge or Circuit to pass sentence according to the preceding Clause, and refer the trial to the Nizamut Adawlut	*Third.* If in any instance the judge of Circuit shall be of opinion, that a further mitigation or remission of punishment is necessary, he shall, provided he concur in the conviction of the prisoner, pass sentence according to the preceding clause, and refer the trial, with his sentiments at large, for the final sentence or order of the Court of Nizamut Adawlut.
Provision for the punishment of knowingly and fraudulently uttering forged instruments, counterfeit stampt papers, coin, bank notes, promissory notes or other securities for money.	X. *First.* The provisions of Regulation II, 1807, not including the offence of fraudulently issuing and publishing as true, or otherwise fraudulently giving effect or attempting to give effect, to fabricated deeds and papers, knowing the same to be false and fabricated; or the offence of using, issuing, selling or otherwise disposing of, or attempting to dispose of, counterfeit stamp paper, bearing the imitation of a public stump, knowing the same to be counterfeit, or the offence of paying, or tendering in payment, counterfeited coin, bank notes, promissory notes, or other securities for money, knowing the same to be counterfeit the following additional provisions are enacted for the punishment of these offences respectively.
Sentence to be passed on	*Second.* If any person shall be convicted before a Court of Circuit, or the Court of Nizamut Adawlut, of any of

the offences specified in the above clause, he shall be sentenced to imprisonment for such period, not exceeding seven years, as the judge of Circuit may deem adequate to the nature and circumstances of the case: and shall also, in all instances of an aggravated nature, or of a repetition of the offence, after being once convicted and discharged, be sentenced to public exposure by tusheer. In every instance of a repetition of the offence, after a previous conviction and discharge, the judge of Circuit may further at his discretion, sentence the offender to receive corporal punishment, not exceeding thirty stripes, with a corah or ratan. If a person twice convicted and discharged, be again found guilty of any of the offences specified in the preceding clause, and the judge of Circuit shall be of opinion that he ought to be imprisoned for a longer period than seven years, he shall refer the trial, with his sentiments, for the sentence of the Court of Nizamut Adawlut, in pursuance of the seventh clause of Section II, Regulation LIII, 1803.	persons convicted before a Court of Circuit or Nizamut Adawlut of any of the above offences. In cases of an aggravated nature, or a repetition of the offence after first conviction and punishment, and the judge of Circuit may adjudge tusheer and stripes. Rules in cases of third conviction after discharge from former convictions.
Third. The provisions in the above clause are further declared applicable to persons convicted of clipping, filing, drilling, defacing, or debasing the gold or silver coin of the British Governments in India, or any coin usually received as money within the British possessions in India; the whole of which offences, in the Regulations for the coinage, are already made cognizable by the Criminal Courts, and declared punishable as the law may direct.	Provisions in the above clauses applicable to persons convicted of clipping, filing, drilling, defacing or debasing the gold or silver coin.
XI. If any person, subject to the jurisdiction of a zillah or city magistrate, shall be convicted of having in his, or her possession, without lawful or satisfactory excuse, any counterfeited coin, or stampt paper, bearing an imitation of any current coin, or public stamp, and shall not shew good and sufficient cause for having such counterfeit coin, or stampt paper in his or her possession, the persons so convicted shall be sentenced by the magistrate to pay a fine equal to four times the nominal value of such counterfeit coin, or stampt paper, in his or her, possession, one moiety of which fine shall, on receipt of it, be given to any informer, or informers,	Persons convicted before a magistrate of having in possession counterfeit coin or stampt paper, without lawful excuse, punishable by fine or 3 months imprisonment.

	who may have given information of the offence, and established the truth of it. In the event of such fine not being paid, the person convicted shall be confined for such period as the magistrate may direct, not exceeding six months. The counterfeit coin or stampt paper, shall also, in every instance, be forwarded to the mint master or superintendent of stamps respectively.
	xx xx xx xx

Appendix A.28

A.D. 1817 REGULATION XXV

A REGULATION for fixing the Weight of the Pice struck at the Calcutta Mint, and for giving general circulation to Pice struck at any of the Mints subordinate to this Presidency.—PASSED by the Vice-President in Council on the 9th December 1817, corresponding with the 25th Aughun 1224 Bengal era; the 16th Aughun 1225 Fussily; the 26th Aughun 1225 Willaity; the 1st Aughun 1874 Sumbut, and the 29th Moherrem 1233 Higeree.

WHEREAS it has been deemed expedient to adopt some precise rules for the coinage and currency of the copper pice struck in the mint of Calcutta, and also for extending the circulation of those pice, as well as the pice struck at the mints of Benares and Furruckabad, the following rules are therefore enacted, to be in force from the date of their promulgation throughout the provinces immediately dependent on the presidency of Fort William.	Preamble
II. The copper pice struck at the Calcutta mint, shall be of pure copper, and of the weight of 100 grains troy.	Specification of the weight of copper pice struck at the mint at Calcutta.
III. The inscription shall be on one side, One Pie Sicca, in the Bangalee, Persian and Nagree characters, and the date on the obverse.	Inscription and date.
IV. The pice shall be issued from the mint and public treasuries at the rate of sixty-four to one sicca rupee, at which rate they will be received again by the public officers in payment of the fractional parts of a rupee, and they shall also be legal tender in payments of the same nature, at the rate of sixty-four to a rupee of the local currency throughout the provinces subject to the presidency of Fort William.	Rate at which the pice shall be issued and received.

The pice struck at the mint of Benares and Furruckabad to circulate equally with the pice of Calcutta coinage, throughout the provinces.	V. The pice struck at the mints of Benares and Furruckabad, agreeably to the provisions of Regulation X, 1809, Regulation VII, 1814, and Regulation XXI, 1816, shall also be considered as circulating equally with the pice of Calcutta coinage throughout the above-mentioned provinces, and shall in like manner be received as a legal tender in payment of the fractional parts of a rupee of the local currency, at the rate of sixty-four pice for each rupee.

Appendix A.29

A.D. 1817 REGULATION XXVI

A REGULATION for authorizing the circulation of Furruckabad Rupees, coined in either of the Mints of Calcutta, Furruckabad, or Benares, or at any other Mint, established by Order of the Governor General in Council.—PASSED by the Vice-President in Council on the 10th December, 1817; corresponding with the 3rd Poose 1224 Bengal era; the 23rd Aughun 1225 Fussily; the 4th Poose 1225 Willaity; the 8th Aughun 1874 Sumbut, and the 6th Suffer 1233 Higeree.

WHEREAS it may from time to time be found expedient to coin rupees of the weight and standard of the Furruckabad Rupee at the mints of Calcutta or Benares, it has been deemed advisable to rescind so much of Section II of Regulation XLV, of 1803, as tends to limit the coinage of Furruckabad Rupees to the mint of Furruckabad; and to direct that the following enactment be henceforward in force.	Preamble
II. The silver coin denominated the Furruckabad Rupee, and of the weight and standard prescribed by Section II, of Regulation III, 1806, struck at the mints of Calcutta, Furruckabad or Benares, or at any other mint, established by order of the Governor General in Council, is hereby declared to be the established and legal silver coin in the Ceded and Conquered Provinces.	Furruckabad Rupee coined in any of the mints, to be the established and legal silver coin in the Ceded and Conquered Provinces.

Appendix A.30

A.D. 1818 REGULATION XIV

A REGULATION for altering the Standard of the Calcutta Sicca Rupee and Gold Mohur, and for further modifying some of the rules in force respecting those Coins.—PASSED by the Governor General in Council, on the 24th December 1818; corresponding with the 11th Poose 1225 Bengal era; the 12th Poose, 1226 Willaity; the 12th Poose 1875 Sumbut; and the 25th Suffer 1234 Higeree.

Preamble	THE high standards established for the Gold Mohur and Sicca Rupee, having been found productive of many inconveniencies, both to individuals and the public, inasmuch as they are ill calculated to resist the wear and defacement to which coins are necessarily exposed, and as they are only to be obtained by having recourse to the expensive process of refining, diminishing consequently the productiveness of most of the sorts of Bullion imported into the Company's territories; and it being desirable also, that as much uniformity as can be established between the currencies circulating at the different Presidencies, should be introduced,—consequently that an approximation of the standard of the Calcutta Coins to the standard of those current at Madras and Bombay should be effected,—it has been resolved to rescind the provisions of former Regulations relative to the standard of the Gold Mohur and nineteenth Sun Sicca Rupee, and to coin in future money of the proportions hereafter to be specified. As a reduction in the value of the Sicca Rupee from its being in great measure the money of account, both in private and public transactions, would necessarily change the terms of all existing contracts, and might be productive of embarrassment and trouble, it has been determined to leave the Rupee unaltered in this respect and the new Calcutta Sicca Rupee will consequently contain the same quantity of fine Silver, as that heretofore struck, and being of the same intrinsic value, will circulate on the same terms. The Mint proportions of Silver and

Gold being, it is believed, inaccurately estimated at present, and it being also desirable, that an uniformity in this respect should be introduced at the three Presidencies of Calcutta, Madras and Bombay, it has been thought advisable to make a slight deduction in the intrinsic value of the Gold Mohur, to be coined at this Presidency, in order to raise the relative value of fine Gold to fine Silver, from the present rates of 1 to 14,861, to that of 1 to 15. The Gold Mohur will still continue to pass current at the present rate of Sixteen Rupees. For the purposes and objects above enumerated, the following provisions are hereby enacted, and declared to be in force from the 1st of January, 1819.	
I. First. So much of Section II Regulation XXXV, 1793, as fixes the weight and standard of the Nineteenth Sun Sicca Rupee and Gold Mohur, is hereby rescinded.	Part of Section II, Regulation XXXV 1793 rescinded.
Second. The weight and standard of the Calcutta Sicca Rupee and Gold Mohur and their respective divisions, shall be as follows.	Specification of the weight and standard of the Calcutta Sicca Rupee and Gold Mohur.

	Gold.	*Fine Gold.*	*Alloy.*
Gold Mohur Weight.			
Grs. - - - - - - -	204.710	187.651	17.059
Half ditto, - - - - -	102.355	93.825	8.529
Quarter ditto, - - - -	51.177	46.912	4.264
	Silver.	*Fine Silver.*	*Alloy.*
Sicca Rupee Weight			
Grs. - - - - - - -	191.010	175.923	15.993
Half ditto, - - - - - -	95.953	87.961	7.997
Quarter ditto, - - - -	47.979	43.981	3.998

II. All Calcutta Sicca Rupees and Gold Mohurs of the weight and standard specified in Section I which may be coined in the Calcutta Mint after the 1st of January, 1819, and also their halves and quarters, are to be considered as legal tender of payment in all public and private transactions throughout the provinces of Bengal, Behar and Orissa, in like manner as the Nineteenth Sun Sicca Rupees and Gold Mohurs, and the fractional parts of them now in circulation, and any Native officer of Government refusing to receive them, shall be subject to the penalty prescribed in Section III Regulation XXXV, 1793.	Sicca Rupees and Gold Mohurs of the weight and standard specified in the preceding section, to be considered as legal tenders.

Section II Regulation II 1812, rescinded.	III. First. The following provisions shall be substituted for those of Section II Regulation II 1812, which are hereby rescinded.
Duty to be levied on bullion or coin delivered into the Calcutta Mint for coinage.	Second. All silver bullion or coin (not being struck at the Calcutta Mint) which may be delivered into that Mint for coinage, shall be subject to a duty at the rate of two per cent on the produce of such bullion or coin, in Sicca Rupees of the above weight and standard, and the amount of the said duty shall be accordingly deducted from the return to be made to the proprietor.
Duty to be levied if the proprietor shall desire to have his bullion or coin converted into halves or Quarters of rupees.	Third. Individuals who may be desirous of it, shall be at liberty to have their bullion or coin converted into halves or quarters of the above Rupee, on condition of paying a duty at the rate of one per cent in addition to the duty of two per cent established by the preceding Clause.
Duty to be levied if such coin shall consist of Calcutta Siccas.	Fourth. Should however the coin brought to the Mint for that purpose, consist of Calcutta Siccas of the former or present weight and standard, the proprietors shall only be subject to the additional duty of one per cent and not to the duty on all other coin and bullion.
Course of proceeding to be observed when silver bullion or coin, shall be delivered into the Mint.	Fifth. On delivery of the silver bullion or coin into the Mint, the Mint Master shall grant to the proprietor a receipt, entitling him to a certificate from the Assay Master, for the net produce of such bullion or coin, agreeably to the Table subjoined to this Regulation, and marked No. 1 payable at the General Treasury at Calcutta, at the expiration of ten days, if the produce be deliverable in whole Rupees; and at the expiration of twenty days, if the produce be deliverable in halves or quarters of a Rupee, from the date of such certificate. In the latter case, the additional duty established by Clause Third Section IV of this Regulation, is of course to be deducted from the net produce.
Application of Section III, Regulation II, 1812, to Rupees, half and quarter Rupees,	IV. Section III. Regulation II 1812, is hereby declared applicable to Rupees, half and quarter Rupees, coined in conformity with the provisions of this Regulation, provided however that all such Rupees, halves and quarters, shall be receivable in all public and private

transactions, if, when separately weighed, the deficiency in point of weight, be not more than two pice, or grains Troy 1,999 per Rupee.	coined in conformity with this Regulation.
V. *First.* The following rules shall be observed in lieu of the Third and Fourth Clauses of Section V, Regulation II 1812, which are hereby rescinded.	Clauses 3rd and 4th, Section V, Regulation II, 1812, rescinded.
Second. For all gold bullion or coin equal to, or better than the standard prescribed for the Gold Mohur by this Regulation, which may be brought to the Mint for coinage, a number of the new Gold Mohurs, or of the halves and quarters of such Mohurs, equal to the produce of such bullion, shall be returned to the proprietor, after deducting the duty of $2\frac{1}{2}$ per cent as mentioned in Clause Second, Section V, Regulation II, 1812.	Mode of proceeding when gold bullion or coin brought to the Mint for coinage, shall be equal to or better than standard prescribed for the Gold Mohur by this Regulation.
Third. All gold bullion or gold coin, being under the above specified standard, which may be delivered into the Calcutta Mint for coinage, shall, in addition to the duty of two Rupees eight Annas per cent fixed by Clause Second, Section V Regulation II 1812, be subject to a charge, on account of the loss and expense of refining agreeably to Table No. II annexed to this Regulation, together with the established deduction, on account of the inferiority of standard.	Mode of proceeding when it may be inferior to the above specified standard.
VI. Such parts of Regulation XXXV of 1793, and Regulation II 1812, as are not repealed by the above Regulation, shall be considered as still in force.	Certain provisions of Regulation XXXV 1793 and Regulation II 1812, to be still in force.

[NO. 1.]

TABLE OF THE PRODUCE OF SILVER BILLION IN THE CALCUTTA MINT, COMMENCING THE 1ST OF JANUARY 1819.

Standard	Decimal addition or Deduction per cent	Charges for Refining	Total Deduction	Produce in Sa. Wt.	Produce in Sa. Rs.	Duty of 2 per cent on Coinage	Nett Produce Sicca Rupees
Dwts.							
20 Br.	9.091	"	"	109.091	102.128	2.013	100.085
19½ Br.	8.864	"	"	108.864	101.915	2.038	99.877
19 Br.	8.636	"	"	108.636	101.702	2.034	99.668
18½ Br.	8.409	"	"	108.409	101.489	2.030	99.459
18 Br.	8.182	"	"	108.182	101.277	2.026	99.251
17½ Br.	7.955	"	"	107.955	101.064	2.021	99.043
17 Br.	7.727	"	"	107.727	100.851	2.017	98.834
16½ Br.	7.500	"	"	107.500	100.638	2.013	98.625
16 Br.	7.273	"	"	107.273	100.426	2.008	98.418
15½ Br.	7.045	"	"	107.045	100.212	2.004	98.208
15 Br.	6.818	"	"	106.818	100.000	2.000	98.000
14½ Br.	6.591	"	"	106.591	99.787	1.996	97.791
14 Br.	6.364	"	"	106.364	99.575	1.991	97.584
13½ Br.	6.136	"	"	106.136	99.361	1.987	97.374
13 Br.	5.909	"	"	105.909	99.149	1.983	97.166
12½ Br.	5.682	"	"	105.682	98.936	1.979	96.957
12 Br.	5.455	"	"	105.455	98.724	1.974	96.750
11½ Br.	5.227	"	"	105.227	98.510	1.970	96.540
11 Br.	5.000	"	"	105.000	98.298	1.966	96.332
10½ Br.	4.773	"	"	104.773	98.085	1.962	96.123
10 Br.	4.545	"	"	104.545	97.872	1.957	95.915
9½ Br.	4.318	"	"	104.318	97.659	1.953	95.706
9 Br.	4.091	"	"	104.091	97.447	1.949	95.498
8½ Br.	3.864	"	"	103.864	97.234	1.945	95.289
8 Br.	3.636	"	"	103.636	97.021	1.940	95.081
7½ Br.	3.409	"	"	103.409	96.808	1.936	94.872
7 Br.	3.182	"	"	103.182	96.596	1.931	94.665
6½ Br.	2.955	"	"	102.955	96.383	1.928	94.455
6 Br.	2.727	"	"	102.727	96.170	1.923	94.247
5½ Br.	2.500	"	"	102.500	95.957	1.919	94.038
5 Br.	2.273	"	"	102.273	95.745	1.915	93.830
4½ Br.	2.045	"	"	102.045	95.531	1.911	93.620
4 Br.	1.818	"	"	101.818	95.319	1.906	93.413
3½ Br.	1.591	"	"	101.591	95.106	1.902	93.204

Standard	Decimal addition or Deduction per cent	Charges for Refining	Total Deduction	Produce in Sa. Wt.	Produce in Sa. Rs.	Duty of 2 per cent on Coinage	Nett Produce Sicca Rupees
Dwts.							
3 Br.	1.364	"	"	101.364	94.894	1.898	92.996
2½ Br.	1.136	"	"	101.136	94.680	1.894	92.786
2 Br. Eng. Std.	.909	"	"	100.909	94.468	1.889	92.579
1½ Br.	.682	"	"	100.682	94.255	1.885	92.370
1 Br.	.455	"	"	100.455	94.043	1.881	92.162
½ Br.	.227	"	"	100.227	93.830	1.877	91.953
Standard.	.000	"	"	100.000	93.617	1.872	91.745
½ W.	.227	"	.227	99.773	93.404	1.868	91.536
1 W.	.455	"	.455	99.545	93.191	1.864	91.327
1½ W.	.682	"	.682	99.318	92.979	1.860	91.119
2 W.	.900	"	.909	99.091	92.766	1.855	90.911
2½ W.	1.136	"	1.136	98.864	92.554	1.851	90.703
3 W.	1.364	"	1.364	98.636	92.341	1.847	90.494
3½ W.	1.591	"	1.591	98.409	92.128	1.843	90.285
4 W.	1.818	"	1.818	98.182	91.915	1.838	90.077
4½ W.	2.045	"	2.045	97.955	91.708	1.834	89.869
5 W.	2.273	"	2.273	97.727	91.489	1.830	89.659
5½ W. Sp. Dr. Std.	2.500	"	2.500	97.500	91.277	1.826	89.451
6 W.	2.727	"	2.727	97.273	91.064	1.821	89.243
6½ W.	2.955	.297	3.252	96.748	90.573	1.811	88.762
7 W.	3.182	.445	3.627	96.373	90.222	1.804	88.418
7½ W.	3.409	.592	4.001	95.999	89.871	1.797	88.074
8 W.	3.686	.744	4.380	95.620	89.517	1.790	87.727
8½ W.	3.864	.901	4.765	95.235	89.156	1.783	87.373
9 W.	4.091	1.058	5.149	94.851	88.797	1.776	87.021
9½ W.	4.318	1.064	5.382	94.618	88.579	1.771	86.808
10 W.	4.545	1.072	5.617	94.383	88.359	1.767	86.592
10½ W.	4.778	1.078	5.851	94.149	88.139	1.763	86.376
11 W.	5.000	1.088	6.088	93.912	87.918	1.758	86.160
11½ W.	5.227	1.100	6.327	93.673	87.694	1.754	85.940
12 W.	5.455	1.112	6.567	93.433	87.469	1.749	85.720
12½ W.	5.682	1.125	6.807	93.193	87.244	1.745	85.499
13 W.	5.909	1.138	7.047	92.953	87.020	1.740	85.280
13½ W.	6.136	1.150	7.286	92.714	86.796	1.736	85.060

Standard	Decimal addition or Deduction per cent	Charges for Refining	Total Deduction	Produce in Sa. Wt.	Produce in Sa. Rs.	Duty of 2 per cent on Coinage	Nett Produce Sicca Rupees
Dwts.							
14 W.	6.364	1.161	7.525	92.475	86.572	1.731	84.841
14½ W.	6.591	1.173	7.764	92.236	86.349	1.727	84.622
15 W.	6.818	1.186	8.004	91.996	86.124	1.722	84.402
15½ W.	7.045	1.196	8.241	91.759	85.902	1.718	84.184
16 W.	7.273	1.208	8.481	91.519	85.677	1.713	83.964
16½ W.	7.500	1.220	8.720	91.280	85.454	1.709	83.745
17 W.	7.727	1.233	8.960	91.040	85.229	1.704	83.525
17½ W.	7.955	1.250	9.205	90.795	85.000	1.700	83.300
18 W.	8.182	1.268	9.450	90.550	84.770	1.695	83.075
18½ W.	8.409	1.287	9.696	90.304	84.540	1.691	82.849
19 W.	8.636	1.305	9.941	90.059	84.311	1.686	82.625
19½ W.	8.864	1.321	10.185	89.815	84.082	1.682	82.400
20 W.	9.091	1.339	10.430	89.570	83.853	1.677	82.176
20½ W.	9.318	1.357	10.675	89.325	83.623	1.672	81.951
21 W.	9.545	1.373	10.918	89.082	83.396	1.668	81.728
21½ W.	9.773	1.404	11.177	88.823	83.153	1.663	81.490
22 W.	10.000	1.434	11.434	88.566	82.913	1.658	81.255
22½ W.	10.227	1.466	11.693	88.307	82.670	1.653	81.017
23 W.	10.455	1.496	11.951	88.049	82.429	1.648	80.781
23½ W.	10.682	1.526	12.208	87.792	82.188	1.644	80.544
24 W.	10.909	1.555	12.464	87.536	81.949	1.639	80.310
24½ W.	11.136	1.585	12.721	87.279	81.708	1.634	80.074
25 W.	11.364	1.615	12.979	87.021	81.466	1.629	79.837
25½ W.	11.591	1.649	13.240	86.760	81.222	1.624	79.598
26 W.	11.818	1.683	13.501	86.499	80.978	1.620	79.358
26½ W.	12.045	1.717	13.762	86.238	80.733	1.614	79.119
27 W.	12.273	1.751	14.024	85.976	80.488	1.610	78.878
27½ W.	12.500	1.800	14.300	85.700	80.230	1.605	78.625
28 W.	12.727	1.850	14.577	85.423	79.970	1.599	78.371
28½ W.	12.955	1.900	14.855	85.145	79.710	1.594	78.116
29 W.	13.182	1.950	15.132	84.868	79.451	1.589	77.862
29½ W.	13.409	2.010	15.419	84.581	79.182	1.584	77.598
30 W.	13.636	2.068	15.704	84.296	78.915	1.578	77.337
30½ W.	13.864	2.128	15.992	84.008	78.646	1.573	77.073
31 W.	14.091	2.183	16.274	83.726	78.382	1.568	76.814
31½ W.	14.318	2.240	16.558	83.442	78.116	1.562	76.554
32 W.	14.545	2.296	16.841	83.159	77.581	1.557	76.294
32½ W.	14.773	2.349	17.122	82.878	77.588	1.552	76.036

Standard	Decimal addition or Deduction per cent	Charges for Refining	Total Deduction	Produce in Sa. Wt.	Produce in Sa. Rs.	Duty of 2 per cent on Coinage	Nett Produce Sicca Rupees
Dwts.							
33 W.	15.000	2.398	17.398	82.602	77.330	1.547	75.783
$33\frac{1}{2}$ W.	15.227	2.444	17.671	82.329	77.074	1.541	75.533
34 W.	15.455	2.485	17.940	82.060	76.822	1.536	75.286
$34\frac{1}{2}$ W.	15.682	2.511	18.193	81.807	76.585	1.532	75.053
35 W.	15.909	2.536	18.445	81.555	76.349	1.527	74.822

[NO. 2.]

TABLE OF THE PRODUCE OF GOLD BILLION IN THE CALCUTTA MINT, COMMENCING THE 1ST JANUARY 1819.

New Standard			Decimal Addition or Deduction per cent	Charges for Refining	Total Deduction	Produce in Sicca Weight	Produce in Gold Mohurs	Duty of $2\frac{1}{2}$ per cent on Coinage	Nett Produce Sicca Rupees
Carats	Grains	Qrs.							
2.	”	Br.	9.09091	”	”	109.09091	95.74485	2.39362	93.35123
1.	3.	$\frac{3}{4}$ Br.	8.80682	”	”	108.80682	95.49551	2.38739	93.10812
1.	3.	$\frac{1}{2}$ Br.	8.52273	”	”	108.52273	95.24618	2.38115	92.86503
1.	3.	$\frac{1}{4}$ Br.	8.23864	”	”	108.23864	94.99684	2.37492	92.62192
1.	3.	0 Br.	7.95455	”	”	107.95455	94.74751	2.36869	92.37882
1.	2.	$\frac{3}{4}$ Br.	7.67046	”	”	107.67046	94.49817	2.36245	92.13572
1.	2.	$\frac{1}{2}$ Br.	7.38636	”	”	107.38636	94.24883	2.35622	91.89261
1.	2.	$\frac{1}{4}$ Br.	7.10227	”	”	107.10227	93.99949	2.34999	91.64950
1.	2.	0 Br.	6.81818	”	”	106.81818	93.75016	2.34375	91.40641
1.	1.	$\frac{3}{4}$ Br.	6.53409	”	”	106.53409	93.50082	2.33752	91.16330
1.	1.	$\frac{1}{2}$ Br.	6.25000	”	”	106.25000	93.25149	2.33129	90.92020
1.	1.	$\frac{1}{4}$ Br.	5.96591	”	”	105.96591	93.00216	2.32505	90.67711
1.	1.	0 Br.	5.68182	”	”	105.68182	92.75282	2.31882	90.43400
1.	0.	$\frac{3}{4}$ Br.	5.39773	”	”	105.39773	92.50349	2.31259	90.19090
1.	0.	$\frac{1}{2}$ Br.	5.11364	”	”	105.11364	92.25416	2.30635	89.94781
1.	0.	$\frac{1}{4}$ Br.	4.82956	”	”	104.82956	92.00483	2.30012	89.70471
1.	0.	0 Br.	4.54545	”	”	104.54545	91.75547	2.29389	89.46158
0.	3.	$\frac{3}{4}$ Br.	4.26136	”	”	104.26136	91.50614	2.28765	89.21849
0.	3.	$\frac{1}{2}$ Br.	3.97727	”	”	103.97727	91.25680	2.28142	88.97538

0.	3.	¼ Br.	3.69318	”	”	103.69318	91.00747	2.27519	88.73228
0.	3.	0 Br.	3.40909	”	”	103.40909	90.75813	2.26895	88.48918
0.	2.	¾ Br.	3.12500	”	”	103.12500	90.50880	2.26272	88.24608
0.	2.	½ Br.	2.84091	”	”	102.84091	90.25946	2.25649	88.00297
0.	2.	¼ Br.	2.55682	”	”	102.55682	90.01013	2.25025	87.75988
0.	2.	0 Br.	2.27273	”	”	102.27273	89.76079	2.24402	87.51677
0.	1.	¾ Br.	1.98864	”	”	101.98864	89.51146	2.23779	87.27367
0.	1.	½ Br.	1.70455	”	”	101.70455	89.26213	2.23155	87.03058
0.	1.	¼ Br.	1.42045	”	”	101.42045	89.01278	2.22532	86.78746
0.	1.	0 Br.	1.13636	”	”	101.13636	88.76345	2.21909	86.54436
0.	0.	¾ Br.	.85227	”	”	100.85227	88.51411	2.21285	86.30126
0.	0.	½ Br.	.56818	”	”	100.56818	88.26478	2.20662	86.05816
0.	0.	¼ Br.	.28409	”	”	100.28409	88.01544	2.20039	85.81505
Standard			.00000	”	”	100.00000	87.76611	2.19415	85.57196
0.	0.	¼ W.	.28409	.50000	.78409	99.21591	87.07794	2.17695	84.90099
0.	0.	½ W.	.56818	.50000	1.06818	98.93182	86.82861	2.17072	84.65789
0.	0.	¾ W.	.85227	.50000	1.35227	98.64773	86.57927	2.16448	84.41479
0.	1.	0 W.	1.13636	.50000	1.63636	98.36364	86.32994	2.15825	84.17169
0.	1.	¼ W.	1.42045	.50000	1.92045	98.07955	86.08060	2.15202	83.92858
0.	1.	½ W.	1.70455	.50000	2.20455	97.79545	85.83126	2.14578	83.68548
0.	1.	¾ W.	1.98864	.50000	2.48864	97.51136	85.58193	2.13955	83.44238
0.	2.	0 W.	2.27273	.50000	2.77273	97.22727	85.33259	2.13331	83.19928
0.	2.	¼ W.	2.55682	.50000	3.05682	96.94318	85.08326	2.12708	82.95618
0.	2.	½ W.	2.84091	.50000	3.34091	96.65909	84.83392	2.12085	82.71307
0.	2.	¾ W.	3.12500	.50000	3.62500	96.37500	84.58459	2.11461	82.46998
0.	3.	0 W.	3.40909	.50000	3.90909	96.09091	84.33525	2.10838	82.22687

New Standard			Decimal Addition or Deduction per cent	Charges for Refining	Total Deduction	Produce in Sicca Weight	Produce in Gold Mohurs	Duty of $2\frac{1}{2}$ per cent on Coinage	Nett Produce Sicca Rupees
Carats	Grains	Qrs.							
0.	3.	$\frac{1}{4}$ W.	3.69318	.50000	4.19318	95.80682	84.08592	2.10215	81.98377
0.	3.	$\frac{1}{2}$ W.	3.97727	.50000	4.47727	95.52273	83.83659	2.09591	81.74068
0.	3.	$\frac{3}{4}$ W.	4.26136	.50000	4.76136	95.23864	83.58725	2.08968	81.49757
1.	0.	0 W.	4.54545	.50000	5.04545	94.95455	83.33791	2.08345	81.25446
1.	0.	$\frac{1}{4}$ W.	4.82955	.50000	5.32955	94.67045	83.08857	2.07721	81.01136
1.	0.	$\frac{1}{2}$ W.	5.11364	.50000	5.61364	94.38636	82.83923	2.07098	80.76825
1.	0.	$\frac{3}{4}$ W.	5.39773	.50000	5.89773	94.10227	82.58990	2.06475	80.52515
1.	1.	0 W.	5.68182	.50000	6.18182	93.81818	82.34057	2.05851	80.28206
1.	1.	$\frac{1}{4}$ W.	5.96591	1.00000	6.96591	93.03409	81.65240	2.04131	79.61109
1.	1.	$\frac{1}{2}$ W.	6.25000	1.00000	7.25000	92.75000	81.40307	2.03508	79.36799
1.	1.	$\frac{3}{4}$ W.	6.53409	1.00000	7.53409	92.46591	81.15373	2.02884	79.12489
1.	2.	0 W.	6.81818	1.00000	7.81818	92.18182	80.90440	2.02261	78.88179
1.	2.	$\frac{1}{4}$ W.	7.10227	1.00000	8.10227	91.89773	80.65506	2.01638	78.63868
1.	2.	$\frac{1}{2}$ W.	7.38636	1.00000	8.38636	91.61364	80.40573	2.01014	78.39559
1.	2.	$\frac{3}{4}$ W.	7.67045	1.00000	8.67045	91.32955	80.15639	2.00391	78.15248
1.	3.	0 W.	7.95455	1.00000	8.95455	91.04545	79.90705	1.99768	77.90937
1.	3.	$\frac{1}{4}$ W.	8.23864	1.00000	9.23864	90.76136	79.65771	1.99114	77.66627
1.	3.	$\frac{1}{2}$ W.	8.52273	1.00000	9.52273	90.47727	79.40838	1.98521	77.42317
1.	3.	$\frac{3}{4}$ W.	8.80682	1.00000	9.80682	90.19318	79.15904	1.97898	77.13006
2.	0.	0 W.	9.09091	1.00000	10.09091	89.90909	78.90971	1.97274	76.93697
2.	0.	$\frac{1}{4}$ W.	9.37500	1.00000	10.37500	89.62500	78.66037	1.96651	76.69306
2.	0.	$\frac{1}{2}$ W.	9.65909	1.00000	10.65909	89.34091	78.41104	1.96028	70.45076

2.	0.	$\frac{3}{4}$ W.	9.94318	1.00000	10.94318	89.05682	78.16170	1.95404	76.20766
2.	1.	0 W.	10.22727	1.00000	11.22727	88.77273	77.91237	1.94781	75.96456
2.	1.	$\frac{1}{4}$ W.	10.51136	1.00000	11.51136	88.48864	77.66304	1.94458	75.72146
2.	1.	$\frac{1}{2}$ W.	10.79545	1.00000	11.79545	88.20455	77.41370	1.93534	75.47836
2.	1.	$\frac{3}{4}$ W.	11.07955	1.00000	12.07955	87.92045	77.16436	1.92911	75.23525
2.	2.	0 W.	11.36364	1.00000	12.36364	87.63636	76.91502	1.92288	74.99214
2.	2.	$\frac{1}{4}$ W.	11.64773	1.50000	13.14773	86.85227	76.22686	1.90567	74.32119
2.	2.	$\frac{1}{2}$ W.	11.93182	1.50000	13.48182	86.56818	75.97752	1.89944	74.07808
2.	2.	$\frac{3}{4}$ W.	12.21591	1.50000	13.71591	86.28409	75.72819	1.89320	73.83499
2.	3.	0 W.	12.50000	1.50000	14.00000	86.00000	75.47885	1.88697	73.59188
2.	3.	$\frac{1}{4}$ W.	12.78409	1.50000	14.28409	85.71591	75.22932	1.88074	73.34878
2.	3.	$\frac{1}{2}$ W.	13.06818	1.50000	14.56818	85.43182	74.98018	1.87450	73.10568
2.	3.	$\frac{3}{4}$ W.	13.35227	1.50000	14.85227	85.14773	74.73085	1.86827	72.86258
3.	0.	0 W.	13.63636	1.50000	15.13636	84.86364	74.48151	1.86204	72.61947
3.	0.	$\frac{1}{4}$ W.	13.92045	1.50000	15.42045	84.57955	74.23218	1.85580	72.37638
3.	0.	$\frac{1}{2}$ W.	14.20455	1.50000	15.70455	84.29545	73.98284	1.84957	72.13327
3.	0.	$\frac{3}{4}$ W.	14.48864	1.50000	15.98864	84.01136	73.73350	1.84334	71.89016
3.	1.	0 W.	14.77273	1.50000	16.27273	83.72727	73.48417	1.83710	71.64707
3.	1.	$\frac{1}{4}$ W.	15.05682	1.50000	16.55682	83.44318	73.23488	1.83087	71.40396
3.	1.	$\frac{1}{2}$ W.	15.34091	1.50000	16.84091	83.15909	72.98550	1.82464	71.16086
3.	1.	$\frac{3}{4}$ W.	15.62500	1.50000	17.12500	82.87500	72.73616	1.81840	70.91776
3.	2.	0 W.	15.90909	1.50000	17.40909	82.59091	72.48683	1.81217	70.67466
3.	2.	$\frac{1}{4}$ W.	16.19318	1.50000	17.69318	82.30682	72.23749	1.80594	70.43155
3.	2.	$\frac{1}{2}$ W.	16.47727	1.50000	17.97727	82.02273	71.98816	1.79970	70.18846
3.	2.	$\frac{3}{4}$ W.	16.76136	1.50000	18.26136	81.73864	71.73882	1.79347	69.94535
3.	3.	0 W.	17.04545	1.50000	18.54545	81.45455	71.48949	1.78724	69.70225
3.	3.	$\frac{1}{4}$ W.	17.32955	2.00000	19.32955	80.67045	70.80131	1.77003	69.03128

New Standard			Decimal Addition or Deduction per cent.	Charges for Refining	Total Deduction	Produce in Sicca Weight	Produce in Gold Mohurs	Duty of $2\frac{1}{2}$ per cent on Coinage	Nett Produce Sicca Rupees
Carats	Grains	Qrs.							
3.	3.	$\frac{1}{2}$ W.	17.61364	2.00000	19.61364	80.38636	70.55198	1.76380	68.78818
3.	3.	$\frac{3}{4}$ W.	17.89773	2.00000	19.89773	80.10227	70.30264	1.75757	68.54507
4.	0.	0 W.	18.18182	2.00000	20.18182	79.81818	70.05331	1.75133	68.30198
4.	0.	$\frac{1}{4}$ W.	18.46591	2.00000	20.46591	79.53409	69.80398	1.74510	68.05888
4.	0.	$\frac{1}{2}$ W.	18.75000	2.00000	20.75000	79.25000	69.55464	1.73887	67.81577
4.	0.	$\frac{3}{4}$ W.	19.03409	2.00000	21.03409	78.96591	69.30531	1.73263	67.57268
4.	1.	0 W.	19.31818	2.00000	21.31818	78.68182	69.05597	1.72640	67.32957
4.	1.	$\frac{1}{4}$ W.	19.60227	2.00000	21.60227	78.39773	68.80664	1.72017	67.08647
4.	1.	$\frac{1}{2}$ W.	19.88636	2.00000	21.88636	78.11364	68.55730	1.71393	67.84337
4.	1.	$\frac{3}{4}$ W.	20.17045	2.00000	22.17045	77.82955	68.30797	1.70770	66.60027
4.	2.	0 W.	20.45455	2.00000	22.45455	77.54545	68.05862	1.70147	66.35715
4.	2.	$\frac{1}{4}$ W.	20.73864	2.00000	22.73864	77.26136	67.80929	1.69523	66.11406
4.	2.	$\frac{1}{2}$ W.	21.02273	2.00000	23.02273	76.97727	67.55995	1.63900	65.87095
4.	2.	$\frac{3}{4}$ W.	21.30682	2.00000	23.30682	76.69318	67.31062	1.68277	65.62785
4.	3.	0 W.	21.59091	2.00000	23.59091	76.40909	67.06123	1.67658	65.38475
4.	3.	$\frac{1}{4}$ W.	21.87500	2.00000	23.87500	76.12500	66.81195	1.67030	65.14165
4.	3.	$\frac{1}{2}$ W.	22.15909	2.00000	24.15909	75.84091	66.56261	1.66407	64.89854
4.	3.	$\frac{3}{4}$ W.	22.44318	2.00000	24.44318	75.55682	66.31328	1.65788	64.65545
5.	0.	0 W.	22.72727	2.00000	24.72727	75.27273	66.06394	1.65160	64.41234

Appendix A.31

A.D. 1819 REGULATION V

A REGULATION for modifying certain parts of the rules in force, in regard to the conduct of the business of the Mints subordinate to this Presidency.—PASSED by the Governor General in Council on the 25th June, 1819; corresponding with the 12th Assaur 1226 Bengal Era; the 17th Assaur 1226 Fussily; the 13th Assaur 1226 Willaity, the 3rd Assaur 1876 Sumbut, and the 1st Ramzan 1234 Higeree.

BY Regulation II 1812, and Regulation XIV, 1818, fixed periods are prescribed for the payment of certificates, granted to individuals in exchange for bullion or coin, delivered into the Mints of Calcutta, Benares and Furruckabad: but the importations of bullion may at times be so heavy, as to preclude the possibility of coining it, as tendered for that purpose, within the fixed period; while the exigencies of the state may render it inconvenient to provide for the payment of mint certificates, before the bullion for which they are granted, can be coined:—It has become expedient therefore to rescind the said rules, and to reserve to Government the power of fixing from time to time, by public notice, the periods within which the certificates aforesaid shall be payable.—It further appears expedient to reserve to the Governor General in Council the power of altering, in like manner, the form and inscription of the coins to be struck at the said mints;—provided always, that no diminution be made with regard to the quantity of pure bullion, purported to be contained in each piece of coin respectively.—It has likewise been deemed proper to fix the duty to be levied on the coinage of gold bullion and coin, at the same rate as has been established for silver:—The following rules have accordingly been enacted, to be in force from the present date, within the provinces immediately dependent on the presidency of Fort William.	Preamble

Rescinding certain rules of former Regulations which prescribe that certificates gratned at the different mints for bullion or coin should be payable within the periods therein specified.	II. So much of Clause Fourth, Section VIII and Section XXXI, Regulation II, 1812, and Clause Fifth, Section III Regulation XIV, 1818, as prescribes that the mint certificates granted at the mints of Furruckabad, Benares and Calcutta, for bullion or coin, delivered into those mints, shall be payable within the periods therein severally specified,—is hereby rescinded and annulled.
The Governor General in Council will determine the periods for which such certificates should run, and such determination to be made public.	III. The Governor General in Council will from time to time determine the periods for which the certificates aforesaid shall run; such determination to be made public by advertisement in the Government Gazette, and by a notice to be affixed in a conspicuous part of the mint to which the order may refer.
The Governor General in Council reserves to himself the power of altering the form mid inscription of coins.	IV. The Governor General in Council further reserves to himself the power of altering, in like manner, the form and inscription of the coins struck at the said mints.
Modifying former rules and enacting that a duty of two per cent only be deducted from the produce of gold bullion or coin brought for coinage to the Calcutta mint.	V. In modification of the rules contained in Section V, Regulation II 1812, and Section V Regulation XIV 1818, it is hereby enacted, that from and after the promulgation of this Regulation, a duty of two per cent only shall be deducted from the produce of gold bullion or coin which may be brought for coinage to the Calcutta mint, in lieu of the duty specified in Table 2 annexed to the last mentioned Regulation.

Appendix A.32

A.D. IX 1819 REGULATION XI

A REGULATION for discontinuing the Coinage of the Benares Rupee; for declaring the Furruckabad Rupee the legal Currency of the Province of Benares; for altering the Standard of the Furruckabad Rupee, and for defining the rate at which that Rupee is to be received within the province of Benares.—PASSED by the Governor General in Council on the 31st December, 1819, corresponding with the 17th Poose 1226 Bengal Era; the 30th Poose 1227 Fussily; the 18th Poose 1227 Willaity; the 15th Poose 1878 Sumbut; and the 13th Rubbee-ul-awul 1235 Higeree.

THE existence of different local currencies in a country subject to one common authority, must obviously impede that constant intercourse by which its several provinces are necessarily connected, and considerable inconvenience from that cause has been experienced in the intercourse between the several provinces subordinate to this Presidency.—Great difficulties, however, oppose the immediate establishment of one currency throughout all those provinces. On the one hand, the Calcutta Sicca Rupee having been long established throughout the extensive provinces of Bengal, Behar and Orissa, all private engagements have been made in that coin: the land revenue payable by the zemindars, which (with partial exceptions) has been fixed in perpetuity throughout those provinces, as well as the whole of the registered debt of this country, are likewise expressed in the Calcutta Rupee; any alteration in its value would therefore occasion great embarrassment and perplexity. On the other hand, the Furruckabad Rupee forms the currency of the whole of the ceded and conquered provinces, and the influence of any change in regard to it would be proportionably important and extensive. In it all payments on account of the public revenue within those provinces are received, and the pay of the troops and of all public establishments therein stationed is discharged; the price of articles of ordinary consumption has necessarily been regulated with reference to the local	Preamble

coin. If therefore the Calcutta Sicca Rupee were rendered the local currency of those provinces, while Government must of course allow to the zemindars an abatement in their revenue, equivalent to the difference between the, Calcutta and Furruckabad Rupee, and would therefore be compelled to issue the former at its intrinsic value, the troops and other public establishments might be subject, temporarily at least, to considerable loss and inconvenience, by receiving payment in a coin that might not immediately bear its full value in the market, compared with articles of ordinary consumption. It has thence appeared necessary, for the present at least, to maintain the currencies now established in the provinces of Bengal, Behar and Orissa, and in the ceded and conquered provinces respectively. The legal circulation of the Benares Rupee is confined to a single province—that coin has long been issued to the troops and other public establishments as equivalent to the Furruckabad Rupee. It circulates generally at par with that Rupee when employed beyond the limits of the province of Benares; though exceeding it in value to the extent of two and a quarter per cent. The land revenue of Benares is indeed, like that of Bengal, Behar and Orissa, fixed in perpetuity; and any alteration in the nominal amount of the jumma, being likely to lead to serious misapprehension, Government deem it right, in introducing into Benares the inferior currency of the western provinces, to relinquish the claim which they might in strictness assert to the difference between the two Rupees, rather than to give the slightest occasion for any doubt or alarm in regard to the stability of an arrangement guaranteed by the public faith. The amount however of the land revenue in question is comparatively limited, and the public advantage likely to result from a simplification of the currencies of those provinces, appears to counterbalance the partial loss which Government must sustain in receiving the Furruckabad Rupee at par with the Benares Rupee: the adjustment of private engagements in a single province will be comparatively easy, and while the community will be saved from the loss which they have heretofore sustained, whenever they carried the Benares Rupee beyond the limits of that province, the difference between the two coins amounting only to two and a quarter per cent will

have little or no perceptible influence on the market price of articles consumed by the lower orders of the people; more especially, since the value of the two Rupees in copper money has for some time past been equalized. It appears therefore that the discontinuance of the coinage of the Benares Rupees while it will greatly simplify the monetary system of this Presidency, and will otherwise essentially promote the trade and general prosperity of the country, will be attended with little inconvenience, and that only temporary and partial. The Governor General in Council has accordingly resolved to limit the legal currencies in the territories subordinate to this presidency to two, namely, the Calcutta and the Furruckabad Rupee. With the view of still further simplifying the system of coinage in the said territories, and of facilitating the conversion of the above mentioned currencies, the one into the other, it has been also determined to reduce them to one general standard : so that, though differing in intrinsic value, yet as they will contain the same proportions of pure metal and alloy, no charge, for refinage, nor for the trouble of adjusting the standard will be incurred in the coinage of the one currency into the other. To give effect to the above arrangements, and at the same time to fix the rate at which, the Furruckabad Rupee is to be received in the province of Benares, in liquidation of existing engagements between Individuals, the following rules have been enacted by the Governor General in Council to be in force from the date of their promulgation.	
II. The coinage of the Benares Rupee shall be discontinued from the date of this Regulation.	Coinage of the Benares Rupee discontinued.
III. The Furruckabad Rupee shall be considered the legal currency of the province of Benares.	Furruckabad Rupee declared legal currency of Benares
IV. The Furruckabad Rupee shall be a legal tender in all the territories under the Bengal Government, with the exception of Bengal, Behar and Orissa, whether struck at the Mints, of Calcutta, Benares or Furruckabad, or at any other Mint that may be hereafter established within the aforesaid limits, under the authority of the British Government.	Such Rupee to be a legal tender in all places under this Presidency, exception to Bengal, Behar and Orissa,

Specification of the value and standard of the new Farruckabad Rupee.	V. The Furruckabad Rupee to be struck at any of the Mints before mentioned, shall be of the value of the present Furruckabad Rupee, and of the standard of the present Calcutta Rupee; that is to say, it shall be of the following weight and fineness: Weight, ...Troy Grains 180.234 Pure Silver, ... 165.215 Alloy, ... 15.019 Being 11-12th pure, and 1-12th alloy.
Rates of charge for coining Bullion.	VI. Individuals bringing Bullion for coinage into the new Furruckabad Rupee, to either of the Mints above specified, shall have it so coined, agreeably to the rates of charge and produce stated in the accompanying Table.
Rates of charge on recoinage of Rupees.	VII. Individuals bringing to the same Mints, Calcutta, Benares or Furruckabad Rupees, either of the old or new coinage, but coined at one of the Honorable Company's Mints, shall have them converted into the new Furruckabad Rupee, at a total charge of no more than one per cent.
At what rate Government engage to receive and pay the old and new Furruckabad Rupee, in the province of Benares.	VIII. Government will receive Furruckabad Rupees of the old or new standard, at par with the present Benares Rupee, in payment of the land revenue, and in liquidation of all other public demands, and will pay them at the same valuation with in the province of Benares.
The preceding rule declared Inapplicable in certain cases.	IX. The preceding rule shall not apply to bills payable in Benares Rupees, and drawn previously to the 1st March 1820, nor to sums due to individuals under specific engagements in Benares Rupees, contracted previously to that date.
All money engagements in Benares entered into after the 1st March, 1820, to be expressed and	X. Bonds or other engagements, and all agreements, written or verbal, which may be entered into within the province of Benares after the 1st March 1820, shall be expressed in Furruckabad Rupees, and if any such deed or agreement shall stipulate for the payment of Benares Rupees, such stipulation shall not be enforced by the

courts of judicature; but the amount shall Rates of charge for coining Bullion.	paid in Furruckabad Rupees.
XI. With regard to engagements entered into previously to the 1st of March next, the Furruckabad Rupee shall be held a legal tender, at the rate of 102¼ Furruckabad Rupees for 100 Benares Rupees.	Rate at which payments are to be made when engagements are dated prior to the 1st March, 1830.
XII. All the rules affecting the coinage of the Mints of Benares and Furruckabad, which are not abrogated by the foregoing enactments, shall continue in force.	Former rules, if not, rescinded by this Regulation, to remain in force.

TABLE OF THE PRODUCE OF SILVER BULLION IN THE FURRUCKABAD MINT, COMMENCING THE 2ND OCTOBER 1819

New Standard	Decimal Addition, or Deduction per cent	Charges for Refining	Total Deduction	Produce in Sa. Wt.	Produce in Furruckabad Rupees	Duty of 2 per cent on coinage	Nett Produce Furruckabad Rupees
Dwts.							
20 Br.	9.091	"	"	109.091	104.712	2.094	102.618
19½ Br.	8.864	"	"	108.864	104.495	2.090	102.405
19 Br.	8.636	"	"	108.636	104.276	2.086	102.190
18½ Br.	8.409	"	"	108.409	104.058	2.081	101.977
18 Br.	8.182	"	"	108.182	103.840	2.077	101.763
17½ Br.	7.955	"	"	107.955	103.622	2.072	101.550
17 Br.	7.727	"	"	107.727	103.403	2.068	101.335
16½ Br.	7.500	"	"	107.500	103.185	2.064	101.121
16 Br.	7.273	"	"	107.273	102.967	2.059	100.908
15½ Br.	7.045	"	"	107.045	102.749	2.055	100.694
15 Br.	6.818	"	"	106.818	102.531	2.051	100.480
14½ Br.	6.591	"	"	106.591	102.313	2.046	100.267
14 Br.	6.364	"	"	106.364	102.095	2.042	100.053
13½ Br.	6.136	"	"	106.136	101.876	2.038	99.838
13 Br.	5.909	"	"	105.909	101.658	2.033	99.625
12½ Br.	5.682	"	"	105.682	101.440	2.029	99.411
12 Br.	5.455	"	"	105.455	101.222	2.024	99.198
11½ Br.	5.227	"	"	105.227	101.004	2.020	98.984
11 Br.	5.000	"	"	105.000	100.786	2.016	98.770

New Standard	Decimal Addition, or Deduction per cent	Charges for Refining	Total Deduction	Produce in Sa. Wt.	Produce in Furruckabad Rupees	Duty of 2 per cent on coinage	Nett Produce Furruckabad Rupees
Dwts.							
10½ Br.	4.773	,,	,,	101.773	100.568	2.011	98.557
10 Br.	4.545	,,	,,	104.545	100.349	2.007	98.342
9½ Br.	4.318	,,	,,	104.318	100.131	2.003	98.128
9 Br.	4.091	,,	,,	104.091	99.913	1.998	97.915
8½ Br.	3.864	,,	,,	103.864	99.695	1.994	97.701
8 Br.	3.636	,,	,,	103.636	99.476	1.990	97.486
7½ Br.	3.409	,,	,,	103.409	99.259	1.985	97.274
7 Br.	3.182	,,	,,	103.182	99.011	1.981	97.060
6½ Br.	2.955	,,	,,	102.955	98.823	1.976	96.847
6 Br.	2.727	,,	,,	102.727	98.604	1.972	96.632
5½ Br.	2.500	,,	,,	102.500	98.386	1.968	96.418
5 Br.	2.273	,,	,,	102.273	98.168	1.963	96.205
4½ Br.	2.045	,,	,,	102.045	97.949	1.959	95.990
4 Br.	1.818	,,	,,	101.818	97.731	1.955	95.776
3½ Br.	1.591	,,	,,	101.591	97.513	1.950	95.563
3 Br.	1.364	,,	,,	101.364	97.296	1.946	95.350
2½ Br.	1.136	,,	,,	101.136	97.077	1.942	95.135
2 Br. } Eng. Std.	0.909	,,	,,	100.909	96.859	1.937	94.922
1½ Br.	0.682	,,	,,	100.682	96.641	1.933	94.708
1 Br.	0.455	,,	,,	100.455	96.423	1.928	94.495
½ Br.	0.227	,,	,,	100.227	96.204	1.924	94.280
Standard	0.000	,,	,,	100.000	95.986	1.920	94.066
½ W.	0.227	,,	.227	99.773	95.768	1.915	93.853
1 W.	0.455	,,	.455	99.545	95.550	1.911	93.639
1½ W.	0.682	,,	.682	99.318	95.332	1.907	93.425
2 W.	0.909	,,	.909	99.091	95.114	1.902	93.212
2½ W.	1.136	,,	1.136	93.864	94.896	1.898	92.998
3 W.	1.364	,,	1.364	98.636	91.677	1:894	92.783
3½ W.	1.591	,,	1.591	98.409	94.459	1.889	92.570
4 W.	1.818	,,	1.818	98.182	94.241	1.885	92.356
4½ W.	2.045	,,	2.045	97.955	94.023	1.880	92.143
5 W.	2.273	,,	2.273	97.727	93.805	1.876	91.929
5½ W.	2.500	,,	2.500	97.500	93.587	1.872	91.715
6 W.	2.727	,,	2.727	97.273	93.369	1.867	91.502
6½ W.	2.955	.297	3.252	96.748	92.865	1.857	91.008
7 W.	3.182	.445	3.627	96.373	92.505	1.850	90.655
7½ W.	3.409	.592	4.001	95.999	92.146	1.843	90.303

New Standard	Decimal Addition, or Deduction per cent	Charges for Refining	Total Deduction	Produce in Sa. Wt.	Produce in Furruckabad Rupees	Duty of 2 per cent on coinage	Nett Produce Furruckabad Rupees
Dwts.							
8 W.	3.636	.744	4.380	95.620	91.782	1.836	89.946
$8\frac{1}{2}$ W.	3.864	.901	4.765	95.235	91.413	1.828	89.585
9 W.	4.091	1.058	5.149	94.851	91.044	1.821	89.223
$9\frac{1}{2}$ W.	4.318	1.064	5.382	94.618	90.820	1.816	89.004
10 W.	4.545	1.072	5.617	94.383	90.595	1.812	88.783
$10\frac{1}{2}$ W.	4.773	1.078	5.851	94.149	90.370	1.807	88.563
11 W.	5.000	1.088	6.088	93.912	90.143	1.803	88.340
$11\frac{1}{2}$ W.	5.227	1.100	6.327	93.673	89.913	1.798	88.115
12 W.	5.455	1.112	6.567	93.433	89.683	1.794	87.889
$12\frac{1}{2}$ W.	5.682	1.125	6.807	93.193	89.453	1.789	87.664
13 W.	5.909	1.138	7.047	92.953	89.222	1.784	87.438
$13\frac{1}{2}$ W.	6.136	1.150	7.286	92.714	88.993	1.780	87.213
14 W.	6.364	1.161	7.525	92.475	88.763	1.775	86.988
$14\frac{1}{2}$ W.	6.591	1.173	7.764	92.236	88.534	1.771	86.763
15 W.	6.818	1.186	8.004	91.996	88.304	1.766	86.538
$15\frac{1}{2}$ W.	7.045	1.196	8.241	91.759	88.076	1.762	86.314
16 W.	7.273	1.208	8.481	91.519	87.846	1.757	86.089
$16\frac{1}{2}$ W.	7.500	1.220	8.720	91.280	87.616	1.752	85.864
17 W.	7.727	1.233	8.960	91.040	87.386	1.748	85.638
$17\frac{1}{2}$ W.	7.955	1.250	9.205	90.795	87.151	1.743	85.408
18 W.	8.182	1.268	9.450	90.550	86.916	1.738	85.178
$18\frac{1}{2}$ W.	8.409	1.287	9.696	90.304	86.679	1.734	84.945
19 W.	8.636	1.305	9.941	90.059	86.444	1.729	84.715
$19\frac{1}{2}$ W.	8.864	1.321	10.185	89.815	86.210	1.724	84.486
20 W.	9.091	1.339	10.430	89.570	85.975	1.720	84.255
$20\frac{1}{2}$ W.	9.318	1.357	10.675	89.325	85.740	1.715	84.025
21 W.	9.545	1.373	10.918	89.082	85.507	1.710	83.797
$21\frac{1}{2}$ W.	9.773	1.404	11.177	88.823	85.258	1.705	83.553
22 W.	10.000	1.434	11.434	88.566	85.011	1.700	83.311
$22\frac{1}{2}$ W.	10.227	1.466	11.693	88.307	84.763	1.695	83.068
23 W.	10.455	1.496	11.951	88.049	84.515	1.690	82.825
$23\frac{1}{2}$ W.	10.682	1.526	12.208	87.792	84.268	1.685	82.583
24 W.	10.909	1.555	12.464	87.536	84.023	1.680	82.343
$24\frac{1}{2}$ W.	11.136	1.585	12.721	87.279	83.776	1.676	82.100
25 W.	11.364	1.615	12.979	87.021	83.528	1.671	81.857
$25\frac{1}{2}$ W.	11.591	1.649	13.240	86.760	83.278	1.666	81.612
26 W.	11.818	1.683	13.501	86.499	83.027	1.661	81.366
$26\frac{1}{2}$ W.	12.045	1.717	13.762	86.238	82.777	1.656	81.121

New Standard	Decimal Addition, or Deduction per cent	Charges for Refining	Total Deduction	Produce in Sa. Wt.	Produce in Furruckabad Rupees	Duty of 2 per cent on coinage	Nett Produce Furruckabad Rupees
Dwts.							
27 W.	12.273	1.751	14.024	85.976	82.525	1.651	80.874
27½ W.	12.500	1.800	14.300	85.700	82.260	1.645	80.615
28 W.	12.727	1.850	14.577	85.423	81.994	1.640	80.354
28½ W.	12.955	1.900	14.855	85.145	81.728	1.635	80.093
29 W.	13.182	1.950	15.132	84.868	81.462	1.629	79.833
29½ W.	13.409	2.010	15.419	84.581	81.186	1.624	79.562
30 W.	13.636	2.068	15.704	84.296	80.913	1.618	79.295
30½ W.	13.864	2.128	15.992	84.008	80.636	1.613	79.023
31 W.	14.091	2.183	16.274	83.726	80.366	1.607	78.759
31½ W.	14.318	2.240	16.558	83.442	80.093	1.602	78.491
32 W.	14.545	2.296	16.841	83.159	79.821	1.596	78.225
32½ W.	14.773	2.349	17.122	82.878	79.552	1.591	77.961
33 W.	15.000	2.398	17.398	82.602	79.287	1.586	77.701
33½ W.	15.227	2.444	17.671	82.329	79.025	1.581	77.444
34 W.	15.455	2.485	17.940	82.060	78.766	1.575	77.191
34½ W.	15.682	2.511	18.193	81.807	78.524	1.570	76.954
35 W.	15.909	2.536	18.445	81.555	78.282	1.566	76.716
35½ W.	16.136	2.560	18.696	81.304	78.041	1.561	76.480
36 W.	16.364	2.583	18.947	81.053	77.800	1.556	76.244
36½ W.	16.591	2.605	19.196	80.804	77.561	1.551	76.010
37 W.	16.818	2.626	19.444	80.556	77.323	1.546	75.777
37½ W.	17.046	2.646	19.692	80.308	77.085	1.542	75.543
38 W.	17.273	2.665	19.938	80.062	76.849	1.537	75.312
38½ W.	17.500	2.683	20.183	79.817	76.613	1.532	75.081
39 W.	17.727	2.700	20.427	79.573	76.379	1.528	74.851
39½ W.	17.955	2.716	20.671	79.329	76.145	1.523	74.622
40 W.	18.182	2.731	20.913	79.087	75.913	1.518	74.395

Appendix A.33

A.D. 1820 REGULATION VI

A REGULATION for modifying a Part of a Provision contained in Regulation X, 1809, respecting the copper coinage of the Province of Benares.—PASSED by the Vice President-in-Council on the 25th August, 1820; corresponding with the 11th Bhadoon 1227 Bengal era; the 2nd Bhadoon 1227 Fussily; the 12th Bhadoon 1227 Willaity; the 2nd. Bhadoon 1877 Sumbut and; the 15th Zekaad 1229 Higeree.

WHEREAS it being deemed no longer expedient to continue to individuals the privilege of tendering copper for coinage at the mint at Furruckabad, the following rules have been enacted to be immediately in force from the date of its promulgation.	Preamble
II. Sections 46, 47, and 48, Regulation XLV, 1803, are hereby rescinded.	Sections 46, 47, and 48 Regulation XLV, 1803 rescinded.

N.B.: Superseded with Regulation XLV, 1803, by Regulation II, 1824.

Appendix A.34

A.D. 1821 REGULATION V

A REGULATION for settling the rates at which Benares and Furruckabad Rupees shall be received in payment of the Revenue of Malgoozars, whose engagements are expressed in Gohurshahee or Tirsoolee Rupees.—PASSED by the Governor General in Council on the 23rd November 1821; corresponding with the 9th Aughun 1228 Bengal Era; the 14th Aughun 1229 Fussily; the 10th Augun 1229 Willaity; the 14th Aughun 1878 Sumbut, and the 27th Suffer 1237 Higeree.

Preamble	IT is enacted by Regulation XI 1819 that the Furruckabad rupees shall be received within the province of Benares at par with the Benares rupees: but no provision has been made for, regulating the exchange in account between the said rupees and the Gohurshahee, and Tirsoolee rupees, in which it appears that the engagements of many malgoozars are expressed: moreover the batta to be taken from such malgoozars has hitherto been arbitrarily fixed, and considerable abuses have consequently prevailed. The intrinsic value of the coins having been now ascertained by a careful assay, whence it has appeared that the rupee denominated Chorah Gohurshahee exceeds, and the other descriptions of Gohurshahee rupees equal the Furruckabad rupee in value, and that the latter coin is 3:11:7 per cent superior in value to the Tirsoolee rupee, the revenue officers have been directed to adjust their demands on the said malgoozars according to the results of the assay, subject to the general principle of receiving the Furruckabad rupee at par with the Benares rupee, and without any demand of batta on account of its inferiority in value below the local currency. In pursuance of the orders already issued in this matter, and for the purpose of making generally known the results of the assays, and of removing all doubts as to the rate at which rupees denominated Gohurshahee and Tirsoolee are to be valued, the following rules have been enacted, to be in force from the date of their promulgation.

II. The Benares and Furruckabad rupees, which are now received as of equal value in all payments of the Government revenue shall be paid and received in lieu of the Gohurshahee rupees, and at par with the same in liquidation of all demands on any malgoozar or other person who may have entered into engagements with Government, expressed in any description of Gohurshahee rupee. The Gohurshahee rupee shall be held and considered as of equal value with the Furruckabad and Benares rupees in the adjustment of all claims or demands, on account of revenue arising out of such engagements as aforesaid, which may be suspended or unsettled, and no malgoozar or other person aforesaid shall be entitled to any deduction or allowance by way of batta, or the like on account of payments made or tendered by him in Benares or Furruckabad rupees, in fulfilment (*sic*) of engagements expressed in Gohurshahee rupees: provided always that in cases in which such deduction or allowance may have been made, and receipts granted or credit given accordingly, nothing in this Regulation shall be understood to authorize the officers of Government or individuals to make any demand on account of such deduction or allowance; nor shall any such demand be held valid.	In what cases the Benares, Furruckabad and Gohurshaee rupees to be considered of equal value, and to be received and paid without any allowance or deduction on account of batta. Proviso.
III. All malgoozars or other persons whose engagements are expressed in Tirsoolee rupees, shall be allowed a batta of rupees 3: 11: 7 per cent on payments made in Furruckabad or Benares rupees: that is to say, on the payment of rupees 96: 4: 5 of the Furruckabad or Benares currency, the said persons shall have credit for 100 Tirsoolee rupees, in liquidation of demands under engagements expressed in that description of rupee: provided always that all suspended or unsettled demands or accounts shall be adjusted on the same principle, but no fresh demands shall be admitted on account of any deduction or allowance made in the settlement of accounts already adjusted.	Persons whose engagements are made in Tirsoolee rupees to be allowed a certain batta or percentage on payments in Furruckabad or Benares rupees. Proviso.
IV. All mehals held in farm within the province of Benares, whereof there may be no ancient proprietors forthcoming entitled to re-enter, subject to the payment of the jumma already fixed, being open to re-settlement on the death of the farmers, it is hereby declared and enacted that the collectors within the said province shall	Certain cases in which engagement for lapsed mehals within the province of

Benares are to be made in Furruckabad rupees. And others in which the payment if expressed in Gohurshaee or Tirsooli rupees, is to be converted into Furruckabad rupees.	hereafter adjust the assessment of such estates with reference to the assets estimated in Furruckabad rupees, and that the engagements of the malgoozars of such estates shall be uniformly expressed in that currency. In like manner in cases wherein the ancient zemindars may be entitled to re-enter, subject to the payment of the jumma already fixed, the said jumma, if expressed in Gohurshahee or Tirsoolee rupees, shall be converted into Furruckabad rupees at the rates herein before specified, and the engagements of the proprietors shall be expressed in the last mentioned currency.

Appendix A.35

A.D. 1824 REGULATION II

A REGULATION for abolishing the Furruckabad Mint, and for modifying some of the Rules in force relative to the Furruckabad Rupee.—PASSED by the Right Honorable the Governor General in Council on the 5th February 1824, corresponding with the 24th Maug 1230 Bengal era; the 20th Maug 1231 Fussily; the 25th Maug 1231 Willaity; the 5th Maug 1880 Sumbat; and the 4th Juma-dee-us-Sanee 1239 Higeree.

WHEREAS provision has been made by Regulation XXVI 1817 for the coinage of the Furruckabad Rupee, at any of the Mints established by Government: and it appears to be no longer necessary to continue the Mint at Furruckabad for the coinage of the said Rupee;—And Whereas it is expedient to modify the existing Rules relative to the currency of Furruckabad Rupees, in conformity with the principle already applicable to the Calcutta Sicca Rupee, under the provisions of Section I Regulation XIV 1818, the following Rules here been enacted to be in force from the date of their promulgation.	Preamble
II. The Mint established at Furruckabad under Regulation XLV 1803, shall be abolished; and all Rules which require or can be construed to require, that any Money or Bullion shall be sent to or received for coinage at the said Mint, are hereby, rescinded: Provided, however, that all persons, who, previously to the promulgation of this Regulation, may have brought coin or bullion to the said Mint for coinage, shall be entitled to receive the produce thereof under the Rules of Regulation II 1812, or an equivalent sum.	The Mint at Furruckabad abolished. Proviso in regard to coin or bullion brought to the mint for coinage previously to the promulgation of this Regulation.
III. In modification of the Rules contained in Sections XXXIII and XXXV Regulation XLV 1803, it is hereby enacted that all Furruckabad Rupees, and Half and Quarter Rupees, shall be receivable in all public and	Furruckabad Rupees, and Half and Quarter Rupees,

shall be receivable in all public and private transactions, if not below certain weight.	private transactions, if, when separately weighed, the deficiency in point of weight be not more than two pies, or grains Troy 1.875 per Rupee.

Appendix A.36

A.D. 1825 REGULATION XV

A REGULATION to make certain alterations in the Rates of Duty charged, and Drawbacks allowed on Goods imported or exported by Sea at the Port of Calcutta, or any other Place within the Territories immediately subordinate to the Presidency of Fort William; and to amend and consolidate the Rules in force relative to such Duties and Drawbacks.—PASSED by the Governor General in Council on the 14th July 1825, corresponding with the 32nd Assaur 1232 Bengal era; the 14th Sawun 1232 Fussily; the 1st Sawun 1232 Willaity; the 13th Sawun 1882 Sumbut; and the 26th Zekaada 1240 Higeree.

WHEREAS in pursuance of a Treaty recently concluded between the British Government and the Government of the Netherlands, it has become necessary to alter the Rates of Duty chargeable on Goods imported and exported on Foreign Bottoms: and whereas it has also appeared to be expedient to reduce, in certain cases, the Duties now levied or retained on Goods imported and exported on British Bottoms; and whereas it will essentially promote the public convenience, to consolidate and simplify the existing Rules (modified as aforesaid) relative to the Duties and Drawbacks to be charged or allowed, on Imports and Exports by Sea, the following Rules have been enacted to be in force from the date of their promulgation.	Preamble
II. *First.* Such parts of the Rules contained in Regulation IX 1810, Regulation III 1811, Regulation XII 1818, Regulation IV 1814, Regulations XV, XVI and XXI 1817, Regulation V 1820, and Regulation V 1823, as have reference to the Rate of Duty to be levied, or the Drawback to be allowed, on Goods imported or exported by Sea at Calcutta, or any other Port or Place within the Territories immediately subordinate to the Presidency of Fort William, are hereby rescinded.	Rescission of existing provisions.

Ditto.	*Second.* Regulation X 1816, is also hereby rescinded.
Certain provisions to continue rescinded or modified.	*Third.* The several Provisions which were rescinded or modified by the Rules above-mentioned shall continue to be respectively rescinded or modified, as before the enactment of this Regulation.
Imports by Sea to be charged with duties, specifed in Schedule No. I, annexed to this Regulation. Proviso	III *First.* Goods imported by Sea into Calcutta or any other Port or Place belonging to the Presidency of Fort William, on British or on Foreign Bottoms) shall be severally Subject to the Duties specified in the Schedule No. 1, annexed to this Regulation, with the exceptions therein stated. Provided, however, that the Rules contained in Section V, Regulation XXI, 1817, shall still be applicable to Goods, which may be originally imported by Sea on a British Bottom, at any Port in the Territories subject to the British Government in India; and shall afterwards be re-exported to Calcutta, or any Port immediately dependent on this Presidency.
Re-exports to be allowed a drawback as specified in Schedule No. II.	*Second.* Goods imported by Sea as aforesaid, and charged with an Import Duty under the above Rule, shall, on re-exportation, be allowed a Drawback at the several Rates, specified in the Schedule No. II, annexed to this Regulation: and no Drawback of Import Duty shall be granted, excepting as therein specifically allowed.
Duties chargeable & drawbacks allowed on articles, the produce and manufacture of the country, when exported by Sea, to be regulated by Schedule No. III.	*Third.* Articles, the produce or manufacture of Calcutta, or of the Interior of the Country, shall, on Exportation by Sea, be respectively passed Free, or subjected to Duty, or allowed a Drawback, according to the directions contained in the Schedule No. III, annexed to this Regulation; and the said Schedule, together with those mentioned in the two preceding Clauses, shall be, and be considered, a part of this Regulation.

SCHEDULE NO. I.
RATES OF DUTY CHARGEABLE ON GOODS IMPORTED BY SEA INTO CALCUTTA, OR ANY PORT OF PLACE BELONGING TO THE PRESIDENCY OF FORT WILLIAM.

Enumeration of Goods	Imported on a British Bottom	Imported on a Foreign Bottom
1st. Goods, the Produce or Manufacture of the United Kingdom.		
1. Bullion and Coin	Free.	Free.
2. Horses,	Free.	Free.
3. Marine Stores,	Free.	$2\frac{1}{2}$ per cent.
4. Metals, wrought and unwrought,	Free.	$2\frac{1}{2}$ per cent.
5. Opium,	24 Rs. a seer of 80 Sa. Wt.	48 Rs. a seer of 80 Sa. Wt.
6. Precious Stones and Pearls,	Free.	Free.
7. Salt,	3 Rs. a maund of 82 Sa. Wt. per seer.	6 Rs. a maund of 82 Sa. Wt. per seer.
8. Spirituous Liquors,	10 per cent	20 per cent.
9. Tobacco,	4 Annas a maund of 80 Sa. Wt. per seer.	8 Annas a maund of 80 Sa. Wt. per seer.
10. Wines,	10 per cent	20 per cent.
11. Woollens,	Free.	$2\frac{1}{2}$ per cent.
Articles not included in the above Eleven Items	$2\frac{1}{2}$ per cent	5 per cent.
2nd. Goods, the Produce of Foreign Europe, or of the United States of America.		
1. Arrack at a fixed valuation of £30 per Cask of 126 Gallons	10 per cent.	20 per cent.
2. Bullion and Coin,	Free.	Free.
3. Horses,	Free.	Free.
4. Opium,	24 Rs. a seer of 80 Sa. Wt.	48 Rs. a seer of 80 Sa. Wt.
5. Precious Stones and Pearls,	Free.	Free.
6. Salt,	3 Rs. a maund of 82 Sa. Wt. per seer.	6 Rs. a maund of 82 Sa. Wt. per seer.
7. Spirits,	10 per cent.	20 per cent.
8. Tabacco,	4 Annas a maund of 80 Sa. Wt. a seer.	8 Annas a maund of 80 Sa. Wt. per seer.
9. Wines,	10 per cent.	20 per cent.
Articles not included in the above Nine Items	5 per cent	10 per cent.

Enumeration of Goods	Imported on a British Bottom	Imported on a Foreign Bottom
3rd. Goods, the Produce or Manufacture of Places, other than the United Kingdom, Foregin Europe, or the United States of America.		
1. All Spice,	10 per cent	20 per cent.
2. Aloe Wood,	7½ ditto	15 ditto.
3. Altah,	7½ ditto	15 ditto.
4. Alum,	10 ditto	20 ditto.
5. Ambergris,	7½ ditto	15 ditto.
6. Arrack, Batavia,	55 Sa. Rs. per Leagur.	110 Sa. Rs. per Leagur.
7. Arrack, from Foreign Territories in Asia,	30 Sa. Rs. per Leagur.	60 Sa. Rs. per Leagur.
8. Arsenic, White, Red, or Yellow	10 per cent.	20 per cent.
9. Assafoetida,	10 ditto.	20 ditto.
10. Awl Root, or Morinda	7½ ditto	15 ditto.
11. Beads, Malas or Rozaries,	7½ ditto	15 ditto.
12. Beetle Nut, (Customs)	7½ ditto	15 ditto.
Ditto, (Town Duty)	5 ditto.	10 ditto.
13. Benjamin, or Loban,	7½ ditto	15 ditto.
14. Brandy, from Foregin Territories in Asia,	30 ditto	60 ditto.
15. Brass, wrought and unwrought,	10 per cent.	20 per cent
16. Brimstone	10 ditto.	20 ditto.
17. Brocades and Embroidered Goods,	7½ ditto.	15 ditto.
18. Baltera, or Myrobolan,	10 ditto.	20 ditto.
19. Buckum, or Sappan Wood,	7½ ditto.	15 ditto.
20. Bullion and Coin,	Free.	Free.
21. Calizeerah, or Nigellah	7½ ditto.	15 per cent.
22. Camphire,	10 ditto.	20 ditto.
23. Canvas,—Excepting Canvas made of Sunn or Henap or other Material the Growth or Manufacture of places subject to the Government of the East India Company, which is exempted from charge of Duty on Importation by sea,	5 ditto.	10 ditto.
24. Cardamoms,	7½ ditto.	15 ditto.
25. Carriages and Conveyances,	7½ ditto.	15 ditto.
26. Cassia,	10 ditto.	20 ditto.
27. Chanks,	7½ ditto.	15 ditto.
28. Cherayta,	10 ditto.	20 ditto.
29. China Goods, or Goods from China, not otherwise enumerated in this Table,	7½ ditto.	15 ditto.

Enumeration of Goods	Imported on a British Bottom	Imported on a Foreign Bottom
30. Cloves,	10 ditto.	20 ditto.
31. Cochineal, or Crimdanah,	$7\frac{1}{2}$ ditto.	15 ditto.
32. Coffee,	$7\frac{1}{2}$ ditto.	15 ditto.
33. Coir, the Produce of Places not subject to the Government of the East India Company in India,	5 ditto.	10 ditto.
34. Coin and Bullion,	Free.	Free.
35. Columbo Root,	10 per cent.	20 per cent.
36. Coosum Fool, or unwrought	$7\frac{1}{2}$ ditto.	15 ditto.
37. Copal or Kahroba,	10 ditto.	20 ditto.
38. Copper, wrought and unwrought	10 ditto.	20 ditto.
39. Coral,	10 ditto.	20 ditto.
40. Cordage,—Excepting Cordage made of sunn, Hemp or other Material, the produce of Places subject to the Government of the East India Company which shall be exempt from the charge of Duty on Importation by Sea.	5 ditto.	10 ditto.
41. Crimdanah, or Cochineal,	$7\frac{1}{2}$ ditto.	15 ditto.
42. Dhye Flower,	$7\frac{1}{2}$ ditto.	15 ditto.
43. Elephant's Teeth,	$7\frac{1}{2}$ ditto.	15 ditto.
44. Embroidered Goods and Brocades,	$7\frac{1}{2}$ ditto.	15 ditto.
45. Frankincense, or Gundiberoza,	$7\frac{1}{2}$ ditto.	15 ditto.
46. Galbanum,	10 ditto.	20 ditto.
47. Galingall,	$7\frac{1}{2}$ ditto.	15 ditto.
48. Ghee (Customs)	5 ditto.	10 ditto.
Ditto (Town duty)	10 ditto.	20 ditto.
49. Gin, from Foreign Territories in Asia,	30 ditto.	60 ditto.
50. Goopee Muttee, or Yellow Ochre,	10 ditto.	20 ditto.
51. Goomootoo, Sunn and Hemp,	Free.	Free.
52. Gum Arabic,	10 per cent.	20 per cent.
53. Gundiberoza, or Frankincense,	$7\frac{1}{2}$ ditto.	15 ditto.
54. Hemp, Sunn or Goomootoo,	Free.	Free.
55. Hurrah, or Myrobolan,	10 per cent.	20 per cent.
56. Horses,	Free.	Free.
57. Hursinghar Flower,	$7\frac{1}{2}$ ditto.	15 ditto.
58. Hurtaul, or Orpiment, or Yellow Arsenic,	10 ditto.	20 ditto.
59. Iron, wrought or unwrought,	10 ditto.	20 ditto.
60. Ivory,	$7\frac{1}{2}$ ditto.	15 ditto.
61. Juttamunsee, or Spikenard,	10 ditto.	20 ditto.
62. Kullinjun,	$7\frac{1}{2}$ ditto.	15 ditto.

Enumeration of Goods	Imported on a British Bottom	Imported on a Foreign Bottom
63. Lead, pig, sheet, milled, and small shot,	10 ditto.	20 ditto.
64. Loadh,	$7\frac{1}{2}$ ditto.	15 ditto.
65. Loban, or Benjamin,	$7\frac{1}{2}$ ditto.	15 ditto.
66. Mace,	10 per cent.	20 per cent.
67. Madder, or Munjeet,	$7\frac{1}{2}$ ditto.	15 ditto.
68. Mahogany, and all other sorts of wood used in Cabinet-work,	$7\frac{1}{2}$ ditto.	15 ditto.
69. Mastick,	10 ditto.	20 ditto.
70. Minium, or Red Lead,	10 ditto.	20 ditto.
71. Morinda, or Awl Root,	$7\frac{1}{2}$ ditto.	15 ditto.
72. Munjeet, or Madder,	$7\frac{1}{2}$ ditto.	15 ditto.
73. Musk,	$7\frac{1}{2}$ ditto.	15 ditto.
74. Myrobolans, viz. Buhera, Hurra and Ownla,	10 ditto.	20 ditto.
75. Myrrh,	10 ditto.	20 ditto.
76. Nutmegs,	10 ditto.	20 ditto.
77. Oils, Vegetable or Animal (Customs),	$7\frac{1}{2}$ ditto.	15 ditto.
Ditto, (Town duty)	5 ditto.	10 ditto.
78. Oil Seeds (Customs),	$7\frac{1}{2}$ ditto.	15 ditto.
Ditto (Town duty),	5 ditto.	10 ditto.
79. Oils, perfumed or essential or Otter and Fooleyl Teyll,	$7\frac{1}{2}$ ditto.	15 ditto.
80. Opium, Foreign,	24 Rs. per seer of 80 Ca. Sa. Wt.	48 Rs. per seer of 80 Ca. Sa. Wt.
81. Orpiment, or Yellow Arsenic or Hurtaul,	10 per cent.	20 per cent.
82. Otter, or Essential Oils,	$7\frac{1}{2}$ ditto.	15 ditto.
83. Ownla, or Myrobolan,	10 ditto.	20 ditto.
84. Pepper, Black and White,	10 ditto.	20 ditto.
85. Piece Goods—Cotton, Silk, and partly Cotton and partly Silk, the Manufacture of the Hon'ble Company's Territories in India	$2\frac{1}{2}$ ditto.	5 ditto.
86. Ditto ditto ditto, when not the Manufacture of the Hon'ble Company's Territories in India,	$7\frac{1}{2}$ ditto.	15 ditto.
87. Pimento, or All Spice,	10 ditto.	20 ditto.
88. Pipe Staves,	$7\frac{1}{2}$ ditto.	15 ditto.
89. Precious Stones and Pearls,	Free.	Free.
90. Prussian Blue,	10 per cent.	20 per cent.
91. Putcha Paut,	$7\frac{1}{2}$ ditto.	15 ditto.
92. Quick Silver,	10 ditto.	20 ditto.

Enumeration of Goods	Imported on a British Bottom	Imported on a Foreign Bottom
93. Rattans,	7½ ditto.	15 ditto.
94. Red Sandal Wood,	7½ ditto.	15 ditto.
95. Red Lead, or Minium,	10 ditto.	20 ditto.
96. Rose Water,	7½ ditto.	15 ditto.
97. Rum, from Foreign Territories in Asia,	30 ditto.	60 ditto.
98. Saffron,	10 ditto.	20 ditto.
99. Safflower, or Coossoom Fool,	7½ ditto.	15 ditto.
100. Sago,	7½ ditto.	15 ditto.
101. Salt, Foreign,	3 Rs. per maund of 82 Sa. Wt. per seer.	6 Rs. per maund of 82 Sa. Wt. per seer.
102. Sandal Wood, Red, White or Yellow,	7½ per cent.	15 per cent.
103. Sappan, or Buckum Wood,	7½ ditto.	15 ditto.
104. Senna,	10 ditto.	20 ditto.
105. Soonamookey Leaf,	10 ditto.	20 ditto.
106. Spikenard, or Juttamunsee,	10 ditto.	20 ditto.
107. Spirituous Liquors, not otherwise described in this Table,	10 ditto.	20 ditto.
108. Steel, wrought and unwrought,	10 ditto.	20 ditto.
109. Storax,	10 ditto.	20 ditto.
110. Stones (precious) and Pearls,	Free.	Free.
111. Sugar, wet or dry, including Joggry and Molasses (Customs),	5 per cent.	10 per cent.
Ditto ditto (Town duty),	5 ditto.	10 ditto.
112. Sulphur, or Brimestone,	10 ditto.	20 ditto.
113. Sunn, Hemp and Goomootoo,	Free.	Free.
114. Tape,	7½ per cent.	15 per cent.
115. Taizepaut, or Malabathrum Leaf,	10 per cent.	20 per cent.
116. Tea,	10 ditto.	20 ditto.
117. Teak Timber,	Free.	Free.
118. Thread,	7½ per cent.	15 per cent.
119. Tin and Tin Ware,	10 ditto.	20 ditto.
120. Tobacco (Customs),	4 Annas per maund of 80 Sa. Wt. per seer	8 Annas per maund of 80 Sa. Wt. per seer.
Ditto (Town duty,)	10 per cent.	20 per cent.
121. Toond Flower,	7½ ditto.	15 ditto.
122. Tugger Wood,	7½ ditto.	15 ditto.
123. Turmeric (Customs),	5 ditto.	10 ditto.
Ditto (Town duty),	5 ditto.	10 ditto.
124. Tutenague,	10 ditto.	20 ditto.
125. Ugger, or Aloe Wood,	7½ ditto.	15 ditto.

Enumeration of Goods	Imported on a British Bottom	Imported on a Foreign Bottom
126. Vermilion,	10 ditto.	20 ditto.
127. Verdigrease,	10 ditto.	20 ditto.
128. Wax and Wax Candles,	10 ditto.	20 ditto.
129. Wines and Spirits, not otherwise provided for,	10 ditto.	20 ditto.
130. Wood, of all sorts used in Cabinet-work,	$7\frac{1}{2}$ ditto.	15 ditto.
131. Yellow Ochre, or Goopee Mattee,	10 ditto.	20 ditto.
132. Articles not enumberated above	5 ditto.	10 ditto.

Appendix A.37

A.D. 1826 REGULATION VII

A REGULATION for transferring the Control of the Benares Mint, from the Board of Revenue in the Central Provinces, to a Local Committee.—PASSED by the Governor General in Council on the 13th July, 1820, corresponding with the 30th Assar 1233 Bengal Era; the 24th Assar 1233 Fussily, the 31st Assar 1233 Willaity; the 9th Sawun 1883 Sumbat, and the 6th Zehijja 1241 Higeree.

WHEREAS it will conduce to the public convenience, to vest the Superintendence of the Benares Mint in a Local Committee, according to the principle already acted upon in regard to the Calcutta Mint, the following rules have been enacted to be in force, from the date of their promulgation.	Preamble
II. Sections XV and XVII, Regulation II, 1812, and so much of any other Regulation in force, as vests the Board of Revenue in the Central Provinces, with the Superintendence of the Benares Mint, are hereby rescinded: The Mint and Assay Masters of the said Mint, and the subordinate Officers, shall be subject to the authority of a Local Committee, consisting of such Officers as the Governor General in Council may, from time to time, appoint, and the said Committee shall be guided by such rules as may be prescribed by Government.	The Benares Mint to be subject to the authority of a Local Committee.

Appendix A.38

A.D. 1831 REGULATION III

A REGULATION for legalizing the circulation of Copper Half Ana and Single Pie Pieces.—PASSED by the Vice President in Council on the 18th October 1831, corresponding with the 3rd Cartick 1238 Bengal Era; the 12th Assin 1239 Fussily; the 4th Cartick 1239 Willaity; the 12th Assin 1888 Sumbut and the 11th Jmnadee-ul-uwal 1247 Higeree.

Preamble	WHEREAS great Public convenience is expected from the circulation of Copper Coins of various denominations, in addition to the Copper Currency now in use, it is hereby enacted—
One copper Half Ana Piece and One copper Pie to be coined.	II. That besides the Copper Pice now current, which shall remain unchanged, there shall be coined One Copper Half Ana Piece, and One Copper Pie, or One-twelfth of an Ana.
The copper Half Ana Piece to be of a certain weight, and to bear on each face a distinctive Legend. Its value to be One for Two Pice.	III. The Copper Half Ana Piece shall weigh twice the weight of the present Pice, or 200 Grains Troy; and shall bear on one face the Legend Half Ana in Persian and Nagari, and on the other the same in English and Bengalee. The Exchangeable value of this Coin shall be Two for One Ana, or One for Two Pice.
The copper Pie to be of a certain weight, and to bear on each face a distinctive legend. The value to be Twelve for One Ana or Three for One Pice.	IV. The Twelfth of an Ana Piece, or One Pie, shall weigh Troy Grains 33-333, and shall bear on one face the Legend One Pie in Persian and Nagari, and the same on the other in English and Bengalee. The Exchangeable value of this Coin shall be Twelve for One Ana, or Three for One Pice.
To be current in all the Provinces under the Bengal Presidency.	V. These Coins shall be current at the above rates in the above provinces under the Bengal Presidency.

Appendix A.39

A.D. 1833 REGULATION VII

A REGULATION for altering the weight of the new Furruckabad Rupee and for assimilating it to the legal currency of the Madras and Bombay Presidencies; for adjusting the weight of the Calcutta Sicca Rupee, and for fixing a standard Unit of weight for India.—PASSED by the Governor General in Council on the 13th July 1833, corresponding with the 31st Assar 1240 Bengal Era; the 12th Assar 1240 Fussily; the 32nd Assar 1240 Willaity; the 11th Assar 1890 Sumbut; and the 24th Suffer 1249 Higeree.

BY a Resolution of the Governor General in Council, dated the 10th of September 1824, the Furruckabad Rupee was ordered to be coined of 180 Grains, 165 fine and 15 alloy, and was declared the legal currency of the Saugor and Nerbuddah Territories. It is considered expedient to adopt this Weight and Standard for the Furruckabad Rupee at the Calcutta as well as at the Saugor Mint, instead of that described in Section V Regulation XI, 1819, from which it differs very slightly, and to make the Furruckabad Currency correspond in weight and intrinsic value with the new Currency of the Madras and Bombay Presidencies. It is likewise convenient to make a trifling alteration in the weight of the Calcutta Sicca Rupee, as prescribed by Clause 1, Section I Regulation XIV 1818. It is further convenient to introduce the weight of the Furruckabad Rupee as the Unit of a general system of Weights for Government transactions throughout India under the Native and well known denomination of the Tola. The following Rules have accordingly been enacted by the Governor General in Council to be in force from the date of their promulgation:	Preamble
II. So much of Clause 2, Section I, Regulation XIV, 1818, as fixes the Weight and Standard of the Nineteenth Sun Sicca Rupee, and of Regulation XI 1819, as fixes the Weight and Standard of the Furruckabad Rupee, is hereby rescinded.	Parts of former Regulations rescinded.

The Weight and Standard of the Calcutta Sicca Rupee and of the Furruckabad Rupee, and of their respective subdivisions, declared.

III. The Weight and Standard of the Calcutta Sicca Rupee and its subdivisions, and of the Furruckabad Rupee, shall be as follows:

	Weight. Grains.	Fine. Grains.	Alloy. Grains.
Calcutta Sicca Rupee, ...	192	176	16
Ditto Half, ...	96	88	8
Ditto Quarter, ...	48	44	4
Furruckabad Rupee, ...	180	165	15

and its fractions, in proportion, being 11-12ths pure and 1-12th alloy.

The use of the present Sicca Weight to be discontinued at the Mints of Government.

IV. The use of the Sicca Weight of 179.666 Grains hitherto employed for the receipt of Bullion at the Mint, being in fact the weight of the Moorshedabad Rupee of the old Standard, which was assumed as the Sicca Currency of the Honorable Company's Provinces of Bengal, Behar and Orissa, shall be discontinued; and in its place the following Unit, to be called the Tola, shall be introduced, which, from its immediate connection with the Rupee of the Upper Provinces, and of Madras and Bombay, will easily and speedily become universal through the British Territories.

The Tola to be established of 180 Grains Troy in lieu of the Unit of Sicca Weight 179.660 Grains.

A scale of Weights according to this principle, described.

The Tola or Sicca Weight to be equal to 180 Grains Troy, and the other denominations of weight to be derived from this Unit, according to the following scale; viz.

8 Ruttees	= 1 Masha	= 15 Troy Grains.
12 Mashas	= 1 Tola	= 180 ditto.
80 Tolas (or Sicca Weight) 1 Seer	= $2\frac{1}{2}$ lbs. Troy.	
40 Seers	= 1 Mun, or Bazar Maund	= 100 lbs. Troy.

The produce of Bullion at the Mints, how to be calculated.

Subject to Seignorage duty—

And to a further charge for

V. The calculation of produce of Bullion at the Mints of Saugor and Calcutta will be made in accordance with the system herein before set forth, subject to the duty or Seignorage of 2 per cent already provided by the Mint Regulations; and in case of Bullion below Dollar Standard, or more than 6 dwts. worse, subject to a further Mint charge to cover the expense of refining it up to Standard purity, it being optional with the

Proprietor of the Bullion to refine it out of the Mint, or to pay the refinage charge according to established rates. A Table of the produce of Silver Bullion, calculated according to the scale of Tola Weight, and the modification of the Sicca and Furruckabad Rupee herein prescribed, is annexed to this Regulation.	refinage when below Standard purity. The Proprietor may at his option refine his Bullion out of the Mint, or pay the prescribed refinage charge. A Table of the produce of Silver Bullion annexed to the Regulation.
VI. The system of Weights described in Section IV, is to be adopted at the Mints and Assay Offices of Calcutta and Saugor respectively, in the adjustment and verification of all Weights for Government or public purposes, sent thither for examination.	Weights for Government or Public purposes to be adjusted and verified according to the new system prescribed in Section IV of this Regulation.

TABLE OF THE INTRINSIC OR ASSAY PRODUCE OF SILVER BULLION IN FURRUCKABAD AND CALCUTTA RUPEES, TO BE USED AT THE MINTS OF CALCUTTA AND SAUGOR, FROM THE PROMULGATION OF THIS REGULATION.

Weight of Bullion in Tolas or New Sicca Weight	Assay Report	Touch, or Fine Silver in 100 parts	Produce in Furruckabad or Sonat Rupees	Produce in Calcutta or Sicca Rupees
100	20 Dwts. Br.	100.000	109.091	102.273
”	19½ ” Br.	99.792	108.864	102.060
”	19 ” Br.	99.583	108.636	101.846
”	18½ ” Br.	99.375	108.409	101.633
”	18 ” Br.	99.167	108.182	101.421
”	17½ ” Br.	98.958	107.955	101.121
”	17 ” Br.	98.750	107.727	100.994
”	16½ ” Br.	98.542	107.500	100.781
”	16 ” Br.	98.333	107.273	100.568
”	15½ ” Br.	98.125	107.045	100.355
”	15 ” Br.	97.917	106.818	100.142
”	14½ ” Br.	97.708	106.591	99.929
”	14 ” Br.	97.500	106.364	99.716

Weight of Bullion in Tolas or New Sicca Weight	Assay Report	Touch, or Fine Silver in 100 parts	Produce in Furruckabad or Sonat Rupees	Produce in Calcutta or Sicca Rupees
100	13½ ” Br.	97.292	106.136	99.502
”	13 ” Br.	97.083	105.909	99.290
”	12½ ” Br.	96.875	105.682	99.077
”	12 ” Br.	96.667	105.455	98.864
”	11½ ” Br.	96.458	105.277	98.697
”	11 ” Br.	96.250	105.000	98.437
”	10½ ” Br.	96.042	104.773	98.225
”	10 ” Br.	95.833	104.545	98.011
”	9½ ” Br	95.625	104.318	97.798
”	9 ” Br.	95.417	104.091	97.585
”	8½ ” Br.	95.208	103.864	97.372
”	8 ” Br.	95.000	103.636	97.159
”	7½ ” Br.	94.792	103.409	96.946
”	7 ” Br.	94.583	103.182	96.733
”	6½ ” Br.	94.375	102.955	96.520
”	6 ” Br.	94.167	102.727	96.306
”	5½ ” Br.	93.958	102.500	96.094
”	5 ” Br.	93.750	102.273	95.881
”	4½ ” Br.	93.542	102.045	95.667
”	4 ” Br.	93.333	191.818	95.454
”	3½ ” Br.	93.125	101.591	95.241
”	3 ” Br.	92.917	101.364	95.029
”	2½ ” Br.	92.708	101.136	94.815
”	2 ” Br.	92.500	100.909	94.602
”	1½ ” Br.	92.292	100.682	94.389
”	1 ” Br.	92.083	100.455	94.176
”	½ ” Br.	91.875	100.227	93.963
”	Standard.	91.667	100.000	93.750
”	½ Dwts. Wo.	91.458	99.773	93.537
”	1 ” Wo.	91.250	99.545	93.323
”	1½ ” Wo.	91.042	99.318	93.111
”	2 ” Wo.	90.833	99.091	92.898
”	2½ ” Wo.	90.625	98.864	92.685
”	3 ” Wo.	90.417	98.636	92.471
”	3½ ” Wo.	90.208	98.409	92.258
”	4 ” Wo.	90.000	98.182	92.046
”	4½ ” Wo.	89.792	97.955	91.833
”	5 ” Wo.	89.583	97.727	91.619
”	5½ ” Wo.	89.375	97.500	91.406
”	6 ” Wo.	89.167	97.273	91.193

Weight of Bullion in Tolas or New Sicca Weight	Assay Report	Touch, or Fine Silver in 100 parts	Produce in Furruckabad or Sonat Rupees	Produce in Calcutta or Sicca Rupees
100	6½ " Wo.	88.958	97.045	90.980
"	7 " Wo.	88.750	96.818	90.767
"	7½ " Wo.	88.542	96.591	90.554
"	8 " Wo.	88.333	96.364	90.341
"	8½ " Wo.	88.125	96.136	90.127
"	9 " Wo.	87.917	95.909	89.915
"	9½ " Wo.	87.708	95.682	89.702
"	10 " Wo.	87.500	95.455	89.489
"	10½ " Wo.	87.292	95.227	89.275
"	11 " Wo.	87.084	95.000	89.062
"	11½ " Wo.	86.875	94.773	88.850
"	12 " Wo.	86.667	91.545	88.636
"	12½ " Wo.	86.458	94.318	88.423
"	13 " Wo.	86.250	91.091	88.210
"	13½ " Wo.	86.042	93.864	87.998
"	14 " Wo.	85.834	93.636	87.784
"	14½ " Wo.	85.625	93.409	87.571
"	15 " Wo.	85.417	93.182	87.358
"	15½ " Wo.	85.208	92.955	87.145
"	16 " Wo.	85.000	92.727	86.932
"	16½ " Wo.	84.792	92.500	86.719
"	17 " Wo.	84.583	92.273	86.506
"	17½ " Wo.	84.375	92.045	86.292
"	18 " Wo.	84.167	91.818	86.079
"	18½ " Wo.	83.958	91.591	85.867
"	19 " Wo.	83.750	91.364	85.654
"	19½ " Wo.	83.542	91.136	85.440
"	20 " Wo.	83.333	90.909	85.227

and so on for Bullion of inferior quality.

All Bullion or Foreign Coin brought to the Mint for Coinage is subject to a Seignorage of Two per Cent; but upon the Re-coinage of Rupees struck at any of the Honorable Company's Mints, a duty of One per cent only is levied.

Upon all Bullion of a quality inferior to Standard, (unless the same be required at the Mint for the purposes of allegation), a charge is made for the expence of refining the said Bullion up to the quality of the Rupee, at the rate of .04 per cent. per dwt. of worseness in the Assay Report. Thus, upon Bullion reported 12½ dwts. worse, the charge for refinage will be

12½ multiplied by .04 = 0.50 or one-half per cent. Upon 20 Wo. it will be 20 × .04 = 0.80 per cent.

And so on for Silver of other qualities, as in the following Table:

TABLE OF REFINING CHARGE ON SILVER BULLION.

Assay	Refining Chage per cent	Assay	Refining Chage per cent	Assay	Refining Chage per cent
0½ Wo.	0.02	6½ Wo.	0.26	12½ Wo.	0.50
1 Wo.	0.04	7 Wo.	0.28	13 Wo.	0.52
1½ Wo.	0.06	7½ Wo.	0.30	13½ Wo.	0.54
2 Wo.	0.08	8 Wo.	0.32	14 Wo.	0.56
2½ Wo.	0.10	8½ Wo.	0.34	14½ Wo.	0.58
3 Wo.	0.12	9 Wo.	0.36	15 Wo.	0.60
3½ Wo.	0.14	9½ Wo.	0.38	15½ Wo.	0.62
4 Wo.	0.16	10 Wo.	0.40	16 Wo.	0.64
4½ Wo.	0.18	10½ Wo.	0.42	16½ Wo.	0.66
5 Wo.	0.20	11 Wo.	0.44	17 Wo.	0.68
5½ Wo.	0.22	11½ Wo.	0.46	17½ Wo.	0.70
6 Wo.	0.24	12 Wo.	0.48	18 Wo.	0.72

* By the practice of the Calcutta mint, the charge for refineage is usually remitted up to 6 Wo; at the Saugor mint, it is levied on all denominations of Bullion inferior to Standard.

Appendix A.40

A.D. 1835 ACT XVII

ACT XVII.—PASSED by the Honourable the Governor-General of India in Council, on the 17th August, 1835.

I. BE it enacted, that from the 1st day of September, 1835, the undermentioned silver coins *only* shall be coined at the mints within the territories of the East India Company: a rupee, to be denominated the Company's rupee; a half-rupee, a quarter-rupee, and a double rupee; and the weight of the said rupee shall be 180 grains troy, and the standard shall be as follows: $\frac{11}{12}$ or 165 grains of pure silver, $\frac{1}{12}$ or 15 grains of alloy; and the other coins shall be of proportionate weight and of the same standard.	Weight standard and denomination of silver coins.
II. And be it enacted, that these coins shall bear on the obverse the head and the name of the *reigning* sovereign of the United Kingdom of Great Britain and Ireland, and on the reverse the designation of the coin in English and Persian, and the words "East-India Company" in English, with such embellishment as shall from time to time be ordered by the Governor-General in Council.	What impression to bear.
III. And be it enacted, that the Company's rupee, half-rupee, and double rupee, shall be a legal tender in satisfaction of all engagements, provided the coin shall not have lost more than two per cent in weight, and provided it shall not have been clipped or filed, or have been defaced otherwise than by use.	What may be a legal tender.
IV. And be it enacted, that the said rupee shall be received as equivalent to the Bombay, Madras, Furruckabad, and Sonat rupees, and to fifteen-sixteenths of the Calcutta sicca rupee; and the half and double rupee respectively shall be received as equivalent to the half and double of	Relative value of the Company's with other rupees.

	the above-mentioned Bombay, Madras, Furruckabad, and Sonat rupees, and to the half and double of fifteen-sixteenths of the Calcutta sicca rupee.
How the quarter-rupee may be legally tendered.	V. And be it enacted, that the Company's quarter-rupee shall be a legal tender only in payment of the fraction of a rupee.
Provisos.	VI. Provided, that if in any contract for the payment of Calcutta sicca rupees it shall have been specially stipulated, that if payment be made in the territories of the Madras, Bombay, or Agra presidency, it shall be made in the rupee now current in those presidencies respectively, at a different rate from that above provided with reference to the Calcutta sicca rupee, the contract shall be satisfied by payment within those presidencies of Company's rupees of the amount of Furruckabad, Madras, or Bombay rupees so especially stipulated. Provided also, that if payment of the principal or interest of the public debt be made for the convenience of creditors at any public treasury other than as stipulated in the notes and engagement of the Government, it shall be competent to the Government to make such payments at the same exchange as heretofore.
Weight and standard of gold coins.	VII. And be it enacted, that the undermentioned gold coins only shall henceforth be coined at the mints within the territories of the East India Company. *First.* A gold mohur or 15-rupee piece of the weight of 180 grains troy, and of the following standard, viz.: $\frac{11}{12}$ or 165 grains of pure gold, $\frac{1}{12}$ or 15 grains of alloy. *Second.* A five-rupee piece equal to a third of a gold mohur. *Third.* A ten-rupee piece equal to two-thirds of a gold mohur. *Fourth.* A thirty-rupee piece or double gold mohur; and the three last-mentioned coins shall be of the same standard with the gold mohur, and of proportionate weight.

VIII. And be it enacted, that these gold coins shall bear on the obverse the head and name of the *reigning* sovereign of the United Kingdom of Great Britain and Ireland, and on the reverse the designation of the coin in English and Persian, and the word, "East-India Company" in English, with such embellishment as shall from time to time be ordered by the Governor-General in Council, which shall be different from that of the silver coinage.	What impression to bear.
IX. And be it enacted that no gold coin shall henceforth be a legal tender of payment in any of the territories of the East India Company.	Gold coin not a legal tender.
X. And be it enacted, that it shall be competent to the Governor-General in Council, in his executive capacity, to direct the coining and issuing of all coins authorized by this Act; to prescribe the devices and inscriptions of the copper coins issued from the mints in the said territories, and to establish, regulate, and abolish mints, any law hitherto in force to the contrary notwithstanding.	Powers of the Governor-General in Council as to coinage and mints. Copper Coinage.

Appendix A.41

A.D. 1835 ACT XXI

ACT XXI.—PASSED by the Honourable the Governor-General of India in Council, on the 7th December, 1835.

Weight of Copper coins in Bengal.	I. BE it enacted, that from the 20th day of December 1835, the following copper coins only shall be issued from any mint within the presidency of Bengal: 1. A pice, weighing ... ... 100 grains troy. 2. A double pice ... ... 200 " 3. A pie, or one-twelfth of an anna-piece ... ... $33\frac{1}{3}$ " with such devices as shall be fixed for the same by the Governor-General in Council, according to the provisions of Section X of Act XVII of 1835.
Value of Copper coins in Bengal.	II. And be it enacted, that from the said 20th day of December, 1835, the said pice shall be legal tender for $\frac{1}{64}$ of the Company's rupee, and the said double pice for $\frac{1}{32}$ of the Company's rupee, and the said pie for $\frac{1}{192}$ of the Company's rupee.
When Copper coins may be legally tendered.	III. Provided always, that after the said 20th day of December, 1835, no copper coin shall in any part of the territories of the East India Company be legal tender, except for fractions of a rupee.

B. Madras Regulations

Appendix B.1

A.D. 1803. REGULATION IX

A REGULATION for Levying a Duty on the imports and exports of merchandize by Sea at the Port of Madras, for determining the amount of duty and for defining the Rules under which that duty shall be collected.—PASSED by the Governor-in-Council of Fort St. George, on the 12th of August 1803.

xx xx xx xx	
XXVII *First*. The following articles shall be exempt from the payment of Duty.	Articles exempt from duties
xx xx xx xx	
Copper purchased at the Company's sales at any other Presidency in India, if sold on the condition of being exempt from the payment of duty.	
xx xx xx xx	
Treasure and Bullion	
xx xx xx xx	
Second. The Collector of Customs shall nevertheless register the quantity of Goods imported free of duty.	Register top be kept of Goods imported Duty free

Appendix B.2

A.D. 1803. REGULATION X

A REGULATION for Levying a Duty on the imports and exports of merchandize by Land into the Town of Madras and circumjacent villages and on articles manufactured or produced within the said Town and villages; for determining the amount of duty and for defining the Rules under which that duty shall be collected.—PASSED by the Governor-in-Council of Fort St. George, on the 12th of August 1803.

	xx xx xx xx
Articles exempt from duties	XIX. The following articles imported into the limits of the Madras Land Custom House, shall be exempt from the payment of Duty and Commission.
	All goods the property of the Honourable Company, on the production of a Certificate from a Competent authority
	Treasure
	Bullion
	xx xx xx xx
The first seven articles to be Registered.	*Second.* The first seven articles of merchandize passed duty free, shall nevertheless be registered by the Collector of Customs.

N.B.: Town duties introduced.

Appendix B.3

A.D. 1803. REGULATION XI

A REGULATION for Levying a Duty on imports and exports by Sea at the several Ports in the Provinces subject to the authority of Fort St. George and for determining the amount of duty and defining the Rules under which that duty shall be collected.—PASSED by the Governor-in-Council of Fort St. George, on the 12th of August 1803.

xx xx xx xx	
XXIII. The following articles shall not be liable to import and export Duties.	Articles exempt from Import and Export duty.
xx xx xx xx	
Goods the property of the Honourable Company, on the produce of a Certificate to that effect.	
Copper purchased at the Company's sales at any other Presidencies; if proved to have been sold on the condition of being exempted from duty.	
xx xx xx xx	
Treasure and Bullion	
xx xx xx xx	

Appendix B.4

A.D. 1803. REGULATION XII

A REGULATION for Levying a Duty on imports and exports by Sea at the several Ports in the Provinces subject to the authority of Fort St. George and for determining the amount of duty and defining the Rules under which that duty shall be collected.—PASSED by the Governor-in-Council of Fort St. George, on the 12th of August 1803.

	XX XX XX XX
Articles exempt from payment of frontier and town duties.	XXX. The under mentioned articles, whether imported or exported, shall be exempt from the payment of frontier and town duties, throughout the territories subject to the Presidency of Fort St. George.
	Goods the property of the Honourable Company, on the production of a Certificate from the Commercial Officer.
	XX XX XX XX
	Treasure and Bullion
The first seven articles nevertheless to be Registered.	*Second.* The first seven articles of merchandize passed free of duty, shall, nevertheless be registered.
	XX XX XX XX

N.B.: Rescinded by Regulation I of 1812.

Appendix B.5

A.D. 1827. REGULATION VI

A regulating for explaining the provisions of Clause First, Section V, Regulation XV, 1803, and Clause Fourth, Section III, Regulation VI, 1822; for making farther provisions against the offence of counterfeiting the coin; for Declaring magistrates empowered to take recognizances and security for keeping the peace in certain cases; for Enlarging the power granted to magistrates by Clause First, Section III, Regulation II, 1822; for Modifying and amending the rules in force relating to the requisition of security for good behaviour; and for subjecting to compulsory labour persons unable to find the security required.—PASSED by The Governor in Council of Fort St. George, on the 15th May, 1827.

IT is provided by Clause First, Section V, Regulation XV, 1803, that in cases of secret theft, or larceny without open violence, the Mohummudan law with the modifications of it in the existing Regulations and the rules contained in Section II of the said Regulation XV, 1803, shall govern the sentences of the Courts of Circuit as well as of the Foujdaree Udalut in any cases referred to that Court. In the construction of this Clause it has been doubted whether the Courts of Circuit and the Foujdaree Udalut, in commutation of a sentence of Hud under the Mohummudan law in cases of theft, are competent to adjudge stripes in addition to imprisonment for the term of seven years prescribed by Section XXI, Regulation VII, 1802; and it is necessary to remove all doubts on this point, and to declare the competency of the said Courts to adjudge stripes in addition to imprisonment for the prescribed term of seven years in all aggravated cases of theft—Moreover the construction given to the provisions of Clause Fourth, Section III, Regulation VI, 1822, having injuriously operated to abridge the discretion of the Criminal Judges in proportioning punishment to crime in the cases therein specified, and to take away from the Magistrates and	Preamble

Heads of District Police the power intended to be left with them of punishing in petty cases of cattle-stealing: an explanation of those provisions has become necessary. *It has also been deemed necessary for the further prevention of the offence of counterfeiting coin, to declare the making, mending, buying, selling, concealing, or possessing of implements used exclusively in coining, without lawful authority or sufficient excuse, to be a misdemeanour and to prescribe the punishment to which persons convicted thereof shall be liable.* Moreover the Regulations in force contain no express provision empowering Magistrates to take personal recognizances for the maintenance of the peace in their respective jurisdictions, nor expressly sanction the requisition of security to keep the peace, except from persons charged with criminal offences, whilst the charge is under examination, although it has been the established usage to require such personal recognizances, and also securities for keeping the peace in cases other than those expressly provided for; and it has been deemed expedient to declare that nothing contained in the existing Regulations was intended to preclude the Magistrates from the exercise of a discretion so necessary to the due maintenance of the peace in their respective jurisdictions, and also to provide that the orders of the Magistrates in the exercise of this discretion shall be liable to revision by the Judges on Circuit.—Further the power vested in Magistrates by Section III. Regulation II, 1822, to take from vagrants and others security for their appearance when required has been found insufficient to accomplish the object for which that power was granted, and in order effectually to restrain such persons from the practice of their evil habits it has been deemed necessary to vest Magistrates with authority to require from them security for their good behaviour; And all these and other cases in which security may lawfully be demanded it is expedient that the responsibility incurred by sureties should be defined; that the term for which persons unable to find the security required are to be imprisoned should, except in particular cases, be limited in the order requiring it, and that persons confined in default of security, should be subjected under certain restrictions to compulsory

labour.—The Honorable the Governor in Council, therefore, for the several reasons and purposes abovementioned, has enacted the following rules.	
xx xx xx xx	
IV. First. From and after the First day of October One thousand eight hundred and twenty seven, it shall be unlawful for any person subject to the jurisdiction of the Courts in the Provinces, except by the direction or under the authority of the Officers of Government, knowingly to make or mend, or to buy or sell, or conceal, or to have in his possession any tool or instrument used exclusively for coining money, or any stamp, or mould, or dye, or other implement whatsoever capable of producing the exact impression, or so near a resemblance as to be mistaken for the impression of any of the gold, silver, or copper coins of the British Governments in India, or of any coin usually received as money in the British possessions in India; and it is hereby declared that every such act shall, be punishable as a misdemeanour under the following rules.	The making, mending, buying, selling, concealing, or having possession of implements for coining declared a punishable offence.
Second. On receiving a charge of any of the acts mentioned in the preceding Clause, the Magistrate or the Head of District Police shall, proceed as is directed in all other cases of misdemeanour under the general Regulations; and if there shall be reasonable grounds, to believe the charge well-founded, he shall forward the prosecutor, the witnesses, and the accused, with all the proceedings in the case to the Criminal Judge of the Zillah.	Mode of procedure on charge of this nature.
Third. Any person who shall be convicted before the Criminal; Judge of any of the acts mentioned in Clause First of this Section, without shewing lawful authority or sufficient: excuse for the same, shall be sentenced to imprisonment, and hard labour in irons for a term, not exceeding one year for the first offence; and for a second offence, committed after, his conviction of the first, he shall be sentenced to receive corporal punishment not exceeding thirty stripes with a rattan and to be imprisoned and kept to hard labour in irons for a, term not exceeding eighteen months.	Punishment for an offence. Punishment for a second offence.

Punishment for a third or subsequent offence.	Fourth. For a third or any subsequent offence under this Section, the offender, shall be committed for trial before the Court of Circuit; and on conviction thereof shall be sentenced, to receive corporal punishment not exceeding thirty-nine stripes with a rattan, and to be imprisoned and kept to hard labour in irons, in banishment at the discretion of the Judge, for a term not exceeding seven years.

C. Bombay Regulations

Appendix C.1

A.D. 1805 REGULATION I

A REGULATION for amending Regulation VI of 1799 and adding additional Rules for the collection of Bombay Customs.—PASSED by the Governor-in-Council on the 14th of May, 1805 (answering to the 1st of Vysack Vud, 1861 Sumbut, and 14th Suffer 1220 Hejry).

xx xx xx xx	
XVII. No treasure, bullion, or pearls, of any description, to be permitted to be imported or exported, but upon manifests by the importers or exporter; and all treasure, bullion, pearls and jewels, as above imported, to be opened at the Custom-house, in order to enable the Custom-Master to send in correct returns of the same, agreeable to the orders of Government.	All imports of treasure or pearls and the like to be opened and registered at the Custom-house
xx xx xx xx	

Appendix C.2

A.D. 1810 REGULATION I

A REGULATION for the re-establishment of a Town Duty.—PASSED by the Governor-in-Council on the 1st of May, 1810 (corresponding with the 13th of Chyter Vud, Sumbut, or Vikramajit Era 1866, Salbahan, 1732; and 26th Ruby ul avul, 1225 Hejry).

	XX XX XX XX
	III *Fifth.* The following additional articles to be assessed both to the customs and the town duties: pearls and precious stones, hitherto omitted to be charged with either; and jewellery, which has heretofore paid only the rate of customs.
	XX XX XX XX

N.B.: Collection of Town duties that had ceased from the end of April 1805, were renewed by the orders of the Court of Directors. Bullion not mentioned.

Appendix C.3

A.D. 1812 REGULATION I

A RULE, Ordinance and Regulation for the good order and Civil Government of the Island of Bombay.—PASSED in Council on the 25th day of March, 1812 and registered in the Court of the Recorder of Bombay on the 20th day of May 1812.

xx xx xx xx	
TITLE NINTH *OF COINING*	
ARTICLE I. All persons who, without authority from Government, shall make or attempt to make, any coin current in this island, or without such authority shall have in their possessions, instruments for making such coin, or who shall utter such coin knowing it to be made here otherwise than in the Mint, and by authority of Government, or who shall debase such coin, or utter it knowing it to be debased, shall be punishable by the Court of Petty Sessions, and may, on this Regulation, which becomes a part of the Statute of the 47th of George III, to be prosecuted for a misdemeanour in the Recorder's Court.	Coining, how to be punished.
xx xx xx xx	

N.B.: Passed under authority of 'a statute passed in the forty-seventh year of His present Majesty King George the Third, entitled: 'An Act for the better Government of the Settlements of Fort St. George and Bombay.'

Appendix C.4

A.D. 1813. REGULATION X

A REGULATION for the conduct of the Trade of Foreign Nations with the Ports and Settlements in the East-Indies; and for defining the Duties to which such Trade shall be subject at such of the said Ports and Settlements as are immediately dependent on the Presidency of Bombay, and for prohibiting the export of Woollens to China, defining the duties to be levied on provisions imported on account of His Majesty's Navy, and directing the levy of a duty on the export of Bullion to Europe or America.—PASSED by the Governor-in-Council on the 4th September, 1813 (corresponding with the 9th Bhadrapud, Sood, Sumbut, or Vekramajit Era 1869, Salbahan, 1735; and 8th Rumzan, 1228 Hejry).

	xx xx xx xx
Duty to be levied on the exportation of coin or bullion to Europe or America.	IX. A Duty shall be levied on all coin or bullion exported from Bombay, or from any port subordinate thereto, either to America or Europe, at the rate of three per cent if exported on British vessels, and six per cent if exported on foreign bottoms.
Exception	Provided, however, that nothing contained in the present or in any former Regulation shall be construed to authorize the collection of any duty on the exportation of coin or bullion to any other place, excepting Europe and America, as provided.
	xx xx xx xx

Appendix C.5

A.D. 1827. REGULATION XIV

A REGULATION for defining Crimes and Offences, and specifying the Punishments to be inflicted for the same.—PASSED by the Governor-in-Council, on the 1st January, 1827.

WHEREAS the principles of justice require that the punishments to be inflicted on criminals, and the offences by which those punishments are respectively incurred, should be publicly promulgated; and whereas, in conformity with this object and with the enactments of the British Legislature, it has been the practice of the British Government of Bombay to apply to its subjects respectively their peculiar laws, modified and amended as necessity required by Regulations passed and published, the courts of justice ascertaining the native law in each case, as it occurred, by a reference to the law officer of the religion of the offender; and whereas an enactment, which should enumerate various offences, and specify their respective punishments, the same being the general result of the practice of the courts, founded on the successive expositions of the law officers consulted, must, to a considerable extent, secure the more steady observance of the principle of administering to individuals the law of their religion, by avoiding the probable variation in the expositions of different officers given each at the moment when the law is about to be applied; and whereas such an enactment will also combine the great advantages of superior publicity to the law, and of substituting a suitable discretion for the indefinite power conferred in numerous instances on the court by the expositions of the law officers, while it will also provide a code easy of access for those individuals of the community to whom, as not being subject to any specific national or religious code of criminal law, the English law has, with considerable inconvenience, been hitherto applied;—the following Rules are therefore enacted, to	Preamble

	have effect from such date as shall be prescribed in a Regulation to be hereafter passed for that purpose.
	CHAPTER I. A GENERAL DESCRIPTION OF THE ACTS WHICH ARE TO BE CONSIDERED CRIMINAL, WITH REFERENCE TO THE MODE IN WHICH EACH IS PUNISHABLE.
Specification of penal acts.	I. First. Actions such as those hereafter enumerated are declared to be liable to the punishments respectively assigned:
Offences against the State.	1. Offences committed against the state in its domestic or foreign relations, as defined with the punishments to which they are liable in Chapter III.
morality, and the community at large.	2. Offences against morality, or the community at large, as defined with the punishments to which they are liable in Chapter IV.
	xx xx xx xx
	CHAPTER IV. OF OFFENCES AGAINST MORALITY On THE COMMUNITY AT LARGE, AND THE PUNISHMENTS TO WHICH THEY ARE LIABLE; COMPRISING— *Perjury;* *Forgery;* *Coining;* *Issuing base coin;* *Selling poisons;* *Disguising the appearance of valuable articles;* *Fraudulent use of weights or measures;* *Fraudulently describing articles offered for sale;* *Violation of local police rules;* *Escape from custody;* *Resistance of legal process.*
	xx xx xx xx

XVII. First. Any person who shall counterfeit or fabricate any document or written instrument, or any signature, seal, or mark, upon such, or shall alter or efface the same, or any part thereof, with the intent of applying the same to a fraudulent purpose, shall be deemed to have committed forgery.	Forgery.
Second. Any person who shall make a fraudulent use of a document or instrument so forged, knowing it to be so, shall be liable to the punishment prescribed for forgery.	and the wilful application of forgery to purposes of fraud.
Third. Forgery shall be punishable by fine, imprisonment not exceeding five years, flogging not exceeding fifty stripes, [*or public disgrace,*] or any of these combined.	how punished.
XVIII. Any person coining money without authority from Government, or wilfully injuring the legal coin of the country, or furnishing tools knowing that they are to be applied to the said purposes, shall be punishable with fine, ordinary imprisonment not exceeding eight years, or flogging, or any of these combined.	Unlawful coining or injuring the legal coin, how punished.
XIX. First. Any person who may issue money which he knows to be base and unlawfully coined, shall, if the amount be greater than ten rupees, or if he have previously been convicted of the said offence, be liable to the punishment prescribed for unlawful coining in the preceding section.	The issue of unlawful coin, how punished in serious cases.
Second. But if the amount do not exceed ten rupees, and the culprit have not before been convicted of the offence, he shall be punishable by fine, not exceeding three times the amount of the sum issued, or attempted to be issued, commutable to ordinary imprisonment, without labour, for a period of two days for each rupee of fine.	and how in more trivial ones.

II: WEIGHT SYSTEM

A. IMPERIAL WEIGHTS

Imperial Troy Weight

The Troy pounds and its subdivisions were used for coins and precious metals. This system was introduced in England by Henry VIII in 1527. The name Troy is derived from the city of Troyes (Champagne—France) where the system is believed to have originated. It was abolished in England on 6 January 1879.

1 **grain** or gr.		(= 64.79891 mg)
24 grains	= 1 **pennyweight**[1] or dwt.	(= 1.55517384 g)
20 pennyweights	= 1 **ounce** or oz.[2]	(= 31.1034768 g or 480 grains)
12 ounces	= 1 **pound** or lb.[3]	(= 5760 grains or 373.2417216 g)

Note: For conversion of weights in Troy grains mentioned in the original sources referred to in this work, the following formula has been applied:

Grains ÷ 15.432 = Grams.

1 ÷ 15.432 = 0.064 g.

Imperial Carat

Carat (or ct.) is derived from *qirat*, Arabic for the seeds of the carob tree, which were used as weights on precision scales because of their reputation for having a uniform weight.

In the context of coinage the carat was used only for gold and in the analysis of this precious metal *vis-à-vis* the alloy contents, in twenty-four parts, e.g. a 22 carat gold contains 22/24 gold or 91.7 per cent pure gold and 0.3 per cent alloy, generally silver.

In England the carat was divisible into four grains, and the grain was divisible into four quarts.

1 Carat	=	4 grains
1 Grain	=	4 quarts

Thus, a gold alloy of $\frac{381}{384}$ fineness (that is, 99.2 per cent purity) could have been described as being *23-carat, 3-grain, 1-quart* gold.

B. INDIAN WEIGHT

8 **chowals** (or grains of rice)	=	1 **ratti**
8 *rattis*	=	1 **masha**
12 *mashas*	=	1 **tola**
80 *tolas*	=	1 **ser**
40 *sers*	=	1 **man** (or maund)

Sicca Weight (established by Regulation XXXV of 1793)

10 *mashas*		or $179\frac{2}{3}$ (or 179.666) grains Troy	
		or 11.642 g.	
= 16 *annas*	∴	1 *anna*	= 179.666 ÷ 16
			= 11.229 grains Troy
			or 0.727g.
= 12 *pice*	∴	1 *pice*	= 11.229 ÷ 12
			= 0.935 grains Troy
			or 0.060 g.

NOTES

1. So called because it was the weight of a silver penny.
2. From Italian *onza* – meaning ounce.
3. From the Roman *libra* meaning a weight or a balance, whose weight was anything between 4944 and 5220 grains.

Sources

The importance of archival sources for the purpose of writing economic history has been well realized by scholars. According to K.N. Chaudhuri, 'For the economic historian, the archives of the English East India Company provide one of the most comprehensive sources of information for the reconstruction of the commercial history of Europe and Asia in the pre-modern age.'[1]

The present work is primarily based on the records of the East India Company housed in various archival repositories. Besides, unpublished (manuscript) records housed in these repositories, a motley assortment of original source material available in a printed/published form, have also been utilized. A list of primary and secondary sources is given below.

PRIMARY SOURCES

Unpublished Records

a. National Archives of India
b. Tamil Nadu State Archives, Madras
c. Maharashtra State Archives, Bombay
d. West Bengal State Archives, Calcutta
e. Asia, Pacific and Africa Collection (formerly India Office Library & Records [IOLR]/ Oriental and India Office Collection [OIOC]), British Library, London

Printed Published Records

a. Selections from Records, etc.
b. Act, Regulations, Codes, etc.
c. Parliamentary Papers
d. Other Official Publications, viz., *Gazettes*

Contemporary Works

a. Tracts, Pamphlets, etc.
b. Travelogues
c. Newspapers and Chronicles
d. Calendars, Almanacs and Directories

SECONDARY SOURCES

See Select Annotated Bibliography (pp. 495-504) and Bibliography (pp. 505-35)

PRIMARY SOURCES

UNPUBLISHED RECORDS

a. National Archives of India, New Delhi

Records pertaining to:

i. Public Department, 1748-1810
ii. Foreign Department, 1748-1835
iii. Financial Department, 1810-35
iv. Mint Committee, 1792-1835
v. Mint, 1835
vi. Mint (Bengal), 1835
vii. Financial Department (Bengal), 1834-5

b. Tamil Nadu State Archives, Chennai

i. Madras Mint Records, 1744-1835

c. Maharashtra State Archives, Mumbai

i. Public (General) Department, 1720-1835
ii. Commercial Department, 1786-1835
iii. Financial Department, 1811-35
iv. Mint Department, 1830-5

d. West Bengal State Archives, Kolkata

i. Board of Trade (Commercial) Proceedings, 1774-1833
ii. Board of Revenue (Misc.) Proceedings, 1788-93

e. Asia, Pacific and Africa Collection (formerly India Office Library and Records [IOLR]/Oriental and India Office Collection [OIOC]), British Library, London

i. Home Miscellaneous Volumes.
ii. Mint Coinage Account Current (Madras), 1784-1801.
iii. New Mint Journals and Ledgers (Madras), 1807-33.
iv. Mint Masters Journals and Ledgers (Bombay), 1829-35
v. Calcutta Mint Account Current, 1809-31 & 1835

PRINTED/PUBLISHED RECORDS

a. Selections from Records

Datta, K.K. (1968), *Selection from the Judicial Records of the Bhagalpur District Office (1792-1805)*, Patna: State Central Records Office.

Forrest, G.W. (1891-3), *Bengal and Madras Papers* [*1671-1785*], 3 vols., Calcutta: Imperial Record Department.
——— (1887), *Selections from the Letters, Despatches, and Other State Papers, Preserved in the Bombay Secretariat—Home Series*, 2 vols., Bombay: [Bombay Government].
——— (1910), *Selection from the State Papers of the Governor-General of India, Warren Hastings*, 2 vols., Oxford: B.H. Blackwell.
Hill, Samuel Charles (1905), *Bengal in 1756-1757: A Selection of Public and Private Papers Dealing with the Affairs of the British in Bengal during the Reign of Sirajuddaula*, 3 vols., London: John Murray.
Long, J. (1869), *Selections from Unpublished Records of Government for the Years, 1748 to 1767*, vol. 1, Calcutta: Superintendent of Government Printing.
Love, H.D. (1913), *Vestiges of Old Madras, 1640-1800*, 4 vols. London: John Murray.
FWIHC (1949-85), *Fort William India House Correspondence, 1748-1800*, 21 vols. (vols. 1-13: Public series, 1748-1800; vols. 15-18: Foreign and Secret series, 1752-1800; vol. 19-21: Military series, 1787-1800), New Delhi: National Archives of India.
——— (1949), vol. V, Public, 1767-9, ed. N.K. Sinha.
——— (1955), vol. XVIII, Foreign, Political and Secret, 1792-5, ed. Y.I. Taraporevala.
——— (1957), vol. II, Public, 1758-9, ed. H.N. Sinha.
——— (1958), vol. I, Public, 1748-58, ed. K.K. Datta.
——— (1959), vol. IX, Public, 1782-5, ed. B.A. Saletore.
——— (1959), vol. XIII, Public, 1795-1800, ed. P.C. Gupta.
——— (1960), vol. VI, Public, 1770-2, ed. Bisheswar Prasad.
——— (1962), vol. IV, Public, 1764-6, ed. C.S. Srinivasachari.
——— (1963), vol. XV, Foreign and Secret Letters, 1782-6, ed. C.H. Philips and B.B. Misra.
——— (1968), vol. III, Public, 1760-3, ed. R.R. Sethi.
——— (1969), vol. XXI, Military, 1792-6, ed. A.C. Banerjee.
——— (1969), vol. XXII, Military, 1797-1800, ed. S.R. Kohli.
——— (1971), vol. VII, Public, 1773-6, ed. R.P. Patwardhan.
——— (1972), vol. X, Public, 1786-8, ed. Raghubir Sinh.
——— (1974), vol. XI, Public, 1789-92, ed. I.B. Banerjee.
——— (1974), vol. XIX, Foreign, Political and Secret, 1798-1800, ed. Fr. H. Heras.
——— (1975), vol. XX, Military, 1787-91, ed. Bisheswar Prasad.
——— (1976), vol. XVII, Foreign, Secret and Political, 1787-91, ed. S.H. Askari.
——— (1978), vol. XII, Public, 1793-5, ed. Amales Tripathi.
——— (1981), vol. VIII, Public, 1777-81, ed. H.D. Gupta.
——— (1985), vol. XIV, Secret and Secret Committee, 1752-81, ed. Amba Prasad.

North Western Provinces (1868), *Selections from the Records of the Government, North-Western Provinces: Mr. Thompson's Despatches,* vol. 1, Allahabad: North Western Provinces Government Press.

b. Acts, Regulations, Codes, etc.

Annand, Alexander (1832), *Brief Outline of the Existing System for the Government of India; to which is Annexed a Tabular Statement of Legislative Enactments from 1773 to 1826*, London: Saunders & Benning.

Clarke, Richard (1848), *The Regulations of the Government of Fort St. George, In Force at the End of 1847: To Which are Added, the Acts of the Government of India in Force in that Presidency,* London: J.&H. Cox.

——— (1854), *The Regulations of the Government of Fort William in Bengal, In Force at the End of 1853: To Which are Added, the Acts of the Government of India in Force in that Presidency,* 3 vols., London: J.&H. Cox.

Colebrooke, James Edwards (1807), *Supplement to the Digest of the Regulations and Laws Enacted by the Governor General in Council for the Civil Government of the Territories under the Presidency of Bengal; Containing a Collection of the Regulations Enacted Anterior to the Year MDCCXCIII, and Completing Each Article of the Digest to the Close of the Year MDCCCVI,* 3 vols., Calcutta: [Company's Press].

Harington, John Herbert (1814-17), *An Elementary Analysis of the Laws and Regulations Enacted by the Governor General in Council, at Fort William, in Bengal, for the Civil Government of the British Territories under that Presidency,* 6 vols., Calcutta: Company's Press.

Sutherland, D. (1862), *Regulations of the Bengal Code in Force in September, 1862 with a List of Titles and Index,* Calcutta: Bengal Printing Co.

White, Henry (1820), *Regulations and Laws Passed by the Governor General in Council for Civil Government,* 6 vols.

c. Parliamentary Papers

House of Commons (1803), *Reports from Committees of the House of Commons, 1715-1801,* 15 vols., London.

Vol. III: *Five Reports from the Select Committee on East India Company Affairs, 1772-3* (Col. Burgoyne).

Vol. IV: *Nine Reports from the Secret Committee on East India Company Affairs, 1772-3* (Lord North).

——— (1846), *Calcutta Mint: A Copy of the Rules and Regulations of the Calcutta Mint and an Abstract of the Operations of the Mint in Each Year since its Reform [1831-32].* Return Dated: 10 March 1846, vol. 31, paper no. 117.

——— (1857-8), *East India (Coinage etc.): Copies of all Acts, Notifications and Proclamations of the Government of India Concerning the Coinage, Currency and Legal Tender of the Territories under the said Government from 1st day of May 1834 to the date of the Latest Accounts Received.* Return Dated: 22 March 1858, vol. 53, paper no. 152.

——— (1898), *East India (Currency): Copy of the Despatch Addressed by the Court of Directors to the Governments of Bengal and Madras on the 25th day of April 1806 Dealing with the Coinage of India.* Return Dated: 23 March 1898, vol. 61, paper no. 127.

Ferminger, W.K. (1984), *Affairs of the East India Company (Being the Fifth Report from the Select Committee of the House of Commons 28 July 1812)*, 3 vols., rep. Delhi: Neeraj Pub. House.

d. Gazettes

Calcutta Gazette, 1793-1835
Fort St George Gazette, 1802-35
Bombay Government Gazette, 1831-35

CONTEMPORARY WORKS

a. Tracts, Pamphlets, etc.

Anon (1767), *An Attempt to Pay off the National Debt by Abolishing the East India Company of Merchants*, London: S. Bladon.

Colquhoun, Patrick (1788), *Observations Relative to the Resources of the East India Company for Productive Remittance: And the National Loss Occasioned by the Importation of the Same Species of Cotton Which Can Be Manufactured in Great Britain* [London].

[Crawfurd, John] (1837), *A Sketch of the Commercial Resources and Monetary and Mercantile System of British India, with Suggestions for their Improvement, by Means of Banking Establishments*, London: Smith, Elder and Co. [rpt. in Chaudhuri 1971: 217-316, who assigns the authorship of this anonymous tract to John Crawfurd (1783-1868), see pp. 14-15].

Dalrymple, A. (1794), *Observations on the Copper Coinage wanted for the Circars*, London: George Bigg.

Hall, Robert (1813), *An Address to the Public on an Important Subject Connected with the Renewal of the Charter of the East India Company*, London: W. Button and Son.

Liverpool, Charles, Earl of (1805), *A Treatise on the Coins of the Realm; In a Letter to the King*, Oxford: Oxford University Press.

McMulloch, J.R. (1856), *A Select Collection of Scarce and Valuable Tracts on Money*, London: Political Economy Club.

Milburn, William and Thomas Thornton (1825), *Oriental Commerce, or,*

The East India trader's complete guide containing a geographical and nautical description of the maritime parts of India, China, Japan, and neighbouring countries, including the Eastern Islands, and the trading stations on the passage from Europe, with an account of their respective commerce, productions, coins, weights, and measures, their port regulations, duties, rates, charges &c., and a description of the commodities imported from thence into Great Britain, and the duties payable thereon, together with a mass of miscellaneous information, collected during many years' employment in the East India service, and in the course of seven voyages to India and China. London: Kingsbury, Parbury, and Allen.

Pattullo, Henry (1772), *An Essay upon the Cultivation of the Lands, and Improvements of the Revenues of Bengal*, London: T. Becket and P.A. de Hardt.

Prinsep, George Alexander (1823), *Remarks on the External Commerce and Exchange of Bengal, with Appendix of Accounts and Estimates*, London: Kingsbury, Parbury and Allen [rpt. in Chaudhuri 1971: 51-167].

Steuart, James (1772), *The Principles of Money Applied to the Present State of the Coin of Bengal: Being an Inquiry Into the Methods to be Used for Correcting the Defects of the Present Currency; for Stopping the Drains Which Carry off the Coin; and for Extending Circulation by Means of Paper-Credit*, London: East India Company.

——— (1805), *The Works, Political, Metaphysical and Chronological, of the Late Sir James Steuart of Coltness, Bart., Now First Collected, with Anecdotes of the Author, by his Son, General Sir James Denham Steuart*, 6 vols., London: T. Cadell and W. Davies.

Tucker, Henry St. George (1825), *A Review of the Financial Situation of the East India Company in 1824*, London: Kingsbury, Parbury and Allen.

Verelst, Harry (1772), *A View of the Rise, Progress, and Present State of the English Government in Bengal: Including a Reply to the Misrepresentations of Mr. Bolts, and Other Writers*, London: J. Nourse.

Warring, John Scott (1771), *Observations on the Present State of the East India Company and on the Measures to be Pursued for Ensuring its Permanency, and Augmenting its Commerce*, London: J. Nourse.

b. Travelogues

Buchanan, Francis (1807), *A Journey from Madras through the Countries of Mysore, Canara and Malabar, 1800 (23 April 1800 to 6 July 1801)*, 3 vols., London: T. Cadell and W. Davies.

——— (1925), *Journal of Francis Buchanan Kept during the Survey of the Districts of Patna and Gaya in 1811-1812*, Patna: Superintendent, Government Printing, Bihar and Orissa.

Hodges, William (1799), *Travels in India During the Years 1780, 1781, 1782, and 1783*, London: J. Edwards.

Manucci, Niccolao (1907-8), *Storia do Mogor: or Mogul India, 1653-1708*, 4 vols., London: John Murray.

Pillai, Ananda Ranga (1904-28), *The Private Diary of Ananda Ranga Pillai, 1736-1761*, 12 vols., ed. J. Fredrick Price (vols. 1-2); H. Dodwell (vols. 3-12), Madras: Government Press.

c. Newspapers and Chronicles

i. *Annual Register*
ii. *Bombay Chronicle*, 1825+
iii. *Bombay Halkaru* and *Vartaman* (Gujarati), 1833+
iv. *Bombay Weekly Guide* (1832-3)
v. *Bombay Messenger* (1831)

SECONDARY SOURCES: SELECT ANNOTATED BIBLIOGRAPHY

For a general survey of India's economic life during the eighteenth century, apart from *Cambridge Economic History of India*, vol. II: *c.* 1757-1970 (1982) and the contributions of classical economic historians like Dada Bhai Naoroji, Romesh C. Dutt, etc., works such as Jadunath Sarkar's *Economics of British India* (1909); K.K. Datta's *Survey of India's Social Life and Economic Conditions in the Eighteenth Century 1707-1813* (1st edn. 1961; 2nd rev. edn. 1978); A.I Chicherov's *India: Economic Development in the 16-18 Centuries* (1971); Satish Chandra's *The 18th Century in India* (1982) [esp. Section Two 'Trade, Market and Economy']; Dietmar Rothermund's *An Economic History of India from Pre-Colonial Times to 1986* (1988); and Deepak Lal's *The Hindu Equilibrium: Cultural Stability and Economic Stagnation, c. 1500 BC-AD 1980*, vol. II (1989) [esp. part II—'The Colonial Centuries'] provide the essential backdrop for perceiving the Indian economic scenario during the period of our review.

During the last decade or so, there has been a renewed interest in various aspects of the eighteenth century. P.J. Marshall edited a volume *The Eighteenth Century* (1998) 'The Oxford History of the British Empire' series. An anthology of articles previously published by different authors on various aspects of the eighteenth century—*The Eighteenth Century in India* (2002) was brought out by Seema Alavi. Close on its heels was another one from the same publisher and with an almost homonymous title, *The Eighteenth Century in Indian History: Evolution or Revolution* (2003). This volume, also edited by P.J. Marshall who wrote a new introduction for this book, repeats at least two essays from Alavi's anthology. All these compilations, containing the contributions of Frank Perlin, Burton Stein, M. Athar Ali, Rajat Kanta Ray, Irfan Habib and others, underline various issues and controversies surrounding the study of this period.

A relatively large number of specialized studies on various aspects of the economic activities of society are now available as an aid for analysing various issues connected with the central theme of our work, viz., the role of the changing monetary structure on different aspects of the economic life of the people.

In this category, we may include works on trade, especially the studies of Charles Hamilton (1924), Durga Prashad (1932), K.N. Chaudhuri (1978) and Holden Furber (1948 and 1976), all dealing with India's external trade, especially with England; Ole Feldback (1978) on Danish trade; Kristof Glamann (1958), C.R. Boxer (1965) and Om Prakash (1994) on Dutch trade; C.R. Boxer (1969), F.C. Danvers (1988) and Sanjay Subrahmanyam (1990) on Portuguese trade; R.B. Morse (1926) and Michael Greenberg on Chinese trade; and Ian Bruce Watson (1980) on English private trade in India, all revolving round the general theme of European expansion in Asia.

Another dimension of available writings on the economic history of India can be seen in the form of studies of various regions during the period of the development and consolidation of colonial power in India. In this category, works on Bengal far outnumber those on any other region. Here, we have some general economic surveys like J.C. Sinha's *Economic Annals of Bengal* (1927) covering a period from 1707 to 1793, K.K. Datta's *Studies in the History of the Bengal Subah, 1740-70* (1936); H.R. Ghoshal's *Economic Transition in the Bengal Presidency, 1793-1833* (1950); N.K. Sinha's *Economic History of Bengal: From Plassey to Permanent Settlement* [esp. vols. I & III] (1956 and 1978); P.J. Marshall's *East Indian Fortune* (1976) and *Bengal: The British Bridgehead* (1982), etc. Studies on trade and commercial organizations in Bengal include Amales Tripathi's *Trade and Finance in Bengal Presidency 1783-1833*, (1956) and Susil Chaudhury's *Trade and Commercial Organisations in Bengal, 1650-1720* (1975), to name just a few.

Similarly, for south India, A.V. Raman Rao's *Economic Development of Andhra Pradesh, 1766-1957* (1958), A. Sardaraju's *Economic Conditions in the Madras Presidency, 1800-1850* (1961), Ashin Dasgupta's *Malabar in Asian Trade 1740-1800* (1967), R.N. Banerjee's *Economic Progress of the East India Company on the Coromandel Coast, 1702-1746* (1974), C. Ramachandran's *East India Company and South Indian Economy* (1980) and S. Arasaratnam's *Merchants, Companies and Commerce on the Coromandel Coast, 1650-1740* (1986); for western India, Holden Furber's *Bombay Presidency in the Mid-eighteenth Century* (1965) and Pamela Nightingale's *Trade and Empire in Western India, 1784-1806* (1970); for northern India, Rudrangshu Mukherjee's *Trade and Empire in Awadh, 1765-1802* (1977) and a more comprehensive study by C.A. Bayly, viz., *Rulers, Townsmen and Bazars* (1983) both on the doab region, and for Rajasthan, B.L. Gupta's *Trade and Commerce in Rajasthan during the 18th Century* are some of the works that provide a detailed survey of the economic life of specific regions.

Coming more precisely to monetary history, it is observed that questions concerning money and credit are usually discussed only in specialist publications. As technical details such as statistical data and quantitative analysis are involved in these studies, this subject has often discouraged students of history and, as a result, has not been very well-integrated in surveys of economic history. This problem is more glaring especially for the period selected for the present study. Even in the otherwise well-documented *CEHI*, vol. II, we do not find any discussion on monetary policies and institutions during the eighteenth century. However, a few works by economists on the historical process of the development of various economic ideas and institutions are now available. They provide a theoretical analysis of various economic doctrines. We have William Barker's *British Economic Thought and India, 1600-1858* (1975) where he discusses various schools of economic thought that were prevalent in Britain and their overall impact on the economic policies of the English East India Company. Another economist, S. Ambirajan's two important works, viz., *Political Economy and British Policy in India* (1978) and more precisely his *Political Economy and Monetary Management, India; 1766-1914* (1984) discuss various monetary experiments carried out by the British in India as a result of changing economic doctrines in England and Europe.

As for the actual discussion on the eighteenth and nineteenth centuries, monetary structure in India, D.B. Mitra's *Monetary System in Bengal Presidency 1757-1835* (1991); Frank Perlin's *The Invisible City: Monetary, Administrative and Popular Infrastructure in Asia and Europe, 1500-1900* (1993) and also his *Unbroken Landscape: Commodity, Category, Sign and Identity, their Production as Myth and Knowledge from 1500* (1994), and a recent work by Anirban Biswas—*Money and Markets from Pre-Colonial to Colonial India* (2007), directly touch upon the subject of monetary policies, practices and institutions of the pre-colonial and colonial economy.

A noteworthy trend in recent writings on economic history is the publication of a number of thematic editions containing contributions of different scholars. In the field of the monetary history of Asia in general and India in particular, a number of such studies are available. Notable among these are the works edited by John F. Richards, *Precious Metals in the Later Medieval and Early Modern Worlds* (1983) [esp. the contributions of John S. Deyell, Joseph J. Brenning and John F. Richards], E. Van Cauvenberghe and F. Irsigler, eds., *Minting, Monetary Circulation and Exchange Rates* (1984), E. Van Cauvenberghe, ed., *Precious Metals, Coinage and the Change of Monetary Structures in Latin America, Europe and Asia (Late Middle Age-Early Modern Times)* (1989), containing papers presented at a conference on monetary history held at Leuven University; and also *Money, Coins and Commerce: Essays in the Monetary History of Asia and Europe (from Antiquity to Modern Times)* (1991) [esp. articles by Om Prakash and Frank Perlin]; W. Fischer et al., eds., *Emergence of a World Economy 1500-1914*, vol. I (1986), wherein various aspects of the flow of precious metals from Europe to Asia have been discussed by D.O. Flynn, K.N. Chaudhuri and Om Prakash; H. Pohl, ed., *European Discovery of the World and its Effect on Pre-Industrial Society* (1990) [esp. the contribution of Frank Perlin on financial institutions and business practices] and Sanjay Subrahmanyam's *Money and the Market in India, 1100-1700* (1994), which is a compilation of articles published in the *Indian Economic and Social History Review*.

To these cited works may be added a hoard of research papers dealing with economic issues and covering themes such as money changers and indigenous fiscal practices, banking, the bullion trade, the history of prices and exchange, various currencies and coinages, the operation of mints, etc. Among these are the contributions of Irfan Habib, Asiya Siddiqi, Shireen Moosvi, E.I. Brodkin, K.K. Datta, Susil Chaudhury, K.N. Chaudhuri, Om Prakash, Sanjay Subrahmanyam, Frank Perlin, P.J. Marshall, Najaf Haider, Rajat Datta, etc.

Finally, we have numismatic studies on the coinages of the British. The monumental work by F. Pridmore, *The Coins of the British Common Wealth of Nations to the End of the Reign of George VI, 1952, Part 4; India*, 2 vols., 1975 & 1980 documents various series of coins issued by the British for their Indian territories. This may be supplemented by a number of articles by numismatists, viz., C.H. Biddulph, Peter Snartt, Michael Mitchner, K.W. Wiggins, Paul Stevens, Shailendra Bhandare, etc.

NOTE

1. Chaudhuri 1978: Preface, xv.

Bibliography

BOOKS

Anon (1982), *Bombay Mint: 150th Anniversary Celebration Souvenir*, Bombay: India Government Mint.

——— (1986), *The Bombay Mint,* Bombay: India Government Mint.

Abdus Sadeque (1938), *The Problem of the Standard of Indian Currency: Its History and Solution*, Calcutta: Fatima Sadeque.

Adams, Brooks (1896), *The Law of Civilization and Decay: An Essay on History*, New York: The Macmillan Company.

Aldenham, Lord (1900), *A Colloquy on Currency*, London: Effingham Wilson.

Alam, Muzaffar (1986), *The Crisis of Empire in Mughal North India: Awadh and Punjab, 1707-1748*, New Delhi: Oxford University Press.

Alavi, Seema (2002), *The Eighteenth Century in India*, New Delhi: Oxford University Press.

Ambedkar, B.R. (1925), *The Evolution of Provincial Finance in British India: A Study in the Provincial Decentralisation of Imperial Finance*, London: P.S. King & Son Ltd.

——— (1947), *History of Indian Currency and Banking*, Bombay: Thacker and Company.

Ambirajan, S. (1978), *Classical Political Economy and British Policy in India*, Cambridge: Cambridge University Press.

——— (1984), *Political Economy and Monetary Management, India, 1766-1914*, Madras: Affiliated East-West Press.

Arasaratnam, S. (1986), *Merchants, Companies and Commerce on the Coromandel Coast, 1600-1750*, New Delhi: Oxford University Press.

Atkins, James (1889), *The Coins and Tokens of the Possessions and Colonies of the British Empire*, London: Quaritch.

Bagchi, Amiya Kumar (1981), *Merchants and Colonialism*, Calcutta: Centre for Studies in Social Sciences.

——— (1982), *Money and Credit as Areas of Conflict in Colonial India* (Mimeographed), Calcutta: Centre for Studies in Social Sciences.

——— (1987), *The Evolution of the State Bank of India, The Roots, 1806-1863, Parts I & II*, New Delhi: Oxford University Press.

——— ed. (2002), *Money and Credit in Indian History: From Early Medieval Times*, New Delhi: Tulika.

Bal Krishna (1924), *Commercial Relations between India and England, 1601-1757*, London: G. Routledge & Sons.

Banerjea, Pramathanath (1922), *Fiscal Policy in India*, Calcutta: Macmillan & Co.

——— (1928), *Indian Finance in the Days of the Company*, London: Macmillan & Co.

——— (1940), *A Study of Indian Economics*, Calcutta: Macmillan & Co.

Banerji, R.N. (1974), *Economic Progress of the East India Company on the Coromandel Coast, 1702-1746*, Nagpur: Nagpur University

Barbour, Sir David (1913), *The Influence of the Gold Supply on Prices and Profits*, London: Macmillan & Co.

Barendse, R.J. (2002), *The Arabian Sea: The Indian Ocean World of the Seventeenth Century*, New Delhi: Vision Books.

Barker, William J. (1975), *British Economic Thought and India, 1600-1858: A Study in the History of Development Economics*, London: Oxford University Press.

Bayly, C.A. (1983), *Rulers, Townsmen and Bazaars: North Indian Society in the Age of Expansion, 1770-1870*, Cambridge: Cambridge University Press.

——— (1989), *Imperial Meridian: The British Empire and the World, 1780-1830*, London: Longman.

Beaglehole, T.H. (1966), *Thomas Munro and the Development of Administrative Policy in Madras, 1792-1818*, Cambridge: Cambridge University Press.

Bearce, George D. (1861), *British Attitude Towards India, 1784-1858*, London: Oxford University Press.

Bhargava, Brijkishore (1935), *Indigenous Banking in Ancient and Medieval India*, Bombay: D.B. Taraporevala Sons & Company.

Bhatt, V.V. (1963), *Aspects of Economic Change and Policy in India, 1800-1960*, Bombay: Allied Publishers.

Bhattacharya, Dhires (1972), *A Concise History of the Indian Economy, 1750-1950*, Calcutta: Progressive Publishers.

Bhattacharya, S. (1954), *The East India Company and the Economy of Bengal, from 1704 to 1740*, London: Luzac & Co.

——— (1971), *Financial Foundations of the Raj: Men and Ideas in the Post Mutiny period of Reconstruction of Indian Piublic Finance, 1858-1872*, Simla: Indian Institute of Advanced Study.

——— ed. (1987), *Essays in Modern Indian Economic History*, Delhi: Munshiram Manoharlal.

Bipan Chandra (1966), *The Rise and Growth of Economic Nationalism in India: Economic Policies of Indian National Leadership, 1880-1905*, New Delhi: People's Publishing House.

Biswas, Anirban (2007), *Money and Markets from Pre-Colonial to Colonial India*, New Delhi: Aakar Books.

Blusse, L. and F. Gaastra, eds. (1981), *Companies and Trade: Essays on Overseas Trading Companies during the Ancien Régime*, Leiden: Leiden University Press.

Bowen, H.V. (1991), *Revenue and Reform: The Indian Problem in British Politics, 1757-1773*, Cambridge: Cambridge University Press.

——— et al., eds. (2002), *The Worlds of the English East India Company*, Suffolk (UK): Boydell Press.

Cameron, Rondo (1989), *A Concise Economic History of the World: From Paleolithic Times to the Present*, New York: Oxford University Press.

Cauwenberghe, E. van, ed. (1989), *Precious Metals, Coinage and the Changes of Monetary Structures in Latin America, Europe and Asia (Late Middle Ages–Early Modern Times*, Leuven: Leuven University Press.

——— (1991), *Money Coins and Commerce: Essays in the Monetary History, Asia and Europe (from Antiquity to Modern Times)*, Leuven: Leuven University Press.

Cauwenberghe, E. van and F. Irsigler, eds. (1984), *Minting, Monetary Circulation and Exchange Rates*, Trier: Verlag Trierer Historische Forschungen.

Chakraborti, Phanindra Nath (1994), *Rise and Growth of East India Company: A Study of British Mercantile Activities in Mughal India*, Calcutta: Punthi Pustak.

Challis, C.E. ed. (1992), *A New History of the Royal Mint*, Cambridge: Cambridge University Press.

Chalmers, R. (1893), *A History of Currency in the British Colonies*, London: Her Majesty's Stationery Office.

Chaterjee, Kumkum (1996), *Merchants, Politics and Society in Early Modern India: Bihar, 1733-1820*, Leiden: E.J. Brill.

Chatterjee, Nandalal (1939), *Verelst's Rule in India*, Allahabad: Indian Press.

Chaudhuri, K.N., ed. (1971), *The Economic Development of India Under the East India Company, 1814-58: A Selection of Contemporary Writings*, Cambridge: Cambridge University Press.

——— (1978), *The Trading World of Asia and the East India Company, 1660-1760*, Cambridge: Cambridge University Press.

——— (1985), *Trade and Civilisation in the Indian Ocean: An Economic History from the Rise of Islam to 1750*, Cambridge: Cambridge University Press.

Chaudhuri, Sushil (1975), *Trade and Commercial Organisation in Bengal, 1650-1720*, Calcutta: Firma K.L. Mukhopadhyay.

——— (1995), *From Prosperity to Decline: Eighteenth Century Bengal*, New Delhi: Manohar.

Chaudhury, Sushil and Michel Morineau, eds. (1999), *Merchants, Companies and Trade: Europe and Asia in the Early Modern Era*, New York: Maison des Sciences de l'Hommes and Cambridge University Press.

Chicherov, A.I. (1971), *India: Economic Development in the 16th-18th Centuries, Outline History of Crafts and Trade*, Moscow: Nauka Publishing House.

Chitnis, K.N. (1979), *Socio-Economic Aspects of Medieval India*, Poona: R.K. Chitnis.

Choksey, R.D. (1945a), *Selections from the Deccan Commissioners' Peshwa Daftar: Period of Transition (1818-1826)*, Poona: pub. by the author.

——— (1945b), *Economic History of Bombay Deccan and Karnatak, 1818-1868*, Poona: pub. by the author.

——— (1950), *Aftermath*, Based on original records, 1818-1826, Bombay: New Book Co.

——— (1968), *Economic Life in Bombay Gujarat, 1800-1839*, London: Asia Publishing House.

Clough, Shepard B. (1975), *European Economic History: The Economic Development of Western Civilization*, 3rd edn., New York: McGraw-Hill.

Cooke, C.N. (1863), *The Rise, Progress and Present Condition of Banking in India*, Calcutta: Bengal Print Co.

Court, W.H.B. (1954), *A Concise Economic History of England since 1750-1959*, Cambridge: Cambridge University Press.

Craig, Sir John (1953), *The Mint: A History of the London Mint from AD 287 to 1948*, Cambridge: Cambridge University Press.

Curzon, Marquis (1925), *British Government in India*, 2 vols., vol. II, London: Cassell & Co.

Datta, Rajat (2000), *Society, Economy, and the Market: Commercialization in Rural Bengal, c. 1760-1800*, New Delhi: Manohar.

Das Gupta, Ashin (1994), *Merchants of Maritime India, 1500-1800*, Aldershot (UK): Variorum.

Das Gupta, Ashin and M.N. Pearson (1987), *India and the Indian Ocean, 1500-1800*, Calcutta: Oxford University Press.

Datta, K[ali] K[inkar] (1936), *Studies in the History of the Bengal Subah, 1740-1770: Social and Economic*, Calcutta: University of Calcutta.

——— (1978), *Survey of India's Social life and Economic Condition in the Eighteenth Century (1707-1813)*, 2nd rev. edn., New Delhi: Munshiram Manoharlal.

Day, John (1987), *The Medieval Market Economy*, Oxford: Basil Blackwell.

De, Barun (1989), *Problems of the Study of Indian History: With Particular Reference to Interpretation of the 18th Century* (Mimeograph), Calcutta: Centre for Studies in Social Science.

Desai, Tripta (1984), *The English East India Company: A Brief Survey from 1599 to 1857*, New Delhi: Kanak Publications.

Digby, William (1901), *'Prosperous' British India: A Revelation from Official Records*, London: Unwin.

Dutt, Romesh Chandra (1902), *Economic History of India*, vol. I, London: Trübner & Co.

Duckenfield, Mark, ed. (2004), *The Monetary History of Gold: A Collection of Historical Documents, 1660–1999*, London: Pickering & Chatto.

Edwards, Michael (1967), *British India, 1772-1947: A Survey of the Nature and Effects of Alien Rule*, London: Sidgwick & Jackson.

Einzig, Paul (1964), *Monetary Policy: Ends and Means*, Harmondsworth: Penguin Books.

Embree, Ainslee T. (1962), *Charles Grant and British Rule in India*, London: G. Allen.

Eraly, Abraham (2000), *Emperors of the Peacock Throne: The Saga of the Great Mughals*, New Delhi: Penguin Books.

Feldback, Ole (1978), *Indian Trade under the Danish Flag, 1772-1808: European Entreprise and Anglo-Indian Remittance and Trade*, London: Curzon Press.

Ferminger, W.K. (1917), *Historical Introduction to the Bengal Portion of the Fifth Report*, Calcutta: R. Cambray and Company (rpt. in *Indian Studies Past and Present*, Calcutta, 1962).

Fetter, F.W. (1965), *Development of British Monetary Orthodoxy, 1797-1875*, Cambridge, Mass.: Harvard University Press.

FICCI (1999), *Footprints of Enterprise: Indian Business through the Ages*, New Delhi: Oxford University Press.

Fisher, Irving (1922), *The Purchasing Power of Money, its Determination and Relation to Credit, Interests and Crises*, rev. edn., New York: Macmillan, (online edn. http://oll.libertyfund.org/title/1165; last accessed on 3 September 2007).

Fisher, Michael H., ed. (1993), *The Politics of the British Annexation of India, 1757-1857*, New Delhi: Oxford University Press.

Fischer, W. et al., eds. (1986), *The Emergence of a World Economy, 1500-1914*, Wiesbaden: In Kommission bei F. Steiner.

Flores, J.M., ed. (1991), *The Asian Seas, 1500-1800: Local Societies, European Expansion and the Portuguese*, Macao: Revista de Cultura.

Floud, R. and D.N. McCloskey (1981), *The Economic History of Britain since 1700, Vol. I: 1700-1860*, Cambridge: Cambridge University Press.

Foster, William W. (1902), *The Founding of Fort St. George, Madras*, London: Eyre & Spottiswoode.

——— (1906), *A Note on the First English Coinage at Bombay*, London: Royal Numismatic Society.

——— (1924), *The East India House: Its History and Associations*, London: John Lane.

Furber, Holden (1965), *Bombay Presidency in the mid-Eighteenth Century*, Bombay: Asia Publishing House.

——— (1980), *Rival Empires of Trade in the Orient, 1600-1800*, New Delhi: Oxford University Press.

Garg, Vipin K. (1984), *Trade Practices and Traditions: Origin and Development in India*, Delhi: Allied Publishers.

Ghoshal, Hari Ranjan (1950), *Economic Transition in the Bengal Presidency, 1793-1833*, Patna: Patna University.

Gleig, G.R. (1830/5), *The History of the British Empire in India*, 4 vols. (vol. 1: *1830*; vols. 2-4: *1835*), London: John Murray.

Goldsmith, Raymond W. (1983), *The Financial Development of India, 1860-1977*, New Haven: Yale University Press.

Goor, J van, ed. (1986), *Trading Companies in Asia, 1600-1830*, Utrecht: HES Uitgevers.

Greenberg, Michael (1969), *British Trade and the Opening of China, 1800-1842*, Cambridge: Cambridge University Press.

Grierson, Philip (1975), *Numismatics*, London: Oxford University Press.

Griffiths, Percival (1952), *The British Impact on India*, London: MacDonald.

Gupta, B.L. (1987), *Trade and Commerce in Rajasthan during the 18th Century*, Jaipur: Jaipur Publishing House.

Gupta, Brijen K. (1966), *Sirajuddaulah and the East India Company, 1750-1757*, Leiden: E.J. Brill.

Gupta, O.P. (1935), *Central Banking in India, 1773-1934, with special examination of the Reserve Bank of India Act, 1934, in the light of laws, charters and statutes regulating over thirty banks of issue in different parts of the world*, Delhi: Hindustan Times Press.

Habib, Irfan (1987), *Caste and Money in Indian History*, Bombay: University of Bombay.

——— (1995), *Essays in Indian History: Towards a Marxist Perception*, New Delhi: Tulika.

——— ed. (2005), *India: Studies in the History of an Idea*, New Delhi: Aligarh Historians Society and Munshiram Manoharlal.

Hamilton, C.J. (1919), *The Trade Relations between England and India, 1600-1896*, Calcutta: Thacker, Spink and Co.

Hand, J.R. (1894), *Early English Administration of Bihar, 1781-85*, Calcutta: Bengal Secretariat Press.

Hicks, Sir John (1969), *A Theory of Economic History*, Oxford: Clarendon Press.

Hintze, Andrea (1997), *The Mughal Empire and its Decline: An Interpretation of the Sources of Social Power*, Aldershot (UK): Ashgate Publishing Company.

Horsefield, J.K. (1960), *British Monetary Experiments, 1650-1710*, London: Bell.

Hossain, Hameeda (1988), *The Company Weavers in Bengal: The East India Company and the Organisation of Textile Production in Bengal, 1750-1813*, New Delhi: Oxford University Press.

Huq, Marharul (1964), *The East India Company's Land Policy and Commerce in Bengal, 1698-1784*, Dacca: Asiatic Society of Pakistan.

Irvine, William (1922), *Later Mughals*, 2 vols., ed. Jadunath Sarkar, Calcutta: M.C. Sarkar & Sons.

Iyer, G. Subramania (1988), *Economic Aspects of British Rule in India*, Delhi: Gian Publishers.

Jevons, William Stanley (1875), *Money and the Mechanism of Exchange*, London: C. Kegan Paul (online edn. www.econlib.org/library/YPDBooks/Jevons/jvnMME.html, last accessed on 24 April 2011).

Kedia, K.L. and A. Sinha (1987), *Roots of Underdevelopment: A Peep into India's Colonial Past*, New Delhi: Indian Council for Social Sciences Research.

Keith, Arthur Berriedale (1937), *A Constitutional History of India, 1600-1935*, 2nd edn., London: Methuen & Co. Ltd.

Keynes, J.M. (1923), *A Tract on Monetary Reform*, London: Macmillan & Co.

Khan, Shafa'at Ahmed (1923), *The East India Trade in the XVIIth Century in its Political and Economic Aspects*, London: Humphrey Milford.

——— ed. (1927), *John Marshall in India: Notes and Observations in Bengal, 1668-1672*, London: Oxford University Press.

Kirby, C.F. (1867), *Adventures of an Arcot Rupee*, London: Saunders, Otley and Co.

Kling, Blair B. and M.N. Pearsons, eds. (1979), *The Age of Partnership: Europeans in Asia before Dominion*, Honolulu: University of Hawaii.

Kruger, Horst, ed. (1969), *Kunwar Mohammad Ashraf, An Indian Scholar and Revolutionary, 1903-1962*, Delhi: Peoples Publishing House.

Kumar, D., ed. (1983), *The Cambridge Economic History of India*, vol. II: *c. 1757-1970*, Cambridge: Cambridge University Press.

Kutty, G. Krishnan (1985), *Colonialism in India: Roots of Underdevelopment*, Delhi: Ashish Publishing House.

Lal, Deepak (1988-89), *The Hindu Equilibrium: Cultural Stability and Economic Stagnation, India, c. 1500 BC-AD 1980*, 2 vols., Oxford: Clarendon Press.

Lane Poole, S. (1892), *The Coins of the Moghul Emperors of Hindustan in the British Museum*, ed. Reginald Stuart Poole, London: The British Museum.

Less, W. Nassau, (1864), *The Drain of Silver to the East and the Currency of India*, London: W.H. Allen & Co.

Linecar, H.W.A. (1959), *British Commonwealth Coinage*, London: E. Benn.

Little, J.H. (1967), *House of Jagat Seth*, Calcutta: Calcutta Historical Society.

Logan, W. (1879), *A Collection of Treaties, Engagements and Other Papers of Importance Relating to British Affairs in Malabar*, Calicut: printed by A. Manuel.

Lombard, Denys and Jean Aubin, ed. (2000), *Asian Merchants and Businessmen in Indian Ocean and China Sea*, Chennai: Oxford University Press.

Mallick, B.S. (1991), *Money, Banking and Trade in Mughal India*, Jaipur: Rawat Publications.

Markovits, Claude (2000), *The Global World of Indian Merchants, 1750-1947: Traders of Sind from Bukhara to Panama*, Cambridge: Cambridge University Press.

Marshall, P.J. (1976), *East India Fortunes: The British in Bengal in the Eighteenth Century*, Oxford: Clarendon Press.

——— (1987), *Bengal: The British Bridgehead—Eastern India, 1740-1828*, Cambridge: Cambridge University Press.

——— (1993), *Trade and Conquest: Studies on the Rise of British Domination in India*, Aldershot (UK): Variorum.

——— ed. (1998), *The Oxford History of the British Empire*, vol. II: *The Eighteenth Century*, Oxford: Oxford University Press.

——— (2003), *The Eighteenth Century in Indian History: Evolution or Revolution?*, New Delhi: Oxford University Press.

Mazumdar, P.C. (1905), *Musnad of Murshidabad, 1704-1905*, Murshidabad: Sarodar Ray.

McGuire, John, Patrick Bertola and Peter Reeves, eds. (2001), *Evolution of the World Economy: Precious Metals and India*, New Delhi: Oxford University Press.

McMinn, C.W. (1904), *Indian Trade and Bullion Import in the Eighteenth Century*, Calcutta: Baptist Mission Press.

Mishra, Girish (1994), *An Economic History of Modern India*, Delhi: Pragati Publishers.

Mitra, Debendra Bijoy (1991), *Monetary System in the Bengal Presidency, 1757-1835*, Calcutta: K.P. Bagchi.

Moosvi, Shirin (1987), *Economy of the Mughal Empire, c. 1595: A Statistical Study*, New Delhi: Centre of Advanced Study in History, Aligarh Muslim University and Oxford University Press.

Morse, H.B. (1926-29), *Chronicles of the East India Company Trading to China, 1635-1834,* 5 vols., Oxford: Clarendon Press.

Mukherjee, Ramakrishna (1955), *The Rise and Fall of the East India Company*, Berlin: Deutscher Verlag der Wissenschaften.

Mukherjee, Rudarangshu (1977), *Trade and Empire in Awadh, 1765-1804*, Calcutta: Centre for Studies in Social Science.

Mukherjee, Rudrangshu and Lakshmi Subramanian, eds (2000), *Politics and Trade in the Indian Ocean World: Essays in Honour of Ashin Dasgupta*, New Delhi: Oxford University Press.

Mukund, Kanakalatha (1999), *The Trading World of the Tamil Merchant: Evolution of Merchant Capitalism in the Coromandel*, Hyderabad: Orient-Longman.

Nair, P. Thankappan (1999), *James Prinsep: Life and Works*, vol. I: *Background and Benares Period*, Calcutta: Firma K.L. Mukhopadhyay.

Nightingale, Pamela (1970), *Trade and Empire in Western India, 1784-1806*, Cambridge: Cambridge University Press.

NMML (1980), *Seminar on Aspects of the Economy, Society and Politics in Modern India, 1900-1950* (Mimeographed), New Delhi: Nehru Memorial Museum & Library.

Om Prakash (1994), *Precious Metals and Commerce: The Dutch East India Company in the Indian Ocean Trade*, Aldershot (UK): Variorum.

——— (1997), *European Commercial Expansion in Early Modern Asia*, Aldershot (UK): Variorum.

Om Prakash and Denys Lombard, eds. (1999), *Commerce and Culture in the Bay of Bengal*, New Delhi: Manohar and Indian Council of Historical Research.

Pant, D. (1978), *The Commercial Policy of the Mughals*, rpt., Delhi: Idarah-e-Adabiyat.

Pargellis, S. and D.J. Medley, eds. (1977), *Bibliography of British History: The 18th Century, 1714-1789*, Sussex (UK): Harvester Press.

Parkinson, C. Northcote (1937), *Trade in the Eastern Seas, 1793-1813*, Cambridge: Cambridge University Press.

Parshad, I. Durga (1932), *Some Aspects of Indian Foreign Trade, 1757-1893*, London: P.S. King & Son.

Perlin, Frank (1993), *The Invisible City: Monetary, Administrative and Popular Infrastructures in Asia and Europe, 1500-1900*, Aldershot (UK): Variorum.

——— (1994), *Unbroken Landscape: Commodity, Category, Sign and Identity: Their Production as Myth and Knowledge, from 1550*, Aldershot (UK): Variorum.

Philips, C.H. (1961), *The East India Company, 1784-1834*, Bombay: Oxford University Press.

Pohl, H., ed. (1990), *The European Discovery of the World and its Economic Effects on Pre-Industrial Society*, Verlag, Stuttgart: Franz Steiner.

Prabhakaran, M.P. (1990), *The Historical Origin of India's Underdevelopment: A World System Perspective*, USA: Lanham (MD).

Pridmore, Major F. (1975), *The Coins of the British Commonwealth of Nations to the End of the Reign of George VI, 1952:* pt. 4: *India*, vol. 1: *East India Company Presidency, Series, c. 1642-1835*, London: Spink and Son.

——— (1980), *The Coins of the British Commonwealth of Nations to the End of the Reign of George VI, 1952:* pt. 4: *India*, vol. 2: *East India Company 1835-58; Imperial period 1858-1947*, London: Spink and Son.

Prinsep, James (1858), *Useful Tables illustrative of the Coins, Weights and Measures of British India*, ed. Edward Thomas, London: John Murray

Rae, John (1895), *Life of Adam Smith*, London: Macmillan

Ramachandran, C. (1980), *East India Company and South Indian Economy*, Madras: New Era Publications.

Raman Rao, A.V. (1958), *Economic Development of Andhra Pradesh (1766-1957)*, Bombay: Popular Book Depot.

Ranade, Mahadev Govind (1915), *Miscellaneous Writings of Late Mr. Mahadev Govind Ranade, published by Mrs. Ramabai Ranade with an introduction by D.E. Wacha*, Bombay: The Manoranjan Press.

Ray, Rajat K., ed. (1992), *Entrepreneurship and Industry in India, 1800-1947*, New Delhi: Oxford University Press.

Raychaudhuri, Tapan, ed. (1960), *Contributions to Indian Economic History*, vol. I, Calcutta: Firma K.L. Mukhopadhyay.

Raychaudhuri, Tapan, and Irfan Habib, eds. (1982), *The Cambridge Economic History of India*, vol. I: *c. 1200-c. 1750*, Cambridge: Cambridge University Press.

Richards, D., ed. (1970), *Islam and the Trade of Asia*, Philadelphia: University of Pennsylvania Press and B. Cassirer.

Richards, John F., ed. (1983), *Precious Metals in the Later Medieval and Early Modern Worlds*, Durham: Carolina Academic Press.

——— ed. (1987), *The Imperial Monetary System of Mughal India*, New Delhi: Oxford University Press.

——— (1993), *Power, Administration and Finance in Mughal India*, Aldershot (U.K.): Variorum.

——— (1995), *The New Cambridge History of India*, vol. 1.5: *The Mughal Empire*, Cambridge: Cambridge University Press.

——— (2003), *The Unending Frontier: An Environmental History of the Early Modern*, California: University of California Press.

Rodgers, Charles J. (1894), *Catalogue of Coins of the Indian Museum Calcutta*, Part II: *The Mughal Emperors of India, the East India Company, the Native States, the Indian Empire Medals and Tokens*, Calcutta: Indian Museum.

Ross, R. and G.J. Telkamp, eds. (1984), *Colonial Cities: Essays in Urbanism in a Colonial Context*, Derdrecht (The Netherlands): Martinus Nijhoff.

Rothermund, Dietmar (1981), *Asian Trade and European Expansion in the Age of Mercantilism*, New Delhi: Manohar.

——— (1983), *The Indian Economy under the British Rule and Other Essays*, New Delhi: Manohar.

——— (1988), *An Economic History of India, From Pre-colonial Times to 1986*, New York: Routledge.

Roy, Tirthankar (2000), *The Economic History of India, 1857-1947*, New Delhi: Oxford University Press.

Sandes, E.W.C. (1935), *The Military Engineer in India*, 2 vols., Chatham (UK): The Institution of Royal Engineers.

Sanyal, Suprakash (1979), *Benaras and the English East India Company, 1764-1795*, Calcutta: World Press.

Sarda Raju, A. (1961), *Economic Conditions in the Madras Presidency, 1800-1850*, Madras: Madras University Press.

Sarkar, Jadunath (1917), *Economics of British India*, Calcutta: M.C. Sarkar & Sons.

——— (1988), *Fall of the Mughal Empire*, vol. 1: *1739-1754*, 4th edn., New Delhi: Orient Longman.

——— (1991), *Fall of the Mughal Empire*, vol. 2: *1754-1771*, 4th edn., New Delhi: Orient Longman.

——— (1991), *Fall of the Mughal Empire*, vol. 3: *1771-1788*, 4th edn., New Delhi: Orient Longman.

——— (1992), *Fall of the Mughal Empire*, vol. 4: *1789-1803*, 2nd edn., New Delhi: Orient Longman.

Satish Chandra (1972), *Political letters of a Kingmaker at Delhi during 18th Century (Balmukund Nama) by Mehta Balmukund*, Bombay: Asia Publishing House and Centre for Advanced Studies, Aligarh Muslim University.

——— (1982), *The 18th Century in India: Its Economy and the role of the Marathas, the Jats, the Sikhs and the Afghans*, Calcutta: K.P. Bagchi.

——— ed. (1987), *Essays in Medieval Indian Economic History*, Delhi: Munshiram Manoharlal.

Sen, Ranjit (1988), *Economics of Revenue Maximization in Bengal, 1757-1793*, Calcutta: Nalanda Publications.

Sen, S.R. (1957), *The Economics of Sir James Steuart*, London: London School of Economics and Political Science, University of London.

Sen, Sudipta (1998), *Empire of Free Trade: The East India Company and the Making of the Colonial Market Place*, Philadelphia: University of Philadelphia Press.

Sen, Sunil Kumar (1969), *Edmund Burke on Indian Economy*, Calcutta: Progressive Publishers.

Seshadri, R.K. (1985), *The Indian Financial System: With Particular Reference to Currency, Government, Exchange and Other Connected Accounts*, Madras: Institute for Financial Management and Research.

Sharif, K.N. (1979), *Hundred Years of Indian Coinage*, Bangalore: Libra Publishing House.

Siddiqi, Asiya, ed. (1995), *Trade and Finance in Colonial India, 1750-1860*, Delhi: Oxford University Press.

Singh, O.P. (1975), *Surat and its Trade in the Second half of the 17th Century*, Delhi: University of Delhi.

Singh, Paras Nath (2007 VS/1943/44 AD), *Jagat Seth Aur Bengal mein Angrezi Rajya ki Neevein* (in Hindi), Prayag: Bharati Bhandar.

Sinha, H. (1927), *Early European Banking in India*, London: Macmillan & Co.

——— (n.d.), *Banking in the Days of Hastings*, n.p.

Sinha, J.C. (1927), *Economic Annals of Bengal*, London: Macmillan & Co.

Sinha, N.K. (1956), *Economic History of Bengal*, vol. I: *From Plassey to Permanent Settlement*, Calcutta: Firma K.L. Mukhopadhyay.

——— (1970), *Economic History of Bengal*, vol. III: *1793-1848*, Calcutta: Firma K.L. Mukhopadhyay.

Sinha, Nirmal Chandra (1946), *Studies in Indo-British Economy Hundred Years Ago*, Calcutta: A. Mukherjee.

Spear, Percival (1978), *The Oxford History of Modern India, 1740-1975*, 2nd edn., New Delhi: Oxford University Press.

Spengler, Joseph J. (1972), *Indian Economic Thought*, Durham: Duke University Press.

Spufford, Peter (1988), *Money and its Use in Medieval Europe*, Cambridge: Cambridge University Press.

Stein, Burton (1980), *Peasant State and Society in Medieval South India*, New Delhi: Oxford University Press.

——— ed. (1992), *The Making of Agrarian Policy in British India, 1770-1900*, New Delhi: Oxford University Press.

Sturges, R.P. (Comp.) (1975), *Economists' Papers, 1750-1950: A Guide to Archive and Other Manuscript Sources for the History of British and Economic Thought*, Durham: Duke University Press.

Subrahmanyam, Sanjay (1990), *The Poilitical Economy and Commerce: Southern India, 1500-1650*, Cambridge: Cambridge University Press.

——— ed. (1990a), *Merchants, Markets and the State in Early Modern India*, New Delhi: Oxford University Press.

——— (1994), *Money and the Market in India, 1000-1700*, New Delhi: Oxford University Press.

Subramanian, Lakshmi (1996), *Indigenous Capital and Imperial Expansion: Bombay, Surat and the West Coast*, New Delhi: Oxford University Press.

Supple, Barry E. (1959), *Commercial Crisis and Changes in England, 1600-1642: A Study in the Instability of a Mercantile Economy*, Cambridge: Cambridge University Press.

Sutherland, Lucy R. (1952), *The East India Company in Eighteenth Century Politics*, Oxford: Clarendon Press.

Tandon, Prakash (1989), *The Banking Century: A Short History of Banking in India and the Pioneer—Punjab National Bank*, New Delhi: Penguin.

——— ed. (1991), *The Political Economy of Merchant Empires: State Power and World Trade, 1350-1750*, New York: Cambridge University Press.

Tchitcherov, Alexander I. (1998), *India: Changing Economic Structure in the Sixteenth to Seventeenth Centuries: Outline History of Crafts and Trade*, New Delhi: Manohar.

Temple, Richard (1883), *Oriental Experience: A Selection of Essays and Addresses Delivered on Various Occasions*, London: John Murray.

Thomas, Edward (1866), *The Initial Coinage of Bengal*, Hertford: Stephen Austin.

Thomas, P.J. and B.N. Pillai (1933), *Economic Depression in Madras Presidency, from 1820-1854*, Madras: Madras University.

Thompson, Peter R. (2010), *The East India Company and its Coins*, Devon (UK): Token Publishing.

Thornton, Edward (1854), *A Gazetteer of the Territories under the Government of the East-India Company, and of the Native States on the Continent of India*, London: William H. Allen and Company.

Thurston, Edgar (1890), *History of the Coinage of the Territories of the East India Company in the Indian Peninsula and Catalogue of the Coins in the Madras Museum*, Madras: Government Press.

Tracy, James (1990), *Rise of the Merchant Empires: Long-Distance Trade in the Early Modern World, 1350-1750*, New York: Cambridge University Press.

Tripathi, Amales (1979), *Trade and Finance in the Bengal Presidency, 1793-1833*, Calcutta: Oxford University Press.

Tripathi, Dwijendra, ed. (1987), *State and Business in India: A Historical Perspective*, New Delhi: Manohar.

——— (1991), *Business and Politics in India: A Historical Perspective*, New Delhi: Manohar.

Vickers, D. (1960), *Studies in the Theory of Money, 1690-1776*, London: Peter Owen Ltd.

Vilar, Pierre (1976), *A History of Gold and Money, 1450-1920*, London: Atlantic Highlands.

Watson, Ian Bruce (1980), *English Private Trade in India, 1659-1760*, New Delhi: Vikas.

Whiteway, R.S. (1967), *The Rise of the Portuguese Power in India, 1497-1550*, London: Susil Gupta.

Williams, Judith Blow (1972), *British Commercial Policy and Trade Expansion, 1750-1850*, Oxford: Clarendon Press.

Wilson, Charles (1966), *Anglo-Dutch Commerce and Finance in the Eighteenth Century*, Cambridge: Cambridge University Press.

Wilson, Charles and Geoffrey Parker, eds. (1977), *An Introduction to the Sources of European Economic History, 1500-1800*, vol. 1: *Western Europe*, London: Weidenfeld and Nicolson.

Wright, H.R.C. (1961), *East Indian Economic Problems in the Age of Cornwallis and Raffles*, London: Luzac & Co.

Yang, Anand (1998), *Bazar India: Markets, Society and the Colonial State in Gangatic Bihar*, California: University of California Press.

Yule, Henry and A.C. Burnel (1886), *Hobson-Jobson: being a glossary of Anglo-Indian colloquial words and phrases, and of kindred terms; etymological, historical, geographical, and discursive*, London: John Murray.

ARTICLES*

Ambirajan, S. (1986), 'The Pattern of Our Past: How the Economic History of India is being Written', *IBR*, vol. 17.2, pp. 26-39.

*Including chapters contributed in edited works.

Anon (1908), 'The Monopolies of the East India Company', *Modern Review*, vol. 4.2, pp. 95-100.

——— (1884), 'Asiatic Copper Coins struck under British influence', *Scott's Coin Collector's Journal (USA)*, vol. 9, pp. 97-119, 135-148, 169, 177.

Arasaratnam, S. (1979), 'Trade and Political Dominion in South India, 1750-1790: Changing British-Indian Relationships', *MAS*, vol. 13.1, pp. 19-40.

Ali, M. Athar (1975), 'The Passing of Empire: The Mughal Case', *Modern Asian Studies*, vol. 9.3, pp. 699-710.

Awasthi, D. (1979), 'Landmarks in the Development of Indian Coinage in Modern Times', *JAINS*, vol. 2, p. 36.

Bagchi, Amiya Kumar (1985), 'Transition from Indian to British Indian Systems of Money and Banking, 1800-1850', *MAS*, vol. 19.3, pp. 501-19.

——— (1997), 'Contested Hegemonies and Laissez Faire: Controversies over the Monetary Standard in India at the High Noon of the British Empire', *Review*, vol. 20.1, pp. 19-76.

Bamzai, P.N.K. (1931), 'Kashmir During the Mughal Period: An Economic Survey', *IJE*, vol. 11.4, pp. 365-8.

——— (1932), 'Kashmir under the Sikhs (1819-1846): An Economic Survey', *IJE*, vol. 13.1, pp. 35-58.

Banerji, D.N. (1934), 'Some Aspects of the Post-Diwani Land Revenue System in Bengal and Bihar (between 1765 and 1769) Part I', *IJE*, vol. 14.3, pp. 321-38.

——— (1936), 'Some Aspects of the Post-Diwani Land Revenue System in Bengal and Bihar (in 1772) Part II', *IJE*, vol. 16.4, pp. 643-57.

——— (1991), 'Administration in British Territories in India (1707-1818)' in *The History and Culture of the Indian People*, vol. VIII: *The Maratha Supremacy*, 2nd edn, ed. R.C. Majumdar and V.G. Dighe, Bombay: Bhartiya Vidya Bhavan, pp. 578-639.

Banerji, P.N. (1927), 'Deficits and Surpluses in the Accounts of the East India Company', *IJE*, vol. 8.1, pp. 1-26.

Barbour, V. (1930), 'Dutch and English Merchant Shipping in the Seventeenth Century', *EHR*, vol. 2, pp. 261-90.

Basu, D. (1973), 'The Banian and the British in Calcutta, 1800-1850', *BPP*, vol. 92, pp. 157-70.

Basu, K.K. (1944), 'Currency and Coinage in Bihar under the Hon'ble Company', *JBRS*, vol. 30, p. 237.

Bayly, C.A. (2004), 'Pre-Colonial Indian Merchant and Rationality', in *India's Colonial Encounter: Essays in Memory of Eric Stokes*, 2nd revised and enlarged edn, ed. Mushirul Hasan and Narayani Gupta, New Delhi: Manohar, pp. 39-60.

Bhandare, Shailendra (2007), 'Money on the Move: The Rupee and the

Indian Ocean Region', in *Cross Currents and Community Networks: The History of the Indian Ocean World*, ed. Himanshu Prabha Ray and Edward A. Alpers, New Delhi: Oxford University Press, pp. 206-44.

——— (2000), 'Bangalore—A New Mint for the East India Company Coinage', *ONSNL*, no. 164, pp. 26-7.

Bhandare, Shailendra and Paul Stevens (2002), '"Bombay Billys": The British Coinage for the Malabar Coast—A Reappraisal', *ONSNL*, Supplement no. 172, pp. 1-22.

Bhandarkar, D.R. (1930), 'Shipping in Bombay in 1795-96', *PIHRC* (Patna Session), vol. 13, pp. 73-84.

Biddulph, C.H. (1959), 'Rupees issued by the English and French East India Companies and the Nawabs of Arcot in the 18th and 19th centuries', *JNSI*, vol. 21, p. 146.

——— (1959a), 'Tokens resembling coins of the East India Company', *JNSI*, vol. 21.2, pp. 176-8.

——— (1959b), 'Coin-weights of the East India Company', *JNSI*, vol. 21.2, pp. 179-80.

——— (1960), 'Coin-weights of the East India Company', *JNSI*, vol. 22, pp. 293-4.

——— (1966), 'Copper coins of the East India Company of Chinapatam (Madras) Mint issued in the name of Aurangzeb Alamgir', *JNSI*, vol. 28, pp. 223-5.

Borpujari, Jitendra G. (1973), 'The Impact of the Transit Duty System in British India', *IESHR*, vol. 10.3, pp. 218-41.

Bowen, H.V. (1988), 'A Question of Sovereignty? The Bengal Land Revenue Issue, 1765-67', *JICH*, vol. 16, pp. 155-76.

——— (2002), 'Sinews of Trade and Empire: the Supply of Commodity Exports to the East India Company during the late Eighteenth Century', *EHR*, vol. 55.3, pp. 466-86.

Brenning, Joseph J. (1977), 'Merchants and the European Enclaves of Seventeenth Century Coromandel', *MAS*, vol. 11.3, pp. 321-40.

Brodkin, E.I. (1973), 'British India and the Abuses of Power: Rohilkhand under Company Rule', *IESHR*, vol. 10.2, pp. 129-56.

Brown, Victor (1971), 'The Origin and Significance of the East India Company's Balemark and its Application to Company's Coinage', *SCMB*, vol. 635, 248-50.

Chakrabarti, Shubhra (1994), 'Collaboration and Resistance: Bengal Merchants and the English East India Company, 1757-1833', *SIH*, vol. 10.2, pp. 105-29.

——— (1997), 'Intransigent Shroffs and the East India Company's Currency Reforms in Bengal', *IESHR*, vol. 34.1, pp. 69-94.

——— (2004), 'The English East India Company and the Indigenous Sloop Merchants of Bengal: Akrur Dutta and His Family, 1757-1857', *SIH*, vol. 20.1, pp. 131-57.

——— (2005), 'Colonized Trade: Major Shifts in India's Trade and Commercial Organizations, 1700-1860', in *History of Science, Philosophy and Culture in Indian Civilization*, vol. VIII, part 3: *Economic History of India from Eighteenth to Twentieth Century*, ed. Binay Bhushan Chaudhuri, New Delhi: Centre for Studies in Civilizations, pp. 57-106.

Chaloner, W.H. (1975), 'Currency Problems of the British Empire, 1814-1914', in *Great Britain and her world, 1750-1914: Essays in honour of W.O. Henderson*, ed. Barrie M. Redcliff, Manchester: Manchester University Press, pp. 179-208.

Chandra, Bipan (1981), 'Karl Marx, his Theories of Asian Societies, and Colonial Rule', *Review*, vol. 5.1, pp. 13-91.

Chaterjee, Kumkum (1993), 'Collaboration and Conflict: Bankers and Early Colonial Rule in India, 1757-1813', *IESHR*, vol. 30.3, pp. 283-310.

Chaterjee, Suranjan (1985), 'Economic History or an Apologia for Colonialism', *Social Scientist*, vol. 13.1, pp. 54-70.

Chaudhuri, Binay Bhushan (1975), 'Land Market in Eastern India, 1793-1940, Part I: The Movement of Land Prices', *IESHR*, vol. 12.1, pp. 1-42.

Chaudhuri, K.N. (1963), 'The East India Company and the Export of Treasure in the Early Seventeenth Century', *EHR* (Second Series), vol. 16.1, pp. 23-38.

——— (1966), 'India's Foreign Trade and the Cessation of the East India Company's Trading Activities, 1828-40', *EHR* (Second Series), vol. 19.2, pp. 345-63.

——— (1968a), 'Treasure and Trade Balances: The East India Company's Export Trade, 1660-1720', *EHR* (Second Series), vol. 21.3, pp. 480-502.

——— (1968b), 'India's International Economy in the Nineteenth Century: A Historical Survey', *MAS*, vol. 2.1, pp. 31-50.

——— (1975), 'The Economic and Monetary Problem of European Trade with Asia during the Seventeenth and Eighteenth Centuries', *JEEH*, vol. 4, pp. 323-56.

——— (1981), 'The World-System East of Longitude 20: The European Role in Asia, 1500-1750', *Review*, vol. 5.2, pp. 219-45.

Chaudhuri, Sushil (1970), 'The Myth of the East India Company's Trading Privileges in Bengal, 1651-1686', *BPP*, vol. 89, pp. 287-92.

——— (1971), 'The Financing of Investments in Bengal: 1650-1720', *IESHR*, vol. 8.2, pp. 109-33.

——— (1971), 'Bengal Merchants and Commercial Organisation in the Second Half of the Seventeenth Century', *BPP*, vol. 90.2, pp. 182-216.

——— (1988), 'Merchants, Companies and Rulers: Bengal in the Eighteenth Century', *JESHO*, vol. 31.1, pp. 74-109.

Chaudhury, Vasant and Parimal Ray (1980), 'A Curious Quarter Pagoda of the East India Company', *JNSI*, vol. 42.1, pp. 55-7.

Cheesman, David (1982), 'The Omnipresent Bania: Rural Moneylenders in Nineteenth-Century Sind', *MAS*, vol. 16.3, pp. 445-62.

Chung, Tan (1973), 'The Britain-China-India Trade Triangle, 1771-1840', *PIHC* (Chandigarh Session), vol. 34.2, pp. 77-92.

Cohn, B.S. (1964), 'The Role of Gosains in the Economy of 18th and 19th Century Upper India', *IESHR*, vol. 1.4, pp. 175-82.

——— (2003), 'Political Systems in Eighteenth-Century India: The Banaras Region', in Marshall (2003), pp. 123-36.

Conell, A.K. (1896), 'Financial Condition of India and the Closing of the Mints', *JEIA*, vol. 28.5, pp. 33-46.

Cribb, Joe (1978), 'East India Company Arkat rupee of Muhammad Shah', *ND*, vol. 2.2, pp. 79-82.

Cunningham, Alexander (1840), 'Notice of Some Counterfeit Bactrian Coins', *JASB*, vol. 9, pp. 393-6, 543-4.

——— (1840a), 'Second Notice of Some Forged Coins of Bactrians and Indo Scythians', *JASB*, vol. 9, pp. 1217-30.

Dale, L.J. (1948), 'The East India Company and its Coinage', *The New Zealand Numismatic Journal*, vol. 4.3, pp. 81-90.

Das, Harihar (1926), 'Sir William Norris at Masulipatam', *JIH*, vol. 5.2, pp. 210-34.

Das, Nabagopal (1933), 'A Glimpse of Banking Activities in India during the First half of the Nineteenth Century', *IJE*, vol. 14.1, pp. 29-52.

Dasgupta, Ashin (1968), 'Some Attitudes among 18th Century Merchants', in *Ideas in History* [Proceedings of a Seminar on Ideas, Motivating Social and Religious Movements and Political and Economic Policies during the 18th and 19th Centuries], ed. Bisheshwar Prasad, London: Asia Publishing House, pp. 165-72.

Datta, K.K. (1931), 'Markets and Prices of Articles in Bengal (1740-1765)', *IJE*, vol. 9.4, pp. 669-82.

——— (1935), 'Economic Importance of Behar during the mid-Eighteenth Century', *IJE*, vol. 15.4, pp. 505-9.

——— (1951), 'India's Trade with Europe and America in the Eighteenth Century', *JESHO*, vol. 2.3, pp. 313-23.

——— (1961), 'Evidence of a newly discovered Hindi Manuscript about the Jagat Seths', *PIHRC* (Chandigarh Session), vol. 36.2, pp. 135-8.

——— (1961), 'Historical Importance of Some Unpublished Bhagalpur Records', *BPP*, vol. 80.1, pp. 1-15.

Datta, Rajat (1999), 'From Medieval to Colonial: Markets, Territoriality and Transition in Eighteenth Century Bengal', *MHJ*, vol. 2.1, pp. 143-67.

——— (2003), 'Commercialisation, Tribute and Transition from Late Mughal to Early Colonial India', *MHJ*, vol. 6.2, pp. 259-91.

——— (2004), 'Eighteenth Century in Indian History', in *History of Indian Economy*, Block 5: 'Expansion and Growth of Medieval Economy, part 2', New Delhi: Indira Gandhi National Open University, pp. 83-106.

Dayal Das (1958), 'First Uniform Currency for India', *PIHRC* (Bhubaneswar Session), vol. 33.2, pp. 65-71.

De, Amalendu (1965), 'Some Facts on the Early History of Saving Banks in Bengal', *The Modern Review*, vol. 47, pp. 195-8.

De, Sushil (1952), 'The Cowrie Currency in India', *OHRJ*, vol. 1.1, pp. 1-10.

——— (1954), 'British Conquest of Orissa and Early British Administration, Parts 1 & 2', *OHRJ*, vol. 3.2, pp. 118-26, 157-62.

De Ligt, L. (2003), 'Taxes, Trade and the Circulation of Coin: The Roman Empire, Mughal India and T'ang China Compared', *MHJ*, vol. 6.2, pp. 231-48.

Deshpande, Y.K. (1929), 'Revenue Administration of Berar in the Reign of Aurangzeb (1679 A.D.)', *PIHRC* (Gwalior Session), vol. 12, pp. 81-7.

Deyell, John S. (1976), 'Numismatic Methodology in the Estimation of Mughal Currency Output', *IESHR*, vol. 137.3, pp. 393-401.

——— (1987), 'The Development of Akbar's Currency System and Monetary Integration of the Conquered Kingdoms', in Richards (1987), pp. 13-67.

——— (2010), 'Cowries and coins: The dual monetary system of the Bengal Sultanate', *IESHR*, vol. 47.1 (2010), pp. 63-106.

Deyell, John S. and R.E. Frykenberg (1982), 'Sovereignty and the "SIKKA" under Company Raj: Minting Prerogative and Imperial Legitimacy in India', *IESHR*, vol. 19.1, pp. 1-25.

Divekar, V.V. (1982), 'The Emergence of an Indigenous Business Class in Maharashtra in the Eighteenth Century', *MAS*, vol. 16.3, pp. 427-43.

Dodwell, Henry H. (1921), 'Substitution of Silver for Gold in South India', *IJE*, vol. 3.2, pp. 183-204.

Dyroff, Jan M. (1978), 'East India Company Provided Chapter in Coin History', *Canadian Coin News*, vol. 16.8, p. 11.

Esteban, Javier Cuenca (2001), 'The British Balance of Payments, 1772-1820: India Transfers and War Finance', *EHR*, vol. 54.1, pp. 58-86.

Flynn, Dennis O. (1991), 'A Model of Minting and Melting Coins', in Cauwenberghe (1991), p. 521.

Furber, Holden (1940), 'The United Company of Merchants Trading into the East Indies, 1783-1796', *EHR*, vol. 10, p. 138.

——— (1953), 'East India Company's Financial records', *The Indian Archives*, vol. 7.2, pp. 100-4.

——— (1967), 'Glimpses of Life and Trade in 1720-1770', *BPP*, vol. 86.2, pp. 13-23.

Ganguli, B.N. (1965), 'Dadabhai Naoroji and the Mechanism of "External Drain"', *IESHR*, vol. 2.2, pp. 85-102.

Garg, Sanjay (1990), 'Establishment of Calcutta Mint, 1757', *PIHC*, 51st Session, Calcutta, pp. 383-92.

——— (1992), 'The Closure of Delhi Mint, A.D. 1818', in *Indian Numismatics, History, Art and Culture: Essays in Honour of Dr. Parmeshwari Lal Gupta*, ed. D.W. MacDowall, Savita Sharma and Sanjay Garg, vol. 2, Delhi: Agam Kala Prakashan, pp. 233-40.

——— (1998), '"Sikka" and the Crown: Genesis of the Native Coinage Act, 1876', *IESHR*, vol. 35.4, pp. 359-80.

——— (2001), 'Prinsep and the Currency Reform', *JAS*, vol. 43.3, pp. 40-55.

——— (2007), 'Non-metallic Currencies in Indian Ocean Trade and Economies', in *Cross Currents and Community Networks: The History of the Indian Ocean World*, ed. Himanshu Prabha Ray and Edward A. Alpers, New Delhi: Oxford University Press, pp. 245-62.

Ganguli, B.N. (1958), 'India: A Colonial Economy (1757-1947)', *Enquiry* (Old Series), vol. 1, pp. 50-61.

Ghosh, Kalpana (1980), 'A new East India Company token', *JNSI*, vol. 42.1, pp. 49-51.

Ghoshal, H.R. (1947), 'Currency Situation in Bengal at the End of the 18th Century', *JBRS*, vol. 33, p. 170.

——— (1962), 'Interesting details from Bengal Board of Trade Records (1793-1803)', *PIHRC* (Poona), vol. 37.2, pp. 55-60.

Glamann, Kristof (1957), 'Bengal and the World Trade about 1700', *BPP*, vol. 76, pp. 30-9.

Gokhale, B.G. (1973), 'Virji Vora', *IBR*, vol. 6.3-4, pp. 22-31.

Guha, Sumit (1996), 'Potentates, Traders, Peasants in Eighteenth Century Western India, *c.* 1700-1870', in *Institutions and Economic Change in South Asia*, ed. Burton Stein and Sanjay Subrahmanyam, New Delhi: Oxford University Press, pp. 71-84.

Gupta, P.L. (1959), 'Silver Coins of Bombay in the Name of William II and Mary', *JNSI*, vol. 21, p. 174.

——— (1977), 'An Unknown Rupee Pattern of East India Company', *ND*, vol. 1.2, p. 66.

Gupta, R.K. and C. Ramachandran (1972), 'The Land Revenue Policy of the East India Company in Madras Presidency', *IBR*, vol. 5.4, pp. 55-60.

——— (1973), 'The Ryotwari System of the East India Company', *IBR*, vol. 6.1, pp. 82-7.

——— (1974), 'The Revenue Policy of the East India Company in Madras', *IBR*, vol. 7.1-2, pp. 78-83.

Gupta, V.B. (1991), 'Imports of Treasure and Surat's Trade in the 17th Century', in Cauwenberghe (1991), pp. 455-72.

Habib, Irfan (1960), 'Banking in Mughal India', Raychaudhuri 1960, pp. 1-20.

——— (1960a), 'Merchant Communities in Pre-colonial India', in Tracy (1960), pp. 371-99.

——— (1961), 'The Currency System of the Mughal Empire, 1556-1707', *MIQ*, vol. 4, pp. 1-21.

——— (1963), Problems of the Study of the Economic History of Medieval India, in *Problems of Historical Writings in India* [Proceedings of the Seminar held at the India International Centre, New Delhi], pp. 76-81.

——— (1969a), 'Potentiality of Capitalist Development in the Economy of the Mughal India', *JEH*, vol. 29.1, pp. 32-78.

——— (1969b), 'Usury in Medieval India', *CSSH*, vol. 6.4, pp. 393-419.

——— (1972), 'The System of Bills of Exchange (Hundi) in the Mughal Empire', *PIHC* (Muzaffarpur Session), vol. 33, pp. 290-303.

——— (1975), 'Colonialization of Indian Economy', *Social Scientist*, vol. 3.32, pp. 23-53.

——— (1985), 'Studying a Colonial Economy without Perceiving Colonialism', *MAS*, vol. 19.3, pp. 355-81.

——— (1987), 'A System of Trimetallism in the Age of the "Price Revolution": Effects of the Silver Influx on the Mughal Monetary System', in Richards 1987, pp. 137-70.

——— (2003), 'The Eighteenth Century in Indian Economic History' [presented at the Conference 'The Eighteenth Century as a Category in Asian History', 1995], in Marshall 2003, pp. 100-22.

Haider, Najaf (1996), 'Precious Metal Flows and Currency Circulation in the Mughal Empire', *JESHO*, vol. 39.3, pp. 298-364.

——— (1997), 'The Disappearance of Coin Production in 1580s?: A Note on the Alf Coins', in *Akbar and his India*, ed. Irfan Habib, New Delhi: Oxford University Press, pp. 55-65.

——— (1999), 'The Quantity Theory and Mughal Monetary History', *MHJ*, vol. 2.2, pp. 309-48.

——— (2002), 'The Monetary Basis of Credit and Banking Instruments in the Mughal Empire', in Bagchi 2002, pp. 58-83.

——— (2003), 'Mughals and Mahmudis: The Incorporation of Gujarat into the Mughal Monetary Syatem', in *Negotiating India's Past: Essays in Memory of Partha Sarthi Gupta*, ed. B. Pati, B.P. Sahu and T.K. Venkatasubramanian, New Delhi: Tulika Books, pp. 134-52.

——— (2004), 'Business Practices and Monetary History', in *History of Indian Economy*, Block 5: 'Expansion and Growth of Medieval Economy, part 2', New Delhi: Indira Gandhi National Open University, pp. 16-36.

——— (2005), 'The Monetary Integration of India under the Mughal Empire', in Habib 2005, pp. 129-43.

——— (2007), 'The Network of Monetary Exchange in the Indian Ocean Trade, 1200-1700', in *Cross Currents and Community Networks*, ed. Himanshu Prabha Ray and Edward A. Alpers, New Delhi: Oxford University Press, pp. 181-205.

——— (2009), 'Standardization and Empire: A Study of the Exchange Rates of Mughal Currencies', in *Mind Over Matter: Essays on Mentalities in Medieval India*, ed. D.N. Jha and Eugenia Vanina, New Delhi: Tulika Books, pp. 40-56.

Hall, Kenneth R. (1999), 'Coinage, Trade and Economy in Early South India and its Southeast Asian Neighbours', *IESHR*, vol. 36.4, pp. 431-59.

Hamashita, Takeshi (1991), 'Asian Trade network and Silver Circulation', in Cauwenberghe 1991, pp. 47-54.

Hariharan, Shantha (2003), 'Town Revenues and Taxes in Eighteenth Century Gujarat: An English East India Company Document', *South Asia Research*, vol. 23.2, pp. 171-9.

Harrison, F.C. (1893), 'The Past Action of the Government of India with Regard to Gold', *EJ*, vol. 3.9, pp. 52-61.

Hasan, Aziza (1969), 'The Silver Currency Output of the Mughal Empire and the Prices in India during the 16th and 17th Centuries', *IESHR*, vol. 6.1, pp. 85-116.

——— (1970), 'Mughal Silver Currency: A Reply', *IESHR*, vol. 7.1, pp. 151-60.

Hatekar, Neeraj (2002), 'Indian Political Economy and the Early British Industrial Revolution: A Fresh Look for 1753-1794', *IESHR*, vol. 39.4, pp. 397-415.

Hatherly, N.J. (1977), 'The Coinage of India: East India Company Issues', *American Numismatic Journal*, vol. 17.1, pp. 67-71.

Jackson, R.P. (1908), 'Some Copper Coins Issued by the East India Company and Other European Powers in Southern India', *BNJ*, vol. 5, pp. 341-46.

Jha, J.S. (1959), 'Some Unpublished Records on the State of Currency in Bihar', *PIHC* (Gauhati Session), vol. 22, p. 390.

Johnston, J.M.C. (1903), 'Coinage of the East India Company', *NC* (4th Series), vol. 3, pp. 71-98.

Kala, Satish Chandra (1947), 'A Rude Imitation Coin of Heliokles', *JNSI*, vol. 9.1, p. 26.

Kale, V.G. (1934), 'Economic Conditions in Maharashtra at the Advent of British Rule', *IJE*, vol. 16.3, pp. 474-80.

——— (1937), 'Money Market in Maharashtra Two Centuries Ago', *IJE*, vol. 17.3, pp. 241-8.

Kotwal, C.E. (1921), 'A Bombay half-rupee of Charles II', *NS*, vol. 35, p. 17.

Kulkarni, A.R. (2002), 'Money and Banking under the Marathas: Seventeenth Century to AD 1848', in Bagchi (2002), pp. 93-117.

Lawson, P. (1982), 'Parliament and the First East India Enquiry, 1767', *Parliamentary History*, vol. 1, pp. 99-114.

Leonard, Karen (1979), 'The "Great Firm" Theory of the Decline of the Mughal Empire', *CSSH*, vol. 21.2, pp. 151-67.

——— (1981), 'Indigenous Banking Firms in Mughal India: A Reply', *CSSH*, vol. 23.2, pp. 309-13.

Lingen, Jan (1979), 'Note on Earlier Madras Pagoda Struck by the British East India Company', *Num. Cir.*, vol. 87.1, pp. 2-3.

——— (1980), 'Rupees with Mint Name Arkat', *SCMB*, vol. 737, pp. 12-15.

Mahapatra, Manorama (1952), 'General Economic Conditions of Orissa', *OHRJ*, vol. 1.2, pp. 171-7.

Malik, Zahiruddin (1967), 'Financial Problems of the Mughal Government during Farrukhsiyar's Reign', *IESHR*, vol. 4.3, pp. 265-76.

——— (1990), 'The Core and the Periphery: A Contribution to the Debate on the Eighteenth Century', *PIHC* (Calcutta Session), pp. 169-99 [also published in *Social Scientist*, vol. 18.11-12, pp. 3-35].

Mallick, B.S. (1981), 'Currencies and their Exchange Value in Seventeenth Century Gujarat and Bengal', *IHR*, vol. 7.1-2, p. 116.

——— (1986), 'English Trade and Indigenous Finance in Bengal and Gujarat in the Seventeenth Century', *SIH* (New Series), vol. 2.1, pp. 31-44.

Manickam, J.K. (1966), 'Sources and Problems of Business History in India from 1600 to 1900', *PIHRC* (Poona), vol. 37:2, pp. 102-4.

Marshall, P.J. (1967), 'Private British Investment in Eighteenth Century Bengal', *BPP*, vol. 86, pp. 52-67.

——— (1975), 'Economic and Political Expansion: The Case of Oudh', *MAS*, vol. 9.4, pp. 465-82.

——— (1975a), 'British Expansion in India in the Eighteenth Century: A Historical Revision', *History*, vol. 60, pp. 28-43.

——— (1976), 'British Merchants in Eighteenth Century Bengal', *BPP*, vol. 95, pp. 151-63.

——— (1987), 'Empire and Authority in the Late Eighteenth Century', *JICH*, vol. 15, pp. 105-17.

Menger, Carl (1892), 'On the Origins of Money', *EJ*, vol. 2, pp. 239-55.

Menon, P.K.K. (1958), 'Malabar Coinage in the 18th Century', *PIHC* (Trivandram Session), vol. 21, pp. 633-9.

Mishra, K.P. (1973), 'The Role of the Benaras Bankers in the Economy of Eighteenth Century Upper India', *PIHC* (Chandigarh Session), vol. 34.2, pp. 63-77.

Mitchiner, Micheal (1979), 'The British East India Company Arkat Rupee of Muhammad Shah: A Possible Candidate', *SCMB*, vol. 732, pp. 254-5.

——— (1979), 'An East India Company Nazarana Rupee of Murshidabad Dated AH 1180/RY 8 (AD 1766/67)', *Num. Cir.*, vol. 87.9, p. 384.

——— (1980), 'An East India Company Weight for Farrukhabad Rupees of AD 1806-1818', *ONSNL*, no. 65, p. 4.

Mitra, K.P. (1938), 'Currency in Orissa', *PIHRC* (Poona Session), vol. 15, pp. 114-26.

——— (1943), 'East India Company's Enquiries about Economic Resources', *PIHRC* (Aligarh), vol. 20, p. 42.

Mitra, R.C. (1950), 'A French Account of Commerce in India in 1774', *PIHRC* (Nagpur Session), vol. 27.2, pp. 22-5.

Mirza, Osman Haider (1956), 'Bills of Exchange in Medieval India (1600-1650), *JUPHS*, vol. 4.1-2, pp. 51-64.

Moosvi, Shirin (1987), 'The Silver Influx, Money Supply, Prices and Revenue-Extraction in Mughal India', *JESHO*, vol. 30.1, pp. 47-94.

——— (1999), 'Trade in Mughal India', in *Footprints of Enterprise*, FICCI, edn, pp. 70-7.

——— (2002), 'A Note on Interest Rates in the Seventeenth and Early Eighteenth Century', in Bagchi 2002, pp. 84-92.

Morris, Morris D. (1968), 'Towards a Re-interpretation of Nineteenth Century Indian Economic History', *IESHR*, vol. 5.1, pp. 1-15.

Mukerji, B.B. (1935), 'The East India Company and Silk Industry (1800-1840)', *IJE*, vol. 15.4, pp. 459-75.

——— (1935a), 'Internal Transit Duties under the East India Company', *IJE*, vol. 15.4, pp. 477-87.

Mukerji, Kshitimohan (1963), 'Price Movements in India between 1823 and 1871', *Artha Vigyana* (in Hindi), vol. 5.4, pp. 326-36.

Mukherjee, Nilmani and Robert Eric Frykenberg (1983), 'The Ryotwari System and Social Organisation in Madras Presidency', *IBR*, vol. 10.2, pp. 45-50.

Mukherjee, Rudrangshu (1982), 'Trade and Empire in Awadh 1765-1804', *Past and Present*, vol. 94, pp. 85-102.

Murti, V.N. (1961), 'Indian Economy during the British Rule', *IJE*, vol. 41.4, pp. 331-6.

Nahar, P.C. (1923), 'Genealogy of the Jagat Seths of Murshidabad', *PIHRC* (Calcutta Session), vol. 5, pp. 18-27.

Nanavati, Manilal B. (1944), 'Banking in India', *Annals of the American Academy of Political and Social Science*, vol. 233, pp. 152-60.

Narayanaswamị Naidu, B.V. (1933), 'Rural Economic Conditions in South India, (1800-1890)', *IJE*, vol. 14.3, pp. 419-38.

——— (1934), 'Economic Conditions in South India at the Advent of British Rule', *IJE*, vol. 14.4, pp. 481-93.

Natarajan, B. (1938), 'Regulation of Interest in the Madras Presidency, 1800-1855', *IJE*, vol. 18.4, pp. 581-91.

Nettles, Curtis (1931), 'British Policy and Colonial Money Supply', *EHR* (Series 1), vol. 3.2, pp. 219-45.

Om Prakash (1964), 'The European Trading Companies and the Merchants of Bengal, 1650-1725', *IESHR*, vol. 2.3, pp. 37-63.

——— (1976), 'Bullion for Goods: International Trade and Economy of Early Eighteenth Century Bengal', *IESHR*, vol. 13.2, pp. 159-88.

——— (1987), 'Foreign Merchants and Indian Mints in the Seventeenth and Early Eighteenth Centuries', in Richards 1987, pp. 171-92.

——— (1988), 'On Coinage in Mughal India', *IESHR*, vol. 25.4, pp. 475-91.

——— (1991), 'Sarrafs, Financial Intermediation and Credit Network in Mughal India', in Cauwenberghe 1991, pp. 473-90.

——— (1991a), 'Precious Metal Flows, Coinage and Prices in India in the 17th and Early 18th Century', in Cauwenberghe 1991, pp. 55-74.

——— (2002), 'The System of Credit in Mughal India', in Bagchi 2002, pp. 40-57.

Om Prakash and J. Krishnamurty (1970), 'Mughal Silver Currency: A Critique', *IESHR*, vol. 7.1, pp. 139-50.

Parsons, H.A. (1951), 'Some Major Unpublished Coins of British India and Sumatra', *Num. Cir.*, vol. 59, p. 169.

Patel, Surendra J. (1947), 'British Economic Thought and the Treatment of India as a Colony', *IJE*, vol. 27.4, pp. 367-71.

Perlin, Frank (1980), 'Pre-colonial South Asia and Western Penetration in the Seventeenth to Nineteenth Centuries: A Problem of Epistemological Status', *Review*, vol. 4.2, pp. 267-306.

——— (1983a), 'Growth of Money Economy and Some Questions of Transitions in Late Pre-Colonial India', *Social Scientist*, vol. 10.11, pp. 27-38.

——— (1983b), 'Proto-Industrialization and Pre-Colonial South Asia', *Past and Present*, No. 98, pp. 30-95.

——— (1987), 'Money Use in Late Pre-Colonial India and the International Trade in Currency Media', in Richards 1987, pp. 232-373.

——— (1988), 'Disarticulation of the World: Writing India's Economic History, A Review Article', *CSSH*, vol. 30.2, pp. 379-87.

——— (1991), 'World Economic Integration Before Industrialisation and the Euro-Asian Monetary Continuum: Their Implications and Problems of Categories, Definitions and Method', in Cauwenberghe 1991, pp. 239-74.

——— (1994), 'Changes in production and circulation of money in seventeenth and eighteenth century India: An essay on monetization before colonial occupation', in Subrahmanyam, ed., 1994, pp. 276-308 [originally published in Cauwenberghe and Irsigler 1984].

——— (1999), 'The other 'species' world: speciation of commodities and moneys, and the knowledge-base of commerce, 1500-1900', in Chaudhury and Morineau, eds., 1999, Cambridge, pp. 145-72.

Prasad, Durga and P.L. Gupta (1956), 'Clay Moulds of Punch Marked Coins from Mathura', *JNSI*, vol. 16.2, pp. 166-76.

Pridmore, F. (1961), 'First Silver Coinage of the Madras Mint, 1688', *Num. Cir.*, vol. 69.9, p. 184.

——— (1962), 'Major Varieties of East India Company's Coins Issued between 1835-1862', *Num. Cir.*, vol. 70.9, p. 183.

——— (1962a), 'The East India Company's C's Fanams, *c.* 1674-1730', *Num. Cir.*, vol. 70.3, p. 55.

——— (1962b), 'The East India Company's Coinage, 1835-1862', *Num. Cir.*, vol. 70.4, p. 81.

——— (1962c), 'The East India Company's Trisul Pice of the Mufussil or Provincial Mints of the Bengal Presidency', *Num. Cir.*, vol. 70.6, p. 137.

——— (1963), 'The East India Company's Copper Coinage Struck at the Royal Mint in 1824-25', *Num. Cir.*, vol. 71.12, p. 251.

——— (1963a), 'A Study of Mint Marks: The Bengal Presidency Mints of the Period 1792-1797', *Num. Cir.*, vol. 71.3, p. 50.

——— (1967), 'Gold Ingot Currency of India, 1853-1899', *SCMB*, vol. 585, p. 188.

——— (1968), 'The Silver Coinage of the Bombay Presidency, AD 1800-1835', *Num. Cir.*, vol. 76.6, p. 189.

——— (1968a), 'Notes on Colonial Coins: Mr. A.P. Spencer, Artist, Engraver, His Majesty's Mint, Calcutta and the re-designated Coinages of King George VI, British India, 1938-1947', *BNJ*, vol. 37, pp. 158-74.

——— (1969), 'The Initial 'S' on the Gold and Silver Coins issued by the East India Company during the period 1840/41-1850/51', *Num. Cir.*, vol. 76.6, p. 200.

——— (1970), 'East India Company's Coinage of the Bengal Presidency: Murshidabad or Calcutta Mint', *SCMB*, vol. 625, p. 311.

——— (1971), 'The East India Company's Silver Fanams of the Madras Presidency, 1689-1807', *SCMB*, vol. 639, pp. 285-8.

——— (1971a), 'British Indian Coinage', *SCMB*, vol. 640, pp. 445-7.

——— (1972), 'Bombay Copporoons or Pice, 1672-1703', *Num. Cir.*, vol. 80.3, pp. 100-2.

——— (1972a), 'The East India Company's Bell Metal Coinage of Manipur, 1838', *SCMB*, vol. 652, pp. 477-81.

——— (1974), 'Proof/Patterns and suggested designs for the Imperial Coinage of British India', *Num. Cir.*, vol. 82.1, pp. 7-10.

——— (1976),'The Kandhahar Fulus or Paisa', *Num. Cir.*, vol. 84.12, pp. 455-6.

——— (1976a), 'South India, Arkat 1/5th Rupee or Fanam', *Num. Cir.*, vol. 84.4, pp. 138-40.

——— (1978), 'Two Pattern Rupees of Edward VII, 1901', *SCMB*, vol. 628, pp. 441-3.

——— (1978a), 'The East India Company's Nuzzer Rupees', *Num. Cir.*, vol. 86.2, pp. 67-8.

Rajendran, N. (1997), 'History of Coinage under the East India Company', in *Studies in South Indian Coins*, vol. 7, pp. 159-63.

Ramachandran, C. (1970), 'Madras Currency Under the Early British Rule', *IBR*, vol. 2.3 pp. 42-9.

——— (1970a), 'The Madras Mint Under Early British Rule', *IBR*, vol. 3.2, pp. 34-51.

Ramachandran, C. and R.K. Gupta (1971), 'A Brief History of the Madras Government Bank in the Early Nineteenth Century', *IBR*, vol. 4.2, pp. 33-9.

——— (1971a), 'East India Company and Irrigation Development in Madras Presidency', *IBR*, vol. 4.3, pp. 34-43.

——— (1972), 'Land Revenue Policy of the East India Company in Madras Presidency', *IBR*, vol. 5.3, pp. 55-60.

——— (1976), 'Industrial Policy of the East India Company in Madras', *IBR*, vol. 8.1-2 pp. 96-104.

Ramsbotham, R.B. (1923), 'Some Aspects of the Revenue Collection in Bengal Immediately Before the Assumption of Diwani', *PIHRC* (Calcutta Session), vol. 5, pp. 35-44.

Rau, B. Ramachandra (1929), 'Organised Banking in the Days of John Company', *IJE*, vol. 10.1, pp. 1-49.

Ray, Rajat Kanta (1995), 'Asian Capital in the Age of European Domination: The Rise of the Bazaar, 1800-1914', *MAS*, vol. 29.3, pp. 449-54.

——— (2002), 'Indigenous Banking and Commission Agency in India's Colonial Economy', in Bagchi 2002, pp. 118-30.

Reddy, Varikuti Venkata Subba (1983), 'A Gold Pagoda of English East India Company', *JNSI*, vol. 45.1-2, p. 79.

Reeppeteau, L.V. (1974), 'The Riddle of Portullis Money', *Coin News*, vol. 28.4, pp. 103-6.

Rhodes, Nicholas (1999), 'Bengal: East India Company, the First Copper Coins for Bengal', *ONSNL*, no. 159, pp. 15-16.

——— (2001), 'A Garhwal Takka Struck in the Name of the East India Company', *ONSNL*, no. 166, pp. 17-18.

Richards, J.F. (1981), 'Mughal State Finance and the Premodern World Economy', *CSSH*, vol. 23.2, pp. 285-308.

Rothermund, Dietmar (1970), 'An Aspect of the Monetary Policy of British Imperialism', *IESHR*, vol. 7.1, pp. 91-108.

Roy, Rama Devi (1987), 'Some Aspects of the Economic Drain from India during the British Rule', *Social Scientist*, vol. 15.3, pp. 37-47.

Roy, Sourin (1972), 'A Rare Document on Delhi Wheat Prices, 1763-1835', *IESHR*, vol. 9, pp. 91-9.

Rudner, David (1989), 'Banker's Trust and the Culture of Banking among the Nattukottai Chettiars of Colonial South India', *MAS*, vol. 23.3, pp. 417-58.

Sainthill, R. (1856), 'Unpublished Pattern Rupee of William IV [1834]', *NC* (1st Series), vol. 17, p. 75.

Samant, Vanashree (2002), 'Coins of the East India Company: As the East India Company pursued spices and other imports, it established trading posts in India and indelibly influenced both a coinage and a culture', *The Numismatist*, vol. 115.10, pp. 1178-83 and 1249-52.

Sarkar, Smriti Kumar (2005), 'Social Organisation of Artisan Production in India: Changing Role of the Market Technology, and Merchant-Creditor, 18th to 20th Centuries', in *History of Science, Philosophy and Culture in Indian Civilization,* vol. VIII, part 3: *Economic History of India from Eighteenth to Twentieth Century*, ed. Binay Bhushan Chaudhuri, New Delhi: Centre for Studies in Civilizations, pp. 107-356.

Sastry, Ch. Sitarama (1935), 'The Economic Disintegration in the First Half of the Nineteenth Century', *IJE*, vol. 15.4, pp. 511-21.

Selle, Johannes (1969), 'Coinage "Feud" between Aurangzeb and the East India Company', *JNSI*, vol. 31, p. 63.

Siddiqi, Asiya (1981), 'Money and Prices in the Earlier Stages of Empire: India and Britain, 1760-1840', *IESHR*, vol. 18.3-4, pp. 231-62.

Singh, Dilbagh (1974), 'Role of the Mahajans in the Rural Economy in Eastern Rajasthan During the 18th Century', *Social Scientist*, vol. 22, pp. 20-31.

Sinha, H.C. (1927), 'Indigenous Banking in Bengal', *IJE*, vol. 7.3, pp. 211-26.

——— (1968), 'First Limited Liability Bank in India', *IBR*, vol. 1.10, pp. 31-4.

Sinha, J.C. (1921), 'History of Indian Commerce, 1765-1813', in *Sir Asutosh Mookerjee Silver Jubilee Volumes*, vol. 1 (Arts and Letters), Calcutta: Calcutta University, pp. 245-62.

——— (1924), 'Some Currency Reforms of Hastings', *PIHRC* (Madras), vol. 6, pp. 74-8.

——— (1925), 'Economic Theorists among the Servants of John Company (1766-1806)', *EJ*, vol. 35.137, pp. 47-59.

——— (1925a), 'Earliest Currency Committee in India, 1787', *PIHRC* (Lahore), vol. 8, p. 183.

——— (1926), 'The Company's Trade in Bengal in the days of Cornwallis', *PIHRC* (Lucknow Session), vol. 9, p. 62.

——— (1927), 'Currency in Early British Days', *IJE*, vol. 7.3, pp. 166-75.

——— (1930), 'The Beginning of Jute Export to England', *PIHRC* (Patna), vol. 13, pp. 93-8.

——— (1940), 'Economic Conditions of the Ceded Districts, 1800-07', *PIHRC* (Baroda), vol. 17, p. 56.

Sinha, N.K. (1952), 'Drain of Wealth from Bengal in the Second Half of the 18th Century', *BPP*, vol. 71, pp. 34-43.

——— (1954), 'East India Company's Investment Policy in the 18th Century', *BPP*, vol. 73, pp. 25-44.

——— (1966), 'Sources and Problems of Business History in India in the First Half of the Nineteenth Century', *PIHRC* (Poona Session), vol. 37, pp. 75-9.

Smith, M.A. (1885), 'East India Silver Coinage', *The Numismatist*, vol. 8, p. 39.

Snartt, Peter G. (1974), 'The East India Company's Bell Metal Coinage of Manipur', *Num. Cir.*, vol. 82.10, pp. 384-5.

——— (1976), 'Some unpublished varieties of East India Company's Madras Coins', *Num. Cir.*, vol. 84.9, p. 319.

——— (1976), 'The Rarity of East India Company's Coins', *SCMB*, vol. 691, pp. 78-80.

——— (1976), 'The Rarity of East India Company's Coins', *SCMB*, vol. 700, pp. 468-9.

——— (1977), 'The Rarity of East India Company's Coins', *SCMB*, vol. 707, p. 249.

——— (1977a), 'The Rarity of East India Company's Coins', *SCMB*, vol. 708, pp. 282-5.

——— (1977b), 'The Rarity of East India Company's Coins', *SCMB*, vol. 711, pp. 391-4.

——— (1978), 'The Rarity of East India Company's Coins', *SCMB*, vol. 713, pp. 36-42.

——— (1978a), 'The Rarity of East India Company's Coins', *SCMB*, vol. 716, pp. 112-14.

——— (1978b), 'The Rarity of East India Company's Coins', *SCMB*, vol. 718, pp. 176-9.

——— (1978c), 'The Rarity of East India Company's Coins', *SCMB*, vol. 721, pp. 270-1.

——— (1978d), 'A Curious East India Company Overstrike', *SCMB*, vol. 722, pp. 300-1.

——— (1979), 'The Rarity of East India Company's Coins: Bombay Coinage', *SCMB*, vol. 729, pp. 154-5.

——— (1979a), 'The Rarity of East India Company's Coins: Bombay Coinage', *SCMB*, vol. 730, pp. 186-96.

Sohoni, S.V. (1971), 'Portcullis Money of the East India Company', *INC*, vol. 9, pp. 90-5.

Spooner, Frank C. (1978), 'The Three Functions of Money: Accounts, Exchanges, and Assets', *Diogenes*, vol. 26, pp. 105-37.

Stagg, H. (1930), 'A Brief History and Description of His Majesty's Mint, Calcutta', *NS*, vol. 43, pp. 15-22.

Stevens, P[aul]. J.E. (1992), 'The Coins of the British in India: Silver Fanam

Coinage of the Madras Presidency, 1689-1807', *ONS*, Occasional Paper, no. 27.

——— (2003), 'A Pattern Cash Struck at Soho for Use in Madras', *Num. Cir.*, vol. 111, p. 246.

——— (2003a), 'Imperial and Colonial Coinage', *BNJ*, vol. 73, pp. 148-60.

——— (2004), 'The Reformation of the Coinage of Madras Early in the Nineteenth Century', *BNJ*, vol. 174, pp. 121-44.

——— (2004a), 'The Coins of the Bombay Presidency: The Bankot Mint', *JONS*, no. 179, pp. 28-32.

——— (2004b), 'The Coins of the Bombay Presidency', *JONS*, no. 180, pp. 27-31.

——— (2004c), 'The Coins of the Bombay Presidency: The Transitional Mints of the Deccan', *JONS*, no. 181, pp. 24-9.

——— (2004d), 'The Coins of the Bombay Presidency: The Mints of the Northern Districts', *JONS*, no. 182, pp. 25-32.

——— (2005),'The Company's Crown, An Unrealised Proposal of 1837', *JONS*, no. 186, pp. 42-3.

——— (2006), 'The Coins of the Ceded and Conquered Provinces of the Bengal Presidency', *JONS*, no. 188, pp. 18-23.

——— (2006a), 'The Introduction of the 1835 Quarter Annas (Pice) as part of the Uniform Coinage of British India', *JONS*, no. 189, pp. 22-9.

——— (2007a), 'The Coinage of the Ceded and Conquered Provinces of the Bengal Presidency: The Farrukhabad Mint', *JONS*, no. 190, pp. 37-43.

——— (2007b), 'Rupees of Farrukhsiyar, The First Official Mughal-style Coinage of the Bombay Presidency', *JONS*, no. 191, pp. 31-2.

——— (2011), 'John Prinsep's Copper Coinage', in *Felicitas: Essays in Numismatics, Epigraphy and History in Honour of Joe Cribb*, ed. Shailendra Bhandare and Sanjay Garg, Mumbai: Reesha Books International, pp. 365-84.

Subrahmanyam, Sanjay (1991), 'Precious Metal Flows and Prices in Western and Southern Asia, 1500-1750: Some Comparative and Conjectural Aspects', *SIH*, vol. 7.1, pp. 78-105.

Subramanian, Lakshmi (1985), 'Capital and Crowd in a Declining Asian Port City: The Anglo-Bania Order and the Surat Riots of 1795', *MAS*, vol. 19.2, pp. 205-37.

——— (1987), 'Banias and the British: The Role of Indigenous Credit in the Process of Imperial Expansion in Western India in the Second Half of the Eighteenth Century', *MAS*, vol. 21.3, pp. 473-510.

——— (1991), 'The Eighteenth Century Social Order in Surat: A Reply and an Excursus on the Riots of 1788 and 1795', *MAS*, vol. 25.2, pp. 321-65.

Swaminathan, Saroja (1970), 'A Triangular Contest over a Treasure', *IBR*, vol. 2.3, pp. 35-6.

Thakur, U. (1958), 'Currency of Tirhut during the Early Years of the Company's Rule', *JNSI*, vol. 20, p. 205.

Thavaraj, M.J.K. (1968), 'The Economic Policies of the Colonial Government in India during 1700-1900, in *Ideas in History* [Proceedings of a Seminar on Ideas, Motivating Social and Religious Movements and Political and Economic Policies during the 18th and 19th Centuries], ed. Bisheshwar Prasad, London: Asia Publishing House, pp. 211-19.

Thomas, Edward (1882), 'The Coinage of the East India Company at Bombay, under the Charters of Charles II, with a note on the Indian exchanges of the period', *IA*, vol. 9, p. 313.

Thomas, P.J. and B. Natarajan (1936), 'Economic Depression in the Madras Presidency (1825-54)', *EHR*, vol. 7.1, pp. 67-75.

Thurston, Edgar (1893), 'Note on the History of East India Company Coinage from 1753-1835', *JASB*, vol. 62, pp. 52-84.

Torri, Michelguglielmo (1982), 'In the Deep Blue Sea: Surat and its Merchant Class during the Dyarchic Era (1759-1800), *IESHR*, vol. 19.3-4, pp. 267-99.

——— (1987), 'Surat during the Second half of the Eighteenth Century: What kind of Social Order?: A Rejoinder to Lakshmi Subramanian', *MAS*, vol. 21.4, pp. 679-710.

——— (1998), 'Mughal Nobles, Indian Merchants and the Beginning of British Conquest in Western India: The Case of Surat 1756-1759', *MAS*, vol. 32.2, pp. 257-315.

Tripathi, Dwijendra (1966), 'Sources and Problems of Business History in India from 1600 to 1900', *PIHRC* (Poona Session), vol. 37, pp. 96-101.

——— (2002), 'Rise of Modern Banking in the Princely States of India: The Case of the Bank of Baroda', in Bagchi 2002, pp. 131-48.

Umar, Muhammad (1972), 'Foreign Trade of India during the Eighteenth Century', *Medieval India: A Miscellany*, vol. 2, pp. 227-48.

Upadhyaya, S.C. (1949), 'Copper Coins in Bombay Mint, 1669-1677', *JNSI*, vol. 11, pp. 39-40.

Venkateshwara, S.V. (1918), 'Mughal Currency and Coinage, *IJE*, vol. 2.2, pp. 169-79.

Vijayaraghavan, K.R. (1955), 'The Old Star Pagoda of Madras', *JNSI*, vol. 17, p. 109.

W.D.H. (pseud.) (1837), 'New India Rupee [of 1835]', *Numismatic Journal* (London), vol. 1, p. 137.

Westcott, A. (1899), 'The Copper Coinage of Madras Presidency, *IA*, vol. 28, p. 270.

——— (1900), 'The Copper Coinage of Madras Presidency', *IA*, vol. 29, p. 172.

Wiggins, K[ennith W]. (1977), 'Some Unpublished Coins of the East India Company', *Num. Cir.*, vol. 85.5, p. 201.

——— (1980), 'Two Unsuccessful Mints of the East India Company', *Num. Cir.*, vol. 88.10, pp. 349-50.

——— (1991), 'East India Company Copper Coins of Chinapatan', *Num. Cir.*, vol. 99.2, pp. 41-2.

——— (1994), 'Some New and Unpublished Coins of the East India Company', *Num. Cir.*, vol. 102.6, p. 255.

——— (1996), 'The Acquisition of Indian Mints by the English East India Company', in *Numismatic Panorama: Essays in the Memory of Late Shri S.M. Shukla*, ed. K.K. Maheshwari and Biswajeet Rath, New Delhi: Harman Publishing House, pp. 327-44.

Wilson, Charles (1949), 'Treasure and Trade Balances: The Mercantile Problem', *EHR*, vol. 2, pp. 152-61.

——— (1951), 'Treasure and Trade Balances: Further Evidence', *EHR*, vol. 4, pp. 231-42.

Wodak, E. (1956), 'Balemarks of the East India Company and Coins', *South Australian Numismatic Journal* (Adelaide), vol. 7.2, pp. 9-11.

——— (1958), 'John Prinsep's Copper Coins for Bengal, I', *Num. Cir.*, vol. 66.1, pp. 36-9.

——— (1958a), 'John Prinsep's Copper Coins for Bengal, II', *Num. Cir.*, vol. 66.2, pp. 61-3.

Zambaur, E.V. (1918), 'The Oldest British Murshidabad Rupee', *NS*, vol. 31, p. 483.

Index*

*Excluding the Appendices.